D0206533

WEEK BY WEEK

PLANS FOR DOCUMENTING CHILDREN'S DEVELOPMENT

FOURTH EDITION

Join us on the web at
EarlyChildEd.delmar.com

THOMSON
DELMAR LEARNING

WEEK BY WEEK

PLANS FOR DOCUMENTING CHILDREN'S DEVELOPMENT

FOURTH EDITION

BARBARA ANN NILSEN
Retired, Broome Community College
Binghamton, NY

THOMSON
DELMAR LEARNING
Australia Brazil Canada Mexico Singapore Spain United Kingdom United States

THOMSON
DELMAR LEARNING

Week by Week: Plans for Documenting Children's Development
Barbara Ann Nilsen, Ed.D.

Vice President, Career Education Strategic Business Unit:
Dawn Gerrain

Director of Learning Solutions:
John Fedor

Assistant to the Director of Learning Solutions:
Anne Orgren

Managing Editor:
Robert L. Serenka, Jr.

Acquisitions Editor:
Erin O'Connor

Editorial Assistants:
Alison Archambault and Stephanie Kelly

Director of Production:
Wendy A. Troeger

Production Manager:
Mark Bernard

Content Project Manager:
Angela Iula

Technology Project Manager:
Sandy Charette

Director of Marketing:
Wendy E. Mapstone

Channel Manager:
Kristin McNary

Marketing Coordinator:
Scott A. Chrysler

Art Director:
Joy Kocsis

© 2008 Thomson Delmar Learning, a part of the Thomson Corporation. Thomson, the Star logo and Delmar Learning are trademarks used herein under license.

Printed in
1 2 3 4 5 XXX 10 09 08 07

For more information contact
Delmar Learning,
5 Maxwell Drive, PO Box 8007, Clifton Park, NY 12065-2919.

Or you can visit our Internet site at
http://www.delmarlearning.com.

ALL RIGHTS RESERVED. No part of this work covered by the copyright hereon may be reproduced or used in any form or by any means—graphic, electronic, or mechanical, including photocopying, recording, taping, Web distribution or information storage and retrieval systems—without written permission of the publisher.

For permission to use material from this text or product, submit a request online at http://www.thomsonrights.com
Any additional questions about permissions can be submitted by email to thomsonrights@thomson.com

Library of Congress Cataloging-in-Publication Data

Nilsen, Barbara.
Week by week : plans for documenting children's development /
Barbara Ann Nilsen. — 4th ed.
p. cm.
Includes bibliographical references and index.
ISBN 1-4180-7275-3
1. Behavioral assessment of children.
2. Observation (Psychology) 3. Observation (Educational method) 4. Child development.
I. Title.
BF722.N53 2007
370.15—dc22

2007017381

NOTICE TO THE READER

Publisher does not warrant or guarantee any of the products described herein or perform any independent analysis in connection with any of the product information contained herein. Publisher does not assume, and expressly disclaims, any obligation to obtain and include information other than that provided to it by the manufacturer.

The reader is expressly warned to consider and adopt all safety precautions that might be indicated by the activities herein and to avoid all potential hazards. By following the instructions contained herein, the reader willingly assumes all risks in connection with such instructions.

The Publisher makes no representation or warranties of any kind, including but not limited to, the warranties of fitness for particular purpose or merchantability, nor are any such representations implied with respect to the material set forth herein, and the publisher takes no responsibility with respect to such material. The Publisher shall not be liable for any special, consequential, or exemplary damages resulting, in whole or part, from the readers' use of, or reliance upon, this material.

The authors and Thomson Delmar Learning affirm that the Web site URLs referenced herein were accurate at the time of printing. However, due to the fluid nature of the Internet, we cannot guarantee their accuracy for the life of the edition.

Contents

Preface

Week by Week is a documentation system guidebook for students and practitioners in early childhood education who work with toddlers through second grade children. Each chapter has two main parts: the documentation method and the child development overview. The third part, the plans that integrate the method to document children's development, is in the Bind-in-Book CD. The purpose is to organize and plan deliberately, week by week, to build a Portfolio for each child, filling it with various documents that testify to the child's development and behavior. *Week by Week* presents a manageable plan that will help you gather documentation on *all* the children in the class or group in *all* the developmental areas.

The first three editions of *Week by Week* have been used in a number of ways. Freshman students in associate degree programs use the text for a course in techniques of documentation. Students in subsequent semesters in both associate degree and bachelor degree programs use the text for child development study and in field experiences. The text has been used in baccalaureate and master's teaching preparation programs. Classroom teachers have used the text as a tool to help them organize their observations into meaningful Portfolios that document their children's development. It has also been used in Head Start, Even Start, child care, and nursery-school settings. In this fourth edition, the Bind-in-Book CD provides users with electronic copies of all the forms as well as the week-by-week calendar, which can be adapted to the semester for students or the program year for classroom teachers. By "going digital," we move toward electronic Portfolios, which have several advantages:

1. *Usability*—Forms can be personalized and used over and over.
2. *Confidentiality*—In a computer file, children's information is kept more secure.
3. *Professional presentation*—Printed documents can be spellchecked and formatted into a document suitable to share with families and other professionals.

How This Book Came to Be Written

My original idea for the book was to share my system of child observations with practitioners like myself. The title, *Week by Week,* describes a year-long systematic plan for teachers to document each child's development by forming an extensive Portfolio that shows each child's progress in all areas of development. As my teaching venue changed from the preschool classroom to the college classroom, the book became a textbook. As a college textbook, it introduces students to those methods—in the context of child development—that can be used and practiced in periodic visits into a classroom. It may be used for the sole purpose of observing, or as students participate in a field experience. It has been well received by students, and it is my hope that they will keep the book and renew their acquaintance with it when they get a classroom of their own. Then the full *Week by Week* plan will take on new meaning. There have been times when I've rediscovered books from my college days, and it is like meeting an old friend—we take up where we left off.

Users of *Week by Week*

This book is written for two audiences. It is a textbook for students in preparation programs (as well as being a resource for those same students when they have a classroom of their own) and for practitioners in the field.

***WEEK BY WEEK* FOR THE STUDENT.** As a college textbook this book will be used for 13, 15, or 16 weeks. Each week you will be introduced to a different method and will be given one assignment to practice the method. If you are in a field placement for the whole semester, you can incorporate the *Week by Week* plan as you participate in the classroom activities. If you are taking a course in observation methods, you can make weekly visits just for observation, or you may be able to plan three or four longer visits and do several of the practice assignments in each visit. In either of these two plans, you will miss the day-to-day interactions. This is just for practice, a simulation of what you will be doing when you have a classroom of your own. CAUTION: Seeing children intermittently makes it impossible to draw decisive conclusions about their development. Also, it is important *not to talk specifically* about a child, teacher, or program by name when you are in your college classroom, dorm, or out with friends. **Confidentiality** is a part of the ethical responsibility of professionals. You will practice this recording method by following the assignment on the Bind-in-Book CD. You or your instructor may need to modify this depending on your field placement situation.

***WEEK BY WEEK* FOR THE PRACTITIONER.** Maybe you used this book in your college class and now have your own classroom. Or perhaps you found this book and are making a commitment to better organize your contributions to each child's Portfolio. The Bind-in-Book CD provides information on how to schedule a manageable number of observations each week over the school year, returning to each developmental area several times. You will find a calendar on the Bind-in-Book CD that will help you. Some additional forms are also included there for your use in organizing the Portfolio and using it to individualize the curriculum. After all, that's what observing is all about. You observe, you assess, you plan, you implement, you observe, you assess, you plan. Well, you get the idea by now. Remember that when you are totally responsible for the classroom, you will have to steal moments to write things down. That is the biggest hurdle to observing and recording. For help with this, note especially the "How to Find the Time" sections in each chapter. To achieve the goal of gathering a fairly equal amount of documentation on each child, use various methods, and revisit developmental areas three times over a school year. An organizational system can be used to ensure that you are gathering an approximately equal distribution of Portfolio documentation on all children.

The teacher using the *Week by Week* system will gain skill in using various methods of recording observations and will be reviewing child development and good teaching practices. Knowledge of child development, observation methods, and curriculum are not separate from each other but are interdependent. One must know what to look for in order to be a good observer, and mindful teachers make decisions based on what they see. The *Week by Week* system will enable the teacher to document important information about each child, information that is usable for measurement and reporting, as well as accurate and objective.

Chapter Organization

Each chapter has two major sections, with the third on the Bind-in-Book CD.

USING THE . . . First, we introduce a **recording** method and acquaint you with its uses. Observing and recording has been a challenge for early childhood teachers. Gathering meaningful data that can be used for several purposes is a skill that can be learned, but just as with any other artisan, there are different tools for different tasks. Each chapter presents a documentation tool, a description and illustration of its use, the advantages and disadvantages of the tool, pitfalls to avoid when using it, and hints for incorporating technology that can make the job easier, and suggestions on how to find the time to accurately record events while in a busy classroom. This book, however, is more than just a manual to teach observation methods. There are many of those out there. It is designed to be a system, organizing observation methods and child development into a manageable schedule, equitable to each child.

LOOKING AT . . . Each chapter then reviews an area of development that can be assessed using this particular method of recording. People have asked why so much emphasis on child development in this text on observation methods. You never can know too much about child development, and we need to know what to look for in order to see it. It is always a danger to divide child development into pieces, so this comes with the reminder that every area or domain is interdependent and affects every other, but that there still has to be some way to divide it into segments to make it manageable. That philosophy fits in very well with the *Week by Week* objective: to take the huge task of gathering meaningful developmental data in a natural setting, over time, to build a Portfolio that depicts what the child knows and can do. That is the purpose of this book, this system.

THE BIND-IN-BOOK CD contains the weekly observation plans, along with forms and a way to divide the group into small segments to assure that every child is observed in every developmental area at least three times during the school year. Each of the plans has instructions for both students and for practitioners, making this book a *keeper* for students to use later. Each of the week's plans includes instructions on "What to Do with It." This suggests where to file the documentation, how to use it in conversations with the child and the family, and actions. Actions are suggestions for adding to the curriculum in this particular area, including Read a

Book, a listing of related children's books; In the Environment; In the Curriculum; and In the Newsletter. All of these are resources to use the documentation not just for recording progress but for individualizing learning. A part of the weekly plan also includes a Reflective Journal, which poses open-ended questions to guide the teacher to looking inward. These are for the writer's own consideration of the events of the week, personal attitudes, self-analysis, and promises for the future. These are private journal entries, not a part of the child's records.

Chapter Features

Each chapter has additional segments that illustrate a principle, amplify the topic, or raise points for the reader to consider.

EXERCISES. Scattered throughout the book are interactive sections inviting the reader to answer a question or formulate a list. They are called exercises since the benefit is personal and dependent on participation, becoming active in the learning process.

THINK ABOUT IT. Similar to the Exercises, these are critical thinking questions that ask the reader to think about the concept and compare new information to prior knowledge and experience.

TOPICS IN OBSERVATION. These are discussions on issues related to observing and recording children's development. They are intended to help the reader gain a broader understanding of a specific topic in teaching, learning, or authentic assessment. These essays offer a deeper consideration of a certain aspect of the field of observing and recording.

IT HAPPENED TO ME. These vignettes illustrate points about child development from children I have known and mistakes I have made that taught me what not to do. Some are observations my college students have written. Others are humorous stories related to me. All are stories, incredible, yet true. There are millions that *got away* because I never wrote them down!

HELPING ALL CHILDREN. Every child is unique, as different from one another as observers are. There are sometimes special considerations when observing the widely diverse populations in today's early childhood programs. Inclusion of children with special abilities in schools and programs calls for attention to staff training, adaptability of facilities and environments, and inclusive practices. These are supported in this book by the emphasis on individual assessment, documentation, and individualizing the curriculum based on that assessment. At the risk of reinforcing stereotypes, this section is included to suggest insight relevant to the developmental area or the observation and recording process. It is a reminder that all children are children first, with circumstances that cannot be ignored. Recognizing their individuality influences the responses of thoughtful practitioners.

HELPING PROFESSIONALS. When working with children and families, teachers are often the resource or intermediary between people who need specialized advice and services and the professionals and agencies. This section is included in each chapter to acquaint the reader with the terminology of specialists to whom the teacher may refer the family. Each program should have a list of specific referral agencies and professionals from which the family can select, with guidance from the people they trust.

OTHER METHODS. The recording method and developmental areas are linked in this book to familiarize you with both. However, once you have learned about the methods, you will see that development may be recorded and assessed using several different methods. At the conclusion of each chapter, there is a feature that suggests which other methods would be suitable for documenting the developmental area featured in the chapter.

@ it happened to me

Soliciting YOUR "It Happened to Me" Stories

Each of you, as you work with children and as you read my "It Happened to Me" stories, will have some of your own. Delmar Thomson Learning has set up an e-mail address where you can submit them: WeekbyWeek@thomsonlearning.com. I will be reading them and selecting some for the next edition of *Week by Week.* I'll give you a prompt in each chapter to think about an incident that illustrates a concept in the chapter. These are more than funny, entertaining stories because they demonstrate the child's thinking or our own actions or mistakes that we can laugh at. I look forward to hearing yours!

KEY TERMS. Throughout the chapter, important words appear in red, bold type to draw your attention. They are listed at the end of each chapter; you can use this list as a self-check to be sure you understand their meaning. Each term is listed and defined in the Glossary at the end of the book.

New to This Edition

There are always new studies, new editions of old favorites, and issues that I didn't know about just a few years ago. This new edition makes the text current and hopefully more relevant and useful for the reader with updated information throughout the text.

FAMILIES. In an effort to reflect the lives of many children today, the term *family* has been used throughout the book rather than *parent*. This is not meant to negate the importance of parents in the lives of children but to broaden the importance of those other significant people in the child's life that vary for each child. At times it seems awkward and contrived, but its concept is so important that I invite you to join me in this retraining of ourselves.

STANDARDS. A standard is a recognized measurement, and standards within the education field have proliferated; there are now many federal, state, and association standards for programs, staff, and every aspect of curriculum. This is not to standardize (make all alike), but to improve the quality of children's experiences by what has been determined by the field to be the best practices. Selected standards from various sources are included in each chapter to acquaint the reader with standards that have been developed by many different professional associations and organizations.

THE BIND-IN-BOOK CD. The BIG change with this issue is the Bind-in-Book CD that accompanies the text. This enables us to provide many more documents, electronic copies of forms, calendars for individualizing your observation plan, helping you to move toward electronic Portfolios on children in the future. There are PowerPoint slides to fill in as you read or your professor lectures, learning activities, reflective journal questions and links to internet resources. I hope you will find it useful. The Bind-in-Book CD icon appears within the chapter to prompt you to take advantage of the many features provided.

WEEK BY WEEK PLANS. Earlier I explained the dual purpose for this book. It is primarily a textbook to introduce early childhood students to the importance of documenting children's development and for students and a manual for practitioners to build individual child Portfolios for authentic assessment and curriculum planning, all within the context of child development milestones. On the Bind-in-Book CD, you will find a systematic plan for each week. Each week's plan is divided into parts (Part A, Part B, etc.). In previous editions of this text, the parts were referred to as Plan A, Plan B, etc. The move to the word *Parts* instead of *Plan A, B,* and *C* was so there would be no misunderstanding that the term "Plan B" was the next best alternative. That is not so; Plan B and Plan C are all important parts of the system.

BOOKS IN SPANISH are included in the Read a Book area of the Action section on the Bind-in-Book CD. There are expanded resources for working with children with special needs, sensitivity to multicultural issues, and consideration for family child care providers.

Ancillaries

PROFESSIONAL ENHANCEMENT TEXT. A new supplement to accompany this text is the Observation and Assessment Professional Enhancement handbook for students. This resource, which is part of Thomson Delmar Learning's Early Childhood Education Professional Enhancement series, focuses on key topics of interest for future early childhood directors, teachers, and caregivers. Becoming a teacher is a process of continuing to grow, learn, reflect, and discover through experience. The Professional Enhancement text helps tomorrow's teachers along their way. Students will keep this informational supplement and use it for years to come in their early childhood practices.

The Observation and Assessment Professional Enhancement text provides you with:

- Child development stages and developmental alerts
- Explanation of the difference between watching and observing
- Reasons for why each child is different from another
- Awareness of yourself and its impact on observation
- Common methods used to record/document what you observe
- Uses for what you have observed and recorded that assist in advancing each child's development

- Uses of classroom documentation and assessment for reporting and accountability
- How to manage all the paperwork you collect on each child
- Reminders about the ethics of gathering information on children

eResource E-RESOURCE FOR INSTRUCTORS

THE INSTRUCTOR'S E-RESOURCE. New to this edition is an instructor's e-Resource CD containing a chapter-by-chapter instructor's manual as well as instructor PowerPoint slides, a computerized test bank, grading rubrics, and more.

The students have the same PowerPoint lectures without key points that they can use to guide them in the chapter reading or following the instructor's lecture. Because these are electronic, they can also be used in online courses.

The e-Resource also contains a computerized test bank comprised of true/false, multiple choice, short answer, and completion questions for each chapter. Instructors can use the computerized test bank software to create sample quizzes for students. Refer to the CTB User's Guide for more information on how to create and post quizzes to your school's Internet or Intranet.

Acknowledgments

My thanks and love to family who are my biggest supporters, my friend Carol, who loves me like a sister, my colleagues near and far who dedicate themselves to the care and education of America's children, and to my students who teach me something every day.

Sincere appreciation to Erin O'Connor, who believes in my work, Stephanie Youngers-Kelly, Anne Orgren, and the staff at Delmar for their assistance, patience, and creativity in putting my ideas into reality. Thanks to my favorite librarian, Karen, who helped me search for resource gems that helped me learn more than I ever knew before. A special "thank you" to the reviewers who provided valuable feedback and helped to shape the final work:

Alice D. Beyrent
Hesser College
Manchester, NH

Beverlyn Cain
School of Education and Psychology
Elizabeth City State University
Elizabeth City, NC

Irene Cook
California State University
Bakersfield, CA

Jorja Davis
Blinn College
Bryan, TX

Karyn Gramley
Penney's Child Care Center, LLC, and Child Care 101, LLC
Waunakee, WI

Elizabeth A. Jenkins
Orlando Tech, Orange County Public Schools
Orlando, FL

Michaelene Ostrosky
University of Illinois at Urbana-Champaign
Champaign, IL

Brenda Schin
Child Care Consultant
Ballston Spa, NY

Gail Laubscher Summer
Lenoir-Rhyne College
Hickory, NC

About the Author

Barbara Nilsen retired in 2006 as professor and chair of the Teacher Education and Early Childhood Department at Broome Community College, Binghamton, New York, where she taught in the classroom and on-line. She continues her on-line teaching and community, state, and national involvement in early childhood. She was also the grant director of NYSECEONLINE and the Early Learning Opportunities collaborative project for Building Brighter Futures for Broome. The author received her Ed.D. in Early and Middle Childhood from Nova University. She has been active in local, state, and national early childhood professional development initiatives such as New York State Career Pathways, New York State Children's Program Administrator Infant/Toddler, Family Child Care Credentials, and NAEYC'S Early Childhood Associate Degree Program Accreditation project. She is coauthor, with Virginia Albertalli, of *An Introduction to Learning and Teaching: Infants through Sixth Grade,* and the author of the *Observation and Assessment Professional Enhancement* text.

This text is dedicated to the busy hands, open minds, and caring hearts of all who work with young children. You bear the worthy name: Teacher. I welcome your communication by e-mail at WeekbyWeek@thomsonlearning.com.

Introduction: Getting Started

IN THIS INTRODUCTION

THE 15 WHYS OF OBSERVING

EXERCISE **Observe (or imagine):**

- a clock
- the inside of a refrigerator
- a traffic light

Exactly what do you see? What are your observations telling you? What will you do as a result of what you see? Write down what decisions you might make based on those observations.

The word *observe* brings to mind the action of looking, seeing, not participating but viewing the action as an outsider. In any context, **observing** is just the first step in determining action. The first stage, taking in information, occurs simultaneously with evaluation and selection of a course of action. The clock is observed, usually not to admire the design, but to determine the time. Looking inside a refrigerator may indicate a trip to the store is needed or that the source of a foul odor should be investigated. The traffic light is a lovely shade of green, but its meaning is more important. That observation produces action: Go!

Everything we see is not just observed but immediately interpreted for meaning. A decision is made either to do nothing or to act. The observation may be so insignificant that it is sensed but not acted upon. Later it might prove to be important, like that traffic light that was green but the car in the cross

Figure I–1 Why observe?

Figure I–2 Common activities yield knowledge of the child.

Figure I–3 Observing a child's work, as well as the child as she works, gives valuable information.

street came through the intersection anyway. When filling out the accident report, those details are important.

Why Observe?

When a teacher observes a child, information is collected and could be measured against a whole body of knowledge about child development in general and that child in particular (Figure I–1). Information is then used to make decisions about the next actions. Someone has estimated that a teacher makes thousands of decisions in a day. And each decision is based on observations evaluated for meaning and most appropriate responses. This *observe-decide-act* sequence is repeated over and over again throughout the day.

Let's observe a child painting at the easel and see what we can see in Figure I–2.

SAFETY. The most important reason for watching children is to keep them safe. Seeing a potentially dangerous situation and rushing to prevent an injury is the most basic example of observe-decide-act. A child waiting to paint may be observed trying to wrestle the brush away from the painter. With angry looks and harsh words, she is trying to gain control of the painting area. The teacher rushes over and intervenes before the painter is knocked aside or a brush is poked into someone's eye.

PHYSICAL HEALTH. Recognizing the signs of sickness or disease is another reason to observe, decide, and act. This also can protect the physical health of others. The teacher may notice a few small red spots behind the painter's ear. She casually pats the child's arm and feels bumps beneath the skin. These observations, along with the knowledge that the child's brother had chicken pox two weeks ago, prompts the teacher's decision to isolate the child and call the child's family to take the child home. For chicken pox, of course, it's already too late. Everyone's been exposed! Figure I–3 shows art work that child painted upon her return to school after having chicken pox.

ASSISTANCE. Observation may indicate that help is needed. A child is observed preparing to paint at the easel. The teacher sees that the paper supply is gone. He gets more from the cupboard and shows the child how to attach the sheets with the big clips and where to hang the painting to dry.

DISCOVER INTERESTS. The adult observes the child choose a play area and talks with the child about the play. This observing, remembering, and affirming is a friendly thing to do. It also is another way of building bridges from interests to planning, from home to school, and of making the curriculum relevant. The theme of animals (in the beginning stages of drawing recognizable objects!) emerges in the painting. The observer remembers the home visit where this child showed a menagerie of pets, who might be potential classroom visitors!

LEARNING STYLES AND TEACHING STRATEGIES. Watching a child reveals personality, learning styles, and could give clues to teaching strategies. By observing the painter, learning styles are indicated that will work better for her, maybe verbal directions, or being shown, or trial and error. Reflective observation of the student's learning process leads the teacher to adapt teaching strategies to the child's styles and needs.

CURRICULUM PLANNING. Teaching is building bridges, making connections between new information and old. The teacher plans related experiences and activities. The group has enjoyed and mastered easel painting, so the teacher plans that next week he will introduce watercolors, demonstrating the technique of washing the brush between colors.

EXTEND CHILDREN'S LEARNING. Through observations, teachers can see that teachable moment, that budding interest, that blossoming skill. Providing materials, activities, and opportunities to build on that observed development will capitalize on it. From observing the painting filled with alphabet letters, the teacher decides this is a good time to bring out the alphabet magnets and invite the painter to play with them.

COMMUNICATION WITH THE CHILD. Teachers should talk with every child, and what better subject to discuss with them than the child's activities? Every child deserves the individual attention of the teacher. By discussing what the teacher observes with the child, the child can give the reason or explanation in a way that makes sense only if the teacher asks the child. That is the basis for Piaget's cognitive questioning method (Piaget & Inhelder, 1969), to delve more deeply into children's "wrong" answers. In that way, thinking processes are explored. Results or answers are not simply evaluated. Woodward (1993) calls this "negotiated evaluation." This process involves discussing observations with the child, and also the family.

The teacher says to the painter, "You worked hard on that painting. You used red, blue, and yellow, and you made straight lines and curved lines. Would you like to tell me how you did it? What did you do first?"

GUIDANCE. Prevention is always better than remedy. Redirection is better than discipline or punishment. From observations, potential problems can be averted. The painter's brush is approaching the wall. The teacher reminds the child, "Paint on paper," guiding the brush back to the paper on the easel.

MEASURE PROGRESS. Children change so quickly. Based on knowledge of child development, certain changes are expected and anticipated. Comparisons over time can measure that development. The teacher observes that the painter moved from experimentation with line and color to painting recognizable objects. She proclaims the smiling face with dots is a picture of her brother who is just getting over the chicken pox. The teacher can see her control of small muscles and the frustration when the paint does not flow in the way the painter thinks it should. The child's social world is portrayed in the pictures she paints. Many areas of development can be observed in this one activity and in changes from paintings done a few weeks ago.

ASSESSMENT. Teachers watch children to gather information. That is **assessment**, the process of documenting a child's skills and development. Assessment may take many forms but the premise here is that observation is the best method. Information is gathered to measure the child's development against accepted stages or a set of developmental norms. Assessment measures where the child is at this point and indicates what stage comes next. It alerts the observer to unusually delayed or accelerated development. The painter paints first with the right hand, then switches to the left and back again. The observer assesses the lack of "handedness" at this point in the child's development. Alphabet letters emerge from the painter's strokes as the observer watches. Ah ha!

EVALUATION. **Evaluation** is the decision-making step of assessment. Woodward (1993) uses the following definition: "Evaluation is the collection and analysis of data, from a variety of sources and perspectives, which will contribute to

- making judgments of merit and worth
- making decisions about future planning
- informing learning" (p. 2)

The observer of the painter has collected paintings over several weeks and judges that this child is in the stage when children are beginning to represent thought, not just experimenting with the materials. A sticky note as to the importance of this example may be placed on the back of the painting, noting, "She has moved from making circles and controlled straight lines to painting faces, and was smiling and singing while painting." The teacher may decide to bring out a plastic skeleton for the Science Area or read a story about sick children to give the painter ideas about anatomy. A copy of this drawing is filed in the child's Portfolio to make later comparisons.

For all of these very good reasons, teachers observe children. That informed observation, measuring what is seen against what is known, is assessment and evaluation of the child's development and behavior.

REFERRAL. Sometimes questions or even red flags arise when a teacher observes a child. Certain behaviors, actions, skills, or lack of them, will send an alert calling for a closer look at a developmental area.

From the child's paintings, the teacher observes some alarming messages. The teacher may ask a probing question, such as, "Would you like to tell me about your painting?" and the child's answers may lead only to more questions.

Further reflection and closer observation of behavior over time may warrant the discussion of a concern first with the family or other professionals within the agency, and then perhaps a suggested referral to the family. The **referral** may be for further evaluation in a specific area, such as hearing, speech, physical, or cognitive development. Family involvement and decision making in the referral process are the pivotal factors. Families are recognized and deferred to as the authority on the child.

There may be situations where it is necessary to report suspicions of neglect or abuse. Knowledge, careful judgment, empathy, and consideration are important skills for the teacher in all of these circumstances, both referrals and reporting.

COMMUNICATION WITH THE FAMILY. Talking with the **family** about the child's daily activities communicates the following to them:

- Their child is under a watchful eye.
- This teacher observes and relates important development in their child's actions, rather than giving the family a test score they might not understand how to evaluate.
- The family is included in the world that the teacher and their child share.

Unfortunately, many children and families have come to expect to receive only bad reports, phone calls, and notes from school, bringing a sense of dread. Too often, the only communications they receive about their child relate misbehaviors, failure to perform to expectations, or commands to the child or family to take remedial action. In contrast, discussing the observations from the day's observed activities or documentation from the Portfolio with the child's family gives positive, substantive information about the child's progress, compared only to her previous work, not anyone else's. Observation gives descriptive accounts of the child's behavior and skills from the point of view of achievement rather than deficit, what she can or has done rather than cannot or will not. Observations are shared with families in formal and informal ways.

The paintings in the child's Portfolio previously were scribbles, then become pages filled with lines and deliberate designs. The teacher and child show her family the collection in the Portfolio. The family realizes the teacher *knows and observes* their child's work from a different point of view.

SELF-REFLECTION OF TEACHING METHODS. Observing is not just looking at a child but thinking about our influence on the child and the child's effect on us. The teacher notices that no one is painting anymore and wonders what the cause could be. By observing and recording, questions can be answered and the teacher's own effectiveness can be measured. The interest a child has in the planned activities will indicate to the teacher if the activities are appropriate. Activities that are not challenging or are too difficult will be avoided or abandoned by the child. By closely observing what keeps a child involved, the observer can learn what skills the child is working on and then modify activities to meet those needs.

This type of observation is active research, constantly accumulating data to analyze for its meaning. Yetta Goodman (1989) says "kid watching" involves "teachers who interact with students and who monitor class activities in order to understand more about teaching and learning, mostly learning."

ACCOUNTABILITY. Is the teacher, curriculum, or school doing what it says it will do? Proof is needed to show that children are learning and meeting the standards and expected outcomes. "This child's painting shows increases in small muscle control, attention span, interest in alphabet, and is increasingly detailed." The teacher's notes on the back of the painting relate the significance of this work in the light of developmental progress. It shows the child is learning. Documentation of all types can

- provide evidence of children's learning in all domains.
- provide insight into learning experiences.
- provide a framework for recording each child's interests and developmental progress.
- emphasize learning as an interactive process.
- show advantages of concrete activities and materials as opposed to group testing situations.
- enable teachers to assess knowledge and abilities in order to increase the challenge to match the child's level. (Helm, Beneke, & Steinheimer, 1997)

Why Write It Down?

EXERCISE Using a separate sheet of paper, list the kinds of writing you do in a day. Jot down the reason for each.

"I'll remember this and write it down later." Everyone has said this and then did not write it down. It is lost with all the other details of life that intercede and blur the image, blotting out specifics and erasing the exact words. **Recording** is used here to refer to a written account or notation of what has been observed. What are the reasons for writing down what has been seen? See Figure I–4.

Figure I–4 Why write?

Figure I–5 Write to remember.

TO REMEMBER. The grocery list (Figure I–5), even if it is left home on the refrigerator door, sticks in the memory longer because it was written down. Many students copy their notes over or condense them as a study technique. There is a connection between writing and memory. The words that are written form a visual and kinetic or physical connection in the brain, assisting memory and recall even when the visual cues are not present.

TO COMPARE. A child's height is measured with a line on the wall, and it is surprising a few months later how much she has grown without anyone realizing it. If that mark had not been made, the change would not have been noticed. Children are expected to change, so a mark of comparison is needed. Relying on the memory of the child one, three, or six months ago is inaccurate and unreliable. By writing observations down, teachers have tangible comparison points. Portfolios, collections of the child's work and written observations, are becoming an accepted method of documenting a child's progress. Written observations that are thorough, objective, regular, and done during daily routines and child-initiated play are accurate measures of the child's progress.

TO AMPLIFY LATER. Sometimes there is no time to write the whole incident, so a few strategic notes written and dated at the time can be just enough to jog the memory for a longer, more complete narrative written later.

The teacher shows a new song chart and has just said, "Look up here, all eyes on the chart." Andrew asks, "What's sixteen plus sixteen?" A puzzled look comes over the teacher's face, followed immediately by one of irritation for the interruption. Andrew repeats his question louder. "Thirty-two, now let's look at this new song chart." Andrew replies, "Oh, you want all thirty-two eyes looking at the chart." This tells us about Andrew's thinking, his beginning understanding of math concepts, and causes the teacher to vow to listen more closely to children's questions. This is a wonderful incident to relay to Andrew's family to demonstrate his thinking and his humor. The teacher just had time to write "eyes, 16, 32" with the ever-present pad and pen. That was enough to enable the teacher to fully write about the incident later.

TO CATCH AND PRESERVE DETAILS. Details are quickly forgotten. Insurance companies want auto accident reports written at the scene because of the frailty of human memory. Fine details that seem so clear or seem so unimportant now can best be preserved by writing them down. These details can give clues to trends or correlations that are not seen at the time. Upon closer examination and comparison later, they gain significance. For example, keeping some data on which areas of the classroom the child spends their free time in and how long they stay there gives much information about the child. Without some method of tracking, there is no way to recall details like this that can yield important information.

TO SERVE AS A LITERACY ROLE MODEL. Children need to see adults writing. Literacy is an important concept to teach young children. The importance of the written word is emphasized when children see its usefulness and practical application by their role models, the adults in their lives. When an adult writes something down, a child often asks, "What are you doing?" A reply such as, "I'm writing this down so I won't forget" is laying literacy foundations for the child (Figure I–6). It shows that writing is a way to help memory, that what is written is constant, and it stirs the child's desire to want to write himself. Accessible writing materials encourage him to do just that (Figure I–7).

TO DOCUMENT. Reliable research demands hard data. It is necessary to preserve in writing—to **document**—what has been observed to substantiate it. Recording methods that include facts rather than inferences along with date and time of the recording are essential to meaningful documentation. The details must be preserved to see progress, trends, and correlations.

It is especially critical if a child discloses an incident of abuse. The reports must be accurate and show that the child was not led or influenced in order for the disclosure to be supportable evidence. One would like never to deal with this, but for the

Figure I–6 Busy teachers jot short notes to amplify later.

Dramatic Play Area—paper and pencil next to the play phone, sheets cut for grocery lists attached to a pad on the play refrigerator, calendars on which children can write important events to remember

Block Area—paper, markers, tape for signs on buildings

Large Motor—paper, markers, tape for signs signifying what the climber is today (a rocket ship, a house on fire, Jenny's house)

Sand/Water—paper and pencil nearby to write down a mark at what sinks or floats, draw pictures of what has been found hidden in the sand; paper to list who is waiting for a turn

Cubbies—paper and pencil to list what children say they want to do outside today, to decide which toys to load in the wagon

Group Area—chart paper, markers to take surveys of favorite things, lists of things to remember contributed by the group, safety rules

Figure I–7 A Literacy-Rich Environment.

protection of the child it is important not to jeopardize the testimony by failure to document or inaccurate records. You will read more about this in Chapter 12.

Why Use Different Methods?

EXERCISE How many ways can you cook a chicken? Make a list. Here's a start:

- fry
- broil
- stew
- microwave

Why are there so many ways to cook a chicken? Because there are different end results from each method. The cook may be looking for a certain consistency, lowering calories, tenderizing, or working within a short period of time. Similarly, there are many different methods of recording observations because the end result from each method is different. Yes, they are all based on observing the child and measuring the observation against standards in order to make decisions about immediate and future actions, but they differ in technique, content, and approach. *Week by Week* presents many different methods, along with a review of a developmental area, but the method is not limited to recording only that particular area. In the cooking example above, once the technique of frying or stewing or microwaving is mastered, it can be applied to other foods and modified for a variety of desired results. Just like cooking, once the recording technique is mastered, it can be applied to other developmental areas and modified to fit the recorder's style and selected outcome. The recording methods can be classified using the web design (Figure I–8).

Each method is a technique to focus on a behavior, skill, or action of an individual child or the whole group. The **narrative** recordings, such as Anecdotal Recordings, Running Records, and Interviews, tell a story. They bring the reader along by providing the actual details of actions, words, and results. The **criterion-referenced** recordings, such as Class List Logs, Checklists, and Rating Scales, provide a predetermined skill or standard to look for and measure against. The **quantitative** recordings, such as Time Samples and Frequency Counts, provide a numerical count of individual or group actions that then can be interpreted in various ways. These methods lose most of the raw data, the actual details that narratives preserve, but are useful for certain purposes.

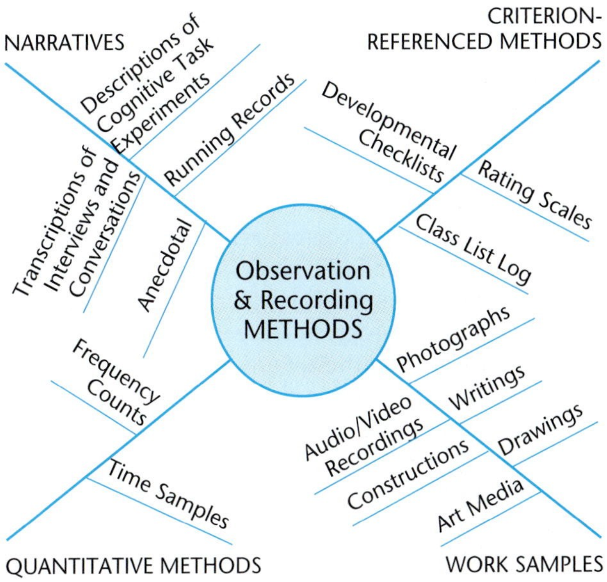

Figure I–8 Methods Web.

The **Work Samples**, such as drawings, writings, constructions, sculptures, and media-preserved work (audio or video recordings or photographs), give a visual account of the child's activities from which assessments are made. Each category and method within the category is distinctive and useful, with its own specific technique, advantages and disadvantages, and best applications. These methods will be presented, practiced, and recommended for specific purposes throughout this book.

PORTFOLIOS

The systematic gathering of information about the child is **Portfolio** assessment. Portfolios are more than a scrapbook or folder full of unrelated pieces of paper. Gronlund (2003) states, "Simply collecting samples of students' work and putting it in a file does not constitute a Portfolio. Much greater care is required in the development of a Portfolio that will be useful in instruction and assessment" (p. 159). Portfolios provide information on each child as an individual, on child development in general, and on the diversity of children. Portfolios give the opportunity for family involvement through communication centered on the child's work, and they help the family become involved in the curriculum. From building Portfolios, teachers learn to assess and plan a curriculum for each child individually, see progress over time, and reflect on teaching practices (Shores & Grace, 2005).

Danielson and Abrutyn (1997) describe three types of Portfolios. *Display* Portfolios are scrapbooks of photographs of children's activities and learning experiences in the classroom without teacher comment or showing progress over time. *Showcase* Portfolios are the best pieces of the child's work, either self- or teacher-selected and without evaluation or information about progress or affecting the curriculum. *Working* Portfolios include selected but typical Work Samples along with teacher documentation to show the child's progress, as well as the teacher's observations. It is on these Portfolios that curriculum is based and future actions planned for the child, with input from the child, the family, and other professionals if needed. *Week by Week* guides the teacher in the collection of documents for this last type, the **Working Portfolio**.

Portfolios draw from multiple information sources and are gathered in the child's natural surroundings by persons familiar with the child and the environment. They are collected over time so they clearly show the child's progress.

What Is in the Portfolio?

A Portfolio is an individual folder for each child in the class. Eventually it may hold many pieces of the child's work, teachers' observations, photos, and video or audio recordings, so it should be expandable. All Portfolios should be stored in a locked file cabinet or file box. This assures they are accessible only to authorized people, including the staff working with the children and the director. The Portfolio is available to the family upon request and to the child.

McAfee and Leong (2002) suggest that the following types of items are appropriate for Portfolios:

- Work products done on paper—samples of cutting, drawing, and any art medium; printing; practice papers; pasting; writings (initial drafts, editing, final drafts). Dictations by nonwriters.
- "Journals" for math, science, writing—children's drawings, scribbles, collages reflecting their experiences and growth.
- Records of data collection and presentation in math, science, social studies, health.
- Sketches of a child's work, made by the child or an adult (block structure, pattern blocks, sand, any 3-D work). Sketches of the plan for that work.
- Photographs of a child engaged in significant work or play.
- Photographs of exhibits and displays prepared by child or group.
- Audio tapes and video tapes.
- Printouts of work done on computer—draw/paint, math, writing programs, games.
- Participation chart—what a child did on a given day or during a given period. Include qualitative information.
- Logs of activities and results (books read to or by child; family can help).
- Time sample or count of what a child did on a given day or period.
- Interviews—audio/video/written. Elicit reports or descriptions of a process, such as how to make a favorite food, get to school, make friends, or play a game; or "favorite" activities, books, or things to do. The child can draw it and then dictate the explanation to an adult.
- Structured observation, performance assessment, or dynamic assessment results. Do one or two children a day.
- Anecdotal records or jottings grouped according to the Portfolio categories and/or affixed in chronological order. Use Post-its, gummed labels, or quarter sheets of recycled office paper (tape them on).
- Awards, certificates, citations.
- Families' comments and goals, notes from family–teacher and child–teacher conferences; drawings and dictated or written messages to families from children. (p. 99)

(From McAfee, *Assessing and Guiding Young Children's Development and Learning, 3e.* Published by Allyn and Bacon, Boston, MA. Copyright © 2002 by Pearson Education. Reprinted by permission of the publisher.)

The systematic plan to build the Portfolio will gather information from multiple sources (Figure I–9):

CHILD. The child contributes Work Samples, such as drawings, art work, samples of writing and language. Media, such as audio and video recordings and photographs, also can be included. The Portfolio is a book about the child so from a very early age, the child has a voice in the included works.

FAMILIES. Families, the true authority on the child—since they know the child better than anyone—submit information to the Portfolio on forms and written comments.

TEACHERS. Teachers who see the child regularly submit formal observations using a variety of methods to best record different kinds of data in the most objective styles. Informal observations are included

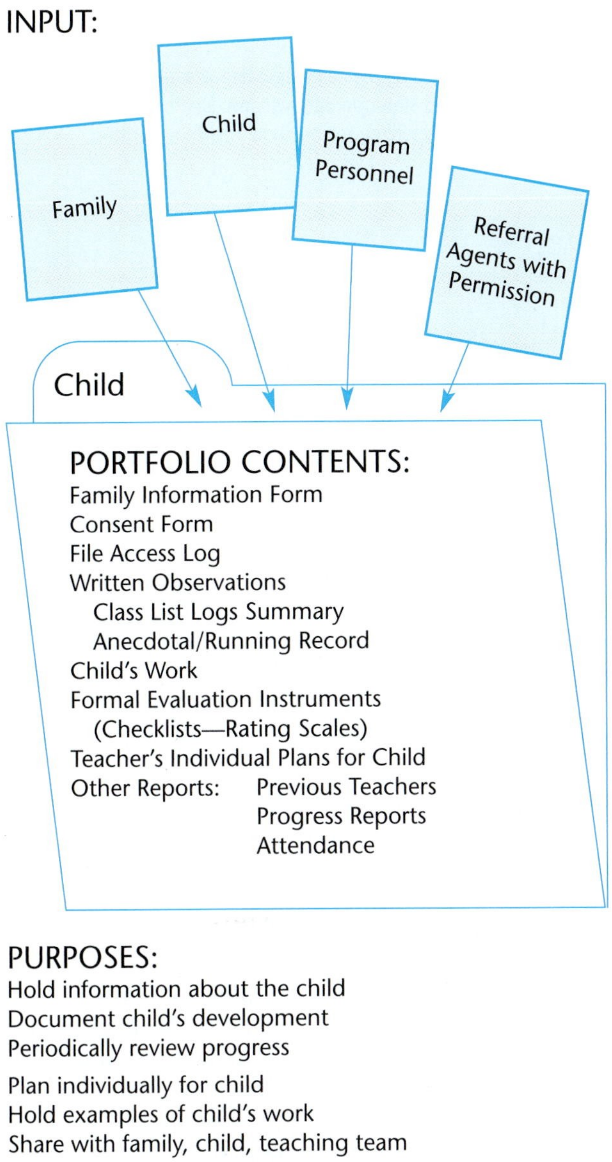

Figure I–9 Portfolios contain information from multiple sources.

as important events worthy of remembering for a variety of reasons.

STAFF. Staff in the program who have contact with the child may write a submission for the Portfolio. The cook, the bus driver, the nurse, all see the child from a different perspective in different settings and have information to contribute.

PREVIOUS TEACHERS. Previous teachers' records may be passed on in the Portfolio or remain in the Administrator's file, depending on the program or school policy.

REFERRAL AGENTS. With consent forms, the program and referral agencies can exchange information. A release form must be used before information is shared. See Figure I–10. Referral agencies may include reports or suggestions for working with the child in the Portfolio.

What Is Not in the Portfolio?

There is another file accessible to the parents or legal guardian, the teachers, and licensing authority upon request. Those files are kept in an administrative filing cabinet, separate from the child's Working Portfolio that is accumulated by week-by-week records. The contents of the administrative file include extensive medical information and any other confidential information that is not appropriate for the child's Working Portfolio. If there are any suspected, but as yet unsubstantiated, concerns about possible child abuse, those records should be kept in a separate confidential file, separate from the child's health records and Working Portfolio. Any Anecdotal Recordings that document a possible disclosure of child abuse should be placed in this confidential file. A copy of the filed Child Abuse Reporting Form and notations tracking the action should also be retained there. The teacher's Reflective Journal is the writer's private property, not to be kept with children's records (preferably kept at home).

Who Can Read the Portfolio?

The Portfolio includes documentation of all developmental areas for helping, measuring, and reporting the child's progress. Documentation is arranged chronologically and by developmental areas, logged in on an Overview Sheet so that contents are noted. Because of the completeness and intimacy of a Portfolio, its contents must be protected from unauthorized viewers. The National Association for the Education of Young Children's *Code of Ethical Conduct* (NAEYC, 2005) under the section on Ethical Responsibilities to Families reads:

> P-2.7—We shall inform families about the nature and purpose of the program's child assessments and how data about their child will be used.
>
> P-2.8—We shall treat child assessment information confidentially and share this information only when there is a legitimate need for it.

Custodial parents or legal guardians have a right to see and control school records under the Family Educational Rights and Privacy Act (Buckley Amendment) passed by Congress in 1974. In the basic belief that early childhood programs are in partnership with families, the records are subject to

INFORMATION RELEASE FORM

I understand the confidentiality of any personally identifiable information concerning my child shall be maintained in accordance with the Family Education Rights and Privacy Act (P.L.93-380), federal and state regulations, and used only for the educational benefit of my child. Personally identifiable information about my child will be released only with my written consent. With this information, I hereby grant the

____

(Name of program, agency, or person)

permission to release the following types of information:

Medical information ____________________
Assessment reports ____________________
Child histories ____________________
Progress reports ____________________
Clinical reports ____________________
(Other) ____________________

to: ____

(Name of agency or person to whom information is to be sent)

regarding ____________________ ____________ ______

Child's Name Birthdate Gender

____

Signature of Parent or Guardian

____

Relationship of Representative

____

Date

Figure I–10 Information Release Form. (From *Health, Safety, and Nutrition for the Young Child,* 6th edition by MAROTZ/CROSS/RUSH. 2005. Reprinted with permission of Delmar Learning, a division of Thomson Learning: www.thomsonrights.com, Fax 800 730-2215.)

their inspection. The systematic plan of gathering information has nothing to hide, for it seeks to provide objective, descriptive documentation.

As a part of the enrollment process or upon the necessity to make a referral, the family should complete an Information Release Form (see Figure I–10). Permission must be obtained before releasing certain information to outside agencies. The family has the right to know and give permission. This form is kept on file with the child's medical history and records in the administrative office.

Occasionally people who have a need or a right to know may see the contents of the Portfolio. Those people may include a program evaluator who is gathering developmental level data, not on individual children but on an aggregate of all the children; or an accreditation validator looking at how the program records developmental information or seeking proof of a systematic authentic assessment plan. An ethical way to inform the families and the program of who has seen the contents of the file is to include a **file access log** (Figure I–11) in each file. Each person who views the file, other than the teacher(s), signs the log, providing the date, identity, agency represented, and reason for looking at the file.

Program handbooks should inform families that their child's Portfolio is open to them any time. At the end of the year, the family usually makes the determination of whether it will go to the next teacher, next center, on to the public school, or taken home. The school will obtain written permission before releasing any Portfolio document to others. The exceptions are school officials with a legitimate educational interest and officials for use in audit or accreditation associations (with names deleted). In emergencies, the information is used to protect the health of the individual (Berger, 2000).

Why Use Portfolio Assessment Rather than Testing?

Chapter 8 will discuss standardized testing and its use and misuse; this book will guide you in using Portfolios as an authentic, reliable way to assess children's development. Much has been written to

The record of ______________________ was reviewed by the following:
(child's name)

DATE	NAME/TITLE	AGENCY	REASON	SIGNATURE

Figure I–11 File Access Log.

promote Portfolio assessments (Gronlund, 2001; Hanson & Gilkerson, 1999; Martin, 2004; Neisworth & Bagnato, 2004; NAEYC,2003; Pack & Knight, 2000; Wiener & Cohen, 2002). A review of the benefits of Portfolio assessment include its ongoing purposeful assessment done during authentic activities in a naturalistic setting without diverting children from natural learning processes.

Portfolios can be a valid, reliable replacement or augmentation for standardized testing. Organizations like the NAEYC and National Association of Early Childhood Specialists in State Departments of Education (NAECS/SDE) take this position on assessment: "To assess young children's strengths, progress and needs, use assessment methods that are developmentally appropriate, culturally and linguistically responsive, tied to children's daily activities, supported by professional development, inclusive of families and connected to specific, beneficial purposes" (NAEYC, 2003, p. 2). They call for more authentic assessment methods that provide documentation gathered from multiple sources over a period of time in the child's natural environment (Figure I–12).

Here are eight principles for guiding the decision on how to assess children (Neisworth & Bognato, 2004, pp. 204–208):

- *Utility*—Can the assessment be used to guide the individualized curriculum?
- *Acceptability*—Is the assessment socially and culturally relevant?
- *Authenticity*—Does it yield information about the child's typical behavior in natural settings?

Figure I–12 Close observation of routine events helps the teacher evaluate and make decisions.

- *Equity*—Does the assessment collect and interpret findings fairly?
- *Sensitivity*—Does the assessment provide for the measurement of a full range of abilities?
- *Convergence*—Does the assessment look at all the domains of development?
- *Collaboration*—Does the assessment gather information from several sources with the family as the authority on the child?
- *Congruence*—Does the assessment make allowances for differing abilities, evidence based?

The *Week by Week* systematic plan for Portfolio building will enable the user to gather data to meet the need of authentic assessment as outlined in the eight principles above in a manageable way. It meets the guidelines for appropriate assessment for planning instruction and communicating with families, identifying children with special needs, and for program evaluation and accountability. (See the Bind-in-Book CD for the full NAEYC position statement.)

Boehm and Weinberg (1996) remind readers of the valuable work of many social scientists, sociologists, and anthropologists who have gathered observational field data. An ecological view is studying in naturalistic settings. An early childhood setting is not a controlled laboratory but an environment that is just a part of the child's world that centers around the family and the community.

WEEK BY WEEK PLAN

EXERCISE How long do these big projects take? What steps lead to completion of the project?

- Conception to birth:
- Earn a college degree:
- Lose twenty-five pounds:
- Crochet a bedspread:

Some of those projects take months, some take years, some take a lifetime. Each one begins with a plan with small steps along the way, leading to the completion of the project. None can happen overnight. Some may even seem impossible, but when broken down into manageable steps, planned and worked on over a period of time, they can be accomplished. Eventually the desired goal will be reached.

Teachers of young children *know* they should be keeping written records on each child's behavior for many good reasons, but there is one seemingly insurmountable obstacle: *time.* This book begins with the premise that writing down observations of children's activities is the preferred method of assessing and documenting children's development.

"But I don't have time!" Every busy adult working with children has said it. The teacher's priority is to applaud the climb to the top of the ladder, redirect that arm ready to throw a block, or give a thoughtful response to a family member as she hurriedly says on her way out, "He's running a little fever and had a touch of diarrhea this morning, but he says he feels fine." The role of the teacher is to provide physical and psychological safety and intellectual challenge to each child. The teacher also strives to maximize the teachable moment and expand on the child's interests and conversations.

Those two responsibilities, accurate record keeping and responsiveness to the needs of each child, seem incompatible. Time and attention for record keeping is minimal. Teachers who know they should be making written records are caught in a bind. They recognize the importance of keeping accurate records on which to base evaluations or plan individualized curricula. The difficulty, and for some the impossibility, is doing this while interacting with the children.

Major accomplishments require time and planning. A meaningful Portfolio of a child's development and work is not gathered in a few days. Authentic assessment is achieved when each child's development is observed and documented objectively and periodically. The results are strategies to facilitate the child's progress to the next developmental level by individualizing the curriculum. When the teacher knows that one or more children in the class have reached a certain level of development, plans can be specified for them to advance. There is a pattern of observe, assess, plan, implement, evaluate, and record. This is repeated in each developmental area for each child, but only when an authentic performance-based assessment system is in place that allows this to happen efficiently.

In order to accomplish this desirable goal, the task must be broken down into manageable segments, planned, and executed in a systematic manner. Doris Bergen (2004) says, "Developing a systematic way of evaluating every child's performance and carefully recording assessment results is a crucial component of authentic assessment" (p. 102). Neuman and Roskos (1993) point out: "Programs need to *build in* the means and opportunities for all caregivers to watch and record what young children do in some systematic way over time" (p. 22). The teacher can place materials for recording observations in strategic places around the room, thus preplanning and organizing for successful recording of observations. Skills, tools, materials, help, and dedication to the plan are needed to systematically build a Portfolio demonstrating a child's development.

I was teaching a college course in observation techniques but struggling to apply the methods in my own classroom. There were mounds of checklists—one for each child—index cards, and notepads all over the room. When I tried to write a daily journal or mark a checklist, I could not remember children like Johnny who floated all over the room, never doing anything "noteworthy." This plagued me until

TOPICS IN OBSERVATION

The Ecological View of the Child

Urie Bronfenbrenner (1979) reminds us that each human exists in the context of society, illustrated by concentric circles of influence that make that person's life unique from all others. We use this same principle in looking at one aspect of a child's behavior, such as when a teacher observes a small segment of a child's behavior—how the child holds the scissors to cut (Figure I–13). This is reflected against what the teacher knows about stages of normal small muscle development. The teacher recognizes the family influences on the child, both biologically and socially. How are her other small muscle skills and large muscle skills? Has she been allowed to use scissors at home? The family's situation in the community is appraised, along with the political and economic influences. Does this family value independence in a child, or is it so stressed over not having enough food that providing opportunities to write and draw are not a priority? Did this family just emigrate to this country after months of nomadic life? National and world conditions, including historical events, have influenced the life of this family and the development of the child, ultimately bringing the child to this point in time.

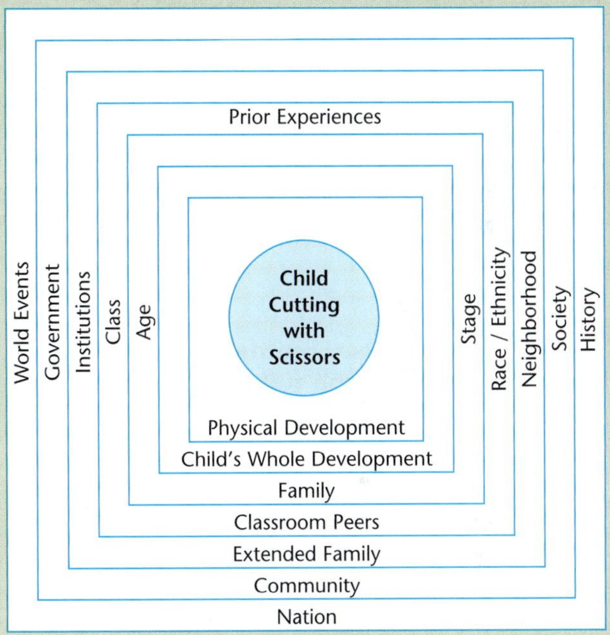

Figure I–13 The Ecological View of the Child from the Teacher's Viewpoint.

The **ecological view** of the child takes a few steps backward to visualize a broader view than just cutting with scissors. This ecological view of development gives the observer multiple perspectives on the child, looking at the big picture.

Scientists do not jump to conclusions based on one view through the microscope. The same is true when observing a child's behavior or skill, frozen in time on a particular day. Other developmental areas overlap to influence that observation. What is observed must be considered in context of the whole child, this child in particular, and added to the body of knowledge about children, families, and the society around them.

I realized *I had to have a plan.* I went looking for one but had no success. After calculating the weeks in the school year, what I wanted to know, and the appropriate method to record it, I had a systematic plan. That plan, refined through many years of teaching and research, is presented in this book.

In *Week by Week,* when the word *teacher* is used, it refers to the recorder who is documenting the child's behavior. It may be the early childhood student in a practicum experience, teacher in a child care setting, or teacher in a classroom setting. The recorder may have the minimum required hours of in-service training, a CDA (Child Development Associate), associate degree to advanced degrees, or teacher certification. Whatever the qualifications on paper, the children call this person "teacher" because she is in the teacher role, and she will be called by that worthy name in this text.

NOW YOU CAN GET STARTED

Every chapter has two main parts plus the Bind-in-Book CD. In each of the next 14 chapters, a recording method is presented and practiced.

Throughout the book are Exercises, interactive sections inviting the reader to answer a question or formulate a list. Readers should write their "answers" in pencil to be erased for privacy or on a separate sheet of paper. These exercises are designed to introduce a concept that is applied in the following portion of the text. These are called exercises because they serve to strengthen the reader's understanding.

Using the . . .

EXERCISE A house builder uses many tools. Next to each of the following, write its purpose:

- Hammer:
- Screwdriver:
- Saw:
- Tape measurer:
- Sandpaper:

Just as a builder has many tools, each with a distinctive purpose, so should the teacher have many recording tools and observation methods to use for specific purposes. There are several different kinds for different occasions or situations. Some are better than others at capturing certain kinds of behaviors, skills, and activities. If it were physical development we were observing and recording, then a developmental checklist would be more efficient than a narrative describing every action of the child's movements. Speech and language are best captured on an audio recording but can also be recorded efficiently on a checklist, but then we lose the exact words, inflections, and context of the situation. Each chapter will present a method or technique along with a description and examples of that method linked to one of the developmental areas in which it can be used. That is not the *only* method for that development area, nor is that method only to be used in that developmental area.

ADVANTAGES AND DISADVANTAGES. A hammer is not adequate to turn a screw; likewise, a screwdriver does not efficiently drive in a nail (although some of us have attempted to do so). We present an observation in each chapter, described and illustrated with examples. Some are methods that will be familiar, some will be new. Some will be simple to grasp and use, while others will take more practice. Some are used often, whereas others are used periodically or only in special circumstances.

PITFALLS TO AVOID. With every one of the builder's tools, incorrect use may result in a dangerous situation or an outcome that is less than desirable. Using a stiff paintbrush leaves unwanted streaks in the paint or varnish, for example. The description of the observation method will also include some cautions about the method or its use. These are not necessarily disadvantages, but they are presented to raise awareness of misuse or common mistakes and are included to maximize the usefulness of the method.

USING TECHNOLOGY. New products and electronic devices can be used to more efficiently manage documenting children's development. This section in each chapter will suggest some products or applications that could be used to collect, organize, store, and report the documentation. Some are inexpensive and handy, while others may require financial investment and a change in practice. Teachers are change agents, seeking to facilitate change in others, so we, of all people, should be open to change ourselves.

HOW TO FIND THE TIME. In this section there will be some suggestions for how to find the few minutes that it takes to accomplish the documenting of children's behavior while managing the classroom at the same time. I repeat, it can be done!

Time? When is there time to write? A developmentally appropriate classroom for young children dedicates blocks of time to children's choice of activities. These are self-initiated, with materials and equipment available on shelves the children can reach themselves. Whole group activities are limited to very short periods, if at all. That leaves the teacher with time, once the environment is prepared, to observe, make notes, and even closely follow and document a child's play. If there is no time for this, the teacher should look at the environment, the schedule, the ratio of children to adults, the curriculum, and the teaching practices. Program and school administrators who support time given to observation value it with resources that empower the teacher. Perhaps there is work to be done in those areas before observation techniques can be implemented.

If you are a student using the recording method to complete an assignment, you have a luxury. Time. You can concentrate on children's movements and listen and write down their exact words without interruption. Now imagine yourself as the teacher trying to capture the same information using the same method while supervising the whole room for safety, reading a book, wiping a nose, washing your hands, and keeping track of the time to transition to the next part of the daily routine. It is tough, but it can be done. However, it takes time-management skills, flexibility, concentration, classroom organization, and cooperation from the other adults in the classroom.

REVIEW BOX. At the end of each recording method section is a short definition of the method and other areas of development or behavior on which it can be used now that you have a working knowledge of the method's procedure, advantages, and disadvantages.

At the end of each child development section, other recording methods are suggested for documenting the progress in that area. This demonstrates that the methods and areas of development are linked in *Week by Week* and are not exclusive of each other. Using some kind of reliable, regular documentation system is the goal.

Looking at . . .

The other half of each chapter is a discussion of one area of child development. That is what you are recording, each child's development, so you need to know what to look for. When the radiologist shows the X-ray of a broken bone to the parents of the crying child, they look at it but may not *see it as she does.* Without her specialized knowledge, they look at the same visual image but understand it at a different level. The teacher needs the specialized knowledge base of child development in order to understand the recorded events (Figure I–14).

Without it, behavior is observed, seen, but not recognized for its importance. For that reason, each chapter includes an overview of a developmental area discussing influences, milestones, terminology, and key theories. There is an emphasis on the child's observable skills and behaviors that demonstrate progress.

STANDARDS. Almost every profession has established standards for itself and its constituents to describe the

Figure I–14 Observation is based on a knowledge of child development.

guiding principles and practices: the Association for Childhood Education International (ACEI), the National Association for the Education of Young Children (NAEYC), National Association for Family Child Care (NAFCC), Division for Early Childhood—Special Education (DEC), along with many others with standards for particular segments such as teacher preparation, curriculum areas, and federal, state and local standards. The United States Department of Health and Human Services has developed Head Start Program Standards as well as Child Outcomes Standards. Included in *Week by Week* are selected examples of relevant standards that apply to the chapter topics (See Figure I–15). As we approach professional preparation in the area of observation and assessment of children's development, we are guided by the National Association for the Education of Young Children's *Preparing Early Childhood Professionals: Standards for Initial Licensure, Advanced, and Associate Degree Programs* (Hyson, 2003). Section three of these standards is all about observing, documenting, and assessing: Well-prepared early childhood professionals

- understand the purposes of assessment.
- use effective assessment strategies.
- use assessment responsibly, to positive influence children's development and learning.

Week by Week seeks to assist professionals in meeting these standards. Standards guiding early childhood program administration, teacher preparation, and curriculum areas such as physical, social, emotional, language, literacy, and creativity will be introduced in each chapter. These standards are often available on the Internet and in publications from the organizations that will be referenced in the Resource Area of each chapter. (The Bind-in-Book CD will also have links to them.)

Selected Examples of STANDARDS/ACCREDITATION CRITERIA featured in each chapter

Chapter	NAEYC Early Childhood Program Standards and Accreditation Criteria	Child Development Associate—Council for Early Childhood Professional Recognition	Head Start Program Performance Standards	Head Start Child Outcomes	Division of Early Childhood Recommended Practices	National Association of Family Child Care Accreditation	NAEYC Professional Early Childhood Preparation Standards	Content Associations and Others
Intro							Section 3 Observation and Documentation	NAEYC Code of Ethical Conduct
1		Functional Area: Physical						American Academy of Pediatrics, Caring for our Children 2.004
2					Self-Assessment: Child-Focused Interventions			American Academy of Pediatrics, Caring for our Children 4.024
3								American Academy of Pediatrics, Caring for our Children 2.009; National Associations of Sports and Physical Education
4								National Council for Social Studies, Association of Childhood International
5			1304.24 Work with families for emotional health			1.21 Understanding Feelings		
6				Language: Speak & Comm Standard Area 1				Teachers of English as a Second Language TESOL #1 Communication for social and learning

7	2B03 Emotional Development				Practice 2 Environment design for physical & emotional health			
8							4.b Teachers' approaches	National Council of Teachers of Mathematics Counting
9				Domain 2 Literacy—phonological awareness				International Reading Association 4.3 Model reading
10		Functional Area 7: Creative		Creative Arts Area 5				
11					Technology applications			McREL Compendium of Standards and Benchmarks—Theater
12	Code of Ethics P1:8-11							
13			Management 1304.51 Program Assessment			5.14 Business and Professional Practices		
14		Functional Area 11 Relationships with families						NAEYC Code of Ethical Conduct—Sharing information with families

Figure I–15 Standards Chart.

It Happened to Me

Vignettes of my classroom experiences are scattered throughout the book. These anecdotes illustrate points about child development from children I have known and mistakes I have made that taught me what not to do. Some are observations my college students have written. Others are humorous stories related to me. All are stories, incredible yet true. There are millions that *got away* because I never wrote them down! Many of these are remembered because after reflection on the real meaning of the incident, they taught me a lesson. Why is it that we often learn best from our mistakes? Many events became more important than I thought they were at the time. I hope you will begin to collect your own stories that have taught you lessons about teaching and life.

Do you have an IT HAPPENED TO ME story? I'm gathering them and would love to read yours and possibly use it in future editions. Please send it to me at WeekbyWeek@thomsonlearning.com

WEEK BY WEEK PLANS. In the Preface, and earlier in this chapter, I explained the dual purpose for this book. It is primarily a textbook to introduce early childhood students to the importance of documenting children's development and building individual child Portfolios for authentic assessment and curriculum planning, all within the context of child development milestones. In the Bind-in-Book CD is a student assignment to complete during that week of field experience. Alternatively, several chapter assignments could be combined and completed in three or four lengthy visits over a semester.

FOR THE STUDENT. You will practice this recording method by following the assignment in the Bind-in-Book CD. You or your instructor may need to modify this depending on your field placement situation.

FOR THE PRACTITIONER. To achieve the goal of gathering a fairly equal amount of documentation on each child, use various methods and revisit developmental areas three times over a school year. An organizational system can be used to ensure that you are gathering an approximately equal distribution of Portfolio documentation on all children.

The monumental task of documenting every child in the class will become a series of small weekly plans, using the methods learned in each chapter to observe the developmental area that has been reviewed. *Week by Week* is a systematic plan to gather documentation on each child, in every developmental area, over a period of time, using a variety of recording methods. Some methods record small specific bits of information on all the children in the class. Other methods focus on one child, gathering detailed information. The Week by Week Plan usually gathers both kinds of information each week, rotating developmental areas and individual children. The children are arbitrarily divided evenly into four observation groups (A, B, C, D) so that selection of children for individual focus is by predesigned plan (Figure I–16). This gives every child a fair representation rather than depending on attention-getting behavior as the documentation cue, resulting in large folders on some children and thin ones on others.

You will notice that new methods are introduced each week and preceding ones are used again, perhaps in a different developmental area and on a different group of children. This shows the versatility

@ it happened to me

Why Doesn't Johnny Paint?

Early in my preschool teaching career, a mother asked me after class, "Why doesn't my Johnny ever paint? He never has any paintings to bring home." I thought, "Of course he paints! Everyone paints at the easel. There are always children on both sides for more than an hour every day. We use gallons of paint and reams of paper every year. Of course, he paints!" I started watching Johnny closely. Sure enough, he never chose easel painting. Even more revealing from my closer observation was how little I knew about what Johnny ever did. He was one of those children who did not draw attention to himself by negative behavior. He played and followed the rules of the classroom. At the end of the day, I had no idea what Johnny, and many others like him, had done. This is why we need to plan observations to include all children, not just those who demand our attention.

Do you recall an incident about a child or yourself regarding record keeping, assessment, referrals, your attempts at systematically gathering child data, or slip ups in confidentiality? Send it to me at WeekbyWeek@thomsonlearning.com

WEEK	METHOD	AREA	ON WHOM
1	Class List Log	Separation and Adjustment	All
	Work Samples	Art	All
	Reflective Journal		Self
2	Anecdotal Record	Self-Care	Group A
	Class List Log	Self-Care	All
	Reflective Journal		Self
3	Checklist	Physical Development	All
	Anecdotal Record	Physical Development	Group B
	Reflective Journal		Self
4	Running Record	Social Development	Group C
	Class List Log	Social Play Stage	All
	Reflective Journal		Self
5	Frequency Count	Emotional Development	All
	Anecdotal Record	Emotional Development	Group D
	Reflective Journal		Self
6	Interview and Checklist	Speech and Language	Group A
	Class List Log	Speech and Language	All
	Reflective Journal		Self
7	Time Sample	Attention Span	All
	Interview and Checklist	Speech and Language	Group B
	Reflective Journal		Self
8	Developmental Checklist	Cognitive	Choice
	Checklist	Math and Science	All
	Interview and Checklist	Speech Language	Group C
	Reflective Journal		Self

(continued)

Figure I–16 Week by Week Plan.

of various methods while assuring that all children are recorded equally and in all developmental areas. The Bind-in-Book CD includes an extended chart so that the teacher can continue to plan past the first 14 weeks, following them to build a meaningful progressive Portfolio on which to base curriculum decisions and to chart achievement.

WHAT TO DO WITH IT. This phrase will become familiar to the reader. At the end of each chapter presenting a recording method, a filing place is suggested along with a Portfolio Overview Sheet (Figure I–17) on which to note its presence, similar to a table of contents. These recordings are the teacher's contributions to the Portfolio being built on each child. The child, the family, and other program personnel also may contribute meaningful data to the Portfolio. Again, the goal is not just a collection of papers but a working, growing body of knowledge about the child for the purposes of

- documenting progress
- documenting typical and atypical behavior for intervention
- planning curriculum and classroom environment changes

WEEK	METHOD	AREA	ON WHOM
9	Rating Scale	Literacy	All
	Interview and Checklist	Speech and Language	Group D
	Reflective Journal		Self
10	Work Samples	Creative	All
	Anecdotal Record	Creative Process	Group A
	Progress Reports*		Group A
	Reflective Journal		Self
11	Media	Dramatic Play and Blocks	All
	Running Record	Dramatic Play	Group B
	Progress Reports*		Group B
	Reflective Journal		Self
12	Class List Log	Self-Esteem	All
	Anecdotal Record	Self-Identity	Group C
	Progress Reports*		Group C
	Reflective Journal		Self
13	Setting Observation	Environment	Visit
	Class List Log	Group Interactions	All
	Anecdotal Record	Group Interactions	Group D
	Progress Reports*		Group D
	Reflective Journal		Self
14	Class List Log	Interactions with Adults	All
	Checklist	Physical Development	All
	Progress Reports		Group D
	Reflective Journal		Self
	*See Week 14, Assignment C		

Figure I–16 (Continued).

Much has been written in the last 10 years concerning Portfolio building. The lack of a systematic plan for gathering that information, using a variety of methods, has led to this book. The purpose of the methods, rationale, instruction, and child development is to come to *know the whole child.* By knowing, then reflecting on this knowing, the teacher can truly plan and assess learning and progress.

SHARING WITH THE CHILD AND THE FAMILY. At the end of the day or session, what the teacher observes can be related to the child. What a wonderful send-off when the teacher says, "You painted a long time at the easel today" or "Today was a good day of sharing toys for you." The teacher shows by specific *positive* reference to the child's action that what they did today was noticed and important. This is not the time for reminders of misdeeds or warnings about tomorrow. This is also an opportune time to share that same kind of positive information with the family member picking the child up. If the routine does not provide that face-to-face contact, a note (even in the form of a quick e-mail, perhaps with a digital photo attached) or a phone call (even to an answering

PORTFOLIO OVERVIEW SHEET

NAME ______________________________ BIRTH DATE ______________

SEPARATIONS AND ADJUSTMENT

Documentation Type	Filed in: Child's Portfolio / Class File / Other	Observer/ Writer	Date

SELF-CARE

Documentation Type	Filed in: Child's Portfolio / Class File / Other	Observer/ Writer	Date

PHYSICAL DEVELOPMENT

Documentation Type	Filed in: Child's Portfolio / Class File / Other	Observer/ Writer	Date

SOCIAL DEVELOPMENT

Documentation Type	Filed in: Child's Portfolio / Class File / Other	Observer/ Writer	Date

EMOTIONAL DEVELOPMENT

Documentation Type	Filed in: Child's Portfolio / Class File / Other	Observer/ Writer	Date

SPEECH AND LANGUAGE

Documentation Type	Filed in: Child's Portfolio / Class File / Other	Observer/ Writer	Date

MEMORY AND ATTENTION SPAN

Documentation Type	Filed in: Child's Portfolio / Class File / Other	Observer/ Writer	Date

COGNITIVE DEVELOPMENT

Documentation Type	Filed in: Child's Portfolio / Class File / Other	Observer/ Writer	Date

LITERACY DEVELOPMENT

Documentation Type	Filed in: Child's Portfolio / Class File / Other	Observer/ Writer	Date

CREATIVITY— ART AND BLOCKS

Documentation Type	Filed in: Child's Portfolio / Class File / Other	Observer/ Writer	Date

CREATIVE—DRAMATIC PLAY

Documentation Type	Filed in: Child's Portfolio / Class File / Other	Observer/ Writer	Date

SELF-IDENTITY

Documentation Type	Filed in: Child's Portfolio / Class File / Other	Observer/ Writer	Date

GROUP INTERACTIONS

Documentation Type	Filed in: Child's Portfolio / Class File / Other	Observer/ Writer	Date

INTERACTIONS WITH ADULTS

Documentation Type	Filed in: Child's Portfolio / Class File / Other	Observer/ Writer	Date

OTHER DOCUMENTATION

____

____

REPRODUCED WITH THE PERMISSION OF AUTHOR: Nilsen, B. (2008). *Week by Week: Plans for Documenting the Development of Young Children, 3E.* Clifton Park, NY: Thomson Delmar Learning.

Figure I–17 Portfolio Overview Sheet.

machine) communicates to the family that the teacher has been carefully watching their child and saw something important. It builds relationships between child, family, and school, and the self-esteem of all. Examples of this type of communication are included in each of the weekly observation plans.

As a student, most likely it will not be your role to communicate with the family, although it depends on your field experience situation. Examples are included for those who do have this responsibility and as a model for those who will someday have direct communication with families. Communication with the child and family members about what we see as teachers is an important part of our job yet one for which little preparation exists. Reading this section will help you begin to formulate your own family communication attitudes and practices.

By now you have probably noticed the shift in language from *parent* to *family* as explained in the Preface. This term includes the parents and close family members who provide primary care for the child. Chapter 14 contains a further discussion of this rationale when it addresses sharing the Portfolio in family conferences (formerly Parent Conferences).

ACTIONS. Because observations are meant to stimulate a decision, a section called *Actions* is included with *Read a Book* suggestions of a few books to read with children about the area of development. The *In the Environment* section suggests small changes or additions to the environment to help stimulate this area of development. *In the Curriculum* gives a few ideas about curriculum projects based on children's interests. Read *Engaging Children's Minds: The Project Approach* (Katz & Chard, 2000) for a full description of this topic. This section also includes ways to individualize the curriculum. The section *In the Newsletter* suggests topics for newsletter articles or ways of sharing anecdotes or children's work.

THE REFLECTIVE JOURNAL. For each week, a group of open-ended questions are provided to guide the teacher in looking inward. These are for the writer's own consideration of the events of the week, personal attitudes, self-analysis, and promises for the future. These are private journal entries, not a part of the child's records. These will be discussed again in Chapter 1. These are found on the Bind-in-Book CD, usually in Part C of each week's plan. Please keep them in a safe place because they should be your honest self-reflection, and a log that you keep week by week.

RESOURCES. Resources listing helpful books and articles on selected topics are included at the end of the chapters following the references.

The Week by Week Plan

The Week by Week Plan guides the student so that all developmental areas are observed at least once. In real life, the areas must be revisited repeatedly to accomplish the objective of seeing change over time, so the plans are extended to 40 weeks in the total plan on the Bind-in-Book CD. Care has been taken to observe each child equally in all developmental areas using a variety of methods. (See the Bind-in-Book CD, Section B, for an overview of that plan.) The weekly plans for the rest of the year are included on the Bind-in-Book CD so it can be a manual for use in an early childhood program throughout the year. Adaptations for class size and situation are explained.

That is how this book is arranged. It is meant to be a weekly plan for recording observations of each child's development and used as a basis for planning curriculum. The outcome of the plan is a meaningful, comprehensive Portfolio.

You will need a new file folder for each child in your class, plus a few extras for new children through the year. Write names on tabs, last name first, and place the folders in alphabetical order. Place in the file any information supplied by the parents.

A Portfolio Overview Sheet is a summary of all the recordings in the Portfolio so the reader can see at a glance what is contained there, a type of table of contents. You will duplicate the one supplied at the end of Chapter 1 to place in each Portfolio.

This introduction sets the stage, gives you the background, and acquaints you with the format of the book. The next steps are yours. Complete the exercises and adapt the plans for your particular group of children. At the end of 14 weeks, you will have accumulated sizable Portfolios on each child, with documentation in each developmental area. If you continue the plans throughout the year (see Section C of the Bind-in-Book CD, you will see the progress the children make and will become a better observer, recorder, and teacher.

A WORD ABOUT ETHICS AND CONFIDENTIALITY

Ethics of Documentation

Ethics should guide documentation in the following ways.

ACCURACY. With every method of observation there is a responsibility to record the raw data (facts) as accurately as possible. This is done by making notes as completely and promptly after observing as possible.

As time passes, our memory dims and details slip away. The best recording is done *as the behavior is observed.* Some methods you will learn about are strictly factual, while others do have elements of judgment inherent in them. Carefully choose those methods and use them wisely.

OBJECTIVITY. Methods that preserve the raw data (just record the facts) are more **objective** (without bias or opinion) than others. That does not mean that one method is better than another or that biases and opinions can't enter into any recording. It is the responsibility of the recorder to capture what is seen and heard without interpretation. Again, the methods will contribute to the recording of data or interpretation. Be aware of that possibility.

Another aspect of objectivity is selecting children to document. By leaving it solely to the observer, it is possible to end up with thick files on children who have challenging behavior, resist classroom routines, or have social difficulties with other children or teachers. Such children are interesting to write about, for we are drawn to negative examples. However, there are children who follow the rules, flow with the routines, and get along with other children and adults. These children seldom are chosen for specimen recordings, but all children deserve an equal representation in observing practices. The Week by Week Plan seeks to make that selection of subjects more arbitrary, thus equalizing the number and topic of the documentation added to each child's Portfolio.

LABELING. We all sort and categorize the information we take in. That is how we attempt to make sense of the world. It is important not to draw premature conclusions or diagnoses about a child based on limited information, or to label a child or behavior. Our observation methods are designed to document the facts and to try to avoid categorizing a child as "bold," "hyperactive," or "shy." Our role as observers is to describe, document, and measure progress, not to draw conclusions about the isolated behavior we observe at any one time.

INTENDED PURPOSES. Students are writing about children for the purpose of observing and interpreting milestones in child development, to see theories in action, and to practice recording methods. The actual files should be destroyed once the course is completed since their purpose has been served. The child's work within the student's practice Portfolio could be given to parents, but the observations and child study should be cleared with the instructor and classroom teacher before it is given to the family. Unintentional breaches of **confidentiality** or inferential and biased statements could be made by the practicing student.

Practitioners' purpose in recording is to document a child's behavior, assess, and plan for that child accordingly. Documenting should not be used to build a case against a child for any reason or to threaten or humiliate a child or family.

SHARING WITH THE FAMILY. For students, sharing with the family is only done under the direction of and with the approval of the teacher. For practitioners, observations should be related to parents using tact and much deliberation about how they will be received. Occasionally, what the teacher thinks is a triumph is seen in a different light by the family because of a different perspective or value. The teacher shows the painting to the family member and relates, "She stayed there a long time and painted over the whole page." The family member looks at it and says, "But it doesn't look like anything."

Talking to the child in front of the family should also be done with consideration. Sometimes children want privacy and a sense of being a person apart from the family. The teacher could ask the child, "May I tell your family about how long you painted today as we show them the painting?" Sometimes the child needs to hear their accomplishments related to their family. Discussing misdeeds or concerns, however, should be done in private, away from the child, and other families, of course.

Confidentiality

Students will mask the identity of the children they observe by using only initials or some other neutral identifier. No last names should ever appear on any student's recording. Permission from a family member may be required by the school or program. It is the student's responsibility to inquire about the policy and abide by it. The file must keep the documentation private from anyone other than the instructor, the child, the child's family, and those who have a legal "right to know."

Writing enhances memory. That point has been strongly emphasized as the reason for writing observations. It is also true that what is remembered is discussed. As one becomes a better observer and recorder, it will also be only natural that conversations will be full of anecdotes. Cute stories, interesting quotes, and even concerns and *inside* information are on the observer's mind and sometimes lips.

Discussions outside the classroom with friends, or one's own family, require discretion. Sometimes stories are related for illustration, but they should never include children's names nor details that could identify the child or their family. Complaining, satirizing, or criticizing children or families is unprofessional.

Professional behavior is guided by wisdom, kindness, and most of all, respect for an individual's privacy. Let's make a commitment to uphold NAEYC'S *Code of Ethical Conduct* (NAEYC, 2005).

KEY TERMS

assessment	narrative
confidentiality	objective
criterion-referenced	observing
document	Portfolio
ecological view	quantitative
ethics	recording
evaluation	referral
family	Work Samples
file access log	Working Portfolio

Go to the Bind-in-Book CD for:

- The week's plan (Parts A and B) for observing and recording individual children and the whole group on a specific developmental domain. This includes the forms you will need. You can print them off or fill them out on the computer or hand-held device.
- What to Do with It—where to file the week's documentation.
- Sharing with the Child and Family—suggestions on the way to discuss your observations.
- Actions—curriculum suggestions for reading specific titles of children's books to enhance that developmental area, changes or additions to the learning environment, curriculum activities, and suggestions for your newsletter for family activities to reinforce the learning.

Part C is the Reflective Journal for you to fill in and keep private.

REFERENCES

Week by Week is based on research in the fields of assessment, child development, and professional practice. Each chapter will include references used in the chapter. I invite you to explore the subject more thoroughly by reading the sources listed here for a fuller explanation of a topic.

Bergen, D. (1993/94). Authentic performance assessments. *Childhood education, 70* (2), 102.

Berger, E. (2000). *Parents as partners in education: Families and schools working together.* Upper Saddle River, NJ: Merrill.

Boehm, A. E., & Weinberg, R. A. (1996). *The classroom observer: Developing observation skills in early childhood settings* (3rd ed.). New York: Teachers College Press.

Bronfenbrenner, U. (1979). *The ecology of human development.* Cambridge, MA: Harvard University Press.

Danielson, C., & Abrutyn, L. (1997). *An introduction to using Portfolios in the classroom.* Alexandria, VA: Association for Supervision and Curriculum Development.

Goodman, Y. M. (1989). Evaluation of students. In K. S. Goodman, Y. M. Goodman, & W. J. Hood (Eds.), *The whole language evaluation book.* Portsmouth, NH: Heinemann.

Gronlund, G., & Engel, B. (2001). *Focused portfolios: A complete assessment for the young child.* St Paul, MN: Redleaf Press.

Gronlund, N. E. (2003). *Assessment of student achievement* (7th ed.). Boston: Allyn and Bacon.

Hanson, M. F., & Gilkerson, D. (1999). Portfolio assessment: More than ABCs and 123s. *Early Childhood Education Journal,* (27) 2, 81–86.

Helm, J. H., Beneke, S., & Steinheimer, K. (1997). Documenting children's learning. *Childhood Education, 73* (4), 200–205.

Hyson, M. (2003). *Preparing early childhood professionals: NAEYC's Standards for initial licensure, advanced, and associate degree programs.* Washington, DC: National Association for the Education of Young Children.

Katz, L., & Chard, S. (2000). *Engaging children's minds: The project approach.* Norwood, NJ: Ablex Publishing Corporation.

Marotz, L. R., Corss, M. Z., & Rush, J. M. (2005). *Health, safety and nutrition for the young child* (6th ed.). Clifton Park, NY: Thomson Delmar Learning.

Martin, S. (2004). *Take a look: Observation and Portfolio assessment in early childhood* (3rd ed.). Toronto Canada: Addison Wesley Pub Ltd.

McAfee, O., & Leong, D. J. (2002). *Assessing and guiding young children's development and learning* (3rd ed.). Boston: Pearson Allyn and Bacon.

NAEYC. (2003). Position statement. Early childhood curriculum, assessment and program evaluation: Building an effective, accountable system in programs for children birth through age 8. Joint position statement of the National Association for the Education of Young Children (NAEYC) and the National Association of Early Childhood Specialists in State Departments of Education (NAECS/SDE). Washington, DC: Author.

NAEYC. (2002). *Early learning standards: Creating the conditions for success. Executive summary.*

Washington, DC: National Association for the Education of Young Children.

Neisworth, J. T., & Bagnato, S. J. (2004) The mis-measure of young children: The authentic assessment alternative. *Infants and Young Children*, (17) 3, 198, July–Sept. 2004)

Neuman, S. B., & Roskos, K. A. (1993). *Language and literacy learning in the early years: An integrated approach.* New York: Harcourt Brace Jovanovich.

Pack, J. A., & Knight, M. E. (2000). Developing a school portfolio: A tool for staff development. *Young Children* (55) 5, 42–46, Sept. 2000.

Piaget, J., & Inhelder, B. (1969). *The psychology of the child.* New York: Basic Books.

Shores, E. F., & Grace, C. (2005). *The Portfolio book: A step-by step guide for teachers.* Upper Saddle River, NJ: Pearson Education.

Wiener, R, B., & Cohen, J. (2002). New paradigms for familiar concepts: Portfolios and conferencing as performance based assessment tools. *Journal of Early Education and Family Review, 9* (3), Jan.–Feb. 2002.

Woodward, H. (1993). *Negotiated evaluation: Involving children and parents in the process.* Portsmouth, NH: Heinemann.

RESOURCES

For more on Portfolios and documentation, see:

Bredekamp, S., & Rosegrant, T. (1992). *Reaching potentials: Appropriate curriculum and assessment for young children, Vol I.* Washington, DC: National Association for the Education of Young Children.

Helm, J. H., Beneke, S., & Steinheimer, K. (1998). *Windows on learning: Documenting young children's work.* New York: Teachers College Press.

Hyson, M. (Ed.). (2003). *Preparing early childhood professionals: NAEYC standards for programs.* Washington, DC: National Association for the Education of Young Children.

Shores, E. F., & Grace, C. (2005). *The Portfolio book: A step-by-step guide for teachers.* Upper Saddle River, NJ: Pearson Education.

CHAPTER 1

Using the Class List Log to Look at Separation and School Adjustment

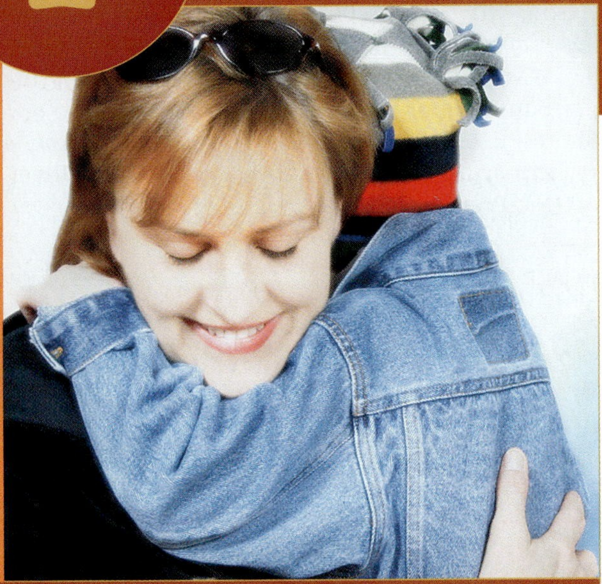

IN THIS CHAPTER

- Using the Class List Log
- Using the Reflective Journal
- Topics in Observation: Why Not Use a Daily Log or Daily Journal?
- Looking at Separation and School Adjustment
- Helping All Children with Separation and School Adjustment
- Helping Professionals for Separation and School Adjustment Concerns

USING THE CLASS LIST LOG

EXERCISE Make a list of all the people you have had contact with today. Note what color shirt each person was wearing.

Some assumptions can be made about the list in the preceding exercise. It may be difficult to list every person one is with but easy to remember more significant people. It also may be difficult to remember the color of the shirt each person wore, especially for casual contacts. It would have been easier if one knew at the beginning of the day what the assignment was and noted it as it occurred. At the end of the day, or after the fact, recall is more accurate concerning some people and some facts than others. Memory might fail regarding people who demanded no attention and received none.

The teacher's clearest recollection at the end of the day is usually of those children who did memorable things. The memory might be a child splashing paint across the room or one singing every song from the latest Disney movie. Children who cause no trouble or draw no attention to themselves might not be remembered at the end of the day.

A method is needed to guide the teacher to record information about every child in the class. The same category of information should be recorded for every child in the group on the same day: It is more equitable to standardize the criteria and collect data on all the children in the group. Memory cannot be trusted for accuracy or remembering each child.

The **Class List Log** is a method or format to record one or more short, specific pieces of information about each child present on that day. It is designed to be quick and easy (something every teacher is looking for). However, it provides information on every child in the group. It records facts that may be interpreted later or incorporated into another type of developmental comparison over time. The Class List Log criterion is determined in advance and is the same for each child (Figure 1–1).

Blank forms are made by alphabetically arranging the first names of the children. This arrangement allows for the quickest way to find the space to jot a note. There is a line at the top for the date. Using a date stamp is a good routine to follow. This assures the date is on every recording, including the year. Leave as much space between names as possible. Two forms may be made vertically on one page and kept on hand for various purposes. Bits of information then can be copied over or cut apart and stapled into each child's file. (Blank Class List Logs are provided on the Bind-in-Book CD, along with directions on how to easily alphabetize the names. A Class List Log is ideal to place on a hand-held computer.) The availability of the Class List Log form is essential to its usefulness.

While the children are engaged in play or work, the recorder uses the Class List Log to record information on one skill or behavior for each child in the group. This provides a natural information-gathering process. For example, cutting could be observed by placing children's scissors on a table with interesting papers to cut, such as gift wrap, wallpaper samples, or comics. The observer sits nearby with a Class List Log and makes notes as each child works in that area. As another example, large motor skills could be observed easily as children go through a maze that

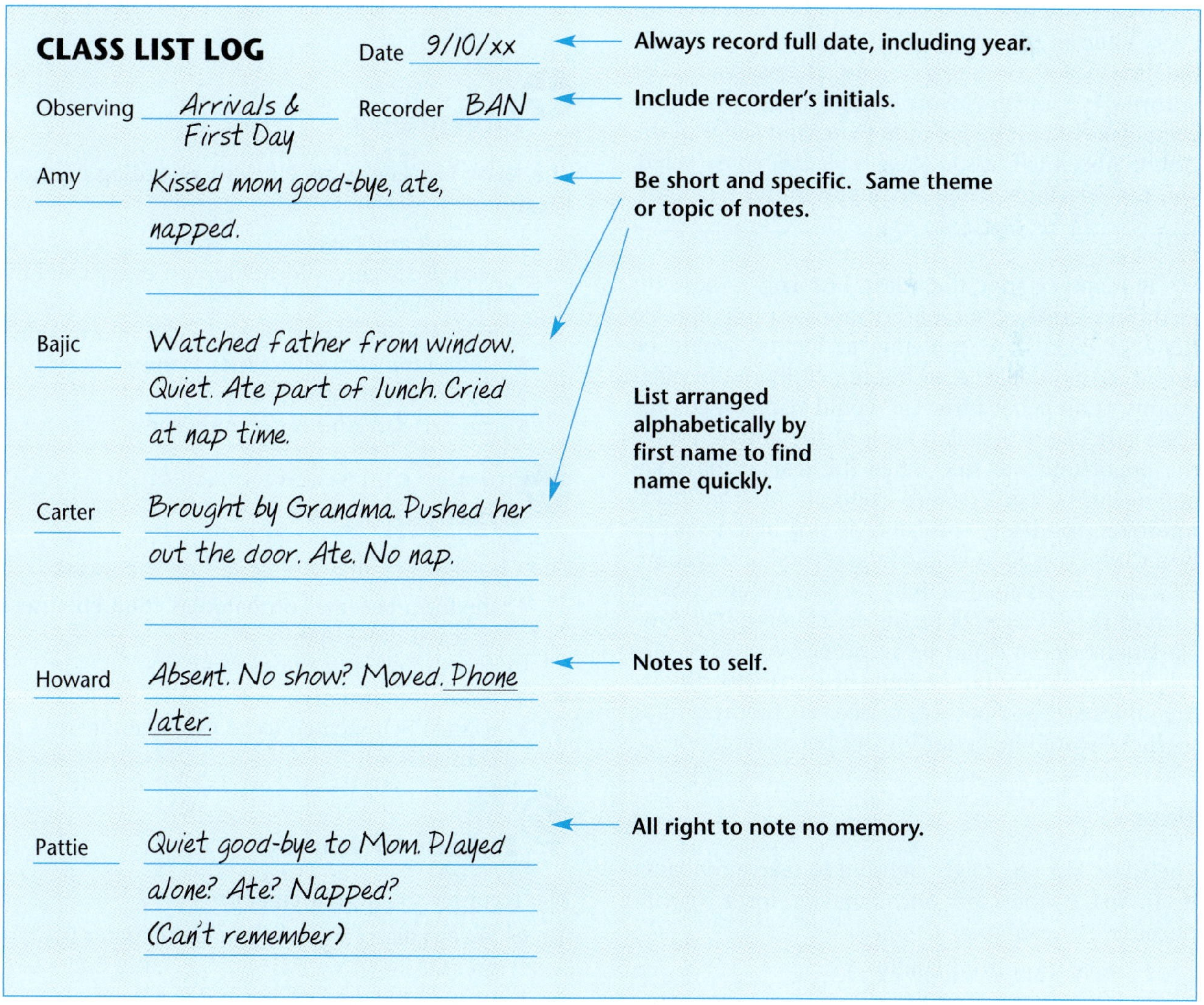

Figure 1–1 Class List Log Example.

includes climbing, balancing, throwing, jumping, and crawling skills. It is important to date every observation, including the year.

EXERCISE **Mark the following *Yes* or *No* for suitability of Class List Log criteria.**

_____ has toileting accidents
_____ is able to cut
_____ listens to story
_____ pours own juice, usually without spilling
_____ sleeps at rest time
_____ considerate of others' feelings
_____ can pedal a tricycle
_____ understands concepts of front/back, up/down, loud/soft
_____ uses words to resolve conflicts
_____ follows classroom rules

Now go back to the list and record in which setting or activity this most easily could be observed for every child in the group in one class session. Divide the list into two categories, direct observation or **summative observation** (those things that have been observed in the past and your knowledge of the child). Since the Class List Log is teacher constructed, you can select items that are important for *your* class.

Remember that the Class List Log is best for recording on-the-spot observations or memorable frequent events, so "toileting accidents" would be useful in the toddler class but hopefully not in older groups. "Can pedal a tricycle" could be recorded on a Class List Log if that day most of the children have the opportunity to ride while the teacher observes and records. "Understands concepts of front/back, up/down, loud/soft" probably is not best recorded by a Class List Log. It would take several observations or a specific planned activity to observe and record each of these concepts on all the children. "Follows classroom rules" could be recorded on a Class List Log from memory, but it would be untrustworthy (as memories are) and possibly biased, so other recording methods would be better for this behavior.

Uses

The Class List Log might be used to take attendance or to make notes on one behavior for a specific purpose. For example:

- separation from family
- large motor: specific skills such as climbing, standing on one leg for five seconds, walking the length of the balance beam, alternating feet coming down stairs, or hopping
- small motor: cutting with scissors, printing first name, rolling a ball, folding a napkin or paper in half, or putting together an eight-piece puzzle
- language: reciting nursery rhymes; responding to vocabulary of over, under, small, bigger, biggest
- literacy: looking at a book from front to back, "reading" pictures
- math: rote counting, using one-to-one correspondence
- science: placing items in sequence, sorting items by color or size
- art: painting lines, circles, human figures, alphabet letters (use Class List Log at the easel to tally each time a child chooses to paint in a week)
- blocks and dramatic play: note level of play, role in dramatic play, or type of constructions made

Advantages

The Class List Log is an efficient recording method because it

- is quick and easy.
- records specific information on every child in the group.
- gives specific, dated, brief, factual information.
- can be transferred to other forms of recording as base information.
- can be used later for comparison.

Disadvantages

The Class List Log may not be desirable because

- the form becomes outdated as children enter or leave the group.
- rewriting is time consuming.
- limited information or data is recorded.
- it must be repeated to be valuable for comparison.

Pitfalls to Avoid

The recorder should remember to

- always date each entry (a stamp dater is great).
- include the time of day and setting, if pertinent.

- select an observable criterion.
- write short, factual notes.

Using Technology

Technology refers to tools that make a task easier. While we may think the term refers only to electronic equipment, it also includes any object or supply that helps make a job easier or more efficient. Here are some tools that will help you manage information you gather with a Class List Log.

CLIPBOARDS. Sometimes we neglect to think of the most obvious. A clipboard holding paper, with pencil or pen attached, or several brightly colored ones placed strategically around the room will make it convenient to jot down details as they happen.

INDEX CARDS AND STICKY NOTES. Who can be without these? Tuck them in your pocket, along with pen or pencil, and be ready to jot down notes to be filed or transferred to more amplified documentation later on.

MAILING LABELS. These can be used to efficiently transfer information gathered in a Class List Log format. By preparing sheets of labels with children's first names in alphabetical order, either by hand or on the computer, the important developmental information gathered from observations can then be transferred to a sheet of paper in each child's Portfolio.

DATE STAMP. Small stamp-pad tools with moveable dates are invaluable to help with one of the most important and basic pieces of information we gather. How many of us have photos from past years without dates on the back, making it difficult to remember when they were taken? The date stamp can be used on each of the mailing labels, on Portfolio entries, and on children's work as it is added to the Portfolio. They are inexpensive and can be placed in many areas of the classroom. Children can be taught to date their own paintings and artwork.

HAND-HELD COMPUTER. A personal digital assistant (PDA) can be very useful for the Class List Log. Using the program Documents to Go, the Class List Log can be produced on the computer, then transferred to the hand-held computer where notes can be entered. Later, the information is transferred back to the main computer and sorted into individual children's files in a matter of minutes. You won't have to copy notes over, cut up lists and tape them into file folders, or even use address labels. The Portfolio Overview Sheet (on the Bind-in-Book CD) can then be used as the outline for storing each piece of documentation according to developmental area. This week's recording on separations or adjustments (discussed later in the chapter) would be electronically pasted under that heading with the date; others later in the year will be added there for a cumulative record.

Using Technology for the Reflective Journal

If you find that you can think and write better at the computer, you can open a new document window, note the date, and let your thoughts flow. Save it in a folder or copy it to a disk where only you can access it. Blogs are online reflections (some deep and some superficial), but they are public, posted online. Because of this, they are inappropriate for keeping such records. A Reflective Journal entry is only for you.

How to Find the Time

Having the forms already made and available around the room (on those clipboards mentioned earlier) make Class List Logs easy to use. Because they are designed to record one small piece of data—the same one on each child—they are not time consuming. By carefully selecting the observable, important developmental task or behavior that you are recording, information can be gathered on every child in the group in a relatively short period of time.

What to Do with This Information

On the Portfolio Overview Sheet, note the type of documentation that provides information for this developmental area (e.g., Class List Log by entering "CLL"). If it is a recording on the individual child, it is filed in the child's folder. If it is a recording method that includes the whole class or a group of children, it is filed in the Class File. The individual's information may either be copied into the child's file, appear as a summary in the child's file, or be referred to directly from the Class File. The recorder's name and date are noted (Figure 1–2). If bits of data are on mailing labels, these are attached to a page in each child's Portfolio with the date. Class List Log sheets can be cut apart and each child's portion stapled, taped, or pasted on a sheet in the Portfolio. Later, observations in this category will be added to this page. Remember, this is your index of all pieces of data you have on the child.

SEPARATIONS AND ADJUSTMENT			
Documentation	Location	Recorder	Date
CL		BAN	9/7
CL		BAN	2/14
CL		MS	4/5
RR		BAN	5/9

Figure 1–2 Portfolio Overview Sheet Example.

If the program uses a developmental checklist or criteria from the state's standards, the bits of information can be transferred to the checklist category in the child's Portfolio with the date and specifics. For example, Class List Log information gathered on cutting may be transferred to a developmental checklist on small muscle development.

Information gathered with the Class List Log could be shared with the family verbally at the end of the day. "Today, Aillio used the scissors to cut up the funny papers. He worked hard at cutting along the lines." A written happy note (Figure 1–3) could be sent home informing families, "Today, Aillio worked hard at cutting."

If a skill below the expected level of development at this age or stage is observed, a curriculum plan is implemented to address this area. This gives the child the opportunity to practice and advance the skill.

The Class List Log is an effective method to use in the first week of school to record observations. This method recognizes that the teacher's first priority is making relationships with the child and family. The observations of separations and first impressions are important ones to record, however, providing an understanding of the foundations and outward manifestations of attachment and separation. The Class List Log provides a quick, easy format on which to record first observations without consuming much of the recorder's time.

Figure 1–3 Happy notes are a method of communicating with families.

EXERCISE **Mark these phrases *S* for subjective or *O* for objective.**

______ jumped from 18 inches
______ very smart
______ nice boy
______ grabbed toy and said, "Mine!"
______ doing fine
______ she's a challenge
______ polite
______ counted to 8
______ recognized nametag
______ called someone a bad name
______ clapped to "Bingo" song
______ enjoyed music time

Check yourself: OSSOSSSOOSOS

USING THE REFLECTIVE JOURNAL

EXERCISE **Which of the following things would you rather discover yourself than have someone else tell you?**

______ You have bad breath.
______ You are unzipped or unbuttoned.
______ You have food stuck between your teeth.
______ You are prejudiced against something.
______ You are acting unprofessionally.

The **Reflective Journal** is a teacher's place for recording personal thoughts. It is like a **diary** in that it is private, with the word *reflective* bringing the image of deliberating, wondering, pondering, thinking, and rethinking. Its purpose is not to provide documentation of children on which to assess their development; rather, it is a place to think about yourself in the daily interactions with children. Teachers need to also be learners, and that learning begins within, inquiring about one's own motivations, influences, molding experiences, culture and cultural biases, values, and beliefs (Balaban, 1995).

Observing children in their natural setting includes the observer as a participant and a partner in the research (Swick, DaRose, & Pavia, 1998/99).

TOPICS IN OBSERVATION

Why Not Use a Daily Log or Daily Journal?

EXERCISE On a separate piece of paper (for your eyes only) describe what you did yesterday, all the people you met, what you did and said.

Many people working with children know they should write about the children. Many even have written diligently in a notebook or in each child's file every day. The difficulty comes when the days get busy, some children's behavior is more memorable than others, and objective assessment-type information is needed. An entry in a **daily log or journal** written at the end of the day is likely to omit details in sequence (Figure 1–4). Exact conversations and movements, which give so much important information to the assessment of children's development, are forgotten. At the end of the day, the strongest memories are those frustrations and difficulties. When it comes to remembering what each child did, the few who were the most difficult are most vividly recalled. Some are remembered at the end of the day because of an unexpectedly advanced skill or a novel, cute incident. The problem occurs when trying to remember the children in the middle. Those are the children who cause no trouble, who quietly abide by the rules, float through the day, doing nothing out of the ordinary to attract attention. Informal diary writing leaves those children out day after day after day.

This same difficulty occurs when writing in each child's page in a notebook. At the end of the day, try as one might, some children are not memorable. How can a teacher say to the family member, "I don't know what your child did today. I can't remember a thing." So instead, general comments are made, not based on hard data. The child is cheated out of being the focus of the observer's attention. It is not out of malice but because of the unsystematic way this type of recording is done. There is no hard data. Observations are written from memory, after the event.

The other shortcoming of the daily log or journal as an observational method is its subjectivity. People have used diaries traditionally for writing their innermost thoughts and feelings. **Subjective** recordings are those that are influenced by state of mind, point of view, or inferences in to the meaning of events. The opposite is objective recordings, which are detached, impersonal, and unprejudiced, recording facts rather than feelings and generalities. For the purpose of fair assessment and documentation of each child's development in all areas, objective methods should be used. The goal is an objective measurement system for each child. Daily log entries do not help the teacher meet that goal.

Analyze your entry written in the preceding exercise. Can you separate the objective and subjective parts?

Thinking and wondering about the child, the teacher's role, the classroom environment, and the policies of the child care center all help the teacher to evaluate and transform what needs to be changed or modified. Teachers need opportunities to inquire into their own experiences and tell their own stories as a method of action research, collecting and analyzing data, and coming to conclusions. These **reflections** may be very private or may be shared with a mentor and discussed for further reflections. The following are some fascinating examples of such inquiries:

- *Going Against the Grain: Supporting the Student-Centered Teacher* (Aaronsohn, 1996) presents a dialogue between a mentor and a beginning teacher who is bearing up under pressure to abandon developmental teaching philosophies.

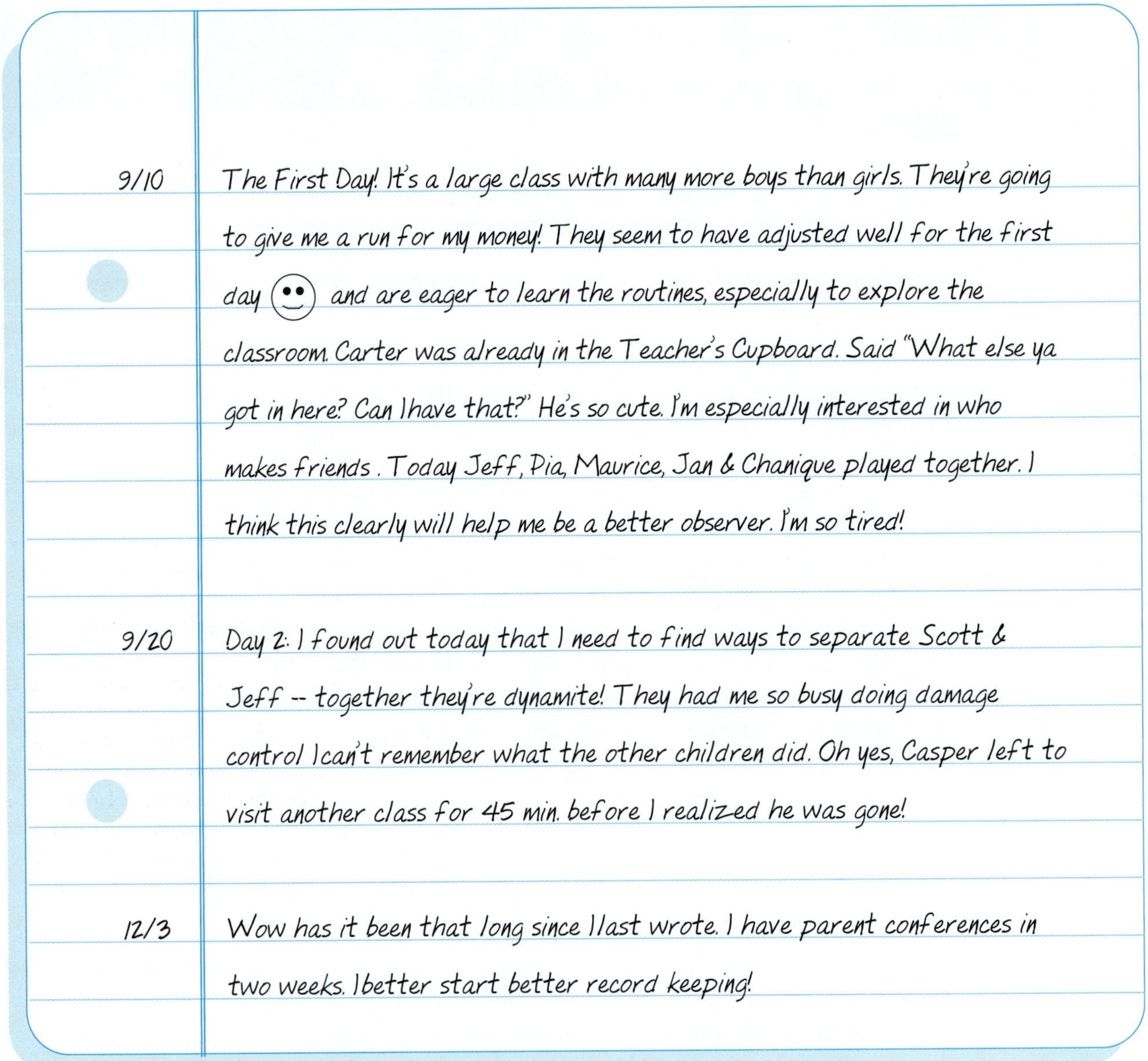

Figure 1–4 This diary example was written at the end of the day. It was difficult to remember details about every child.

- *First Steps Toward Teaching the Reggio Way* (Hendrick, 1997) features stories of how teachers implemented the philosophies of the Reggio Emilia schools in the United States.
- *When Teachers Reflect* (Terte, Klein, & Jewett, 1998) includes several teachers' journeys with self-doubts and evolving practices into inclusion and individualizing curriculum. These reflections are valuable as written documentation of the teachers' private thoughts.

The Reflective Journal is like looking into a mirror (Figure 1–5):

- *External view*—When looking into a mirror, the viewpoint is from the outside, as others see the person. The Reflective Journal is an opportunity to explore the view that others see and compare it to the inner, deeper meaning. It helps the observer see as others see.
- *Quick check*—Often the mirror is used for a quick, overall glance to see that clothes and hair are satisfactory. A Reflective Journal can be a place for a cursory overview of performance, feelings, or events of the day without getting into deep analysis.
- *See changes*—Changes in appearance are identified by looking in the mirror. Grey hairs (or disappearing ones) or extra pounds are noticed visually when reflected in the mirror. The Reflective Journal can help the writer notice changes about thinking and attitudes.

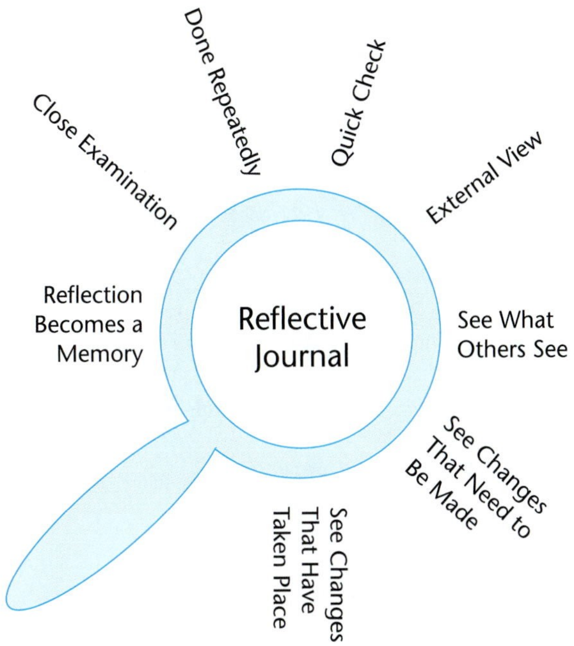

Figure 1–5 The Reflective Journal is like a mirror.

- *Close examination*—The mirror can be used for a concentrated examination of a certain area. It may be a changing spot on the skin, clothing alignment, or a new wrinkle that has appeared overnight. The Reflective Journal can be a private place to self-examine a troublesome area. It may be premature or too private to discuss with someone else. An attitude toward a child or coworker, a creeping doubt about one's ability, or a prejudice that has come into one's consciousness can be closely examined in a journal.
- *Make changes*—When a look in the mirror shows something is askew, missing, or undone, the resultant action is an adjustment to correct the problem. Reaction to visions in the mirror is one of the purposes of looking. Writing in a Reflective Journal raises issues that call for change and presents the opportunity to resolve to take action. The Reflective Journal becomes an agent of change.
- *Done repeatedly*—Glances in the mirror are done many times a day, sometimes using substitutes such as windows in storefronts to re-examine certain areas. The Reflective Journal brings the teacher to inward examination again and again, whether in writing or in thinking.
- *Reflection becomes a memory*—The vision in the mirror is remembered. Looking internally through a Reflective Journal to examine values, beliefs, and feelings also forms memories. Those become as real as physical experiences. Reflection is more than daydreaming. It can be a life-changing experience.

EXERCISE **Try some Reflective Journal writing:**

When I enter a new place for the first time I feel . . .
Writing about myself is . . .
An area I would like to explore about myself is my . . .
I chose to work with children because . . .

What Is Its Purpose?

Just like a personal diary, the teacher's Reflective Journal is a place to express emotions, make judgments, and form hypotheses (Figure 1–6). It is not a part of the child's file but the personal property of the writer, providing a healthy outlet for emotions. "A reflective journal can document your professional journey. It is a place where you record your thinking about complex issues. . . . Writing may generate ideas and emotions about changing yourself and the organization you work in" (Forrest & McCrea, 2002). This type of recording must be kept separate from the assessments of the development of the child. *For privacy, it must be kept at home, away from the work site.*

Uses

The Reflective Journal is useful

- to express emotions or questions; to let off "steam"; to express anger, frustration, or elation; or to express worry concerning a child or the child's family, a coworker, supervisor, or self.
- for self-examination of attitudes, biases, or prejudices.
- to pose theories about a child's behavior that are from intuition.
- to explore remedies, strategies, advantages, and disadvantages of possible solutions.

Advantages

The Reflective Journal is useful as

- an outlet for emotions.
- a vehicle to work through theories and to clarify and expand thinking.
- a record of professional development.

9/10 I'm so excited about the first day of school. I wonder if having so many boys in the class will affect behavior & class management? Hey -- do I expect a difference? I guess I do! How can I keep my "active boy" bias from influencing what I see? Maybe these new methods of recording will help. I think I'll look for some things to read about sex differences and behavior.

9/13 I heard Mary & Ted next door talking about my new room arrangement breaking down the barrier between blocks and dramatic play. Do I let blocks go in the "oven"? Or in purses & briefcases? What about high heels and cowboy boots in the block area? We'll see!

9/20 Boy, this nit-picking is getting to me. Today Mary made me so angry when she said to the director, "my orderly classroom."

Figure 1–6 Reflective Journal Example.

Disadvantages

The Reflective Journal is not useful for assessing children's development, because it is

- written after the event when facts are lost.
- highly inferential and emotionally based.
- not comprehensive in recording information remembered on each and every child, only those who stand out.

What to Do with the Reflective Journal

Because of the confidential, subjective nature of the Reflective Journal, it must be

- kept secure and private, away from the workplace.
- used as an emotional release that may not be possible in any other form.
- used to take a measurement of your personal and professional development in working with children and their families and with coworkers.
- used to explore questions, develop theories, and examine biases.
- reviewed at intervals to examine changes in thinking and attitudes, and measure professional development.

Pitfalls to Avoid

The Reflective Journal is very personal. It is important to maintain trust that what is written there will not be read by anyone. Keep it at home. Get in the habit of writing in it every week. Go beyond the

@ it happened to me

Picky Mother

Was she ever a picky mother! I had strict instructions on how the child's socks needed to be pulled up over the snowsuit legs before the boots were put on. The mittens were to be on before the snowsuit so the cuffs were pulled down over the mittens. The hat had to be snugly down over the ears before the hood was pulled up. And be careful not to knot the scarf on top of the snowsuit too tightly and to move the knot and the ends to the back of the hood. Can you believe it! And we had 15 other children to get ready as well. It helps just to write about recalling the irritation I felt (still, after 20 years!). That's the value in writing a Reflective Journal, the place where your feelings can be expressed and dissipated, somewhat.

Do you have an IT HAPPENED TO ME story about getting acquainted? I'd love to read it. Send it to WeekbyWeek@thomsonlearning.com

guided questions and use it to vent your feelings, questions, ideas, and theories. Keep it safe.

Using Technology

Many people now are in the habit of reading their e-mail once a day. Getting in the habit of entering a Reflective Journal entry is a convenient way to record thoughts, preserving them in a computer document, and printing them out periodically to review them.

How to Find the Time

The Reflective Journal, because it is personal and not used for direct assessment, takes personal time. This is done after the work day has ended, or at home.

REVIEW

CLASS LIST LOG

Alphabetical first name list to record small, specific pieces of information on each child in the class.

Types of Information to Record

- single elements of adjustment to routines
- single elements of self-care
- single elements of physical development
- social development stage
- clear articulation of speech
- single elements of understanding math, science concepts
- single elements of literacy development
- frequency of choices of learning centers (one Class List Log in each center for logging choice), such as painting easel, dramatic play area, computer blocks

REFLECTIVE JOURNAL

Personal diary kept separate and private from children's recording.

Types of Information to Record

- thoughts
- expressions of emotion
- questions
- self-evaluation
- reminders

For many people, writing is a chore; for those people, this task may be difficult. For others, writing is therapeutic and this task may be enjoyable. In either case, setting aside the time is well spent.

LOOKING AT SEPARATION AND SCHOOL ADJUSTMENT

A smooth transition from home to school at the beginning of the year or as a child enters a program provides for the child's immediate comfort and contributes to later success.

Attachment's Relationship to Separation

EXERCISE Using a separate sheet of paper, make a list of objects that are important to you. How did they become so valued? How would you feel if they were destroyed in a fire, lost, or stolen?

People form an **attachment** to objects and other people for a variety of reasons. An object might be something attained after hard work and much preparation. It may be a gift received as an expression of love. Sometimes the longer an item is possessed, the more valuable it becomes. Strong attachment or value makes it hard to part with that object or person. Familiarity provides comfort. Separation brings a feeling of loss.

The infant's relationship with adults begins at birth as needs are met (Figure 1–7). This attachment to the family emerges from built-in survival techniques and responses. In the early weeks, the provider of those needs is irrelevant to the infant, as long as the needs are met. The infant begins to focus on the face, voice, and smells of those close to him, and he begins to form mental images of those who hold him. Bowlby (1969), Yarrow (1964), Shaffer and Emerson (1964), and Ainsworth, Blehar, Waters, and Wall (1978) have all done important studies of this process of attachment. These studies are the basis for guiding expectations and practices. The professional caregiver's role is to build the child's bond to the family as the primary adults and to the teacher as a trustworthy substitute.

In the first few weeks of life, the infant responds to and attends to any nearby caregiver. This is the survival instinct: Without adult provision of needs, the infant could not live.

Between eight weeks and six months, the infant begins to discriminate between familiar people, such as the family, and unfamiliar people. The child is more responsive, and smiles and vocalizes more, to familiar people than to unfamiliar people. There are implications for infants entering child care prior to being six months old. As the infant is beginning to differentiate between self and significant others, the primary caregivers should be consistent people who are responsive to the infant's needs. Infants may exhibit **stranger anxiety** as they are increasingly aware of the difference between close family and other people. However, Shaffer and Emerson (1964) found that most infants are capable of forming a number of attachments at the same time. The role of the teacher

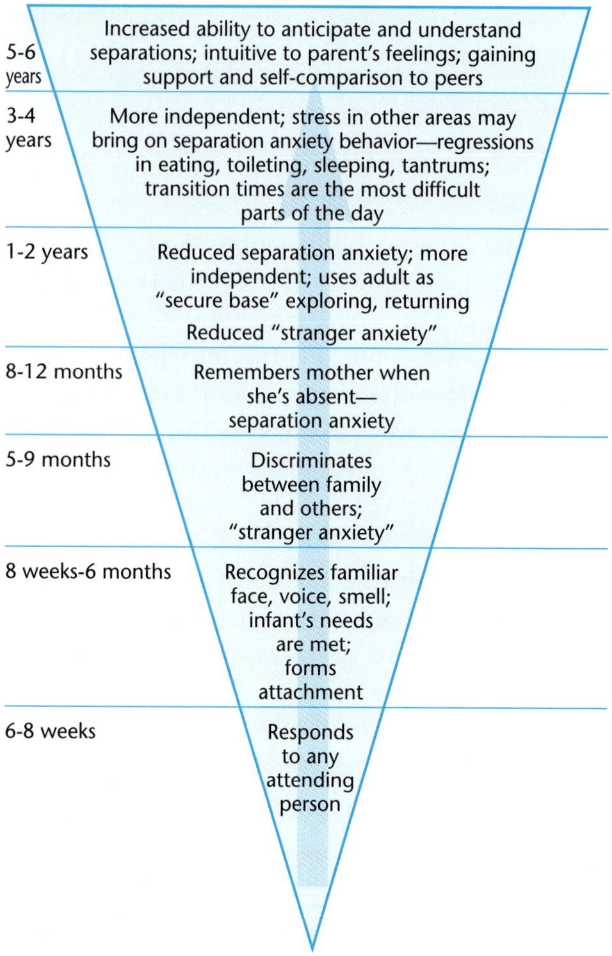

Figure 1–7 Development of Independence—Separation and Adjustment to Out-of-Home Experiences.

is to support the infant attachment to the family. This can be done by providing reminders of the family. Images (photographs), voices (tapes), and smells (belongings) surrounding the child during the day at the center will help to maintain that attachment during the family's absence. This gives assurance to the family and the child that their bond is the primary one. The caregiver maintains that bond during their hours away from each other.

Iinfants and toddlers maintain contact or stay near the attached person throughout the day in child care by creeping, walking, and following those important people. The child uses vocal signals—cooing, crying, and eventually words—to maintain contact. Older infants and toddlers begin to anticipate the coming separation at the end of the day. This may happen when they see their coat and diaper bag being readied by the caregiver, or when they see the family member arrive. This is what is called **separation anxiety**. This is a normal part of development but is distressing to all involved. The family member may see it as a sign of rejection but should be assured that it indicates that the child can have a secure attachment to more than one person and that the transition from one to another is sometimes difficult. The intensity of this stage is dependent on many factors: attachment to the family, temperament of the child, and experiences with consistent responsive caregivers. It can be minimized by establishing those **good-bye rituals** that Balaban speaks about in a very helpful book on this subject, *Learning to Say Good-bye* (1995). She advises families to establish a good-bye routine such as a high-five, rubbing noses, or three quick hugs, a ritual that is consistent every time they part (Figure 1–8). It serves as a dependable signal that leads the child to trust that the family member will return, even though parting may be full of tears and anger.

As the child has experiences outside of the security of home and family, the basic need to feel a sense of belonging and comfort is challenged. Life in group care is different from life at home. Adjusting to discontinuity between home and the center may be stressful. The child may use separation anxiety as a tool to receive special attention and special promises that may result in a relaxation of standards of behavior. The family member may feel guilt or ambivalence for leaving. The teacher's responsibility is to provide the child with a sense of security, build a sense of school family as well as home family, and empower the family member to leave without guilt or losing a battle. Good-bye routines, once established, work very well at helping to ease tension.

Figure 1–8 Good-bye rituals help the child and the family with the transition and separation.

Why all the attention to this area? Research has indicated some serious long-term consequences from separations of families and children. Bjorklund and Bjorklund (1992) summarized the attachment research of Bowlby (1969), Ainsworth et al. (1978), and others to suggest that securely attached children

- are more independent (than unattached children).
- have a more positive self-image.
- engage in positive social interactions with peers.
- have fewer behavioral problems.
- are able to negotiate in conflicts.
- score higher in IQ and standardized tests.
- are more socially competent, self-directed, and attentive at age 35.
- are more curious, flexible, and persistent.
- have better impulse control. (pp. 321–323)

With important outcomes associated with attachment, giving attention and developing strategies to assist in this important developmental area are critical.

Preparation for Entering Programs and Schools

EXERCISE **Using a separate sheet of paper, list important "first" events in a lifetime (such as birth, first step, first tooth, first date).**

Beginnings are memorable events. They are celebrated with much thought, preparation, and anticipation. Photographs, videos, and certificates are concrete remembrances of the occasion. Memories are recited in detailed stories of the process. Lengthy discussions relate what went well and reflect on what did not and how it could have been done differently.

Beginning a new school year, entrance to a new child care center or school, or even the beginning of every day are important events. These beginnings are worthy of careful preparations, thoughtful processes, and detailed recording. Making smooth transitions into the program, whether for the first time ever or the first time that day, begins long before the adult and child come through the door.

IMPORTANT INFORMATION GATHERING PRIOR TO THE FIRST DAY. Every program has its own information-gathering form for facts about the child from the family. The type of program, the objectives, and state regulations prescribe the type of information gathered on this form. A copy is placed in the child's Portfolio for the teacher's reference. The original is kept in the program office.

EXERCISE **On a separate sheet of paper, make a list of information you think should be included on a family information form.**

Refer to the family information form (Figure 1–9) and see how many pieces of information you thought of and which ones you feel are the highest priority.

The family is the most important source of information for assessing the child's development. By requesting developmental information, the program is recognizing the family unit as the child's first teachers, the ones who know the child best. In special education programs where children have been formally evaluated, Bloch (1987) stresses the importance of collaboration with families as information gatherers. She makes the point that "a radical rethinking of the way professionals work with families is required" (p. 4). Bloch's parent assessment component in the Five P's (Parent Professional PreSchool Performance Profile) program (p. 5) teaches them to do the following:

- learn to observe their child's behavior
- systematically collect data about their child's performance at home
- understand early childhood development
- acquire rating skills
- recognize behaviors that interfere with learning
- share and compare assessments with the school
- develop more realistic expectations for their child

Many questionnaires have been developed for families to assess their own child's development, used as a screening device to identify those children who may have developmental delays. The *Ages and Stages Questionnaires System* (Bricker, 1999) is an especially easy tool to use, along with home visits. It has a few selected questions in developmental areas at 11 intervals between 4 months and 4 years of age.

Families should be consulted concerning their goals for the child and expectations of the program. This can be done in an informal conversation, a more formal interview, or in a questionnaire. McAfee and Leong (2002) recommend these procedures for eliciting information from families:

- Be respectful of family and community culture, customs, and language.
- Advise families about what information will be helpful.
- Use existing communication opportunities.
- Be able to get needed information related to a problem or concern.
- Have parents do some assessment and documentation. (pp. 62–63)

PERSONAL MEETINGS. Building a relationship with the child and the families begins before the first day at school. This can be done in a variety of ways, depending on the program, the timing, and the age of the child.

EXERCISE **Check the ways you get acquainted with someone:**

______ phone conversations
______ reading a questionnaire they have answered
______ visiting one another's home
______ introductions
______ work on a task together
______ have a common interest

HOME VISITS. One of the best ways to get to know the child in the family context is to make a home visit. This can be used to fill out the necessary paperwork and begin to establish a bond with the child in the child's surroundings. A home visit is not to inspect or to judge but to better understand the family situation. It is usually done in pairs by the people who will be directly interacting with the child. It often helps to bring an activity or some piece of the school's equipment along, such as a toy or a book. Families and children would be interested in an album of photographs of school activities and people. It is important to provide time for the family and child to ask questions and tell stories of their family. The visitors will not only talk but listen.

This is a friendly, short visit to get acquainted. It can determine the families' needs of assistance from the program or school. Families can ask questions or express concerns they may have. And they can

THE B.C. CENTER
FAMILY, HEALTH, AND DEVELOPMENT FORM

Child's Name:______________________ Date of Birth: ______________________

HEALTH HISTORY

Type of Birth: ______________________ Was the child preterm?______________________

Does your child have a history of the following:

Frequent Colds: _______ Frequent Diarrhea:_______ Asthma: _______ Nosebleeds: _______

Ear Infections: _______ Stomach Aches: _______ Seizures: _______ Headaches: _______

Urinary Infections: _______ Please indicate what brings on the above conditions if you know: ______________________

____

____

What illness(es) has your child had? At what age?

Chicken Pox: _______ Scarlet Fever: _______ Hepatitis: _______ Diabetes: _______ Mumps: _______

Measles:_______ Other: ______________________

Does your child vomit easily? __________ Does your child run high fevers often? ______________

Has your child had any serious accidents? If so, please explain: ______________________

____

Does your child have allergies? __________ If so, how are they manifested?

Asthma: __________ Hay Fever: __________ Hives:__________ Other: __________

What causes the allergy? ______________________

Does your child have any <u>food allergies</u>? ______________________

Does your child receive any medication regularly? ______________________

Do you have any concerns in these areas: Speech: __________ Physical: ______________ Hearing: ________

DEVELOPMENTAL HISTORY

Please answer to the best of your memory!

At what age child: crept __________ sat alone __________ walked alone __________

named simple objects __________ spoke in sentences __________ slept through the night __________

dressed self __________ began toilet training __________

Words child uses for urination/bowel movement: ______________________

Are there any eating problems? ______________________

Any dietary restrictions (vegetarian, etc.)?______________________

How would you describe your child's personality? ______________________

Are there other child care arrangements during hours when the child does not attend this center?

____

How does your child respond to other children? ______________________

Has your child had any other group play experiences? ______________________

How does your child cope with separation? ______________________

Have there been any recent family changes that we should be aware of? ______________________

What do you find best comforts your child? ______________________

Does your child have any fears that you are aware of? ______________________

How does your child show stress and what do you do to relieve it?______________________

Do you have any concerns about your child's development? ______________________

____

Is there any other information you wish to share with us regarding your child? ______________________

____

____

____

Figure 1–9 Family Information Form (Courtesy of and reproduced with permission, BC Center, Broome Community College, Binghamton, NY)

Figure 1–10 A home visit is a way to establish a relationship between the teacher, the child, and the family. (Courtesy of B. Nilsen)

explore ways in which they can be involved in the life of the program. A home visit can be an excellent opportunity to explain the typical arrival and departure procedures, to inform the family and the child of the daily schedule, and to suggest to the family what they should provide (Figure 1–10).

The visitor talks and begins to make friends with the child by smiling and making gestures of friendship without overpowering or demanding their participation. The family watches the developing relationship. Reactions may vary depending on their knowledge and trust of the program and their feelings about the impending separation. Some visitors take a photograph of the family that will greet them on the first day. Giving the child a photograph of the teachers will begin the acquaintance on a visual level also. Having the child draw and then posting the drawing in the classroom for the child to look for on the first day is also a good strategy. Of course, notes about the visit are written and placed in the Class File or program's file and are confidential, open only to those directly responsible for the child, including the parents.

There are many well-known home visitation programs that deliver parenting education and seek to reduce child abuse. The most successful are those that do less modeling and more family support and take advising roles during the visit (Peterson, 1999). Early Head Start attributes its success to effectively engaging families with their child in home visits, with families reporting a feeling of partnership with the home visitor and an improved relationship with their child (Roggman, Boyce, Cook, & Jump, 2001). (See the resources list at the end of this chapter for more information about home visits.)

Home visits for public school teachers have been found to be effective in school adjustment, family involvement in the child's learning, and changes in teacher attitudes. "After home visits we found ourselves relating more often, verbally and emotionally, with the children. . . . After talking to parents in such a personal way, we began to view all of the children in our classes more compassionately and with greater understanding" (Gorter-Reu & Anderson, 1998, p. 73). Unfortunately, teacher–family contact, direct and informal and with less negative content, declines once children enter kindergarten (Rimm-Kaufman & Pianta, 1999). It does not need to be so. Schools are seeing the value in positive relationships with parents, and some have instituted some very effective strategies.

VISIT TO THE SCHOOL OR CENTER. Many schools have kindergarten visit days where children come to the classroom, perhaps ride the school bus around the parking lot, and eat lunch in the cafeteria, getting acquainted with the building, the teachers, and other children. Child care centers invite the family to bring the child to visit the center by appointment, so they receive individual attention. After-hours seems to work best. A typical day's routine is reviewed, from arrival through departure. They can take a tour of the center to see the rooms and areas the child will be using. The child can play and become familiar with the room and equipment. This is easier without the distraction of other children and the impending separation from the family. A nutritional snack time with the visitors sets a social atmosphere. An unhurried visit can help the child adjust to the environment.

The child forms a visual image of the center and begins to build positive images of herself at play there. This also builds the relationship of trust with the family. The family sees this is a good place for the child and experiences the center's willingness to be a part of the support system to their family.

FORMAL FAMILY ORIENTATION. Many programs (schools and centers) have a "family only" orientation where staff is introduced, policies are reviewed, and relationships between the family and the program are established. Food, adult chairs, and friendly greetings set the tone of partnership and cooperation. Providing child care during this orientation will not only assist more families to attend but will be one of the first signs that this is a family-friendly place.

A tour of the setting and a short video or slide presentation showing the "action" of the program help establish a positive atmosphere. Families' questions and concerns are anticipated in a short, reassuring presentation. The staff communicates the recognition of the needs of families and the dedication of the program to cooperate and accommodate as

@ it happened to me

Which one is the "teacher?"

A professor was visiting a student teacher in the infant room of a child care center, arriving before the student (oh, no!). While she was waiting for the student to arrive, she observed three women sitting, holding babies, warmly talking with them, jostling them, feeding them. Later in the visit, she learned that one of the three was the mother of an infant who was transitioning the baby to the center. What a complement to the caregivers that the care they were giving was like "mother-care." That's the way it should be. As for the student—well, that's another story.

Do you have an IT HAPPENED TO ME story about making school a comfortable place? Send it to WeekbyWeek@thomsonlearning.com

much as possible. Humor, understanding, and active listening are characteristics that will make this step in the transition smoother. Individual relationship-building between family and staff at this orientation helps alleviate the anxiety for the family, the child, and the staff. This is useful not only on the first day but throughout the year, as situations develop that no one can foresee right now. An opportunity for individual questions or even anonymous questions will help to provide an open forum.

TRANSITIONS FOR INFANTS. One might think that little babies, wrapped up and sleeping, won't even notice who is taking care of them. Wrong! Stress of infants in child care has been measured by their cortisol level (cortisol is a hormone released when the body is under stress). It has been found, however, that if the mothers spent more days adapting their children to child care, attachments remained secure without spikes in the cortisol level (Ahnert et al., 2004). That tells us that child care programs enrolling infants should encourage, if at all possible, the mother to spend several hours for several days at the center with her infant before leaving the infant

Figure 1–11 Building Blocks of Family-Teacher Relationships. Fill in the skills, qualities, and activities that will build strong relationships.

with the teacher. This can be time spent acquainting the child with the teacher, but it also gives the mother assurance that the child will be well cared for. Children sense the parent's ambivalence about leaving, so this would reduce that transference of anxiety from adult to child.

Working with Families for Arrivals and Departures

EXERCISE Think about the necessary foundations or building blocks of family–teacher relationships. Write the characteristics in the blocks in Figure 1–11.

Building blocks help the child adjust to a new environment; they are necessities in growth and development. Qualities such as trust, open communication, respect, a friendly face, approachability, kindness, and understanding might appear in the blocks.

The partnership of families and teachers gives the child the confidence that needs will be met by trustworthy adults. When there are barriers such as jealousy, fear, or differences in value systems that are not addressed, it is more difficult for the child to adjust to and develop in that environment. Open communication between family and program personnel is an important process.

If it is the beginning of the school year and all children are entering for the first time, a staggered first day, or first week, may be possible: Half, or a portion, of the children attend one day or one morning, with the other portion coming on a second day or in the afternoon. The rationale is that children are learning the routine and adjusting to the setting in small groups. This allows the staff to closely observe and interact with fewer children, forming friendships with them. Staff also can anticipate if there may be a separation stage to work through and begin to consult with families about strategies.

Every child should be greeted as they arrive. The greeter or door person sets the mood for the day, letting the child know he is important. The smile communicates acceptance and friendship. Greeting the child by name, and commenting on an event in the day that he particularly will enjoy, helps to prepare him for a good day ahead. This cannot be stated emphatically enough. Every child should be greeted and made to feel welcome!

Think About It . . .

A family member brings his child to your program for the first time. He gets the child interested in the water table, then walks over to you and says, "I'm just going to slip out so he won't cause a scene." What would you say?

"Separation is a natural part of life," says Susan Miller, author of many books on infant and toddler care and education (2002). "When you build strategies with families and children to alleviate anxieties, you're giving everyone the chance to start each day off right."

Families should be encouraged to establish a good-bye routine, stay for a while, and leave firmly. This allows the child to slowly adjust and not feel rushed or rejected. The child can anticipate the family member's departure by dependable cues. Caution should be taken that the child not manipulate the family member into "one more kiss, one more hug, one more. . . ." Sneaking out is discouraged no matter how much the family member sees it as an easier way. The disappearing parent undermines a child's sense of security. This mistrust leads to a fear that every time he gets involved in play or turns his back, the loved one will leave. Families should witness the staff's concern for the child and be assured that the needed comfort is given. The staff assists the family in involving the child in the routines and activities of the classroom and, if necessary, helps the family say goodbye with conviction. A phone call to the family later to say the child is no longer crying will alleviate the anxiety.

Alice Honig (2002) reminds families and caregivers to arrange for comfort spaces and to make the transition into the day gradual and relaxed. She says to look for the sparkle in the child's eyes as a sign that the child is ready to be engaged in play and exploration. Szamreta (2003) relates her experiences using and expanding peekaboo games and materials to help toddlers practice going-away/coming-back behavior, as a motivation for engagement with materials, and to transition from home to school (p. 88).

Planning for the end of the day is an important part of curriculum as well. It helps to have the child's belongings all in one place, like the cubby or a mailbox system, so there is no last-minute hunt for paintings or library books. When dismissal time is the same for everyone, some programs use closing circles, a hand squeeze, or recall and review of the day as a way to signal the transition from the program to home.

If children leave at different but predictable times, it is up to the teacher to give the child a cue that the departure time is approaching so the child can bring closure to the activity and mentally prepare for the change. When the family picks up unpredictably, the teacher can help the child cope with the change by assisting in the closing of the activity and engaging the family member in conversation so the child can work independently to prepare to leave.

Separation Anxiety and Difficulties

EXERCISE Describe an incident of separation difficulty you have witnessed.

As families consider leaving their child in someone else's care, there are psychological issues for all concerned: the family, the child, and the teacher. It is important to know about how a child develops attachments, as well as about the possible effects of separation on those attachments. There are strategies for helping the child and the family cope with the trauma of separation that reinforce the primary family–child relationship.

EXERCISE Describe what feelings each of these people might have upon the first day of school or care in a new program: the family, the child, and the teacher or caregiver.

SEPARATION ANXIETY BEHAVIOR. A child in the midst of a "separation anxiety attack" may display out-of-control behavior. It is embarrassing for the family member, who is fearful that the teacher will judge the child or the family in a negative way. And it is difficult for the teacher to address the emotional needs of an unfamiliar child. The family, and many other children and families as well, may be looking on. It is equally difficult for the child who is distressed and out of control, needing someone to help. These extreme moments call for calm reassurance that the family will return at the end of the day. An established good-bye routine, such as "kiss, kiss, hug, nose rub, bye-bye" and a prompt departure helps the child anticipate the family member's departure and come to rely on the family member's return.

The distressed child, of course, should receive holding and comforting as long as necessary to help overcome the feeling of abandonment. Often the child rejects any physical contact or comforting from this new adult. The teacher respects this but shows reliability of care and interest in the child's difficult moment. The teacher offers choices of activities that may be of interest to the child. The child may be kicking and screaming. This should be ignored if it is hurting no one, or gently restrained if it is aimed at the teacher, other children, or furniture. Removal of the child from the curious stares of other children prevents embarrassment and copycat behavior from others.

Verbal and body language convey understanding for the feelings of loneliness and anger. The child is reassured that the family member will return. The teacher communicates the desire to help the child gain control and have a safe, happy time while she is here. Reading a book, singing a song, rocking, or stroking the back sometimes helps soothe those feelings. Continued violent reactions call for patience, tolerance, and endurance. The child is mourning and grieving for the absence of familiar people. To try to distract is to deny the child's feelings. They will eventually subside. Sometimes the most effective teacher action is just quiet acceptance of the strong emotions without overtures to distract the child. Each child has individual behavior patterns to be learned. The teacher seeks the most effective relaxation techniques for each child. The child builds trust in the family member's return and learns **coping mechanisms.**

EXERCISE What would you say to this child? See Figure 1–12.

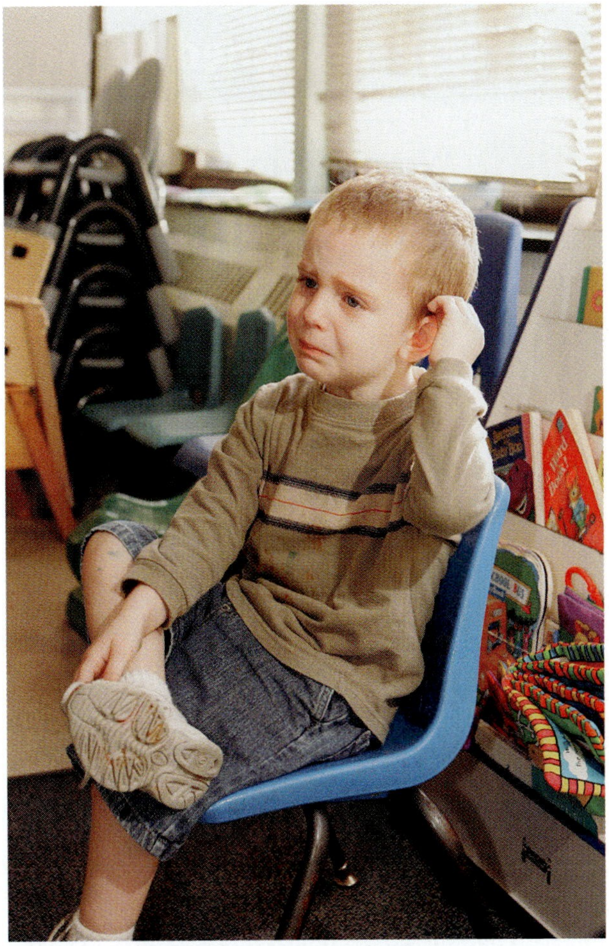

Figure 1–12 What would you say to this child?

Separation Anxiety Warning Signs

Difficulties with separation may not always appear at the beginning of the year, the beginning of the day, or in a violent emotional outburst. Sometimes partway through the day or the year, a child who appeared adjusted to school begins to display some difficulties: Crying at the family member's leaving or the inability to eat, sleep, or play all can happen at any time. What is going on? It may be the maturing process. As the child develops, thinking changes. She may be passing into a new stage. That happy baby who held out her arms wide to the teacher is now burying her head in her dad's coat. She may be the toddler who takes one look at the caregiver, looks at mom, and kicks and shrieks as her coat is removed. The child grabs it back, latches onto her mom's pocketbook strap like it is a life preserver, and will not let go. It may be that child who came happily each day with a smile and a picture she drew for the teacher who now says, "I don't like it here. I wanna go home." It is just as important for the teacher to respond promptly to more subtle separation behavior. Such behavior can take many forms: difficulties in eating, sleeping, toileting, learning, or social difficulties.

EATING. For the infant, refusal to take nourishment is an immediate danger signal. Teachers can try various positions of holding during feeding, and even blocking the infant's view of the family member. Communication with the family member about feeding routines ahead of time, and even a phone

it happened to me

Wrapped in Love

I was visiting in an infant room and saw a baby about six months old wrapped in a large red shawl while the teacher fed him. She later explained he was having difficulty adjusting and would not eat at the center. Through trial and error she and his mother came up with the idea of bringing in something of the mother's from home. Wrapped in his mother's shawl, he was wrapped in the essence of her love and security. Now he could eat.

Do you have an IT HAPPENED TO ME story about a child's separation and adjustment? I'd love to read it. Send it to WeekbyWeek@thomsonlearning.com

call to verify and seek advice, may be helpful. A joint effort of family member and teacher should make this difficulty short-lived. Continued difficulty may need the involvement of the pediatrician and other support personnel.

For toddlers and preschoolers, eating away from home may be distressing, perceived as a betrayal of that very personal time with close family members. A relaxed environment without pressure from teachers, along with familiar foods and utensils, will help ease this time. It usually is just a matter of days until children adjust and join in the sociability of mealtime and look forward to it with enthusiasm. If a child is crying at mealtime, refusing food day after day, or indicating by behaviors that this is a stressful time, the situation demands attention. Family member–teacher communication, sometimes with a referral agent, such as the director or the pediatrician, can usually work this through.

SLEEPING. Environmental changes can affect sleep, so children in new places may have difficulty resting. Other children's schedules and sleep patterns may keep the child from sleeping. The new environment, governed by licensing regulations, may add to the child's difficulty in adjustment to sleeping away from home. The teacher gathers information from the

Figure 1–13 Family members and teachers need to communicate about children's routines.

family on the child's sleep patterns. Upon each day's arrival, family members give information about last night's sleep. Everything possible is done to make the environment conducive to the child's relaxation. Music, favorite toys, books, or a blanket help with sleep routines and should be individual choices for children. Children having adjustment problems to center care may have continued sleep disturbances.

Again, the close observation and responsiveness of the teacher to the individual child's needs will help. Communication with the family for understanding and accommodating the child's needs to the center's practices also helps (Figure 1–13). Sleep deprivation might result in the child's irritable behavior and increased anxiety for the adults.

Making notes on the child's sleepy times of day, indicators of sleep needs, techniques that relax the child, positions of sleep, and toys or physical items normally taken to bed are important pieces of information for the child's file. Sharing and exchanging information such as this with the family will help the child's adjustment to sleeping away from home. It also assists substitute teachers in meeting the child's needs when the regular teacher is absent.

TOILETING. For two-year-olds, managing toilet needs on their own is a big accomplishment, but it is not without its relapses for a variety of reasons. Adjustment to a new place may upset that delicate balance. The child is curious and may frequently use the child-sized toilet as a novelty. The new stimulating environment full of active play areas and new playmates may result in forgetfulness or inattention to toileting cues, leading to accidents. A matter-of-fact attitude by teachers, along with a change into familiar clothing after a toileting accident, usually is all that is necessary to help the child cope with these events.

Some children, however, have a delicate emotional response to new places, making it difficult to eliminate in this new surrounding. A child may hold the genitals, lay over a chair until the urge passes, or even cry from a severe stomachache. It is up to the teacher to be a detective, interpreting these subtle clues. Once the cause is determined, appropriate action can be taken. Again, communication with the family about the child's patterns, times, and physical cues is an important part of making the child comfortable. Family members taking the child into the bathroom and talking about using it should be part of the first visit or first day at the center. Continued disruption in toileting may cause bladder infections or constipation and other disorders. A daily, unobtrusive observation of the child's toileting behavior is also a part of the record-keeping procedure. Any extraordinary behavior should be noted factually and shared at the end of the day with the family member, away from the presence of the child.

PARTICIPATION. The child who is experiencing separation difficulties may not be able to attend to the learning activities that are planned. He may have difficulty making choices or staying with a task. Transitions from one area to another or interacting positively with other children may precipitate crying or tantrums. After a normal adjustment period, if this behavior is observed, it should be recorded. Reference to it later will indicate the stages the child has gone through in the separation process.

SOCIAL INTERACTIONS. When a child is in emotional turmoil, it may affect the child's outward behavior toward others. The child may cling to one teacher, transferring attachment to another adult. That is a healthy coping mechanism in an infant and toddler and, temporarily, for the preschooler. A branching out of friendships and social contacts is expected after a time. Some interventions may be necessary if that is not observed.

Children who are experiencing separation difficulties may be socially withdrawn. The group situation may be overwhelming. The child just needs some time to watch and see how other children are handling it. A sensitive teacher will allow the child this luxury of watching, along with an occasional commentary on what the other children are doing. The child is invited to join the play. The teacher will also be familiar with the stages of play and have realistic expectations for the child's positive social interactions. Communication with the family to know the child's social history will also help to better understand the child's reactions. It would be helpful to know the positive or negative experiences the child has had with siblings and other children who are the same age.

ACTING OUT AS A SYMPTOM OF SEPARATION ANXIETY. For some children, the new environment is so stimulating that their self-control is not strong enough to govern their behavior. The child may be unaccustomed to so many playmates and play areas. Inappropriate and unsafe actions may erupt, which might result in rejection by other children. The teacher redirects or restricts behavior. The staggered first day can help to ease this transition. For the child entering the program once it has already begun, it may be overwhelming. Other children are already established in routines and have formed friendships. The teacher coaches the new child through routines and introduces expectations in various areas to help the child adjust.

The child comes into a new situation not knowing the rules and the people; she feels rejected and abandoned by the family. When the teacher places herself in those little sneakers, it will help to ease the child through these first days.

When the child is sending a signal of distress or going through a new phase, the best defense is that close communication and understanding between family member and teacher. It is helpful to have a talk, outside of the child's hearing, about the change. This may reveal some unusual events at home that are manifested in behaviors of insecurity and separation anxiety. Together, some ideas can be generated about how to help everyone cope with changes or troubled times.

Permanent Departures and Good-byes

Just as beginnings are important, so are endings.

EXERCISE **Using a separate sheet of paper, make a list of ending celebrations, rituals, or customs.**

Bringing closure to a letter, a day, or a life has emotional importance. It closes the circle.

A good-bye party for a child who is moving or leaving the program helps recognize the child for the contribution she made to the class. Classmates can present physical reminders of her friends there. Though it is a sad occasion, it can be a part of learning to say good-bye. By attempting to remain in contact, a sense of the larger community is felt with her as a link to the next city, state, or country. This helps both the child leaving and those remaining.

At the end of the year, a child-centered farewell celebration (as opposed to cap-and-gown commencement for preschoolers) can be planned. This is also a time for remembering (part of the cognitive process); expressing positive feelings for one another (social and emotional development); and drawing, dictating, or writing remembrances (literacy and art activities).

Planning for departures as well as arrivals is an important part of the teacher's responsibilities and also can be opportunities to observe. How does the child organize for the end of the day? What is the child's response to the cue of the approaching end to an activity? How does the child greet the family member at the end of the day? These are possible Class List Log criteria.

HELPING ALL CHILDREN WITH SEPARATION AND SCHOOL ADJUSTMENT

Children with special needs and children from nonmainstream cultures or who may not speak English are entering programs nationwide. The practitioner has the responsibility to be prepared to help these children make the transition into the program as stress-free as possible. Prior knowledge of the child, no matter what the situation, helps this process. Specific knowledge of these special populations is imperative. Family, and professionals providing information, research, and extra observation and patience will all be required.

Children with Special Needs

The Americans with Disabilities Act of 1990 (P.L. 101-336) protects against discrimination based on a person's disability. Children with disabilities must be admitted into settings that have been adapted to accommodate them. When children with special needs are integrated into a group, it is important to have knowledge and information concerning the exceptionality and this child's situation in particular before the first day they come to school. This can be obtained from the family information form, a home visit, or the child's report from helping professionals if the parents have given permission for its release.

The family of a child with a disability may be more anxious about leaving the child in a school setting. That anxiety may be transferred to the child—making separation more difficult for all. Child and family alike need the reassurance that the child will be well cared for and accepted. In fact, inclusive settings often help to foster children's ideas about helping others, the understanding of emotions, and acceptance of individuals with disabilities (Diamond, 2001).

@ it happened to me

Mid-September Reflection

We had gotten through those first days and weeks. All those plans for smooth transitions seemed to have paid off. Each child came ready to play and said good-bye to family willingly. They had fallen into the routine of the day. Today during free play, I could move from area to area, observe their play, comment on their actions, add a prop here and there, and enjoy their absorption with activities of their choosing.

Then I heard a noise, a long sucking in of air with a quiet sort of high-pitched wail. Where did it come from? I looked around the room. Children were climbing and sliding and going in and out the door on the climber, which was their spaceship today. A boy was sitting at the table in the dramatic play area with a police hat on. He was packing a lunch pail with dishes and silverware, talking to another boy who was stirring "soup." Several children were in the block area piling blocks, laying out carpet squares, and standing up farm animals. Sandbox players were pouring, shoveling, and digging for shells they found hidden there. Two children at the easel, a boy on one side and a girl on the other, were busily making lines and circles. There it was again! I looked around again. Same scene as before, but now I could locate the source of the sound. It seemed to be coming from the boy at the easel. As I looked closer, he stared at his paper as his hands moved methodically up and down. He watched the paint as it dripped from the brush, then I heard the sound again and saw his face muscles tense into a frozen stare.

I walked over and placed my hand on his shoulder. The dam broke. He let out all those sobs he had been trying to hold in! He was missing his mom and had tried to hide it for an hour but just could not hold it in any longer. Were there signs I could have seen before it got to this point? Are there others who were feeling this internal sadness, holding it in check but inwardly hurting? Was I being smug and self-congratulating without really addressing the issue of separation with those who were least capable of coping with it—the children? I vowed to be a more empathetic observer and to use more touch as a message to each child that I am here to support and comfort if they need me. Tomorrow I'll read *Are You My Mother?* by Eastman [1988] to stimulate some discussion about separation and the ever-returning parent.

Do you have an IT HAPPENED TO ME story about separation anxiety? I'd love to read it. Send it to WeekbyWeek@thomsonlearning.com

For children with visual impairments, audio recordings about the routines and what to expect from a typical day would be helpful. If the child is hearing-impaired, this could be done through a picture album. The teachers should become familiar with the language the child will be using to communicate. Knowledge of a child's physical impairments will help modify the setting to be more accessible. Of course, the building already meets the guidelines for accessibility under the Americans with Disabilities Act (P.L. 101-336). Modifications may need to be made within the classroom arrangement and in the thinking and approach of the staff. Any modifications for the child preferably are made before the child enters the program. Emotional or behavioral disabilities should be understood thoroughly through conferences with the family and helping professionals so that the teachers are prepared and react in an appropriate and consistent way.

Diverse Cultures

The attachment between family and child varies for different cultures. For some, the infant never is physically apart from an adult, being held, carried, or touched almost constantly. For these children, the physical and emotional separation needs special attention. In other cultures, children are expected to become independent very quickly, so any expectation of separation anxiety is not understood or tolerated. An awareness of cultural parenting styles and the attachment and separation practices will help the teacher adjust expectations and actions.

For the child who is non–English-speaking, it is most helpful if the teacher learns a few of the most important words such as greetings, routines like "Eat," "Toilet," "Mother returning soon," and "I can help you." This can be accomplished by asking the family, working through an interpreter, or researching translations at the library. The child will need time and an environment that is child-centered. When the environment is restricted by teacher's directions and highly emphasizes following directions, the non–English-speaking child will have difficulty adjusting. Play is a universal language, and once the child feels comfortable, the lure of play will help her feel more comfortable.

Meeting the needs of each child as an individual necessitates preparation, understanding, and careful observation skills.

HELPING PROFESSIONALS FOR SEPARATION AND SCHOOL ADJUSTMENT CONCERNS

If a child is having separation or classroom adjustment problems beyond his ability to cope, it may be necessary to consult helping professionals. After consultations with families and the director or program personnel, outside professionals who may help include:

pediatrician—physician specifically trained to care for the health and well-being of children
child psychologist—conducts screenings for diagnosis and treatment of children with emotional, behavioral, or developmental problems
child psychiatrist—provides counseling or consultative services to individuals or families who may be experiencing problems
play therapist—child psychologist who uses play to diagnose and treat children who may be withdrawn, nonverbal, or traumatized

OTHER METHODS

Other Methods to Record Separation and Adjustment:

Anecdotal and Running Records
Checklists/Rating Scales
Conversations and Interviews
Work Samples
Media

STANDARDS

Selected examples of standards for addressing building positive relationships and helping with separations:

Child Development Associate: Assessment System and Competency Standards (1997).
Competency Goal IV
Candidate maintains an open, friendly, and cooperative relationship with each child's family, encourages their involvement in the program, and supports the child's relationship with his or her family.

Standard 2.004
Helping Families Cope with Separation
Caring for Our Children: National Health and Safety Performance Standards: Guidelines for Out-of-Home Child Care Programs (American Academy of Pediatrics (2002). Used with permission.
The staff of the facility shall help the child and parents cope with the experience of separation and loss.
For the child, this shall be accomplished by:

a) Encouraging parents to spend time in the facility with the child;
b) Enabling the child to bring to child care tangible reminders of home/family (such as a favorite toy or a picture of self and parent);
c) Helping the child to play out themes of separation and reunion;
d) Frequently exchanging information between the child's parents and teachers, including activities and routine care information;
e) Reassuring the child about the parent's return;
f) Ensuring that the teacher(s) are consistent both within the parts of a day and across days.

For the parents, this shall be accomplished by:

a) Validating their feelings as a universal human experience;
b) Providing parents with information about the positive effects for children of high quality facilities with strong parent participation;
c) Encouraging parents to discuss their feelings;
d) Providing parents with evidence, such as photographs, that their child is being cared for and is enjoying the activities of the facility.

KEY TERMS

attachment	reflection
Class List Log	Reflective Journal
coping mechanisms	separation anxiety
daily log or journal	stranger anxiety
diary	subjective
good-bye rituals	summative observation

Go to the Bind-in-Book CD Section A Plan Week 1 for:

Class List Log form
Plan Week 1 Part A, Directions for a Class List Log on Separation and School Adjustment, including What to Do with It, Portfolio Overview Example, Sharing with Child and Family, Actions—Read a Book, In the Environment, In the Curriculum, In the Newsletter
Plan Week 1 Part B, Directions for Work Samples for All
Plan Week 1 Part C, Reflective Journal

REFERENCES

Aaronsohn, E. (1996). *Going against the grain: Supporting the student-centered teacher.* Thousand Oaks, CA: Corwin Press.

Ahnert, L., Gunnar, M. R., Lamb, M. E., & Barthel, M. (2004). Transition to child care: Associations with infant-mother attachment, infant negative emotion and cortisol elevations. *Child Development,* (75) 3, 639–650, May/June 2004.

Ainsworth, M., Blehar, M., Waters, E., & Wall, S. (1978). *Patterns of attachment.* Hillsdale, NJ: Lawrence Erlbaum Associates.

American Academy of Pediatrics. (2002). *Caring for our children: National health and safety performance standards: Guidelines for out-of-home child care* (2nd ed.). Elk Grove Village, IL: American Academy of Pediatrics.

Balaban, N. (1995). *Learning to say good-bye: Starting school and other early childhood separations.* New York: New American Library.

Bjorklund, D. F., & Bjorklund, B. R. (1992). *Looking at children: An introduction to child development.* Pacific Grove, CA: Brooks/Cole Publishing Co.

Bloch, J. S. (1987). *The five P's manual.* Syosset, NY: Variety Pre-Schooler's Workshop.

Bowlby, J. (1969). *Attachment.* New York: Basic Books.

Bricker, (1999). *ASQ questionnaire system* (2nd ed.). Baltimore, MD: Brookes.

Council for Early Childhood Professional Recognition. (1997). *The child development associate: Assessment system and competency standards.* Washington, DC: Author.

Diamond, K. E. (2001). Relationships among young children's ideas, emotional understanding and social contact with classmates with disabilities. *Topics in Early Childhood Special Education, 21* (2), 104–114.

Eastman, P. D. (1988). *Are you my mother?* New York: Random House.

Forrest, R., & McCrea, N. (2002, January). How do I relate and share professionally? Child Care Information Exchange, issue *143,* p. 49.

Gorter-Reu, M. S., & Anderson, J. M. (1998). Home kits, home visits, and more! *Young Children,* 53 (3), 73.

Hendrick, J. (1997). *First steps toward teaching the Reggio way.* Upper Saddle River, NJ: Merrill, an imprint of Prentice Hall.

Honig, A. S. (2002). Soothing separations. *Scholastic Early Childhood Today, 17* (1), 20–22.

McAfee, O., & Leong, D. (2007). *Assessing and guiding young children's development and learning* (4th ed.). Boston: Pearson Allyn and Bacon.

Miller, S. A. (2002). Easing the transition from home to school. *Scholastic Early Childhood Today, 17* (1), 33–34.

NAEYC. (2005). *NAEYC early childhood program standards and accreditation criteria.* Washington, DC: Author.

Peterson, E. (1999, Fall). Home-grown advice: Tips on making your program's home visits rewarding for parents and children. *Children and Families, 18* (4), 30–33.

Rimm-Kaufman, S. E., & Pianta, R. C. (1999). Patterns of family–school contact in preschool and kindergarten. *School Psychology Review, 28* (3), 426.

Roggman, L. A., Boyce, L. K., Cook, G. A., & Jump, V. K. (2001). Inside home visits: A collaborative look at process and quality. *Early Childhood Research Quarterly, 16* (1), 53–71.

Shaffer, H., & Emerson, P. E. (1964). The development of social attachments in infancy. *Monographs of the Society for Child Development, 29* (3), serial No. 94.

Swick, K. J., DaRose, D., & Pavia, L. (1998/99). Inquiry as key to early childhood teacher education. *Childhood Education, 75* (2), 66–70.

Szamreta, J. M. (2003). Peekaboo power: To ease separation and build secure relationships. *Young Children, 58* (1), 88.

Terte, E. A., Klein, S. M., & Jewett, J. L. (Eds.). (1998). *When teachers reflect: Journeys toward effective, inclusive practice.* Washington, DC: NAEYC.

Yarrow, L. J. (1964). Separation from parents during early childhood. In M. L. Hoffman & L. W. Hoffman (Eds.), *Review of child development research, Vol. I.* New York: Russell Sage Foundation.

RESOURCES

Aaronsohn, E. (1996). *Going against the grain: Supporting the student-centered teacher.* Thousand Oaks, CA: Corwin Press.

American Academy of Pediatrics. (2002). *Caring for our children: National health and safety performance standards: Guidelines for out-of-home child care* (2nd ed.). Elk Grove Village, IL: American Academy of Pediatrics.

Bailey, B. (2000). *I love you rituals.* New York: Harper Collins.

Balaban, N. (1987). *Learning to say good-bye: Starting school and other early childhood separations.* New York: New American Library.

Blecher-Sass, H. (1997). Good-byes can build trust. *Young Children, 52* (7), 12–14.

Brodkin, A. (1994). "She cries when I leave." *Early Childhood Today, 9* (1), 38–39.

Church, E. B. (1992). Separation: Helping kids and families through the transition. *Pre-K Today,* 7 (1), 62–78.

Hendrick, J. (1997). *First steps toward teaching the Reggio way.* Upper Saddle River, NJ: Merrill, an imprint of Prentice Hall.

Johnson, L., & Mermen, J. (1994). Easing children's entry to school: Home visits help. *Young Children, 49* (4), 62–68.

NAEYC. (2005). *NAEYC early childhood program standards and accreditation criteria.* Washington, DC: Author.

Terte, E. A., Klein, S. M., & Jewett, J. L. (Eds.). (1998). *When teachers reflect: Journeys toward effective, inclusive practice.* Washington, DC: NAEYC.

CHAPTER 2

Using Anecdotal Recordings to Look at Self-Care

IN THIS CHAPTER

USING THE ANECDOTAL RECORDING

Maralyce went into the bathroom in the three-year-old classroom. After considerable time, she could be heard screaming and crying. The teacher rushed to the door to find Maralyce standing by the toilet, pants around ankles, trying to adjust streams of toilet paper to cover the seat. Every time she put one strip on, another would slide off. The teacher asked "What's wrong, Maralyce? Why are you crying?" Maralyce sobbed, "Mommy said I can't go potty 'til I cover the seat, and it won't stay on." The teacher went and quickly got tape and gave it to Maralyce. She taped the paper on the seat, sat down quickly, and let out a "Wooo!" (The teacher saw the still-developing coordination of a three-year-old in conflict with a parental expectation. She was inclined to say, "You don't need that paper. The seat is clean." However, she wanted Maralyce to have a way to do it herself, and did not want to contradict the family's authority and instructions.)

There are incidents that need to be remembered exactly as they happened. They tell a story that lets the reader see, hear, and feel as if he were there. The story contains a factual account of an incident that may be typical or out of the ordinary. The incident, however, is best remembered in its entirety. The most factual recording method is **Anecdotal Recording**. It can be used to

- portray an incident that indicates a child's development in a specific area.

- record a humorous incident to share with families.
- preserve the details of a curious incident for later reflection.
- record the exact details of a child's disclosure of an incidence of abuse.
- exemplify a child's typical behavior.
- record the details of an incident that is totally foreign to the child's typical behavior.

The Anecdotal Recording is a **narrative** account of an incident anywhere from a few seconds to several minutes in length. The Anecdotal Recording recounts the event, telling the reader when, where, who, and what. It does not answer the question *why* in the body of the recording. That conclusion or **inference** is separated from the recording. An inference is an informed judgment or conclusion based on observation. When we see a child crying, our inference is that the child is sad or hurt. We may or may not be correct.

Every newspaper reporter, police officer, and insurance claims adjuster knows that facts written on the scene or very shortly thereafter are the most accurate. When an event occurs that is important to remember, a few notes are jotted down to refer to later. If an interesting conversation is happening, it is recorded word for word. It is written, as much as possible, as it is happening (Figure 2–1). By the end of the day, the notes are amplified and rewritten into a full account while the details are still fresh. It can be written on regular lined paper. It helps to fold the paper in half vertically and write on the left side so that explanatory comments can be written in the right-hand column. In this way, comments of the recorder are placed separately from the recording. The reader then knows the difference between the actual recounting of the incident and the writer's inferences. It also is possible to fold the paper so the comments are not visible. Another reader can then draw independent conclusions about the incident.

Bentzen (2005) calls this an **open method**, a narrative that preserves the details so that different interpretations can be made, determined by the reader's focus. The reader receives a mental picture of that event by reading the words.

An Anecdotal Recording is a written replay of an incident. In Figure 2–1, note the following characteristics of an Anecdotal Recording:

- It sets the stage for the reader: "In cubbies dressing for outdoor play."
- It identifies the characters, the target child by name—Sherita—and the other child by initial for anonymity—D (this may even need to be blotted out later): "Sherita and D and Teacher." Abbreviations are used in the writing for speed.
- The account describes the action in detail: "Sherita bends over with eyes close to D's coat zipper."
- It describes the interaction between the characters. "T bends down and says,"
- It records exact quotes, including pronunciation as it is heard. "I tan't dit it!"
- It concludes with result or reaction between characters. "You're my buddy, right?" Sherita: "Right, Davi."

Separate from that account in the right-hand column, the teacher writes comments, inferences, judgments, questions, and reminders:

- comments on development: "Helper attitude"
- actions: "Talk to speech therapist for an update"
- reminders: "Place Sherita and Davi together at lunch"
- curriculum plans: "Bring in dress-up clothing with separating zippers"

On a separate note, the teacher reminds herself to copy the anecdote for Davi's file, and then she will make appropriate notes in the right-hand column relating to Davi's part in the incident, perhaps blocking out Sherita's name for anonymity.

With the inferences in the right-hand column separate from the actual recording of the incident, it is easily folded back for a fresh viewpoint. Other readers may interpret the incident differently. Inferences or evaluations may differ, depending on the role of the observer. Davi's family might infer she is not getting proper attention from the teacher. Another child's family might wonder why this helpless child is in such an advanced class, demanding time from the teacher. Another teacher might deduce that this child needs some instruction in self-care skills. The speech pathologist might be overjoyed to hear Sherita express herself in nearly recognizable words. The teacher might write a comment to the side, "Sherita is the youngest in her family so seldom has a chance to be the helper. Davi has often excluded Sherita from play, so this may be the beginning of a friendship." All people read the same account, but their inferences are different because of their perspectives.

Frank (1999) calls this "using ethnographic eyes." It is the difference between *note taking* and *note making*. Note taking is the descriptive field notes that give the reader a re-creation of the sensory information (seeing, hearing, feeling, smelling). Note making is the interpretation of what is being observed. In Figure 2–1, the description of zipping the coat and

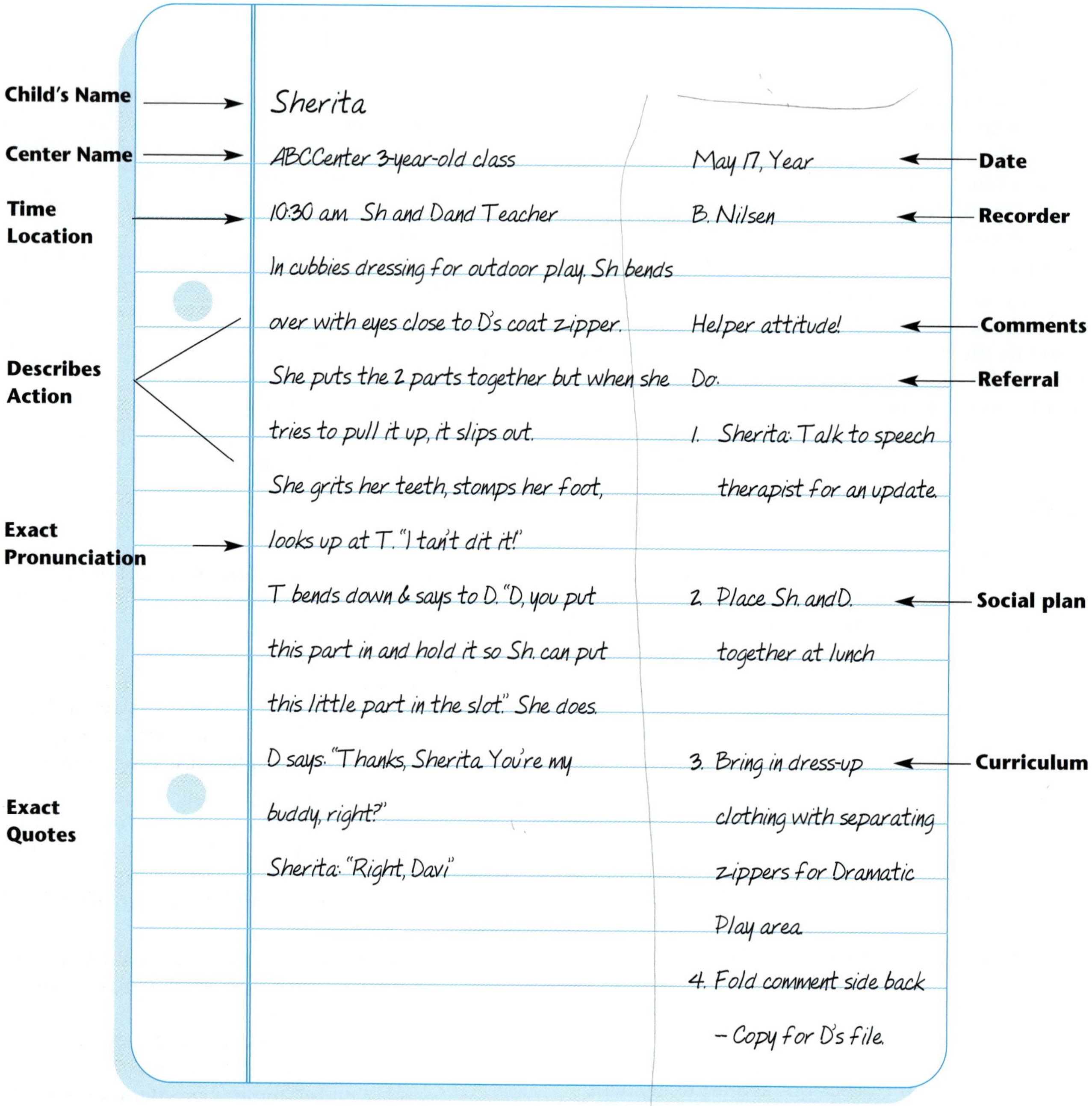

Figure 2–1 Anecdotal Recording Example.

the exact quotes are examples of note taking. "Helper attitude!" is the interpretation—it is note making.

Many people use the term *Anecdotal Recording* when what actually has been written is a diary account (Figure 2–2). This type of recording is true, but it is not factual. It summarizes actions, draws conclusions, and leaves out information that could be useful. Compare Figure 2–2 to Figure 2–1. See that the Anecdotal Recording in Figure 2–1 gives enough detail so that the reader has the feeling of being there. The anecdotal recording relates:

body positions—"bent over, eyes closed"
actions—"puts two parts together," "slips out"
reactions—"grits teeth," "stomps foot," "looks up"
exact words—"Davi, you hold this," "Thanks Sherita"
inflection and pronunciation—"I tan't dit it"

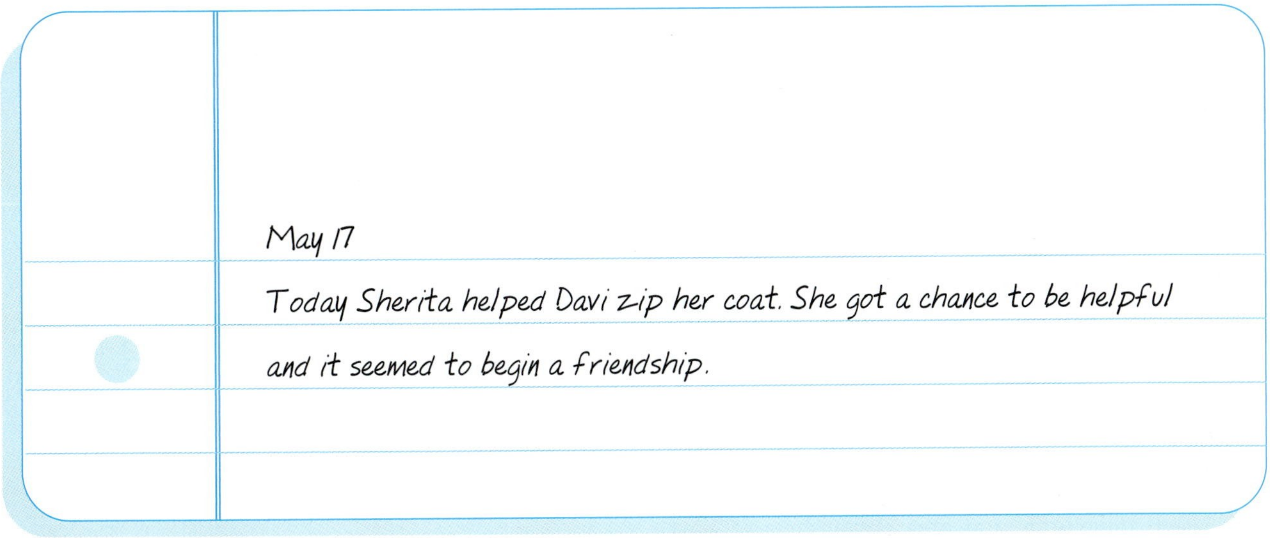

Figure 2–2 Diary Example.

The reader "sees" the incident. She "hears" the conversation along with emphasis as it was spoken. Then, more accurate and individual judgments based on the reader's perspective are made.

Uses

Anecdotal Recordings can be

- used for preserving details about any developmental skill, behavior, or incident for later judgments and reflection.
- given to other people for their independent evaluation.
- used as an accurate, detailed recording method in suspicion or disclosure of child abuse.

Think About It . . .

What advantages and disadvantages do you see in using an Anecdotal Recording?

Read those that follow and see if you agree.

Advantages

Anecdotal Recordings

- need no special forms.
- are preserved facts and details for any reader to draw conclusions.
- give a short, contextual account of an incident.
- give the reader a "sense of being there."
- separate judgments or inferences from details of the incident.
- are useful for recording all areas of development.
- are necessary for capturing exact details for specific purposes, such as speech/language development and child abuse disclosure.

Disadvantages

Some of the shortcomings of Anecdotal Recordings include:

- Choosing which incidents to record gives the writer selectivity that may influence positive or negative collections.
- Intense writing is necessary to capture all details, quotes, body movements.
- Focusing on writing diverts attention from interactions with children.
- The Anecdotal Recording can only focus on a few minutes of action.
- The Anecdotal Recording can only focus on one or two children at a time.

Pitfalls to Avoid

Random selection of children to write about in an anecdotal format presents the same problem as diary entries. There is usually some child performing attention-getting behavior. Others would never have a focused anecdotal record in their file because they are placid, follow the rules, and rarely draw attention to themselves.

This is overcome by the *Week by Week* Portfolio plan. It specifies a few children a week as the focus of in-depth recordings. These children are not selected randomly but from a planned numbering system from the alphabetical Class List Log. In addition, the developmental area to be observed is suggested so that the selection of what and when to write about is more objective and documentation is collected in all developmental areas. With the *Week by Week* plan, information is gathered on all the children every week in a different developmental area. In addition to that, a more focused observation and recording is done on a specified group of children. Over the course of a year, using the *Week by Week* plan, each developmental area is revisited at least three times for each child. Also, each child is the focus of at least three Anecdotal Recordings. The Bind-in-Book CD Section B contains the full *Week by Week* plan. Section D illustrates how the *Week by Week* plan documents the developmental areas for each child in the class.

The most difficult part of Anecdotal Recording is just writing factually. Those little inferences, explanations, reasons, feelings, and biases just slip in. The recorder constantly needs to test if the reader will "see it in the mind." If the recording is not describing an event exactly as it occurred, then the writer is summarizing and it ceases to be an accurate recording. It requires the recorder to stretch vocabulary to describe actions in noninferential, nonjudgmental terms:

"zipped Davi's jacket," not "helped"
"jumped and fell," not "clumsy"
"gave a piece of Play Doh," not "shared"
"eyes widened, mouth open," not "looked surprised"

EXERCISE 1 **Mark the following sentences *Yes* if they fit the criteria for Anecdotal Recording or *No* if they are inferences, explanations, or not exact quotes.**

______ a. Tara ran over to the cubby area.
______ b. She had on a short shirt and wanted to get her jacket.
______ c. Stacey asked her, "Why do you want your jacket on?"
______ d. She said her stomach was cold.
______ e. Tara shrugged her shoulders.
______ f. Stacey went over and zipped the jacket for Tara.
______ g. Tara thanked her.

Answers:

a. Yes. It tells where she went and how she went there.
b. No. How does the reader know what she wanted? Just describe what is visible: "She had on a short shirt. She got her jacket from the hook."
c. Yes. These were the exact words.
d. No. This is not a direct quote. Instead, write, "Tara said, 'My belly is cold.'"
e. Yes. Body motion is described.
f. Yes. Action is described.
g. No. This is not a direct quote. Instead, Tara said, "Thank you, my dear."

EXERCISE 2 **Make a list of descriptive but noninferential, nonjudgmental words to use in place of these to give the reader more information about the nature of how the action was carried out:**

stood
walked
said
cried
laughed

EXERCISE 3 **Look at Figure 2–3. Write an imaginary Anecdotal Recording as if you were there. Remember the technique: description and quotes. Have someone else read it and ask if they can picture exactly what happened from your writing.**

Figure 2–3 Examine this photograph and write an imaginary Anecdotal Record.

EXERCISE 4 **Watch a person performing a routine task, such as walking to and turning on a light, getting something from a purse, or coming into a room and finding a seat. Write an Anecdotal Recording so the reader can mentally visualize exactly the motions of that person. Have someone else read it to determine if it is descriptive and not inferential.**

Using Technology

There are various electronic recording devices that may be used to capture events as they are happening that may be faster and more accurate than writing about the incident while it is happening (or shortly thereafter).

AUDIO RECORDING. Dictating into small tape recorders can be useful for capturing the details that will later help you write an Anecdotal Recording. Transcribing tape-recorded notes can be done quickly by a fast typist into a computer file. The transcription can be placed in the corresponding developmental area of the electronic Portfolio Overview Sheet. Printing out the Anecdotal Record stored in this way also makes it easier for the family or other staff to read.

VIDEO RECORDING. This is the best way to capture all the detail of an incident. Unfortunately, the very advantage—capturing everything—is a disadvantage in that it takes too much time to sift through the material to determine what is mundane and what is important developmental information. It is also difficult to focus the camera on one specific child without the child becoming self-conscious and then changing behavior from natural to unnatural. Filtering out background noise and action is also difficult for all but the most experienced videographers. Video recordings can, however, be useful for practicing Anecdotal Recording skills.

VOICE RECOGNITION SOFTWARE. There are computer programs that are inexpensive, or even free, that allow your speech to be transferred into electronic text. This makes Anecdotal Recording easier to do and easier to read than handwriting.

How to Find the Time

Using the small tape recorder (as discussed above) can save time. Using a voice recognition program (mentioned previously) can also speed the transfer of notes into a detailed account. When you are writing about self-help skills, keep a pad and pen nearby at mealtime, in the cubby area, and in the bathroom; this will enable you to capture those details where they happen.

SELF-CARE

Documentation	Location	Recorder	Date
CL		BAN	9/14
AR		MS	3/15

Figure 2–4 Portfolio Overview Sheet Example.

What to Do with This Information

An Anecdotal Recording preserves specific information that can be used in many ways. It contributes to the overall assessment and evaluation of the child when combined with other information-gathering resources. It is stored in the child's Portfolio (Figure 2–4).

CHILD'S PORTFOLIO. If the incident captured in an Anecdotal Recording involves more than one child, it can be copied and the names of other children blocked out to place in more than one file. Block out names other than the child of this Portfolio. The previous incident could be placed in Sherita's file with Davi's name blocked out. It could be copied for Davi's file with Sherita's name blocked out. In this particular incident, blocking the name may not be necessary, but it does establish a practice of confidentiality. Sometimes it is unpredictable what judgments the reader will make about the other children involved. The teacher's copy in the Class File preserves all names for reference.

In the Portfolio, this Anecdotal Recording will serve as documentation for judgments made about the child: "Sherita is using words in conversations now (language development) and even helping other children (social development)."

This recording can be compared to earlier incidents: "Compare anecdotal record of 2/13 to those of 9/27, 10/14, and 12/20 to see the progress Sherita has made."

CURRICULUM PLANNING. Class activity ideas come from close observations: "I think I'll bring in some clothes with separating zippers for the dramatic play area to give all the children some practice. That sequined vest I got at a garage sale will be a hit."

It can be the basis for making an individual plan: "Sherita is beginning to play near other children. Strategies: Model play and sharing behaviors, connect Sherita with Davi in a cooperative activity, read a book to small group including Sherita, and initiate playmate discussion."

The recorder may decide to further investigate or question a concern: "Listen more closely to Sherita's language and ask the speech pathologist if this is age-appropriate."

OTHER TEACHERS ON THE TEAM. The recording may be read by others on the team to gather their opinions on the meaning of the incident: "Does this incident seem like unusual behavior for Davi from what you've been seeing?" Seeking the advice of colleagues not responsible for the child is also a way to gain the perspective of an uninvolved professional. Of course, the names would all be blocked out. Without written parental permission, records are not shown to anyone outside the team.

SHARING WITH FAMILIES. If you are a student using this textbook, you should not be sharing information directly with the family. That is the teacher's job. However, students may share their written observations with families if they have been cleared by the teacher in charge of the classroom and perhaps the instructor of the course.

When sharing information with the family, the teacher should always be aware of the program's or school's protocol, especially when suggesting there may be a developmental problem and suggesting a referral. Remember, "the child is an extension of the family" and this is a very sensitive area. Suggesting that there might be a problem should not be undertaken without first conferring with a supervisor or thinking through exactly how it should be worded.

Giving the family a copy of the incident provides them with a glimpse into the child's day: "Here's a little incident I wrote down today about Davi getting some help getting ready for outside play. I know you've been working on her manners. She spontaneously said, 'Thank you' and invited the other child to be her friend."

Actions or behavior are recorded descriptively as a way to explain development to the family: "Sherita initiated helping another child today for the first time. I thought you'd like to read about it. We'll be working on helping her develop more ways to play cooperatively."

Factual examples illustrate the teacher's assessment or concern to the family: "Sherita's language seems to be at a younger stage. Here are some examples I tape-recorded. Maybe you'd like to take these to talk with the speech pathologist and see if a full evaluation is recommended."

CONFERRING WITH HELPING PROFESSIONALS. Upon permission from the family, Anecdotal Recordings can be read by helping professionals. This allows people such as the speech and language pathologist, child psychologist, art teacher, and social worker to draw their own conclusions. They evaluate the incident based on their specialized knowledge and area of expertise: "The strategies you've been working on with Sherita in therapy seem to be working. Here's an incident in which she helped another child. What do you think we should do next?"

TALKING WITH THE CHILD. The child can give insight into an incident and also should be aware of the recorder's interest and writing about her actions: "Davi, I wrote down about how Sherita helped you with your jacket today. Then you invited her to be your buddy." The child may respond with an explanation or further conversation.

EVIDENCE TO CHILD PROTECTIVE SERVICES. An Anecdotal Recording is acceptable evidence to document a child abuse disclosure. When a child reveals information that may indicate abuse, it is important to accurately write down how the disclosure came about. The record must contain exact questions and comments of the adult and the child. Behavior or visual indicators may raise suspicions of abuse. The Anecdotal Recording preserves details and factual descriptions without conclusions or judgments.

Go to the Bind-in-Book CD for the forms, plans, and more information about Anecdotal Recording.

LOOKING AT SELF-CARE SKILLS

EXERCISE **On a separate sheet of paper, list the things you do for yourself that give you pride, for example, changing a tire, programming the videocassette recorder, cruising the Internet.**

"I can do it myself!" Those words spoken, sometimes defiantly, stand as a declaration of independence or a statement proclaiming a milestone accomplishment. Why are a child's **self-care** (sometimes called self-help) skills important, other than to free the adult from tasks previously done for the child?

REVIEW

ANECDOTAL RECORDING

Detailed incident on one child (others may interact in the incident), including the setting, action/reaction, exact quotes, and result. It should be detailed enough for the reader to "be there."

Types of Information to Record Using Anecdotal Recording

This method is useful for recording any incident, usual or unusual. It can give information on:

separation and adjustment
self-care skills
physical development
social development
emotional development
language and speech
attention span and interests
cognitive development
literacy creativity
sociodramatic play
child abuse
disclosure self-esteem

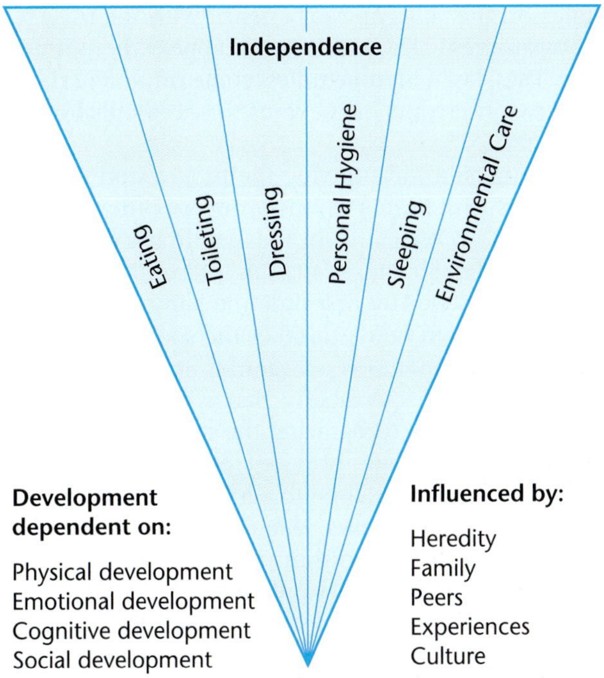

Figure 2–5 Self-Care Development.

The accomplishment of taking care of one's own needs is a progression throughout childhood. It can be viewed as **development**, moving from simple to complex tasks in an orderly, predictable sequence yet at an individual rate for each person. The sequences of self-care skills incorporate many other components of developmental areas and contribute to self-worth and competency. The observer can assess, facilitate, and celebrate those accomplishments (Figure 2–5).

The self-care skills are closely allied to the areas that are affected by separation anxiety. This is probably because they are the tasks a parent does for a child. These are the most tenuous when the parent is no longer present. For the youngest child, they are the basis of survival and comfort. They become common elements in different environments for the older child. They are actions that are expected responsibilities of the caregiver, routines that can be sources of observation and development assessment, and the basis for curricula planning.

Development of Self-Care Skills

The word *development* is an important one to understand. It is more than just change. The changes are

- interdependent on other developmental areas.
- sequential and build on prior learning.
- at varying rates from child to child and within different areas in the same child.
- affected by early experiences.
- from simple to complex.
- influenced by social and emotional contexts.
- actively and culturally transmitted.
- influenced by biological and environmental factors.
- facilitated through play.
- practiced and challenged.
- represented in different modalities. (adapted from Bredekamp, 1997)

The inverted triangle, illustrating the expanding nature of development, is used throughout the book to represent the expansion of skills and knowledge that begins in a limited, crude way but broadens and builds upon prior experiences.

Each self-care skill meets that definition of development. Babies suck before they chew, eat with their fingers before they use a spoon, spoon before fork, fork before knife, knife before melon baller. This series always follows this progression because it depends on physical growth and development and builds on the skills and experience with the preceding attainment. The skills do not appear then disappear. They last a lifetime unless some trauma or drastic event interrupts or prevents the accomplishment of the task.

The reason for knowing the progression of self-care skills is the same as it is for every other area of development. Watching for the first time is a reassurance that development is taking place. It is a milestone, a marker. The first time the baby reaches out to hold her own bottle or takes the spoon and feeds herself is a momentous occasion. It demonstrates an increasing self-responsibility that is an indicator of maturity. Besides recognizing the mastery of a new skill, the adult then provides practice and more opportunities for the child to perform that task independently. The caregiver will also be looking to the next task in the progression and providing experiences for the child to attempt that task.

Once the child has mastered the spoon, the family introduces a little fork and demonstrates the stabbing motion that differentiates a fork from a spoon. This is planning curriculum based on developmental level. The teacher sees that one child is ready for this at 10 months. Another is still working on the spoon at 12 months. This is individualizing the curriculum, developmental education. Families and teachers do it all the time without realizing it.

Self-Care and Autonomy

EXERCISE At what point did you feel independent of your family? List the milestones toward that accomplishment.

Autonomy, the process of governing oneself and providing for one's own needs, is the goal of childhood. For twenty-first-century children, that seems to be a very long process. The human infant is born totally helpless, but by one-and-a-half years, he is mobile and wanting to do more things for himself. Teachers still need to be protective and restrictive while allowing the child opportunities to begin to be more independent. Erikson (1963) describes this conflict as Autonomy versus. Shame and Doubt. To develop autonomy, children need both ability and opportunity. Ability is readiness. A child who has not yet developed small-muscle skills cannot be expected to manage buttons and zippers on clothing. While they want to dress themselves, or more likely undress themselves, their ability may prevent them from doing so. The other aspect of autonomy is opportunity. When a child never is allowed to feed herself because she makes a mess, or to wash his own hands because he doesn't do it thoroughly, the child will be dependent longer and will feel incompetent. Autonomy is also culturally related. Some cultures want children to be dependent for much longer than we do in the United States. In many European, Asian, and African cultures, feeding, dressing, and bathing the child, long after the child is physically capable of doing it herself, is seen as a demonstration of love, caring, and good parenting.

@ it happened to me

Children Need Help Sometimes

I was observing in a very progressive early childhood program where independence was a founding principle. Children served themselves snacks and meals when they were hungry, played inside or outside by choice, napped when they felt tired, and generally went through the day without routines or schedules. I was walking around amazed at how children were spending long periods of time at activities of their choice when I heard a sound from the bathroom. I walked by and saw a little one about 18 months old trying to change messy pants. Unfortunately the job called for extensive clean-up both of clothing, body, and eventually the floor and sink. When I called attention of the teacher to the situation, she indicated that the child should be allowed to do it independently. It didn't seem to me that the child had the physical skills to do so, nor was the inadequate cleanup hygienic for the rest of the children. This is where their ideology and mine collide.

Do you have an IT HAPPENED TO ME story about self care skills? I'd love to read it. Send it to WeekbyWeek@thomsonlearning.com

TOPICS IN OBSERVATION

Using All Our Senses

EXERCISE **Using a separate piece of paper, make a list of what you can observe about a child from senses other than seeing:**

hearing	touching
smelling	tasting

The word *observe* is understood to use sight as the primary source of taking in information; however, all senses are receptors of information on which to base decisions. As observers of young children, all senses can be used to assess and evaluate the child.

SEEING

Visually, information is gathered on the child's physical appearance; size; attributes, such as hair, coloring, features, facial expressions; coordination; actions; location in the room; and choices of activities. From all those visual cues, inferences are made regarding the child (Figure 2–6).

Visual Cues	Inferences
Height, weight, body proportions, coordination, glasses, brace on leg, hearing aid	Physical growth and development, health, developmental delays, physical limitations
Skin color, hair color, eye shape	Racial or ethnic group, health, cosmetic use
Clothing, hairstyle, hygiene	Socioeconomic level, family style and care
Activity level	Emotional state, health factors
Facial expressions and body language	Emotional states, attention, interest
Playmates, interactions	Social stage, personality, sexual preference of playmates, aggressiveness
Approach to play, work, other people	Self-esteem, learning style, cognitive level and style
Mannerisms	Role models—family, TV characters, other children
Evidence of injury	Accident, surgery, abuse

Figure 2–6 Visual cues may lead one to make inferences about children.

HEARING

The adult attunes to the message being communicated, from the first "coos" to intricate stories recounted with sound effects and voice. Many areas of development can be assessed from listening.

emotional state—laughter, crying, whining, teasing, anger, silence

cognitive development—vocabulary, content, grammar, problem-solving strategies, humor, storybook characters

physical development—formation of teeth, tongue, and jaw

health—nasal or bronchial congestion, wheezing, possible hearing difficulties affecting speech, digestive sounds

family—home language, activities, siblings, other family members, other significant people in the child's life, television and video usage

sociability—play stage, themes, playmates, leadership

(continued)

TOPICS IN OBSERVATION *(continued)*

TOUCHING

Some information may not be apparent to sight or sound. The reaction to an adult's soft touch might seem unusual, giving rise to conjecture about the origin of that response.

muscle tone—firm muscle tissue, eating disorders, and some diseases
illness—fever, rashes, cold, clammy skin
stress—tension in the body, trembling, goosebumps
injury—swelling, reaction to touch indicating a tenderness
response to touch—cuddly, withdrawal, rigid

SMELLING

The most obvious information gathered by smelling is that a diaper change is needed. In a one-year-old, that observation is common and demands a standard response. In a six-year-old, that observation, of course, also calls for the action of cleaning up, but it is noteworthy and a red flag indicating further evaluations may be advisable Smelling gives the keen observer clues about

hygiene—cleanliness, tooth decay, bed wetting
illness—respiratory infections, chronic allergies or sinus conditions, diseases such as diabetes that may give off a sweet odor
home odors—smoking, seasonings, animals, perfume
safety—ingestion of a poisonous substance

TASTING

Taste probably would not be used to gather information on the child.

THE "SIXTH SENSE"

The observer's instinct, or "gut" feeling, should receive attention. Sometimes there is something about a child sensed not by eyes, ears, nose, or touch but by a feeling. Professionals must rely on substantive information but often have a heightened awareness. This is not to be used as a measurement but as an indicator that further hard evidence needs to be gathered. The observer makes a closer investigation with detailed documentation for later analysis. This may involve other professionals, with the permission of the parents, such as a social worker, health coordinator, psychologist, or speech therapist.

The keen observer uses all senses to gather information. The knowledge of child development is applied, using multiple methods of documentation of the observations. All of this information-gathering is used to benefit the child and the program.

@ it happened to me

Smelly Clues

A colleague relates that she worked with a student in remedial reading instruction who also had a history of learning difficulties and classroom disruptions. He smelled of nasal congestion. The family was assisted in getting a medical evaluation for him. Tubes in his ears remedied the problem, and he was transformed as a student. All because of a smelling observation!

Do you have an IT HAPPENED TO ME story about observing with other senses? I'd love to read it. Send it to WeekbyWeek@thomsonlearning.com

Older preschoolers and school-age children in what Erikson (1963) calls the Initiative and Industry stages want to take on adult-like activities and are competent and confident in mastering skills and acting independently.

When to Help and When Not To

There is always a fine line between giving assistance and being manipulated. When a child has the small muscle skill to perform self-help skills, she should be encouraged and allowed to do it. When she is in a hurry, not feeling well, or is getting increasingly frustrated, a helping hand is needed. However, some children who can, won't. There may be many reasons for what is sometimes called **learned helplessness**. This may be due to the family interactions with the child, including older siblings, treating the child as a baby, making her feel incompetent. On the other extreme, impossibly high standards which the child feels unable to reach causes her to give up in futility. Some teachers fall into the trap of over-caring for the dependent child so that it becomes a habit. Sometimes children themselves will overdo for another child who they perceive as needy or younger. This sometimes happens when a child with a special need is in the classroom. While we want to encourage caring for one another, both adults and children should do all to help each individual feel competent and confident.

Children who have had no experience of success in becoming independent have a fundamental lack of confidence in their own self-worth. In *Miseducation: Preschoolers at Risk* (1987), David Elkind gives the following practical advice: "Children are just learning these skills, so it is important not to force them. . . . The important thing, as I have tried to suggest, is to find a healthy middle ground between doing everything for children and doing nothing for them and expecting them to cope with the adult-sized world" (p. 111).

Self-Care Skills in the Curriculum

By observing with the developmental progression in mind, observations become assessments and tools for planning curriculum. The area of self-care is not always recognized as a curriculum. It is taken for granted, probably because it develops so naturally. Self-care skills are recognized as a very important part of the curriculum for children with special needs (Bowe, 2004). Occupational therapists often work with young children on these tasks. Upon consideration, taking care of one's own body functions involves many areas of development and contributes not only to physical but also emotional well-being. Both muscle strength and coordination are necessary for these tasks. A great many thinking processes are involved in each skill, beginning with body awareness of the cues of hunger, tiredness, need to eliminate, and feeling cold or hot. The connections between past experiences build and form new thinking patterns.

Certainly self-care skills are necessary for social acceptance. It is part of that whole realm of manners and out-in-public actions. These are learned by observing and imitating role models and from direct instruction. The learning depends on the child's desire to be accepted and liked. There is a feeling of accomplishment and increased self-esteem when one can do something independently, without assistance. Following surgery or an illness, people report how good it feels just to be able to brush their own teeth or go up a few steps. Those actions become so natural, done without thinking or appreciating their complexity. In childhood, they are skills to learn, moving from basic to complex levels.

Individual differences are significant in self-care skills. Predictability of body rhythmicity is seen dramatically in the Thomas and Chess (1977, 1980) longitudinal studies. The studies indicated that feeding, elimination, and sleeping patterns at two months were consistent or at least similar at 10 years old. In addition to physical differences, social, racial, and cultural influences as well as birth order may affect self-care development. Lynch and Hanson (2004) warn, "Expectations for children concerning feeding, sleeping and speaking, as well as the use of discipline, to mention only a few may vary widely across cultural groups" (p. 12). The book reviews many different cultural beliefs important for teachers to know. Information on the child's self-care skills can be gathered from families as well as observed in the natural routines of the day in the group setting. Figure 2–7, taken from Ireton (1995), is a checklist that could be used to assess self-help skills with the ages at which these normally occur. These are part of the developmental process so the observer realizes that each child attains these milestones in an individual timetable.

Self-Care Skills

Self-care skills are points of observing and recording used to recognize milestones, plot and share progress, and plan curriculum. The normal progression of self-help skills of dressing, feeding, toileting and washing, and general is well illustrated in Figure 2–8, which is taken from Allen and Cowdery (2005).

SELF-HELP

Includes eating, dressing, bathing, toileting, independence, and responsibility

Age 1-2

- ❍ Removes socks. 12m
- ❍ Lifts a cup to mouth and drinks. 12m
- ❍ Feeds self with a spoon. 15m
- ❍ Hands empty dish to adult. 15m
- Ⓟ❍ Remembers where things are kept in the house. 15m
- ❍ Uses a small pail or other container for carrying things. Or used to. 15m
- ❍ Tries to put on shoes. Or puts them on. 15m
- ❍ Climbs on chair, stool, or box to reach things. 15m
- ❍ Eats with a fork. 18m
- ❍ Eats with a spoon with little spilling. 21m
- ❍ Takes off shoes and socks. 21m
- ❍ Unzips zippers. 21m

Age 2-3

- Ⓟ❍ Wipes up spills, using cloth or sponge. 2-0
- Ⓟ❍ Takes off unbuttoned shirt/blouse without help. 2-0
- Ⓟ❍ Opens door by turning knob and pulling. 2-0
- Ⓟ❍ Washes and dries hands. 2-6
- Ⓟ❍ Goes around the house independently; requires little supervision. 2-6
- Ⓟ❍ Washes self in bathtub—may need a little help. 2-6

Ages 3-4

- ❍ Puts on a shirt/blouse or jacket without help. 3-0
- ❍ Toilet trained for urine control and bowel movements. 3-0, 2-6
- Ⓟ❍ Brushes teeth without help. 3-0
- Ⓟ❍ Takes responsibility for self in eating, dressing, and washing—but may need a little help. 3-3
- Ⓟ❍ Undresses completely without help. 3-6, 3-0
- Ⓟ❍ Washes face without help. 3-9, 3-3
- Ⓟ❍ Notices when shirt/blouse or pants are inside-out and turns them right-side-out. 3-9
- Ⓟ❍ Dresses and undresses without help, except for tying shoelaces. 3-9, 3-6
- Ⓟ❍ Stays dry all night. 4-3, 3-3

Age 4-5

- ❍ Uses table knife for spreading. 4-3
- ❍ Buttons one or more buttons. 4-3
- Ⓟ❍ Usually looks both ways when crossing streets. 4-6
- ❍ Buttons a shirt, blouse, or coat, having all the buttons in the correct holes. 5-0, 4-3
- ❍ Goes to the toilet without help; wipes self, flushes toilet, and washes hands. 5-0, 4-3
- ❍ Takes care of personal belongings. 5-3, 4-6

Age 5-6

- ❍ Puts shoes on the correct feet. 5-0
- Ⓟ❍ Pours self a drink. 5-0
- Ⓟ❍ Pours dry cereal and milk into a bowl without spilling. 5-3

OTHER SKILLS

- ❍ ______________________________
- ❍ ______________________________
- ❍ ______________________________

PROBLEMS

- ❍ Immature; acts much younger than age
- ❍ Disorganized; messy, careless, irresponsible
- ❍ Can't sit still; may be hyperactive
- ❍ Passive; seldom shows initiative
- ❍ Lacks self-confidence; says "I'm dumb," etc.

Figure 2–7 Self-Help Milestones (Ireton, H. *Child Development Inventory Teacher's Observation Guide,* © 1995. Reprinted by permission of Behavior Science Systems, Inc., Box 19512, Minneapolis MN 55419-9998. 612-850-8700.)

	Dressing	Feeding	Toileting and Washing	General
2 to 3 years	Can take clothes off to put on other articles of clothing but tires easily and gives up. Generally cooperative when helped.	Can use a fork, but still prefers spoon or fingers. Will feed self preferred food. Drinks from glass.	Verbalizes toilet needs in advance. Retention span for urination lengthening—can "hold" longer.	Can open some doors with easy latches or low knobs. Goes up and down stairs, usually holding rail. Can push chair or stool around to climb on and get what is wanted.
3 to 4 years	Undresses self. Can put on most articles of clothing and can manipulate buttons and zippers, depending upon their size and place. Can put clothes away in drawers or hang them up, given right height hooks.	Usually eats with fork. Can pour from pitcher into glass with few mishaps. Enjoys eating with family, but may dawdle.	May insist on washing self in tub but does it imperfectly. Very few toilet accidents. Often wakes up at night and asks to be taken to toilet.	Can tell own age, sex, and first and last name. Can follow two- and three-step directions. Able to stay at preschool without parent.
4 to 5 years	Laces shoes; some children learning to tie. Dresses and undresses with little or no assistance, especially if clothes are laid out. May dawdle excessively over dressing. Can tell front from back but may still have trouble getting some garments on properly.	Uses fork and spoon appropriately; often needs help to cut "tough" meat. Likes to "make" own breakfast and lunches (dry cereal, peanut butter sandwiches).	Can bathe and dry self, at least partially. Can perform toileting, hand washing and drying. May forget sometimes.	Plays with peers with less supervision. Can put toys away but usually needs reminding. Can help with many household chores: set table, empty trash, feed pets. May "forget" some steps.
5 to 6 years	Ties own shoes. Can manage almost any article of clothing. Can assist younger brother or sister in getting dressed.	Can use all eating utensils but is sometimes messy. Aware of appropriate table manners but tends to forget them.	Bathes and dries self with minimal supervision. Usually does not wash own hair, but may help. Totally self-sufficient in toilet routine.	Can make own bed, put soiled clothes in hamper. Learning to distinguish left from right.

Figure 2–8 Examples of self-help skills for various age groups. (From *The Exceptional Child: Inclusion in Early Childhood Education,* 5th edition, by ALLEN, 2005. Reprinted with permission of Delmar Learning, a division of Thomson Learning: www.thomsonrights.com. Fax 800 730-2215.)

EATING. In infancy, the adult is the source of nourishment to the child, whether by breast or by bottle. The infant depends on the adult to provide the acceptable food at regular times and as the infant gives signals of hunger. Reflex actions of rooting (turning toward the cheek that is touched) and sucking once the nipple is felt on the lips are built-in muscle responses. They enable the infant to receive nourishment. By three or four months, the baby will begin to recognize the breast or bottle, reach for it, and hold it firmly. In another month, the baby begins to push it away when full. By six months, the pincer grasp of thumb and forefinger enables the baby to indiscriminately pick up small food items (and fuzz balls) and get them into the mouth. This means the teacher must give extra caution to the cleanliness of the environment. The teacher must be vigilant regarding small ingestible and indigestible items. Soon the teacher will begin to give the baby the opportunity to eat small bits of appropriate food items while the child is securely strapped in a high chair or infant seat.

In the second year, the child begins to assert independence by grabbing the spoon, the bottle, or the cracker. He now has the small motor skills to get them to his mouth fairly accurately and teeth to chew. Three- and four-year-olds gain skill at using utensils: spoon first, then the fork, then the knife. They should be given the opportunity to practice under supervision (Figure 2–9). Gentle reminders and pointers for using the silverware effectively are given. They can efficiently pour, if the pitcher is lightweight and clear, so they can see the liquid approaching the spout. It

Figure 2–9 Pouring takes physical skills, concentration and patience.

helps if the glass or paper cup has a fill line for a visual cue to stop pouring. It helps to place the glass on a tray to catch "over pours" until control is gained.

By late four and early five years, children have the physical mobility and manual dexterity to help themselves to food as it is passed. They love to assist in preparation of peeling foods with proper utensils and supervision. They can set the table, fold napkins, clear the table, and be quite helpful in the whole mealtime routine.

Learning and language connected with eating begins with the recognition of food sources, such as the breast or bottle. Accompanying vocabulary is built as the teacher says, "Here comes the baba, baby hungry?" The creeper finds tidbits on the floor but her ability to discriminate between food and nonfood items is not developed, possibly placing her in danger.

By one year she begins to display likes and dislikes of foods by their appearance or a single taste. As language explodes in the second year, she can recognize and name many foods. The sorting skills of the three- and four-year-old transfer into food groups. It begins with likes and dislikes. Eventually, she can classify meat, vegetables, fruits, drinks, and breads. She is learning the names for the individual items based on visual and aromatic cues.

Think About It . . .

What table rules did you learn as a child? How did you learn them?

The social-emotional aspects of eating are lessons that are learned early. The aura of mealtime lasts a lifetime. It may be a relaxed, social gathering, or a tense, emotion-laden time of restrictions and prohibitions. Adults are responsible for the physical environment of cleanliness, safety, appropriateness of menu,

@ it happened to me

Impatience with Pancakes

We were making pancakes in the preschool room and our foster grandparent was helping the children pour the batter and flip the pancakes. Each child struggled as they carefully slid the spatula under the pancake and at the crucial moment flipped it over, hopefully in approximately the same place it had been on the pan. It was a tedious process, sometimes requiring several tries before each pancake was flipped successfully. Grandma's patience was at its limit. As the umpteenth child tried to flip the pancake, she grabbed the spatula and said, "Oh @$#$, just let me do it!"

Do you have an IT HAPPENED TO ME story about when patience ran out? I'd love to read it. Send it to WeekbyWeek@thomsonlearning.com

cognitive connections, and language and vocabulary expansion. They are modeling table manners and providing an emotional atmosphere where psychological safety and individualism are recognized.

When children participate to their ability with the preparation, of the meal or a particular dish, it builds the feeling of competency. Children learn a lot from measuring, stirring, cutting, and spreading, which enhance small muscle skills. Of course it takes more time and patience but its importance is in the learning process that is taking place.

We often feel that way; we can do it faster and more efficiently, but children need to try in order to succeed. No place is that seen so dramatically as in self-help skills. Sitting at a table that fits them, serving and passing foods, and interacting with peers and adults in pleasant conversation teaches many social lessons. Children develop their taste for new foods in the first six years so providing a variety of nutritious foods from which to choose influences their attitudes toward nutrition.

Children learn they are trusted when they are given autonomy over choices among healthy foods. By participating in the food preparation, serving, and self-feeding they feel competent. When they interact with others during mealtime, they learn skills that they will be using around the table the rest of their lives. Because eating disorders are beginning as early as three and four, close attention should be given to mealtimes and the emotions involved.

In the standards pertaining to nutrition and food service described in *Caring for Our Children: National Health and Safety Performance Standards: Guidelines for Out-of-Home Child Care* (American Academy of Pediatrics, 2002, sec. 4), toddlers are encouraged in self-feeding, mealtimes are conducted in a relaxed atmosphere with furnishings, utensils, and servings all aimed at promoting independence and social skills. School breakfast and lunch programs provide the basic nutrition but many lack adult conversation, modeling, or direct instruction in table manners or social behavior.

TOILETING. Control of body eliminations is truly an illustration of development: from no control with only reflex actions, through the steps dependent on physical growth, to a complex set of controls and releases dependent on many other factors (Figure 2–10).

Of course, the infant has no control over body eliminations, so the adult performs all necessary tasks of absorbing, catching, cleaning, and diapering. This routine function, like any other done with an infant, is not without its effect on the infant's cognitive, language, and social-emotional realm.

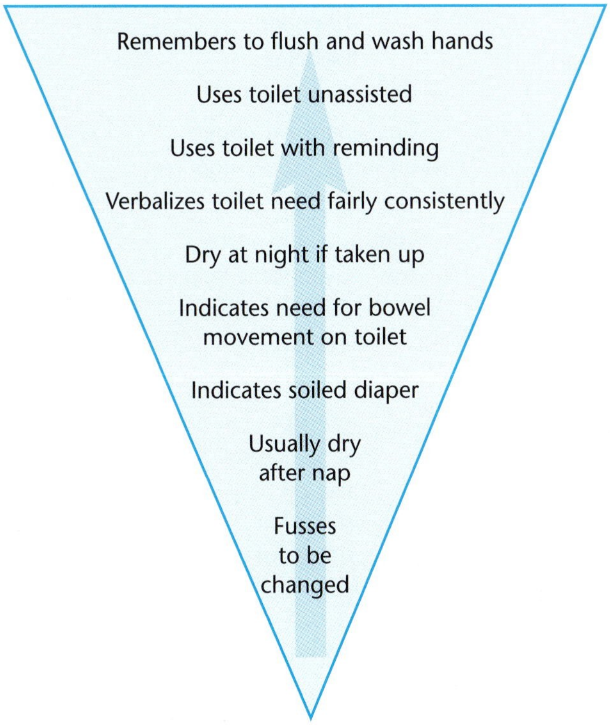

Figure 2–10 Toileting Development.

Adults give many messages to the infant during diapering, such as messages about safety, gentleness, hygiene, acceptance of body elimination, and sexual attitudes. When a teacher expresses unpleasantness at the task by a facial expression of disgust, or verbally such as saying "Yucky," the infant confuses the message. He does not know it is the task, and not him, that is the cause of the unpleasant facial expressions and expressive language.

EXERCISE Ask a parent to recount a toilet-training story (everyone has at least one), and write it down as it is told. Use the criteria for an Anecdotal Recording.

Usually children are well into the second year before they begin to recognize the body signals of an impending bowel movement and, even later, the need to urinate. The physical growth of muscles is occurring, along with the mental attention to body signals. Unfortunately, it is at a time when there is a strong desire to gain more control of the world. In this battle to control the body, the child and the adult are often at opposite poles, making toilet training a chore many adults dread. The struggle can be eased by recognizing the turmoil going on inside the child. She is given control, since the adult cannot control it anyway. Kinnell's practical book *Good Going!* (2004) gives this advice: "It is annoying to have to clean up the child and wash all the clothes, but it is a part of the learning process for the child. Fighting the inevitable accidents or punishing the child for them will certainly slow the process" (p. 13). Curriculum for this area is in environment preparation, positive role models, and sometimes direct instruction.

Environment. The adult's role is to provide an environment that encourages the desired action: potty chair, steps to the toilet, child-sized toilet seat, books, pictures, pleasant room decor. The bathroom often is overlooked as a place where learning occurs. Interesting pictures at the side and back of the toilet give "goers" thought-provoking visual aids. Of course, visual reminders of hand washing will link toileting with personal hygiene.

EXERCISE Toileting is an emotionally charged subject for child and adult. Finish these reflective questions:

The most uncomfortable part for me about working with children surrounding toileting is . . .
I think it is because . . .
Maybe it would be better if I . . .

---

it happened to me

Bad Example

I was observing in a child care center at morning snack time. Some of the children had been doing puzzles and playing with Play Doh at the table while others had been painting, stacking with blocks, shoveling sand, and looking at books. The teacher rattled a box of Cocoa Puffs, and the children came running to sit at the table. She stood behind each child, scooped up a handful of cereal from the box and placed it on the bare table in front of each one. She poured juice from a can into paper cups and set them in front of each child. She said, "OK, eat, and no spilling." She stepped away from the table and ate a candy bar from her pocket.

Do you have an IT HAPPENED TO ME story about self-care? I'd love to read it. Send it to WeekbyWeek@thomsonlearning.com

Think About It . . .

"It Happened to Me: Bad Example" is a true Anecdotal Recording, unfortunately! What was wrong with the teacher's practices?

Role Models. Toileting is sometimes aided by the social aspect in group care because of the child's natural imitative nature. When one child uses the toilet, others will want to do it also. When a child is praised for potty use, it is likely to occur again and again and eventually become a routine.

Direct Instruction. Some children may need to be taught proper use of the toilet and toilet paper. This is best accomplished on an anatomically correct doll. Teachers should avoid performing this task on a child in an enclosed bathroom stall. For children still needing assistance, stalls are without doors or the task is done with the door propped open. This is a precaution against possible child abuse allegations.

As the child is expanding her vocabulary, a consideration of which words to use for body elimination functions should be explored so that families and teachers attain consistency. This also gives a positive rather than negative connotation to the function. The struggle over toilet training is an emotionally and culturally sensitive topic that is enhanced by the teacher's partnership with the family and the child. Lynch and Hanson (2004) give the reminder that "in the United States, toilet training between the child's second and third birthday is a common practice and is highly valued by many families. However, this practice may be viewed by many other cultural groups as unnecessary and too early" (p. 13).

DRESSING. It is always easier to knock down a building than to build it, delete a page of type than to write it, criticize than to praise. So it is with dressing—the first step in self-care is taking clothing off. Parents have all experienced, at least once, the shock of a stark-naked child appearing when they were just fully clothed a few minutes before. Dressing is a developmental progression of skills (Figure 2–11).

Children can be given the power to take off the articles of clothing they can manage. By the time they are two or three years old, they can take off their shoes at nap time, their hat after coming in from outside play, and all their clothes at bath time. They should do what they can do. By selecting clothing that children can manage themselves, such as boxer pants,

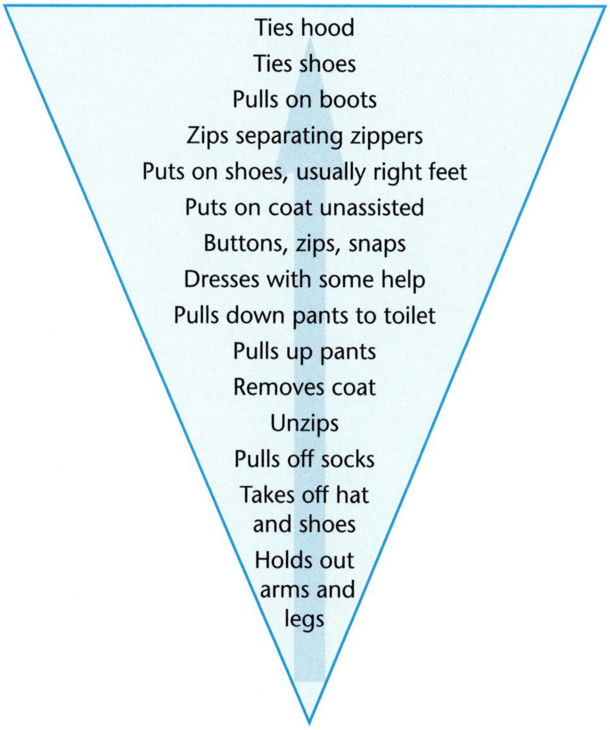

Figure 2–11 Dressing Development.

@ it happened to me

Am I Clean?

This happened to a friend of mine. In a four-year-old class, a child had gone to the bathroom while they were having snack. She waddled back from the bathroom with her pants around her ankles, bent over, and looking through her legs yelled, "Am I clean?" "Yes, you're clean. Good job wiping," said the teacher matter-of-factly. The girl returned to the bathroom, dressed, washed hands, and returned to snack.

Do you have an IT HAPPENED TO ME story about toilet training? I'd love to read it. Send it to WeekbyWeek@thomsonlearning.com

the child finds the task much easier. It is easier than a one-piece jumpsuit or buttons up the back of a dress.

EXERCISE Make a list of clothing fasteners that are difficult even for adults. How could it have been designed differently?

Teachers can add play items with buttons, snaps, zippers, and ties to the curriculum to encourage practice of those skills. It is always amazing how a child can squeeze into a leotard and tutu over a pair of jeans and a sweatshirt and sneakers. If they want it on, they will find a way. Inviting dress-up props stimulate interest and practice skills (Figure 2–12).

Think About It . . .

What does "It Happened to Me: Am I Clean?" tell you about the child's stage of development? Home influence? The teacher?

When helping a child after toileting or getting ready to go outside, the child should be assisted with what they cannot do and encouraged to do what they can. The adult can pull up the pants and let the child pull up the suspenders. The teacher can start the separating zipper and let her finish it, or finish tying the bow after she has crossed the ties. Remember: Never do for children what they can do for themselves.

Figure 2–12 Dress-up clothes give practice in buttoning, zipping, and tying.

PERSONAL HYGIENE. Body cleanliness and care of the infant is, of course, the sole responsibility of the adult (Figure 2–13). It is a physical function that is building associations in the infant between certain events. "They change my diaper and wash my body and hands." "They set me in the high chair, wash my hands, then give me food." "They take me away from the table and wash my face and hands." In the first year, these associations are being made. In the second year, when the child gains mobility and small muscle control, she can go to the sink, which is adapted so she can reach it, and wash her hands. She is taught to do this after going to the toilet or wiping her nose, or before eating. She can manage to turn on the water, wash, dry, and go on with play. In the fourth and fifth years, small muscle control is more developed. The child can now efficiently handle combing hair, brushing teeth, and bathing in the tub with supervision.

Recognition of the need for washing is a difficult lesson for young children to learn because of the "invisiblity" of germs. They are concrete thinkers. When they look at their hands and see no dirt, they find it incomprehensible that they should wash, especially if they did it once today already. It is the social acceptance and cognitive bridging that reinforce the personal hygiene habits until the child is into the elementary school years when microscopic particles are understood.

SLEEPING. Sleep needs and patterns are individual but follow a developmental pattern. Individual differences are seen in the amount of sleep children need, how they get to sleep, how soundly they sleep, and their usual waking-up routines.

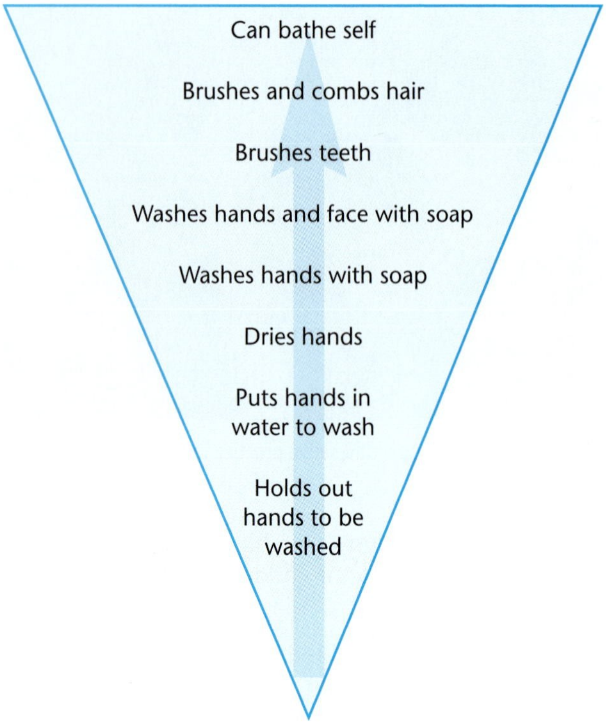

Figure 2–13 Personal Hygiene Skill Development.

Children in group care tend to be overstimulated because of many available playmates and play things. It is lessened by stress reduction throughout the day and by planning for smooth transitions, as well as by alternating active and quiet activity choices. Prior to nap time, consistent routines such as mealtime, teeth brushing, and music listening or a story help to prepare the children for sleep. Attention is given to the program schedule and environment to allow for resting and sleeping time on self-demand. Sleeping arrangements often are strictly mandated by state regulations for safety and supervision. *Caring for Our Children* (American Academy of Pediatrics, 2002), Standard 5.144, mandates children have their own cribs, bedding, feeding utensils, clothing, diapers, pacifiers, and other special comforting objects. Infants' names are used to label every personal item. Individual programs develop routines of backrubs, soft music, and quiet play preceding rest times to help children relax and sleep if they need to (Figure 2–14). Allowances are made for those children who are no longer taking naps to look quietly at books in the napping area or to play in a quiet learning center.

Individual children have their own patterns when it comes to sleep, such as preferred sleeping position or what soothes them into sleep. They may require possessions nearby to fall asleep. By noting a reduction in sleep times, modifications are made for the

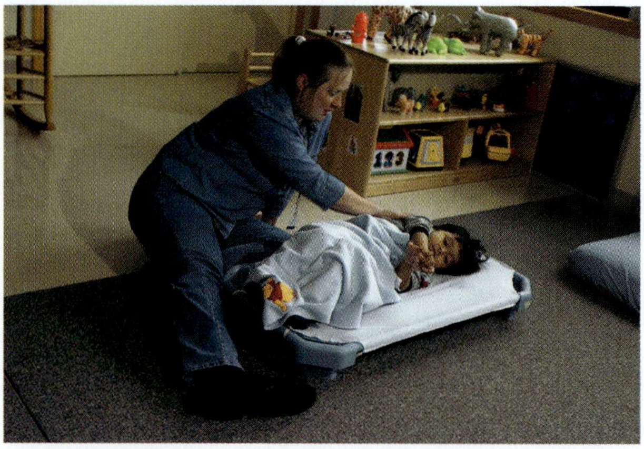

Figure 2–14 Allowances should be made for children's individual sleeping patterns.

child who no longer requires a nap. Communication of daily sleep patterns between home and school assists both family and center in meeting the needs of the child.

Family and staff daily reports are used in most centers to convey this type of information at arrival and departure times. Sharing "what works" benefits the child at home and at the center.

Self-Care in the Classroom

Caring for the classroom environment is another area of development.

EXERCISE Observe the room you are in. What are the items in the room (or the arrangement of items) that encourage self-care? (Example: "Wastebasket available" or "Paper towels at child-level.")

Some observable signs of a child's participation in classroom self-care are

- selects toys for play
- puts a toy back in its place
- plays actively without adult leadership
- follows classroom routines
- cleans up spills
- helps prepare for activity
- can carry breakable objects
- performs "job chart" tasks
- demonstrates safety awareness
- assists another child to do a task

While an occasional newspaper story may highlight a young child's extraordinary competence in an emergency, there have been just as many horror stories of children left alone at a very young age, most

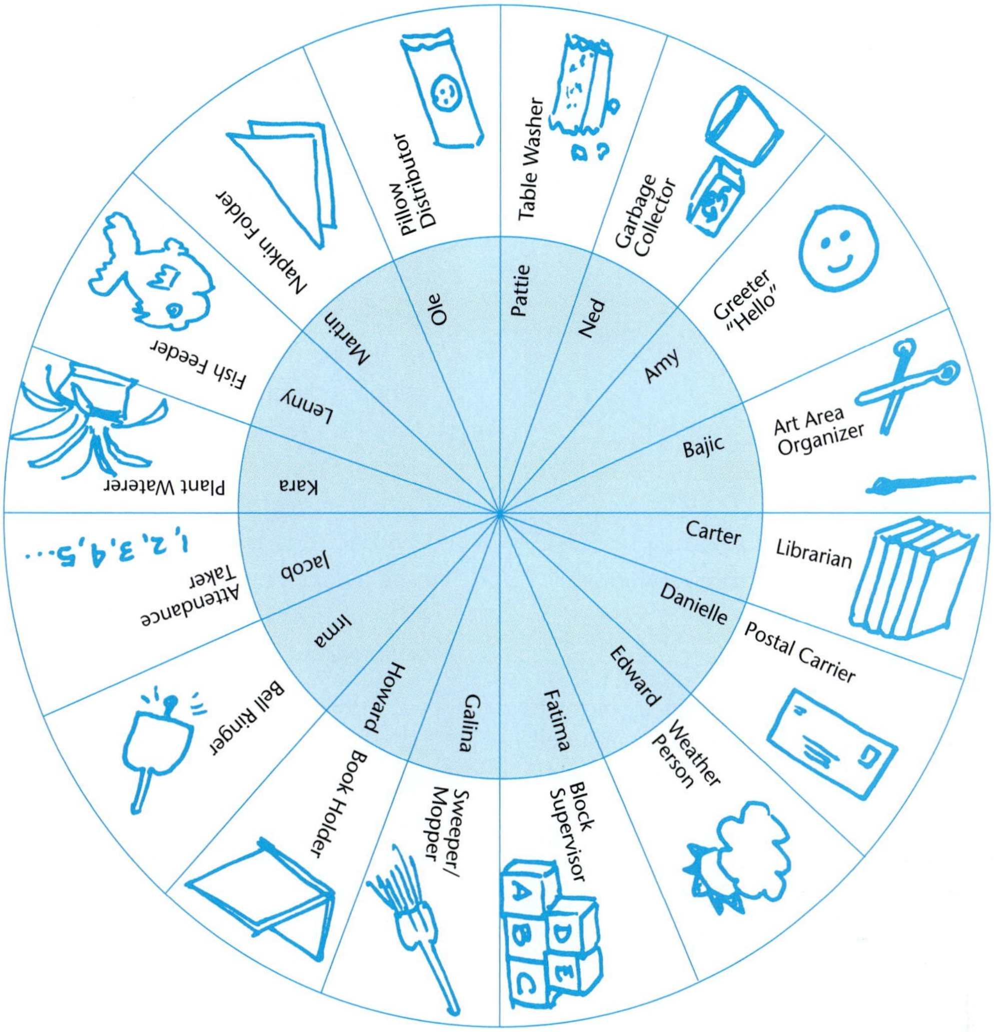

Names (inner circle) move each day.

Figure 2–15 Job Chart. (Reprinted with permission from Carol Fuller, Conklin Presbyterian Preschool, Conklin, NY.)

with dire results. Some of these children are caring for even younger siblings, and often there are tragedies. The concept of self-care is not meant to hurry the child along to independence before he is ready but rather to allow him the freedom and responsibility for self-care. This is done in small, manageable steps that build confidence and competency. Children eventually develop the ability to make safe self-care decisions. The age at which a child can be allowed to play unattended in a room at home, go down the street alone, and eventually stay at home alone for a short time varies with the individual child. It also is affected by the home setting, the neighborhood, and prior experiences. There should be a history of smaller, successful instances of self-care. Parents are in the business of working themselves out of a job and building into the child the competencies for self-care. It is done one day at a time.

Many classrooms and home environments use job charts for daily responsibilities. This is an organized way to ensure care of the environment. It also teaches that each person must do a part for the good of the group (Figure 2–15).

In the classroom as well, children become competent in self-care as they learn the routines. They can meet realistic expectations for cleaning up after themselves and should be given responsibilities for themselves and others. There are children who are so averse to cleaning up that they are reluctant to play with anything so they do not have to put anything away. Clean-up time is easier with the aid of effective transitions. These begin with a warning time that playtime is almost over, which helps to

Pick up, pick up.
Everybody do your share.
Pick up, pick up.
Pick up everywhere.
To the traditional "Today Is Monday" tune:
It's time to pick up.
It's time to pick up.
Mary's picking up blocks.
Jack's sweeping sand.
Tania's finishing her painting.
Soon it will be snack.

Figure 2–16 Pick-up songs help make an orderly environment everyone's responsibility.

prepare children to end play and begin to pick up. Little ritual songs or signals, such as music or a bell, work better than an adult yelling, "Pick-up time!" See Figure 2–16.

Adults can make pick-up time fun by using child-sized brooms, small vacuum cleaners, and toy trucks to transport toys back to their clearly labeled places. Adults can also give children appropriate choices: "Are you going to pick up the blocks or the dolls?" Even when the children played with neither of these choices, this reinforces group participation in taking care of the classroom and initiates the concept of environmental responsibility.

it happened to me

"Woman's Work"

In my classroom we had daily jobs that rotated. One was to wash off the work/snack tables (before the teacher did it with disinfectant). In my young days as a teacher, one day a boy's father arrived when he was washing off the table. The father took the sponge from his son and told me, "That's women's work." The family had immigrated from the Middle East, and I had no idea that was offensive. That was my rude awakening to the home/school conflict of cultural practices. What would you have said or done?

Do you have an IT HAPPENED TO ME story about children's responsibilities in the classroom? I'd love to read it. Send it to WeekbyWeek@thomsonlearning.com

IF THE CHILD IS HAVING DIFFICULTY. The teacher begins with a closer examination of the environment. Modifications are made to help the child, such as low clothes hooks, reduced lighting in the nap area, or steps up to the changing table or toilet. If the environment is appropriate, the expectations for the child may not be reasonable. Other areas of the child's development are considered (language, cognitive, small muscle). Are these self-care expectations realistic? After this, a talk with the family is the next step to find out if they can give advice, insight, or assistance.

The teacher should be aware of the families' expectations for the child at home, how the child does these things at home, and what may be the reason for this inability here. More time may be all that is needed.

THE IMPORTANCE OF SELF-CARE. Children who can care for their own bodies are physically and psychologically strong. It is a progression, though relapses may occur and reminders may be needed. There will likely be some frustration. Families sometimes wonder if their child will be graduating from high school in diapers, sucking on a bottle, with zippers unzipped. That rarely happens; they do learn it along the way. The adult's role is to mediate the environment to be child-friendly and child-accessible, and to provide realistic expectations, positive role models, and direct, specific instructions. Clean-up involves classification, seriation, and organizational skills. It builds a respect for the environment and a sense of responsibility. A model teacher was observed using a variety of creative clean-up strategies. He acted like a human crane, made "dot picker uppers" with masking tape (sticky side up on blocks), created a sympathetic response to a story about a "home for lost toys" to find places for displaced items, and used chairs as bulldozers to push toys to their rightful place (Bauer & Sheerer, 1997). Children then develop these self-care skills that allow them to be independent and socially accepted.

HELPING ALL CHILDREN WITH SELF-CARE SKILLS

It has already been mentioned that cultural differences are seen most in the area of self-care skills. The teacher needs to be sensitive to different attitudes and practices. The family role of providing cultural socialization must be accommodated in the program through the cultural competence of the teachers, clarifying their own values and assumptions (Lynch and Hanson, 2004). This can be done through home visits, research, family questionnaires, and gaining information from watching the child and family together. Adjustment of routines for these differences is the appropriate action, rather than forcing the child to conform. Communication and coordination between school and home must occur for the benefit of the child.

Children with special needs, as previously mentioned, need to be allowed to do all they can for themselves. Self-care routines provide opportunities for assessment, intervention, and development of skills (Benner, 2003). They are frequent, common to all children, and involve identified sequences. They do not interfere with regular programming and do not require additional staff or special training. These routines also need to be coordinated with family life, so collaboration between program and family is necessary for continuity of practice. A survey of the routines of the day and setting specific goals for the child in each routine can be implemented and serve as communication between all team members, family, and the child (Cripe & Lee, 1997). It may mean that some modifications are made to the environment and expectations. All children have the need to feel competent and responsible.

HELPING PROFESSIONALS FOR SELF-CARE SKILLS

Other professionals may be consulted depending on the area of difficulty.

pediatrician—for a thorough physical checkup to rule out any possible physical reasons for difficulties

social worker—for advice on family and center or school practices and expectations

occupational therapist—to examine more closely fine muscle skills involved in self-care

child psychologist—to explore the child's attitudes and reasons for refusing to care for herself

OTHER METHODS

Other Methods to Record Self-Care

Class List Log
Checklists/Rating Scales
Running Records
Frequency Counts
Conversations and Interviews
Work Samples
Media

STANDARDS

Here are selected examples of standards related to self-help skills:

Standard 4.024
Encouraging Self-Feeding by Toddlers
Caring for Our Children: National Health and Safety Performance Standards: Guidelines for Out-of-Home Child Care Programs (2nd ed.). (American Academy of Pediatrics, 2002). Used with permission.
Caregivers shall encourage toddlers to hold and drink from a cup, to use a spoon, and to use their finger for self-feeding

Division of Early Childhood Recommended Practices in Early Intervention/Early Childhood Special Education (2000)
Practices and goals are individualized for each child based on: (a) the child's current behavior and abilities across relevant domains instead of the child's diagnostic category; (b) the family's view of what the child needs to learn; (c) interventionist and specialist views of what the child needs to learn; and (d) the demands, expectations, and requirements of the child's current environments.

KEY TERMS

Anecdotal Recording	learned helplessness
autonomy	narrative
development	open method
inference	self-care

Go to the Bind-in-Book CD for:

Note for Adjusting Week by Week Plan to Your Class
Anecdotal Recording form

Plan Week 2 Part A, Directions for Anecdotal Recording on Self-Care for Group A, including What to Do with It, Portfolio Overview Example, Sharing with Child and Family, Actions—Read a Book, In the Environment, In the Curriculum, In the Newsletter

Plan Week 2 Part B, Class List Log on Self-Care and What to Do With It

Plan Week 2 Part C, Reflective Journal

REFERENCES

Allen, K. E., & Cowdery, G. E. (2005). *The exceptional child: Inclusion in early childhood education* (5th ed.). Clifton Park, NY: Thomson Delmar Learning.

American Academy of Pediatrics, American Public Health Association, and National Resource Center for Health and Safety in Child Care. (2002). *Caring for our children: National health and safety performance standards: Guidelines for out-of-home child care programs* (2nd ed.). Elk Grove Village, IL: American Academy of Pediatrics and Washington, DC: American Public Health Association. Also available at http://nrc.uchsc.edu.

Bauer, K. L., & Sheerer, M. A., with Dettore, E., Jr. (1997). Creative strategies in Ernie's childhood classroom. *Young Children. 52* (6)

Benner, S. M. (2003). *Assessment of young children with special needs: A context-based approach.* Clifton Park, NY: Thomson Delmar Learning.

Bentzen, W. (2005). *Seeing young children: A guide to deserving and rewarding behavior* (5th ed.). Clifton Park, NY: Thomson Delmar Learning.

Bowe, F. G. (2004). *Birth to five: Early childhood special education* (3rd ed.). Clifton Park, NY: Thomson Delmar Learning.

Bredekamp, S. (1997). *Developmentally appropriate practice in early childhood programs.* Revised edition. Washington, DC: National Association for the Education of Young Children.

Cripe, J. W., & Lee, J. M. (1997). Activity-based intervention strategies for serving young children with developmental delays in early childhood programs. In W. H. Brown & M. A. Conroy, *Including and supporting preschool children with developmental delays in early childhood programs.* Little Rock, AR: Southern Early Childhood Association, 49–63.

Division of Early Childhood—Council for Exceptional Children. (2000). *DEC Recommended practices in early intervention/early childhood special education.* Missoula, MT: Author.

Elkind. D. (1987). *Miseducation: Preschoolers at risk.* New York: Alfred A. Knopf.

Erikson, E. (1963). *Childhood and society* (2nd ed.). New York: Norton.

Frank, C. (1999). *Ethnographic eyes.* Portsmouth, NH: Heinemann.

Ireton, H. R. (1995). *Teacher's observation guide.* Minneapolis, MN: Behavioral Science Systems.

Kinnell, G. (2004). *Good going!* St. Paul, MN: Redleaf Press.

Lynch, E. W., & Hanson, M. J. (2004). *Developing cross-cultural competence: A guide for working with young children and their families* (3rd ed.). Baltimore, MD: Brookes.

NAEYC. (2005). *NAEYC early childhood program standards and accreditation criteria.* Washington, DC: Author.

Thomas, A., & Chess, S. (1977). *Temperament and development.* New York: Brunner/Mazel.

Thomas, A., & Chess, S. (1980). *The dynamics of psychological development.* New York: Brunner/Mazel.

RESOURCES

American Academy of Pediatrics. (2002). *Caring for our children: National health and safety performance standards: Guidelines for out-of-home child care programs* (2nd Ed.). Elk Grove Village, IL: Author. http://nrc.uchsc.edu/CFOC/index.html.

Feldman, J. (1995). *Transition time: Let's do something different!* Beltsville, MD: Gryphon House.

Kinnell, G. (2004). *Good going!* St. Paul, MN: Redleaf Press.

Lynch, E. W., & Hanson, M. J. (2004). *Developing cross-cultural competence: A guide for working with young children and their families* (3rd ed.). Baltimore, MD: Brookes.

NAEYC. (2005). *NAEYC early childhood program standards and accreditation criteria.* Washington, DC: Author.

Psaltis, M., & Stonehouse, A. (1990). Toddler-centered routines. In A. Stonehouse. *Trusting toddlers: Planning for one- to three-year-olds in child care centers.* St. Paul, MN: Toys 'n Things Press.

CHAPTER 3

Using Checklists to Look at Physical Development

IN THIS CHAPTER

USING THE CHECKLIST

EXERCISE **Complete the following Checklist.**

- ______ I read Chapters 1 and 2.
- ______ I completed each exercise in Chapters 1 and 2.
- ______ I enjoyed writing in my Reflective Journal.
- ______ I underlined key passages.
- ______ I know the definition of *development*.

A **Checklist** is a predetermined list of criteria against which the recorder answers *yes* or *no*. In Checklist ratings, the recorder reads the criterion, decides on an answer, and makes a checkmark as an indication of an affirmative answer. Some of the preceding criteria are observable, whereas others are judgmental or inferential. Mark those with a *J*. The third and fifth items are not observable.

Bentzen (2005) describes Checklists as a **closed method** because no raw data or evidence is recorded, just the decision (inference) of the recorder about the criterion. Checklists are highly selective, only giving the recorder the opportunity to record a decision concerning the criterion. That does not mean it is not useful or accurate, but the reader has no raw data or details to check the recorder's decision. This is a characteristic of Checklist recording.

A valid child development Checklist records the attainment of accepted developmental milestones of knowledge, behavior, and skills. All Checklists depend on the familiarity of the observer with the criteria and ability to assess the criteria accurately. Therefore, the criteria should be clearly observable, leaving little room for subjective judgments. If not, two raters may see the same child performing a skill, yet rate the skill differently. Checklists' criteria should be closely examined for appropriateness to the population they are assessing and the developmental sequence of the criteria. Many programs and teachers design their own Checklists to fit the goals and objectives of the program and the population the program serves.

The developmental sequence of a Checklist makes it a forecaster or predictor of the skills or behaviors that will appear next. In this way, they help the teacher to individualize the curriculum by suggesting what experiences to provide in the next stage. For example:

__X__ Child sits unassisted.
__X__ Child creeps.
______ Child pulls to a standing position.
______ Child walks holding onto furniture.
______ Child walks alone.

By seeing that the next stage is pulling to a standing position, the teacher will provide an environment that stimulates pulling up to a standing position, such as stable furniture and interesting things to look at above the creeping level. The teacher may plan activities in which the child is lifted to a standing position and supported for short periods of time.

Each criterion should measure the presence or absence of the knowledge, behavior, or skill. Checklists sometimes contain criteria that ask the recorder to judge or summarize groups of actions. For example, a Checklist item on small muscle skills may list:

______ Coordinated eye/hand movements

The teacher observed the child putting puzzle pieces into the correct holes. The meaning or summary of that skill could be inferred as "coordinated eye/hand movements." This type of criterion leaves much room for interpretation and the greater chance that it is subjective rather than factual, objective recording. Valid Checklists list specific knowledge, behaviors, and skills, in developmental sequence, that describe exactly a movement, skill, or behavior. This leaves the recorder only to answer the basic question, "Is the child doing that or not?"

EXERCISE **Mark the following Checklist items O for observed, or I for interpreted.**

______ **1.** Can sit unassisted for two minutes
______ **2.** Uses pincer grasp to pick up small objects
______ **3.** Enjoys pulling self up on furniture
______ **4.** Able to do most small muscle skills
______ **5.** Can walk six feet on a four-inch balance beam
______ **6.** Can cut
______ **7.** Moves gracefully
______ **8.** Increasing strength and dexterity
______ **9.** Gives little attention to small muscle activities
______ **10.** Balances on one foot for five seconds

Check yourself:

1. O—The position is observable, and time is measured.
2. O—How the child picks up the object is observed.
3. I—Whether the child enjoys it or not is interpreted by observing behavior and forming a conclusion. If the criteria were "Pulls self up on furniture," it would be O.
4. I—What are *most small muscle tasks?* It is not clear what they are, and if they are observed or not.
5. O—The length and width of board is a precise measurement, and action is observable.
6. I—The criterion is too broad. More accurate criteria would be "Can cut a straight line" or "Can cut a curved line."
7. I—The observer has much latitude in deciding if the movement is "graceful." An observable criterion is "Moves without bumping into objects in the room" or "Moves to rhythm of music."
8. I—Increasing from what? This is not measurable. An observable criterion is "Can suspend body weight on bars for 10 seconds" or "Can catch an 8-inch ball from 10 feet."
9. I—Judgment of the observer is recorded rather than observed behavior. An observable criterion is "Spends ____ minutes on small muscle activity."
10. O—Position and time measurement is specific. This is an objective criterion.

If Checklists were used for every increment, in every skill or behavior, in every developmental area, the Checklist would be unwieldy. Well-constructed Checklists are specific and limited to observable milestones. They are used with other methods of recording to document the specifics of observations.

The Checklist is reused periodically to measure progress along the developmental continuum. If progress is not indicated by observing criteria farther along the scale, the teacher takes a closer look to be sure the data is correct. The Checklist may indicate significant lags that need to be addressed. A discussion is held with the family, possibly referring them to helping professionals for a full evaluation. The decision may be made just to wait and watch for another period to see if the skills develop.

A Checklist is an effective tool to share with the family. It shows expected developmental progression and the level attained within those expectations. It indicates the dates of the observations and how much progress has taken place over that time. It may reveal accelerated or delayed development in specific areas, showing the child's strengths or areas yet to be developed. The Checklist becomes a permanent part of the child's Portfolio or file.

Checklists, their content or format, can be varied to meet the needs of the recorder or program (Figure 3–1 and Figure 3–2). Some recorders recommend that different colored pens be used for each rating period. Many observers and Checklists are entering the technological age with computer scanning and analysis.

Limitations to Checklists

1. Checklists do not preserve the details of a conversation where vocabulary, tone of voice, and exact words give the essence of the exchange.
2. The observer sees behaviors and skills and makes a decision as to the presence or absence of the criteria. Once the checkmark or indication is made, there is no further notation about the event. You will notice that most of the items in the Checklists in Figure 3–1 and Figure 3–2 (Gober, 2002) are directly observable. These Checklists could be modified by entering the date the behavior was observed instead of just including a checkmark in the box. Beaty, in *Observing Development of the Young Child* (2006), inserts a column next to each criterion to use for note taking in order to make the Checklist more of an open method. Beaty refers to these notes as "evidence" because they retain details of why the observer made that judgment. Of course, it will be necessary to return to the lists periodically to record the child's progress.
3. Some Checklists are sequential (see 0–12 months in Figure 3–1), but others are not (see 6–8-year-olds in Figure 3–2). Nonsequential Checklists are not as useful for anticipating emerging development or in planning curriculum to help the child reach the next milestone.
4. The observer's decision may be influenced by personal biases. The Checklist provides no way for the reader to form an independent opinion. The reader has to trust the recorder's judgment. This shortcoming of Checklists can be overcome by having various individuals recording with the Checklist. This gives more than one person's opinion regarding the criteria.
5. Because of its lack of detail, the Checklist is not a method that is reliable for documentation of suspected child abuse.

EXERCISE Look through the Checklists of physical development in Figure 3–1 and mark each criterion that is based directly on observations with an O, with a J if it is a judgment based on the observation, and a P if it is a perception of the child's inner feelings. Talk about your findings with a classmate.

Uses

The Checklist method of recording

- records the presence or absence of predetermined criteria.
- shows the sequence of developmental progress.
- measures progress.
- can be used as a screening for developmental lags.
- can be used as a curriculum planning tool for individualizing the curriculum.

Advantages

The Checklist is

- time- and labor-efficient.
- comprehensive. (It may cover many developmental areas in one Checklist.)

0–12 Months		
	Observed	**Not Observed**
Physical Growth/Motor Development		
Looks around (2 months)	❑	❑
Laughs aloud (3–5 months)	❑	❑
Controls head movements (about 4 months)	❑	❑
Notices hands/feet and plays with them (3–5 months)	❑	❑
Rolls over (4–6 months)	❑	❑
Sits up without support (6–8 months)	❑	❑
Holds bottle (6–8 months)	❑	❑
Crawls (6–8 months)	❑	❑
Walks with support	❑	❑
Imitates adults' facial gestures	❑	❑
Reaches, grasps	❑	❑
Puts objects in mouth	❑	❑
Picks things up with thumb and finger	❑	❑
Picks up toys that are dropped	❑	❑
Teeth appear (6–12 months)	❑	❑
12–24 Months		
Physical Growth/Motor Development		
Teething continues	❑	❑
Crawls well, stands alone well	❑	❑
Walks without help	❑	❑
Pushes, pulls toys	❑	❑
Sits in chair	❑	❑
Moves to music	❑	❑
Throws, kicks a ball	❑	❑
Crawls down stairs backward	❑	❑
Stacks blocks	❑	❑
Uses a spoon, chews food	❑	❑
Turns book pages	❑	❑
Jumps up and down	❑	❑
Holds glass	❑	❑
Opens doors and cabinets	❑	❑
Scribbles, paints with whole arm	❑	❑
Starts elimination control	❑	❑
24–36 Months		
Physical Growth/Motor Development		
Uses a spoon without spilling	❑	❑
Opens doors	❑	❑
Washes and dries hands	❑	❑
Begins to cut with scissors	❑	❑
Uses one hand consistently	❑	❑
Runs forward, jumps in place, climbs	❑	❑
Stands on one foot	❑	❑
Walks on tiptoes	❑	❑
Kicks ball forward	❑	❑
Rides a tricycle	❑	❑
Marches to music	❑	❑

Figure 3–1 Developmental Checklist, 0–36 Months. (From *Six Simple Ways to Assess Young Children,* 1st edition, by GOBER, 2002. Reprinted with permission of Delmar Learning, a division of Thomson Learning: www.thomsonrights.com. Fax 800 730-2215.)

3-Year-Olds		
	Observed	**Not Observed**
Physical Growth/Motor Development		
Copies circles	❑	❑
Manipulates clay, puzzles, scissors	❑	❑
Builds	❑	❑
Runs around obstacles	❑	❑
Walks on a line	❑	❑
Hops/balances on one foot	❑	❑
Steers and pedals tricycle	❑	❑
Throws ball overhand	❑	❑
Jumps with two feet	❑	❑
Begins to use zippers, buttons to dress	❑	❑
4-Year-Olds		
Physical Growth/Motor Development		
Draws, paints, uses scissors	❑	❑
Dresses and undresses without assistance	❑	❑
Walks stairs alone, alternating feet	❑	❑
Self-reliant in bathroom	❑	❑
Kicks, throws, bounces, catches a ball	❑	❑
Runs, hops, skips, jumps, gallops	❑	❑
Developing eye–hand coordination	❑	❑
5-Year-Olds		
Physical Growth/Motor Development		
Takes care of personal needs (ties shoes, buttons, zips, etc.)	❑	❑
Coordinates body parts (biking, swimming, etc.)	❑	❑
Cuts accurately	❑	❑
Uses pencil and scissors correctly	❑	❑
Basic grasp of right and left, but confuses them	❑	❑
Movements appear smooth	❑	❑
Walks backward	❑	❑
Skips	❑	❑
Right or left handedness is established	❑	❑
Uses glue correctly and easily	❑	❑
6–8-Year-Olds		
Physical Growth/Motor Development		
Rate of growth slows, but growth spurts occur	❑	❑
Enjoys team sports	❑	❑
Repeats skill for mastery (bike riding, skating, swimming, etc.)	❑	❑
Forms letters and numbers well	❑	❑
Loss of teeth	❑	❑
Body develops more proportionately	❑	❑
Visual difficulties may surface	❑	❑
Shows coordination of large and small motor skills	❑	❑
Draws a person with clothes and body parts	❑	❑

Figure 3–2 Developmental Checklist, 3–8 Years. (From *Six Simple Ways to Assess Young Children,* 1st edition, by GOBER, 2002. Reprinted with permission of Delmar Learning, a division of Thomson Learning: www.thomsonrights.com. Fax 800 730-2215.)

- documentation of development.
- individual documentation on each child.
- a clear illustration of the developmental continuum.

Disadvantages

The Checklist

- loses the details of events.
- may be biased by the recorder.
- depends on the criteria to be clearly observable.
- may have many items to check, making it time consuming.

Pitfalls to Avoid

Checklists seem like they can be done from memory, but memories are inaccurate and can be biased. The recordings should be from direct observation.

Checklists can be unwieldy if the recorder is trying to do too much at one time. To actually observe and record on a Checklist, it helps to either select one child to observe over a period of a day in all developmental areas, or one developmental area and observe all children in that area.

Be sure that the Checklist is broad enough to include skills and behavioral milestones at prior levels as well as future ones. Children's development is uneven, and a child may be functioning at a young level in one area and an advanced level in another. The unchecked criteria give guidance about curriculum planning.

Many Checklists are covered by copyright. Either purchase the rating sheets or receive permission to copy them. It's the honest thing to do.

Using Technology

A Checklist can easily be loaded on a personal digital assistant or a small laptop using Documents to Go software. In the classroom, all you have to do is open the document, check what the child has attained, and save the document with the child's name. It can later be downloaded into the child's electronic Portfolio.

How to Find the Time

Checklists are not time consuming if you select only a portion of the Checklist and observe all the children for the chosen developmental area. On another day, select a different developmental area. This procedure will help you to focus your attention on one type of behavior and you can observe each of the children in that particular way.

What to Do with It

Programs usually purchase or develop a Checklist to match program goals and the age range of the children in the program or class. An individual Checklist is kept in each child's Portfolio or file. Periodically, the recorder reexamines each developmental area. It is objective only as long as the Checklist closely describes exact observable behavior rather than vague generalizations that may be interpreted many ways.

Families have access to this Portfolio and the Checklist. It is a good tool to show families the developmental sequence and the documentation of the accomplishments of their child. Focusing on the accomplishments, rather than the areas yet to be attained, is a positive way of evaluating a child's development.

Some Examples of Checklists

Ages and Stages Questionnaires (ASQ), 2nd edition, (Bricker & Squires, 1999) is an age-related series of developmental screening questions answered by parents or primary caregivers and is designed to identify the few infants and young children who require more extensive evaluation (Figure 3–3).

The *Brigance Diagnostic Inventory of Early Development* (Brigance, 2004) is a comprehensive Checklist to assess development and diagnose developmental delay.

The *Child Development Inventory (CDI)* (Ireton, 1992) is a Parent Checklist for ages six months to six years to measure development and identify potential problems for further assessment.

The *Child Observation Record (COR)* (High/Scope Press, 2003) is an ascending Checklist for cognitive, movement, and social-emotional development dependent on anecdotal records (Key Experience Notes) prior to completing the Checklist.

The *Denver Developmental Screening Test II (DDSTII)* (Frankenburg et al., 1990) provides a range of criteria over four domains: social-emotional, fine motor, gross motor, and language. It can be used for screening at-risk children.

GROSS MOTOR *Be sure to try each activity with your child.*

	YES	SOMETIMES	NOT YET	
1. Does your child catch a large ball with both hands? You should stand about 5 feet away and give your child two or three tries.	❑	❑	❑	____
2. Does your child climb the rungs of a ladder of a playground slide and slide down without help?	❑	❑	❑	____
3. While standing, does your child throw a ball overhand in the direction of a person standing at least 6 feet away? To throw overhand, your child must raise her arm to shoulder height and throw the ball forward. (Dropping the ball, letting the ball go, or throwing the ball underhand should be scored as "not yet.")	❑	❑	❑	____
4. Does your child hop up and down on either the right or left foot at least one time without losing his balance or falling?				
5. Does your child jump forward a distance of 20 inches from a standing position, starting with her feet together?	❑	❑	❑	____
6. Without holding onto anything, does your child stand on one foot for at least 5 seconds without losing his balance and putting his foot down? You may give your child two or three tries before you mark the question.	❑	❑	❑	____
	GROSS MOTOR TOTAL			____

FINE MOTOR *Be sure to try each activity with your child.*

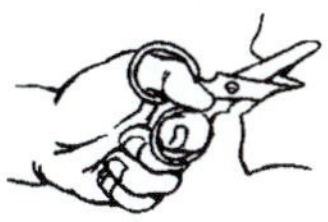

1. Does your child put together a six-piece interlocking puzzle? (If one is not available, take a full-page picture from a magazine or catalog and cut it into six pieces. Does your child put it back together correctly?)	❑	❑	❑	____
2. Using child-safe scissors, does your child cut a paper in half on a more or less straight line, making the blades go up and down? (Carefully watch your child's use of scissors for safety reasons.)	❑	❑	❑	____
3. Using the shapes below to look at, does your child copy at least three shapes onto a large piece of paper using a pencil or crayon, without tracing? Your child's drawings should look similar to the design of the shapes below, but they may be different in size.	❑	❑	❑	____
4. Does your child unbutton one or more buttons? Your child may use his own clothing or a doll's clothing.	❑	❑	❑	____
5. Does your child draw pictures of people that have at least three of the following features: head, eyes, nose, mouth, neck, hair, trunk, arms, hands, legs, or feet?	❑	❑	❑	____
6. Does your child color mostly within the lines in a coloring book? Your child should not go more than 1/4 inch outside the lines on most of the picture.	❑	❑	❑	____
	FINE MOTOR TOTAL			____

Figure 3–3 Reprinted by permission from *Ages & Stages Questionnaires® (ASQ): A Parent-Completed, Child-Monitoring System, Second Edition,* by Diane Bricker and Jane Squires, with assistance from Linda Mount, LaWanda Potter, Robert Nickel, Elizabeth Twombly, and Jane Farrell, Copyright © 1999 by Paul H Brookes Publishing Co. (1-800-638-3775; www.brookespublishing.com).

REVIEW

CHECKLIST

Listing of related criteria against which skills, knowledge, or behavior are measured indicating yes or no, present or not present. Can indicate milestones attained and areas yet to be developed.

Types of Information to Record Using Checklists

- self-care skills
- physical development—large muscle/small muscle skills
- stages of social development
- stages of emotional development
- stages of language development
- stages of cognitive development—specific criteria such as "knows colors, shapes, recognizes numbers"
- stages of literacy development
- stages of creative development
- stages of sociodramatic play
- aspects of self-concept

Developmental Profiles: Pre-Birth Through Twelve, 5th edition (Allen & Marotz, 2007) provides one-page-for-one-year developmental Checklists that give the milestones for that year. The text provides more specific information, learning activities, and developmental alerts.

Observing Development of the Young Child, 6th edition (Beaty, 2006) is a Checklist with an evidence column for three- to six-year-olds with ascending criteria in all developmental areas. Child development and curriculum planning resources.

The Peabody Developmental Motor Scales, 2nd edition (Folio & Fewell, 2000) is an assessment of gross and fine motor skills birth through five years.

The Adaptive Behavior Assessment System, 2nd edition (Harrison & Oakland, 2003) presents criteria from several domains to assess development from birth to five, with separate checklists for parents and for day care providers.

The Work Sampling System (Meisels et al., 1994) has Checklist components in personal and social development, language and literacy, mathematical and scientific thinking, social studies, the arts, and physical development. It assesses children's skills, knowledge, behavior, and accomplishments.

Go to the Bind-in-Book for Checklist forms, plans and resources.

LOOKING AT GROWTH AND DEVELOPMENT

EXERCISE Using a separate sheet of paper, list five phrases to describe your body.

Read the chapter, then return to your descriptions and mark them *G* for growth areas and *D* for development areas.

it happened to me

"BMW vs. Harley"

One year I had two little girls in my preschool class. One whose mother brought her in her BMW, parked at the end of the sidewalk in the No Parking Zone, swooped in on her high heels and full length fur coat. In the same class was another little girl whose mother drove her to school on the back of her Harley. She clanked in wearing full leathers, chain link necklace, tattoos, and feather earrings. Now, looking at those two children without the smudges on my frame of reference because of these facts was very difficult. I had to be honest with myself and trust objective recording methods to filter out those biases.

Do you have an IT HAPPENED TO ME story about hidden biases? I'd love to read about it. Send it to WeekbyWeek@thomsonlearning.com

TOPICS IN OBSERVATION

Your Frame of Reference

Everyone looks at the world through a unique **frame of reference**. That frame of reference can be compared to a picture frame to help understand the concept (Figure 3–4).

A frame is the boundary or outer limits around a picture. The frame around the perimeter of a piece of glass sets the boundaries all around and limits vision beyond. Each person's understanding or "vision" is limited by boundaries different from every other person's. The frame of reference is formed from past experiences but is very influential in viewing the present and the future. For the teacher, the frame of reference must be considered when observing children because it determines how the child is viewed. Some experiences that form the frame of reference follow.

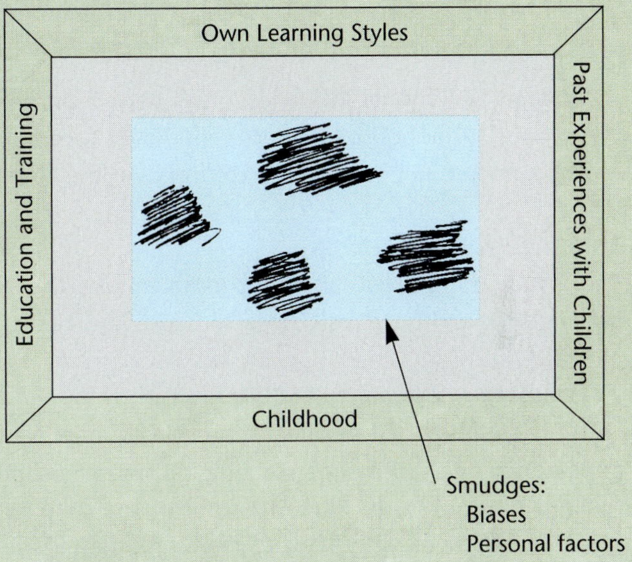

Figure 3–4 Frame of Reference.

Childhood. Each person's childhood is unique, even for children born in the same family, even for twins. Birth order, health, dynamics of personality in interactions with family members, inborn characteristics, and family environment all have an effect on childhood. When observing a child, adults subconsciously reflect on their own childhoods. These are factors in limiting how the adult sees the child. They unconsciously ask themselves, "How is this child like me or different from me as a child? What advantages or disadvantages does this child have that might influence the child in a different way from my own childhood? Can I even relate to the situation of this child because of the kind of childhood I have had?"

Education and Training. The educational level and philosophies learned affect the teacher's perceptions and judgments of the child being viewed. From a psychological background, the viewer may look for the meaning behind the behavior. From a psychosocial background, the viewer may look for conflict between biological and social demands at each maturational stage. From a behaviorist background, the viewer might look for the stimulus and responses reinforced in the behavior.

Past Experiences with Children. Many people working with children have a long history. They may be parents and grandparents or may have started out their career caring for younger siblings, babysitting as a teenager, and now caring for extended family members. The past is the keyhole through which the present is viewed. This observed behavior may trigger memories and situations from the past and send up a warning signal, while other observers ignore the same action or regard it as insignificant. What is seen is always reflected back to what has been experienced in the past. Those new to the profession, with little experience, are going to see behaviors and incidents differently from those with much experience.

(continued)

TOPICS IN OBSERVATION *(continued)*

Own Learning Styles. With the advent of more knowledge of individual learning styles, it becomes clearer that a teacher's learning style is as important as the student's. Depending on the acute sensory reception, the observer will absorb information in different ways:

auditory learner—from language and sounds the child makes
visual learner—from actions, scenes, pictures of the child's behavior
tactile learner—from touching the child

Values. Society has influenced each person differently in the formation of values and viewpoints. The societal influences of socioeconomic level, race, religion, ethnicity, and gender enter into the observation framework. There is little control over the formation until awareness is raised.

SMUDGES ON THE GLASS

The frame of reference is the perimeter, but the viewing is done through the glass. There may be smudges on the glass. Those smudges are biases that keep the observer from seeing the child objectively.

Biases For or Against the Child. Individual **bias** and prejudice are human factors that may interfere with a clear view of the child. Those biases may even be positive ones, such as the child's attractive appearance or charming personality, causing the child's needs to be overlooked because of personal feelings that get in the way. Strengths of the child may be overlooked because of a prejudice or bias that will negatively affect objective observation. Some might be:

sex—may prefer boys or girls
hair color—may love or hate redheads
racial or ethnic—stereotypic beliefs
economic or social status—rich or poor may interfere with how the child is perceived
personality clashes—may love or hate children who are whiny, mischievous, active, sassy, bold, shy
prior contact with the family—older child was in the class
physical attributes—beauty, handicaps, weight
hearsay—prior teachers influence opinion

Personal Factors That Affect Observation. Adults may have their own situations that have nothing to do with the child but may affect the observer enough to interfere with objective recording:

health—headache, awaiting test results, impending surgery, pregnancy, or premenstrual syndrome
stress—financial, personal, or workplace tension
outside pressure—gathering evidence to document a decision or a referral

The observer's consciousness is raised on these issues through reflection. By selecting objective observation methods, communicating and sharing observations and conferences with coworkers and parents, these biases can be minimized.

TOPICS IN OBSERVATION *(continued)*

All of these—the framework, the biases, and the daily situation—influence observation. Because observation is subjective, many criticize it as untrustworthy for evaluation. Many prefer standardized tests as more objective measuring tools. Testing will be discussed in a later section. These warnings regarding the influences of biases and personal factors on observations are discussed here as a prelude to offer evidence for the necessity of carefully choosing recording methods. When limitations are recognized, efforts can be made to overcome the possible negative influences. "Forewarned is forearmed," as the saying goes. "We do, because we know." Some recording methods can be biased. Some days might not be good ones to gather information and make decisions. The professional acts ethically.

Bodies change. They grow and develop. What is the difference? **Growth** refers to changes in size, *quantitative* change, those changes that can be measured in increasing numbers such as height, weight, head circumference, and teeth.

- Most infants range in length from 18 to 21 inches at birth and are expected to grow longer and taller.
- By 36 months, the toddler has molars and a total of 20 "baby" teeth and is expected to grow more.
- The average five-year-old weighs 38 to 45 pounds and is expected to increase in weight as she grows older.
- Between the ages of six and eight, the body takes on a lanky appearance as arms and legs grow longer, with permanent teeth replacing baby teeth, developing more adult-like features.

There are norms, or averages, established by statistical analysis of large groups of people. These are the established ranges for average growth at specific ages (Figure 3–5). Tables like these can alert observers to significant variations that warrant further investigation for the cause.

Other changes can be measured in numbers that are not physical. Vocabulary also "grows" because it can be measured in numbers. The toddler has a vocabulary of 50 to 300 words. The attention span is growing, too. It can be measured in minutes (sometimes seconds) and is expected to increase as the child matures.

Development is also change, but *qualitative change,* increasingly better, more complex, and more coordinated. Development, like growth, occurs in sequential, predictable stages, yet is different for every individual based on several factors. Physical development, involving both large and small muscle coordination, begins with reflex actions and progresses to rudimentary, then fundamental movement quality during the preschool years . It forms the basis for refinements that are used in all active sports.

EXERCISE **List all the factors you can think of that affect physical development.**

Now read on and see how many factors correlate to your list.

Many factors affect growth and development.

- Genetics determines thousands of characteristics of growth and development, such as body size, sex, and coloring.
- Prenatal care, including the mother's nutrition and physical condition, and even age, contribute to prebirth growth and development.
- Health factors, such as preventive care, diseases, illnesses, and accidents in childhood, can affect both the growth and development of the body.
- Environmental factors, such as nutrition, quality of air, and geographic location, affect physical growth and development.
- Age or maturation is a determining factor in the changing body's size and development.
- Social factors, such as opportunities, experiences, and role models, affect development.
- Economic level has an effect on both physical growth and development through nutrition, experiences, and opportunities.

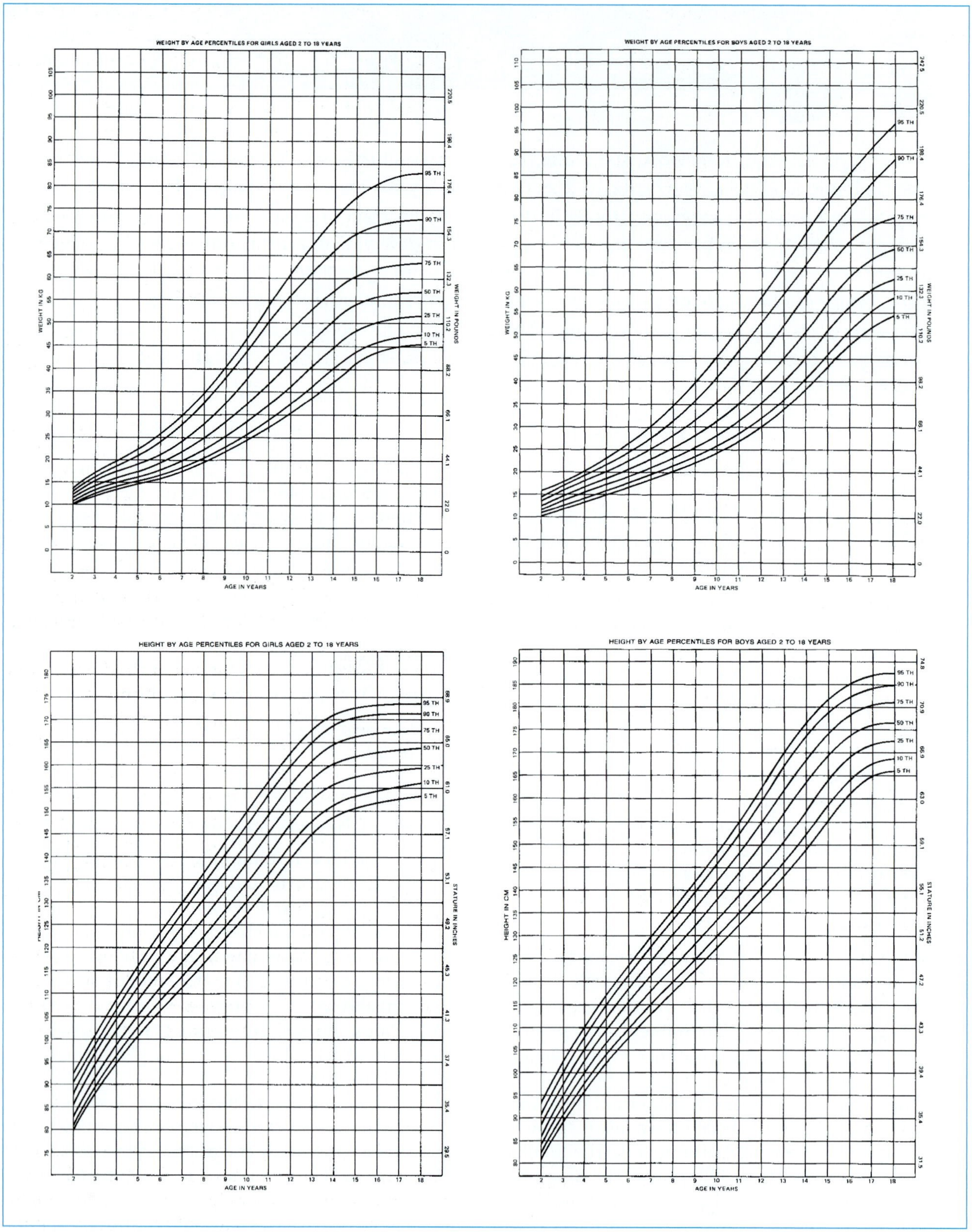

Figure 3–5 Height and Weight Charts.

Other areas of development have a two-way influence.

- Cognitive development affects physical development. As the child's thinking changes to higher levels, her movements change. She can do a more complex puzzle, not just because of physical dexterity but because of the ability to visualize pieces of the whole. It is also through physically manipulating materials that the child's cognitive structures build, experiencing soft and hard, hot and cold.
- Language and physical development are interdependent. As the child physically develops, he also learns new vocabulary words for the movements (jump, skip, pirouette). By following verbal directions, processing language, he learns how to perform physical tasks. "Hold the bat up straighter, away from your body."
- Social interactions with other people encourage physical development. By imitating the actions of others, children learn to perform tasks, such as painting, swinging, and riding a bike. As they perform these actions, they interact with other people, and their physical development is used to play and work cooperatively.
- Emotional deprivation has been known to stunt physical growth (**failure to thrive syndrome** is described in Chapter 12). Emotional development is affected by body growth. Abnormal growth and physical disabilities can affect self-esteem. It influences development because lack of confidence can make someone awkward.

When physical growth or development is adversely affected, whatever the cause, modifications can be made to the environment. This minimizes the social-emotional effects and helps compensate for or improve the skill. This can be accomplished through observation, evaluation, and individualized curriculum planning.

Stages of Physical Development

The common characteristics of development: Predictable sequences with individual differences are very evident in physical development (Figure 3–6).

PREDICTABLE SEQUENCE. Development and coordination (voluntary control of the muscles) occur in predictable directions (Figure 3–7). The infant first gains control of the head by using neck muscles, then the shoulders and torso. When development reaches the thighs and calves and toes, real crawling and creeping are accomplished. This head-to-toe direction of development is described as **cephalocaudal**. The development of physical control from the center of the body outward—control of the shoulders and arms comes before hands, then fingers—is described as **proximodistal**, or near to far (Figure 3–8).

INDIVIDUAL TIMETABLE. Some infants purposefully pick up their head and look for the source of a voice or sound by 1 month. Some do this earlier than others. Some children are walking by 10 months, and others not until 16 months. A baby will not walk until she *can*. An adult cannot make a baby walk before the muscles are strong and coordinated enough to accomplish the task.

READINESS. Physical development vividly illustrates the predictable, sequential, individual aspects of development. In other areas of development, such as emotional and cognitive development, the stages are not as easily observed. This visual reminder is an important concept to apply to curriculum planning in all areas. The child's body and mind must be ready before she can accomplish the skill. All the other steps have come before it to lead the way, serving as a benchmark of readiness for the next step.

By the age of one and a half, a child has accomplished the basic physical skills of mobility (**large muscle** or gross motor) and manipulation (**small muscle** or fine motor). The next 48 months will see vast increases in coordination and integration of all body structures. By the time children are five, they have acquired body control. The skills of walking, running, climbing, balancing, pushing, pulling, lifting, carrying, throwing, catching, and striking prepare them for life functions and all the sports and recreation skills.

EXERCISE **Turn the sound off on a television show. Observe just the facial and body movements of the people you are viewing. What does that tell you about that person?**

Ways of Seeing Beyond Physical Skills. In the provocative book *The Dancing Dialogue: Using the Communicative Power of Movement with Young Children* (Tortora, 2006), the author encourages early childhood professionals to closely observe children's body movements as ways of seeing what the child is thinking and feeling. From the very youngest infant in what Piaget describes as the Sensorimotor Stage, long before language appears or even very much muscle control, we can interpret much from the way the

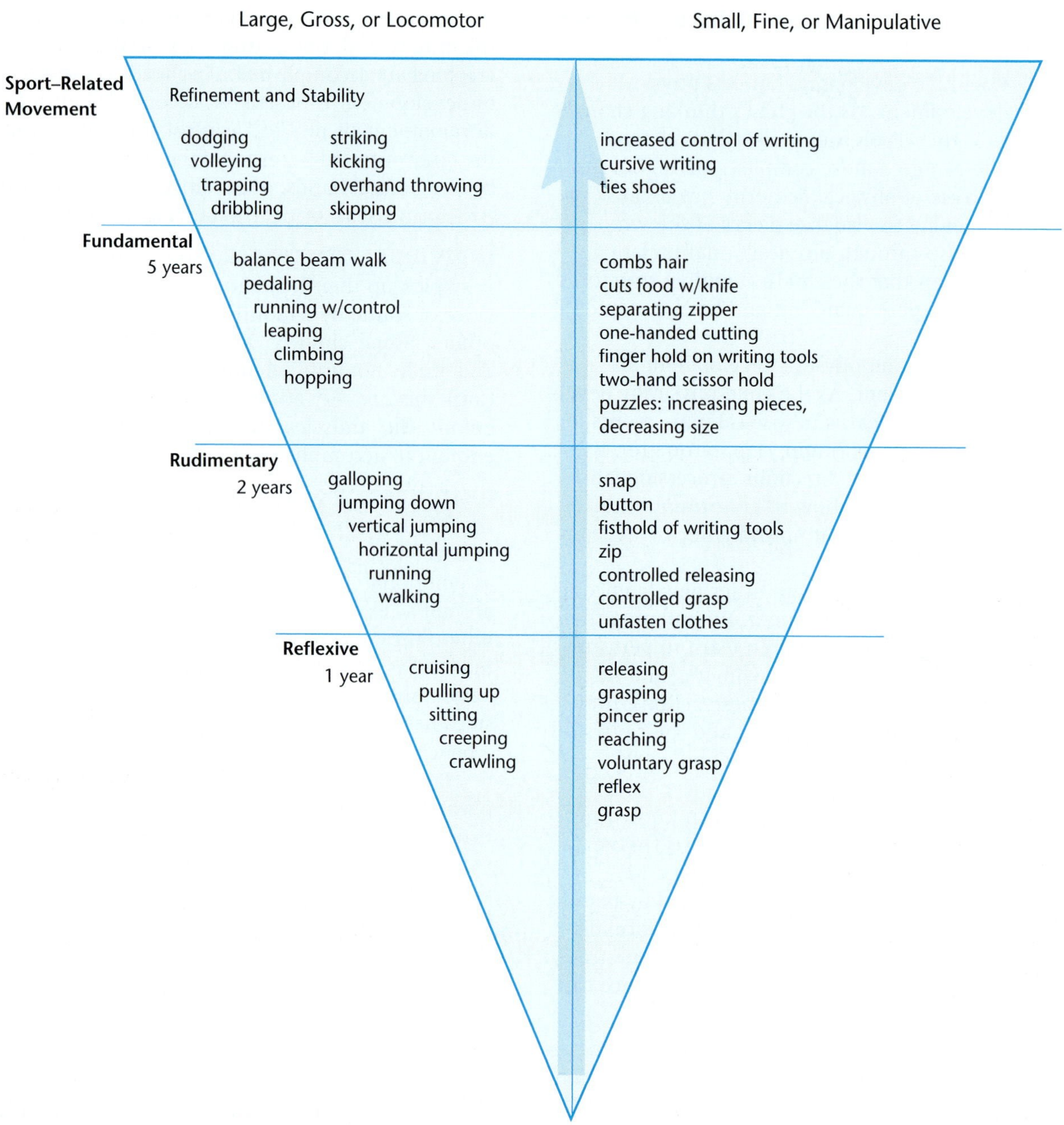

Figure 3–6 Muscle Control and Skill Development.

infant moves. Humans are programmed and learn to interpret others' movements, especially facial expressions, as reflections of themselves. An interesting study comparing the responses of children who had been physically abused with children who had been neglected and children with typical early experiences found that the sensitivity of physically abused children to nuances of body movements was acute, compared with the responses of neglected children, who had a low level of body movement interpretation (Pollak et al., 2000). Not only are adults *observing children's movements and facial expressions, but children are interpreting those they see as well.*

Why Physical Development Is Important

The principle that developmental areas are interrelated is very plainly seen in physical development. Movement and physical activity affect other domains of development, and movement-related concepts can be incorporated into learning activities to positively impact learning. "All domains are interrelated as children develop" (NAECS/SDE, 2002).

PHYSICAL DEVELOPMENT AND HEALTH. Early physical development and fitness affect lifelong health

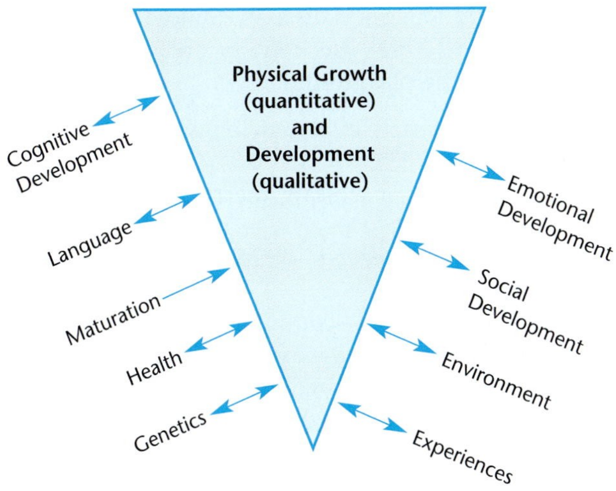

Figure 3–7 Interrelated Factors in Physical Growth and Development.

in areas such as posture, balance, muscular strength, cardiovascular endurance, and body leanness. Declining fitness and increasing obesity are national concerns. Studies have shown that even among children aged three to four years, those who were less active tended to remain less active than most of their peers after age three, so it appears that early experiences have lifelong effects (Pate, Baranowski, Dowda, & Trost, 1996). The alarming increase in rates of heart disease, diabetes, and high blood pressure are connected to physical activity. In 2000, the United States Department of Health and Human Services launched Healthy People 2010, a campaign to advocate and plan for a more active population. It is based on studies of obesity and has concrete plans for changing behavior and measuring success (see http://www.healthypeople.gov/document/ for more information). It is important for families and educators to become positive role models and to be actively involved in physical activity on a regular basis.

There are many theories about the factors leading to this physical decline. Television, video watching and game playing, and computers have been attributed as major contributions to obesity. One study found that 2-, 3-, and 4-year old children were watching 14.9, 16.3, and 18.4 hours per week, respectively (Dennison, 2002). Little research is available on children below the age of 2, but there is increasing concern regarding this link between electronic media (television and videos) and decreasing physical activity. Because it promotes children's inactivity, and because of the prevalence of advertisements for high-calorie, fat-laden foods, television is blamed (Bar-Or, 2000; Crespo et al., 2001; Proctor et al., 2003). This has prompted the American Academy of Pediatrics to issue a policy statement (2001) discouraging ANY viewing for children under 2 and limiting viewing to 2 hours a day for preschoolers. Changes in family structures, with both parents working outside the home and turning child-rearing over to others, or to the children themselves, has been blamed for children not playing actively. Violence in the neighborhood has also kept some children from playgrounds or from playing outside in the street or yard (Burdette, 2005). Schools have been reducing their emphasis on physical education as mandates for improved academic performance and budgetary woes increase.

Health-related physical fitness involves four components that can easily be incorporated into the early childhood curriculum:

muscular strength and endurance (the force both large and small muscles can produce developed from exercising longer)—climbing, jumping, pumping on a swing

flexibility (range of motion in a joint developed by slow stretching and movements)—pretend movements such as climbing, reaching, not bouncing while stretching

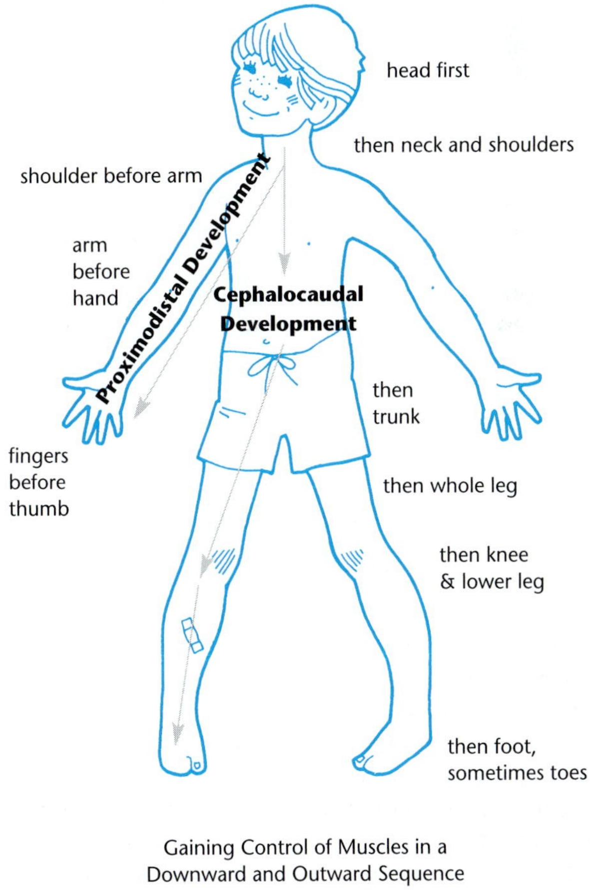

Figure 3–8 Cephalocaudal and Proximodistal Muscle Control Development. (Reprinted from *Active Start: A Statement of Physical Activity Guidelines for Children Birth to Five Years* (2002), with permission from the National Association for Sport and Physical Education (NASPE), 1900 Association Drive, Reston, VA 20191, USA.)

cardiovascular efficiency (heart, lungs, and circulatory system)—walking, playing tag, marching, riding a tricycle, dancing, jumping rope
body composition (ratio of lean tissue to body fat affected by heredity, nutrition, and lifestyle)—nutritious meals and snacks, and physical activity (Graham et al., 2004; Pica, 2006)

Family physicians urge adults to

- moderate the amount of time children spend in front of television, computers, and video terminals.
- encourage spontaneous physical activity during recess and physical education classes.
- provide safe opportunities for play. (Stephens, 2002)

PHYSICAL DEVELOPMENT AND COGNITION. While the importance of early physical activity to lifelong fitness is obvious, researchers are finding its importance to cognitive and emotional development as well. Neuroscientists studying the brain with Positron Emission Tomography (PET) scans observe and measure brain activity levels. Physical movement that involves both hemispheres of the brain, such as creeping and crawling, heighten cognitive functioning (Hannaford, 1995). As the infant's brain is developing, sensory systems such as vision, hearing, taste, smell, touch, balance, and body awareness are functioning at their most primary stage. The body's central nervous system is beginning to integrate these systems. As the infant continues to grow and develop, this integration comes under the control of the infant and responses to senses become automatic and unconscious. This sensory integration allows the brain to then process more complex information. When this integration is interrupted for some reason, it may result in the child acting disorganized, confused, and frustrated, and may ultimately interfere with learning (Bakley, 2001). Early perceptual sensory motor experiences can increase brain functioning and lead to cognitive gains. There is no doubt that exercise and good nutrition are necessary for learning and growing. As the child becomes more mobile, cruising, creeping, toddling, it should not be surprising that their vocabulary is rapidly increasing as they add more nouns in answer to their constant, "Whaddat?" This demonstrates the interplay of physical, cognitive, and language development domains.

Even though physical play is in the social domain, Bjorklund (1998) reminds us that the mechanisms involved expand the realm of cognitive benefits as well. In the position statement on young children and recess, the National Association of Early Childhood Specialists in State Departments of Education (2002) lists content areas that can be explored on the playground.

natural elements—experiencing wind, dirt, water, seasons
physics—using a see-saw, merry-go-round, swings
architecture and design—building with natural materials
math and numbers—counting, keeping score
language development—explaining, describing, articulating, seeking information, and making use of oral language/vocabulary/word power

Therefore, they recommend that all early childhood and elementary schools include periods within the instructional day for free and active outdoor play.

Motor-learning and reading are related (Block, 2001). Auditory comprehension, rhythmical processing, sequencing, and visual processing are common elements of physical development and literacy. Early literacy development of preschool hearing children using sign language can be enhanced (Daniels, 2001).

Hannaford, in *Smart Moves: Why Learning Is Not All in Your Head* (1995), suggests children create their own toys, be encouraged to make up imaginative stories, participate in rational dialogue by the age of four years, honor care of people, pets, and objects, be encouraged to delay gratification, be discouraged from watching TV and play video games, and, above all, take part in lots of body movement opportunities for full limbic system development. It is vital to brain development. The interplay of mind and body is not surprising but is a reemphasis of the importance of physical activity to overall success in learning and living.

PHYSICAL DEVELOPMENT AND SOCIAL-EMOTIONAL DEVELOPMENT. Researchers also point out that large muscle skills have social and emotional effects on children's views of themselves and their perceptions of how others feel about them (Gallahue, 2003; Purkey, 1996; Coakley, 2001). Success-oriented physical education meets not only the child's need for motor skill development but also the social-emotional development qualities of competence, belonging, and self-worth (Weiller & Richardson, 1993).

Obesity can cause children (especially girls) to be ridiculed and rejected, which may cause low self-esteem and lead to unhealthy dieting and food-related problems like bulimia and anorexia (Lowey, 1998).

Cortisol, the hormone released during stress, undermines neurological development and can affect cognitive, motor, and social development. Pica (2000) makes the case for the importance of physical development beyond fitness, emphasizing the relationship to social-emotional, creative, and cognitive development. She relates movement to all curriculum areas.

PHYSICAL DEVELOPMENT AND PLAY. As infants become more social, they interact with objects and other people in play. At first, play is a sensory manipulation. The infant reaches out and takes hold of a rattle or a toy, or grabs his father's nose. As the child's muscles eventually become coordinated through experience, he will discover that he can cause the toy to make a sound, or can make someone smile. In an ever-increasing spiral of complex actions and reactions, the child's play repertoire expands. The child learns that play is pleasurable, self-motivating, not expected to produce a specific outcome, and requires the integration of several different skills to continue. This play is inborn in animals and humans. Playing appears to be linked to social adjustment and improved physical condition (Power, 2000).

As children mature, their physical ability to run, throw, catch, climb, and kick are often channeled into more formal kinds of play, such as sports games with rules. Success in sports depends not only on physical ability but emotional stability, self-control, and social competence. Games for young children, however, should be those in which all children can find success, so there should be no competition. Traditional games such as Duck, Duck, Goose, where only one or two children are moving and the rest are observing, can be embarrassing and discouraging and should be eliminated from organized play (Graham, 2004). Cooperative games, *not* those with one winner and the rest losers, can help young children develop team spirit and encourage them to seek out game-playing for its intrinsic rewards. In addition, losing produces negative feelings that can affect emotional development (low self-esteem) and social development (promoting self over others).

Young children should be given every possible opportunity to build their physical skills. The opposite actually happens in competitive games—those who need the most practice get the least amount of time to play. Children cannot develop their physical skills if they are on the sidelines. In *Active Start: A Statement of Physical Guidelines for Children Birth to Five Years* (NASPE, 2002), specific guidelines address the physical activity needs of children during the first five years. It begins with the following position statement: "All children birth to age five should engage in daily physical activity that promotes health-related fitness and movement skills." It is a misconception, however, that children are just normally engaged in vigorous activity. When children 3–5 years old were observed in various preschool settings, they engaged in 4 to 10 minutes of moderate-to-vigorous physical activity per hour (Pate, 2004), falling far short of the recommended 120 minutes of physical activity a day, half of which should consist of structured activities (Figure 3–9).

Position: All children birth to age five should engage in daily physical activity that promotes health-related fitness and movement skills.

INFANTS	TODDLERS	PRESCHOOLERS
Interact & Explore environment	30 min daily of structured activities	60 minutes daily of structured activities
Safe, unrestricted settings for prolonged periods of time	60 minutes – several hours daily unstructured physical activity. Not sedentary for more than 60 min.	60 minutes – several hours daily unstructured physical activity. Not sedentary for more than 60 min.
Physical activity should promote development of movement skills	Should develop movement skills	Should develop competence in movement skills
Environment that meets or exceeds safety standards for large muscle activities	Indoor and outdoor areas that meet or exceed recommended safety standards for large muscle activities	Indoor and outdoor areas that meet or exceed recommended safety standards for large muscle activities
Responsible individuals should be aware of the importance of physical activity and facilitate the child's movement skills	Responsible individuals should be aware of the importance of physical activity and facilitate the child's movement skills	Responsible individuals should be aware of the importance of physical activity and facilitate the child's movement skills

Figure 3–9 ACTIVE START: A Statement of Physical Activity Guidelines for Children Birth to Five. (Reprinted from *Active Start: A Statement of Physical Activity Guidelines for Children Birth to Five Years* (2002), with permission from the National Association for Sport and Physical Education (NASPE), 1900 Association Drive, Reston, VA 20191, USA.)

The Role of Observation in Physical Development

EXERCISE Watch two people walk across the room. Write a description of how each one walks. What contributed to the differences?

OBSERVATION AND RECORDING FOR ASSESSMENT. Watching children move gives the observer information, leading knowledge, and theories about the contributing factors for the following aspects of physical development:

height—parents' height
weight—nutrition, metabolism, television habits, family's physical fitness
movement—age, experiences, inherited capabilities, self-esteem, physical energy level, possible disabilities

Written observations provide documentation for comparisons over time to show progress. From observations, assessments may be made as to the child's growth and development. Further evaluations may be recommended if assessments indicate results fall below the normal range.

OBSERVATION FOR SAFETY MAINTENANCE. It is the adult's responsibility to prepare a safe environment for children.

EXERCISE Using a separate sheet of paper, list five safety features you would plan if you were designing a room for young children.

Accidents occur frequently in the early years because of increased mobility, lack of coordination, inability to anticipate and avoid dangerous actions, or lack of supervision. The newly mobile infant requires crawling surfaces that are sanitary and free of ingestible objects. Beds and changing tables must have high sides, safety straps, and adult supervision. For the infant and toddler, surrounding equipment must have a stable base as the standing infant pulls himself up. He uses furniture for handles and stabilizers as he begins to walk around. Children are built to run and climb, motivated by curiosity and newfound physical skills. When running and climbing are seen as a form of active learning, physical coordination, and a source of self-esteem, modifications to the environment are made to provide for safe moving. Climbing on objects not meant to be climbed can be dangerous, so the furniture must be secured. Other climbing experiences should be provided, within a manageable range of the child's climbing ability. A soft mat is placed underneath to cushion inevitable falls. Places should be provided for running or jumping in the classroom. Look at where children are running and climbing and make it as safe as you can, altering the environment to eliminate the unsafe conditions. All stairways and doorways must be blocked from the little cruiser.

Frost (1992) has devised a Playground Maintenance Checklist for ages 3 to 8 that features criteria on surfaces, equipment, natural aspects, security, storage, safety, and educational usefulness (Figure 3–10).

EXERCISE Use the Playground Maintenance Checklist to practice Checklist recording and review the criteria for safe environments.

Mobility and coordination increase the risk of accidents. As independence grows from the onset of crawling onward, children have the urge to get things for themselves. Leaving an area, climbing into a cupboard or onto shelves, or attempting tasks beyond their capability and judgment present dangers. Toddlers and preschoolers need an environment with interesting things to do, opportunities to help themselves in learning centers, and adequate supervision for safety and facilitating play. Then the potential for accidents can be reduced.

ASSESSING MUSCLE DEVELOPMENT THROUGH THE ENVIRONMENT. It is the teacher's role and responsibility to provide a safe environment to meet the developmental needs of the children. Usually the classroom space is predetermined, so the teacher makes decisions on furnishings and room arrangement based on teaching philosophies and priorities for space.

Indoor Play. Lack of space is the reason given by many teachers for not designating classroom space for a large muscle area. A climber and space to jump, tumble, and run require open, nonfurnished areas. A clear floor space of 35 square feet per child is the minimum needed for toddlers and preschoolers. Less than 25 square feet of usable space reduces gross motor activity and group play, and may increase aggression.

A designer of innovative developmental environmental facilities for children, Ania Rui Olds (2001) bases designs on four basic environmental needs:

1. to encourage movement
2. to support comfort

Date Detected	Date Repaired	
		• Hard surfaces under and around equipment in fall zones • Resilient surface material pitted or scattered • Insufficient space between equipment • Equipment not sized for age of children • Entrapment areas • Excessive or unprotected heights • Shearing and crushing mechanisms • Cracking, bending, warping, rusting, breaking, or missing components • Pinching actions, open S hooks, deformed rings, links, etc. • Loose or uncapped bolts, nuts, etc. • Worn bearings or axles • Worn swing hangers (swivels) or chains • Metal slides in direct path of sun • Slide beds loose, metal edges accessible to fingers • Heavy swing seats or seats with protruding elements • Exposed or damaged concrete footings • Equipment improperly anchored • Sharp edges and points • Exposed or projecting elements, caps missing • Railings of insufficient height • Railings invite climbing (horizontal instead of vertical) • Exposed metal in tires or swing seats • Suspended elements (e.g., ropes, cables) in movement areas • Deteriorated (splintered, cracked, rotting) wood • Broken or missing railings, steps, swing seats, rungs, deck components, etc. • Slippery footing areas on decks, steps, walkways • Trash (broken glass, foreign objects, etc.) in area • Vandalism (fire damage, broken or missing parts) • Obstacles (rocks, roots, trash, badly placed equipment) in movement area • Poor drainage (standing water) • Accessible electrical apparatus (air conditioners, switch boxes) climbable poles, guy wires, ladders accessing electrical lines • Fence not installed or in need of repair, gates not securable (younger children), extra protection for pools • Signs illegible and in poor repair • Moving parts not lubricated • Toxic materials • Foreign materials or equipment parts in fall zone

Figure 3–10 Maintenance Checklist. (From *Play and Playscapes*, 1st edition, by FROST, 1992. Reprinted with permission of Delmar Learning, a division of Thomson Learning: www.thomsonrights.com. Fax 800 730-2215.)

3. to foster competence
4. to encourage a sense of control (pp. 8–11)

In the physical environment, the adult assures safety, provides opportunities, and gives support. The developing skill determines the environment (Figure 3–11), which includes all the skill opportunities that have already been attained so they can be refined and practiced. New experiences are added to the old.

Traffic, school, and work schedules, less play space, even neighborhood dangers contribute to what Rivkin (1995) calls "vanishing habitats for play." The benefits of outdoor play to physical development—as well as to sensory learning, appreciation for nature, and expending energy—are obvious, but families and teachers seem to give it less and less attention.

Outdoor Play. The outdoor environment should also be considered to maximize development in all areas.

EXERCISE If you were designing a playground for infants, toddlers, preschoolers, or school-age children, what kinds of equipment and surfaces would it have?

Crawlers and walkers need materials that are safe and soft for first crawling and walking efforts indoors and out. Carriage and stroller paths past interesting things to look at begin the infant's outdoor experience. Paths later can be used for toddling, walking, and wheeled toys. Gentle inclines provide climbing and rolling down fun. A variety of natural materials such as grass, sand, wood, and smooth rocks provide sensory experiences in texture. Wind chimes, birdfeeders, and portable tape players provide hearing experiences. The area is enriched with a variety of toys for manipulation, pretend play, and construction (Figure 3–12).

Preschoolers need the same type of equipment and surfaces as the younger children but more challenging and separate. They need climbing apparatus and balancing equipment. They need steep hills to climb and roll down, and movable construction materials. Riding toys, swings, and sports equipment such as balls, bats, nets, and ropes also facilitate physical development.

Environments for early school-age children should provide opportunities to develop noncompetitive activities like dancing, tumbling, skating, swimming, and the supportive skills for sports such as running, throwing, and catching.

Outdoor play can be enhanced by nonpermanent, movable equipment. Griffin and Rinn (1998)

SKILL	ENVIRONMENT
Infants	
Rhythmic movement	Rocking chair, music
Crawling	Clean, cushioned surfaces to crawl on, under, through
Pulling up/standing	Stable furniture to hold
Walking, holding on (cruising)	Furnishings placed close together
Walking alone	Smooth, nonslip carpeted surface
Climbing	Low, padded platforms with padded surface beneath
Pushing, pulling, and lifting	Movable materials, tubs, wheeled toys
Toddlers: Above, plus	
Climbing	More challenging apparatus, three or four stairs with railing
Scooting	Wheeled toys
Running	Clear, carpeted area for running
Jumping	Sturdy, low platforms
Pushing, pulling, and lifting	Heavier, movable equipment
Throwing	Large, lightweight balls
Preschoolers: Above, plus	
Balancing	Climbing and balance apparatus
Pedaling	Tricycles, scooters
Hopping	Floor games and patterns
Throwing and catching	Balls and beanbags, targets
Striking	Bats, rackets, foam balls, wiffle balls suspended from ceiling
Schoolagers: Above, plus	
Dribbling and shooting	Basketballs, baskets, and court
Running races	Team games
Gymnastics	Padded surface, horse, and parallel bars
Dancing	Rhythmic group dancing

Figure 3–11 Developing skills determine the environment.

@ it happened to me

"Pants"

I was observing my preschool children climbing on the climber in the classroom. One boy, taller and heavier than all the rest, had difficulty climbing the ladder. He would try and try. I thought perhaps it was that he just didn't know how, so I tried to talk him through it without lifting him up (I probably couldn't). He still couldn't do it. Then I looked closer. For one thing, his torso was long, his legs were short, making him out of proportion. Also, because he was heavy, in order to purchase pants to fit his waist, his parents had to buy a size so large that the crotch was long, almost to his knees. Ever try to climb a ladder with your knees tied together? It must be what it felt like. I had a little private conversation with his mother, and we thought about possible solutions: shorts, pants with stretch. It wasn't just the pants but his weight, body proportion, and lack of arm strength, but he *wanted* to climb so badly that he eventually could once the clothing barrier was solved. Again, it pays to watch closely, not just check off "No" to "Able to climb a ladder."

Do you have an IT HAPPENED TO ME story about a child's physical development? I'd love to read about it. Send it to WeekbyWeek@thomsonlearning.com

give many examples using such materials as used tires, large boxes, plastic trash barrels, and carpet remnants. The goals of an obstacle course are to

- develop a means for children to understand spatial awareness in connection with their own bodies.
- offer adventure.
- enhance gross motor skills and cooperative skills.

Figure 3–12 Even the littlest ones need an enriched outdoor environment full of sights, sounds, and a variety of textures.

- provide opportunities for experimentation and exploration.
- offer creative and dramatic-play outlets.
- enhance positive self-esteem.
- provide challenge. (p. 18)

Sutterby and Frost (2002), playground researchers, recommend

- playgrounds that include gardening and nature areas.
- fitness homework assignments that involve the family.
- outdoor cooking activities linked to culture.
- dress code for teachers that allows for active participation with children.
- walking to and from school where possible.

In elementary school, recess is usually the one free-play time of the day when children can make choices. As children's opportunities for outdoor play are reduced by busy lives, neighborhood risks, and the culture of inactivity, the need for recess is greater. However, in the climate of pressure for academic performance, recess is sometimes sacrificed for remedial work or disciplinary measures. It is often the time when children are supervised by aides rather than their teachers. If teachers were on the playground, a great deal could be learned about children's physical and social behavior (O'Brien, 2003).

Physically challenged children can use the paths for wheelchairs and raised water and sand play areas for accessibility. Children with visual impairments are provided tactile and auditory stimulation materials. A real garden provides gross motor exercise as it is dug, raked, and weeded; it also encourages science, language, and sensory pleasure.

"Making playgrounds fit for children and children fit on playgrounds is essential for increasing the fitness and improving the health of today's children and tomorrow's adults" (Sutterby & Frost, 2002).

Cognitive and emotional development can have an effect on physical development. Through physical development and achievement, children's self-esteem and confidence are enhanced. Encouraging a healthy and fit lifestyle should begin early in life. The National Association for Sport and Physical Education (NASPE, 1995) has defined standards with benchmarks and assessment examples for young children's physical education. They include motor skills, physical fitness, social behavior in physical activity settings, understanding and respect for differences among people, and physical activity for enjoyment, challenge, self-expression, and social interaction. In order for young children to achieve these standards, the teacher must incorporate a regular, purposeful, physical activity into the curriculum.

OBSERVATION FOR CURRICULUM PLANNING. For infants, body awareness, learning names for the parts of the body, and naming parts as they are washed and moved are the beginnings of the large muscle curriculum. Using the Developmental Assessment Checklist, the adult can see what the child has accomplished and continue to give her practice to refine that skill. If she can roll over, then she is frequently placed on the floor and coaxed, called, lured by a toy, or gently rocked to practice the rolling. She will be sitting up soon, so she can be propped in a sitting position several times a day for short periods to give her a new view. Moving to a beat is an important curriculum goal, so music, rhythm instruments, singing, and dancing are planned daily.

Older infants and toddlers begin the quest to explore beyond their body. Toys and activities to manipulate and move are a necessary part of the curriculum. Activities are planned for interaction with adults and materials chosen to keep interest. The adult models and introduces new ways of playing.

Locomotor movement, such as creeping and crawling, transfers weight from one side of the body to the other. This is a necessary skill for walking because all the more complex skills build on it. To stimulate creeping and crawling, interesting objects and pictures are placed at floor level, not too far away to be frustrating but alluring enough to produce forward motion. Crawlers want interesting things to crawl on, such as unbreakable mirrors or pictures under sheets of plexiglass on the floor. Texture mazes on the floor and up the first two feet of the wall are stimulating environments planned for infant and toddler motor development. Feeling the steady beat, Weikart (2000) believes, is a primary ability to basic motor skill development, so those games of "Patty Cake" and baby rumbas are planned curriculum activities. Reading poetry, repeating fingerplays, and reading stories with repetitive lines provide verbal experiences with rhythm.

To encourage children's physical activity, Pica (2006) suggests:

- arranging the environment to allow for movement
- buying equipment and props with movement in mind
- demonstrating enthusiasm for physical activity
- helping children understand why movement is important.

Planned activities can be documented using different methods to indicate the child's reaction to the experiences and development of skills. Over time, this record becomes valuable evidence of the efforts and celebrations of accomplishments. The developmental Checklists show skills for practicing and improvement and list the next skill that is to be introduced and encouraged. Vygotsky (1978) calls this the zone of proximal development, the "distance between the actual developmental level . . . and the level of potential development . . . under adult guidance or in collaboration with more capable peers" (p. 86). With the help of an adult or another child, the developing child can approximate the skill before he really can accomplish it on his own. This brings the promise, the feeling of success, and builds rapport with those who support the attempt.

The curriculum is individualized by referring to assessments to determine the level of motor development each child has attained. Daily plans for the whole group would include a variety of large muscle activities. They address the key experiences previously discussed. Individual children benefit from specifically focused activities to help them achieve the next level of development. They must, however, have many opportunities for success at their present level without feeling pressured or required to try something they are not sure they will attain. The skillful teacher addresses needs by combining planned activities with the child's interests; like the song line says, "A little bit of sugar helps the medicine go down."

Planning for exceptional children will build on the abilities they do have. The curriculum is adapted so they have the closest match to what the rest of the class is doing. This is what is known as the **least restrictive environment**. If the class is marching, the child in the wheelchair can push along in the parade or beat the drum. The child with a hearing impairment can watch the beat being tapped out and feel the vibration of the drum. The child who does not speak can lead the band. The child who is visually impaired can play an instrument in one location. The child who speaks no English can move and play with everyone else.

SHARE OBSERVATIONS WITH CHILDREN AND FAMILIES. Relating observations to families not only informs them of the child's activity that day but is an opportunity to teach child development principles and raise the child's self-esteem.

EXERCISE **How do you think a child would feel about the following comments?**

"Now you can stand up all by yourself!"
"Look at how you are sitting up! You're so strong."
"You worked so hard at that balance beam today."
"You climbed to the top of the climber today. How did it feel up there?"

Accomplishments, as well as attempts, should be relayed to the child and the family. Telling the family good news in front of the child is a self-esteem booster for everyone. When the formal observation documentation such as Checklists or Anecdotal Records is shown or given to families, they see the progress and become involved in setting goals and strategies for the next skill or level. If the assessment indicates a significant developmental lag or regression, the family is consulted in private. This is to determine if this coincides with what they have observed. Then a follow-up action can be decided. It may be just to wait a while for the skill to develop or to seek further advice depending on the situation and the family's decision.

Differences between Girls and Boys

EXERCISE How are boys and girls different other than anatomically?

It is generally believed that physiologically, men are stronger than women but women have greater endurance. There are other differences seen very early in life. Male one-year-olds already spend more time in gross motor activities, while girls of that age spend more time in fine motor activities.

The social treatment of girls and boys, regarding toys and movement, begins very early. It is virtually impossible to control for that factor. This makes it difficult to determine what indeed is genetic and what is learned. Many studies have shown gender differences in toy selection, adult interactions with girls and boys, fantasy play themes, and types of play. Boys were found to be more aggressive (Figure 3–13) and girls more domestic, boys more physical and girls more verbal. The exact cause of those differences is still under debate.

Think About It . . .

How does Figure 3–13 make you feel? What would you do if you were the adult in charge?

Because early childhood care and education is a field with predominantly female personnel, their own genetic and social predispositions guide play expectations for girls and boys. That subtle bias can be seen in the low priority for large muscle equipment and curriculum in early childhood programs. Often, female personnel give quick responses and attempt to discourage rough-and-tumble play in the classroom. The biases are not so subtle in comments such as "Boys don't cry" or "Young ladies don't do that."

Figure 3–13 Boys are more likely to engage in rough-and-tumble play.

Pellegrini and Smith (1998) have done longitudinal studies of rough-and-tumble play, defined as active physical running and wrestling accompanied by laughter rather than frowning and hitting. Rough-and-tumble play is not about territories or possessions. Participants take turns as victim and victimizer. Their studies found that rough-and-tumble play was engaged in typically by boys who had high social skills. They contend that observation of rough-and-tumble play can be a social competence indicator. It leads to games with rules, role taking, and problem solving. Its use—with established guidelines—is promoted by Porter (1994). He claims it is a safe, fun activity to be encouraged as "a natural expression of children's exuberance, joy, and affection for each other" (p. 45). The implications give early childhood educators issues to consider:

- Does the environment meet the large muscle needs of all the children in the class?
- What is the response of adults when children are spontaneously using large muscles to run, wrestle, or pretend to box in the classroom?
- Is the dramatic play area designed to attract domestic players and not active players, thereby reinforcing the sex stereotypic play?
- Do children wear casual clothing for physical, indoor, and outdoor activities?
- Do adults wear casual clothing for physical, indoor, and outdoor activities?

Small Muscle Development

The coordinated functions of arm, hand, and fingers are often taken for granted.

EXERCISE Pick up each of the following items: chair, book, dime, hair. Perform each of the following tasks: zip a zipper, tie a shoe, write your name. Now perform the above tasks with your nondominant hand. Notice the different movements and functions of your small muscles.

For the first few months of life, the small muscles of hands and feet are moved by **reflexes**, rather than purposeful movements controlled by thought. Apply pressure to the palms of the infant, and her mouth opens and her head flexes forward (Babkin reflex). Stroke her palm, and her hand closes into a grip around the object so strong it can hold her weight. Stroke the sole of her foot, and her toes extend. Over the course of the first year, the infant develops control over these small muscles, first by reaching, corralling, and grasping with the entire hand. By age one, the infant can use the thumb and forefinger in a pincer grasp. Letting go, or releasing, comes later than grasping. This explains why an infant holding onto an earring or a lock of hair has a hard time letting go of it.

These small muscle skills are connected to eye and hand coordination, the cephalocaudal and proximodistal development of the whole body, and thought processes. They will continue to develop into the more specific motions needed to twist, squeeze, pinch, button, snap, zip, pour, pick up small objects, insert, and cut. All of these skills are leading to the achievement of readiness to write. Other developmental skills also signal that the child is ready for writing:

- balance without using the hands
- grasp and release objects voluntarily
- handedness predominates, with one hand leading and the other following
- eye-hand coordination
- construction experiences—putting things together, parts and whole concept
- increased attention span

The developmental sequence is

- scribbling, holding tool in a hammer hold
- scribbling, with finger hold
- control of tool to close a circle shape
- making straight lines
- drawing with the characteristics of writing
- beginning of alphabet letters
- ability to make a square
- printing name—in uppercase letters
- printing name—in upper- and lowercase
- left-to-right progression of letters and words

OBSERVING SMALL MUSCLE DEVELOPMENT. The physical environment includes materials and opportunities for the child to practice small muscle skills. The baby touches and grasps any objects within its reach, appropriate or not, grandpa's glasses, a hot coffee cup, or a dust mote floating through the air. The toddler grabs, carries, dumps, fills, manipulates whatever is movable: toilet paper, stones in the driveway, knickknacks on the coffee table, or items on the supermarket shelf. The preschooler practices writing with whatever tools are available: a stick in the dust, Mommy's lipstick, or a paintbrush in tar. The important observer role is to watch what the child is touching, then evaluate its potential for harm. If necessary, the adult intervenes before damage is done to the child, the object, or the environment.

The observer in an educational setting sees the movements as indicators of development and documents what the child can do on this date so that periodically the record is updated to check if progress is being made. Knowledge of the child's abilities at this stage influences the kinds of equipment, materials, and activities the teacher provides. An infant is given items that are easy to grasp and that give some immediate signal, such as a rattle or a toy with a bell or squeak. The toddler is given items to stack, fill and dump, pound, squeeze, and manipulate such as Play Doh and puzzles with simple, large pieces. The preschooler is provided with smaller manipulatives, such as building bricks, puzzles with smaller pieces,

@ it happened to me

He Sure Can Cut!

We had been working with Andy's small muscle skills, finding ways to interest him in trying some cutting instead of always playing with blocks and on the climber. We found some construction machinery catalogs and invited him to cut and paste to make a book to take home. He worked for several days at it, and we saw those cutting skills improve so dramatically we sent home a "Happy Note" about the news. Mom came in a few days later and said, "You know those cutting skills you've been working on with Andy? He's been working on them at home too. He got the scissors and cut up all the chains in my jewelry box into little pieces!" Gulp! Teaching should come with disclaimers, "We cannot be responsible for the application of newly learned skills in a nonsupervised environment."

Do you have an IT HAPPENED TO ME story about an experience like this? I'd love to hear it. Send it to me at WeekbyWeek@thomsonlearning.com

lacing cards, scissors, and a wide array of writing tools and papers.

Documentation of small muscle development can be made with Checklists, Anecdotal Records, and samples of the child's work on paper. The first scribbles, the first alphabet letters, the first name writing, and the first "I love you" note are precious and graphic illustrations of the small muscle development as it leads to literacy. These are important evidence to be added to the Portfolio and shared with families to illustrate the child's small muscle development. Stages of small muscle development also are integrally involved in both art and literacy, and are discussed again in later chapters.

HELPING ALL CHILDREN WITH PHYSICAL DEVELOPMENT

Adapting the environment for children with special needs already has been addressed. Just as with any other child, the basis for planning the curriculum begins with the assessment of where the child is in that developmental area. More information is usually present about the area of disability, from family information and the child's file with reports from helping professionals. It is in the areas other than the one affected that the observer needs to attune. It sometimes is the bias or unconscious attitude that other developmental areas are similarly affected. That is not true. Other areas could be right at the age or stage level with other children. They could just as easily be advanced. Objective observation and recording, without bias concerning the disability, is important.

Non–English-speaking children and children of diverse cultures are not different physically from others in the group. It may be in the communication of expectations with both groups that any difficulties may arise. Modeling and acceptance will help all children feel the freedom to try physical activities.

HELPING PROFESSIONALS FOR PHYSICAL DEVELOPMENT CONCERNS

If observation and assessment reveal a developmental lag, the family is consulted, following confirmation by others on the team. They can be referred to their medical helper, such as the pediatrician, for evaluation. Others who may become involved in evaluations of physical developmental lags follow:

occupational therapist—a specialist who evaluates activities of daily living (feeding or dressing themselves) and provides therapy for assisting in the mastery of these activities

neurologist—a physician who specializes in the diagnosis and treatment of disorders of the nervous system, treating symptoms of pain and motor impairments

physical therapist—a specialist who evaluates capabilities for standing, sitting, and ambulation and provides therapy for people who have problems with these functions

STANDARDS

Here are selected examples of standards related to children's physical development and health:

> Standard. 2.009
> Indoor and Outdoor play, provision for, space needs, safety
> *Caring for Our Children: National Health and Safety Performance Standards: Guidelines for Out-of-Home Child Care Programs,* 2nd ed. (American Academy of Pediatrics, 2002). Used with permission.
> Children shall play outdoors daily when weather and air quality conditions do not pose a significant health risk. Outdoor play for infants may include riding in a carriage or stroller: however, infants shall be offered opportunities for gross motor play outdoors, as well.
> Weather that poses a significant health risk shall include wind chill at or below 15 degrees F and heat index at or above 90 degrees F, as identified by the National Weather Service
> Children shall be protected from the sun by using shade, sun protective clothing, and sunscreen with UVB-ray and UVA-ray protection of SPF-15 or higher with permission as described in STANDARD 3.081, during outdoor play.

National Association for Sport & Physical Education (NASPE) *Active Start* (2004), see Figure 3–8.

OTHER METHODS

Other Methods to Record Physical Development

Class Log List
Anecdotal/Running Record
Media such as photographs or video recording

KEY TERMS

- bias
- cephalocaudal
- Checklist
- closed method
- failure to thrive syndrome
- frame of reference
- growth
- large muscle
- least restrictive environment
- proximodistal
- reflexes
- small muscle

Go to the Bind-in-Book CD for:

- Check List forms on Physical Development for All
- Plan Week 3 Part A, Directions for a Checklist on Physical Development, including What to Do with It, Portfolio Overview Example, Sharing with Child and Family, Actions—Read a Book, In the Environment, In the Curriculum, In the Newsletter
- Plan Week 3 Part B, Directions for Anecdotal Recording of Physical Development for Group B, including What to Do with It and Sharing with the Child and the Family
- Plan Week 3 Part C, Reflective Journal

REFERENCES

Allen, K. E., & Marotz, L. (2007). *Developmental profiles: Prebirth through twelve* (5th ed.). Albany, NY: Delmar.

American Academy of Pediatrics. (2001). Children, adolescents and television: Policy statement. *Pediatrics, 10* (2), 423–426.

Bakley, S. (2001). Through the lens of sensory integration: A different way of analyzing challenging behavior. *Young Children, 56* (6), 70–76.

Bar-Or, O. (2000). Juvenile obesity, physical activity, and lifestyle changes. *The Physician and Sports Medicine, 28* (11), 51–58.

Beaty, J. (2006). *Observing development of the young child* (6th ed.). Upper Saddle River, NJ: Merrill.

Bentzen, W. R. (2005). *Seeing young children: A guide to observing and recording behavior* (5th ed.). Clifton Park, NY: Thomson Delmar Learning.

Bjorklund, D. F., & Brown, R. K. (1998). Physical play and cognitive development: Integrating activity, cognition and education. *Child Development, 69* (3), 604–606.

Block, B. A. (2001). Literacy through movement: An organizational approach. *The Journal of Physical Education, Recreation, & Dance, 72* (1), Jan. 2001, 39.

Bricker, D., & Squires, J. (1999). *Ages and stages questionnaires (ASQ)* (2nd ed.). Baltimore, MD: Brookes.

Brigance, A. H. (2004). *Brigance diagnostic inventory of early development.* North Billerica, MA: Curriculum Associates, Inc.

Burdette, H., & Whitaker, R. C. (2005). A national study of neighborhood safety, outdoor play, television viewing and preschool children. *Pediatrics, 116* (3), Sept. 2005.

Coakley, J. J. (2001). *Sport in society: Issues and controversies* (7th ed.). St. Louis: Mosby.

Crespo, C. J., Smit, E., Troiano, R. P., Bartlett, S. J., Macera, C. A., & Andersen, R. E. (2001). Television watching, energy intake, and obesity in U.S. children. *Archives of Pediatrics and Adolescent Medicine, 155,* 360–365.

Daniels, M. (2001). *Dancing with words: Signing for hearing children's literacy.* Westport, CT: Bergin & Garvey.

Dennison, B. A., Erb, T. A., & Jenkins, P. I. (2002). Television viewing and television in bedroom associated with overweight risk among low-income preschool children. *Pediatrics, 109* (6), June 2002, 1028–1035.

Folio, M. R., & Fewell, R. R. (2000). *Peabody developmental motor scales* (2nd ed.). Allen, TX: Developmental Learning Materials Teaching Resources.

Frankenburg, W. K., Dodds, J. B., & Fandal, A. W. (1990). *Denver Developmental Screening II (DDST-II).* Denver: Denver Developmental Materials, Inc.

Frost, J. (1992). *Play and playscapes.* Clifton Park, NY: Thomson Delmar Learning.

Gallahue, D. L. (2003). *Developmental physical education for children.* Champaign, IL: Human Kinetics.

Gober, S. Y. (2002). *Six simple ways to assess young children.* Clifton Park, NY: Thomson Delmar Learning.

Griffin, C., & Rinn, B. (1998). Enhancing outdoor play with an obstacle course. *Young Children, 53* (3), 18–23.

Hannaford, C. (1995). *Smart moves: Why learning is not all in your head.* Arlington, VA: Great Ocean Publishers.

Harrison, P. L., & Oakland, T. (2003). *Adaptive Behavior Assessment System,* 2nd ed. *(ABASII).* San Antonio, TX: Harcourt Assessment, Inc.

High/Scope Educational Research Foundation. (2003). *Child Observation Record (COR) and Child Assessment Record (CAR).* Ypsilanti, MI: High/Scope Educational Research Foundation.

Ireton, H. (1992). *Child Development Inventory (CDI).* Minneapolis, MN: Behavioral Science Systems.

Lowey, M. (1998). Suggestions for working with fat children in schools. *Professional School Counseling, 1* (4), 18–23.

Meisels, S., Jablon, J., Marsden, D., Dichtmiller, D., & Dorfman, A. (1994). *The work sampling system.* Ann Arbor, MI: Rebus Planning Associates, Inc.

National Association for Sport and Physical Education. (1995). *Moving into the future: National standards for physical education.* Reston, VA: Author.

National Association for Sport and Physical Education. (2001). *Active start: A statement of physical guidelines for children birth to five years.* Reston, VA: Author.

National Association of Early Childhood Specialists in State Departments of Education. (2002). *Recess and the importance of play: A position statement on young children and recess.* Retrieved May 20, 2006, from http://ericps.crc.uiuc.edu/naecs/position/recessplay.html.

Novak, D. E. (2000). *Help! It's an indoor recess day.* Thousand Oaks, CA: Corwin Press.

Olds, A. R. (2001). *Child care design guide.* New York: McGraw-Hill.

O'Brien, L. M. (2003). The rewards and restrictions of recess: Reflections on being a playground volunteer. *Childhood Education, 79* (3), 161.

Pate, R. R., Pfeiffer, K. A., Trost, S. G., Ziegler, P., & Dowda, M. (2004). Physical activity among children attending preschools. *Pediatrics, 114* (5), Nov. 2004.

Pate, R. R., Baranowski, T., Dowda, M., & Trost, S. G. (1996). Tracking of physical activity in young children. *Medicine and Science in Sports and Exercise 28* (1), 92–96.

Pellegrini, A. D., & Smith, P. K. (1998). Physical activity play: The nature and function of a neglected aspect of play. *Child Development, 69* (3), 577–598.

Pica, R. (2006). Physical fitness and the early childhood curriculum. *Young Children, 61* (3), May 2006.

Pica, R. (2000). *Moving and learning series. Preschoolers & kindergartners.* Clifton Park, NY: Thomson Delmar Learning.

Pollak, S. D., Cicchetti, D., Hornung, K, & Reed, A. (2000). Recognizing emotion in faces: Developmental effects of child abuse and neglect in *Developmental Psychology, 36* (5), Sept. 2000, 679–688.

Porter, R. (1994). Roughhousing as a style of play. *Child Care Information Exchange, 96,* May/June 1994.

Power, T. (2000). *Play and exploration in children and animals.* Mahwah, NJ: Lawrence Erlbaum Associates.

Proctor, M. H., Moore, L. L., Gao, D., Cupples, L. A., Bradlee, M. L., Hood, M. Y, Ellison, R. C. (2003). Television viewing and change in body fat from preschool to early adolescence: The Framingham Children's Study. *International Journal of Obesity, 27* (7). Jul. 2003.

Purkey, W. W., & Novak, J. M. (1996). *Inviting school success: a self-concept approach to teaching, learning and democracy.* Belmont, CA: Wadsworth.

Rivkin, M. S. (1995). *The great outdoors: Restoring children's right to play outside.* Washington, DC: National Association for the Education of Young Children.

Stephens, M. (2002). Children, physical activity, and public health: Another call to action. *American Family Physician, 65* (6), 1033.

Sutterby, J. A., & Frost, J. L. (2002). Making playgrounds fit for children and children fit on playgrounds. *Young Children, 57* (3), 36–41.

Tortora, S. (2006). *The dancing dialogue: Using the communicative power of movement with young children.* Baltimore: Paul H. Brookes Publishing Company.

Vygotsky, L. S. (1978). *Mind in society: The development of higher psychological processes.* Cambridge, MA: Harvard University Press.

Weikart, Phyllis S. (2000). *Round the circle* (2nd ed.). Ypsilanti, MI: High/Scope Press.

Weiller, K. H., & Richardson, P. A. (1993). A program for kids: Success-oriented physical education. *Childhood Education, 69* (3).

RESOURCES

American Academy of Pediatrics (2002). *Caring for our children: National health and safety performance standards: Guidelines for out-of-home child care* (2nd ed.). Elk Grove Village, IL: Author.

Daniels, M. (2001). *Dancing with words: Signing for hearing children's literacy.* Westport, CT: Bergin & Garvey.

Hall, J. T., & Sweeny, N. H. (1976). *Until the whistle blows: A collection of games, dances, and activities for four-to-eight year olds.* Santa Monica, CA: Goodyear Publishing Co.

Novak, D. E. (2000). *Help! It's an indoor recess day.* Thousand Oaks, CA: Corwin Press.

Olds, A. R. (2001). *Child care design guide.* New York: McGraw-Hill.

Rivkin, M. S. (1995). *The great outdoors: Restoring children's right to play outside.* Washington, DC: National Association for the Education of Young Children.

Sanders, S. W. (2002). *Active for life: Developmentally appropriate movement programs for young children.* Washington, DC: National Association for the Education of Young Children.

Weikart, P. S. (2000). *Round the circle* (2nd ed.). Ypsilanti, MI: High/Scope Press.

Weiller, K. H., & Richardson, P. A. (1993). A program for kids: Success-oriented physical education. *Childhood Education, 69* (3), Spring 1993.

Young Children, Vol. 61, No 3, May 2006. Healthy young children: Encouraging good nutrition and physical fitness. Entire issue.

CHAPTER

4

Using Running Records to Look at Social Development

IN THIS CHAPTER

USING RUNNING RECORDS

EXERCISE Read the Running Record that focuses on Larry (Figure 4–1). Cover the right-hand column with a sheet of paper; make comments or inferences about Larry as indicated from this incident.

From the exercise, you see that a **Running Record** uses the same technique as the Anecdotal Recording. It is a factual, detailed, written account over a span of time. Actions are described and quotes are recorded as precisely as possible. Commentary or interpretation about the recording is written separately from the actual account. The recorder decides to observe and write for a period of time, focusing on one child or one play area. A nonselective narrative documents a specimen of that child's or that area's action.

The Running Record is written as the events are happening, while the Anecdotal Recording usually is written shortly after a significant event. The Anecdotal Recording is a little story with a beginning, the action, and an ending. Running Records are indiscriminate, giving a more objective glimpse into a normal (or what may turn out to be an abnormal) segment of time. That is not known, however, before the recorder begins to write. Everything that happens in that time segment is recorded: the mundane, the boring, the unexplained. At the end of a time period, the recording stops. This may not necessarily be at the end of the event. A Running Record is like turning on a video camera and just letting it run for a certain amount of time, recording whatever occurs. A Running Record is the most useful in giving a naturalistic view of a short time in the life of the child.

When a learning center or area of the classroom is the focus of a Running Record, it can evaluate the usefulness of the area and if the area needs any modifications. Particular learning centers or classroom areas are more suitable for viewing specific skills. A Running Record in the large muscle area obviously gives information on children's climbing, running, or jumping skills but also can yield valuable information on social, emotional, and verbal development. Imaginative play, social interactions, and self-concept are illustrated vividly in the dramatic play area as well as the block area. Small muscle skills, literacy development, and social and verbal skills are observed easily in the art area or during play at the sand or water table. Running Records of 10 minutes at any one of these areas can be extremely informative.

The Running Record requires intense concentration and focused attention. Other staff are needed in the room to be sure all children are supervised adequately. Of course, any recording in progress is secondary to a child in need. Any time recording must be interrupted, a line is drawn and the ending and return time is noted. It may be resumed if the situation is now under control.

EXERCISE **On a separate sheet of paper, describe how you might feel if someone were watching you for 10 minutes and writing notes.**

One caution in using the Running Record, or any other recording technique, is the possible effect it may have on the child's behavior (Figure 4–2). It may make them feel uncomfortable or act in an artificial way. The recorder must be sensitive to that self-consciousness. When such behavior is observed, the writing would then stop and efforts be made to be less obvious in the future. In a classroom where observation and recording go on all the time as a natural part of everyday life, children often cease to notice. If they are shown the notes, even if they are not yet able to read, they feel more comfortable about the writing. Talking with them about what was observed helps them understand the purpose behind the writing. When they hear the teacher talk with their family about the episodes from the notes, they realize that their actions are important and meaningful. Warning: Any negative occurrences or difficulties

Time Recording Began — *Recorder*

Nov. 14 10:15 a.m. BAN recorder
LARRY 4 Yrs., 2 mo.

Larry is in the play kitchen with Susan, Allison, and Marie. M: put the eggs in the refrigerator. L. takes 2 dishes and 2 forks and sets the dishes on the table. Hands forks to Andrea, sitting at the table. L. gets another plate and fork and sets it at another chair. Andrea goes by on a big truck and L. gets on the back. A: yells, Get off! L. gets off then stands watching her as she goes on. L. stands watching. Still watching, L. walks into other room where A. went with truck. To Mike: These robbers stole our truck, pointing to A. M. has the gas tank. He just looks up. L: She needs some gas, points to A. A: No, they didn't tell ya. M. holds gas tank to chest. A. rolls towards them. L. puts two hands out to stop the truck. She drives by and he just watches. L. walks back into other room and gets into rocker boat. A. and S. come by on two trucks. A to L: Can you show us the cemetery? L. doesn't answer. H. rocks fast with Lucy and S. gets on. L. rocks fast. They hand him dolls. He holds them. Kevin gets in and rocks. S: You need to get off this boat. Lucy to L: You're our neighbor. L: I can stay on here. Sets dolls down. Picks them up. Lucy purposely falls out of boat. She laughs, gets back in and rocks fast. Lucy: You're making me fall off. L. stops rocking. Steven comes over to get in. L: You're too heavy. K. comes with blocks. L. drops them into trucks parked nearby. L: We need some money. Jumps out. Climbs up climber, runs down slide, back to boat. Chews on fingernail. Other boys dropping blocks into boat. L. laughs loudly. Stands up in boat, smiling. No more money he says loudly. He takes the doll and throws it out, throws out some blocks. L. gets out and throws some blocks back in. 1: More money, more money. Gets back in the boat. Girls in boat tip over backwards on purpose, laughing. He pulls blocks out and takes 2 over to the shelf and drops them nearby. Screws up face, arms out. Too much money. Why are you doing this? Gets into boat and starts stacking the blocks in it. Kevin gets in. They rock and sing, Do, do, do, ya need some gas?
10:26

Use initials after first mention of name for time saving.
Action
Exact Quotes
Follow target child
Comments: Play entry tactic
Comments: Where did this come from?
Asserts himself
Uncertain?
Accepted into the game
Beginning cleanup!
A new friend!
Time ended *Teacher's questions* *(?) Should blocks be allowed in this area? Ask Betty.*

Note: Bare record could be copied for other children's files if no negative events took place or block other names

Figure 4–1 Running Record Example.

Figure 4–2 Observation may change behavior, so the observer attempts to be unobtrusive.

it happened to me

Artist's Model?

I was sightseeing on a bus in a foreign country, feeling very special, looking all around at the scenery, when I felt someone watching me. A young man toward the rear of the bus was sketching on a pad. "Oh," I thought, "he's an artist. This country's full of artists. He must be sketching me." So I turned my best side toward him, sat up straighter in the seat, and sat still with a facial expression I wanted captured on his pad. As he was leaving the bus I craned my neck to see the pad. It was a forest scene, apparently from memory, he was working on. Because I thought he was watching me, I changed my behavior.

Do you have an IT HAPPENED TO ME story about how observation changed behavior? I'd love to read it. Please send it to WeekbyWeek@thomsonlearning.com

observed should not be discussed with the family in the presence of the child.

Uses

The Running Record

- records detailed segments of behavior occurring in a certain time block.
- focuses on an individual child to show a naturalistic view of a part of the day.
- can be analyzed for evaluation of many developmental areas: physical, social, emotional, language, self-concept, attention span, problem solving, memory, learning style.
- documents evaluation of developmental areas for child study.
- can focus on a particular learning center or classroom area to see what typically occurs there.

Advantages

The Running Record is helpful because it

- details a normal segment of time in the day, giving a more natural view.
- reveals many areas of development in one recording.
- can evaluate the effectiveness of a learning center or area.

Disadvantages

The Running Record may

- make the subject feel watched, become uncomfortable, and change behavior, destroying the nature of the recording.
- not show in the time segment what normally occurs.

- make the adult unavailable to facilitate or observe what is happening in the rest of the room because attention is focused on the recording.
- tire and drain the recorder because of its intensity.

EXERCISE **Practice writing a Running Record. Take a separate sheet of paper right now, fold it in half, select a person to watch, and write down everything that person does and says for 10 minutes.**

Rate your Running Record.

- Did you mention the setting so the reader knows where it took place?
- Did you write the date and time you started?
- Did you write your name on it as the recorder?

Look over the words you used and make sure they described actions, not summarized them or gave reasons for them. The words should form mental pictures.

- If you used any of the following words, perhaps you fell in the trap of summarizing: *because, wanted to, tried, saw, played, looked (emotion), noticed, pretended.*
- If more than one person was involved, did you write down the conversation word for word?
- Now go back and in the right column write what judgments you would make about this person's physical, cognitive, social, and emotional development.
- What did this segment of action show about that person? What questions did it raise about why the person acted that way?

EXERCISE **The following pages contain Running Records on which to practice. Find the recorder's mistakes, then return to this point and check yourself.**

In Figure 4–3, the term *plays* is too generic. The recorder should be specific and mention who else is there. "Talks" is not recording exact quotes. This was an example of good action description. How does the

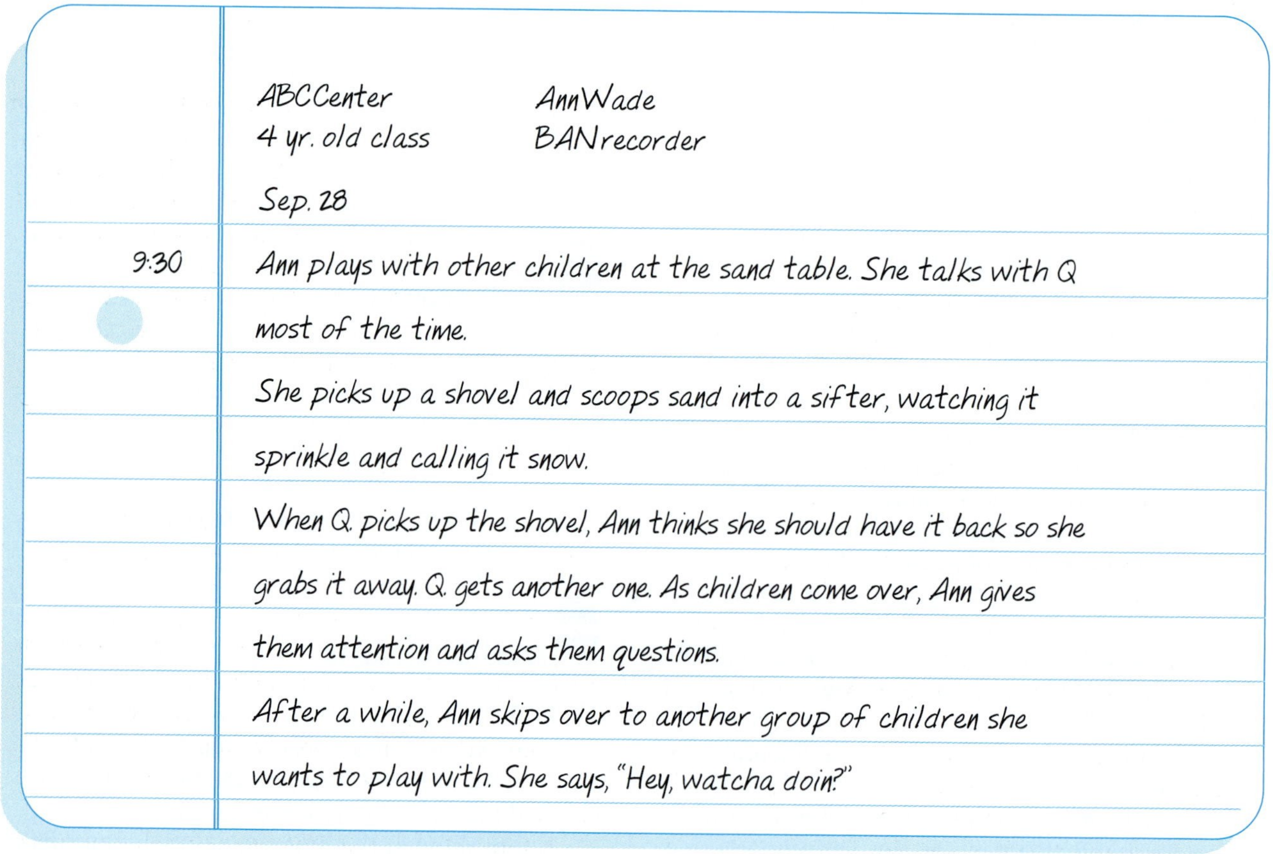

ABCCenter AnnWade
4 yr. old class BANrecorder
Sep. 28

9:30	Ann plays with other children at the sand table. She talks with Q most of the time.
	She picks up a shovel and scoops sand into a sifter, watching it sprinkle and calling it snow.
	When Q. picks up the shovel, Ann thinks she should have it back so she grabs it away. Q. gets another one. As children come over, Ann gives them attention and asks them questions.
	After a while, Ann skips over to another group of children she wants to play with. She says, "Hey, watcha doin?"

Figure 4–3 Find the recorder's errors: Running Record #1.

	ABC Center JimmyFresno 4 yr old class BAN recorder Sep. 29
8:20am.	Jimmy and T. are in the block area where they play a lot together. J. places four longer blocks in a square on the rug and tells T. to go get some more. T. obeys as usual and gets on the big truck, making motor noises. Scoots over to the convenient block shelf. He picks up blocks with each hand, loads the truck, then drives it slowly to where J. has started building. J takes 4 blocks & sets them on end. He decides he doesn't like it so he gives a vicious kick & knocks them down. T. jumps up screaming at J. because he is so angry. The teacher tells J. to help build the building up and he does.

Figure 4–4 Find the recorder's errors: Running Record #2.

observer know what Ann thinks? Exact quotes were not written down. This is 15 minutes of action? The recorder exactly documented pronunciation giving the reader more information about the child.

Read Figure 4–4. "Play a lot" is a summary, there is no documentation. It is a good description of placing blocks, but there are no quotes. "As usual" is an unsubstantiated comment. It could be written in the right-hand column. "Convenient" is a judgment. Perhaps the writer set up the room? Movement on the trucks and blocks was well described. How does the writer know J. does not like it? "Vicious" is a subjective term with some bias showing. "Because" is a red flag. The Running Record, since it is an open method, only describes action. The reasons for the action or reaction can be written in the right-hand column. What exactly did the teacher say? "Go over and apologize and build that back up!" "Look at T.'s face. He is sad. You knocked over his building. Helping him build it back up is a friendly thing to do."

In Figure 4–5, "started playing" is a summary of their actions with no descriptions. Were they just piling them or making the Eiffel Tower? Twenty minutes of playing should contain more details. How did the recorder know what N. wanted? The teacher's words are lost, and it doesn't matter if she loved it. It should be satisfying to the builder unless she commissioned it to be built. "Got bored," what does that *look* like? "Decided" is another red-flag word. A recorder only writes what actually happens, not what is decided. That is determined by the actions.

Running and Anecdotal Records are like written movie scripts, exactly describing actions, facial expressions, and exact words of the players.

Pitfalls to Avoid

Running Records are time and energy intensive, so the recorder must be sure that the children are safely involved and under the supervision of at least one other adult for interaction; only then should a running record be started. Because of the objective technique, it probably is not a method that a volunteer could be asked to do, but the supervision could be assigned. Attention to safety and the interactive needs of children always takes precedence over recording.

Another pitfall is that close observation tends to make the target child feel observed, which can alter

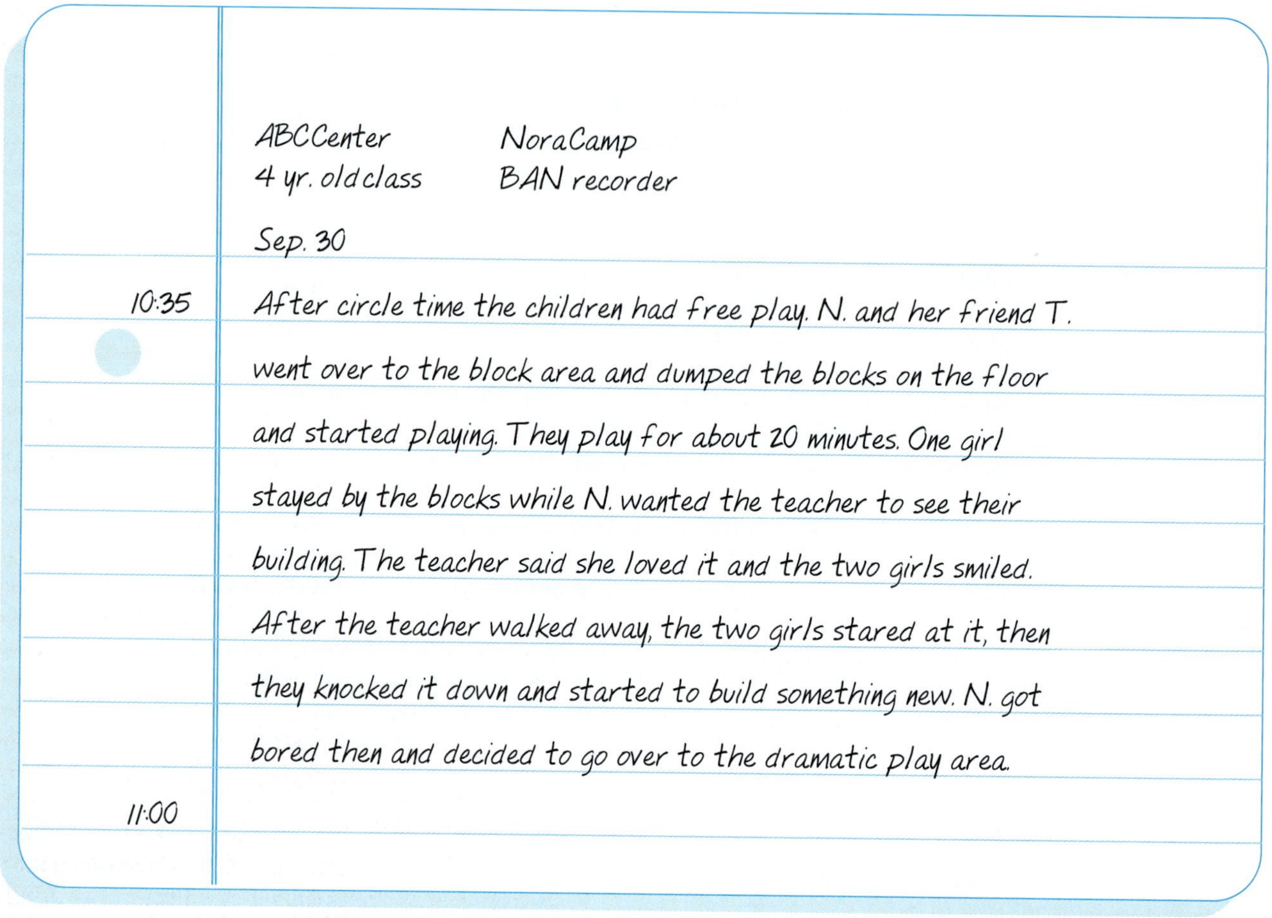

ABCCenter NoraCamp
4 yr. old class BAN recorder
Sep. 30

10:35 After circle time the children had free play. N. and her friend T. went over to the block area and dumped the blocks on the floor and started playing. They play for about 20 minutes. One girl stayed by the blocks while N. wanted the teacher to see their building. The teacher said she loved it and the two girls smiled. After the teacher walked away, the two girls stared at it, then they knocked it down and started to build something new. N. got bored then and decided to go over to the dramatic play area.

11:00

Figure 4–5 Find the recorder's errors: Running Record #3.

behavior. The recorder must be very careful to observe from far enough away so as to not interfere with the child's actions but close enough to hear conversations. Sometimes the location of a chair on the other side of a piece of equipment, behind the child's line of vision but within hearing distance, can be effective.

Often other children enter into the Running Record in interactions with the target child. Because this will be filed in one child's Portfolio, other children's names should be blotted from this particular recording for anonymity.

A Running Record can yield a great deal of insight into a child's usual activities, but it can be so mundane as to seem unimportant. It is not. As a true measure of a child's development and behavior, naturalistic observation like a Running Record is invaluable.

Using Technology

A video camera is a wonderful tool for capturing live action. There is no way a written Anecdotal or Running Record can compare, but using a video camera does take time, patience, and the knack for being in the right place at the right time. Using a video camera can also be intrusive. Whenever anyone but the most experienced model sees a camera aimed their way, they change their behavior. It is very difficult to capture spontaneous, meaningful video footage.

Hand-held computers can accommodate a portable keyboard that unfolds, which can be helpful because many people can type faster than they can write. Using a keyboard also makes it easier to add the Running Record to an electronic file on each child. Electronic files, mentioned in Chapter 3, are easy to manipulate, do not take up classroom storage space, are easier to keep confidential, and can also store artwork and photographs.

How to Find the Time

Running Records are one of the most time-intensive recording methods. To concentrate fully on one child and write accurately and descriptively about the child's every action and conversation takes undivided attention. That means that this recording method, in its purest sense, done as the action is taking place, is not practical for the person who is also responsible for the classroom. A modification can be to jot notes and amplify them later; however, time dulls the accuracy of the memory, so it is never as rich as what really happened. We are therefore faced with the dilemma of how to make time to complete Running Records.

The student teacher or student visitor may have the luxury of doing Running Records and having no other classroom responsibility. This is a wonderful learning experience and one that should be practiced. Not only can it be a great help to the teacher, but it can be a learning experience for the student by sharing the Running Record with the teacher and then discussing the interpretation. Another option is for the program administrator to arrange for coverage of the teacher's classroom for a brief period each day so that the teacher can sit and watch children's play. Or a classroom volunteer could be trained in this method under the direction of the teacher. However it is arranged, Running Records are valuable pieces of documentation, and a 10-minute observation in every developmental area usually provides enough detail or depth to enable the observer and the reader to draw some conclusions about the child's level.

What to Do with It

Following the actual recording, the teacher can make notes in the right-hand column in the same categories as the Anecdotal Record:

- explanations
- comments about development
- questions for further investigation
- plans for the child based on the observation

The Running Record is filed in the target child's Portfolio after noting its presence on the Portfolio Overview Sheet. It may be read to the child at a later date for the basis of a conversation about the child's activities. The teacher can ask questions like, "When you were piling the blocks up and ran out of blocks, you stopped building. Is there something else you could have used to continue playing there?" or "When you were at the Writing Center, I heard you say something about writing a letter and an elephant but I couldn't hear what you said. Do you remember?"

The Running Record that includes other children who interacted with the target child can be copied, with the teacher then making notations in the right-hand column about the second child. When the record is filed in a child's Portfolio, the names of the other children should be blotted out.

Go to the Bind-in-Book CD for Running Record forms, plans, and resources.

LOOKING AT SOCIAL DEVELOPMENT

Two children are pulling on the same toy. "It's mine!" "No I want it!" An adult comes over, takes it away from one and gives it to the other. "You've got to share! Don't be so selfish."

That is not sharing. That is robbery. That is reinforcing the concept that bigger people can take things away from smaller people. True sharing is the willing relinquishing of one's rightful possession to another person. But how do children learn not to be so selfish?

The Need for a Selfless Society

Moving from selfish to selfless takes more than changing a few alphabet letters. It is a total transformation from self-centered, immediate gratification to other-centered, altruistic generosity. The goal of maturity in a moral society is to become less concerned with one's own needs and desires by giving priority to others'. A person, group, or society that only lives for itself is constantly in conflict (Figure 4–6). Often more than one person wants a particular object or for their own opinion to prevail, and everyone cannot be satisfied. From that conflict came the rules of the tribe, then laws. Now laws are so numerous and complex that entire buildings are needed to hold the books that list and interpret them all. People devote their lives to interpreting, enforcing, changing, and even breaking them. There are also some people in a society who cannot fill their own needs, so others are needed to generously help if they are to survive. The task of raising the young to be selfless is necessary for the survival of the society. What a responsibility! This is a long struggle that begins with small steps.

Think About It . . .

Think about how the following laws or rules restrict your freedom for the good of society.

- Only licensed physicians can practice medicine.
- Drive on the right side of the road.

Figure 4–6 Attaining social development is not without its struggles.

REVIEW

RUNNING RECORD

Detailed account of a segment of the child's day, written as it is observed. Includes settings, descriptions of actions and interactions, and exact quotes.

Types of Information to Record Using Running Records

Any segment of the child's day, usual or unusual. It can yield information on:

- separation and adjustment
- self-care skills
- physical development
- social development
- emotional development
- language and speech
- attention span and interests
- cognitive development
- literacy
- creativity
- socio-dramatic play
- self-esteem

- Items in a store must be exchanged for payment.
- Use utensils, not hands, for serving items from the salad bar.
- Buckle up your seat belt in the car.

In caring, teaching, or working with young children, the development of the social domain is a high priority. It does not develop separately from physical, cognitive, or emotional areas but simultaneously moves forward, influenced by many of the same factors of genetics, environment, culture, and society. Helping a child to learn the rules of the tribe will help him function in that group. It is a necessary skill for both physical and psychological well-being.

EXERCISE **List some social rules, not developed naturally, that children must be taught.**

The infant is born concerned only with its own needs, totally dependent on reflexes and signals calling for responses to those signals. The hungry baby never considers the mother's dinner getting cold. The baby crying in the middle of the night pays no heed to parents' early work schedules. The crawler pulls the cat's tail, or the toddler takes a truck from another. The needs and wants of the other person are not deliberated or weighed or even considered at all. Years and much growing and developing must take place before the child sees the point of view of the other person. It takes even longer before she can place the other person's needs ahead of her own with generosity and empathy. She has much growing up to do before living up to society's expectations and taking on the responsibility for others. Along that path there are observable stages—developmental milestones—which are aided in their arrival by interactions with adults.

TOPICS IN OBSERVATION

"The Stew"

Once upon a time a chef set out to make a stew by preparing the ingredients and placing them on the stove to cook. After a period of time, the chef took a deep ladle and sampled a bit of each of the ingredients to judge the progress of the stew. Some needed more time to cook, so the chef extended the cooking time. The broth was lacking in flavor, so the chef added some spices. It was too salty, so the chef added a potato to take away some saltiness. The chef still was unsatisfied with the taste, so a master chef, a stew expert, was called in to give an opinion. More modifications were made to the stew.

The stew was then served to the first diner, the chef's mother, who declared the stew "Marvelous!" The Board of Health inspector closely examined each part of the stew, looking for irregularities, without actually caring about the whole stew. The vegetarian, repulsed by the meat in the stew, stopped eating, vowing to make comments to the cook. One diner thought it needed more salt, while another thought it was too salty. The unserved portions of the stew were refrigerated and reheated the next day with flavors mellowed and texture softer. The smart chef wrote down the recipe so that future stews could be as flavorful, but the chef knew it all depended on the ingredients available. But alas, some of the diners had moved on to other restaurants, so they never got the full, aged taste of the stew. Ah, if they could only taste the stew now.

MEANING

The stew is the child made up of many areas of development. The family brings the child to the teacher with knowledge, skills, and abilities. The teacher works with those to bring them to a certain expected level. A sample of the child's development is made to determine progress in development and further actions. In some areas, nothing is needed but time. In other areas, additions are made in the curriculum to assist in development. Sometimes behaviors that are getting in the way of learning are modified. Expert advice is sometimes needed, so the family and teachers seek the referral and advice of helping professionals.

Hopefully, the family is pleased with the progress of the child, overlooking some areas still developing. Some observers look at specific areas while not seeing the whole child, such as a speech pathologist, dentist, or physical therapist. The child's progress may not be acceptable to some who have special interests or biases. Over time, the child grows, develops, and changes, but past teachers and resource people do not have the opportunity to observe the progress. The family and teachers who have a record of the changes know what worked for that child. Each child is unique, however, and the teacher realizes the necessity for adapting environment and curriculum for each child and group. It is sad that not everyone gets the opportunity to appreciate the transformation.

Theories of Social Development and Their Implications on Early Childhood Professional Practice

Many in the past have pondered the origins of how people relate to one another.

Freud (1953) attributes social behavior to the sexual nature of humans hidden in the subconscious. He saw a strong parental role in developing the superego, or conscience, to balance the id, the unconscious part of the psyche that demands the satisfaction of desires. The parental influences on the child's knowledge and feelings of right and wrong are deeply ingrained and differ from one family to another. It is important for the teacher to know and work cooperatively with parents to reduce the dissonance of differing messages and to cope with them when they do occur. Freudian theory also reminds teachers that the child also has a sexual nature. Although they are very young, basic sex roles and attitudes are forming through experiences in early childhood.

Erikson's psychosocial developmental theory (1963, orig. 1950) looks at not just biology but also at the changing mind and emotions and the effects of society in forming behavior patterns. His "Eight Stages of Man" illustrate the observable, predictable stages through which humans move. The first four stages are explained here, with the last four included to complete the concept.

Stage 1—Infancy: the challenge of trust (versus mistrust). Between birth and about 18 months, infants face the first of life's challenges: to gain a sense of trust that their world is a safe place. Family members play a key role in how any infant meets this challenge.

Stage 2—Toddlerhood: the challenge of autonomy (versus doubt and shame). The next challenge, up to age 3, is to learn skills to cope with the world in a confident way. Failure to gain self-control leads children to doubt their abilities.

Stage 3—Preschool: the challenge of initiative (versus guilt). Four- and five-year-olds must learn to engage their surroundings—including people outside the family—or experience guilt at having failed to meet the expectations of parents and others.

Stage 4—Preadolescence: the challenge of industriousness (versus inferiority). Between ages 6 and 13, children enter school, make friends, and strike out on their own more and more. They feel proud of their accomplishments or, at times, fear that they do not measure up.

Stage 5—Adolescence: the challenge of gaining identity (versus confusion).

Stage 6—Young adulthood: the challenge of intimacy (versus isolation).

Stage 7—Middle adulthood: the challenge of making a difference (versus self-absorption).

Stage 8—Old age: the challenge of integrity (versus despair).

These stages include the developing social role in each stage. Unlike Freud, who looked into the past to find reasons for pathological behavior, Erikson looked to the future, not giving up hope that the past can be overcome. Erikson's theory also stresses the importance of the adults in understanding and meeting children's needs in each stage. This affects how the child feels about himself and interacts with others.

Piaget's work in cognitive theory (Flavell, 1977) has significance for children's social development. Children's thinking governs their actions. As the child takes in new information, the child interprets it differently at different stages. Before the infant reaches **object permanence**, that is, until they acquire the awareness that objects continue to exist outside their sight, the infant will not "miss" his mother. Once he has cognitively reached that stage, other people's faces are compared to his mental image of hers, and that mismatch results in separation anxiety. The young child is described in Piaget's theory as **egocentric**, only able to see things from his own point of view. The child thinks, "I want this ball so I should have it," and takes the ball from another child. When the adult says, "How would you like it if he did that to you?" it has no meaning. The child cannot mentally picture himself with the ball in his hands with another child taking the ball away. This is just too much abstract cognitive processing for his ability at this stage. This is the underlying factor of social actions in the preschool years: the conflict between what one child wants (and thinks he should have) and that of another. Recognizing this, the adults take many actions to account for this, such as having enough duplicate toys so that the need for possession is met. Once the child becomes verbal, the adult repeats phrases children can use. Phrases like "You could say, 'I want to play with that ball when you're done'" or "Tell her 'I don't like it when you take that away from me'" help the child function socially.

Behaviorists' social learning theory (Skinner, 1953; Watson, 1950) describes how learning takes place when it is reinforced either negatively or positively. This behaviorism is the reason that spanking or punishment works (for a while) and that praise or reward encourages behavior to occur again. This is external reinforcement of behavior. Parents and teachers, however, want the child to be *intrinsically motivated,* that is, to do the right thing even when no one is there to say, "Good job," or "No, No." When appropriate recognition for *right* and *wrong* deeds is given, the child sees the results from those actions and forms a thinking process for making choices about right and wrong for next time. Hopefully, the adult does not have to be present for reinforcement for the child to make the *right choice.*

Maslow's work (1970) investigating the causes of behavior also was based on met or unmet needs. His "Hierarchy of Human Needs" chart is familiar to students of psychology (Figure 4–7). It has the most basic survival needs at the bottom of the pyramid, moving up to social needs, and eventually to self-actualization. This is where satisfaction comes from—from serving others rather than self.

From Maslow's work, it is clear that physical and psychological safety are necessary for children to develop. Schools have learned that a hungry child cannot learn, so national programs provide nutritious breakfasts and lunches. Similarly, the physical and aesthetic environment influences behavior, so millions of dollars are spent in homes, schools, restaurants, arcades, and businesses on color, furnishings, lighting, and aesthetics to influence human behavior. The classroom environment is an important factor in learning, since it attends to both the physical and psychological needs of the children and adults. The affective needs of acceptance, recognition, affection, belonging, and love are the work of the curriculum of the social development area. From names on the cubbies to hugs at the end of the day, children thrive socially in the environment that meets their emotional needs.

Hartup (1992) and many others have studied the importance of peer relationships. The critical social purposes of early childhood education are reinforced by his statement:

> Indeed, the single best childhood predictor of adult adaptation is not IQ, not school grades, and not classroom behavior, but rather, the

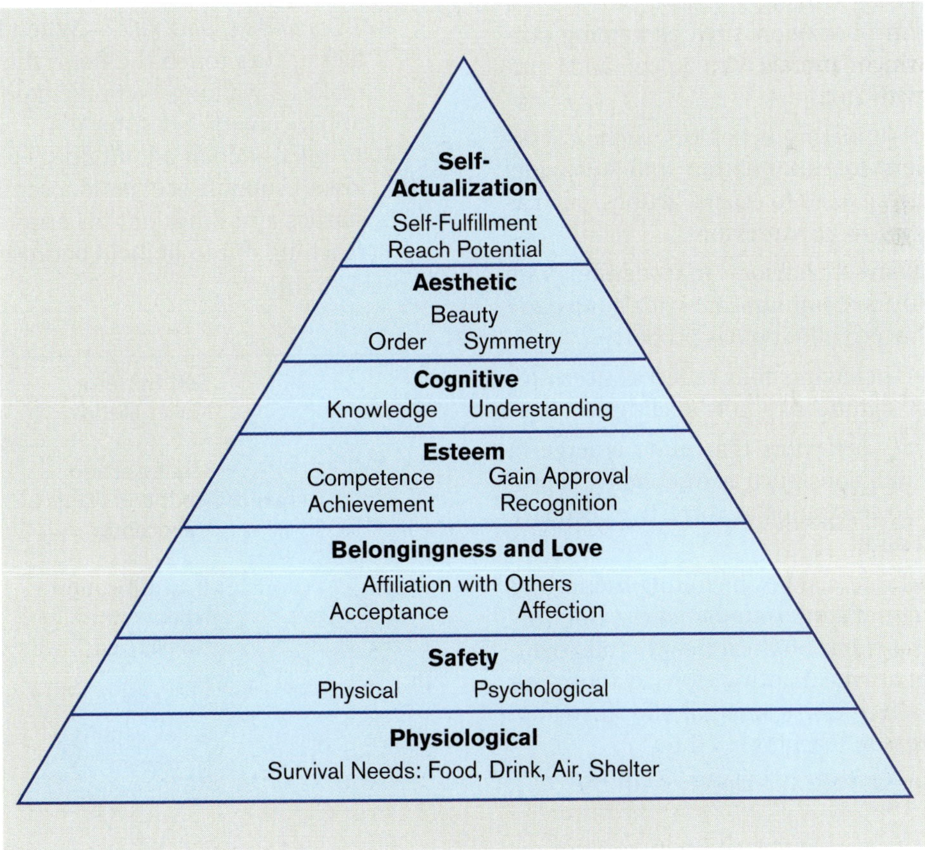

Figure 4–7 Maslow's Hierarchy of Needs. (Adapted from Maslow, A. H., 1970, *Motivation and Personality,* 2nd ed., New York: Harper & Row)

adequacy with which the child gets along with other children. Children who are generally disliked, who are aggressive and disruptive, who are unable to sustain close relationships with other children, and who cannot establish a place for themselves in the peer culture are seriously at risk.

Peer interaction has been identified as an important component of school readiness and a predictor of positive adjustment to school (Birch & Ladd, 1996).

IMPLICATIONS OF SOCIAL LEARNING THEORY ON EARLY CHILDHOOD PRACTICES. In recent years, there has been an increased interest in identifying social factors such as the ability to have friends, maintain interactions, and cultivate **social competence** (Fabes et al., 1999). Children who are able to control their own physiological, emotional, and behavioral responses are socially competent, which enables them to function in a social atmosphere as well as in a learning environment. It is during the preschool years that this regulatory control system is formed (Rothbart & Bates, 1998). Five major clusters of social skill behaviors, with the acronym CARES, have been identified (Elliott, McKevitt, & DiPerna, 2002, p. 1042):

1. *cooperation*—behaviors such as helping others, sharing materials with a peer, and complying with rules
2. *assertion*—initiating behaviors such as asking others for information and behaviors that are responses to others' actions, such as responding to peer pressure
3. *responsibility*—behaviors that demonstrate the ability to communicate with adults and show concern about one's property
4. *empathy*—behaviors that reflect concern for peers' or significant adults' feelings
5. *self-control*—behaviors that often emerge in conflict situations, such as responding appropriately to teasing or to corrective feedback from an adult

Positive social interactions, including friendships between children and adults, are beneficial not only for emotional health but physical health and cognitive development as well. Lacking close relationships can negatively affect every area of life (Lawhon, 1997). For this reason teachers need to

- work cooperatively and closely with the family.
- be aware of sex role formation in young children.
- meet children's needs.
- consider the child's cognitive level in determining realistic social expectations.
- give appropriate recognition for right and wrong deeds, along with resulting consequences.
- assist each child toward social competence.

Stages of Social Development

The word *development* indicates that the change which takes place in the way the child interacts with other people is qualitative. It is a change that can be measured not in numbers but in refinement. It moves from simple to more complex, in a predictable sequence, but at different rates for individual people (Figure 4–8).

SELF. The newborn infant (neonate) has no social competence. Interactions with other people are governed by reflexes:

Rooting reflex—When stroked on the cheek, the neonate turns toward that side. (It is not to see his mother better.)

Babkin reflex—When the palms are stimulated, the neonate's fingers curl around it and grasp it. (It is not to play with daddy's finger.)

Walking and stepping reflex—When held so that feet or toes touch the floor, the neonate makes a walking, stepping motion. (It is not to dance with her sister.)

Moro reflex—When a loud noise, bright light, or loss of support is experienced, the neonate startles and flings out his arms. (It is not reaching out to be held because he was scared.)

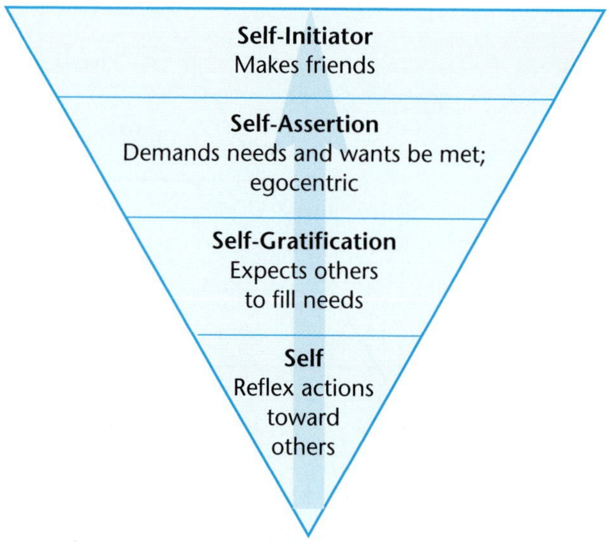

Figure 4–8 Stages of Social Development.

What is the neonate doing socially? The infant can see very well close up, looking at close faces and registering information about what is seen and heard. The baby's kinesthetic sense (body movement and position) is present so the baby senses she is held, rocked, or touched. Babies are usually soothed by motion, crying less when rocked. The baby imitates and matches facial expressions. There is a wonderful example of this in the video *Exploring First Feelings* (1986). An adult is holding a newborn and opens her mouth. The baby gazes intently and matches the movement. Some babies right from the start are more gregarious, responsive to others, and open to friendly overtures (Figure 4–9). Others are much more serious and reserved, limiting social contacts to just a few people. This personality type affects social interactions, and it may be evident throughout the child's life. All areas of development—physical, cognitive, and emotional—are being affected by and are affecting social development.

Figure 4–9 Social development begins with the infant's needs being met.

The implications for social development seem clear. The adult role is to meet the baby's needs, first of all in physical care. The infant who has attention and is prompted to respond to coos and words is being prepared for verbal conversations. The environment stimulates cognitive development. Psychological needs are met by being close and by handling the baby gently and responsively. Interactions are initiated and provide an interesting environment that responds to what the baby indicates she likes. These met needs give the infant a secure base from which to emerge into the social realm with the abilities to function in it.

SELF-GRATIFICATION. During the first year, the infant is focused on receiving what he needs to survive and be happy, whatever that takes. This is the stage of his attachment to his parents, as well as the beginning of his independence from them. During the first months of life, the baby increases imitative behavior with smiles and laughs as the adult feeds, dresses, and cares for him. In the second half of the first year, the baby shows separation anxiety, trying to recapture the presence of the ones who meet his needs. He also begins some social exchanges by reaching out his hands and arms to be held, kicking or making noises to gain attention. He is becoming mobile, so he now can crawl to mother and pull on her leg. He is beginning to learn that he is no longer allowed to cry, sleep, play, eat, or act strictly by his own desires. He may be put down for a nap when he is not "ready," or be told "No" when he reaches for grandpa's glasses. He cries and uses whatever social skills he has learned to get what he wants. He also is beginning to exert social control by withdrawing, by turning away from the spoon, a plaything, or a smiling auntie, pulling back his social self.

The play that infants engage in during the first year is mainly manipulation. They experience the object in every way possible: touching, squeezing, biting, smelling, shaking to listen, and throwing to see the reaction. A favorite game is peekaboo, which builds the cognitive structure of what goes away is not gone forever but returns. This game prepares the infant for separation. Another favorite game is to throw the toy away and have someone return it. It is a social give-and-take, action and response. It also reinforces not only object permanence but also that power over other people to get them to do what he wants them to do. It is the precursor for taking turns, sharing, and playing baseball.

This process over the first two years is moving from being solely focused on the self to the consideration of others. It is dependent on the infant's capabilities and the supportive adult behaviors. Figure 4–10 graphically portrays the stages involved,

PHASE	AGE OF ONSET IN MONTHS	INFANT CAPABILITIES	SOCIAL OUTCOME	ROLE IN INDIVIDUATION PROCESS	ADULT BEHAVIORS THAT SUPPORT INDIVIDUATION
I	0–1	Sucking; visual tracking; grasping; cuddling; vocalizes; social attunement	Reflexes; shared gazing; orienting toward caregiver	Proximity to caregiver	Observation of states; prompt basic care
II	1–2	More time quietly alert; sensory learning about people and objects; molding to caregiver's body; continues interesting activities; coos and goos	Beginning social responsiveness; mutual cueing	Begins differentiation between self and objects; more ways of maintaining proximity	Provide objects; engage in turn-taking play; give prompt basic care; respond sensitively to different states
III	4–8	Sits, grasps; creeps; increased interest in objects; sensory learning: mouthing, manipulating, examining, banging; laughs, yells, and squeals; babbling	Recognizes familiar people; shows clear preferences among people; intentionality limited to previously learned actions; playful; social smile, laughter	Beginnings of social expectations; stranger fear; maintains proximity by following, checking back on caregiver after short excursions	Provide a safe environment for floor exploration; establish limits for child; respond predictably
IV	9–14	Walking, climbing, running; joyful exploration; curious; excited; beginning use of language and gesture; person and object permanence becoming clearer; trial-and-error problem solving; intentions conveyed by language, gesture, and action; makes requests; comprehends words; complex babbling	Strong desire for approval, inclined to comply; self-willed; increased self-control; variety of emotions; social play with adults; interest in events	Maintains proximity by following and calling caregiver; strong preferences for particular people; protests separation; uses caregiver as a "base of operations" and moves outward; recognizes that others act; beginning to cooperate	Protect from hazards (child has mobility without judgment); respond promptly to communicative acts; set and maintain routines and limits; provide opportunity for independence; use language to comfort; explain leaving child with familiar adults; have patience
V	15–24	Increase of all motor tasks; skillful exploration; rapid increase in language and nonverbal communication skills; offers objects to preferred adults; self-recognition and person permanence; pointing, says words, then word combinations	Is likely to cling, then run away; plays "mother chase me!"; self-willed: "No" before compliance; considerable amount of self-control; self-comforting; may show sudden fear after departure from caregiver; may cry from relief at caregiver's return	Realizes caregiver's goals are not own goals; may be ambivalent about dependence/independence; can play happily in absence of preferred person; uses "gifts" of toys in seeking proximity, more language	Verbalize about departures, reassure; tolerate rapid changes in approach and withdrawal; use language to discuss events, relationships, objects, etc.; allow child to control some holding on, letting go; make social expectations clear over and over; have patience
VI	24–30	Good understanding of ordinary language; intentionality well developed; mental problem solving; ability to ask for help based on need; goal-directed behavior; self-definition of gender and age	Increasing interest in other children; peer play and communication stronger; mutually regulated social interactions; pretend play	Realistic sense of self and others; uses a wide array of techniques to maintain proximity (helping, conversation, play stories); can cope well with separations	Continue to reassure, support, and provide affection; praise efforts at self-control and independent behavior; provide experience with another toddler

Figure 4–10 The Individuation Process and Appropriate Adult Responses from *Guiding Children's Social Development,* 5th edition, by KOSTELNIK/WHIREN/SODERMAN/GREGAN, 2006. Reprinted with permission of Delmar Learning, a divison of Thomson Learning: www.thomsonrights.com. FAX 800-730-2215.

the roles of child and adult, as well as the desired outcomes (Kostelnik et al., 2006).

SELF-ASSERTION. In the second year, the child generalizes all other social relationships. She expects that everyone, especially other children, will treat her in the same way as her parents: accepting, acquiescent, providing what she needs and wants. When this does not happen, she cannot understand it.

Language is developing at this time also, so vocabulary and verbal expression come into the social realm. Words and phrases like "No!" "Mine!" and "Gimme" are repeatedly used in social gatherings. "Please" is expected to yield miraculous results, with objects or toys being the lure of toddler friendships.

Stages of Play. Parten's Stages of Social Play (cited in Rogers & Sawyers, 1988) have long been referred to when classifying the development of social play (Figure 4–11). Although we will speak of them as stages, they have been found not to be stages with an ascending level of involvement but rather more like forms of social play seen at all ages at varying times (Ladd, 2005). In **unoccupied play**, the child is not focused on any toy or activity: He follows the adult but does not engage in any sustained way. In **onlooker play**, the child watches other children play but does not get involved. This is used frequently by children in new situations. They scope out the territory. It is also the style of children who are shy, emotionally depressed, or just not feeling like getting involved. The teacher attends to both behaviors, assesses possible causes, and decides if action is indicated. The adult may decide to issue an invitation to play. In this way, she can role-model how to join in the play. The decision may be to allow the child to have control over joining or not.

Solitary play, playing alone or being totally focused on one's own play, is used for manipulation and practice, stress release, or by choice. It is the way of gaining familiarity with a new toy, game, or sports equipment. It is the repetitive motion that makes a skill become natural. Many find this relaxing and rewarding.

In **parallel play**, there is minimal social contact. It is not solitary play, but it is not involved either. It entails companionship but not cooperation, affiliation but not association. The young child at this stage is not developmentally able to sustain a higher level of play.

This stage is mainly manipulative, seeing how things work. The developing small muscles are used to twist, insert, pound, shovel, grasp, release, and pinch. The large muscles are used for climbing, pedaling, running, and jumping. The child, at the beginning of

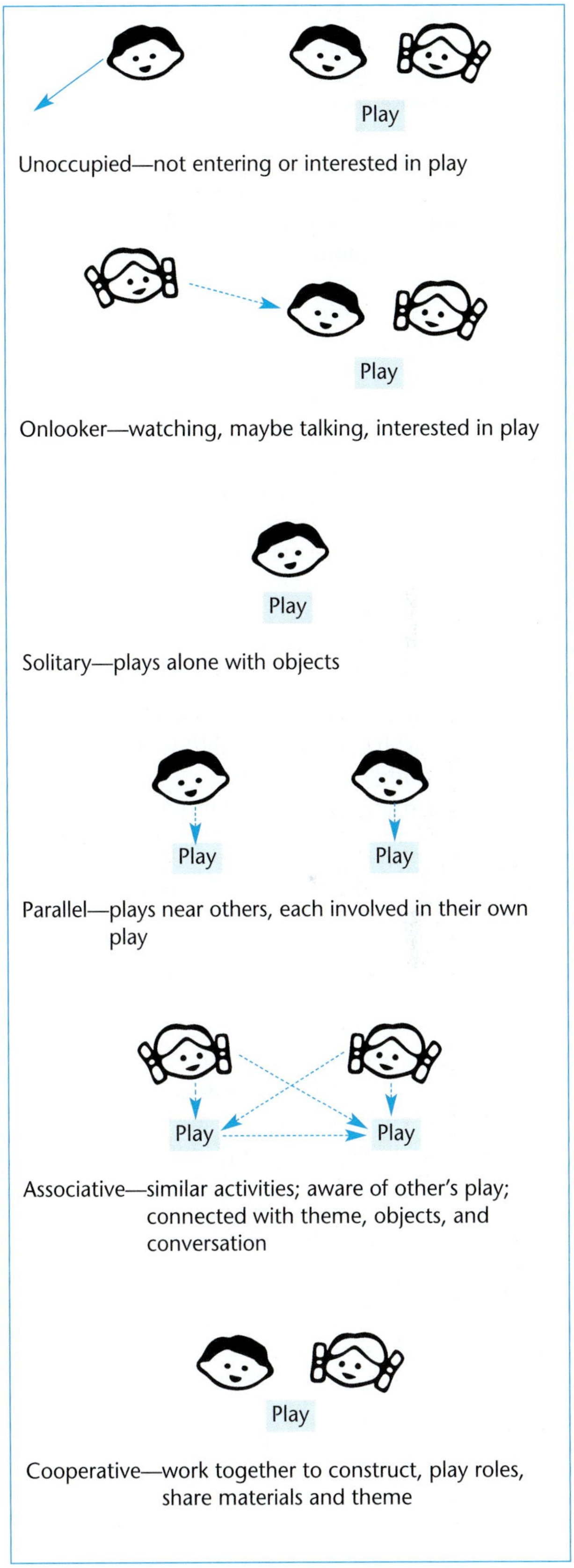

Figure 4–11 The Stages of Social Play.

this stage, cannot sustain interactive play because of limited language and insufficient cognitive, social, and emotional skills. That does not keep the child from seeking out those social contacts. In the second year, walking widens the social world considerably. Now the child can walk over to other children and initiate interactions. Because of social immaturity, however, those overtures to play may be in the form of grabbing a toy, biting, or screaming. The responses may be less than friendly.

By the end of the second year, children have begun to make friends. They recognize other children with whom they have frequent contact. They imitate and initiate overtures of affection, such as hugging, kissing, and giving objects to others. Occasionally, they make eye contact, engaging in little conversations. Mostly they are involved in their own play and play objects. Still possessing immature cognitive, social, and emotional structures, sharing and turn-taking are limited, if present at all. Some very young children have been observed in friendships. In *The Friendship Factor* (2002), Rubin discusses some factors that contributed to these early friendships:

- secure relationships with their mothers
- relationships with older siblings or children
- their mothers were friends
- the children were at similar developmental levels, had similar temperaments and behavioral styles

Children's play can be observed and coded using Rubin's play matrix (Rubin, Maioni, & Hornung, 1976), which consists of Functional Play (explorative, repetitive play), Constructive Play (creating a product), Dramatic Play (pretending), and Play with Rules (game playing), combined with the social stages of solitary (alone), parallel (alongside), and interactive (with others). The stages of play are developmental stages that are attained and built upon for the next stage, but they are revisited again and again throughout life for various reasons. Regression to an earlier stage is not viewed as peculiar or cause for alarm. The setting, the person's style, and the situation determine how the person will interact.

Types of Play. Besides the stages of play, another dynamic enters play. It is the *how* of play. Four categories of play are seen in the social stages of play (Figure 4–12). In **Functional Play**, actions are repeated for practice and exploration. A child paints all over the paper, his hands, and the legs of the easel. Clay is squeezed, patted, rolled, poked, and cut. Blocks are piled and knocked down, containers filled with them, then dumped. No end product is in mind; it is just manipulation of materials. People do this all the time in sporting goods stores as they take practice swings with golf clubs or baseball bats.

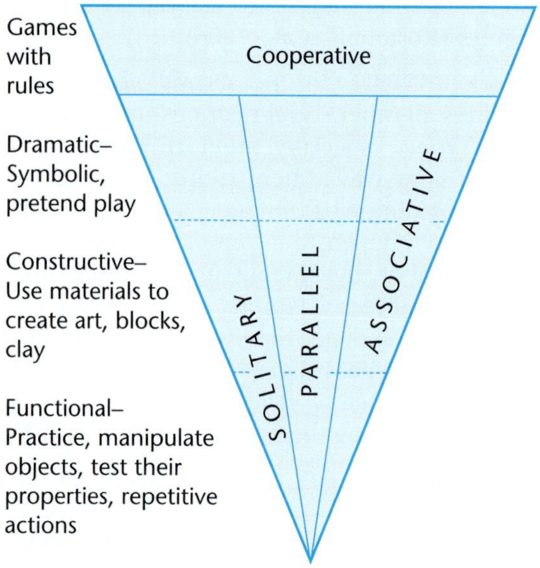

Figure 4–12 Types of Play.

Constructive Play produces a product. That manipulation of the paintbrush turns into a recognizable flower. Clay balls are piled on one another and named a "snowman." Blocks are piled, and the builder calls it "The Umpire (sic) State Building."

Dramatic Play takes the player into the world of pretend. The paintbrush becomes a bee buzzing toward the flower, gathering nectar. The snowman is moved along the table, talking to other clay creations and wondering what will happen when the sun comes out. The builder takes a monkey from the jungle set and has King Kong climbing up the building. Participation, with or without props, in the world of fantasy is classified as this type of play. It is in dramatic play that children exercise power, power over a world that they now can control, over objects, over others (including dolls and action figures).

As children move toward the fifth and sixth years, **games with rules** become part of their play repertoire. This coincides with mathematical reasoning and the social-emotional stage of industry, of putting things in order. By this age, children are bringing themselves into control, passing the egocentric stage, so now they can see from another's point of view. This stage also appears at a time when children's language skills are more developed and they are able to play in a more cooperative way.

SELF-INITIATOR Three-, four-, and five-year-olds are blossoming social beings. At this age, they have

@ it happened to me

"Bad Dolly"

As I observed children in dramatic play episodes, I frequently saw the child who I knew had never been spanked viciously spanking the dolls for "bad" deeds. While we had a "no guns" rule, children were very creative in forming Legos, tinker toys, and even artistically chewed pieces of bread into guns. We later gave up on that rule after reading *The War Play Dilemma* (Carlsson-Paige & Levin, 1987). But what was the motivating factor for violent dramatic play? Power!

Do you have an IT HAPPENED TO ME story about a child exercising power? I'd love to read it. Send it to WeekbyWeek@thomsonlearning.com

the verbal, physical, and cognitive skills to begin to interact more with each other. They engage in **associative play**—doing a similar type of activity, involving the same play theme or with similar types of toys—but in this stage they still are "doing their own thing." They are not working together toward a common goal, they just happen to be near each other, talking about what each of them is doing.

Cooperative play in contrast, produces a common product, such as a block building, a road in the sand connecting areas, or dinner in the dramatic area. All players are working out a common plan. Preschoolers are still in the Preoperational Stage, still egocentric, but they are beginning to engage in this kind of play. The teacher prepares an environment that will enhance social development by providing enough materials so that solitary and parallel play is not thwarted by having to "steal" from others. Cooperation and sharing are planned into the routines and curriculum by such things as helper charts, joint projects, songs, stories, and puppet plays. Competition during this period is not understood, so it is not an appropriate method of group interaction. Games with winners and losers—who can be the best, the fastest, or the neatest—reinforce selfish attitudes. Cooperation and concern for others are the major social tasks of this age. Children who have had experiences in rule-making for the classroom and in their enforcement in an acceptable way get along better. They know and understand the reasons why rules exist. They are careful observers of others who are breaking the rules. This is the beginning of moral development, recognizing right from wrong.

Difficulties between children are best handled not by the teacher as the judge. The teacher's role is as a facilitator for negotiation, helping those involved to tell each other their point of view. The children decide in a democratic manner. This kind of facilitation assists children in cognitive development (problem solving) and moral development (beginning to see someone else's point of view). Because bullying, victimizing another child by exclusion, teasing, or even physical aggression are seen in three- and four-year-old children, the teacher's role is more active than that of a facilitator alone; the teacher must first of all be a protector, then an active encourager of friendship formation through curriculum and intervention (Dunn, 2004).

Excluded children, those who have difficulty being accepted by peers, have some common characteristics. Disliked children often ignore other children's overtures to play, misunderstand peers' emotions, and are aggressive (Kemple, 2004). A strategy to help excluded or disliked children is to pair them with a younger child with whom they can feel more socially confident. Likewise, they may be paired with those who are socially competent as a model. Alternatives to aggressiveness through role plays, books, and puppet plays may give such children problem-solving ideas to be remembered when conflicts arise. Asking provocative questions when children are engaged in good guy/bad guy play is a strategy to divert possible anti-social activities: "How does Spiderman weave the web?" (Jones & Cooper, 2006).

The Importance of Play to Social Development

Think About It . . .

How do you play?

Play is a part of life, not just for children but for adults as well. Some early childhood programs are criticized for allowing play. "They're not learning anything there. All they ever do is just play." The word *play* is used repeatedly in discussing social development and many other areas as well. An understanding of play and its importance is necessary to child observers because it is a vehicle for learning.

The phrase "Play is the child's work," or variations of it, have been the theme or motto for defending play. The Concept Map in Figure 4–13 illustrates the developmental areas involved in play, the kinds of play, its connection with language arts, and the necessary provisions for play. The opposite word from *play* is *work*. The constructivist theory (DeVries & Kohlberg, 1987) contends it is through play and interaction with the environment that children construct mental images and processes. This is *work* in the sense that it has purpose and a definite goal. When an attempt is made to differentiate play from work, the dividing line becomes blurred. Play has been described and researched by many people.

Figure 4–13 Concept Map of Play.

Rubin, Fein, and Vandenberg (1983) formed this description of play:

- Play is intrinsically motivated.
- Play is relatively free of externally imposed rules.
- Play is carried out as if the activity were real.
- Play focuses on the process rather than any product.
- Play is dominated by the players.
- Play requires the active involvement of the players.

The International Association for the Child's Right to Play (IPA) has in its declaration that play, along with the basic needs of nutrition, health, shelter, and education, is vital to develop the potential of all children. Play is instinctive, voluntary, and spontaneous. Play helps children develop physically, mentally, emotionally, and socially. Play is a means of learning to live, not merely a way to pass time.

It is obvious that play can take place without other people, so solitary play is not just a stage but a type of play. Play with other people involved is democratic, without rules. Each player has some authority over the play. By observing, it is evident that not every player has equal power or as much power as they may want. Conflict in play erupts when the social development of the players is uneven. All the other developmental areas—cognitive, language, physical, and emotional—contribute to play's success.

Observing Play and Social Development

The observation of children interacting with each other—or "kidwatching," as Goodman, Goodman, and Hood (1989) term it—can be extremely amusing. They reveal so much of themselves and all areas of development as they play. Information on physical, cognitive, language, emotional, and social development can be gathered as children interact with the environment and other people.

ANECDOTAL AND RUNNING RECORDS. Social play observations are caught vividly with Anecdotal and Running Recordings that capture both the actions and the words. Such a narrative gives a lasting memory of an event that can be fraught with meaning to every reader. One of the foremost kidwatchers is Vivian Paley. Her books of Anecdotal Recordings, many about boys and girls in dramatic play, are not only entertaining but also full of meaning. In *Boys & Girls: Superheroes in the Doll Corner* (1984), she relates a discussion with the children about where the real work of school is happening in the classroom.

Paley is very skillful in asking open-ended questions such as, "How can you tell if you're working or playing?" She accurately records children's conversations as well as her questions that explore their thinking. Reeny, an African American child in *The Girl with the Brown Crayon* (Paley, 1997), joins her

@ it happened to me

"The Overheard Parent Conference"

I was in a conference with the parent of probably the brightest child I ever had in my preschool class. We were talking about his development when he appeared at the door, obviously listening. We invited him in, and we discussed his progress in the various areas of development. In talking about social development, I remarked that I had not seen him playing with any other children. Indeed, he could make elaborate block structures, read books on his own, draw and paint recognizable objects, but he had no friends. He was just a shadow player. He asked, "Am I supposed to play with other children?" His mother explained that he could do all these other things at home, which he did, but at school he had other children to play with and that is why he was here. "Oh, OK." And from that day forward, he moved into play groups, talked with them, interacted, and became a welcome play partner. It was his intellectual ability that helped him be a friend. It taught me a lesson that it helps if children know adults' expectations of them (and to be sure that conferences are private, although this one was all positive and turned out successfully).

Do you have an IT HAPPENED TO ME story about a child learning to make friends? I'd love to read it. Send it to WeekbyWeek@thomsonlearning.com

classmates in a study of the books of Leo Lionni as well as leading them to learn about self-identity. These books are wonderful examples of Anecdotal Recording and thoughtful teaching.

CLASSIFICATIONS OF PLAY. Observers of social development should be able to recognize and label social play using Parten's stages (really forms) of play (unoccupied, onlooker, solitary, parallel, associative, cooperative) and Smilansky's and Piaget's play categories (functional, constructive, dramatic, games with rules).

EXERCISE Using Parten's, Smilansky's, and Piaget's terms, classify the following players.

1. Jake and Donald are sitting across from each other, building with separate Lego sets. Jake and Donald are in the ____________ stage, demonstrating the ____________ type of play.
2. Heather, Greg, and Lisa are putting on a puppet play in a cardboard stage. Louise has been watching for several minutes. Louise is in the ____________ stage, while Heather, Greg, and Lisa are in the ____________ stage, demonstrating ____________ type of play.
3. Piku is at the art table making balls of clay and poking them with a pencil. He is in the ____________ stage of play, demonstrating ____________ type of play.
4. Barry is laying parallel rows of blocks and Birdie is riding a truck back and forth between them. Barry and Birdie are in the ________ stage of play, Barry demonstrating ________ type of play. Birdie is demonstrating ________. She says, "I'm delivering bread to the store." Now her play is ____________.

In checking your understanding of the play stages and types, you should have recognized: (1) parallel, constructive; (2) onlooker, cooperative, dramatic; (3) solitary, functional; (4) associative, constructive, functional, dramatic.

Young Children and Social Studies

When children begin to move out from beyond the family into their own social groups in child care or preschool, their world broadens to include children from other families, other cultures. They learn the rules about the rights of others and about the rule of the majority. They learn about the community, careers, transportation, how goods and services are made and distributed, concepts of time, and historical perspective. These are common themes in the curriculum of the young child as their world expands. In the same way that they learn anything, they learn from their experiences (both planned and spontaneous), from watching others, from books, and from direct instruction. Seefeldt (2006) lists the early childhood content topics based on the National Council for the Social Studies:

culture
time, continuity, and change
people, places, and environment
individual development and identity
individuals, groups, and institutions
power, authority, and governance
production, distribution, and consumption
science, technology, and society
global connections
civic ideals and practices

Looking at the list, common early childhood themes lend themselves to these categories: All About Me, Celebrations in My Family, See How I Grow, People in My Family, Inside/Outside, Transportation, Community Helpers, Playing Store, My Friends and How We Play, We Share, and All Around the World. Wallace (2006) says, "Among the most important elements of the social studies curriculum are the strategies and skills that teach students how to learn, how to make decisions, and how to work effectively with others"(p 8).

CHECKLISTS. Most developmental checklists have a section for social play, usually using the stages and types previously mentioned. One that has been developed to help teachers and parents monitor a child's social behavior is shown in Figure 4–14. It comes with the admonition from the authors, McClellan and Katz, that the intent is not to prescribe "correct social behavior" (1993). Rather, it is to uncover children who may be doing poorly on many items on the list. Those children may have personality and temperament differences that are completely normal for them. Children from diverse cultural and family backgrounds may not *usually* do many of these things. When this checklist shows children are having social difficulties, the teacher assesses the cause and plans for a classroom that is supportive and accepting.

There are two published rating scales with preschool norms: the Social Skills Rating Scale (SSRS) (Gresham & Elliott, 1990) and the Preschool and Kindergarten Behavior Scales (PKBS2nd) (Merrell,

I. Individual Attributes

The child:

1. Is **usually** in a positive mood
2. Is not **excessively** dependent on the teacher, assistant, or other adults
3. **Usually** comes to the program or setting willingly
4. **Usually** copes with rebuffs and reverses adequately
5. Shows the capacity to empathize
6. Has a positive relationship with one or two peers; shows capacity to really care about them, miss them if absent, etc.
7. Displays the capacity for humor
8. Does not seem to be acutely or chronically lonely

II. Social Skill Attributes

The child **usually**

1. Approaches others positively
2. Expresses wishes and preferences clearly; gives reasons for actions and positions
3. Asserts own rights and needs appropriately
4. Is not easily intimidated by bullies
5. Expresses frustrations and anger effectively and without harming others or property
6. Gains access to ongoing groups at play and work
7. Enters ongoing discussion on the subject; makes relevant contributions to ongoing activities
8. Takes turns fairly easily
9. Shows interest in others; exchanges information with and requests information from others appropriately
10. Negotiates and compromises with others appropriately
11. Does not draw inappropriate attention to self
12. Accepts and enjoys peers and adults of ethnic groups other than his or her own
13. Gains access to ongoing groups at play and work
14. Interacts nonverbally with other children with smiles, waves, nods, etc.

III. Peer Relationship Attributes

The child is

1. **Usually** accepted, versus neglected or rejected, by other children
2. **Sometimes** invited by other children to join them in play, friendship, and work.

Figure 4–14 Adapted by permission, from L. B. Katz & D. E. McClellan, *Fostering Children's Social Competence: The Teacher's Role* (Washington, DC: NAEYC, 1997, 106. Reprinted with permissions from the National Association for the Education of Young Children.

2004). These tools can be used for social skills assessment and intervention planning. They contain observable criteria such as:

- smiles and laughs with other children
- is invited to play with other children
- comforts other children when they are upset
- takes turns with toys and other objects

HELPING ALL CHILDREN WITH SOCIAL DEVELOPMENT

Free play in smaller spaces for close proximity play, with teachers providing low structure with minimal rules but a wide variety of toys, provides the best environment for social interactions for children with or without disabilities. While meeting the learning needs of children with disabilities, inclusive settings have been shown to contribute to emotional understanding and acceptance in typically developing children (Diamond, 2001). There seems to be little difference between the number of friendships for children with disabilities and typically developing children in inclusive settings (Buysse, Goldman, & Skinner, 2002). This environment promotes imitation of peers by younger children and those with developmental delays. Some modifications to the environment are made specific to the child's need.

Social interactions depend heavily on communication. For the child with a hearing loss, this is a barrier. Early involvement with hearing children as social role models and alternative communication techniques are helpful in promoting social development. For the teacher, this also means learning some way to communicate with the child to facilitate social interactions with the child's peers and to interpret the classroom environment.

Vision impairment does not necessarily cause social problems, but more likely it is society's reaction to the impairment that has a negative effect. Curiously, the more severe the impairment, the less negative the reaction, possibly because of the sympathy effect. Children with thick corrective lenses may be rejected as a playmate by other children just from appearances. The teacher can inform children of the nature of the child's vision and how it may affect the child in the classroom, inviting other children's assistance and acceptance. The teacher as a role model provides an environment that is safe, but allows all the freedom and challenge other children receive.

Children with physical limitations are now included in regular classrooms, advertisements, and television shows. Familiarity with prostheses, walkers, and wheelchairs is helping to bring about more social peer acceptance in group settings. Children have a desire to be helpful, yet the danger exists for them to do too much, reinforcing learned helplessness. It is important for every child to be included in every classroom activity to the fullest of her ability.

This will go a long way in facilitating peer acceptance as well.

Children from other cultures may have different social styles, depending on their cultural values and practices. The teacher familiarizes himself with the cultures of the children in the group and transfers that awareness to assist the child to feel comfortable socially in the classroom. If a child does not speak English, the teacher, even though he may not speak the child's language, can act as a body language translator and an advocate for the child with the other children. The family, through an interpreter, can supply the teacher with a list of common words and their meanings.

The social climate of acceptance for all children will be extended to any child with differences. Having a friend is one of the most important motivators in learning and feeling successful and happy. The teacher must do all in his power to make that happen.

HELPING PROFESSIONALS FOR SOCIAL DEVELOPMENT CONCERNS

If all the efforts of the staff and observations documented by Anecdotal and Running Records or social checklists indicate a child is having a problem in social development, some action must be taken. In a talk with the family, the teacher can discuss his concerns. This is a sensitive area since no family wants to hear that their child is rejected and friendless. Family dynamics and values are closely woven with social development, so the utmost care should be taken. The family probably already has clues that the child is having difficulty. The child may be reluctant to come to school, with crying and tantrums every morning. The child may be getting into fights, hurting and being hurt. Together, some of the possible causes are explored and some plans agreed upon.

If the problem is prolonged or appears so severe that it is determined inadvisable to delay advising the family and seeking professional help, then helping professionals may be consulted. After the medical personnel have ruled out any possible physical cause, then the psychological causes could be examined. Some of those professionals might include one or more of the following:

social worker—counsels individuals and families, serves as advocate or consultant to agencies or schools

family therapist—psychologist specializing in working with families in the treatment of an individual or family group

play therapist—psychologist or psychiatrist using play for diagnosis, dialogue, and treatment of childhood social-emotional disorders

child psychologist—evaluates, diagnoses, and treats children for emotional, social, cognitive, and behavioral disorders

OTHER METHODS

Other Methods to Record Social Development

Class List Log—who plays with whom

Notation of level of social play stage:

- Anecdotal Recording
- Checklists and Rating Scales
- Frequency Counts—How many play encounters occur with another child during one day? How frequently does a child lead/follow another child during one day?
- Interviews or discussions about friends
- Time Samples—who the child is with during free choice time
- Work Samples—child's friends depicted in art work, collaborative work such as murals, joint buildings
- Photographs, audio or video recordings capturing child's interactions with others

STANDARDS

Here are selected examples of standards related to social development:

National Council for the Social Studies (1994). Expectations of Excellence: Curriculum Standards for Social Studies. IV. Individual Development and Identity:

The teacher will:

- assist learners as they work independently and cooperatively within groups and institutions to accomplish goals

The Association for Childhood Education International has developed *Global Guidelines for the Education and Care of Young Children in the 21st Century* (2006) in an effort to assess the status of early childhood education globally. The guidelines consider the following areas:

- environment and physical space and settings for children

curriculum content and pedagogy
early childhood educators and caregivers
partnership with families and communities
acountability, supervision, and management of programs for children

In the Early Childhood Educators and Communities is a standard directly related to social studies:

#48 Educators/Caregivers respect children, their culture, and family practice.

KEY TERMS

associative play
constructive play
cooperative play
dramatic play
egocentric
functional play
games with rules
object permanence
onlooker play
parallel play
Running Record
social competence
solitary play
unoccupied play

Go to the Bind-in-Book CD for:

Anecdotal/Running Record form
Plan Week 4, Part A, Directions for Running Records of Social Development for Group C, including What to Do with It, Portfolio Overview Example, Sharing with Child and Family, Actions—Read a Book, In the Environment, In the Curriculum, and In the Newsletter
Plan Week 4, Part B, Class List Log of Social Development for All, including What to Do with It and Sharing with Child and Family
Plan Week 4, Part C, Reflective Journal

REFERENCES

Association for Childhood Education International. *Global guidelines for the education and care of young children in the 21st century.* (2006). Retrieved July 6, 2006, from http://www.acei.org/wguides.htm.

Birch, S. H., & Ladd, H. W. (1996). Interpersonal relationships in the school environment and children's early school adjustment: The role of teachers and peers. In K. W. Wentzel & J. H. Juvonen (Eds.). *Social motivation: Understanding children's school adjustment.* New York: Cambridge University Press.

Buysse, V., Goldman, B. D., & Skinner, M. L. (2002). Setting effects on friendship formation among young children with and without disabilities. *Exceptional Children, 68* (4) 503–517.

Carlsson-Paige, N., & Levin, D. E. (1987). *The war play dilemma: Balancing needs and values in the early childhood classroom.* New York: Teachers College Press.

DeVries, R., & Kohlberg, L. (1987). *Constructivist early childhood education: Overview and comparison with other programs.* Washington, DC: National Association for the Education of Young Children.

Diamond, K. E. (2001). Relationships among young children's ideas, emotional understanding and social contact with classmates with disabilities. *Topics in Early Childhood Special Education, 21* (2), 104.

Dunn, J. (2004). *Children's friendships: The beginnings of intimacy.* Malden, MA: Blackwell Publishing

Elliott, S. N., McKevitt, B. C., & DiPerna, J. C. (2002). Best practices in preschool social skills training. In A. Thomas & J. Grimes, *Best practices in school psychology IV.* Bethesda, MD: National Association of School Psychologists.

Erikson. E. H. (1963, orig. 1950). *Childhood and society.* New York: Norton.

Exploring first feelings: Milestones in the emotional development of babies. (1985). [Videorecording]. Washington, DC: Institute for Mental Health Initiatives.

Fabes, R. A., Eisenberg, N., Jones, S., Smigh, M., Guthrie, I., Poulin, R., Shepard, S., & Friedman, J. (1999). Regulation, emotionality and preschoolers' socially competent peer interactions. *Child Development, 70* (2), 432–442.

Flavell, J. (1977). *Cognitive development.* Englewood Cliffs, NJ: Prentice Hall.

Freud, S. (1953). *The standard edition of the complete psychological works of Sigmund Freud* (J. Strachey, Ed. and Trans.). London: Hogarth and the Institute of Psychoanalysis.

Goodman, K. S., Goodman, Y. M., & Hood, W. J. (1989). *The whole language evaluation book.* Portsmouth, NH: Heinemann.

Gresham, F. M., & Elliott, S. N. (1990). *Social skills rating system.* Circle Pines, MN: American Guidance System.

Hartup, W. W. (1992). *Having friends, making friends, and keeping friends: Relationships as educational contexts.* Urbana, IL: ERIC Clearinghouse on Elementary and Early Childhood Education, ED 354 854.

Jones, E., & Cooper, R. (2006). *Playing to get smart.* New York: Teachers College Press.

Kemple, K. (2004). *Let's be friends: Peer Competence and social inclusion in early childhood programs.* New York: Teachers College Press.

Kostelnik, M. J., Whiren, A. P., Soderman, A. K., Stein, L. C., & Gregory, K. (2006). *Guiding children's social development: Theory to practice* (5th ed.). Clifton Park, NY: Thomson Delmar Learning.

Ladd, G. W. (2005). *Children's peer relations and social competence: A century of progress.* New Haven: Yale University Press.

Lawhon, T. (1997). Encouraging friendships among children. *Childhood Education, 73* (4), 228–231.

Maslow, A. H. (1970). *Motivation and personality.* New York: Harper & Row.

McClellan, D., & Katz, L. (1993). *Young children's social development: A checklist.* Urbana, IL: ERIC Clearinghouse on Elementary and Early Childhood Education. EDO-PS-93-6.

Merrell, K. W. (2002). *Preschool and kindergarten behavior scales* (2nd ed.). Austin, TX: PRO-ED.

National Council for the Social Studies. (1994). *Expectations of excellence: Curriculum standards for social studies.* Waldorf, MD: Author.

Paley, V. G. (1984). *Boys & girls: Superheroes in the doll corner.* Chicago: The University of Chicago Press.

Paley, V. G. (1997). *The girl with the brown crayon.* Cambridge, MA: Harvard University Press.

Rogers, C. S., & Sawyers, J. K. (1988). *Play in the lives of children.* Washington, DC: National Association for the Education of Young Children.

Rothbart, M. K., & Bates, J. E. (1998). In N. Eisenberg (Ed.), W. Damon (Series Ed.), *Handbook of child psychology: Vol. 3, Social, emotional and personality development* (pp. 105–176). New York: Wiley.

Rubin, K. H., Maioni, T., & Hornung, M. (1976). Free play behaviors in lower-class and middle-class preschoolers: Parten and Piaget revisited. *Child Development, 47,* 414–419.

Rubin, K., & Thompson, A. (2002) *The friendship factor: Helping our children navigate their social world—and why it matters for their success and happiness.* New York: Penguin.

Rubin, Z. (1980). *Children's friendships.* Cambridge, MA: Harvard University Press.

Seefeldt, C. (2005). *How to work with standards in the early childhood classroom.* New York: Teachers College Press.

Skinner, B. F. (1953). *Science and human behavior.* New York: Macmillan.

Wallace, M. (2006). *Social studies: All day, every day in the early childhood classroom.* Clifton Park, NY: Thomson Delmar Learning.

Watson, J. B. (1950). *Behaviorism.* New York: Norton.

RESOURCES

Association for Childhood Education International. (2006). *Global guidelines for the education and care of young children in the 21st century.* http://www.acei.org.

Katz, L. G., & McClellan, D. C. (1997). *Fostering children's social competence: The teacher's role.* Washington, DC: NAEYC.

Kostelnik, M. J., Whiren, A. P., Soderman, A. K., Stein, L. C., & Gregory, K. (2006). *Guiding children's social development* (5th ed.). Clifton Park, NY: Thomson Delmar Learning.

Levin, D. E. (2003). *Teaching young children in violent times: Building a peaceable classroom.* Cambridge, MA: Educators for Social Responsibility.

Miller, K. (2000). Caring for the little ones: Friendships in the baby room. *Child Care Information Exchange* (133, 62), May/June 2000.

NAEYC Early Childhood Program Standards and Accreditation Criteria (2005).

National Council for the Social Studies (1994). *Expectations of excellence: Curriculum standards for social studies.* Waldorf, MD: Author.

Palmer, D., Neugebauer, B. (2006). *Connecting: Friendships in the lives of young children and their teachers.* Redmond, WA: Exchange Press.

Rogers, C. S., & Sawyers, J. K. (1988). *Play in the lives of children.* Washington, DC: National Association for the Education of Young Children.

Sluss, D. J. (2005). *Supporting play: Birth through age eight.* Clifton Park, NY: Thomson Delmar Learning.

Stephens, K. (2006). *Social skills children need to make and keep friends.* Redmond WA: Exchange Press.

CHAPTER

5

Using Frequency Counts to Look at Emotional Development

USING FREQUENCY COUNTS

EXERCISE **How often did you do each of the following today?**

eat
go to the bathroom
talk on the phone
say your pet phrase ("Oh well," "Basically," or "Whatever")

Much behavior is habitual, done without thinking. Occasionally, those habitual actions become really important. More attention is given to how often and what food is eaten when someone is on a diet. Measuring or counting is a part of decision making. If a person is experiencing an illness, the number of times one goes to the bathroom may be an important symptom. Legislators tally the number of pro and con calls received on an issue. Weight before beginning a diet, the number of phone calls, or an unusual change in body functions is an indicator that provides information for comparison. In behavior modification, a measurement is made, action taken, and then a new measurement is taken to see the significance of the change.

In the classroom, a **Frequency Count** can measure repeated actions of a child, the whole group, or the teacher. It is sometimes necessary to count behaviors that occur often in one day or session, such as hitting, children running, or the teacher saying, "Don't."

IN THIS CHAPTER

Strategies are then implemented to reduce negative actions or behavior, or to increase desirable ones.

EXERCISE Frequently occurring actions that may occur in a group of preschool children follow. What is your estimate of how many times a day each happens? In the following list, place a + next to the ones you would like to increase and a – next to ones you would like to decrease.

______ 1. spills
______ 2. biting
______ 3. punching
______ 4. "Thank you."
______ 5. vomiting
______ 6. using the book area
______ 7. sharing
______ 8. "Don't . . ."
______ 9. "OK, guys."
______ 10. "Teacher, Teacher . . ."

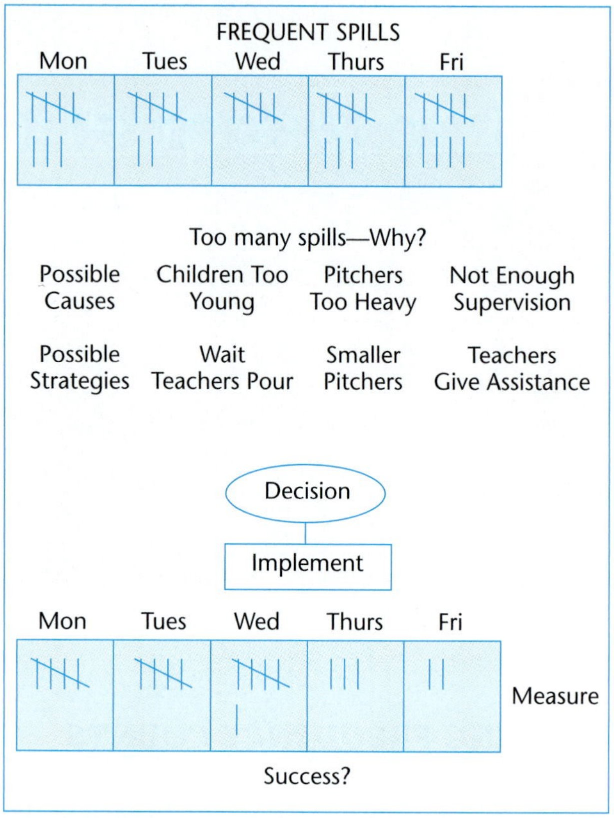

Figure 5–1 Frequency Counts to Measure Reduction of Undesirable Behavior.

Candidates for a reduction are numbers 1, 2, 3, 8, 9, and 10. Numbers 4, 6, and 7 could be increased. Number 5 is an infrequent event and would not be a measurable criterion for a Frequency Count or a reduction plan. It is necessary to note such an incident, however, on a health form or a short Anecdotal Recording. In an infant room, this may be a more frequent event. Number 2 is more likely to occur in a toddler room, because it is an expected behavior. If it were a frequent behavior in a kindergarten room, with an individual child, or many children, the teacher would begin to search for answers, after she applied first aid, of course. Biting is not expected behavior for kindergarten students.

Frequency Counts are a way of seeing just how often an event happens. The purpose is to try to change undesirable behavior. If the action is negative and excessive for the age or stage expectations, then a plan is implemented to try to reduce it. If an expected behavior is not present or not happening often enough, then a plan is made to try to increase it. After a period of time, another Frequency Count is taken to measure the success. The process is documented by a Frequency Count to "prove" if the remedy or theory works.

This is not recommending a program of behavior modification where positive behavior is rewarded so it will increase, and negative behavior is punished so it will decrease. It is more a measurement of the teacher or learning process, like a pretest and a posttest. It assumes a change will take place. The agents of that change may be time, direct instruction, modeling, planned experiences, or self-regulation. Bandura's social learning theory (1977) recognized that the change, called learning, results from an interaction between thinking, acting, and the environment.

Figure 5–1 is an example of a Frequency Count. Spills seem to be happening many times a day in this classroom, and the staff is concerned—beyond being simply irritated—about the messes. They complain, then talk about some possible reasons. The children may be too young to initiate pouring, or the pitchers available are too heavy with no lids and opaque so the liquid comes out unexpectedly for novice pourers. Perhaps the adults are not sitting at the table with the children but using that time to prepare for the next activity. Each of the possible reasons suggests possible strategies. A decision is reached, and the strategy is implemented. A later Frequency Count measures whether the strategy is successful or not.

Using the Frequency Count to Document Frequently Occurring Behaviors

Other classroom situations and possible strategies for Frequency Count measurement follow:

- *decrease aggressive acts*—prosocial or emotional curriculum

it happened to me

The Spilling Song

In a center I visited recently, a spill occurred. Immediately, a teacher jumped up and turned on a record player with a little song about spilling. She later remarked, "That same child deliberately spills every day." I asked about the song. "Oh, they love it." Do you think the teacher's response to spilling increased or decreased spilling at snack time?

Do you have an IT HAPPENED TO ME story about how a well-intentioned plan worked in reverse? I'd love to read it. Please send it to WeekbyWeek@thomsonlearning.com

- *decrease the need for teacher intervention*—more self-help shelves for materials and supplies
- *decrease inappropriate use of materials*—helper chart to encourage responsibility
- *document individual child with transition difficulties*—individual Frequency Count and implementation of special warning before it is time to change activities
- *decrease use of punitive guidance techniques*—training in positive guidance
- *decrease domination of adult voices in the classroom*—tape recorder to monitor and make teachers aware of voice level
- *increase cooperative play*—buddy time when each child and a friend choose an activity to do together
- *increase interactions with families*—weekly happy notes
- *increase eye-level talking with children*—small chairs in each learning center for teacher to sit on while observing play and talking to children
- *increase scanning supervision of whole room*—reminder posters for teachers on every wall that display "SCAN"
- *increase use of learning area*—place an adult there to interact with the children
- *increase self-care*—equip room with cleaning equipment, low shelves, paint smocks with Velcro, dress-up clothes with elastic and Velcro

Using Frequency Counts to Measure Prosocial and Antisocial Behavior

Groups of young children are emotionally and socially immature, resulting in disagreements and a lack of empathy for one another. The goals of adults who work with children are to decrease antisocial behavior and increase prosocial behavior. Frequency Counts can measure the effectiveness of a chosen strategy or intervention, or the progress that children make just from maturation and experience in a group setting.

A Frequency Count tallies each time a specified behavior occurs. The Frequency Count example in Figure 5–2 shows a group of 11 children on a certain day. Huy made no social contacts. What does that mean? We cannot tell from this recording. That means that it is a closed method. All the details except for the name of the child involved and the fact that it occurred are lost. The reader does not know the nature of the action, what precipitated it, any conversation from the incident, or the result. The purpose is solely to count.

EXERCISE Interpret what the information in Figure 5–2 could mean.

What kind of a player is Carol? Solitary, parallel, cooperative (not the traditional meaning, but play stage meaning)?
What do you think Edward did?
What about Huy? Why do you think he has no tallies?

Probably Carol is in the advanced cooperative stage of play but immature emotionally. She had a lot of social contacts, but she may not have her emotions under control.

After reading the rest of the chapter, particularly regarding the difference between girls and boys, come back and think about Edward here. Huy probably is not making many social contacts because of his language barrier. Isolated children are neither prosocial or antisocial. The common definition of an introverted, withdrawn, quiet person is, "He's antisocial." In this case, it probably is not deliberate or willful, just lack of confidence: "When in doubt, do nothing" syndrome.

Prosocial and antisocial Frequency Counts give indicators of the emotional tone of the classroom. Prosocial behavior is the outward manifestation of

FREQUENCY COUNT Date *March 01 Year* Recorder *BAN*

Make a tally mark in the column next to the child's name each time you observe a behavior that you would classify as prosocial or antisocial.

CHILD'S NAME	PROSOCIAL Helping, sharing, hugging, calling another child by a kind name	ANTISOCIAL Hurting, hoarding, bad name calling, rejecting another child
Amy	✓✓	
Bajic	✓✓✓	✓✓✓✓
Carol	✓✓✓✓✓✓	✓✓✓✓✓✓
Danielle	✓	✓✓
Edward		✓✓✓✓✓✓✓
Fatima	✓	
Galina	✓✓✓	
Huy		
Irma	✓✓	✓
Jacob	✓✓	✓✓
Kara	✓✓✓✓	
Totals	*24*	*22*

Figure 5–2 Frequency Count Example.

empathy, caring for another person through an action. In encouraging caring communities, Frequency Counts help the teacher clearly see patterns of individuals who are displaying these behaviors.

Frequency Counts can be used in selected circumstances, not as a usual part of the classroom information gathering. Effectively measuring before and after a strategy or over a period of time gives important documentation of the degree of change during the interval.

Using Technology

If you are counting the frequency of one child's target behavior or actions, you can attach a counter to your belt. If counting a specific behavior of a group of children, the tallies on each child should be separate, so a pencil-and-paper tally sheet would be the most efficient tool.

How to Find the Time

This method takes very little time. It may be one of the least time-consuming methods. Details, quotes, and situations are not recorded; only record the occurrence of the target behavior.

What to Do with the Information

The information gathered from a Frequency Count is more than food for an inquiring mind, although it may indicate that no change is needed. It is a tool to measure a baseline, the commonplace, the usual. It is the basis for judgments about the need for change. A strategy is implemented to attempt the change, then more Frequency Counts are taken to measure progress and success. The process is a kind of mini-research, an experiment in a behavior-modification format. Depending on the topic and subject of the research, it can be shared as a victory in progress with families, other teachers, and the administration. It can be used as a needs assessment for equipment, materials, or teacher training. The post-intervention Frequency Count can be used in reporting to funders or the administration the difference the new equipment or the training has made. Periodic return to the Frequency Count method will measure how long-lasting the effects of the project have been.

Advantages

Frequency Counts are

- a quantitative measurement on which to base strategies for change.
- quick to record, with no details, just tallies to write.
- useful for quantitatively and objectively measuring frequently occurring behaviors.

Disadvantages

Frequency Counts can

- lose the raw data, with no details recorded.
- only measure one kind of behavior, making the results highly selective.
- allow the recorder's bias to enter the recording.

Pitfalls to Avoid

Frequency Counts

- can select behaviors to measure that do not occur often (we hope), such as accidents requiring stitches, incidents of child abuse, and guinea pig escapes.
- infer from one sample that this is normal behavior. (It may have been an unusual day, so results are not indicative of a normal day.)
- allow much interpretation from one recorder to another. (For example, "Was that sharing when Aiko handed Katerina the Play Doh because Katerina demanded it?")
- are an intense recording method that requires the adult to be free from child-interaction responsibilities, which is not always possible.

Go to the Bind-in-Book CD for Frequency Count forms, plans, and resources.

LOOKING AT EMOTIONAL DEVELOPMENT

Stages of Emotional Development

EXERCISE **What emotions would these events stir in you? How would you express it?**

You won the $3 million lottery.
You are asked by your best friend to cosign a $20,000 loan.
You are told the plane has lost power, prepare for a crash landing.
You have lost an heirloom ring that has been in your family for five generations.
You just got a phone call from the lottery office that they made a mistake. You did not win the money after all.

Emotions are not grown. They change over time from simple to complex. Their development occurs in predictable stages but in very individual ways. Development of emotions is in their expression and control. As the human matures, the capacity for distinguishing between various emotions intensifies, and along with it the ability to recognize those same emotions in others. Finding acceptable expressions and control of those emotions is a lifelong struggle for the ability to control the intensity at both ends of the emotional balance.

Studies of emotions have found that there are emotions common to all humans (Figure 5–3). These **core emotions**—fear, rage, and love—were researched in the work of J. B. Watson (1914). These core emotions form the basis for all other emotions, which are just more finite distinctions of fear, rage, and love. Core emotions are, at first, purely responses to stimuli. Within the first year, however, their appearance becomes more deliberate and recognizable (Figure 5–4).

In the infant, these emotions are expressed first by reflexes, varying in intensity. They are usually governed not as much by the situation as by **temperament**. One baby expressing joy or contentment may lie passively, while others may move actively about. Babies differ in the intensity of their crying, which is

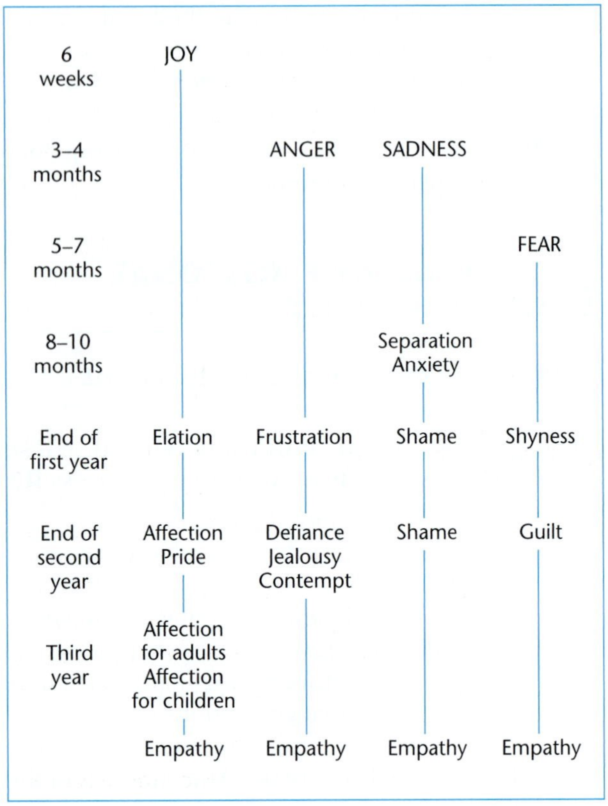

Figure 5–3 Emergence of children's emotions during the first three years of life.

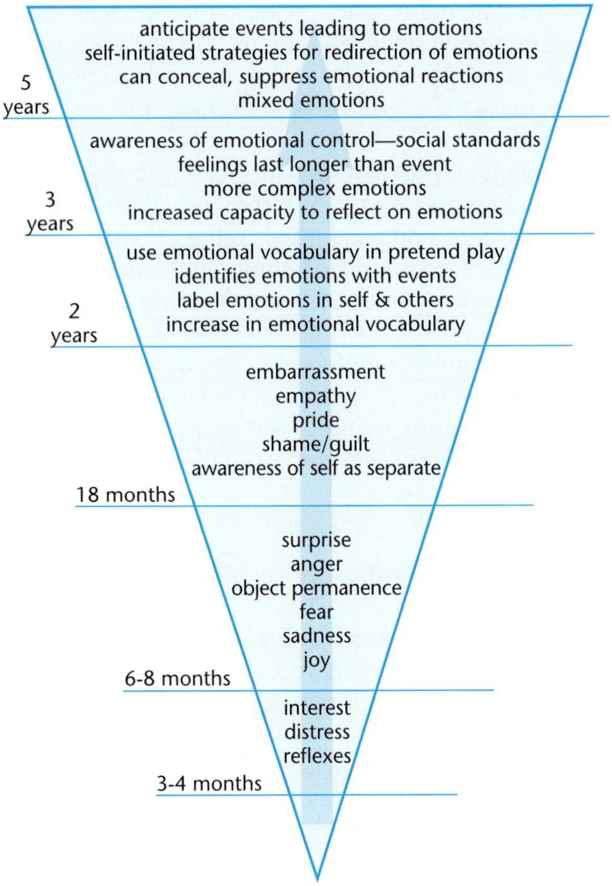

Figure 5–4 Emotional Development.

dependent more on their particular style than the range of their discontent. These temperaments are genetic, but over time other influences will affect change in emotional responses. Parental influence on temperament has been studied by many researchers. Thomas and Chess (1977) have done research on the long-term effects of mother–child interactions on personality and emotional development. They identified nine temperamental qualities that can be observed not only in the infant but continued throughout life:

1. *activity level*—physical motion
2. *rhythmicity*—regularity of biological functions
3. *approach or withdrawal*—initial reaction to new stimulation
4. *adaptability*—flexibility after initial reaction
5. *intensity of reaction*—energy level of responses
6. *threshold of responsiveness*—intensity of stimulation needed to produce a response
7. *quality of mood*—general behavior
8. *distractibility*—outside stimulation changing ongoing behavior
9. *attention span and persistence*—length of time activities are maintained

EXERCISE **Think of yourself and one other person you know well and jot down, on a separate sheet of paper, descriptors in the nine categories of temperament.**

	Self	**Friend**
1.		
2.		
3.		
4.		
5.		
6.		
7.		
8.		
9.		

Examine the differences. Why are you different from your friend? Genetics? Family influences? Experiences with peers?

REVIEW

FREQUENCY COUNT

A recording of predetermined frequently occurring behaviors to quantify their frequency, and later for comparison after a strategy is implemented.

Types of Information to Record Using Frequency Counts

- frequently occurring separation difficulties of individual children
- frequent requests for assistance or reminders of self-care behaviors
- frequent observances of social play stages
- frequent prosocial and antisocial incidents in a period of time
- frequency of language used in a certain function such as to enter play area or solve social difficulty
- frequency of use of book area during free play time
- frequency of choice of creative area—visual arts, blocks, sociodramatic

Socialization of Emotions

Emotional development has several aspects. The first is recognizing and interpreting the emotions of others. This is accomplished very early in life when an infant can distinguish between a smile and a serious face or frown. Infants whose mothers suffer from depression and therefore may lack certain facial expressions, especially friendly, approving ones, may internalize the expressions as displeasure or rejection. This could affect attachment, one of the most basic necessities in future emotional development.

As the child develops a more complex thinking process, he can differentiate the range of feelings from pleasant to elated and select expressive behaviors appropriate to the range. Emotional development, then, is the recognition of the feelings and range of emotions. Most of all, emotional development is learning to control and express emotions in socially acceptable ways. Humans spend the rest of their lives trying to interpret the feelings of others, which in turn has implications for the development of self. Goldman (1995) describes this ability as **emotional intelligence**, recognizing the emotions of others and having the self-awareness and impulse control to manage one's own emotions. School readiness, early school success, and, later, accomplishments in the workplace are dependent on this emotional intelligence or competence (Peth-Pierce, 2000). Intervention programs have been successful in teaching children how to do this, making them better able to function in relationships in school, home, and, ultimately, the workplace.

Infants are born with the basic emotional responses that will become more defined in how they are expressed as other areas of development become more mature. As thinking levels develop, the causes of the feelings and more choices of expression are understood.

Emotional regulation is the ability to display spontaneous reactions and the ability to delay or control reactions as needed. Control and appropriate expression of emotions are learned, just as other skills are, through

modeling—seeing how others react and express emotions

direct instruction—saying something like, "When you feel like that, this is what you can do or shouldn't do . . ."

positive or negative reinforcement—smiles, nods, verbal praise or scowls, stern looks, no-no head shake, or harsh physical touching

Inhibited children repress their emotions, resulting not only in added stress but also the inability to learn how to practice social competencies, not learning how to appropriately express anger, fear, and frustration. Children without social skills and language to express emotions resort to socially unacceptable words and actions that cause them to be rejected by peers and labeled by adults as acting out.

Emotions are socialized or influenced in their recognition and expression by adults in the child's world. Americans display more intense expression of emotions than Chinese and Japanese people. This may cause children from Eastern cultures to be ill at ease in a setting where discussion and free expression of emotions are encouraged.

It is difficult to interpret the inner cause for the outward display of emotions. The observer infers the cause based on prior knowledge of development and behavioral cues. Each individual is different, and before language appears, it is impossible to be certain of the emotions of the observed. Between two and three years old, children use the words *happy, angry,*

@ it happened to me

When Are You Going to Control Your Temper?

My two sons and I were sitting at the dining room table doing homework when they started arguing over a pencil, the way seven- and nine-year-olds will. The argument got more and more heated until the furious nine-year-old flung the pencil at his brother. The pencil seemed to spin in slow motion as it narrowly missed his brother's eye. I was relieved that it missed but outraged that he would do such a dangerous thing. I got right in his face, and yelled, "When are you going to learn to control your temper!?" At that moment I realized I was out of control and he was wise not to say, "When you do, Mother."

Do you have an IT HAPPENED TO ME story about your own emotions out of control? I'd love to read it. Please send it to WeekbyWeek@thomsonlearning.com

and *sad* (in that order)—and later *scared, surprised,* and *disgusted*—to describe their own and others' emotions. Notice the correlation to the core emotions. By five years old, they can match and label a broader range of emotions from pictures (Widen & Russell, 2003).

Help With Emotional Expression

Think About It . . .

How do you feel when someone says, "I know just how you feel"?

Do you want to say, "No, you don't. How can you? Your experience was different from mine. You had different supports to lean on. You are different from me. You can't know how I really feel. I'm only letting you see a bit of what I really feel"?

How do you feel when someone says, "Don't feel that way"?

Will you stop feeling because they said that? Does it make the hurt or anger go away because they commanded it? You *do* feel that way. What you are trying to do is deal with it.

Emotions and their expression are very personal. As much as someone would like to alleviate another's pain, it is one of those times when a person only knows what they feel. The role of the family and teacher is to respect the child's emotions, not deny that they exist. "I can see that you are really sad over that." The adult models an acceptable way to express the emotion, "When I get sad or hurt, I sometimes cry and want to be alone." And everyone needs a friend who offers, "When you are ready to talk about it, or need a hug, I'm here." In the case of angry and aggressive emotions, the same technique can be used. "I can see that you are really angry over that, but I can't let you hurt other people. When you are ready to tell your friend what made you so angry and try to work out the problem, I'll be here to help you. Until then you can paint at the easel or cut Play Doh with scissors to get yourself under control."

Joy, Love, and Happiness

EXERCISE What does happiness look like? What might be some causes of happiness?

The most recognizable characteristic that suggests joy or happiness is smiling. Those first smiles are reputed to be reflex responses to digestion rather than an emotional state. Smiles in response to human voices are seen at three weeks, and to familiar faces by three and a half months. Laughter, in response to physical stimulation like tickling, then to more social situations, begins at four months. The reciprocal sharing of smiles, coos, and laughter is part of the attachment process needed for the coming separation, cognitively and physically. Emotional development is closely aligned with social interactions and cognitive development. When the infant can differentiate between self and others and realizes the primary caregiver is not with her, anger and fear combine to form separation anxiety. The emotional task of infancy is the formation of trust (Erikson, 1950), the confidence that needs will be met, mother will return, and all is well. That is the foundation for mental health (Figure 5–5).

Joy is manifested after the age of one from situations that have favorable results. To young children, that means it satisfies their own desires. As they work on autonomy, the accomplishment of tasks brings joy

Figure 5–5 Joy is easy to recognize!

in the form of pride. As they near four and five years old, happiness is meeting adults' expectations. They are working toward empathy. They can now find joy for what is happening to others rather than self. That is a goal of social development for the benefit of the whole community.

THE ABSENCE OF JOY. Factors that influence this emotion begin, as always, with what is inborn. Some infants just have a generally happy behavior. Others are more irritable and harder to find in a state of satisfaction and calm. That inborn temperament may be the beginning point. Interactions with mother, the primary caregivers, and others are extremely important. In cases studied in which infants were deprived of social interactions, physical, mental, and emotional disorders were seen contributing to the **failure to thrive**. In situations of neglect, conditions of poverty, or physical illness, emotional damage can be seen as well.

Think About It . . .

How do you deal with difficult situations?

Some children display behaviors that will allow them to deal with the absence of joy in their life. First, children may be in denial. They may use fantasy or refuse to recognize the difficult situation by acting as if it were not so. Children use this technique to come through abuse, removing themselves emotionally from the situation until it becomes unreal, a sealed-off part of their life. Children may regress to an earlier stage of behavior to escape the reality of the difficulty. By recording a child's progress, an observation of regression can be a warning that something may be bothering the child. Withdrawal might be used as protection from facing the absence of joy. By not interacting socially, there is less risk of pain. Negative emotional experiences activate the same pain centers in the brain as physical distress (Eisenberger et al., 2003). Emotional distress may be exhibited in physical ailments such as stomachaches or headaches that have no physiological basis. Sadness, withdrawal, low interest level, and physical pain may be symptoms of childhood depression, an increasingly prevalent phenomenon in children ages 2 to 12 (Papalia & Olds, 2004).

By evaluating children's social behaviors against the typical stages, clues may be noticed that suggest a possible emotional trauma. When children act out, there may be many causes. It may be a realistic behavior for this age or stage, an expression of emotional need, or a disregard for others because of the emotional pain the child is experiencing. Observing the indicators of defense mechanisms should be noted and studied further.

When a child displays a lack of joy, the teacher has some steps to take (Figure 5–6). The first one is to recognize the emotion and not show disapproval or denial even if the emotion is not justified. So often adults say, "Smile for me," or "You shouldn't feel that way." The emotion is real to the person feeling it and should not be denied by an outsider. Second, trying to get the child to forget about the feeling is a short-term solution. Pretending happiness does not help when the child is experiencing loneliness from missing the family member who left him at day care. Acting silly to get the child to smile or involving him in an activity only temporarily relieves the difficulty.

Think About It . . .

Think of someone you know who has had a life of really difficult experiences yet appears to have overcome the obstacles and is emotionally whole. What made the difference for that person?

An interesting phenomenon that puzzles researchers, as well as anyone who wonders about

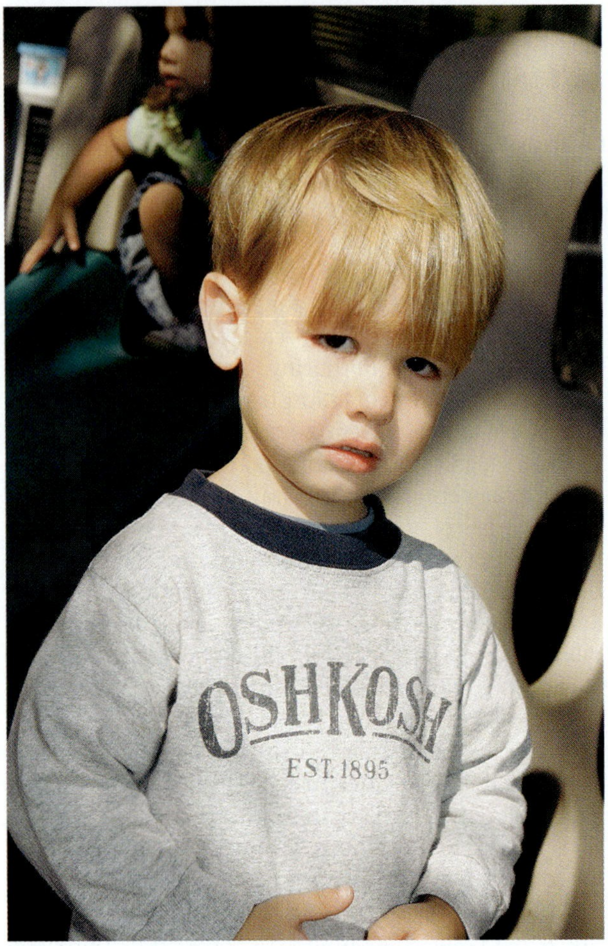

Figure 5–6 A child with an absence of joy is a concern.

cause and effect, is the coping mechanisms that some children develop. Some children can remain emotionally healthy after experiencing traumatic events. Anthony and Cohler (1987) looked at the common factors in the **invulnerable child**, the one who survives and can rise above expected dire outcomes from difficult, seemingly impossible circumstances. Advances in brain science gives indications that the human brain is designed to be resilient, to overcome risk, storing information not as dry facts but as it is connected with emotional experiences. (Brendtro & Longurst, 2005). Children who are resilient exhibit empathy, detachment from the dysfunctional behaviors of others, a sense of humor, and personal power. This can be attributed to what Bendtro, Brokenleg, and Van Bockern (2002) call the Circle of Courage model, involving belonging, mastery, independence, and generosity. Despite the best intentions, families and teachers cannot always protect children from traumatic events in these uncertain times. Dr Stanley Greenspan (2002) gives four basic principles in helping to develop a secure child:

- *spending time together as a family*—establishing warm, nurturing relationships
- *expressing feelings*—assisting children to recognize and give words to feelings with empathy, paraphrasing to extend the conversation and meaning
- *reassurance*—couched in reality that the child can understand at her level
- *contributions and helping others*—adults leading children to gain confidence and overcome helplessness

Teachers have incredible belief in the capacity for the spirit to overcome difficult situations. This leads them to assist every child learning **coping skills**. The child's competency and empowerment will help bring joy and happiness out of deprivation. When children learn coping skills, they can generalize to any situation that is unpleasant. In this way, they can address the difficulty in an emotionally healthy way.

Coping skills are learned in the same ways other skills are learned. The first step is the recognition of the cause of the problem. This will help the child, at her developmental level, understand why she has this feeling. The emotion is named, and the normalcy of these feelings will help the child move toward a solution. For example: "You're not happy today because you didn't want to say good-bye to your dad and see him leave you. Everyone feels sad sometimes when they want to be with someone and they can't. What are some things you could do until he comes back?"

Adults can role model coping mechanisms for children. "I think I'll put on this happy record. It always makes me feel like smiling when I hear this song." Some direct instruction can take place by using discussions following books or puppet scenarios in which characters have similar feelings of sadness or loneliness. Helping children to learn ways to deal with their feelings is a part of the social-emotional curriculum.

Anger and Aggression

EXERCISE Using a separate sheet of paper, list 10 things that make you angry. What do you do when you are angry?

DEVELOPMENTAL STAGES OF ANGER. Anger grows from the unmet needs of the self. When a baby rolls over and gets stuck next to the bars of the crib, that cry is an angry one. She wants to move, but something is preventing her from carrying out that urge to move. That same feeling will overcome her 20 years later when she is late for work but stuck in traffic. The response is usually different (sometimes not). Anger is energizing. It motivates the child to chase down the one who took his tricycle while he was off picking dandelions. It enables the adult to clean the whole house after an argument with a friend. Some of those actions may address the cause of the anger, while others act as a valve to let off steam. This **displacement** of anger's energy has been the subject of much research, with varying results. The major objection to displacement is that it does not solve the problem, just vents the energy.

In the child's second year, she is seeking to be autonomous, to rule herself. She is angry when those attempts are resisted, even if it is for her own safety. Her lack of full language development makes it difficult for her to express her desires or her feelings about being thwarted or denied, so anger and frustration are increased (Figure 5–7). The egocentricism

Figure 5–7 Tantrums are common in toddlers, displaying newly developed emotions without the inner controls to manage them.

contributes to angry feelings. The child can only see her own point of view. She cannot understand why she cannot have the tricycle back after leaving it for 10 minutes, just because she wants it. She wants it, so she believes she should have it. With the struggle for autonomy, it is not surprising that defiance, an angry stance against authority, would begin in the second year. The battle of wills is beginning here, and depending on the child's temperament and the parenting style, it may be a long, difficult one or less severe.

Toward the end of the second year, a more complicated form of anger—jealousy—appears. It could be caused by adult attention diverted away from the child or a desirable object seen in the hands of someone else. A common reaction to this jealousy is a temper tantrum. These are often seen in the grocery store, or the mall, where there is so much visual stimulation. Attractive, desirable objects are all around, but so are restrictions the child cannot understand. They are told not to touch when their mother is touching. They are told they cannot have it when it is placed at eye level and within their reach.

The temper tantrum can be seen in the classroom for just the same reasons. With the teacher's time divided among several children, demands for time and attention are many and are divided. Equipment and materials in the toddler room are well thought out to provide many duplicates so that competition for toys is kept to a minimum. Tantrums will still occur, so the teacher should be prepared to understand their causes and deal with them in an understanding way. He gives attention to the causes and the safety of the child, not the behavior. That prevents it from becoming a battle of wills.

AGGRESSION. Aggression is the display of anger that results in physical or emotional damage to people or property. Most infants begin to use physical aggression between 1 and 2 years of age, peaking by age 3 in competition for limited resources and declining steadily by age 11 (Tremblay, 2004). Aggression has been the subject of much research. Jacquelyn Gentry of the American Psychological Association states, "Kids who see constructive ways to deal with anger, frustration, and disappointment are learning violence prevention" (quoted in Chamberlin, 2000, p. 54). Genetic or biological causes are being researched to learn if medications or genetic manipulation could reduce aggressiveness. Family influence on aggressive behavior is being studied to identify the cycle over the generations and try to intervene in its recurrence. Society's influence, especially violent television programming, has been the focus of a large segment of the aggression research, with much of it pointing to high correlations. The predictability and treatment of childhood aggression as well as the influences of sex differences on aggression are other aspects of these studies. All of these underscore the problematic nature of childhood aggression and the complexity of its effects on behavior. These cannot be minimized or trivialized, but there are some basic understandings about children and aggression that every teacher should recognize.

EXERCISE **What does aggression in the classroom look like? Make a list. Scary, isn't it?**

But adults must understand this: *Aggression is developmental*. Children are aggressive at various predictable stages (Kostelnik, Whiren, Soderman, & Gregory, 2006) (Figure 5–8).

Two- and three-year-olds display aggressiveness mainly to attain or maintain possession of items or territories. They will use physical violence, hitting, kicking, and biting to keep or get what they want. Two-year-old aggressiveness is described as instrumental aggression. It works! Hit the person who has the toy and he lets go. Knock the person off the bicycle so now she can get on. As language skills increase, the child can speak rather than act, and eventually negotiate. However, some factors such as young mothers who smoke, younger siblings, and low income have been found to predict that an aggressive very young child 17–42 months old has a higher risk of more serious antisocial behavior in adolescence (Tremblay et al., 2004). This study of 500 children concluded that interventions in learning less aggressive and more prosocial behaviors at this age would have more of an impact than similar efforts 5 to 10 years later.

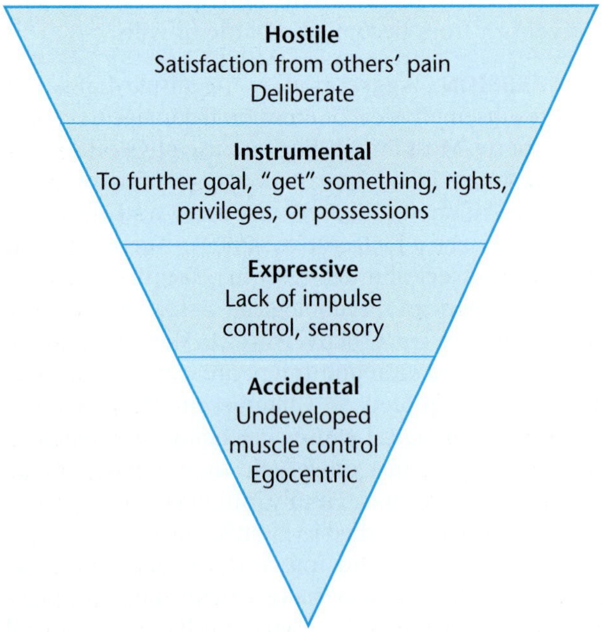

Figure 5–8 Types of Aggression.

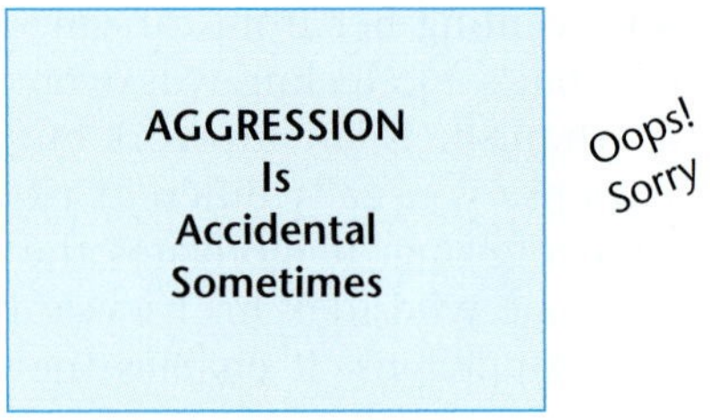

Figure 5–9 Accidental Aggression.

Preschoolers are beginning to use words to express their desires but may still be resorting to grabbing, stealing, or hiding items to keep them. Early school-age children use negotiation more often but shift from physical aggression to verbal aggression. Name-calling, mean talk, and threatening to withdraw friendships are the ways school-age children are aggressive.

Aggression Can Be Accidental. Young children are physically uncoordinated. Much of the hurtful actions take place because they are inaccurate walkers and touchers (Figure 5–9). Stepping on each others' fingers, exploratory touches that end up hurting, and manipulation of materials and equipment in ways that hurt someone else are common. While digging vigorously in the sand, it flies into someone's eyes. While walking through the block area, she knocks down a pile of blocks. A child slides down the slide and knocks down the person standing at the bottom. All are incidents that can be classified as aggression but were unintentional. However, young children cannot understand intentionality. If they are hurt, they interpret it as aggression and feel vindicated in hitting back. When the adult says, "She didn't mean it," those words have little meaning for the young child. The observant adult can only reduce this type of aggression by creating a safe environment and with constant supervision. Positive guidance techniques such as, "Shovel the sand into the bucket," "Build inside these dividing lines," or "Wait to slide down until that person is out of the way" can help preschool children have a little more control over their behavior.

Aggression Can Be Changed to Assertion. The adult will not always be present to prevent scuffles over toys or disagreements over turns or rights. Physical aggression, typical in early childhood, becomes less

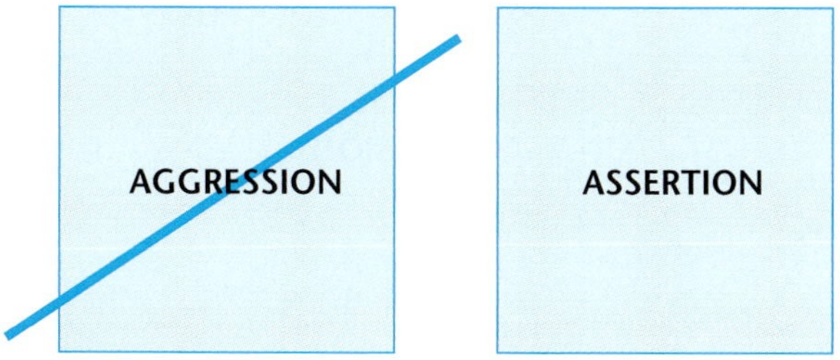

Figure 5–10 Aggression—No! Assertion—Yes!

frequent with development as **executive function** increases. Executive function (Seguin & Zelazo, 2005) is the ability to self-regulate thought, action, and emotion because of the development of cognitive and neural skills. Helping children become more assertive is another of those lessons that have many rewards (Figure 5–10). The child who can express what he wants or needs is more likely to receive it than the child who grabs. The child who can defend himself verbally from aggressors gains self-esteem and prevents himself from becoming a victim. The assertion skills will give the individual the autonomy to make their own needs known. When others must guess, they may do so incorrectly. Assertion, too, is developmental. It progresses from the two-year-old saying, "Mine," to the three-year-old saying, "I had that first," and the four-year-old saying, "Maybe we could take turns."

Aggressiveness Is Not an Outcome of Child Care but of Strict Discipline. Studies by Belsky and others have reported that children in child care are more aggressive than those children reared exclusively at home (Belsky, 2002; Haskins, 1985; Thornburg, Pearl, Crompton, & Ispa, 1990) (Figure 5–11). Caldwell, a researcher with the National Institute of Child Health and Human Development, refutes Belsky's conclusions by pointing out that the high incidence of aggression was correlated with multiple factors, such as maternal sensitivity (2001). A study of more than 3,000 Canadian 2- and 3-year-olds found that those cared for by their own parents but in high-risk families displayed more aggression than those in high-risk families but in child care. This is another example in the growing body of research that shows punitive adult behavior increases child aggression. It calls for families and teachers to develop more appropriate discipline strategies. Children in child care may display increased aggression. When children see the aggressor getting what she wants, getting attention, or other children copying the aggressive behavior, increased aggressive acts result (Goldstein, Arnold, Rosenberg, Stowe, & Ortiz, 2001). Teacher presence and prevention of aggression were cited as important to prevent the chain reaction of aggression.

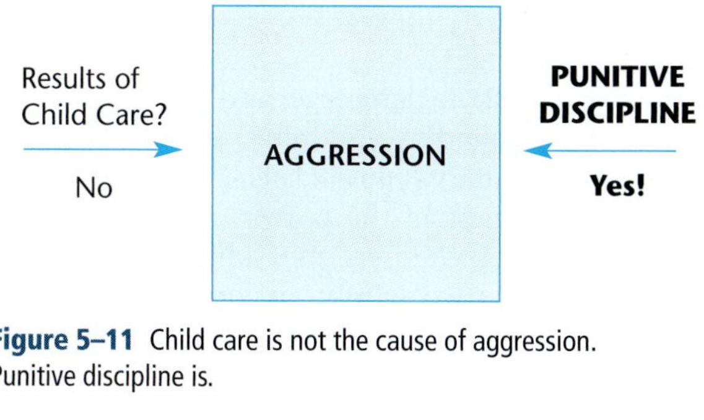

Figure 5–11 Child care is not the cause of aggression. Punitive discipline is.

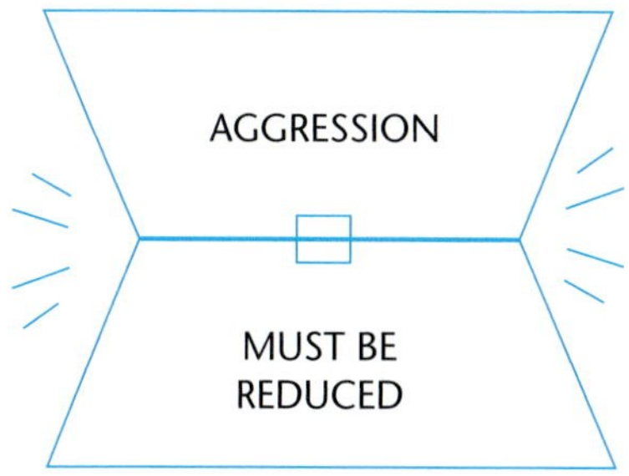

Figure 5–12 Aggression must be reduced!

Aggression Must Be Reduced. The first reason to reduce aggression is safety, in the classroom or at home (Figure 5–12). This is not just for the present, but for the future. Bullying has come into national focus following tragic school violence events. More than 30 percent of school youth reported participating in bullying behavior or being bullied themselves (Nansel et al., 2001), and a majority of former bullies had at least one violent crime conviction. Garbarino (1999), who has studied boys who have been involved in violence, says that they suffer from "emotional illiteracy," a restricted range of emotional expression and a restricted language to express emotions. Many studies have shown that aggressiveness in the early elementary grades predicts aggressiveness in early adulthood (Huesmann, Eron, & Lefkowitz, 1984). This continuity is disturbing yet holds the promise for early childhood education. The goal of emotional control is a critical one. Lowering aggression before the early elementary age can have long-lasting effects. Farrington's study (1991) found high percentages of other causes for aggression. Economic deprivation, family criminality, poor child-rearing behavior, and school failure were all measurable at 8 to 10 years of age. Physically abused and neglected children are at risk of antisocial behavior (Finzi, Ram, Har-Even, Shnit, & Weizman, 2001), and a meta-analysis of the use of violent video games found a correlation to aggressive behavior in children and young adults (Anderson & Bushman, 2001).

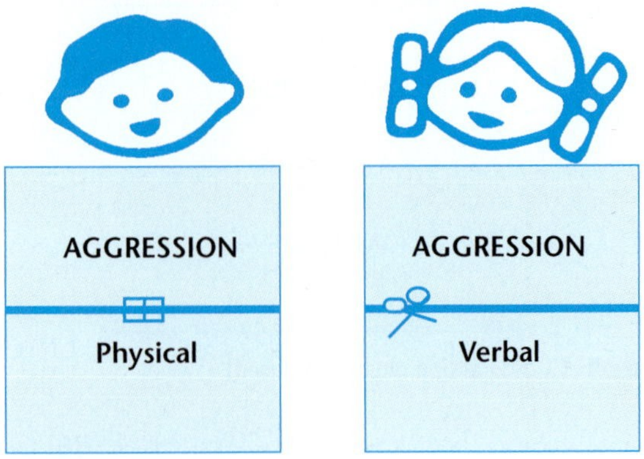

Figure 5–13 Differences in Aggression of Boys and Girls.

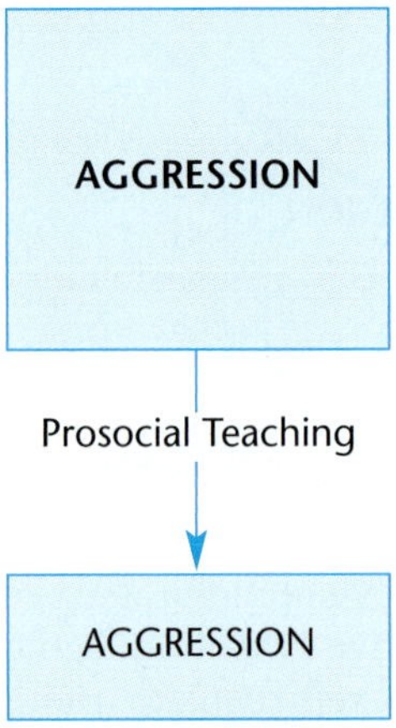

Figure 5–14 Prosocial teaching reduces antisocial behavior, including aggression.

Aggression in Boys and Girls. For many years, research has looked at hostile aggression as a greater problem for boys than girls (Figure 5–13). More boys are reported by teachers and families as aggressive, peaking at three years of age. Archer (2004) studied more than 40 other studies examining physical aggression in boys and girls and analysis showed that boys were more physically aggressive but that aggression declined rapidly after the preschool years. It has been found that first grade is a critical point in boys' pathway to or away from aggression (Kellam, Ling, Merisca, Brown, & Ialongo, 1998), and that girls are actually more aggressive than boys but in relational aggression that is displayed by exclusion: "You can't play with us" (Crick, Ostrov, Appleyard, Jansen, & Casas, 2004). Other researchers suggest that while girls may be less physically aggressive in the school years, the more aggressive girls tended to display more physical aggression in their teens (Tremblay et al., 2004):

- More became adolescent mothers.
- More were single parents.
- They experienced higher levels of psychiatric disorders.
- They had children who were more aggressive.

No matter what the cause, aggression is a problem in group settings of children, in the home, and in society as a whole. A task of the early childhood field, then, is to attempt to reduce the aggression.

Aggression Can Be Reduced. Children can learn to exhibit prosocial behavior through a variety of strategies (Figure 5–14):

1. Label prosocial acts as they occur naturally.
2. Point out instances where unintentional lack of kindness was shown and describe an alternate, prosocial approach.
3. Create opportunities for children to cooperate.
4. Create opportunities for children to help.
5. Use prosocial reasoning when talking with children.
6. Reward prosocial behavior.
7. Administer group rewards.
8. Demonstrate a variety of prosocial behaviors.
9. Demonstrate constructive ways of responding to other people's prosocial behavior.
10. Be positive when engaging in prosocial behavior.
11. Point out the prosocial behaviors modeled by yourself and others.
12. Use positive attribution to increase children's prosocial self-images. (Kostelnik et al., 2006, pp. 435–437)

To promote social and emotional competence, the Teaching Pyramid (Figure 5–15) (Fox, Dunlap, Hemmeter, Joseph, & Strain, 2003) illustrates that positive relationships with children and families is the foundation for early educators. It is supported by an environment of high-quality early education, including social skills curricula, and positive intensive individualized intervention for children with persistent challenges.

Novick (2002), a language and literacy expert, suggests that expanding children's (especially boys') emotional vocabulary helps in social interactions and brings an awareness of the power of words to hurt or heal. Teaching children the skill of negotiation has been used successfully in one Head Start's Fussbusters initiative (Gillespie & Chick, 2001). In it, classroom disputes were discussed at a Peace Table.

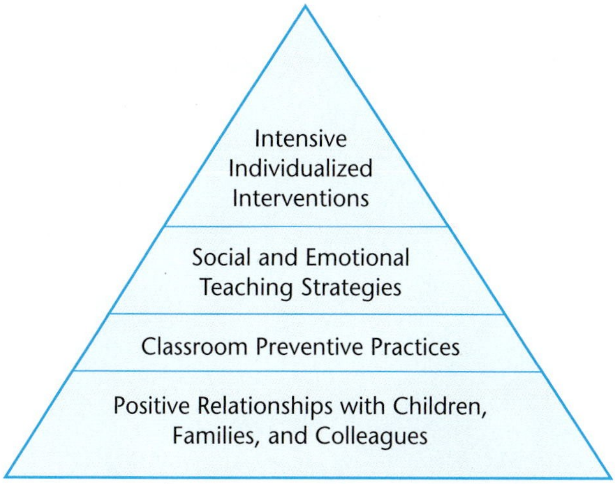

Figure 5–15 Teaching Pyramid. (Courtesy of Fox, L., Dunlap, G., Hemmeter, M. L., Joseph, G. E., & Strain, P. S. (2003). The teaching pyramid: A model for supporting social competence and preventing challenging behavior in young children. *Young Children, 58* (4), 48–52.)

A classmate not in the dispute but chosen by participants mediated the conversation. Children developed their own set of classroom rules, and conflicts were reduced when children took control of their own solutions. In another initiative, a whole-school bullying intervention was found to be more effective than a focus on individual students (Bullying Prevention, 2002). Educators are becoming more aware of the social effects of aggression on learning and are infusing curriculum with social development objectives.

Fear and Shyness

EXERCISE What are you afraid of?

FEAR AND DEVELOPMENT. The first fear is of strangers. That only happens after the child has developed an awareness of separateness from others and has formed mental images of those familiar faces that are seen frequently. Sometimes even these may cause terrified screams. This change, at around six months, signals a changing cognitive development. The infant is constantly matching new pictures with the old. Any discrepancy—glasses/no glasses, hair up/hair down—that does not match the mental image triggers the fear response (Figure 5–16).

Other fears develop around two-and-a-half once a child's thinking is more advanced. Fears develop from the child's inability to make sense of the world. With limited understanding, everything is magic and anything is possible. There could be a grizzly bear under the bed. The house might blow away. The closet might be full of scary things that come out at night. These fears can be planted by tales the child hears from other people, adults included. Television or a fantasy book, read for fun and imagination, can produce fears. Fears of monsters, of nightmares, and of being hurt persist into the sixth and seventh year, when a firmer understanding of reality and fantasy is formed.

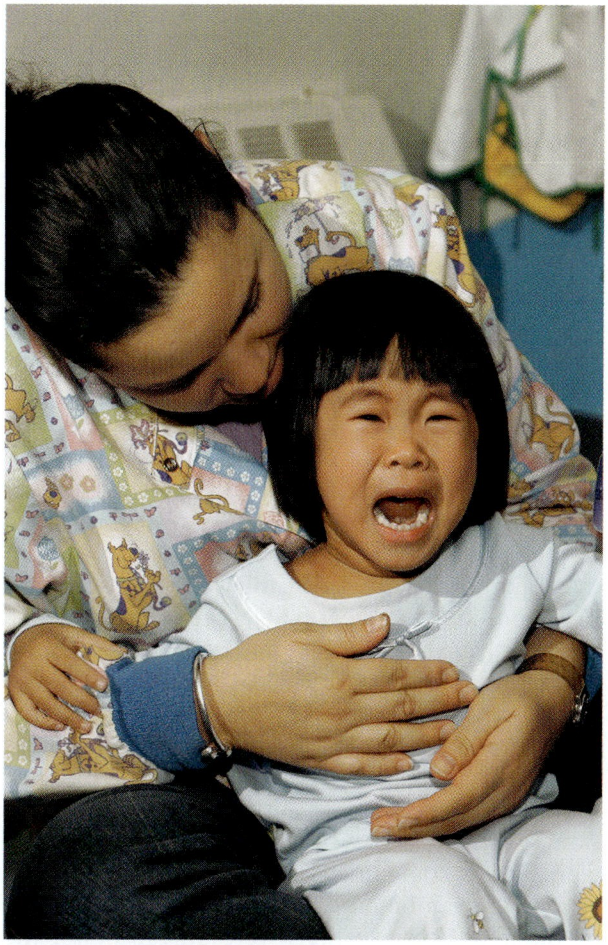

Figure 5–16 Children have many fears.

EXERCISE What does fear look like? Describe the physical changes that take place when you are afraid. How can others tell you are afraid? What helps quell the fear?

Fear is exhibited by wide-open eyes; screaming; crying; rigid body; sometimes uncontrollable trembling; retreat or withdrawal; or seeking adult help.

Some of the same strategies to help the child deal with anger can be used with fear. Talking about the fear by naming the emotion, not denying the feeling, and working together to help the child cope with the feeling are approaches that have been successful. The child can be encouraged to draw or act out the fear, write or dictate a story about it, or eventually face up to it little by little.

SHAME, A FORM OF FEAR. During the second year, when the child is struggling with autonomy, a stronger sense of guilt or shame is developed. This shows that the thinking processes have been categorizing actions as acceptable and not acceptable. This is a necessary step in moral development. When the child does something perceived as unacceptable, feelings of shame develop. These are extremely strong in children who have strong family authority without the opportunity to make decisions for themselves.

Four- and five-year-olds are in what Lickona (1983) calls Stage 1 of Moral Development, "You Should Do What You're Told." Children at this age, he says, believe that "what's right is doing what grown-ups tell you and the reason to do what you're told is you could get in trouble if you don't" (p. 114). Children who develop shame are those who are constantly reminded that they are not doing as they were told. It sometimes leads them to believe there is something inherently wrong with them. It may be the adult's expectations were unrealistic for the child's ability to comply. The feelings of inadequacy and shame are all the child knows in this situation.

Figure 5–17 Children who are labeled "shy" often continue that behavior.

SHYNESS, A FORM OF FEAR. Shyness may be a type of fear that appears at the end of the first year because so many situations and people are new. The child at this age realizes the separateness from parents. The new freedom in mobility and competency is accompanied by feelings of inadequacy. Extra attention causes them discomfort (Figure 5–17). They are often most comfortable observing or withdrawing from the action until they are sure they can function. This should be accepted as a feeling not to be denied, changed, or negated. The adult helps the child find ways to understand and cope with the feeling. Empty praise is not helpful, nor is labeling like "the shy one." Care should be taken to give opportunities without pushing.

Shyness in our culture carries many messages: feminine/masculine, powerful/weak, smart/slow, low/high self-esteem, bold/timid. Swallow (2000) says that 20 percent of children are born shy and another 20 percent develop shyness before adulthood. Possible causes for developing shyness may be a stage the child is going through, a trauma, teasing, moving, poor parenting, or school pressures. He says, "Shyness is a personality style shared by millions" (p. 9). But shyness can interfere with development, school performance, and social experiences. The teacher should

- get to know each child as an individual.
- provide quiet and observation spaces in the classroom.
- make all children aware of the routine and changes.
- use transition techniques that allow for children to conclude previous activity before moving on.
- give choices in participation, allowing observing without embarrassment.
- work with family to determine the best approach for each child.

CHILDREN UNDER STRESS. Stress is most often seen in physical reactions of crying, withdrawal, aggressive outbursts, and self-comforting behavior

@ it happened to me

The Beginning of Conscience

I was talking with the mother of a two-year-old when the mother looked down. Her little girl had a fistful of little pieces of paper. She admonished her, "Don't throw those pieces on the floor." The little girl looked up at her mom, closed her eyes, and opened her hand. This was a great example of a beginning conscience. She only believed something was wrong if someone is watching. She displayed her egocentric thinking: If she did not see it, neither did her mother.

Do you have an IT HAPPENED TO ME story about seeing the beginning of conscience? I'd love to read it. Please send it to WeekbyWeek@thomsonlearning.com

such as hair twirling, thumb sucking, and biting fingernails, but it can also manifest itself in a more internalized way, such as headaches or stomachaches. Young children are more likely to either distance themselves or communicate distress in some way other than verbally, whereas older children learn to try to problem-solve or verbalize the feelings and possible reasons (Jewett & Peterson, 2002). Earlier in the chapter we discussed the resiliency or coping strategies that help children deal with negative feelings, but there are some basic things that teachers can do to assist in this area.

There are three major sources of **stress** for children. The first is within the child, from a temperament that is slow to adjust to change and fearful of new people and experiences. As the child matures and builds confidence, the feeling of stress due to change may dissipate or the child may develop coping mechanisms to alleviate the negative feelings. Stress may cause the child to become more withdrawn, less socially outgoing, and less prone to engage in risky behavior.

The family can be a source of stress for the child. An abusive or neglectful family is stressful and damaging to developing social and emotional well-being. Family situations such as poverty, ill health, death, divorce, remarriage, new siblings, and moving are stressful as well. Even families with no pathology and who only want the best for their child may involve the child in so many scheduled activities that the child has no downtime, no time to relax or unwind naturally, which can be stressful.

The world itself is a stressful place. Instant and graphic images of dramatic, scary events such as war, accidents, disease, and famine play out in every living room, giving the child (and adults too) a feeling of vulnerability, leaving all to question, "Am I safe anywhere? Will it happen to me? Can anybody take care of me and protect me?" It is not surprising that children display signs of stress. Natural disasters and tragic national/international events reach young ears, eyes, and minds. Teachers need to be prepared to support young children and assist their families through these traumas with peaceful classrooms, stress-reducing activities, and secure, reliable relationships and resources.

The Emotionally Secure Environment

The role of the family and early childhood environment is to reduce the effects of negative emotions. They can help the child develop healthy attitudes, inner controls, and acceptable expressions. It begins with an atmosphere of mutual trust between the home and the program or school. There are predictable room arrangements, and routines are reassuring and stress-reducing. The rooms are physically comfortable, without too much sensory stimulation. The curriculum is appropriate for the age and stage of the child, reflecting an attitude of acceptance of mistakes and responsiveness to the individual. Learning activities promote internal satisfaction rather than emphasis on strict obedience or pleasing the adult. The schedule gives freedom to move, make choices, and use creative play outlets. These all contribute to a stress-free environment, control of negative emotions, encouragement of the positive ones of interest, curiosity, and enjoyment. This is accomplished by assessing the children's developmental levels and planning curriculum from topics or themes or projects that come from the children's world.

EXERCISE Using a separate sheet of paper, make a list of prosocial (caring and empathetic) actions you would like to see in your classroom. Now make a list of antisocial actions you probably witnessed but wished you had not. (These are typical behaviors of young children without emotional self-control.)

it happened to me

A Scary Dream

A four-year-old girl came into day care one morning, carrying her blanket and looking very serious. (No one spoke to her father as he dropped her off. No one greeted the little girl or noticed her facial or body expressions.) I was there observing a student teacher involved in an activity, who also did not notice the girl. She walked over to me, a perfect stranger, and laid her head on my shoulder.

"You look like you're still sleepy," I said.

"No, I had a bad dream last night," she said quietly.

"Do you remember what the dream was about?" I asked.

"It was scary. Dreams are what you think about when you're sleeping." That was profound, I thought.

"But dreams aren't real," I replied, thinking that might help.

"I know, but you still wake up scared." How true. I needed a four-year-old to remind me that even unreal things can make us feel real feelings. We trust that someone will notice, care, give voice to our fears, and help us face them not feeling alone. *Listen to the children.*

Do you have an IT HAPPENED TO ME story about a child trying to express emotions? I'd love to read it. Please send it to WeekbyWeek@thomsonlearning.com

This is the connection between emotional development and Frequency Counts on prosocial and antisocial actions. They are done occasionally to take the social-emotional temperature of the room. It gives an objective, quantitative measurement of the environment. It may be the temperature is "normal" and nothing else needs to be done. It may reveal there are "hot zones," certain children who are having difficulty controlling aggressive tendencies. They could benefit from some intervention, since aggressive behavior affects social relationships, self-esteem, and ultimately success in school.

The physical environment is the first area to assess in providing for the emotional and prosocial development of children. An environment that is not safe or comfortable may contribute to stress and misbehavior. Kostelnik et al. (2006) identify possible environmental factors that can affect behavior, such as temperature, cleanliness, equipment, and interior design, including color, displays and textures, sound, and lighting.

The Socialization of Emotional Competence

Denham (1998) stresses three components of the socialization of emotional competence: modeling, coaching, and contingency. This is how children learn to comprehend others' emotions, interpret their own feelings, and express their feelings in appropriate ways.

MODELING. Whenever an adult shows emotion, intentionally or not, the child observes the behavior and adds it to his own storehouse of reactions to replay in later situations. He learns the emotional significance of events and common behaviors associated with expression of emotions such as yelling, swearing, crying, silence, increased activity, talking it out, and coping. *Example:* The car is stalled in traffic and the driver leans on the horn and utters some profanity.

COACHING. Talking about emotions is an important function of language. Discussing feelings and their causes and subsequent actions is a way to teach emotional competence. *Example:* "You were angry when you thought Aaron was taking your toy but then you saw that he had one just like yours and got them mixed up. When you said, 'That's mine,' it made him look closely and see the one in his hand wasn't his. Next time you might say, 'I have one like that. Is that one mine or yours?'"

CONTINGENCY. Adult reactions to a child's emotions reflect to the child the seriousness of the event, the adult's concern over it, and a comforting knowledge that the adult understands and will help. *Example:* The child stumbles and hits her head. The adult looks over, assesses the situation, and continues talking or rushes over and says, "Ouch, that must have hurt. Let me see if you need a bandage." Contingency reactions by the adult are moderated by

@ it happened to me

The Red Telephone Struggle

Two four-year-old girls wanted the red telephone in the dramatic play area. They each had a tight hold on an end of the receiver. This meant they were very close together, struggling in a pulling match. Gritting their teeth, looking eye to eye, they each grunted, "I want it," "I want it." I observed this but waited a few seconds to see what would happen. I could have gotten the other phone and talked to them about it, but I waited. It went on longer and longer. Their faces turned red, and neither showed signs of increasing violence nor of giving up. Minutes went by. I had to restrain myself from entering in, but I knew they could learn from the experience and I was curious as to how it would end. Finally, after many minutes of stalemate, one dropped her end, turned, and flounced away. The one left holding the phone (you guessed it) dropped it and flounced off herself.

Do you have an IT HAPPENED TO ME story about children and their emotions? I'd love to read it. Please send it to WeekbyWeek@thomsonlearning.com

the age of the child. Younger children with limited emotional experience need constant reassurance that the adult is watching and cares about emotional situations. As a child gets older, the adult uses more judgment in when to assist or intervene, or when to allow the child to take control of the situation and work it out on her own.

Through observation, children's emotional and social situations are examined closely. From that examination, the teacher takes actions to assist the child to move on in the developmental stage. The adult helps the child recognize emotional and social states, gain control of behavior, feel more competent, and move on to the next level of social development.

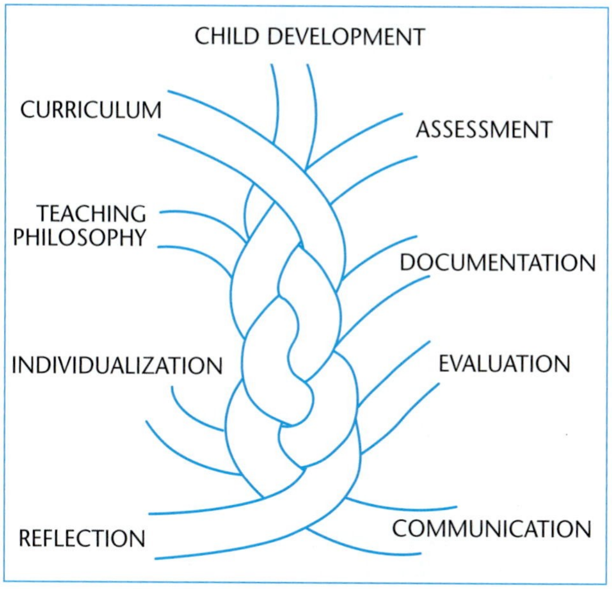

Figure 5–18 Development, assessment, and curriculum are three strands of the braid of appropriate programs for young children.

Observation and recording are closely entwined with curriculum to assist this process. This is similar to making a braid (Figure 5–18).

HELPING ALL CHILDREN WITH EMOTIONAL DEVELOPMENT

Emotional development can be observed in all children as we observe how the classroom environment affects them and how their emotional behaviors affect others. For children who are English language learners, both the culture and the lack of the ability to communicate feelings make it more difficult for the teacher to interpret and understand what the child is feeling. It may be manifested in extreme shyness, unwillingness to participate, or in crying or temper tantrums. The teacher, working with the family, can assess the child's abilities in her first language and then individualize the instruction, accepting non-verbal behavior without pressure, providing for successful solitary play episodes, and interacting with the child in a patient manner, providing a safe way for the child to try out new vocabulary words and short expressions.

For children with developmental delays or disabilities, emotions are a large part of the child's successful adjustment. When children with physical disabilities are included in programs with other children, self-comparisons are made. The other children are also learners with still-developing social skills, understanding, and empathy. Fear, rejection, and curiosity may be the emotions displayed by the

TOPICS IN OBSERVATION

The Assessment and Curriculum Braid

EXERCISE Try making a French braid in a volunteer's hair. Here are the directions: Section the top and separate into three parts. Place the left strand across the center. Bring the center strand to the left, switching their positions. Place the right strand across the center, bring the center strand to the right, switching their positions. Gather additional hair from behind the left ear, and add it to the strand that is now on the left. Place the strand with the added hair across the center strand. Use the right thumb to gather additional hair from the back of the right ear and add it to the strand that is now on the right. Place the strand with the added hair across the center strand. Keep taking additional hair and combining it with the main strands.

Think of development, assessment, and curriculum as the three main strands (Figure 5–18). It all begins with the knowledge of child development; the normal expectations of how the child will change over time physically, socially, emotionally, and cognitively. Every group of children brings its own range of development, interests, and today's reality. Assessing their knowledge and interest will determine the curriculum vehicle. Reggio Emilia's projects (Edwards, Gandini, & Foreman, 1993) are based on children's interests and happenings in their town. The projects about the race or the fountains in town demonstrate how the curriculum was real to the children before the activities began. They could then relate it to prior knowledge. Left on their own, children will play the Olympics *after* rather than *before* they happen. The children have then seen it on television and have heard their parents talk about it. It is a part of their real world. When teachers introduce the Olympic theme weeks before it happens, it is a part of the teachers' world but not the child's.

Knowledge of what two-year-olds—or threes or fours—are like is one of the main strands in the braid. The specific group is observed and assessed through knowledgeable eyes. They are measured against a range of expectations. They also are observed to poll their interests. This makes assessment another strand of the braid. Documentation is the process of writing down what is seen. It will be remembered and used for a variety of purposes. That also will be a strand that runs through the braid, making a formalized record of what is known, done, and questioned.

Curriculum is the strand that carries the experiences and opportunities for exploration and discovery through the senses. By planning activities that children touch, taste, hear, see, and smell, all the developmental areas are being stimulated. If the experiences are familiar to their world, they make associations or matches: "Oh, I tasted this before. It's a sweet pickle." If the experiences are new ones, they seek to find equilibrium: "This is *called* a pickle but it's *made* out of a cucumber?" The association with the cucumber is unbalanced. What makes a pickle a pickle? A worthy curriculum theme? Science is seeing cause-and-effect changes. Math is following the recipe. Language is learning vocabulary and new, fun songs and rhymes about pickles. Visual perception is the comparison of shades of green in varieties of pickles. They appear in drawings and easel paintings. Social interactions take place in exploring who likes dill and who likes sweet pickles. People like different kinds of pickles, and people are different like pickles. Playing "Who's in the Pickle Jar" promotes social and physical development as children run to catch each other. The unstressful, nonacademic theme will produce emotional relaxation through enjoyment and self-esteem: "These are the pickles I made in school today. Bet you can't guess

TOPICS IN OBSERVATION *(continued)*

they're made out of cucumbers." Weaving all these activities together is the web, that very fragile but definite unending thread.

Implementation of curriculum is another strand of the braid. The teacher may have the background training in the "plan, do, review" model of High/Scope (Hohmann & Weikart, 2002). The teacher may follow the Creative Curriculum (Trister-Dodge, 2002), which carries the curriculum through the physical environment. Montessori training may lead the teacher to set up formal lessons with defined procedures for children to follow. If the teacher is like most, the teaching philosophy or professional practice is eclectic. It is a combination of many philosophies that fit into their own learning style, personality, educational background, and also the program goals.

While the curriculum is being carried out, the teacher is the observer. She notes such things as how each child is running in the game, who can count the pickles in the jar, and who has never seen a cucumber before. The teacher writes down the wonderful stories they tell about how the seeds got in there and what will happen if they are swallowed. Every developmental area can be evaluated as children interact with the environment without intrusion or pressure.

There will be children on both ends of the range of normal who will need some adaptation of the environment. The child who has not yet reached the levels of most of the other children will need to have some teacher assistance and facilitation to bridge the gap. This is what Vygotsky calls the **zone of proximal development** (Hills, 1992). It allows the child to approximate a level of competency, held up by the teacher's scaffold or mediation. The observer will document (to remember) what the child knows, what he can do, how he behaves, and how he feels about himself. This is all while observing the pickle game.

The teacher evaluates each child against what is expected for this age or developmental stage. Added to that is what the teacher knows about this particular child's circumstances. Because of that knowledge, a decision is made to modify the curriculum for a particular child. A child may need to have a pickle sign placed in his hand as the signal that it is his turn to chase because he cannot hear his name called. Another may need to hear the word in Spanish. The observer may notice that a particular child is easily frustrated when matching the lids to the pickle jars. She notes to take a closer look at possible vision or small muscle problems. The observer may notice that a child was reading all the ingredients to the recipe chart. That child needs a simple reader about pickles to keep him interested and a way to tape record so that others can listen to it. By writing this down (documenting) the teacher will remember to follow through on the plan, or follow up on questions to be answered.

The evaluations are communicated first to the family. The best way is that face-to-face exchange about specific incidents and their relation to the child's developing knowledge and skill. This is a form of family education about child development and shows the family that the teacher is closely watching and recognizing the accomplishments of their child. The child should also hear of their accomplishments. Empty valuative words like "Wonderful" or "Good" are meaningless compared to specific statements such as, "When you counted those pickles, it was higher than I've ever heard you count before." The communication of evaluations of child development can be used effectively to initiate early intervention. Through careful observation and documentation, developmental concerns are raised that need to be investigated further. After additional observations and consultations with other team members,

(continued)

TOPICS IN OBSERVATION *(continued)*

the validity of the concern is confirmed. The family and teacher can pursue a course of action to address the concern.

The teacher activates the curriculum and evaluates development. Another strand in the braid reflects on the professional and personal efforts of the process. Attitudes are monitored and decisions reconsidered. Receptiveness to change is measured. The reflective practitioner returns to the strands of child development and assessment. The process begins again.

As this braid weaves in all these components, it becomes stronger. When any of the strands is weak, broken, or absent, the result is not as effective. In many programs, the documentation of assessment is the weakest strand, leaving individualization and communication to rely on memory and chance. Those are too important to not be supported by data, collected in a natural way through multiple sources. That is how assessment/documentation/evaluation drives curriculum.

What does observing and recording have to do with curriculum? Everything or nothing—it depends on the program and the teacher. All the methods and assignments in this book could be used to compile a vast and impressive Portfolio on each child. It would be useless if it only showed where the child was at any given point. It becomes dynamic information when it is used to help guide curriculum. "How is that done?" becomes the question.

How is curriculum formed? Schweinhart (1995) studied the use of various curriculum models that are being used by early childhood leaders and how extensively they were used. High/Scope, the Creative Curriculum, and the Bank Street model were the three predominant curriculums studied. Findings suggest that less than one-third espouse any one model while more than two-thirds use parts of some models, though not extensively. Other models such as the Reggio Emilia approach and the DLM (Wright Group) research-based curriculum are being used, though it appears that usually curriculum is individualized for program needs and to fit teaching styles of individual teachers.

Schweinhart's study was undertaken to try to measure and compare the outcomes of various models. With this much variation in how they are used, it is impossible to assess the outcomes of any one model using standardized testing. By observing and assessing individual children, however, the curriculum and the teaching methods can be evaluated, not just measured against a standard, to become the basis for change. That is what Rosegrant and Bredekamp (1991) call transformational curriculum—curriculum that helps bring about change. One strand of the braid is assessment of prosocial and emotional control with a Frequency Count. Another is implementation of curriculum. The third is evaluation of individual children's social interactions and emotional nature and controls. These are woven together in the braid to make a strong, efficient, and neat model.

classmates, causing loneliness, doubt, and low self-esteem in the child with the disability. The teacher prepares the other children in the group, just as the environment is prepared, to receive the child with a disability. Providing adaptive apparatus, such as wheelchairs, walkers, hearing aid cases, and eyeglass frames, the children can experiment with how it feels to use these things. Many more books now include children with differing abilities, both in regular storylines and in nonfiction child-level explanations of disabilities.

Children with emotional disorders in the classroom will affect the emotions of both the staff and other children. Difficult behaviors, aggressiveness, withdrawal, and acting out are always challenges for staff. For the child with chronic emotional disorders, it is an even greater challenge. Acceptance and knowledge of the disorder and approaches to use will be part of the preparation for this child. Information from families, records from other professionals working with the child and the family, and individual research will provide the teacher with a background and strategies to deal with the child. The other children can be informed and helped to understand the nature of this child's needs so that a caring atmosphere is created for all.

HELPING PROFESSIONALS FOR EMOTIONAL CONCERNS

Helping professionals, such as social workers, psychologists, or psychiatrists, may be involved in consultations, assisting in emotional development difficulties. The staff will use each other for resources to seek answers to emotional behavior problems. Discussions with parents in the initial interview and intake process, in open communication opportunities such as open house, parent meetings, and social events give the teacher insight about the child. When all other attempts are not working, a more formalized discussion with the parents may be necessary. The emotional realm is subjective and also personally connected with the families' and teacher's emotions. This conference should be approached sensitively, seeking a partnership of ways to help the child. Caution is taken not to lay blame, make diagnoses, or criticize. The teacher is prepared to suggest referrals for further evaluation. They may include the following:

medical personnel—pediatrician, neurologist (treatment of brain and central nervous system disorders)
mental health professionals—psychiatrists, psychologists, social workers, therapists
support groups—mentor families; family resource centers; cooperative extension agents; school, religious, or community agencies

OTHER METHODS

Other Methods to Record Emotional Development

Anecdotal/Running Records
Developmental Checklist or Rating Scale with emotional development component
Dialogs/Discussions with child about emotions
Media recordings depicting emotions

STANDARDS

Here are selected examples of standards relating to emotional development:

The Head Start Performance Standards (ACF 2005) require programs to work together with families regarding their child's emotional health.

1304.24 Child mental health.

(a) Mental health services.

(1) Grantee and delegate agencies must work collaboratively with parents (see 45 CFR 1304.40(f) for issues related to parent education) by:

(i) Soliciting parental information, observations, and concerns about their child's mental health;
(ii) Sharing staff observations of their child and discussing and anticipating with parents their child's behavior and development, including separation and attachment issues;
(iii) Discussing and identifying with parents appropriate responses to their child's behaviors;
(iv) Discussing how to strengthen nurturing, supportive environments and relationships in the home and at the program;
(v) Helping parents to better understand mental health issues; and
(vi) Supporting parents' participation in any needed mental health interventions

National Association for Family Child Care *Quality Standards for NAFCC Accreditation* (2005)

Part 1. Relationships: The Children with Each Other

1.21 The provider helps children understand their own feelings and those of others.

KEY TERMS

aggression	Frequency Count
coping skills	invulnerable child
core emotions	shyness
displacement	stress
emotional intelligence	temperament
executive function	zone of proximal development
failure to thrive	

Go to the Bind-in-Book CD for:

Frequency Count form
Plan Week 5 Part A, Directions for Frequency Count of Social-Emotional Development, including What to Do with It, Portfolio Overview Example, Sharing with Child and Family, Actions—Read a Book, In the Environment, In the Curriculum, In the Newsletter
Plan Week 5 Part B, Anecdotal Recording of Emotional Development for Group D, including What to Do With It.
Plan Week 5 Part C, Reflective Journal

REFERENCES

Anderson, C. A., & Bushman, B. J. (2001). Effects of violent videogames on aggressive behavior, aggressive cognition, aggressive affect, physiological arousal, and prosocial behavior: A meta-analytic review of the scientific literature. *Psychological Science, 12* (5), 353.

Anthony, J. E., & Cohler, B. J. (Eds.). (1987). *The invulnerable child.* New York: The Guilford Press.

Archer, J. (2004). Sex differences in aggression in real-world settings: A meta-analytic review. *Review of General Psychology*, 8, 291–322.

Bandura, A. (1977). *Social learning theory.* Englewood Cliffs, NJ: Prentice Hall.

Belsky, J. (2002). Quantity counts: Amount of child care and children's socioemotional development. *Journal of Developmental & Behavioral Pediatrics, 23* (3), 167–170.

Bendtro, L., Brokenleg, M., & Van Bockern, S. (2002). *Reclaiming youth at risk.* Bloomington, IN: National Education Service.

Bendtro, L., & Longhurst, J. E. (2005). The resilient brain. *Reclaiming Children & Youth, 14* (1), 52–60, Spring 2005.

Bullying prevention program may reduce aggression. (2002). *The Brown University Child and Adolescent Behavior Letter, 18* (12), 5(1).

Burchard, J. D., & Burchard, S. N. (Eds.). (1987). *Prevention of delinquent behavior.* Beverly Hills, CA: Sage.

Caldwell, B. M. (2001). Déjà vu all over again: A researcher explains the NICHD Study. *Young Children, 56* (4), 58–59.

Chamberlin, J. (2000). Working to create a violence free future for young children. *Monitor on Psychology, 31* (8), 54–55.

Crick, N. R., Ostrov, J. M., Appleyard, K., Jansen, E. A., & Casas, J. F. (2004). Relational aggression in early childhood. In M. Putallaz, & K. L. Bierman (Eds.), *Aggression, antisocial behavior, and violence among girls: A developmental perspective.* New York: Guilford Press.

Denham, S. A. (1998). *Emotional development in young children.* New York: The Guilford Press.

Edwards, C., Gandini, L., & Forman, G. (Eds.). (1993). *The hundred languages of children: The Reggio Emilia approach to early childhood education.* Norwood, NJ: Ablex.

Eisenberger, N., Lieberman, M., & Williams, K. (2003). The pain of social exclusion. *Science, 302,* 290–292.

Erikson, E. H. (1950). *Childhood and society.* New York: Norton.

Farrington, D. P. (1991). Childhood aggression and adult violence: Early precursors and later-life outcomes. In D. J. Furman (1995, January), Helping children cope with stress and deal with feelings. *Young Children, 50* (2).

Finzi, R., Ram, A., Har-Even, D., Shnit, D., & Weizman, A. (2001). Attachment styles and aggression in physically abused and neglected children. *Journal of Youth and Adolescence, 30* (6), 769.

Fox, L., Dunlap, G., Hemmeter, M. L., Joseph, G. E., & Strain, P. S. (2003). The teaching pyramid: A model for supporting social competence and preventing challenging behavior in young children. *Young Children, 49* (4), July 2003.

Garbarino, J. (1999, July/August). *Boys to men: Questions of violence.* Harvard Education Letter Research. Retrieved February 15, 2003, from http://www.edletter.org/past/issues/1999-ja/forum.shtml.

Gillespie, C. W., & Chick, A. (2001). Fussbusters: Using peers to mediate conflict resolution in a Head Start classroom. *Childhood Education, 77* (4), 192–195.

Goldman, D. (1995). *Emotional intelligence: Why it can matter more than IQ.* New York: Bantam Books.

Goldstein, N. E., Arnold, D. H., Rosenberg, J. L., Stowe, R. M., & Ortiz, C. (2001). Contagion of aggression in day care classrooms as a function of peer and teacher responses. *Journal of Educational Psychology, 93* (4), 708.

Greenspan, S. (2002). The secure child: Helping children feel safe and confident in a changing world. Cambridge, MA: Perseus Publishing.

Haskins, R. (1985). Public school aggression among children with varying day-care experience. *Child Development, 56,* 689–703.

Hills, T. W. (1992). Reach potentials through appropriate assessment. In S. Bredekamp, & T. Rosegrant (Eds.), *Reaching potentials: Appropriate curriculum and assessment for young children, Volume 1.* Washington, DC: National Association for the Education of Young Children.

Hohmann, M., & Weikart, D. P. (2002). *Educating young children: Active learning practices for preschool and child care programs.* Ypsilanti, MI: High/Scope Press.

Huesmann, L. R., Eron, L. D., Lefkowitz, M. M., & Walder, L. O. (1984). Stability of aggression over time and generations. *Developmental Psychology, 20,* 1120–1134.

Jewett, J., & Peterson, K. (2002). *Stress and young children.* Urbana, IL: ERIC Clearinghouse on Elementary and Early Childhood Education, ED471911-2002-12-00.

Kellam, S. G., Ling, X., Merisca, R., Brown, C. H., & Ialongo, N. (1998). The effect of the level of aggression in the first grade classroom on the course and malleability of aggressive behavior in middle school. *Development and Psychopathology, 10,* 165–185.

Kostelnik, M. J., Whiren, A. P., Soderman, A. K., & Gregory, K. (2006). *Guiding young children's social development* (5th ed.). Clifton Park, NY: Thomson Delmar Learning.

Lickona, T. (1983). *Raising good children.* New York: Bantam Books.

Nansel, T. R., Overpeck, M., Pilla, R. S., Ruan, W. J., Simons-Morton, B., & Scheidt, P. (2001). Bullying behaviors among US youth: Prevalence and association with psychosocial adjustment. *Journal of American Medical Association, 285,* 2094–2100.

National Association for Family Child Care. (2005). *Quality standards for NAFCC accreditation.* Salt Lake City, UT: Author.

Novick, R. (2002). Learning to read the heart: Nurturing emotional literacy. *Young Children, 57* (3), 84–89.

Papalia, D., Olds, S., & Feldman, R. (2004). *A child's world* (9th ed.). Boston: McGraw Hill.

Peth-Pierce, R. (2000). A good beginning: Sending America's children to school with the social and emotional competence they need to succeed. *Monograph from the Children's Mental Health Foundations and Agencies Network, 9.* Bethesda, MD: National Institute of Mental Health. Available online at http://www.nimh.nih.gov/childhp/fdnconsb.htm.

Rosegrant, T., & Bredekamp, S. (1991). Reaching individual potentials through transformational curriculum. In S. Bredekamp and T. Rosegrant (Eds.), *Reaching potentials: Appropriate curriculum and assessment for young children, Volume 1.* Washington, DC: National Association for the Education of Young Children.

Schweinhart, L. (1995, June). *Early childhood curriculum models: Who needs them?* Research presented at the meeting of the National Institute for Early Childhood Professional Development, San Francisco, CA.

Seguin, J. R., & Zelazo, P. D. (2005). Executive function in early physical aggression. In R. E. Tremblay, W. W. Hartup, & J. Archer, *Developmental origins of aggression.* New York: Guilford Press.

Seligman, J. (July 3, 1995). Testosterone wimping out? *Newsweek,* 61.

Slaby, R. G., Roedell, W. C., Arezzo, D., & Hendrix, K. (1995). *Early violence prevention: Tools for teachers of young children.* Washington, DC: National Association for the Education of Young Children.

Swallow, W. K. (2000). *The shy child: Helping children triumph over shyness.* New York: Warner Books.

Thomas, A., & Chess, S. (1977). *Temperament and development.* New York: Brunner/Mazel.

Thornburg, K. R., Pearl, P., Crompton, D., & Ispa, J. M. (1990). Development of kindergarten children based on child care arrangements. *Early Childhood Research Quarterly, 5,* 27–42.

Tremblay, R. E., Nagin, D.S., Seguin, J. R., Zoccolillo, M., Zelazo, P., Bolvin, M., Perusse, D., & Japel, C. (2004). Physical aggression during early childhood: Trajectories and predictors. *Pediatrics, 114* (1), 43–50, July 2004.

Trister-Dodge, D. (2002). *The creative curriculum for early childhood* (4th ed.). Washington, DC: Creative Associates International, Inc.

U.S. Department of Health and Human Services, Administration for Children and Families. (2005). *Head start performance standards.* Washington, DC: Author.

Watson, J. B. (1914). *Behavior: An introduction to comparative psychology.* New York: Holt, Rinehart, & Winston.

Widen, S. C., & Russell, J. A. (2003). A closer look at preschoolers' freely produced labels for facial expressions. *Developmental Psychology,* 39 (1), 114–128, Jan 2003.

Zimbardo, P., & Radl, S. (1981). *The shy child: A parent's guide to preventing and overcoming shyness from infancy to adulthood.* New York: McGraw-Hill.

RESOURCES

Bailey, R. (2000). *Conscious discipline: 7 basic skills for brain smart classrooms.* Oviedo, FL: Loving Guidance.

Bailey, R. (2000). *Easy to love, difficult to discipline: The 7 basic skills for turning conflict into cooperation.* New York: William Morrow.

Bos, B. (1990). *Together we're better.* Roseville, CA: Turn the Page Press.

Greenspan, S. (2002). *The secure child: Helping children feel safe and confident in a changing world.* Cambridge, MA: Perseus Publishing.

Hyson, M. (2004). *The emotional development of young children* (2nd ed.). New York: Teachers College Press.

Slaby, R. G., Roedell, W. C., Arezzo, D., & Hendrix, K. (1995). *Early violence prevention: Tools for teachers of young children.* Washington, DC: National Association for the Education of Young Children.

Smith, C. A. (1993). *The peaceful classroom: 162 easy activities to teach preschoolers compassion and cooperation.* Mt. Rainier, MD: Gryphon House.

Center on the Social and Emotional Foundations for Early Learning. http://www.vanderbilt.edu/csefel/.

CHAPTER 6

Using Conversations to Listen to Language and Speech

IN THIS CHAPTER

USING CONVERSATIONS AS AN OBSERVATION METHOD

EXERCISE **What might the following sentences tell you about the person speaking?**

"Howdy, y'all."
"I've just had a dialogue with my stock broker . . ."
"When I was in France . . ."
"I'm so stupid . . ."
"Thith ith fun!"
"I ain't got no job."
"Dey gonna come get you bein' bad."
"Wa wa."
"You raise sheep? How do e-w-e do it?" (spells out *ewe*)
"Na na, na na, na."
"You sister him?"

Observing by listening is done naturally all the time. The message received by the listener is not just the words and their meaning. Inferences are made about where the speaker is from, their self-esteem, educational background, social situation, ethnic group, and even mental age. Subtle, and sometimes not so subtle, clues are given about their interests, economics, and experiences. The listener notices teeth formation, facial expression, body language, eye contact, sense of humor, and vocabulary choice. All of these may give more information about the speaker than the actual words spoken.

EXERCISE When you want to know something about the following subjects, whom do you ask?

What postage is due on this package I'm mailing?
How many automobiles were shipped into the United States last year?
How long do I cook a five-pound roast?
What medicine can I take for this cold?
Do I need a haircut?
Where does it hurt?

Figure 6–1 Talking with a child can be interesting and a source of developmental assessment.

To receive a reliable answer to a question, it must be addressed to the person who most likely knows the answer. Scramble the answers to the questions in the preceding exercise to see how foolish it is to ask the wrong person, or even guess the answer. It only makes sense, then, to gather information *about* the child *from* the child. Harste, Woodward, and Burke (1984) use the phrase "the child as the informant." By listening to the child, both what is said and how it is said, information is transferred upon which evaluations are made.

EXERCISE Using a tape recorder, talk to five children of different ages. Try to find a child of one, two, three, four, and five. This tape will be used repeatedly in this chapter to illustrate speech and language development.

Carry on a little conversation beginning with a greeting, "My name is ______. What's your name? How old are you? What are you doing? Where did you get that? What are you going to do with it?"
What differences did you hear in the way children of various ages answered the questions?

Interviewing, or asking children questions to find out what they know or what they are thinking about, is an age-old technique. The early childhood field has a prestigious role model for interviewing children in Piaget (Evans, 1973), who used the "clinical" interview, writing meticulous notes on the questions and answers. He began with his own children but extended his interviews to others to delve deeper into their thinking and understand their wrong answers to questions.

Talking with young children can be interesting and rewarding (Figure 6–1). It also can be frustrating because of their short attention span and egocentricism (only understanding from their own point of view). Sometimes they do not speak clearly enough to be understood. Questioning children brings surprising results: Ask a child, "What color is a banana?" The child may say white or may say yellow. The part we eat is white. Ask a child, "What color is an apple?" The answer may be white. Is that a wrong answer? It probably would be considered wrong on a standardized test, although it is correct technically.

There are many formal tests of speech and language that use picture recognition, imitating letter sounds, comprehension, and sentence completion. These are used primarily by speech and language pathologists in determining a child's level of speech and language ability. The family and the teacher are concerned most of all in communicating with the child. Formal evaluation measures are used only when that communication seems to be hampered by speech or language delays or difficulties.

Social discourse or discussions and questioning methods were first called **action research** by Kurt Lewin in 1948. It is a way for teachers to find out what they want to know and to seek answers about their own classroom. Talking with children and their self-reporting are accepted fact-finding methods (Moxley, Kenny, & Hunt, 1990). Conversations take several forms, depending on the age of the child, situation, and information to be gathered. **Informal conversations** happen all the time in the normal functioning of the child in the environment. As the adult talks with the child about her actions, he asks, "Wow! How did you get that to stand up on that little end like that?" or "Can you think of another way to use these old pieces of plastic someone gave us?" Snack, mealtimes, and discussions after stories are excellent times for informal discussions or interviews. This style allows the conversation to flow in a natural way and to gather spontaneous samples of what the child is doing and thinking. Besides listening to the message, the listener can also examine how the child is using language and the quality of the speech production. It then becomes an informal **diagnostic interview** as well. Interviewing can be a process to confirm a problem that may need remediation. Both casual conversations and structured interviews can be diagnostic.

A more **structured interview** gathers specific information about the child's understanding of certain concepts. The adult sets up items for the child to choose—big/little; short/long; over/under; red/blue—things that go together or things that do not belong. Selected pictures or books often are used to elicit conversation. During the interview, speech and language skills are assessed (Wortham, 2001). An Interest Questionnaire (Almy & Genishi, 1979) can give older children an opportunity to express their likes and dislikes and give insight into a child's happiness or self-esteem, with questions like: "What would you like to know more about?" or "The most interesting thing I have done at our school during the past week is . . ." or "What is your favorite thing to do at school?"

Responses may be written in a log by older children or dictated to the teacher (Figure 6–2). Dictation gives the child a role model for literacy, seeing spoken words translated into permanent print. It also gives the child an opportunity to think and reflect on the past. Through dictation, the child expresses feelings by elaborating on thoughts and feelings. Opinions are stated or interpretations or reasons for an event can be explored. The interview is a little conversation with a purpose. Neuman and Roskos (1993, p. 258) suggest this mini-outline:

A greeting of some kind—"Hello, June."
Expression of interest—"I have some new markers. Would you like to try them?"

Figure 6–2 Children's dictations and drawings give insight into their thinking.

Taking turns at speaking—As June draws, she says, "That's my mom's friend's sister." The teacher asks, "What is she doing?" June replies, "She's going in there . . . shopping. She's meeting her friend and buy something." The teacher asks, "What is she buying?" June says, "Milk . . . and cereal . . . egg . . . and orange!" She smiles broadly. "I see she is carrying something." "Her bag," and pointing to the other hand, "She puts money in there. She's going to bring a flower for her kid."
Some pausing—"No" she says sadly. (pause) "But I get to go the preception!" (pause) "I'm done. I'm going to play now."
Leave-taking, or way to end the conversation—"I enjoyed our little conversation. I'd like to put your drawing and your story about it in our class storybook. May I? I can make a copy of the drawing so you can take the original home." June nods and runs off.

Efficient questioning techniques and skills make the most of the interviewing method. There is a hierarchy of questions (Bryen & Gallaher, 1983) that yield progressively more information while requiring more complex levels of comprehension.

Yes/no questions—"Do you want a drink?"
What (object)—"What's this?"
What (action)—"What are you doing?"
Where (location)—"Where's the dolly?"
What (attributes)—"What color is this?"
Who (persons)—"Who is picking you up today?"
Whose (possession)—"Whose boots are these?"
Which (selection)—"Which cookie cutter do you want?"
When (time)—"When are you going to paint today?"
How (manner)—"How did you make those dots?"
Why (cause-effect)—"Why did that paper rip?" (p. 103)

Each type of question requires more thought, understanding of the *Wh*-questions, and longer, more revealing answers. A **closed question** is one for which the asker already knows the answer and is testing the receiver. All but the last two of the preceding list are closed questions. They may give information about a child's specific knowledge but not about thinking processes or creativity. An **open question** such as "What's another way . . . " or "Can you tell me how . . . ?" gives more insight and are more natural conversation models.

Asking children open-ended questions (those for which the person asking does not know the precise answer) is a technique to help the child think, imagine, and solve problems.

EXERCISE Here are some typical questions. Put a checkmark by the open-ended questions.

- *Observing*—"What do you notice here?"
- *Recall*—"What did you see at the zoo?"
- *Differences*—"How are they different?"
- *Similarities*—"How are these the same?"
- *Ordering*—"Can you order these colors from lightest to darkest?"
- *Grouping*—"Which of these go together?"
- *Labeling*—"What is the name of that group?"
- *Classifying*—"Which cubes here are red?"
- *Concept Testing*—"This cube is blue but does it belong?"
- *Causes*—"Why do you think that happened?"
- *Effects*—"What happens if . . . ?"
- *Feelings*—"How do you think she feels?"
- *Generalizing*—"What usually happens to water in the freezer?"
- *Questioning*—"What could you ask her?"
- *Anticipating*—"What do you think will happen?"
- *Making choices*—"Which one would you like?"

(Adapted from Sigel's Questioning Model in Pelligrini [1991])

All but naming, labeling, classifying, and concept testing are open-ended questions.

Selecting an interview type depends on what the adult wants to know about the child, the child's cognitive level, and the emotional state of the child.

The style of the questioner is also a factor in interviewing. Some people are more comfortable engaging in a conversation that is spontaneous and flows from the exchange between child and adult. Others may prefer a more structured format for uniformity and comparison as well as comfort with the method. Questions for discussion or interviews with preschool children will be provided for the interview assignments, but the observer or recorder is free to record more natural conversations if that is more comfortable.

What Can You Tell About a Child from Listening?

EXERCISE In the following categories, list on a separate sheet of paper what you might learn about a child by listening to speech and language as well as content.

Family:
Culture:
Physical development:
Health:
Age or stage of development:
Socioeconomic level:
Cognitive development:
Self-concept:
Needs:
Temperament:
Activity level:
Humor:
Television viewing habits:
Imagination:
Problem-solving abilities:
Social development:

In each category, there are the obvious bits of knowledge that can be acquired by listening or asking the child questions.

family—manners, attitudes, as well as finding out inside information such as a new baby is on the way

culture—customs, holiday celebrations, common activities

physical development—abilities like riding a bike with no training wheels, interests such as dancing or karate, missing teeth, muscles, or structure of the mouth and jaw

health—nasal congestion, "I threw up before I came to school," "My arm hurts."

age or stage of development—grammatical construction, "Me do it."

socioeconomic level—"We're flying to Disney World," or "We slept in the car last night."

cognitive development—"If I want more cookie I can just break this one up and have lots," "Eight, nine, ten, eleventeen, twelveteen."

self-concept—"Nobody likes me."

needs—"Help me, I can't do it."

temperament—"I CAN'T DO IT!"

activity level—"I'm gonna swing on a swing then I'm gonna ride a bike, then I'm gonna dig in the sand, then I'm gonna . . ."

humor—"Where does a sheep get a haircut? In the baabaa shop."

television viewing habits—"I'm gonna be a Power Ranger."

imagination—"I have this refrigerator and it follows me wherever I go so I can have a cold drink whenever I want it."

problem-solving abilities—"I tried it this way but it didn't work so I tried this and it worked!"

social development—"If you don't give me a turn I won't invite you to my birthday party."

Listen to children talk, sometimes prompted by a few open-ended questions such as:

"Do you want to tell me about . . . ?"
"How'd you do that?"
"Then what happened?"
"What do you think will happen next?"
"Hmmmmm."

Confidentiality Issue

Just a reminder to teachers that the child is the client. In that special relationship, what a child tells a teacher is privileged information, just as with a doctor or a lawyer. It is important not to use this information for a general topic of conversation, only to help the child. In a later chapter, the child's disclosures of possible abuse are discussed.

Advantages of Conversations and Interviews

They can

- yield multitudes of information both in content and in language production from natural situations.
- be analyzed later.
- show progress of speech and language over time.
- raise child's self-esteem as the focus of a one-on-one conversation, with a closely attentive listener.

Disadvantages of Interviews

They are

- time intensive when focusing on one child.
- intimidating, so the child may be reluctant to speak under certain circumstances.
- intrusive and may appear to probe into confidential areas.

Conducting a conversation or interview gives you the opportunity to gather much information about the child that can be used for assessment. Its effectiveness depends on your own conversational skills; you must listen actively and formulate questions based on the child's lead. A language sample can be gathered effectively in this way through a written record of the child's exact spoken words, taken in the context of the child's activity, usually in conversations with you or other children. A dated series of language samples over time can demonstrate the child's growth and progress (Leonard, 1997).

Using Technology

In the context of this book, **record** is taken to mean writing down information. Recording conversations and interviews has a more traditional meaning referring to electronic recording such as audio tape recording. This is an effective method for preserving the conversation for later transcription into words and for a more careful analysis of the child's speech and language. It depends, however, on the comfort zone of both the adult and the child. Tape recording can be intimidating and intrusive. If it is, it modifies the results by changing behavior. Frequent use of the tape recorder for children to record themselves and each other reduces the intimidation and familiarizes them with the tape recorder.

A tape for each child with a collection of recordings made throughout the year is an appropriate addition to the Portfolio. Most children enjoy taping and listening to themselves. The teacher also makes written summaries or notes of the tape recordings. This method is recommended for the beginning interviewer so that concentration is focused on the conversation rather than note taking.

Video recording a child's conversations yields even more information than an audio recording because you also see facial and body expressions. Any kind of overt preservation of a child's behavior—writing, audio, or video recording—has the possibility of altering the behavior, so care must be taken to obtain a natural sample so that it is objective and authentic.

How to Find the Time

The teacher talks with children throughout the day—carrying out the routines and instructions necessary to achieve the goal of getting through the day. However, the amount of time left for one-on-one or even meaningful group conversations seems to be ever smaller. We know, of course, how important verbal exchanges are to knowing each child, learning what they know, and meeting their emotional, social, and cognitive needs. The teacher can look at every aspect of the day and see opportunities for individual conversations. Arrival time offers an opportunity to have a brief conversation with each child, getting feedback on what has happened since they were last together, how the child is feeling, what the teacher has in store for the group that day. A Class List Log near the entryway can help quickly capture important points. While children are working and playing is an ideal time for the teacher to circulate and comment on the play and extend the conversation.

Anecdotal notes, even abbreviated to be expanded upon later, only take a few moments. Class meetings can be an opportune time to have wonderful conversations. The tape recorder or a second person writing notes can preserve these important times that provide developmental information.

Pitfalls to Avoid

Children may be uncomfortable with interviews. When holding individual formal interviews with each child, it is important to emphasize the special conversations will be held with *each* child and *everyone* will have a turn. If a child appears anxious during the interview and is reluctant to speak, the interviewer should stop and observe the child in a more natural setting.

A busy classroom may interfere with the interview, but isolation in another room is not recommended. Find a quiet spot, as free from distractions as possible, within the classroom.

The teacher has an ethical responsibility not to probe into personal family matters and practices. Any information revealed by the child of a personal nature should not be recorded unless it is a child abuse disclosure. (See Chapter 12 for a full discussion of this subject.) Of course, all personal conversations with children are confidential, not to be shared with others without the child's permission. This is a very sensitive area.

What to Do with It

The Structured Interview questions and answers are filed in the child's Portfolio. Anecdotal notes or jottings from conversations or Informal Interviews are also filed in the Portfolio. Significant parts can be highlighted with a marker to draw attention. The information yielded can be noted in respective categories on the overview sheet, such as cognitive, social, self-identity, or emotional.

Tape recordings are also filed in the Portfolio. A sheet is attached to the tape, listing the dates and subject (and counter number, if possible) of each recording. Full transcriptions are not necessary unless there is some reason to amplify documentation of a developmental area or to provide the raw data/exact wording for a referral.

The tape-recorded conversations or interviews make excellent resources for listening closely to a child's speech and language. The next section, on speech and language development, gives guidelines for listening and evaluating, both from live and tape-recorded conversations.

REVIEW

CONVERSATIONS OR INTERVIEWS

Recording a child's verbal interactions either in writing or in audio recording.

Types of Information to Record Using Conversations or Interviews

- Informal conversations that are planned or spontaneous.
- Interviews that are structured for a specific purpose.
    - child's viewpoint on school adjustment
    - child's self-responsibility views
    - child's self-evaluation of physical skills
    - child's self-evaluation of friendships and social interactions
    - child's self-evaluation of emotional difficulties
    - to listen carefully to child's speech and language
    - to assess child's attention span for conversations
    - to assess child's cognitive development:
        - physical knowledge
        - logico-mathematical knowledge
        - social knowledge
- to assess child's literacy development
- to discuss a child's creative work or play

Go to the Bind-in-Book CD for plans and resources for this week.

LISTENING TO LANGUAGE AND SPEECH

"Listen before you speak" is not just wise advice but actually the progression of language development. Listening is also described as **receptive language**.

Receptive and Expressive Language

An important principle of language development is that the receptive language always is greater than the **expressive language** (Figure 6–3). The one-year-old

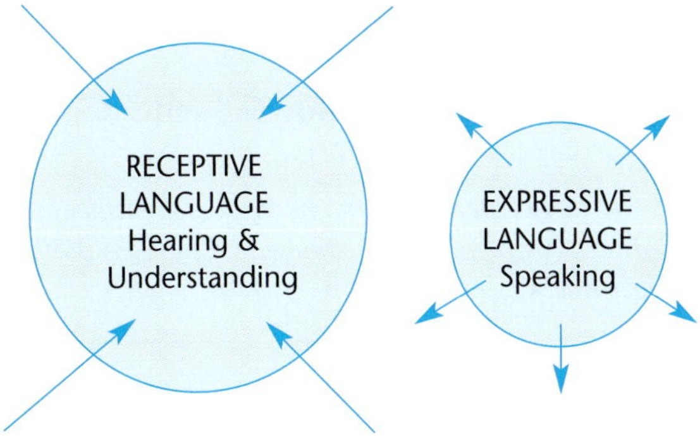

Figure 6–3 Receptive language is always greater than expressive language.

is told, "Go give grandma a kiss." The infant crawls, or walks, to grandma and gives her a kiss. He cannot say anything close to, "I want to kiss my grandma," but from his actions that is interpreted. He can understand the words of the request, act on them, but not say or express the words himself. When people are learning a second language, they always can understand far more than they are able to actually say themselves. This principle is also displayed when a person has a thought or idea but has difficulty explaining it to someone else. They say, "I know what I mean, but I just can't explain it." Receptive language, understanding verbal communication, is always greater than the ability to express thoughts verbally.

This has some direct implications for anyone around young children. The phrase, "Little pitchers have big ears" comes from this principle. Although children are physically small, unsophisticated, and unable to speak themselves, they are "taking in" what they hear. It will eventually be expressed. Not only is this a warning for adults to monitor their conversations in the presence of young children, but it is a reminder that this is a fertile learning time. All that is said, read, and sung is received. It emphasizes the importance of adults talking to babies who cannot yet communicate back. The foundations for vocabulary and language not yet present are laid in these early months and years.

Language Acquisition

Exactly how language is acquired has been the focus of much study and controversy. As infants say their first words—*ma, da, see, bye, hi, no*—they get positive reinforcement to repeat those meaningful sounds when the adults around them smile and repeat the word back to the infant. Behaviorists and social learning theorists, such as Skinner (1957) and Bandura (1977), say this imitation and positive response is how language develops. Children who are deprived of hearing language can end up permanently incapable of learning and using language. Noam Chomsky's (1965) work broadened the view of how language is acquired with studies that indicated that children from all cultures develop language skills in the same sequence at close to the same time, supporting a biological approach to language. His idea is that there is a Language Acquisition Device (LAD) present in all humans, but not animals. Proof of this are the choices in grammar that children make automatically. No one teaches a child to say "goed." It comes from the internalization of language. The process converts to a past tense using an untaught rule. It also causes the switch from "goed" to "went" a little later. Interactionist theorists, such as Bruner (1983), agree that there are behavioral and biological aspects, but they emphasize the role of an environment in which adults support language learning and use. Developmentalists like Chomsky (1968) believe that

@ it happened to me

Lily Patio

I was observing in a classroom of two-year-olds, always a delightful experience except when more than one of them is having a temper tantrum. The teacher laid out large pieces of green felt to resemble lily pads on the rug, and the children were singing the "Speckled Frog" song. As twos will do, one little girl was doing her own thing, jumping from one lily pad to another. She jumped with great gusto and proclaimed, "I'm on my lily patio." This reinforced for me again that language meaning is regulated by experience. She knew what a patio was, something you sit on, but she had no experience with lily pads so this must be a lily patio. "That silly teacher was saying it wrong." Makes sense to me!

Do you have an IT HAPPENED TO ME story about a child's logical made-up word? I'd love to read it. Please send it to WeekbyWeek@thomsonlearning.com

intelligence precedes language acquisition, as illustrated by the parallel development of cognition and language, whereas Vygotsky (1962) disagrees and believes children are speaking internally to solve difficult problems.

Three key findings from the new brain research relate to language development in the following ways:

- Biology (nature) blueprints the brain for language, but positive interaction with nurturing adults (nurture) is also necessary for effective communication.
- Early experiences and interactions stimulate brain circuitry and affect spoken and written language.
- Brain development is dependent on experiences at optimal times for acquiring different kinds of knowledge and skills.

By early experiences, positive interactions, and communication with others, a child learns language, the key to lifelong learning (Willis, 1998). Hart and Risley (2004) found some astounding results in a study that measured the language experiences of children of different socioeconomic classes in the first four years of life. Children between one and four years old in families that were on welfare heard 13 million words, children in working-class families heard 26 million words, and in professional homes children heard 45 million words (p. 198). There were also proportional differences in vocabulary used in naming and recalling people, places, and objects; words used to ask or demand; and responsiveness to the child during interactions. The differences that Hart and Risley found at three years of age were strongly linked to school performance at age nine. They concluded that a part-day preschool program at four years of age for children in language-deficient homes could not make up the difference. A conclusion from this study is that language intervention needs to be a priority of every infant/toddler out-of-home program, as well as the focus of family education. The study also concludes that preschool may be too late to make an appreciable difference in a child's language development.

The adult role in language acquisition cannot be denied. When children are provided an environment where people are talking to them, they talk sooner. When adults respond to babies' early sounds, those sounds occur more frequently. Reinforcement, encouragement, expectation, and rewards for language stimulate development. Probably, it is a combination of all of these factors working together. The important principle for parents and teachers of young children is the recognition and response to each child's attempts to communicate.

Speech Development

EXERCISE **Read the following sentence out loud:**

"Eres el/la heredero de una herencia. Ve inmediatemente a Madrid y pregunta por el alcalde. Él te va a indicar lo que debes hacer."

You have just spoken Spanish. You have the speech. You have the sounds, but you do not have the language unless you know the meaning. Have you communicated in Spanish? Only if the hearer or receiver knows the language. (The sentence means: "You are the heir of a fortune. Go at once to Madrid and ask for the mayor. He will direct you.") It would be important to be able to receive that message!

As explained in Chapter 1, the words *growth* and *development* often are used interchangeably. However, they have different meanings. The words *speech* and *language* are so often used together that most people think they are the same also (Figure 6–4). Not so! **Speech** is the sound produced to make the words. The reason that the tip of the triangle—Beginning Sounds—in Figure 6–4 is outside the language circle is that the child makes sounds before they are language, experimenting, playing with tongue and voice. Once those sounds become "mama" with the expectation that mama will respond, then those sounds become language. **Language** is the term for words and phrases that convey meaning. There can be speech without language (just making random

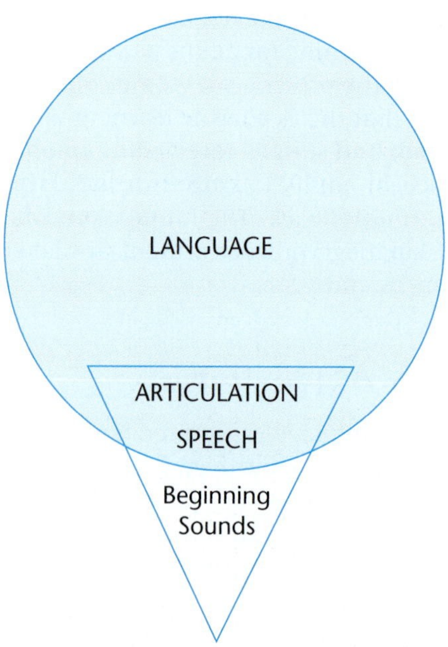

Figure 6–4 Speech as a part of language development.

sounds). There can be no audible language without speech. Nonverbal communication is body language or gestures, the way of conveying messages without speaking.

The smallest units making the sounds of the words are the **phonemes**, the sounds of speech. These are phonemes: /u/, /o/, /a/, /m/, /p/, /b/, /t/, /n/, /k/, /ng/, /y/, /g/, /f/, /v/, /sh/, /zh/, /l/, /rth/, /ch/. These are in the order in which they typically appear developmentally. Along with vowels to link them, words are formed. These are called **morphemes**, small units of sound that have meaning. It is interesting that /m/ is one of the first sounds an infant can make, and in most languages of the world, the word for the person who bore them begins with the /m/ sound: *mother, mama, mamone* (Ouseg, 1962).

The infant begins to make sounds at birth, crying, not purposefully but by reflex, just like reflex actions in other developmental areas. Within the first month, the crying becomes more differentiated, so the teacher can begin to tell the difference between the hungry cry and the painful cry. During that first month, preverbal infants can even differentiate between the sounds of /ba/ and /pa/ (de Villiers & de Villiers, 1986).

During the second month, more purposeful and pleasant sounds emerge: cooing and squealing. Those can be written down because the sounds are phonemes that are recognizable as vowels. As the infant gains muscular control of the lips and tongue, the consonants appear in babbling and, later, in imitation of adult talking. "Ba ba, ma ma, da da, pa pa," understandable approximations of longer words, are usually frequent by the end of the first year.

Infants can make and hear all the sounds found in every language. The "click" sound in southern African languages or the sound made by blowing through his lips like a cross between a /p/ and an /f/ in the Japanese language are made but later lost by English-speaking children. These sounds are heard in babbles of all babies around the world but disappear or are added by one year of age, depending on the language they are learning. Kuhl (1993) calls infants "citizens of the world" at this stage. This accounts for the difficulty adult learners have with certain sounds of the second language they are learning. The ability to make those sounds has disappeared from their repertoire. It also makes the case for exposing infants and toddlers to other languages to help preserve those sounds.

The precise articulation or production of phonemes, the sounds of language, is a long developmental period (see Figure 6–5). Some of the more difficult combinations of sounds may not be present until six or seven years old.

@ it happened to me

"A reem a ivd i a re"

The speech of a child in my preschool class was almost unintelligible. One day at class meeting, he had something to say to the group. It sounded like this:

"A ha a rem us ite n a reem a ivd i a re"

The child's mother and grandmother assured me that his father had spoken just like this when he was four and that he grew out of it. I'm not a speech therapist, but I was concerned about how his speech might interfere with his ability to relate socially to other children. Amazingly, they were able to understand him easier than I and he got along well for quite a few months until one day when the mother was in the classroom and saw his frustration at not being understood. He was evaluated and started speech therapy.

Oh, you want to know what he was saying? "I had a dream last night and I dreamed I lived in a tree."

Do you have an IT HAPPENED TO ME story about a child with difficulty speaking? I'd love to read it. Please send it to WeekbyWeek@thomson learning.com

EXERCISE Listen to the tape you made in the tape-recording exercise again, listening closely and looking at the following articulation chart. This outlines the usual progression and expectation of acquiring certain sounds. Did the children you listened to produce these sounds clearly?

p, w, h, m, n (usually by three years)
b, k, g, d, y (usually by four years)
f, ng, t, r, l (usually by six years)
ch, sh, j, s, z, v, th, zh, br, tr (clear by seven to eight years)

LEVEL	AGE RANGE	ASSOCIATED SKILLS
Prespeech	Birth to 10 months	Development of sound (perception and production) Development of gestures Concomitant changes in nonlinguistic development Rapid development of sound perception; infant a few weeks old can distinguish phonological contrasts in human speech; speech production rooted in infant's crying and vegetative noises; play with speech sounds including reciprocal speech sounds with others begins after three months; between 6 to 10 months consonant and consonant-vowel imitations are evident in babbling
First Words: Emergence of naming	10 to 13 months	Single-word comprehension Single-word production Individual differences in single-word use Gestures that function as words Attention can be directed with object names ("see the dog," "Amy, dog"); by 13 monhts receptive vocabulary from 17 to 97 words; as speech production increases, gestures decrease
Word combinations	18 to 24 months	Transition between production of single words with complex meanings to multiword phrases Nature of word combinations and individual differences Parallel developments in other developmental domains Use of word combinations initiates shift into sentence use; size of spoken vocabulary undergoing rapid acceleration and expansion of types of words, especially verbs; parallel development includes gestural imitation, classification of objects, and multigesture strings in play indicating the need for accompanying cognitive development to allow language development
Grammaticization	20 to 30 months (fundamentals of grammar) 36 months (competent speaker)	Acquisition of rules of morphology and syntax Speed of morphemic acquisition Nature and sequence of grammatical development Uniqueness of language development for this age Application of rules Mastery of irregular patterns and rules Requires a baseline of cognitive and language development

Figure 6–5 Four Levels of Language Development (Courtesy of S. M. Benner; *Assessment of Children with Special Needs,* 2003, p. 141. Clifton Park, NY: Thomson Delmar Learning.)

By the time children are four years old, they have usually developed the vocabulary, language structure, and grammatical rules needed to communicate about their world. Because young children are learners, their speech and language will be imperfect. They still may have **articulation** (sound) errors, which will continue to develop into the seventh year, especially those combinations like *wh* (whether), *rth, ch, sz.* Those imperfections can be categorized but are not necessarily cause for alarm. Some of the common mispronunciations in the preschool years are

substitutions—"wabbit" for "rabbit"
omissions—"tar" for "star"
distortions—"caaa" for "car"
additions—"pisghetti" for "spaghetti"
lisps—"thith" for "this"

Speech and language screening in the preschool years is recommended and especially indicated if the child is very difficult to understand. The role of the early childhood educator is one of facilitator, interpreter, and responder rather than remediator. Content and meaning are the most important aspects when talking with young children.

STUTTERING. Dysfluent, repetitive speech, or stuttering, "I, I, I, I want it," occurs frequently in the four- and five-year-old. It is for most children a temporary, often short-lived, disorder that disappears without formal intervention. Stuttering persists and requires assistance in only a minority of cases (Yairi, 1999). The adult listener should listen patiently without telling the child, "Now, just slow down" or "Don't talk so fast" or "Your ideas just get ahead of your tongue." Statements like these draw the child's attention to the stuttering and add to the stress. Avoid placing the child in the spotlight to speak or in a situation where they feel the pressure of the whole group waiting on them. If this does not pass in a few weeks, further investigation may be needed to look for stressors or other factors. A private conversation with the family should begin the investigation, along with notes on when the stuttering began and the child's reaction to it.

The Development of Language

After a child's first birthday, vocabulary grows (because it can be measured in numbers) at a fantastic rate (Figure 6–6). Listen again to the taped conversations: Count the number of different words each child said. Did it increase with age? Look at the explosive increase in vocabulary from the ages of 18 months through 6 years shown in Figure 6–7.

EXERCISE Here is a mathematical problem for you. Using Figure 6–7, what is the percentage rate of vocabulary growth between one year (use 15 words) and six years?

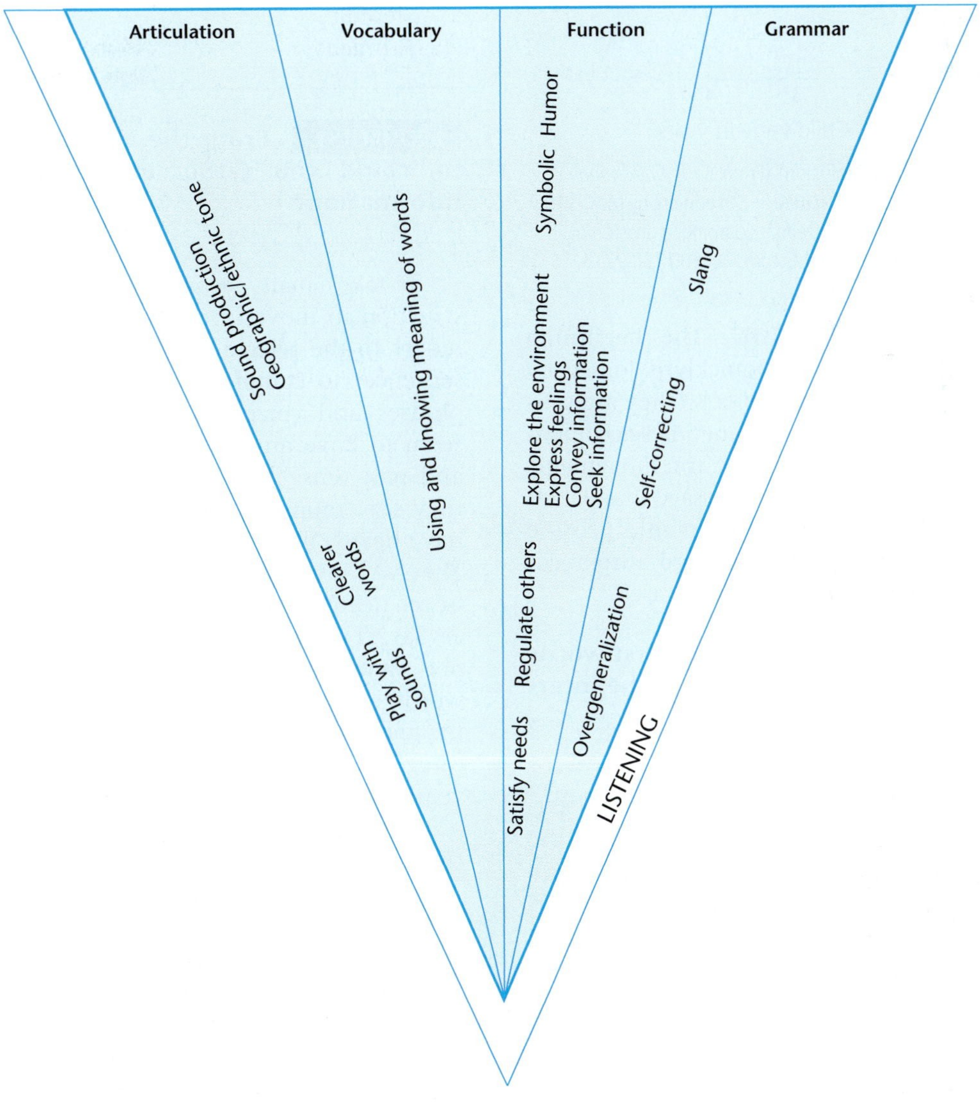

Figure 6–6 Speech and Language Development.

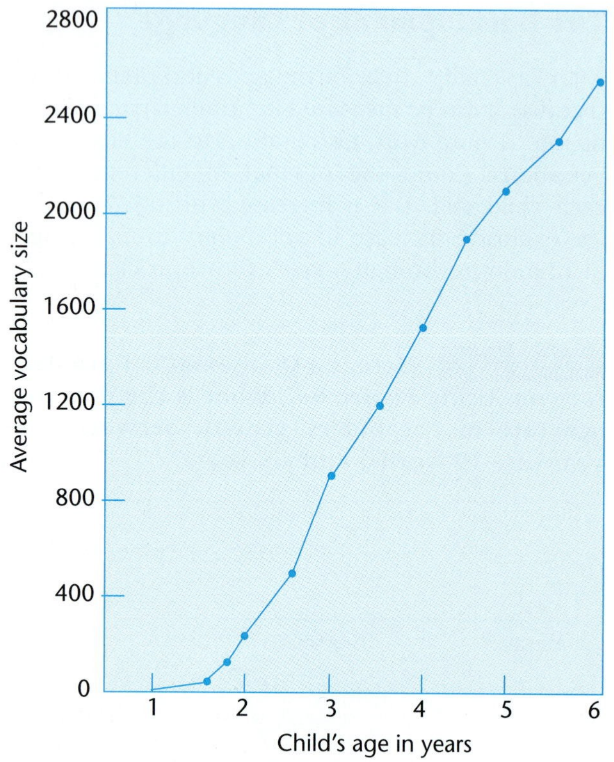

Figure 6–7 The Vocabulary Explosion! (From *Early Childhood Experiences in Language Arts, Early Literacy*, 8th edition, by MACHADO, 2007. Reprinted with permission of Delmar Learning, a division of Thomson Learning: www.thomsonrights.com. Fax 800 730-2215.)

BEGINNING COMMUNICATION. The beginning talker starts with one word. It quickly is joined by others, all names for people or objects. They are spoken with various inflections and sometimes accompanied by gestures, such as pointing or arm movements that convey a more sophisticated message than labeling. Single words between 12 and 18 months become requests or questions. These one-word utterances that have meaning are **holographic** phrases.

EXERCISE "Mama" is one of the first words a baby says. How many meanings can be interpreted by the way you say it?

These are soon followed by short two-word sentences called **telegraphic** phrases. Examples of the telegraphic phrases are "Doggie gone," and "Look baby." When telegraphic phrases occur, the child has acquired language. She is expressing herself using the sounds of speech.

EXERCISE Listen to the children on the tape. Did any of them use just one word to convey a whole thought?

Language is developing, changing from simple to complex in a predictable pattern but at individual rates. The child is developing a sense of **syntax,** the order of words in a sentence that make it understandable to others: "Mama go," "Baby ba ba." His language is the combination of heredity, social interactions, and emotional environment. Cognitive or learning ability and physical development all combine to make this happen. The interdependence and simultaneous development of many areas are vividly illustrated in language development.

EXERCISE Describe how speech or language might be affected by:

Hearing:
Muscle development:
Geography:
Abuse:
Siblings:
Heredity:
Ethnicity:

EXERCISE From the children you listened to, could you gather any of the preceding information?

It takes many years for the grammatical construction to move from one-word holographic sentences to the telegraphic but meaningful few-word sentences to complex sentences with prepositional phrases and correct tenses and plurals. Children seem to have an inner sense of picking up plurals and past tense from hearing adults speak. At first they say "mouses," instead of "mice," because they have heard "houses" meaning more than one house. They will say, "I *goed* to the store," though they have never heard anyone say that. They have heard others say, "I *washed* the dishes." This application of simple grammatical rules to all plurals and past tense words is **overgeneralization.** Children internalize the grammatical rule and apply it to all words in that category. Over time, this self-corrects, usually by five years of age.

The development of grammatical construction (Bryen & Gallaher, 1983) follows this progression:

uses correct word order (by two-and-a-half)
uses pronouns (by two-and-a-half)
gives name (by three)
uses plurals and some prepositions (by three)
tells day's schedule in sequence (by four)
can tell an imaginative story about a picture (by four)
speaks in adultlike sentences (by four)

EXERCISE **How complex were the sentences in the tape recording of conversations? Were there any examples of overgeneralization?**

LANGUAGE AND LITERACY CONNECTION. The critical role that early education plays in language and literacy development was emphasized in the National Academy of Sciences report *Preventing Reading Difficulties in Young Children* (Snow, Burns, & Griffin, 1998). In seeking solutions to readying children for school success, researcher David Dickinson points out that language is a literacy activity that provides the vocabulary, structure, and meaning verbally which will be found later in the printed word. In the Home-School Study (2001), Dickinson and Tabors learned much about the linkage between language and literacy. The income level, vocabulary, the opportunity to hear books read and learn the concept of words and books, and child care quality all have correlations to later school success. This has implications for teachers of young children. Families and child care staff can maximize language use throughout the day.

To encourage children's language development:

- At snack and meals, sit with children and have family-style mealtime conversations.
- Encourage discussions about non-immediate events, remembering details from the past.
- Encourage children to use new vocabulary words learned during class lessons.

When reading to the group:

- Identify important words and concepts.
- Encourage children to talk about aspects of the story.
- Respond to children's questions.
- Link books to themes and other activities.
- Avoid long stretches of talk and stay on the subject.

During free play:

- Children need opportunities to talk with each other.
- Minimize interruptions—teacher involvement in dramatic play tends to disrupt and disengage the players.
- Engage individual children in conversations using a variety of words, especially novel words. (Dickinson & Tabors, 2001, 252–254)

FUNCTIONS OF LANGUAGE. Children develop in the more complex use of language. Their first single words convey recognition and description, "Ma ma," "Ba ba." Very quickly, they learn that their language can be used to influence others. Those same words can now call others to communicate a need. "Ma ma," "Ba ba." As they gain vocabulary and willfulness, the communication takes the form of commands like "Go" and "No bath." With mobility and experience in a wider environment, their language expands not only in vocabulary but in using it to describe what they see, "My ball." They convey information, "Ball all gone," as they watch the ball going down the toilet. They seek information in their second year with incessant "Where Daddy go?" "Where doggie go?" and in the third and fourth years with the constant "Why?" questions. They begin to express feelings—"So sad" after a scolding, the "So sorry" that softens a grandma's heart. By four and five years old, cognitive development is moving toward the symbolic stage, when reading and writing develop. The symbolic stage appears in language too, "I have an idea." Humor emerges in double meanings of words and puns. By five, the concept of rhyming appears.

SOCIAL AND NONVERBAL LANGUAGE. Acredolo and Goodwyn (2000) point out that nonverbal gestures as signs or signals come before words. A baby with arms outstretched is making an understandable

@ it happened to me

"The French Waiter"

We had set up a restaurant in our classroom for dramatic play, complete with picture menus, order pads, aprons, and tableware. It was well used, indicating the children had experience in ordering and eating in a restaurant. One child's experience went far beyond our expectations when he took on the role of the waiter with towel over his arm and carried on the whole dialog with an affected French accent. What a surprise!

Do you have an IT HAPPENED TO ME story about how a surprising language experience? I'd love to read it. Please send it to WeekbyWeek@thomsonlearning.com

but silent plea. Asking a one- to two-year-old, "Where's your nose?" elicits a knowledgeable response months before the child can say the word "nose." *Sometimes biting is the nonverbal gesture for young children who may not have the language development to express feelings like frustration but also excitement and happiness.* By observing gestures, providing vocabulary for feelings, and also listening for words, the caregiver can learn about the child's needs, what he knows, and even what he is thinking. Kinnell (2002) warns teachers and parents alike: "Despite even the best efforts of the best teachers to prevent it, biting still (unfortunately) does happen. When it does occur, teachers must be prepared to respond appropriately and effectively" (p. 7).

Very young children without hearing impairments can learn to communicate using sign language even before they can speak. Daniels, in a fascinating study (2001), tells of infants learning to convey important messages such as *more, yes, no, come* months before they could say the words. She also studied the effects of hearing children learning sign language, showing positive results on later reading scores.

Children show social and cognitive skills in their language as well. Think about each of the children on your tape as they talked with you.

Did they demonstrate a "turn-taking" kind of conversation where they knew they were to speak, then you would have a turn, or was it more of a monologue?
Did they make eye contact?
What was the facial expression as they spoke?
What gestures did they use, if any?
What could you tell from the tone of voice that just writing down the words would not convey?

EXERCISE **Practice your ability to place bits of language in chronological order of their normal development. Number the following from the earliest to the latest in the progression of development:**

_____ "Want milk"
_____ "Waader"
_____ "When I grow up, I'm gonna be a ballerina."
_____ "No"
_____ "mum mum mum mum mum"
_____ "I goed to the store."
_____ "Wha's dat?"
_____ "ah-ah-ah"

The sequence of normal development is vowels, consonants and vowels, approximations of words,

@ it happened to me

He Shared His Expertise

Jason was a very quiet four-year-old when he started preschool. Several weeks went by while he just watched other children, without interacting or speaking in the classroom. Some children just need more time to adjust to a situation. We spoke to him about the day, what he was doing, greeted him at the door without pressuring him to speak or commenting on his silence. In private talks with his mother, she said that was his way of coping with new situations. She assured us he was very verbal at home. This continued for weeks and into months, with his mother assuring us this was his little game. He did begin to play with objects in the classroom, first the sand and blocks. He eventually began to interact with other children, but still without speaking. We still tried not to draw attention to it but spoke to him as we did all the other children in conversation as they played.

One day in February, when dinosaurs were the project theme, he brought in a book from home. At the door he held it open to me and said, "This is a stegosaurus." I was shocked and the children even commented saying, "He talked!" I said, "Jason, that's the first thing you've ever said to me. I wonder why you chose today to talk." He said matter-of-factly, "I wanted to share my expertise about dinosaurs with you." (Exact words, I swear.) From that day on, he talked occasionally with peers and teachers as he played. I often marvel at the strength of will he had all those weeks. His willpower held us all hostage to his little game.

Do you have an IT HAPPENED TO ME story about a child who wouldn't talk? I'd love to read it. Please send it to WeekbyWeek@thomsonlearning.com

telegraphic speech, questions, refusals (this can come anytime after consonants and vowels), imperfect grammar, and adult-like but self-centered.

Answers are: 8, 5, 2, 4, 1, 7, 6, 3.

FACILITATING LANGUAGE. Children learn language through interaction with adults. Adults initiate and respond in a way that demonstrates listening, understanding, expanding, and modeling. By opening the *circles of communication* (Bardige & Segal, 2005), teachers respond by giving one more turn on the circle by repeating, expanding, or asking questions. Kratcoski and Katz (1998) suggest these strategies:

Expansion—respond, expanding holographic and telegraphic sentences
C: "Doggie eat." T: "Yes, the doggie is eating."
Extensions—response and addition of new information
C: "Doggie eat." T: "Yes, the doggie is eating. Doggie is hungry."

Figure 6–8 The adult should always return the conversational ball.

Figure 6–9 Poor examples of language role models.

Repetition—repeats phrase
C: "Doggie eat." T: "Eat, doggie. Eat, doggie."
Parallel talk—describes child's action
C: "Doggie eat." T: "Yes, doggie is eating. You feed the doggie her food."
Self-talk—describes own action
C: "Doggie eat." T: "Yes, doggie is eating. I gave the doggie her food."
Vertical structuring—uses questions to facilitate longer sentences
C: "Doggie eat." T: "Yes, the doggie is eating. Does she want a drink?"
Fill-ins—conversation structured for child to provide word to complete the statement
T: "Doggie wants a drink. Let's get her some _____." C: "Water!"
Play "conversational ball"—the conversation goes back and forth between the two parties. The child is a learner, so may drop the ball. The adult always catches or picks it up and tosses it back (Figure 6–8).

LANGUAGE ROLE MODELS. Adults are language role models for children (Figure 6–9).

EXERCISE Set up a tape recorder in the classroom or wear a small portable one in your pocket. Tape a 30- to 60-minute sample of yourself "for your ears only." Analyze it for your common language habits, and see if any changes need to be made in the language role model you are presenting to children.

Teachers of young children fall into some habits that are not helpful to children. Some are reviewed here to alert the reader to consider the impact on the child.

The Tester. Many teachers of young children know the way to find out what children know is to ask questions. Unfortunately, they translate this into a series of test questions: "What color is the coat you are wearing today?" "Is it sunny or rainy?" "How many colors in your picture?" "What month is it?" The child might answer sarcastically, "You're supposed to be the teacher and you don't know so you're asking a little kid?" As language role models and empathetic humans, adults should speak to children in the same manner they speak to peers. An adult would not ask a bystander, "What color is your shirt?" or a friend, "How many bracelets are you wearing today?" Questions asked of children should be motivated by natural interest and desire to explore the child's thinking, rather than checking if the child knows.

The Helper. Adults fall into the trap of speaking of themselves by name in sentences spoken to young children, like the much criticized "we" of the health profession. Often teachers say, "Let Mrs. M. help you with your boots" or "Do you want Miss Barbara to push you on the swing?" If a child said of herself, "Mary can do it," it would be considered an irregular language pattern, not using personal pronouns. As language models, teachers can and should use pronouns when speaking of themselves in sentences. "Would you like me to help you with your boots?" A neighbor would think it odd if a person spoke of themselves when saying, "Mrs. Smith (the speaker) heard your dog barking all night."

"Use Your Words." The underlying reason for this phrase is to encourage children to verbalize their feelings. Unfortunately, these words do not help the child do that. Neither does its accompanying, "Tell him you don't like it when he. . . ." It tells the child what she should do but does not give assistance in how to do it. If she knew how to use her words to tell him, she would have said it already. A more appropriate and helpful phrase might be, "Tell him, 'I don't like it when you. . . .'" It reminds the child that words are preferred to hurtful actions. The child is given the exact words to say. She also does not have to make the shift from "you" to "I" when using the sentence. Imagine a car stopped at the red light, and the driver behind it sounds his horn. The first driver leans out and says sweetly, "Use your words."

"How Would You Like It if She Did That to You?" One of the major characteristics of the egocentric, preoperational child is the inability to see a situation from another's perspective, the inability to put oneself on the receiving end of the action or word. This phrase then becomes meaningless and useless to the child under five or six. A more understandable phrase might be, "Remember when you got sand in your eyes from someone flipping the shovel? That's what you just did to Lois. It hurt your eyes and now her eyes are hurting in the same way. How else could you use the shovel?"

Incorrect Grammar, Slang, and Lazy Articulation. The disagreement of noun and verb plurals is a common grammatical habit. Saying, "We was" rather than "We were" gives children a poor example of grammar. Calling all the children "Kids" or "Guys" rather than by their names is disrespectful. Dropping the /g/ at the end of those *-ing* words is a habit adopted by language learners. By listening to a tape of themselves, teachers can become aware of those habits and try to correct 'em (them). Teachers with an awareness of the potential for misunderstanding or imitation become better language role models for young children.

Tone and Volume. Each person's voice is unique, and we use it in various ways by habit and necessity.

EXERCISE **Say this sentence in many different tones and loudness:**

"Please pick that up."

List the various meanings you have conveyed.

It could be a polite request, a stern command, an impatient order, a descriptive sentence focusing attention on a particular toy. Verbal tone and volume can add to the aggressiveness of the classroom atmosphere by conveying anger, displeasure, and even dislike. If the goal is to reduce aggression in the classroom, it begins by treating and talking to children with respect, modeling not just the words and meaning but also the tone we want the children to use.

HELPING ALL CHILDREN WITH LANGUAGE DEVELOPMENT

Society is increasingly culturally and linguistically diverse as well as aware of differing abilities. It is advisable for teachers to be bilingual, whether in a second cultural language or sign language.

Accepting Other Languages and Dialects

Schools and teachers must be ready to receive a child speaking a language other than English (Figure 6–10).

Figure 6–10 Teachers must be ready to receive families of diverse cultures.

The following statistics may be surprising, but they underscore the reality of the United States—it is becoming more and more diverse, and teachers need to prepare for non–English speakers in classrooms. This increasing diversity has important ramifications for our teaching.

- Spanish is the predominant native language of 79% of the English as a second language (ESL) learners in the United States (Kindler, 2002).
- According to the United States National Clearinghouse for English Language Acquisition Web site, in 2004–2005 there were more than five million English language learners in grades PreK through 12 (2006).
- The states with the highest increase in residents speaking English as a second language are surprising: Georgia 210%, South Carolina 127%, Indiana 88%, North Carolina 84%, Wisconsin 75%, Arkansas 57%, Minnesota 64%, and Missouri 58% (Padolsky, 2002).
- The states with the highest number of ESL students enrolled were California, Texas, Florida, New York, Illinois, and Arizona (Padolsky, 2002).

Bilingualism is a great advantage for teachers. There are so many different languages spoken in many classrooms, however, it would be impossible to have teachers fluent in all of them. Therefore, sensitivity to the child's needs is called for when the child does not speak the language of the classroom or the teacher. It may be the child speaks a dialect such as African American/Black English (AAE/BE), or **Ebonics**, shown to have its own structure and eligible for language remediation (Cloud, Genesee, & Hamayan, 2000). Many group settings include children whose home language is not English. ESL students frequently come into the group knowing no English at all. Many schools have labeled these children Limited English Proficient (LEP), seeing their lack of English as a deficit rather than recognizing their proficiency in the language they have already learned. In the past, assessments given in English indicated major delays and mistakenly prescribed remediation for many of these children.

More tolerant approaches have been developed to help the child become bilingual, not pushing to be monolingual, nor attempting to extinguish the first language. The approach is described as additive, supporting the native language while adding a second. This can be accomplished by

- making a commitment to use their language(s) throughout the classroom.
- labeling classroom items in English and in languages spoken by families in the class or school.
- learning phases, songs, or greeting words in spoken languages.
- having classroom charts written in two or more languages.
- including books in other languages.
- learning the numbers in different languages.
- inviting family members or other persons to teach a simple poem or song to the class.

A basic early childhood principle is the acceptance of each child. Acceptance provides an environment, experiences, and support to help the child progress to the next level. Children learning a second language will progress through the same language development stages as an infant and toddler, beginning with single important words, then to telegraphic stages. They proceed through them with the same stage predictability of any other child learning language. The same techniques of teaching and observation are used regardless of the language the child speaks. See more about assessment and culture in this chapter's "Topics in Observation."

Children with Differing Abilities in Regular Classrooms

Children with differing abilities in speech, language, or hearing may be placed in regular classrooms. Other children become their role models, and communication skills become more functional in the responsive environment. The same strategies that are recommended for effective therapy carried on in the classroom are applicable to any early childhood

TOPICS IN OBSERVATION

Diversity

EXERCISE In a crowded place—at the supermarket, at the fair, on a bus—just take a look around. Do you see any two people who are alike? Look at noses. Just noses. Are any exactly the same shape or size? People-watching is a fascinating pastime.

Every person is different and yet the same. All have two ears and a nose that are parts of the whole. Because all people are members of the same species, there are expectations of how the parts work and how they change over time. Genetics, age, environment, or trauma cause the variations in the basic mold of a human.

Generalities help to make sense of the whole. Averages have been calculated based on large numbers of people, but even then some will not fit within the range of average. Assessments and professional practice are based on averages that may not represent valid measurements for some children. How can a teacher measure vocabulary when the teacher and child do not speak the same language? How can a teacher write down how long the child can stand on one leg when the child is in a wheelchair? How can a teacher comment on the child's separation and adjustment to the classroom when the child has been in eight foster homes in three years? The dilemma is real!

Diversity is a fact of life, but thinking and attitudes sometimes are so narrow that the truth is overlooked. Adults are supposed to be past the egocentric stage, so they should understand statements such as, "How would you like it if . . .

. . . no one learned how to pronounce your name?"
. . . there never were any pictures of people who looked like you around in your classroom?"
. . . the food never had familiar flavors and spices?"
. . . no one would hold your hand in a circle?"
. . . the teacher planned activities that were always too difficult for you to do?"
. . . you had to have money for school tomorrow for a field trip and your family didn't have it?"
. . . letters always went home addressed to parents and you didn't have two parents (or any)?"
. . . everyone else was thin and you were fat?"

Different notes in a song, colors in a rainbow, or flowers in a field are valued. Why not individual differences? They are often rebuffed, ignored, and rejected, causing disharmony and hurt feelings. While working with children, observing and evaluating their development, comparisons to norms must be done very cautiously. The environment should represent and reflect everyone's individuality, and an attitude of acceptance of all must prevail. Here are some practical ways of accomplishing this.

Individual Differences

While norms give a range of expected growth and development, there will always be some children at both ends of the range that demand attention and decision making about that difference. No child will be at the same developmental level as another. Even within each child, the level of development may be different in different areas. The child may be more advanced in language, less advanced in large muscle development, in the mid-range of emotional development, and off the map in cognitive development.

TOPICS IN OBSERVATION *(continued)*

Those differences deserve to be observed, evaluated, and acted upon if needed, but not seen as unusual or strange.

Special Needs

Some children have not developed within the normal range of expected levels. A strengths model looks at the abilities of the child as decision points for the placement. The role of the program is to keep the areas of special need from interfering with other normally developing skills. This opposes the deficit model, which focuses on the need. Instead, the child should be placed where the child can function to capacity wherever possible, and assisted in areas of lesser ability. Authentic assessment, for every child, looks at the individual areas of development to note the highest level of achievement rather than what the child cannot yet do.

Cultural/Ethnic Diversity

Caution is advised when broadly accepting any standard of evaluation or professional practice. It might be in conflict with the values or style differences in culture or ethnicity. Developmental and behavioral norms and professional practice are based on the majority culture and may be diametrically opposed to those of a minority culture. Familiarity and sensitivity to the cultural and ethnic differences of the population of the classroom is the only way to meet each child's needs. For example, the separation, independence and move toward autonomy described in Chapter 1 may not fit the interdependence highly valued in Middle Eastern families.

Toilet training (Chapter 2) is a topic with great cultural variation and should be approached with the family's preferences in mind. Communication differs between cultures. Some cultures use more body language and implicit cues. Other cultures respond more to precise, direct language. Cultural differences must be considered when talking to families about their child. Family decision makers vary between cultures, as do expectations for girls and boys. Acting honestly with a heightened awareness of the differences will help the child. By displaying a willingness to learn and a desire not to offend, families and teachers will build a partnership for the child.

What's in a Name?

Throughout this book you will notice children's names, when used as examples, are from a variety of nationalities. A deliberate effort sought out the most popular names in many different cultures from a baby name book. It is extremely important to learn the correct pronunciation of the first and last names of all the families in the class, not giving them American nicknames unless the family especially requests it. It is a learning experience for the teacher and the other children to learn to pronounce ethnic names and can be a point of teaching tolerance, understanding, and cultural awareness. It must begin with the teacher's attitude.

teacher. Cook, Klein, and Tessier (2004) make the following suggestions:

- Listen attentively.
- Do not ask quiz-like questions—"What color is your shoe?"
- Talk about the here and now.
- Speak in a calm, normal tone of voice.
- Expand sentence length as the child's understanding expands. (p. 298)

The choice between sign language, or manual communication, and speech reading (commonly called lip reading) is decided between experts and families of the hearing impaired. The family makes the decision about their child. The early childhood program responds to that decision just as it would to any other family decisions, with sensitivity and willingness to adapt to meet the needs of the child.

HELPING PROFESSIONALS FOR SPEECH AND LANGUAGE CONCERNS

Speech and language disorders are often first diagnosed in early childhood programs. As children develop, families expect their verbal skills to be emerging but often are not aware, or choose to ignore, what may be a problem in this area. It is not life-threatening; it often is compensated by the parent and other children in the family; and it can be cute and entertaining.

A speech and language screening is routinely administered to preschool children to detect possible difficulties. Informal interviews may act as that screening.

When to Seek Help in Speech and Language

The family is consulted if the child is nearing three years old without much language. Documented observations over a time showing little progress when compared to a chart of norms can help explain the concern. The teacher presents options for referrals to professionals who will conduct preliminary screenings or full evaluations. That referral should begin with medical personnel or the pediatrician. Chronic ear infections often go unnoticed and can cause hearing loss that may affect language development. There are many other possible causes. Early detection for diagnosis and possible intervention is recommended. This dialogue takes place with empathy for the family's feelings and also with a knowledge of community resources. If potential problems are indicated, a full evaluation usually is recommended either by the child's pediatrician or the program team. Teachers and early childhood programs should have referral lists from which the family can choose an agency or professional to perform this evaluation. Some of the following helping professionals that may become involved:

audiologist—conducts screenings and evaluations and diagnoses hearing problems; assesses hearing aids and teaches clients to conserve hearing and to use residual hearing

speech and language pathologist—conducts screenings, evaluation, diagnosis, and treatment of children with communication disorders

otolaryngologist—physician who specializes in diagnosis and treatment of ear, nose, and throat disorders; sometimes known as an ENT (ear, nose, and throat) physician

American Sign Language interpreters—translate spoken language into sign language and vice versa for people with hearing impairments

OTHER METHODS

Other Methods to Record Speech and Language Development

Class List Log—a screening device for specific aspects of speech such as clarity, or language such as "talks freely with peers"

Anecdotal/Running Records—exact quotes are included (as they should be), obtaining a sample of the child's speech and language

Checklists/Rating Scales—formal evaluation instruments can evaluate progress in development

STANDARDS

Here are selected examples of standards for language and speech:

Head Start Child Outcomes (U.S. Health and Human Services, 2003)

Speaking and Communicating

- Indicator 1: Develops increasing abilities to understand and use language to communicate information, experiences, ideas, feelings, opinions, needs, questions; and for other varied purposes.
- Indicator 2: Progresses in abilities to initiate and respond appropriately in conversations and discussions with peers and adults.
- Indicator 3: Uses an increasingly complex and varied spoken vocabulary.
- Indicator 4: Progresses in clarity of pronunciation and towards speaking in sentences of increasing length and grammatical complexity.

- Indicator 5: For non–English-speaking children, progresses in speaking English.

Teachers of English to Speakers of Other Languages (TESOL) PreK–12 English Language Proficiency Standards in the Core Content Areas.

Standard 1: English language learners communicate for social, intercultural, and instructional purposes within the school setting.

KEY TERMS

action research	language
articulation	morphemes
closed question	open question
diagnostic interview	overgeneralization
diversity	phonemes
dysfluent	receptive language
Ebonics	record
expressive language	speech
holographic	structured interview
informal conversations	syntax
	telegraphic

Go to the Bind-in-Book CD for:

Plan Week 6 Part A, Directions for annotating informal conversations, including What to Do with It, Portfolio Overview Example, Sharing with Child and Family, Actions—Read a Book, In the Environment, In the Curriculum, In the Newsletter

Plan Week 6 Part B, Directions Class List Log of Speech and Language on All (Checklist included)

Plan Week 6 Part C, Reflective Journal

REFERENCES

Acredolo, L. P., & Goodwyn, S. W. (2000). *Baby minds: Brain-building games your baby will love to play.* New York: Bantam Books.

Almy, M., & Genishi, C. (1979). *Ways of studying children.* New York: Teachers College Press.

Bandura, A. (1977). *Social learning theory.* Englewood Cliffs, NJ: Prentice Hall.

Bardige, B. S., & Segal, M. M. (2005). *Building literacy with love.* Washington, DC: Zero to Three.

Benner, S. M. (2003). *Assessment of children with special needs.* Clifton Park, NY: Thomson Delmar Learning.

Bruner, J. S. (1983). *Child's talk: Learning to use language.* New York: Norton.

Bryen, D. N., & Gallaher, D. (1983). Assessment of language and communication. In K. D. Paget & B. A. Bracken (Eds.), *The psychoeducational assessment of the preschool child.* New York: Grune & Stratton.

Chomsky, N. (1965). *Aspects of the theory of syntax.* Cambridge, MA: MIT Press.

Chomsky, N. (1968). *Language and mind.* New York: Harcourt, Brace and World.

Cloud, N., Genesee, J., & Hamayan, E. (2000). *Dual language instruction: A handbook for enriched education.* Boston: Heinle & Heinle.

Cook, R. E., Klein, M. D., & Tessier, A. (2004). *Adapting early childhood curricula for children in inclusive settings* (6th ed.). Upper Saddle River, NJ: Pearson Education.

Daniels, M. (2001). *Dancing with words: Signing for hearing children's literacy.* Westport, CT: Bergin & Garvey.

de Villers, P. A., & de Villers, J. G. (1986). *Early language.* Cambridge, MA: Harvard University Press.

Dickinson, D. K., & Tabors, P. O. (Eds.). (2001). *Beginning literacy with language: Young children learning at home and school.* Baltimore, MD: Brookes.

Evans, R. I. (1973). *Jean Piaget: The man and his ideas.* New York: E. P. Dutton.

Harmes, T., Cryer, D., & Clifford, R. M. (2003). *Infant/toddler environment rating scale* (rev. ed.). New York: Teachers College Press.

Harste, J., Woodward, V., & Burke, C. (1984). *Language stories & literacy lessons.* Portsmouth, NH: Heinemann.

Hart, B., & Risley, T. R. (2004). *Meaningful differences in the everyday experiences of young American children.* Baltimore, MD: Brookes.

Kindler, A. (2002). *Survey of the states' limited English proficient students and available educational programs and services, 2000–2001.* Washington, DC: National Clearinghouse for English Language Acquisition and Language Instruction Educational Programs.

Kinnell, G. (2002). *No biting: Policy and practice for toddler programs.* St. Paul, MN: Redleaf Press.

Kratcoski, A. M., & Katz, K. B. (1998). Conversing with young language learners in the classroom. *Young Children, 53* (3), 30–33.

Kuhl, P. K. (1993). Developmental speech perception: Implications for models of language impairment. *Annals of the New York Academy of Sciences, 682,* 248–263.

Leonard, A. M. (1997). *I spy something: A practical guide to classroom observations of young children.* Little Rock, AR: Southern Early Childhood Association.

Lewin, K. (1948). *Resolving social conflicts, selected papers on group dynamics (1935–1946).* New York: Harper.

Machado, J. M. (2003). *Early childhood experiences in language arts* (7th ed.). Clifton Park, NY: Thomson Delmar Learning.

Moxley, R. A., Kenny, K. A., & Hunt, M. K. (1990). Improving the instruction of young children with self-recording and discussion. *Early Childhood Research Quarterly, 5,* 233–249.

Neuman, S. B., & Roskos, K. A. (1993). *Language and literacy learning in the early years.* Fort Worth, TX: Harcourt, Brace Jovanovich.

Ouseg, H. L. (Ed.). (1962). *International dictionary in twenty-one languages.* New York: Philosophical Library.

Padolsky, D. (2002). *How many school-aged English language learners (ELLs) are there in the U.S.?* National Clearinghouse for English Language Acquisition. Retrieved March 16, 2003, from http://www.ncela.gwu.edu/askncela/01leps.htm.

Pelligrini, A. D. (1991). *Applied child study: A developmental approach.* Hillsdale, NJ: Lawrence Erlbaum Associates.

Skinner, B. F. (1957). *Verbal behavior.* New York: Appleton-Century-Crofts.

Snow, C., Burns, M. S., & Griffin, P. (Eds.). (1998). *Preventing reading difficulties in young children.* Washington, DC: National Academy Press.

Teachers of English to Speakers of Other Languages (2006). *PreK-12 English language proficiency standards in the core content areas.* Alexandria, VA: Author.

U.S. Clearinghouse for English Language Acquisition. (2006). FAQ: How many school-aged English language learners (ELLs) are there in the U.S.? Retrieved March 20, 2007, from http://www.ncela.gwu.edu/expert/faq/01leps.html.

U.S. Department of Health and Human Services, Administration for Children and Families. (2003). *The Head Start child outcomes framework.* Washington, DC: Author.

Vygotsky, L. S. (1962). *Thought and language.* New York: John Wiley.

Willis, C. (1998). Language development: A key to lifelong learning. *Child Care Information Exchange 121,* May/June 1998, 63–65.

Wortham, S. C. (2001). *Assessment in early childhood education* (3rd ed). Upper Saddle River, NJ: Merrill Prentice Hall.

Yairi, E., & Ambrose, N. G. (1999). Early child stuttering persistency and recovery rates. *Journal of Speech, Language and Hearing Research, 22* (5), 1097.

RESOURCES

Coppel, C. (2003*). A world of difference: Readings on teaching young children in a diverse society.* Washington, DC: National Association for the Education of Young Children.

Derman-Sparks, L. (1988). *Anti-bias curriculum: Tools for empowering young children.* Washington, DC: National Association for the Education of Young Children.

Hall, N. (1999). *Creative resources for the anti-bias classroom.* Clifton Park, NY: Delmar Thomson Learning.

Hildebrand, V., Phenice, L. A., Gray, M. M., & Hines, R. P. (1996). *Knowing and serving diverse families.* Englewood Cliffs, NJ: Prentice Hall.

Kinnell, G. (2002). *No biting: Policy and practice for toddler programs.* St. Paul, MN: Redleaf Press.

Lynch, E. W., & Hanson, M. J. (2004). *Developing cross-cultural competence* (3rd ed.). Baltimore, MD: Brookes Publishing Co.

Tabors, P. O. (1997). *One child, two languages.* Baltimore, MD: Paul H. Brookes Publishing.

York, S. (2003). *Roots and wings* (rev. ed.). Beltsville, MD: Redleaf Press.

CHAPTER 7

Using Time Samples to Look at Attention Span

IN THIS CHAPTER

- Using Time Samples
- Looking at Cognitive Development
- Helping All Children with Attention Span
- Topics in Observation: Attention Span and Autism
- Helping Professionals for Attention Concerns

USING TIME SAMPLES

Think About It . . .

How much time did you spend in the last week sewing? reading? golfing? shopping?

When is your attention span the longest?

Think about the choices you make. When there is a choice of activities, it is governed by some assumptions:

- You are more likely to do what you *like* to do rather than what you *have* to do.
- You do what you have the opportunity to do. Your sewing machine may be broken. You have no new novel to read. You have no money for golfing or shopping. You would if you could.
- If your first choice, your favorite pastime, is not available, you may choose a related activity. Your sewing machine is broken, so maybe you do some hand sewing. You have no new book to read, so you reread an old one. Instead of golfing or shopping, you read about it in magazines or the newspaper.
- If you have finished all the sewing projects, read all the books, played that course, or shopped that mall already, you may be bored with those choices.
- If you have a new pattern you want to try, a bestseller waiting, a new golf course or mall

just opened, you cannot wait to try it and will avoid all other choices, people, or tasks.

- You are more likely to do it if you feel you will be successful or challenged but not frustrated. You know you can sew a dress, so perhaps you decide to try a jacket. You will work on it until you get to a difficult part. Depending on your personality, you may work at it, rip it apart, and start over, or abandon the project altogether. If you are a slow, deliberate reader, then probably reading is not a favorite pastime. If you feel awkward at physical things, then golfing may not be your forte. A person planning to lose weight before the next season might be frustrated with shopping and leave the store after trying on only one bathing suit.
- You may choose your activity because your friends are doing it too. They call and say, "Let's go golfing or shopping." You had not planned to, but you want to be with them and so you join them.
- While you are at a task of your choosing, time passes quickly. You look up at the clock and cannot believe you have spent four hours working on that garment, reading that book, playing that golf game, or shopping at that mall. The total absorption in the activity also resents intrusions and any attempt to draw you away. The phone rings, you let the answering machine get it. It is time for lunch, so you grab a sandwich and eat it while you are reading. You hurry home from the golf course or shopping and pick up a pizza for dinner. If someone comes and tells you it is time to stop and to come do something else, it makes you angry. You may ignore the first call, the second, and the third.

Factors Influencing Children's Attention Span

What does **attention span** have to do with observing young children? When they have their choice, where, what, and with whom do they choose to spend their time? By observing children's choices of activities, a spectrum of information is gathered. The same principles lead children's activity choices.

The child's choices reveal interests. Avoidance or cursory completion of assigned or chosen tasks may suggest lack of competence. Bessie just loves painting at the easel, so she rushes to get there first, puts on her smock, and gets ready. Miss Jones says, "Bessie, before you start painting I want you to come and paint this hand plaque for your mother." Bessie reluctantly goes to the table, quickly paints the plaque, and returns to the easel, where she paints for the next 15 minutes. Miss Jones wonders to herself, and maybe even writes on her Class List Log, "Short attention span, painted part of plaque and left." Was Bessie interested in painting and does she have a long or short attention span? What made the difference?

The child may select related activities when their first choice is not available. William headed straight for the water table after he hung up his jacket. It was closed. He moved to the climber, but it was taken down, replaced by a writing center. He went into the bathroom, ran water in the sink, wadded up paper towels, and blew them around in the water. Someone had to use the bathroom, so he came out. He climbed up on the shelf and jumped off, three times, before the teacher came over and tried to get him to come to the new writing center. He refused. She wondered, "Why is he doing these things today?" Children will find a way to do what they want and need to do. William found water play soothing, and climbing helped him work off extra energy. Those were two activities his body, temperament, and development needed but were denied by the environment, so he manufactured them himself.

Novel, new activities attract children's interest (Figure 7–1). The next day when William came to the classroom, he saw that there was a computer in the writing center. He ran right over and started touching the keys. Marvella showed him how to turn it on and asked him if he wanted to use the dinosaur program to write a story with her. "Sure." Miss Jones wondered, "I couldn't get William over here yesterday. I wonder what made the difference?"

Children will choose and give attention to activities where they find success. Bessie may have rejected the teacher's painting project, preferring her own.

Figure 7–1 New activities attract attention.

Maybe she never painted a plaque before and was afraid to try. She had trouble controlling the small brushes the teacher provided, but she knew how to use the big brushes and many colors at the easel. Easel painting she knew would be successful. William was not lured by the teacher's invitation to the writing center. He had tried to write his name when his mother made him practice, and he could not do it to please her. If he went to the writing center, he probably would have to write. "No way! Stay away! I'll just stick with water play and climbing and jumping. I know I'm good at those."

Children are sometimes influenced by their friends' choices of activities. Bessie looked over at the art table. "Oh, my friends are all at the art table with shells and twigs and leaves and stones and bottles of glue. They're calling me over. I've never used glue before. My mom says it's too messy." She joins them and watches for a few minutes. "Now I know how to do it!" She works as long as they are there. When they leave, she may decide to finish her collage or leave it and follow them to the next activity they choose. She may choose an activity because that is where the adult is. She likes to be near Mr. Jim. If he had invited her to do the plaque, she would have stayed there longer.

Children involved in an activity may be reluctant to bring it to a close. Timmy's block building is growing taller and wider. He gets more blocks and makes a road up to the building's door. He gets out the little animals and builds a pen for them. Then he gets a tub of cars and drives it up the road to deliver new animals. The teacher says, "Time for everyone to come to circle time." Timmy keeps building. She says, "Timmy, put the blocks away and come to circle time. You have played there a whole hour." There are too many blocks and animals and cars to put away and the building does not yet have a roof or a barn for the animals. It is not finished, and he realizes he did not even have time to play in the water table yet, and he always plays in the water table before circle time. He has been in the block area the whole free choice time.

Measuring Attention Span with Time Samples

One of the characteristics commonly used to describe young children is "short attention span." Families will often report that children who cannot sit still one minute at the dinner table will sit for two hours watching a video and never move. (Is it any wonder that families do not fully cooperate with "Television Turn-Off Day"?) From the preceding adult and children's examples, there are many variables that determine the length of attention span. By watching children as they choose and participate in the activities, a wide spectrum of development and behavior can be assessed and evaluated.

The **Time Sample** is an efficient recording method that tracks children's choices, their playmates, and the time they spend in one area. It is a method suitable for children three years old and older in group settings. It may be a mixed age group or homogeneous age group. Obviously, if it is recording the children's choices, it is only used in a program and at a time when children have choices. That assumption is based on developmentally appropriate practice for young children from birth through eight years old (Bredekamp & Copple, 1997).

> *Infants*—Observing the infant's cues, the adult is able to judge when the baby would like to be held, carried to a new place, or shifted to a new position (p. 72).
> *Toddlers*—Adults adapt schedules and activities to meet individual children's needs within the group setting (p. 84).
> *Three- through five-year olds*—Teachers allocate extended periods of time (at least one hour at a time) for children to engage in play and projects. (p. 126)
> *Six- through eight-year olds*—A variety of work places and spaces is provided and used flexibly (p. 165).

Here is an example of a Time Sample (Figure 7–2). A segment of the free choice time is selected. One-half hour works well, begun after the children have all arrived and are actively engaged. The learning centers or choices are listed down the left margin. Five-minute intervals are filled in across the top from when the recording is begun. The recorder looks at each area and writes down the names of the children who are in that area at that moment. After a quick glance, a circle can be drawn around the names of the children who are playing cooperatively. That does not refer to the absence of arguments but to the social stage of working together for a common goal, as described in Chapter 4. The recorder notes also if an adult is in that area, then looks on to the next area to be observed. The areas are all scanned, and names of players are written down. A category at the bottom designates the names of children not in any area at the time, perhaps in transition, perhaps wandering around not involved in play.

When the next five-minute period begins, the process is repeated. If the recorder knows a child remained in the area for the last five minutes, a

TIME SAMPLE

Class Red Class a.m. (fours) Date 2/26/0_ Recorder B. Smith

TIMES (at 5-minute intervals)

	9:20	9:25	9:30	9:35	9:40	9:45
Puzzles new floor puzzle	Amy Carter Howard Jenny	Amy → → TA Ole	 → → → TA	Martin Kara	Jacob	Bajic
Art/ Collage	Ole Irma Patty TA	Jacob	Amy → Jenny	Carter → Ned → FV Bajic →	→ → FV →	 FV
Easel	Kara	Irma Patty	Irma	Howard		Galina/Jacob
Lg. Muscle - Climber	Edward Fatima	Galina	Jacob	Irma Jenny	Galina Kara Ole TA	Irma Patty
Blocks	Galina Martin	Edward → Fatima →	 Galina	→ → →	Irma Patty	Kara Martin
Sand Table	Jacob	Kara Jenny Martin →	Ole → TA	Ole Fatima → Patty TA	Amy → → Edward →	→ → → Ole TA
Dramatic Play (shoe store)		Amy		Jacob	Martin	
Book Area	Danielle → Ned → FV →	 Bajic →	Patty → → →		 Jenny TA	Irma → TA
Watching	Bajic					

(oval) denotes cooperative play — (arrow) denotes continued play — (starburst) denotes play difficulty

FV family volunteer — TA teacher assistant

Figure 7–2 Time Sample Example.

straight line is drawn, saving a few seconds. If the child left and returned, the name is rewritten. Children do move quickly. Every five minutes the process is repeated.

EXERCISE From the Time Sample example, choose one child and follow the child for a one-half-hour segment. Draw some conclusions about the following:

- the child's interests
- where the child feels competent (probably is most developed)
- where the child may not feel competent (may be the least developed area)
- the stage of play
- the length of attention span
- if the child is teacher-dependent or avoids the adults
- what questions it still leaves in your mind about this child

---

Of course, a total evaluation of a child's development is not drawn from one recording, any more than it should be drawn from one test score. Time Samples should be done periodically to see trends and to amplify other documentation methods.

Analysis of the Time Sample Example

Who do you think is the oldest child in the class?
Probably Edward. He appears to have the longest attention span and is a cooperative player.

Who is probably the youngest?
It might be Bajic, or possibly he is just new to the class.

Whose family member was most likely the volunteer (see FV for family volunteer)?
The FV was probably related to Bajic, or else he is the most dependent.

Who likes to be with the teacher assistant (TA)?
Ole.

What are the most popular areas of the classroom?
Large motor and sand.

What is the least popular area?
Dramatic play. What might be a remedy? Add new props.

What strategy did the TA use?
The TA went to where the most children were.

Where was the teacher (T)?
The teacher possibly was recording the Time Sample.

What child is missing halfway through the Time Sample?
Danielle. She might have gone home sick or gone to a pull-out program such as speech. It is possible she was in transit between areas or just missed. Mistakes do happen.

Who is the child who needed the teacher's attention?
Jenny. What finally worked? The book area.

What well-used area did not sustain long periods of play?
Large muscle. What might be the reason? Too difficult or too easy.

How long would you expect four-year-olds to stay at a task?
A rule of thumb is one minute for each year of age *unless* one of the preceding variables affects it.

A Time Sample is a closed method because the recorder writes down where children are at that moment (raw data) but does not include details of what they are doing, how they are doing it, or what they are saying. The symbols indicate inferences the observer makes as notes are recorded, such as: circles for cooperative play, arrows for uninterrupted play, and a jagged circle for aggressive play. A Time Sample is a very revealing method of gathering and recording information that can be interpreted for many purposes. It even reveals where the adults spend their time and the most and least used areas of the room. Evaluation of children, adults, and curriculum choices all can be made from the Time Sample.

Advantages of the Time Sample Method

The Time Sample is helpful because it

- gathers information on all the children in the class at one time.
- gives quantitative (numerical) information about attention span. (Cindy spent ______ minutes at the easel.)
- indicates the child's play and interest preferences.
- gives clues as to children's strongest areas, inferred by choices.
- gives clues about the child's less-developed areas, inferred by avoidance.
- can indicate the stage of play the child is in.
- can show preferred playmates.
- can track adult positions in the room.
- shows which areas of the classroom are most used.

- shows which areas of the classroom are underutilized.

The recorder can develop abbreviations and adapt the form and method to meet the individual program.

Disadvantages of the Time Sample Method

The Time Sample

- records no details about the nature of the play.
- may not capture children moving while recorder is writing.
- makes inferences that may not be accurate.
- is time intensive for the recorder.
- is effective only where a long period of free choice play is offered.
- is not as effective for toddlers because most play is solitary or parallel, and movement from area to area is more frequent due to the children's shorter attention spans.
- must be done periodically, or it is too judgmental.

Pitfalls to Avoid

Time Samples should be repeated every few weeks so that too much credence is not placed on one isolated Time Sample (as in the exercise interpreting this Time Sample).

The Time Sample is very time consuming, but it is a method that a family member or a volunteer, a nonparticipant observer, could be assigned.

Children must have free choice of activity areas for the Time Sample to be effective. If there is a teacher-led activity during that free choice time, it can be indicated.

Using Technology

A timer is a useful tool to remind the recorder to scan the room again and note where each child is working. Hand-held computers with timers can be used as well. The Time Sample form can be loaded on a computer using the Documents to Go program and can then be used to electronically record the names of the children. Later, when the completed form is downloaded, summary results of each child's activities can be stored in an electronic Portfolio for each child.

How to Find the Time

The Time Sample can be time consuming, but on a day when free play or free choice time is going smoothly, the teacher, assistant, or volunteer is only briefly occupied and can perform other tasks between the recording periods. By carefully planning self-directed projects and curriculum, adult intervention is minimized, leaving time for this kind of record keeping.

What to Do with It

Once a Time Sample is completed, it is stored in the teacher's Class File. Since it has information on all of the children present on that day, it is not copied for individual children's Portfolios. Information can be summarized on each child and placed in that child's Portfolio.

> *Example:* From the Time Sample in Figure 7–2.
> Amy—At the beginning of the day Amy moved around the room frequently, stopping at puzzles and dramatic play. She painted and worked at the Sand Table for longer periods of time. Her play was solitary. 2/26/06
> Edward—Edward and a friend moved together from the climber to an involved block-building project that occupied them for more than 10 minutes. They then moved to the Sand Table, where they played cooperatively. 2/26/06

These summaries give information on play choices, movements, and level of social play. Subsequent Time Samples will be used for comparison to see if the child is in a consistent pattern of play or is moving among the choices in the classroom. These comparisons can be used to measure progress in development as well as to make individual plans for a child who may need some encouragement to extend or experience other choices offered.

Go to the Bind-in-Book CD for Time Sample forms, plans, and resources.

LOOKING AT COGNITIVE DEVELOPMENT

EXERCISE Try the exercise to determine your learning style.

You've purchased a new appliance or piece of equipment. Do you

- read the directions before starting to put it together?
- lay out all the parts and fit them together and refer to the directions if you get stuck?
- have someone help you, reading you the directions while you put it together?
- leave it for later if it doesn't go together on the first try?

These represent visual, tactile, auditory, and tactile attention span and learning styles.

One of the fundamental requirements for learning is a focused attention span. People with brain dysfunctions that prevent them from focusing and filtering all the stimuli that come into the brain at once have difficulty learning. Cognitive development begins with attention span and is the topic of this chapter and continues into the next.

Learning is not just a matter of memorizing information. It is highly complex and individually different. Some people learn best by hearing, reading, and memorizing, whereas others learn best by touching, moving, and interacting either with materials or with people. The art of teaching does not begin with knowing the pupil, but with knowing oneself. Recognizing that others learn in ways different from ourselves profoundly affects understanding and teaching. Teaching then becomes the orchestration of experiences for all modalities or ways of learning. The traditional method of "recite, memorize, and test" has been unsuccessful for many people. The development of cognition—thinking processes—is observable and an area for teachers to consider in environment and schedule planning as well as daily lesson planning.

The development of cognition entwines all other areas already discussed—attachment and separation, physical development, language, and social and emotional development. In the next few chapters, it will be the focus of a closer look. Observers need knowledge and clues to examine closely the changes that take place in children's mental processes. Whether the process is called knowledge, imagination, creativity, reasoning, problem solving, classification, logic, symbolizing, or logico-mathematical reasoning, it all is relevant to cognitive development. The following divisions are for ease of categorization and description, not to imply that these processes are separate from one another.

REVIEW

TIME SAMPLE

Documentation of the duration of a child's chosen activity. Can be compiled on an individual child or an entire class by noting each child's location in the room at regular intervals of time.

Types of Information to Record Using Time Samples

Location of child at regular intervals. It can also yield information on the following:

- interests
- areas of strength
- patterns of behavior
- areas that may not be developed by noting activities the child never selects
- playmates
- social play stage
- child's selection or avoidance of adults in the classroom
- length of time a child stays in one area

Piaget and Cognitive Development

No discussion of cognition can be complete without a review of the work of Jean Piaget (1896–1980) and his interpreters (Flavell, 2002; Furth, 1969; Ginsburg & Opper, 1969). He described the kinds of knowledge and the stages of children's cognitive development.

Piaget was a Swiss scientist, psychologist, and epistemologist (a person who studies the methods and foundations of knowledge). His early work studied the adaptation of mollusks (related to the clam) to different types of water; he was trained in exacting observation skills. He had to look closely to see changes in a mollusk. His life changed dramatically, as most do, when he became a parent. He then transferred those observation skills to a more fascinating subject, his own children, looking and theorizing the source and meaning of each movement and new skill. Out of those close observations and 60 years of study (talk about a long attention span!) came the foundation for most of what is known about infant and young child maturation cognitive processes.

KINDS OF KNOWLEDGE. Piaget categorized not only the stages of cognitive development but the types of knowledge developed as well (Figure 7–3).

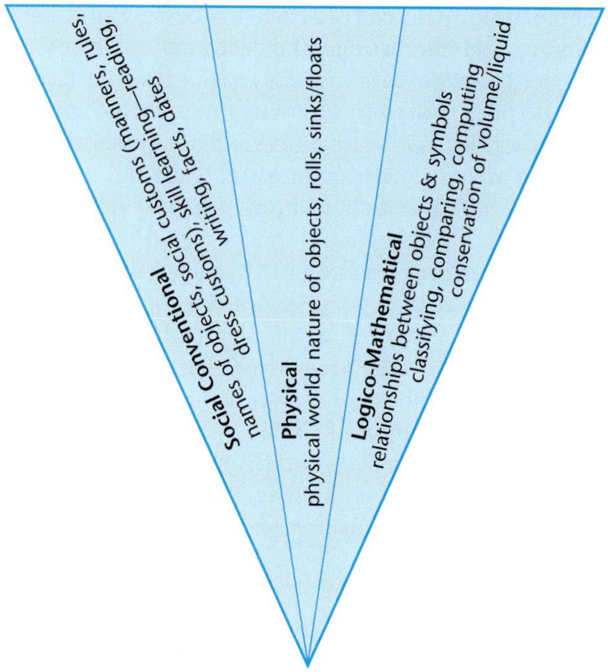

Figure 7–3 Kinds of Knowledge (adapted from Peterson, R., & Felton-Collins, V. 1986. *The Piaget Handbook for Teachers and Parents.* New York: Teachers College Press).

Figure 7–4 Physical knowledge is acquired through experiences with real objects.

Social Conventional Knowledge. **Social conventional knowledge** is described as "the rules of the tribe." It is the type of knowledge that parents teach by instruction and example. These are the accepted social and cultural norms for dress, behavior in different settings, greetings, and ways of addressing others. Some might call this category manners or customs. Language development is another major cognitive category in conventional knowledge. The interactions with other people affect language directly, but certain cognitive processing must be possible before language can appear.

Physical Knowledge. **Physical knowledge** is the accumulation of facts about how the world works. As the child rolls, scoots, crawls, stands, cruises, and climbs, she is inspecting her environment (Figure 7–4). She finds that pushing a ball makes it roll, but pushing a block does not have the same effect. She soon adapts her hand movements and expectations of results when she pushes round objects and grasps square ones. During the sensorimotor stage, the child is gathering data about the properties of all that is around her by manipulating it and watching the results.

Logico-Mathematical Knowledge. **Logico-mathematical knowledge** is the primary area usually associated with cognitive development, the processing of information to draw conclusions, either verbal or mathematical. Seeking relationships is the main task of this type of processing. It is all about the observation of similarities, differences, and commonalities. Variables are manipulated and the results measured. These abstract concepts are clarified when we watch as a child plays with blocks:

- *Similarities and **matching***—He places the same size blocks on top of each other.
- *Commonalities and **classification***—He places all the blocks together and all the toy animals together.
- ***Cause and effect***—He tries to stand the toy horse on the small block too small for all four feet. Then he tries to stand it up on the large block, which succeeds.
- *Measuring and **seriation***—He places the animals in a line according to size.
- ***Rote counting***—He orally counts, perhaps inaccurately, or out of order, "1, 2, 3, 6, 8."
- ***One-to-one correspondence***—He points to each animal as he accurately counts, "1, 2, 3, 4."
- *Object permanence*—He knows that if one of the animals falls off the table, out of his sight, it still exists. If he looks for it, he can find it.
- ***Conservation***—He knows if he sawed one of the two blocks in half, the two halves would weigh the same as the whole block.

These three areas of cognitive development—social conventional knowledge, physical knowledge, and logico-mathematical knowledge—change in a predictable pattern from simple to complex, over a period of time, at individual rates. They have implications for curriculum planning and assessment.

Piaget's Stages of Cognitive Development

INFANCY—SENSORIMOTOR STAGE (BIRTH TO 24 MONTHS). What Piaget's terms the **Sensorimotor Stage**, birth through 24 months old, gives clues of how the infant is processing information through the senses and acting on information with developing large and small muscles (Figure 7–5). Vision in a newborn is at the legally blind level (Flavell, 2002) because of the inability to focus or fixate. However, the newborn is able to distinguish between light and dark contrast (figure-ground) about 7 to 8 inches away, and discern shape and contours. That is just what is needed to look at a human face at close distance. Visual acuity increases rapidly, and by six months it is at the adult level. Hearing is at a near-adult level at birth. Some research suggests an infant can discriminate the mother's voice from others if it is in "motherese," the up-and-down quality that adults naturally use with babies. The infant has been found able to discriminate between "pa" and "ba" sounds at an early age as well. Touch is well developed, especially the sensors for receptive touch, which have caused an interest in baby massage. Those perceptions, along with taste and smell, are present at birth, though at rudimentary levels. Their rapid development necessitates families and teachers to provide sensory-rich environments and experiences for even the youngest infant. In this way, they have a healthy start on the road to cognitive development.

Piaget described intricate substages in which information processing takes circular pathways. Each new piece of information goes through this chain, trying to make a match. Piaget called this constructing knowledge. This basic principle is the foundation for professional practice. The child is involved actively in exploration and experimentation to form his own knowledge. Knowledge is not the transfer of abstract information but the formation of associations based on information from the senses.

To help you become familiar with this theory, Figure 7–6, Figure 7–7, and Figure 7–8 illustrate your own cognitive processes as you read this passage. If you already know and understand Piaget's concept of association, as you read this and look at

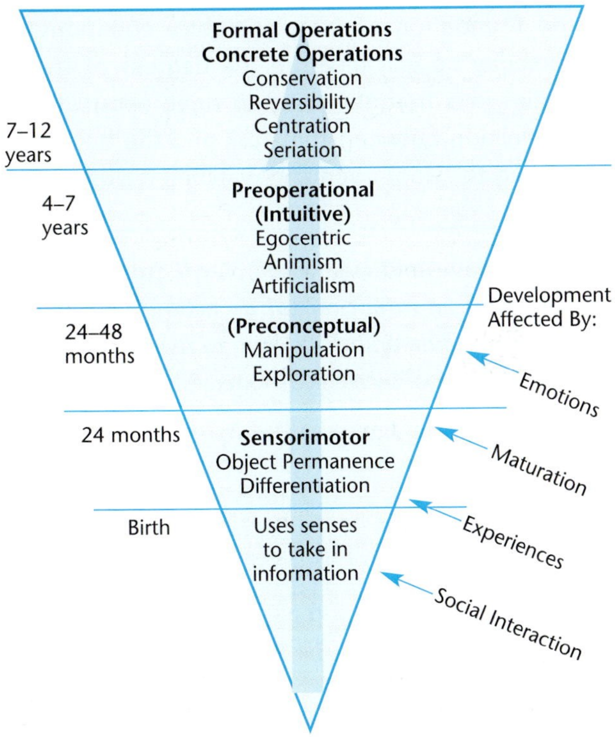

Figure 7–5 Piaget's Stages of Cognitive Development.

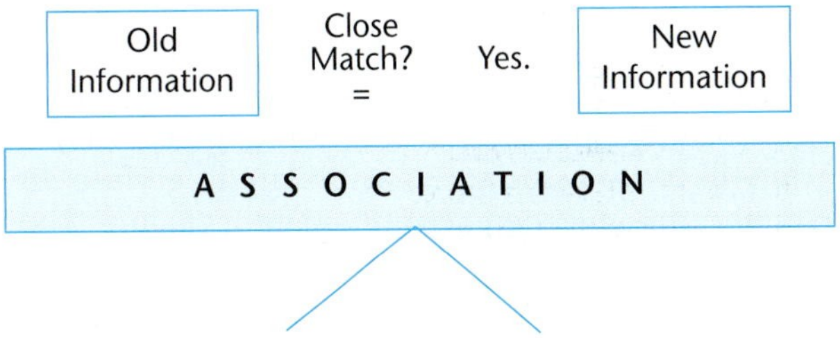

Figure 7–6 Association.

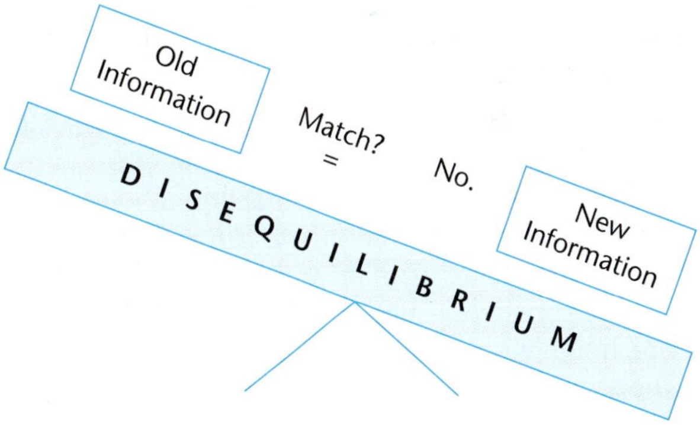

Figure 7–7 Disequilibrium.

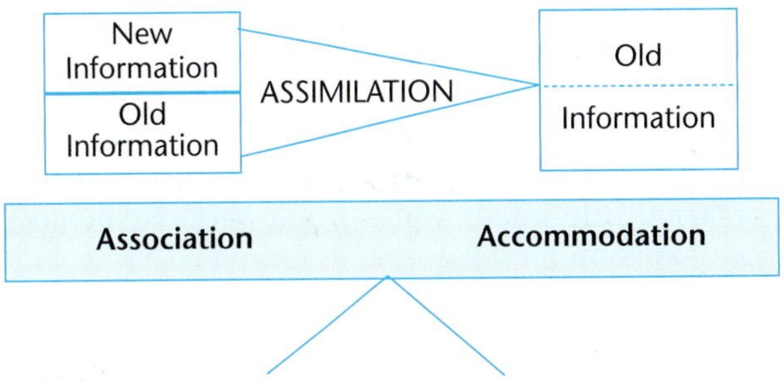

Figure 7–8 Assimilation.

Figure 7–6, your brain is processing, comparing this new information with what you already knew (old information), and you make an association. This is an "aha, I know that" moment.

If it is new information for you, for example, if you realize that this use of the word **association** is different from your previous understanding of the definition, you are in **disequilibrium** (mental confusion or imbalance) until you make a match (Figure 7–7). Taking in the information and forming a bridge or relationship to what you already know is called **assimilation**. You have added another building block—or schema—to existing information or deepened your understanding.

When the new information is associated, assimilated, and added to the old information, you have achieved **accommodation**. You have somewhat changed the structure of what you previously knew, forming new ideas or blocks of knowledge. That is the process of assimilation. Now all of that becomes old information to begin the process all over again the next time a new piece of information is received. You will try to associate it, assimilate it, go into disequilibrium, and then accommodate it (Figure 7–8).

Here is an example: An infant suckles her mother's breast and receives milk. She builds an association between sucking and milk. As she is rolling around in her crib a few months later, the blanket brushes her lips. The reflex motion causes her to suck. "Ugh! I'm not getting milk!" She could not make a match between the milk she received previously and this new substance. She has tried to associate the substance to what she already knew, but it was lint instead of milk. She was in disequilibrium. She spit the blanket out and now has another action or reaction to sucking. She can continue or she can spit it out. She can now assimilate, or make a judgment, and decide on a new course of action, accommodation. She may decide that it is a second-best alternative and continue to chew on it when the nipple is not available.

This process occurs thousands of times a day in nanoseconds (one billionth of a second) without any awareness or conscious decision of the thinker.

The cognitive tasks of the Sensorimotor Stage are self-differentiation and object permanence. Around six months of age, the infant forms the concept that he is a separate entity from the crib, from the car seat, but most of all from the humans around him. This has implications when adults leave the room and the infant wants them back. Remember the discussion on separation in Chapter 1?

Very closely allied is the knowledge that items and people still exist even when out of sight. If a child drops a spoon over the side of the high chair tray, she will look for it. When her teacher leaves the room, she may whine or cry until he comes back. By the end of the second year, infants have both mental representations, which are leading them into the development of language and on into the Preoperational Stage.

Of course, stages are not like stair steps but more like escalators, transitions to the next stage in a smooth yet sequential pattern.

@ it happened to me

Beginning Geometry

A group of parents and toddlers were gathered to share stories, frustrations, and advice. A less-than-two-year-old toddled over to a swinging door with an automatic closer. When he leaned against it, it opened a little way, then closed with a hissing sound. He seriously looked at the door and tried it again. Push, close, hiss. Push, close, hiss. All this time he was looking up at the top of the door jamb. Mom came running over, "Come away from there." She was probably concerned about pinched fingers and what would happen if he pushed too hard and went on through the doorway. I was fascinated that he was not tempted to do that. He was mesmerized by the action and reaction of the door.

As we took his point of view and looked up as he was, we saw the ceiling produced a bright changing triangle as the door closed. He formed a mental image (schema) of triangles and their changing shapes that day that will be the foundation of later geometry equations. Someday he will measure the degrees of the angles in a triangle. I like to think about the connection between that task and the day he pushed the door open and watched it close.

Do you have an IT HAPPENED TO ME story about observing an infant repeat an action over and over to find meaning? I'd love to read it. Please send it to WeekbyWeek@thomsonlearning.com

The Preoperational Stage (Two to Seven Years)

The **Preoperational Stage** consists of the Preconceptual Period (two to four years old) and the Intuitive Period (four to seven years old).

According to Piaget (Peterson & Felton-Collins, 1986) there are four factors that guide development from one substage to the next:

1. emotions that create feelings and motivate learning
2. maturation of physical growth, including the nervous system
3. experiences (own learning and self-discovery)
4. social interaction and influence of parents, teachers, and peers (p. 4)

Having an understanding of these factors assists the early childhood educator to assess and plan for an environment and curriculum that meets the cognitive needs of this stage.

In the Preconceptual Period, the child is an active participant in learning, intentionally acting on the environment and finding how things work. Problems are attacked mostly through trial and error and by manipulation of materials. Instead of just using a spoon to feed herself, she will use it to feed her dolly. This moves her from the function performed on herself to acting on another. She may even move to the symbolic or dramatic use of the play, as when she uses the spoon as a microphone like she saw the singer use on television last night. Throughout this substage, the major task is classification, making connections by physically and mentally placing items in pairs and groups. The vocabulary is rapidly building, and grammar is expanding. Now sentences convey messages and control the environment and other people.

In the Intuitive Period (four to seven years old), as described by Piaget, the reasons the child gives for phenomena are based on appearances or intuition rather than understanding. There are many mental processes the child cannot do until the next stage (the Concrete Operational Stage). Flavell (2002) and others, however, have looked at the Intuitive Period in a more positive light, finding that children in this stage have built large knowledge structures. Although these structures are present, the child may not yet represent them in either language or art. The receptive processes are greater than the expressive. The child understands much more than he can convey either in words, drawings, or writing.

Some classic terminology and experiments demonstrate what a Preoperational child will attain in the next stage:

Egocentrism—The child believes that everyone thinks and feels as he does. (A small screen separates the child and a toy from the examiner, who asks, "Can I see the toy?" If the child can see it, she will answer, "Yes," even if a screen blocks the examiner's view.)

Conservation—The child does not understand the variables that can make quantity look different although the volume is unchanged. (There are two glasses of water with the same level of liquid.) The examiner asks, "Are they the same?" Then liquid is poured from one glass into a tall, thin beaker. The examiner asks, "Are they the same now?" The Preoperational child, without the understanding of the properties of volume, will say, "No. This one has more." The child will answer by appearance.

Reversibility—The child is not yet able to mentally reverse an operation. (The examiner asks, "What will happen if I pour this back? Then will it be the same?")

Centration—The Preoperational child is only able to focus on one attribute at a time. (If the child is sorting by color but the blocks also have different shapes, he will have difficulty centering [concentrating] on sorting by color, ignoring the shape.)

Seriation—The Preoperational child is not able to place items in a series according to a rule such as height or weight. (They can probably pick out largest and smallest but have difficulty with those in between.)

The Preoperational child makes cognitive errors based on appearance, not reasoning, such as:

Animism—The child believes that all objects have properties of being alive. ("My book will be lonely if I leave it home.")

Artificialism—The child believes that natural phenomena are man-caused. ("Daddy, make it stop raining so we can go on our picnic.")

CONCRETE OPERATIONAL STAGE (SEVEN TO ELEVEN YEARS). All the processes that the Preoperational child is developing come to bloom in the **Concrete Operational Stage**. Children now can use logical and rational thinking to understand and explain the properties of volume and number, classifying, seriating, centering, and reversing. It does not occur all at once as they celebrate their seventh birthday; it happens in small, incremental steps as major neurological changes take place. Around seven years old, the ways of thinking have changed. The child is now ready physically, socially, emotionally, and cognitively to apply the experiences of the past seven years to the serious business of learning.

The task of sorting and classifying, recognizing similarities and differences, is *the* recurring curriculum theme. This is not to be interpreted that ways of learning change from those experiential, hands-on explorations. Piaget's theory is complex and full of terminology, but it has practical application for methods, materials, environment, and curricula in any early childhood program. The environment and curriculum allow each child to construct knowledge through exploration, manipulation, and the sensory experiences the adults provide. The role of the adult is still to prepare the environment, facilitate the exploration, support and scaffold approximations of development, and record the progress. If the first roles are fulfilled, there will be progress to record.

Attention

"Attention is the focusing of the individual's perceptual processes upon a specific aspect of the environment. Learning cannot take place unless the individual is able to focus attention" (Cook, Klein, & Tessier, 2004, p. 328). To focus attention, the child must concentrate on the object or task at hand while also ignoring other, insignificant stimuli. This is a skill that is being refined from birth and is critical to school performance, social interaction, and even survival. It is one of the three basic processes used in information processing: attention, perception, and memory.

Jensen, in *Teaching with the Brain in Mind* (1998), gives understandable insight into the workings of the brain. He discusses the purpose of attention for survival and to extend pleasurable states. It provides sensory information on which to base decisions about our next actions. The pathways of attention consist of alarm, orientation, identification, and decision. A child may see the flicker of fire, but without prior experiences on which to base a decision, the attention and decision to seek it out may prove very dangerous. On the other hand, when a child is absorbed in play and the teacher flicks the lights, the decision point is whether to continue the pleasure of play or give attention now to the teacher's agenda. Is it any wonder that children get hurt or in trouble?

The visual system provides 80 percent of the information needed for this process to take place. The brain has to process or sort out irrelevant data and amplify the relevant data. Chemical changes take place during this process, assisting in heightened attention during times of stress and threat. Attention also flows in cycles from high to low throughout the day and night, with periods of inattention of great importance for processing time. When teachers see children gazing out the window or standing and watching, a common response is, "Pay attention." If teachers heeded Jensen's explanation of the processing time, those inactive moments would be seen in a new light. Everyone has experienced profound thoughts that come long after a discussion or experience. The brain just needed that time to process the information and make sense and meaning.

Memory

During the Sensorimotor and Preoperational stages, the child interacts with real objects and builds memory of the properties of these objects and how they react. This assimilation and accommodation is stored in the memory. John Flavell, whose whole career has been devoted to studying cognitive development, reinforces the importance of providing young children with experiences that will increase their knowledge of the world in which they live. He says, "What the hand knows has an enormous effect on what the head learns and remembers" (Flavell, 1987, p. 213). Memory is the construction material of cognitive development.

Those who compare memory to an information processing system say there are three components of the hardware: the sensory memory that receives input from the environment, the working memory that is the site of ongoing cognitive activity, and the long-term memory, a permanent storehouse of knowledge that is present but sometimes hard to access. As children get older, they acquire more efficient strategies to solve problems and are able to inhibit distractions, and some cognitive processes become virtually automatic, aiding in faster processing of information. Kail (2001) sees these as smoother transitions between the cognitive stages than Piaget's steps.

EXERCISE **Respond to the following statements about yourself:**

I have a (bad/good) memory.
It helps me to remember if I . . .

There are many different aspects of memory. Recognition is the most basic. Piaget's term for it was *association*. It is that matching to a past piece of information. Studies of infants and young children show this basic ability is very high early in life. Eliot reviewed early brain development in the book *What's Going on in There?* (1999) and documents incredible changes in the first five years. A fascinating study of 360 infants and toddlers less than three years old found that long-term memory does exist, especially when accompanied by verbal reminders and tangible related items (Bauer, Wenner, Dropik, & Wewerka, 2000). This adds evidence to the importance of verbal repetition and presenting children with connected sensory experiences to assist memory. Sensory experiences are usually messy ones that teachers or families are reluctant to allow. However, they are more than fun and mess, they are important to brain development. The sensory object that infants younger than 12 months are most familiar with is their food. Cultural values about playing with food come into conflict with the educational value of sensory experiences. This dilemma must be resolved with sensitivity and an acceptable solution. Other sensory experiences for infants include massage, bathing, rocking, and patting—all done most naturally without thought as to their cognitive development implications.

Visual recognition has very high rates of memory. "Ah, yes, I've met you before but don't remember your name." Recall, the next phase after recognition, is more difficult, placing the name with the face recognized. The strategy used to help in that recall or retrieval of information is mnemonics. Figure 7–9 illustrates six keys that might be used to "unlock" memory:

- *Wait time*—One of the most natural keys, used by all ages, involves waiting for a period of time and letting the mind work.

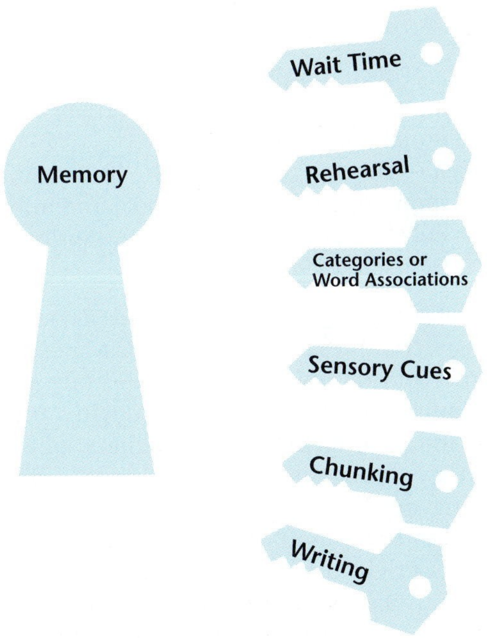

Figure 7–9 Keys to Unlock Memory.

- *Rehearsal*—Repeating, either aloud or silently, is a technique that experimenters have taught young children to use (Kail, 1990). However, it is not long lasting, nor does it become spontaneous.
- *Categories or word associations*—Older children and adults use this technique to put words into categories to aid in retrieval.
- *Sensory cues*—Kail (1990) found that young children use visual and sensory retrieval cues. This reinforces the emphasis on an active, real approach for teaching young children, using multisensory experiences. For example, reading a story about an apple, accompanied by eating one, will help children remember the story about the apple.
- *Chunking*—Memory is aided by breaking strings of information down into smaller parts, such as Social Security numbers, telephone numbers, or song lyrics. (For example, "two, forty-eight, eleven, seventy-nine, seventy-six" for 248-11-7976, or 1-800-FORKIDS for 1-800-367-5437.) Teachers who use rebus charts to teach children song lyrics use visual cues and teach small portions of the song at a time.
- *Writing*—Writing words down helps implant them in the memory and aids in recall. That is the major reason for *written* observations.

The awareness of the need to remember begins in the Preoperational period. Preschoolers were found to be inaccurate predictors of what they could remember, and ill-equipped to develop or act on strategies. By the time they were seven, however, they could group material into similarities or categories to help them remember. They used common aids like making lists or placing items to remember by their coat (Kail, 1990).

The strategies that different people use to learn and remember have been explored from a number of theories. Multiple intelligences and learning styles are ones that have caught the interest of researchers. Educators also see the profound differences between children, bringing that recognition to the next step, which is adopting an individualized curriculum and expectations based on each child's learning style and strengths.

BRAIN DEVELOPMENT. Research on brain development came to the forefront in the late 1990s with the use of new brain imaging technologies coupled with growing concern about the status of children in America. The outcome was a heightened awareness in the media, and among policymakers and families, of what many teachers of the very young knew all along, that these are critical times for learning and growing.

The studies prove it is the interplay of "nature" and "nurture" that is necessary for maximum development and that early care has a long-lasting impact on ability to develop, learn, and relate to others. Timing is crucial, and negative experiences have serious and sustained effects. In *From Neurons to Neighborhoods* (2000), scientists looked at child development through the lens of brain development and early childhood relationships to make a case for the policy and practice of early education and intervention. The research reinforced the concept that it is all about making connections between what has been experienced in the past and how this new experience is alike and different from that. As more is known about the lasting neurological effects of positive early experiences at critical times, as well as exposure to negative influences like poor nutrition and drug and alcohol use by the mother, early education becomes a priority and an investment (Shonkoff & Phillips, 2000).

Multiple Intelligences and Hemisphericity

Howard Gardner (1983) has looked beyond learning styles and identified various different types of intelligence that he calls Frames of Mind. He criticizes schools that only measure and value some while ignoring others. He has identified eight of these **multiple intelligences**:

1. *Linguistic intelligence*—remembering what one hears and reads
2. *Logical-mathematical intelligence*—figuring things out logically using reasoning and problem solving
3. *Spatial intelligence*—recreating what one sees, imagines, visualizes, or creates
4. *Bodily-kinesthetic intelligence*—using one's body to learn, interact, and express oneself
5. *Musical intelligence*—innate musical talent
6. *Interpersonal intelligence*—understanding, cooperative, and communicative with others
7. *Intrapersonal intelligence*—comfortable with self, works best alone, and pursues one's own interests
8. *Naturalist intelligence*—ability to discriminate among living things and a sensitivity to other features of the natural world.

In a later book, *Intelligence Reframed* (1999), Gardner goes beyond these, presenting the idea that there may be any number of others. Attempts have been made to assess individuals for various intelligences, but Gardner resists this "assessment mentality" because tests tend to be biased toward some intelligences and thus would not be a true measure. He has worked instead to "observe children at play (or at work) systematically and to arrive at a quantitative description of their intelligences" (p. 138). This work is called Project Spectrum.

EXERCISE **List the people you know who fit into each of the multiple intelligences. Where are your strengths or gifts?**

By observing and recognizing each child's cognitive style, the teacher can better understand and individualize the curriculum. An environment providing for all modalities sounds very much like a developmentally appropriate early childhood classroom, one that provides the following:

- language-based, print-rich materials
- real objects to explore, manipulate, and experiment with
- art and construction materials to create without models
- music, rhythm, and songs for transitions
- large muscle equipment and opportunities for creative movement
- cooperative activities and a social atmosphere
- alone spaces and individual activities

Another related theory is **brain hemisphericity**. The two hemispheres, or sides, of the brain deal with information and behavioral functions in different ways.

Left—This hemisphere of the brain is analytical, logical, sequential, orderly, verbal, computational, linear, concrete.

Right—This hemisphere of the brain is intuitive, spontaneous, random, casual and informal, holistic, sensory, metaphoric. (Springer & Deutsch, 1998)

The study of the brain continues as neurological testing techniques advance. Scientists are still sorting out the contributions of nature and nurture to the functioning of the brain and studying the effects when injury or illness affects one hemisphere.

Many researchers feel traditional educational teaching and testing methods ignore the sensory, visual, and intuition functions of the brain. The labeling of right-brained learners as learning disabled is an injustice that learning-styles theorists seek to eliminate (Armstrong, 2000). The developmentally appropriate curriculum includes reading, writing, listening, and speaking at the children's level; open-ended building materials; puzzles; music for listening, producing, and moving to; materials and environment for using large and small muscles; attention to receptive and expressive emotions; opportunities for self-reflection; and incorporating plants, animals, and the physical world into the environment both indoors and outside.

HELPING ALL CHILDREN WITH ATTENTION SPAN

Cognitive development, with respect to memory and attention span, is affected by physical, emotional, and cultural influences.

Mental Processing Difficulties

Different causes such as birth defects, maternal drug use, and poor nutrition may result in difficulties in the basic cognitive processes.

ATTENTION DEFICIT. Attention is defined as the ability to focus on a specific aspect of the environment and ignore the other stimuli. Some children with extremely short attention spans, difficulty concentrating, and high distractibility have been diagnosed with **Attention Deficit** Hyperactivity Disorder **(ADHD)** or Attention Deficit Disorder **(ADD)** without hyperactivity. Children with these disorders have been mislabeled sometimes as emotionally disturbed, mentally retarded, or autistic. It is the nature of young children to be impulsive and easily distracted, especially when the classroom does not provide outlets for their energy or appropriate curriculum. This makes the disorder difficult to diagnose. Is it the environment, the curriculum, or the child? Diagnosis begins with gathering information regarding physical, mental, and social-emotional development from families, medical professionals, and teachers. Federal laws, such as the Individuals with Disabilities Education Act (IDEA) and Section 504 of the Rehabilitation Act of 1973 provide coverage for children with ADD (Council, 1992).

The Time Samples of the group will give a quantitative recording of attention behavior. It also will compare the child in question to his peers. (The word *his* is selected purposefully here because more boys than girls are diagnosed with ADHD.)

Running Records focusing on the child will also aid helping professionals in the diagnosis. Even though a child has a short attention span, high distractibility, high activity, and impulsivity, he may not have ADHD.

@ it happened to me

Pay Attention

One of my first-semester college students who worked in an out-of-school program related a story in class one day about a boy with autism in her group. She said she had to speak to the father when he picked up his son. She told the father that the boy was causing a problem because he wouldn't pay attention and follow the rules. She told the father that he should work with his son about that.

What do you think that revealed about the young woman? Did she lack knowledge of a disorder that she knew affected a child in her charge? Did her ignorance lead her to lay a burden on a parent beyond the one he already had? What strategies do you think she had been using to get the boy to pay attention? What would you have said to her if you were the instructor?

Do you have an IT HAPPENED TO ME story about rushing to a conclusion without all the facts? I'd love to read it. Please send it to WeekbyWeek@thomsonlearning.com

It is important for the family or school staff not to impose a label or a diagnosis, leaving that to the professionals. There are brain functioning tests and a breakthrough link to identify the specific gene, discovered at the University of Chicago (*Advance*, 1995, p. 2). Most children with this disorder respond favorably to a stimulant that paradoxically increases attention and decreases impulsivity and activity, along with child and family counseling. There is a national information support group: CHADD (Children and Adults with Attention-Deficit/Hyperactivity Disorder), http://www.chadd.org.

PERCEPTION. Perception is the ability to interpret the objects and events stimulating the senses. For children with a limited ability in hearing, sight, taste, smell, or touch, the intake of information limits their

TOPICS IN OBSERVATION

Attention Span and Autism

Autism is characterized as a "pervasive developmental disorder" (Kauffman, 1997) because it affects all areas of functioning, such as communication, social, physical, and cognitive development. It occurs in 1 in 400 children, occurs in more boys than girls by a ratio of 4:1 boys, and has a neurological basis, perhaps with genetic links (Mauk, Reber, & Batshaw, 1997; Pericak-Vance, 2003; Powers, 2000). There is some evidence that it appears in clusters (Bertrand et al., 2001; Yeargin-Allsopp et al., 2003). While there is no objective measure for diagnosing autism, its effect on the attention span can be an important clue. In contrast to many other cognitive disabilities, such as ADD or ADHD, its onset can be recognized before the age of three. Autism is a spectrum disorder ranging from high-functioning Asperger syndrome to classic autism to mixed autism associated with other conditions such as sensory integration disorder and mental retardation.

Between year one and year two, and certainly by year three, there is a noticeable attention span difference in a child with autism. The child may give little attention to other people, peers, or family. Instead, the child can be preoccupied with an object or a routine to the exclusion of all other interactions and stimuli. The child's behavior can be extreme in response to altered routines or the denial of the obsessive object. Children with autism have been known to attach to vacuum cleaners, ceiling fans, and spinning toys to the exclusion of social interaction, failing even to make eye contact. They can attend to their chosen item to such a degree that all other outside happenings are completely ignored. Many children with autism who have a less severe attachment to specific objects still have difficulty focusing attention on the relevant stimuli in a task. For example, the child with autism who is listening to a story may be so fascinated by the pattern in the rug on which he is sitting that he never gets the context of the story. Language may be affected by echolalia (repeating a phrase over and over) but ignoring the answer, giving attention only to the question, never noticing or listening to the response.

Asperger syndrome is on the high-functioning end of the autistic spectrum. It is classified with autism because it too is a pervasive developmental disorder, one that can range from mild to severe, affecting several domains of development. It often involves the physical domain, particularly balance and coordination. The child may be sensory sensitive (profoundly aware of sensory stimuli such as touch or sound), have irrational fears, and be easily obsessed about things that might happen in their world that would not be stressful to typical children. This can put children with Asperger syndrome in a terrible state of anxiety. It especially involves their social development because of the inability to understand social cues, their own emotions, or the emotions of others. However, expressive language development for those with Asperger syndrome is often very advanced, and the child may display a large vocabulary and savant knowledge about an obscure subject.

You as the observer may recognize symptoms of autism spectrum disorder that otherwise may be described as stubbornness, distractibility, precociousness, or shyness. It is not your role to diagnose but to observe, take specific, accurate information, and share the results with the person who needs to know. Remember, students, it is not for you to approach a family member with any of your suspicions. That must be very carefully done by the teacher or special-services personnel. (This was written with the consultation of Liz Smithmeyer and Michael Logalo.)

cognitive processing. The other modalities may compensate for the limited ones but only as much as the cognitive capacity is able to accommodate. Young children especially depend on sight to cue all kinds of behavior with less attention to verbal language. They carefully watch and imitate rather than listen and do.

Perception depends on the ability to discriminate between appearances, sounds, and textures. With impairments of the receptors or the cognitive structures to process the information, these sensory cues go unrecognized and ignored. The teacher of children with such impaired sensory abilities makes adaptations for the other senses to receive a similar message, such as tapping a rhythm that cannot be heard or associating textures with the words *cool, warm, rough,* and *soft.*

Memory is the third basic cognitive process, received through attention and perception. It is stored in the central nervous system in the various categories of short-term, long-term, visual, rote, recognition, and recall. Children with nervous system difficulties, such as muscular dystrophy or multiple sclerosis, as well as children with limited cognitive ability, may experience memory difficulties.

As with all cognitive, physical, or emotional disorders, families, teachers, and those on special education committees seek to place the child in the least restrictive environment, that in which the child can maximize the abilities which are present and making modifications and allowances for the areas of lower functioning.

Cultural Differences in Memory and Attention Span

Research regarding attention span in various cultures has had mixed results. The assessment of cognitive development must consider the cultural context. When memory tasks used for assessment are unrelated to the child's world, children do poorly (Rogoff, 1990). But when tests were culturally relevant, few differences in memory are found (Mandler, Scribner, Cole, & DeForest, 1980). This is consistent with the principles of fair testing: The test should be culturally relevant to be a valid measurement of ability.

HELPING PROFESSIONALS FOR ATTENTION CONCERNS

If a difficulty with memory, attention span, or cognitive processing is observed, those concerns are addressed by the teaching team, the supervisor, and then brought to the attention of the family of the child with tact and sensitivity. Such difficulties are nebulous and often extremely difficult to diagnose, and even more difficult to treat and strategize. People who may be able to help are described here:

pediatrician—physician specifically trained to treat children

psychologist or psychiatrist—professionals trained in areas of emotional disorders

neurologist—physician specifically trained in sensory or motor responses due to nervous system impairments

special educators—specialists with knowledge or normal and atypical children's development and appropriate education strategies

OTHER METHODS

Other Methods to Record Attention Span

Anecdotal/Running Records—In recording an incident or sample of behavior, attention span may be observed and noted.

Checklist/Rating Scales—Criteria may be included where an inference about attention span is noted.

Frequency Count—An individual child could be the focus of a Frequency Count, noting every time the child changes activity by choice, inferring a long or short attention span depending on the number of changes over a certain period.

Conversations or Interviews—When talking with a child, the child's ability to sustain the conversation or tendency to wander and not be able to concentrate could give indications of attention span.

Work Samples—The child's work may show a short or long attention span—one swipe with a paint brush, one block placed on end, compared to page-covered paintings or intricate block buildings.

Media—Photographs showing the child concentrating, audio recordings of involved conversations, or video recordings following the child from choice to choice can document attention span.

STANDARDS

Here are selected examples of standards related to attention span:

NAEYC Standards for Accreditation (2003)

2.B. Areas of Development: Social-Emotional Development 2.B.03

Universal
Children have varied opportunities to learn the skills needed to regulate their emotions, behavior, and attention span.

Division for Early Childhood Recommended Practices (Sandall et al., 2005)
Practice 2: Child-focused interventions

Adults design environments to promote children's safety, active engagement, learning, participation, and membership.

1. Physical space and materials are structured and adapted to promote engagement, play, interaction, and learning by attending to children's preferences and interests, using novelty, using responsive toys, providing adequate amounts of materials, and using defined spaces.

KEY TERMS

accommodation
ADD
ADHD
animism
artificialism
assimilation
association
attention deficit
attention span
autism
brain hemisphericity
cause and effect
centration
classification
Concrete Operational Stage
conservation
disequilibrium
egocentrism
logico-mathematical knowledge
matching
multiple intelligences
one-to-one correspondence
physical knowledge
Preoperational Stage
reversibility
rote counting
Sensorimotor Stage
seriation
social conventional knowledge
Time Sample

Go to the Bind-in-Book CD for:

Plan Week 7 Part A, Directions for a Time Sample on Attention Span, including What to Do with It, Portfolio Overview Example, Sharing with Child and Family, Actions—Read a Book, In the Environment, In the Curriculum, In the Newsletter
Plan Week 7 Part B, Conversations with Group B for Speech and Language
Plan Week 7 Part C, Reflective Journal

REFERENCES

Armstrong, T. (2000). *In their own way.* New York: Jeremy P. Tarcher/Putman.

Bauer, P. J., Wenner, J. A., Dropik, P. L., & Wewerka, S. S. (2000). Parameters of remembering and forgetting in the transition from infancy to early childhood. *Monograph of the Society for Research in Child Development, 65* (4).

Bertrand, J., Mars, A., Boyle, C., Bove, F., Yeargin-Allsopp, M., & Decoufle, P. (2001). Prevalence of autism in a United States population: the Brick Township, New Jersey, investigation. *Pediatrics, 108* (5). Retrieved April 1, 2003, from http://www.pediatrics.org.

Bredekamp, S., & Copple, C. (Eds.). (1997). *Developmentally appropriate practice in early childhood programs, revised edition.* Washington, DC: National Association for the Education of Young Children.

Cook, R. E., Klein, M. D., & Tessier, A. (2004). *Adapting early childhood curricula for children in inclusive setting* (6th ed.). Upper Saddle River, NJ: Pearson Education.

Council for Exceptional Children. (1992). *Providing an appropriate education to children with attention deficit disorder.* ERIC Digest ED352747-92.

Eliot, L. (1999). *What's going on in there?: How the brain and mind develop in the first five years of life.* New York: Bantam Books.

Flavell, J. H. (1987). *Cognitive development* (2nd ed.). Englewood Cliffs, NJ: Prentice Hall.

Flavell, J. H., Miller, P. H., & Miller, S. A. (2002). *Cognitive development.* Upper Saddle River, NJ: Prentice Hall.

Furth, H. G. (1969). *Piaget and knowledge.* Englewood Cliffs, NJ: Prentice Hall.

Gardner, H. (1983). *Frames of mind: Theory of multiple intelligences.* New York: Basic Books.

Gardner, H. (1999). *Intelligence reframed: Multiple intelligences for the 21st century.* New York: Basic Books.

Ginsburg, H., & Opper, S. (1969). *Piaget's theory of intellectual development.* Englewood Cliffs, NJ: Prentice Hall.

Jensen, E. (1998). *Teaching with the brain in mind.* Alexandria, VA: Association for Supervision and Curriculum.

Kail R. (1990). *The development of memory in children* (2nd ed.). New York: W. H. Freeman & Co.

Kail R. V. (2001). *Children and their development* (2nd ed.). Upper Saddle River, NJ: Prentice Hall.

Kauffman, J. M. (1997). *Characteristics of emotional and behavioral disorder of children and youth* (6th ed.). Upper Saddle River, NJ: Merrill.

Mandler, J. M., Scribner, S., Cole, M., & DeForest, M. (1980). Cross-cultural invariance in story recall. *Child Development, 51,* 19–26.

Mauk, J. E., Reber, M., & Batshaw, M. L. (1997). Autism and other pervasive developmental disorders. In M. L. Batshaw (Ed.), *Children with disabilities* (4th ed.). Baltimore, MD: Brookes.

National Association for the Education of Young Children (2005). *NAEYC early childhood program standards and accreditation criteria.* Washington, DC: Author.

Pericak-Vance, M. A. (2003). Discovering the genetics of autism. *USA Today Magazine, 131,* January 2003, 56.

Peterson, R., & Felton-Collins, V. (1986). *The Piaget handbook for teachers and parents; Children in the age of discovery, preschool–third grade.* New York: Teachers College Press.

Powers, M. D. (2000). What is autism? In M. D. Powers (Ed.), *Children with autism: A parents' guide* (2nd ed.). Bethesda, MD: Woodbine House.

Researchers identify specific gene for ADHD. (1995, April 24). *ADVANCE for Speech Pathologists, (5),* 16.

Rogoff, B. (1990). *Apprenticeship in thinking: Cognitive development in social context.* New York: Oxford University Press.

Sandall, S. R., Hemmeter, M. L., Smith, B. J., & McLean, M. E. (2005). *DEC recommended practices: A comprehensive guide.* Denver, CO: Sopris West.

Shonkoff, J. P., & Phillips, D. A. (Eds.). (2000). *From neurons to neighborhoods: The science of early childhood development.* Washington, DC: National Academy Press.

Springer, S. P., & Deutsch, G. (1998). *Left brain, right brain: Perspectives from cognitive neuroscience* (5th ed.). New York: W. H. Freeman and Company.

Yeargin-Allsopp, M., Rice, C., Karapurkar, T., Doernberg, N., Boyle, C., & Murphy, C. (2003). Prevalence of autism in a US metropolitan area. *Journal of American Medical Association, 289* (1), 87–89.

RESOURCES

Armstrong, T. (2000). *In their own way.* New York: Jeremy P. Tarcher/Putman.

Cushner, K. H., McClellan, A., & Safford, P. L. (2002). *Human diversity in education: An integrative approach* (4th ed.). New York: McGraw-Hill.

Grisham-Brown, J., Hemmeter, M. L., Pretti-Frontczak, K. (2005). *Blended practices for teaching young children in inclusive settings.* Baltimore, MD: Paul Brookes.

Jensen, E. (1998). *Teaching with the brain in mind.* Alexandria, VA: Association for Supervision and Curriculum.

CHAPTER 8

Using Standardized Measurements to Look at Cognitive Development

IN THIS CHAPTER

- Using Tests
- Topics in Observation: Measuring Cognitive Development—Why Not Test?
- Looking at Cognitive Development: Math, Science, and Technology
- Helping All Children with Cognitive Development
- Topics in Observation: "Real" Curriculum
- Helping Professionals for Cognitive Concerns

USING TESTS

Every family wants to know how their child is doing. Some want to know how their child is doing compared to the rest of the children in the class. Teachers want to know if the children in their class are learning what they have been teaching. Some people (such as school administrators or policymakers) want to know if the children in a class/school/state/nation are learning what they should be learning at a particular age. Politicians want to know if tax dollars are being used efficiently to produce the desired outcomes.

A World of Tests

We live in a world of tests. Our driving skills are tested before we can obtain a driver's license. Doctors are tested before they can perform surgery or dispense medications. Teachers in most states must take a test before they can be licensed to teach. Manicurists or beauticians must pass a test before they can perform their skills on a person's nails or hair. Tests are administered for specific purposes.

- to gain information on which to act—such as medical tests
- to certify a certain level of competence in order to issue a license
- to assess knowledge and skills learned in a particular environment

There have always been tests in school to assess knowledge, either developed by the teacher (directly connected to what the teacher taught), or developed for the broader purpose of measuring students against students in other classes, across the state, or against a sample of similar students. In the twenty-first century, there are movements to test children at younger and younger ages using tests that are developed to compare results on nationwide standards. It is important for the early childhood teacher to understand the use of tests in measuring children's development. It is even more important for teachers to become knowledgeable about when and where tests are appropriate and to advocate on behalf of children when tests are not appropriate.

Since the first edition of this textbook was written in 1995, there has been an increase in the use of formal assessments and **standardized tests**. These are being used to make "high-stakes" decisions about children. They have been used to determine "readiness" and "placement" in various levels of kindergarten. Some say they have been used to unfairly penalize children who are poor, of a racial or ethnic minority, whose first language is not English, or who are divergent and creative thinkers (Children's Defense Fund, 2005). In testing children in the second grade and younger, Neisworth and Bagnato (2004) call this movement "the mismeasure of young children," using tests designed for older children with no evidence base in early childhood. They are being used for screening, eligibility for special programs, and to determine teachers' and schools' effectiveness, with much riding on the results. Often, instruction time is focused toward test-taking techniques and test content rather than allowing children to construct knowledge in a way that is relevant to them. This chapter is not designed to teach "how to" use standardized tests but to familiarize the reader with their uses and misuses (Figure 8–1) and ultimately, of course, to make the case for "authentic assessment" by observation and documentation as a valid and reliable way of finding out what children know and can do.

Figure 8–1 Testing has become the accepted measure of child, teacher, and curriculum accountability but Portfolios show what a child knows and can do.

No Child Left Behind

Here is a very brief overview of a very complex and controversial educational law. The purpose behind this federal law was to require states, school districts, and schools to focus on the outcomes of teaching, holding schools accountable for improving student achievement in reading and math. According to the law, schools must set measurable milestones to show they are achieving *adequate yearly progress* by the 2013–2014 school year. They must show that they are providing "highly qualified" teachers and funding for low-achieving students in reading. The law mandates annual testing of primary and middle school students (grades 3 through 8) in reading and math. It also requires that schools use "scientifically based research" in establishing curricula, as measured by statistical (quantitative) research methods, primarily standardized tests. There are numerous conditions, penalties, and threats for *schools in need of improvement*.

This sounds like a reasonable plan; however, in reality, critics say the goals are unachievable and unfair. It is a great burden on schools to find, hire, and retain qualified teachers, especially in rural, inner-city, and high-poverty areas. There are few or no provisions or accommodations for children with special needs and non-native English speakers. And especially for our purposes here, the reliance on standardized test scores, especially for young children (third grade and younger) is inappropriate and not an accurate measure of the child's progress, the teacher's competence, or the school's effectiveness (Neil, 2006; Yell et al., 2006).

The Standards Movement

A **standard** is a statement that defines a goal or practice written by authorities in the field. They are developed with three principles in mind: to give clarity to the breadth and depth of the subject matter, to set expectations for achievement and performance, and to set **benchmarks** for accountability (Kendall &

Marzano, 2004). Early childhood had not historically been included in many of the subject standards. However, since the rise of the school reform movement following the publication of the National Commission on Excellence in Education's *A Nation at Risk: The Imperative for Educational Reform* (1983), which included an imperative for "school readiness," things began to change. Most sets of standards now address the preschool population. There are thousands of educational standards in various disciplines, but most content experts in the field agree that integrating the curriculum among subject areas is necessary. Most people in early childhood are familiar with *Developmentally Appropriate Practice in Early Childhood Programs* (Bredekamp, 1997), setting standards for quality early childhood education practices, but many may be less familiar with other organizations or content-monitoring associations that delineate standards for specific content areas, such as the following:

Art: *National Visual Arts Standards*—National Art Education Association (http://www.naea-reston.org)

Inclusive Education: *Division for Early Childhood—DEC Recommended Practices: A Comprehensive Guide* (http://www.dec-sped.org)

English: *Standards for the English Language Arts*—National Council of Teachers of English and International Reading Association (http://www.ncte.org)

English as a Second Language: *ESL Standards for Pre-K–12 Students*—Teachers of English to Speakers of Other Languages (http://www.tesol.org)

Head Start: *Head Start Child Outcomes Framework*—Department of Health and Human Services (http://www.headstartinfo.org)

Health and Safety Standards for Child Care: *Caring for Our children: National Health and Safety Performance Standards: Guidelines for Out-of-Home Child Care Programs*—American Academy of Pediatrics (http://nrc.uchsc.edu)—Go to Caring for Our Children, Second Edition.

Health Education: *National Health Education Standards*—American Association for Health Education (http://www.aahperd.org)

High/Scope: *Key Experiences*—High/Scope (http://www.highscope.org)

Mathematics: *Principles and Standards for School Mathematics*—National Council of Teachers of Mathematics (http://www.nctm.org)

Compendium of K–12 Standards McRel—Mid-Continent Research for Education and Learning. A compendium of standards and benchmarks from many different arenas arranged by content area. (http://www.mcrel.org)

Music: *Benchmarks in Action: A Guide to Standards-Based Assessment in Music*—The National Association for Music Education (http://www.menc.org)

Physical Education: *Active Start: A Statement of Physical Activity Guidelines for Children Birth to Five Years*—National Association for Sport & Physical Education (http://www.aahperd.org)—Go to National Association for Sport and Physical Education.

Science: *Benchmarks for Science Literacy*—American Association for the Advancement of Science (http://www.project2061.org)

Social Studies: *Expectations of Excellence*—National Council for the Social Studies (http://www.ncss.org)

Technology: *National Educational Technology Standards*—International Society for Technology in Education (http://www.cnets.iste.org)

There are standards by which programs can be assessed. (See Chapter 13 for a discussion of these.)

There are also standards for early childhood professionals and preparation programs.

DEC Recommended Practices in Early Childhood Intervention/Early Childhood Special Education (www.dec-sped.org)

Head Start Program Performance Standards (www.acf.hss.gov)—Go to performance standards in the search box.

Family Child Care Accreditation Standards—National Association of Family Child Care (http://nafcc.org)

NAEYC Professional Preparation Standards at Associate Degree, Initial Licensure and Advance Degrees—National Association for the Education of Young Children (http://www.naeyc.org)

Program Standards—National Council for Accreditation of Teacher Education (http://www.ncate.org)

National Board Certification Standards—National Board for Professional Teaching Standards (http://www.nbpts.org)

Child Development Associate Competencies—Council for Professional Recognition (http://www.cdacouncil.org)

With so many standards, it can be difficult to evaluate how to apply and integrate them into a particular curriculum or program. Seefeldt (2005) gives these suggestions for negotiating the standards:

- From these standards what is meaningful for the children I teach?
- What elements from these standards set the foundation for further learning?
- What do children already know and what do I want them to learn?
- How can I develop firsthand experiences in this subject area for children to be active learners?
- How can I integrate this with what children already know?

Difficulty in Assessing Young Children

Considering the standards movement and the reliance on standardized testing from a cautionary perspective, the National Association for the Education of Young Children (NAEYC) and the National Association of Early Childhood Specialists in State Departments of Education (NAECS/SDE) have developed a position statement that includes curriculum, assessment, and program evaluation (2002). It recognizes that learning standards can be valuable in young children's educational experiences but only "if early learning standards (1) emphasize significant, developmentally appropriate content and outcomes; (2) are developed and reviewed through informed, inclusive processes; (3) use implementation and assessment strategies that are ethical and appropriate for young children; and (4) are accompanied by strong supports for early childhood programs, professionals and families" (NAEYC & NAECS/SDE 2002).

Preliterate (birth to age 8) children cannot be assessed through written answers on a sheet of paper. The purpose of this book is to provide other methods of gathering information about each child's development in order to assess and plan. The change in children's physical, social, linguistic, cognitive, creative, and emotional development is rapid. Because they do not understand the goals of formal testing ("Do your best," "Do it by yourself without help," or "Keep at it until it's finished"), results of pencil-and-paper tests are not accurate assessments. Naturalistic measures such as the ones presented in this text are more accurate methods for describing each child's development, but they do not make it easy to compare children across classrooms, schools, states, or the nation. There are several reasons put forth for making such comparisons:

- identification of children who need more help in school to succeed
- holding teachers and administrators accountable to carry out the responsibility of helping children to learn
- determining the best practices so they can be applied by others to get better results
- conserving or investing public funding wisely in efficient methods

Those are logical reasons for using formal assessment, and there may be times when formal measuring instruments need to be used. This section is designed to be a guide.

Formal Assessment Measures

Fairness is a quality that most people would hold in high esteem. Fairness in assessing children may have even greater appeal.

EXERCISE **Consider the following:**

- **This bag of potato chips holds 11.2 ounces and is priced at $1.89. Another bag of potato chips holds 8 ounces and is priced at $1.69. Which is a fairer price?**
- **You take a class and the final exam has 100 questions and 10 essays. Your friend takes the same class taught by another teacher and the final is a take-home exam. In evaluating which of you learned more, is one testing approach fairer than the other?**
- **You have been waiting in line to order food. A clerk opens a new line. Another customer walks up and is waited on before you. "It's not fair!"**

Trying to determine what is fair necessitates a standard measure. To calculate the best value, you need to convert the price to cost per ounce, a standard comparison. To assess how much you each learned from the class, a common exam would be given. To serve customers in the order in which they came to the counter, the store would need a number system or require clerks to call out, "I'll help the next person in line." Standard measures ensure fairness. The difficulty comes in assessing fairly what one child knows against what another child knows and using a test given on any specific day. To what do we attribute a high or low score? Was it the teacher? Was it the child on that particular day? Was it the family? Fair assessment is always difficult.

Standardized Tests

The word "standardized" means to apply the same measure in the same way to determine an individual result compared to an expected response. It is *conventional* in that all test materials, which may be supplied in a kit or gathered by the tester, are the same and each child is expected to use them in the same way, indicating a level of development. A standardized test is constructed by a content specialist, and it is designed to measure specific aspects of development or behavior. It is usually administered by a trained tester using a specific set of procedures and must be completed in a limited time. It has a **quantitative scoring** system. The results are scored against the **norm**, the group on whom the test was researched, identified by age, gender, race, geographic region, and socioeconomic status. The norm group's average scores then become the scores against which later test-takers are compared. There are three types of standardized tests.

Standardized achievement tests measure what children know or can do at a particular age or grade. These outcomes are determined from a cross section of the population and scored in comparison to that population. The more the children are like that group, the closer the scores will be to the average. *Standardized screening and diagnostic tests* are used to identify a potential learning problem or developmental delay. They are based on broad abilities that most children will possess, revealing only those children who may need further evaluation (McAfee & Leong, 2002; Pellegrini & Bjorklund, 1998).

The checklists discussed in Chapter 3 are standardized based on common expectations for a child of a certain age, based on maturation. All children of that age are measured by the same scale because human development has been studied and determined to be fairly "standard."

STANDARDIZED TESTING AS AN ASSESSMENT METHOD. Before any standardized test is given, some questions should be answered:

1. What is the purpose of the test? The test should have a clear benefit to the child or the program.
2. What is the design of the test? Is it **valid**? In testing terms, valid refers to whether the test measures what it's supposed to measure. If a test's purpose was to measure the ability to multiply but only asked addition questions, it would not be valid. What is the **reliability** of the test? Would the same score be obtained on subsequent tests of the same nature? Because it is difficult to obtain valid and reliable data, especially on cognitive abilities of children under six, only trained professionals with a specific need to know should administer that type of test. Standardized tests must fit the developmental level of the child, be administered individually (not in a group) for children under six, be short in duration, and be given in the child's natural setting (home or school), preferably by a person known to the child.
3. How will the results be used? No single test should be the basis for an important decision regarding the child's placement or diagnosis. Other methods of data collection should be considered, such as input from the family, observational data from the school, and direct information from the child.

APPROPRIATE USES OF EARLY CHILDHOOD ASSESSMENTS. The National Educational Goals Panel (see Shepard, Kagan, & Wurtz, 1998) was formed to "improve methods of assessing the readiness of children for school that would lead to alternatives to currently used early childhood assessments" (Figure 8–2).

Purpose 1. *Assessing to promote children's learning and development.* The classroom teacher, along with the family, know the child best. Seeing a child day after day, alongside other children the same age, viewed through a lens suffused with the knowledge of child development, an accurate assessment of the child's learning and development can be made without a purchased, standardized test. Observations such as those supported by this book can provide an **authentic assessment** of what the child knows and can do (Neisworth & Bagnato, 2004; Meisels, Bickel, Nicholson, Xue, & Atkins-Burnett, 2001). These are "low-stakes" assessments because significant intervention is *not* taking place based on these assessments. They are used as benchmarks for development and for curriculum planning purposes.

Purpose 2. *Assessing to identify children for health and special services.* Federal legislation—the Individuals with Disabilities Education Act (IDEA), passed in 1975—mandated early **screening** for the identification of children with disabilities. Later amendments required family involvement and earlier screenings of infants and toddlers. Screening involves testing large numbers of individuals in a short amount of time to find those who need to be further evaluated. The act provided the definition of developmental delay, supported by performance on a standardized assessment instrument

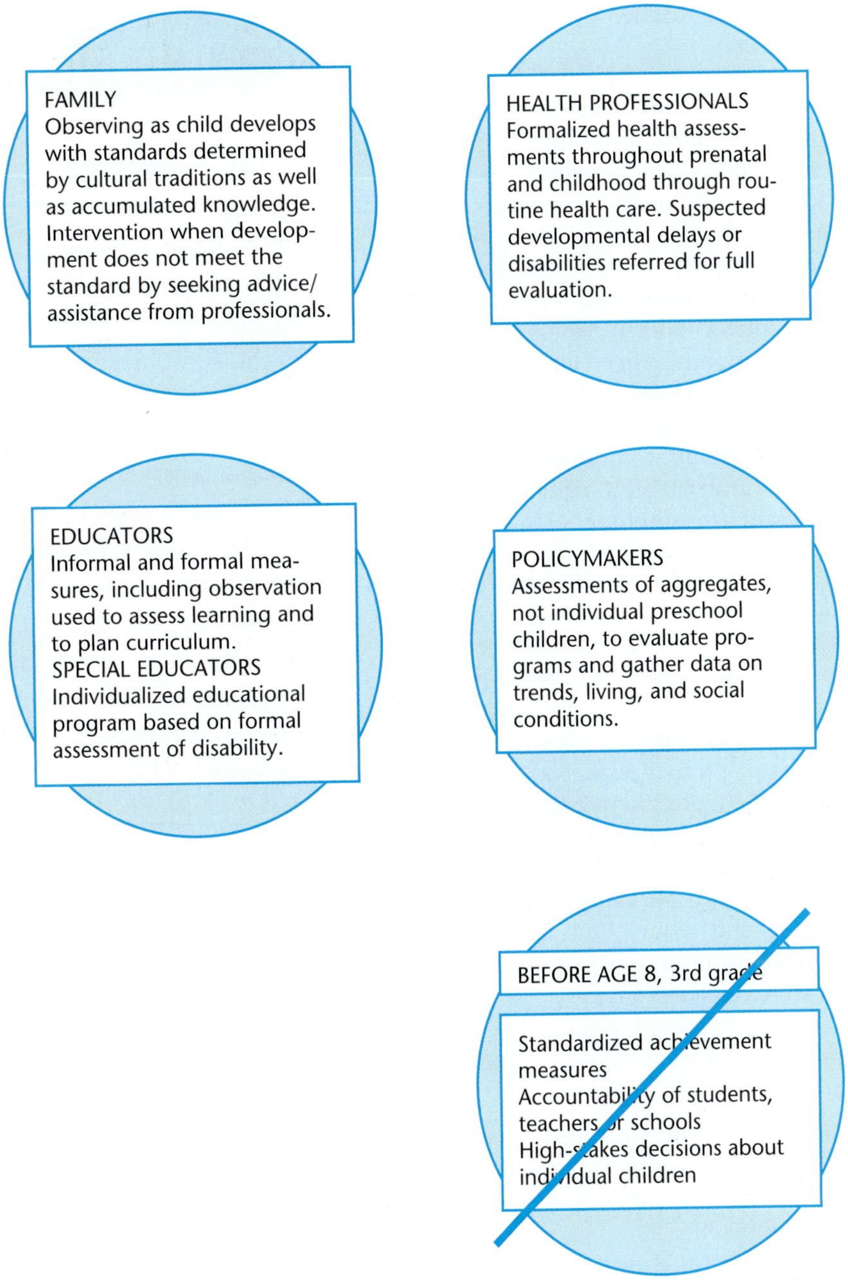

Figure 8–2 Appropriate Assessments of Children. (Adapted from Shepard, L., Kagan, S. L., & Wurtz, E. (1998) *Principles and Recommendations for Early Childhood Assessments.* Washington, DC: National Education Goals.)

and specific observations in developmental domains. After a full evaluation, indicated by the screenings, the law mandates school districts to provide appropriate services. Some screening instruments commonly used are the Hawaii Early Learning Profile (HELP) (VORT Corporation, 1995) and Ages and Stages (Bricker, Squires, & Mount, 1995). Some full-evaluation instruments commonly used are the Bayley Scales of Infant Development II (Bayley, 1993) and the Brigance Diagnostic Inventory of Early Development—Revised (Brigance, 1991). Most of these require prior training by the person administering the test. These are known as **high-stakes tests** because they may be used to make classification and intervention plans. To fairly represent the abilities of the child, it is important to rely on multiple sources for information, and consensus on an intervention plan must be reached by the family and a range of professionals.

Purpose 3. *Assessing to monitor trends and evaluate programs and services.* The Goals Panel recommends that preschool programs and services be assessed on a state or national level, focusing only on the conditions of learning, such as the percentage of low-income children who attend quality preschool programs. Early childhood education trends in early learning should be assessed not on individual children's scores but on a matrix or sampling of a nonintrusive standardized test (Shepard, Kagan, & Wurtz, 1998). Individual program assessments are important for quality assurance for the program itself and as an indicator of quality for consumers, families, and funders. See Chapter 13 for a full discussion of program assessment.

Purpose 4. *Assessing academic achievement to hold individual students, teachers, and schools accountable.* This too is considered high-stakes testing, because these test scores are used to make decisions about the retention of individual students, teachers' tenure, and schools' allocation of funding. The Goals Panel recommends that there be "no high-stakes accountability testing of individual children before the end of third grade" (Shepard, Kagan, & Wrutz, 1998, p. 21). They recommend that instructionally relevant assessments be part of the educational program in kindergarten through second grade. Prior to third grade, only the teachers and programs should keep records of individual student achievement.

Meisels and Atkins-Burnett (2000) proposed principles of appropriate assessment for young children. Assessments should be used

- for assessing all areas of development through multiple sources of information.
- with repeated opportunities to demonstrate developmental competence.
- with the involvement of the most trusted caregiver.
- as a framework of developmental timetables but recognizing differences among children.
- emphasizing real abilities, not artificial situations.
- for identifying strengths and abilities.
- collaboratively between families and professionals.
- as a first step in potential intervention.
- for group and individual planning.
(pp. 231–257)

@ it happened to me

The "Wrong" Answer

Well, this didn't happen to me but to a colleague. She was required to give a standardized test to her class of inner-city kindergartners. One of the questions the tester had to read was the following: "Here are several dogs. What is this one called?" as she pointed to a collie. The child answered "Lassie," and she had to mark it wrong. In that same test, the child had to correctly identify a *doily.* In many homes, children have never seen a *doily*. In another assessment the child is asked, "What color is a banana?" The child answers "white"—wrong—a banana is yellow. Mine are more likely black! Do you see how arbitrary some standardized tests can be?

Do you have an IT HAPPENED TO ME story about how an inappropriate question can skew a test? I'd love to read it. Please send it to WeekbyWeek@thomsonlearning.com

THE CASE AGAINST STANDARDIZED TESTS. There are many strong voices against standardized testing for young children from birth through second grade. Bagnato says the mantra should be "No table-top testing," meaning that assessment based on observation and not standardized tests should be the standard in early childhood. Shepard and Kagan (1998) say that "what works for older children or adults will simply not work for younger children." Sam Meisels, author of the Work Sampling System, a method of performance assessment using Portfolios, says that parents must be convinced that performance assessments, using observations and the children's work, are as trustworthy as standardized tests (2001). Alfie Kohn is another vocal opponent of standardized tests as an extension of his work on rewards and punishments. He describes several problems with testing young children, including the following:

- Standardized testing sets the unrealistic expectation that everyone at the same age acquires the same set of capabilities.

TOPICS IN OBSERVATION

Measuring Cognitive Development—Why Not Test?

EXERCISE **Imagine that you took a test and found out you failed. Jot down how each of the possible reasons that follows might have been the cause of your failure:**

The room:
The person giving the test:
The subject matter of the test:
The importance of the test to you:
The new format of the test:
The way the test was scored:
Your health:
You are physically challenged:
You are in big trouble that has nothing to do with the test:
Your native language is Russian. The test is in English:
Your mother left you here in this strange building to take the test, but you do not know how you will find her later:

These same influences affect the outcomes of a young child taking a test, only more so because they are not able to understand, rationalize, or adjust. This section is intended as a policy statement to defend and uphold authentic assessment methods over standardized or achievement tests. There are three major issues in testing young children: the test itself, the child, and the use of the test.

A standardized test is an evaluation instrument written for a definite purpose and application. When it indeed does measure what it proposes to measure, it is described as valid. Early forms of the test are tried out on a segment of the population that will be taking the test eventually. This early test group is the norm group against which the rest of the scores are measured. If the norm group is significantly different from the subjects taking the test then, the scores will be inaccurate. For example, suppose the norm group in the tryout of a new test consists of 10 children. There are eight boys and two girls, ranging in age from five to eight years old, living in south Florida, all attending the same school. Two children are African American, three are Puerto Rican, and one has been sexually abused. Their scores on the test will set the standard against which children in Idaho, Connecticut, and Minnesota will be measured. This is an extreme example to demonstrate the point, but, unfortunately, it is not far from reality. It is difficult to select a norm group that represents all the variables in exact proportions to the subjects taking the test. Standardized tests have a high risk of being discriminatory because of the scoring against the norm group. The results may be skewed by factors such as geographic region, level of development (urban, suburban, or rural), and different socialization experiences due to culture, economic situation, family dynamics, and native language.

The second major concern in using standardized tests on young children is the nature of the child. Because young children are just that—young—taking tests may be a new experience for them. The way that children confront new experiences varies from child to child. Some just observe, watch, and wait,

(continued)

TOPICS IN OBSERVATION *(continued)*

paralyzed by the novelty. Others will manipulate it and play with it, not recognizing the purpose. They may not understand or follow directions but explore and adapt it to their own style. If the child takes another form of the same test again in a short time, the score may be drastically different. Now they have experience, or have thought of other ways to try it out.

The expectation of standardized tests is that the same subject taking the same type of test in a reasonable period will obtain a similar score. This is known as test reliability. Many standardized tests for young children are not reliable. Children are easily influenced by the test setting, which may be new to them. The examiner may be a stranger to them. They are separated from their family and may not know how to take a test. They lack the ability to screen out noises, hunger, or fear that may divert their attention.

The original intelligence test developed in France by Binet was for a noble purpose, to provide adequate education for children who were mentally retarded. Many tests administered to children today are for a similar purpose, to identify handicapping conditions for which early intervention would be provided.

Many federal and state laws mandate such testing. P.L. 94-142 (1975) provides a free and appropriate public education for children with disabilities between the ages of 3 and 21. P.L. 99-457 (1986) includes infants and toddlers and their families in comprehensive early intervention services. To implement these mandates, it was necessary to identify children who needed services. This was accomplished through a screening, an initial step in identifying those children who had a high probability of developmental delay. Once a screening indicates there might be a delay or problem, a full evaluation or follow-up provides the diagnosis. The diagnosis will determine the type of intervention needed to provide services for the child in the least-restrictive environment. These laws have been effective in helping many children and families receive the services they need.

The problem arises when the screenings and tests developed for one purpose are used for other, possibly less helpful ones. Meisels (1987) has criticized the Gesell Preschool Readiness Test as an invalid predictor of success in kindergarten. Many schools use this as a developmental screening tool. Based on its results, a recommendation may be made to delay school entrance or for the child to spend a year in a transitional grade between kindergarten and first grade. Meisels contends this is a misuse of a test that lacks reliability and validity. Tests are misused when they are the sole factor in decisions to place a child in special education or to label them as an individual with a handicapping condition. NAEYC's *Developmentally Appropriate Practice in Early Childhood Programs, Revised Edition* (1997) emphasizes the role of observation: "Decisions that have a major impact on children, such as enrollment or placement, are never made on the basis of a single developmental assessment or screening device but are based on multiple sources of relevant information, particularly observations by teachers and parents" (p. 21).

The NAEYC position and constructivist writings, such as Kamii and Kamii (1990) in *Achievement Testing in the Early Grades: The Games Grown-Ups Play,* enumerate the abuses of testing:

- Results of standardized tests might be inappropriately used as readiness screening tests for placement decisions.
- Standardized testing increases the academic emphasis of the curriculum, which should be localized, not centralized.

TOPICS IN OBSERVATION *(continued)*

- Achievement tests frequently do not reflect current theory or research about how children learn.
- Many schools "teach to the test" to raise school scores.
- Standardized tests cannot predict how well students will do in the future.
- Below third grade, development is uneven and still emergent.
- Racial, cultural, and social biases are evident.
- Numerical results are not useful in curriculum planning for individual students.

How can the effectiveness of teachers and schools be measured if children are not tested? How can a teacher know if the child is learning? How could school boards and voters know their education tax dollars were well spent but still be sensitive to the population it was examining?

Authentic assessment assumes that children in a supportive setting will initiate and direct their own learning, constructing knowledge at their own rate physically, emotionally, socially, and intellectually. It also assumes that learning proceeds from concrete to abstract. Children learn by interacting with an enriched environment that recognizes and values different intelligences and is facilitated by an adult who has specialized training and skills. Teaching is individualized and in small groups. Individual learning needs are acknowledged based on objective evaluation of each child's strengths, moving the child forward in the continuum of learning through relevant curriculum. Assessment is rooted in principles of child growth and development and involves a collaboration of child, teacher, family, and other professionals as needed (Puckett & Black, 2000).

The form of that assessment is in question. Teachers ask, "How can a test manufactured in New Jersey measure what the children have learned about magnets in my class in Nevada? How can the test maker in New Jersey even know if my class in Nevada has worked with magnets?" The test can only measure it if the teachers know what is on the test and make sure that it is taught in the classroom. In this way, it is the test determining the curriculum, instead of measuring achievement. Methods of authentic assessment, then, must be locally based to measure progress of a distinct group of children. This is done by "keeping track" (Kamii & Kamii, 1990, pp. 120, 121) of their work on three levels:

1. Descriptive data about each child that can be analyzed by the teacher as well as outside evaluators
2. Summaries and interpretations of that data by the teacher to evaluate the effectiveness of teaching methods and the individual progress of the child
3. Quantitative information that gives statistical analysis of the whole group, against which individual children may be compared to adjust the curriculum

These principles of performance assessment are consistent with the knowledge of child growth and development, as well as with developmentally appropriate practice. Assessment by observation and recording using multiple techniques is repeated in a systematic way. The Portfolio documents the child's progress and is shared with the parents and the child. That describes what can be achieved by *Week by Week* assessment planning.

- Standardized assessments cannot produce an accurate picture of what a child can do.
- The stress on young children to perform on the tests interferes with accurate results. (Kohn, 2001)

He encourages teachers to take an organized stand against testing through advocacy with families and administration. Groups such as the National PTA, the National Association of Early Childhood Specialists in State Departments of Education, the Southern Early Childhood Association, and the American Educational Research Association have issued policy statements of caution regarding group standardized, high-stakes tests for young children.

"Accountability shovedown" is the term Hatch (2002) uses to describe the standards movement, stating it is "so pervasive across educational settings today [it] is threatening children in early childhood in the same ways as the curriculum shovedown movement did in the 1980s" (p. 457). He sees child observation changing from a strategy for shaping curriculum to a device for monitoring student progress. Among the troubling results of this trend, Hatch includes the following:

increasing pressure on children
increasing pressure on teachers
narrowing of experiences
accountability as punishment rather than motivation for improvement
teacher deprofessionalization
an emphasis on performance over learning
individual devaluation
an emphasis on sameness versus diversity
questionable benefits to school improvement
increasing corporate mentality

He challenges teachers with this statement: "Our accountability comes from an ethical commitment to do what is right for every child, not from measuring productivity according to an arbitrary set of narrowly defined outcomes."

Stress indicators such as wiggling, chewing on pencils, twisting hair, playing with clothes, complaining of feeling tired, and crying were observed in kindergartners during standardized tests (Fleege, Charlesworth, Burts, & Hart, 1996). These behaviors had not been present in observations done weeks before the California Achievement Test was administered to groups of 10 children. In addition to the stress, other behaviors such as copying, refusing to continue, calling out answers, and asking for reassurance of correct answers indicated that children did not understand nor could they comply with test-taking rules. Increased stress and inaccurate results due to the developmental level of children are two of the main arguments against group-administered standardized tests for young children. Neuman and Roskos (2000) state:

> Many of our young children are evaluated, screened, and labeled each year using standardized measures that describe what children do against prescribed developmental markers or average norms. Particularly during these early years, standardized paper-and-pencil measures are not effective in measuring what children know and do not know. Because children's knowledge and skills are in constant motion, these tests tend not to be reliable or valid measures of what children can do in typical situations. (p. 24)

What's a Teacher to Do

The TRACE Center for Excellence in Early Childhood Assessment, funded by the U.S. Department of Education, conducts research on evidence-based early childhood assessments and the validity and reliability of authentic assessment (Neisworth & Bagnato, 2004). Their guidelines coincide very closely with the *Week by Week* system—using multiple observers, over time, in real settings, for the purpose of discovering progress and individualizing the curriculum.

IF YOU HAVE TO ADMINISTER A STANDARDIZED TEST. Because tests are becoming a fact of life for early educators, here is some advice for teachers and families with young children (Benner, 2003; Greenspan & Meisels, 1994; Kohn, 2001; Puckett & Black, 2000; Shepard & Kagan, 1998):

1. No testing of young children should occur unless it can be shown to lead to beneficial results.
2. Know child development ages, stages, and milestones, understanding the range of individual rates and styles for those stages. This will give you a basis against which to measure each child's progress. A red flag should go up when a child does not appear to be progressing in development. Then an evaluation with a standardized instrument may be necessary.
3. If a formal assessment is used, the content, form, validity, and standards for interpretation should match the purpose of the assessment.

4. If a diagnostic test is called for to determine the cause or extent of a developmental lag, the following considerations should be made:
   - The test should be administered by a qualified professional using carefully selected tests (preferably more than one).
   - The child should not be forced to separate from the parents, causing undue stress, which could negatively affect the results of the test.
   - Tests that consist of isolated tasks resulting in a score do not give a complete picture of how the child uses those skills in the context of everyday interactions, so the assessment should consist of a wider range of criteria.
   - The tests should not carry more weight for decisions about the child than testimony from families and teachers and direct observations of the child in familiar environments.
5. The test's purpose should be to improve performance, not just to monitor it for measuring the effectiveness of a program, teacher, or school.
6. The test should be individually administered. Young children are still developing the skill of following directions, so a group-administered test is not appropriate.
7. Formal tests should be skill based rather than verbal or written, allowing the child as much time as needed to complete the tasks and feel supported by the person administering the test.
8. Do no more preparation than necessary. Time spent in preparation for tests is time not spent on subjects children want to know about. Families and teachers prepping children on items to be tested may also skew test results.

The National Association for the Education of Young Children (2003) has developed a set of guidelines regarding appropriate curriculum content and assessment in programs serving children ages three through eight. In Chapter 14, these guidelines are applied to the *Week by Week* observation and recording plan.

Advantages

Standardized tests, **used appropriately,** may be

- fair, objective assessments of a child's capabilities.
- recognized tests and scores used by intervention professionals.
- **must be** used with other forms of information about the child, to contribute to an overall picture of the child.

Disadvantages

Standardized tests are used inappropriately when

- children feel pressure during testing.
- norms may not match the child's cultural and socioeconomic circumstances.
- young children's performance assessment is affected by the child's lack of experience with testing protocol.
- they are used to make decisions about the child based on a false reading.
- test results punish economically disadvantaged children and children whose first language is not English.

Pitfalls to Avoid

Advice for the use of standardized tests:

- Do not allow testing that places children under stress.
- Be sure the test is administered by a trained professional.
- Advocate for multiple sources of information about the child be used in any decision about placement, readiness, or intervention.

Go to the Bind-in-Book CD for plans and resources.

LOOKING AT COGNITIVE DEVELOPMENT: MATH, SCIENCE, AND TECHNOLOGY

Dear reader, by now you should understand that cognitive development, just as every other developmental domain, is interdependent on each other. Also, I am sure you realize that even though the rest of this chapter focuses on math and science, those subjects are but a few of the areas that are affected by cognitive development. Math and science have been selected for this chapter because of their growing importance, and sorry to say, their neglected emphasis in many early childhood classrooms.

Think About It . . .

How do you feel when you read these words?

Mathematics
Physics
Geometry
Hypothesis

In looking further at **cognitive** development, it is important to consider not just the knowledge of the subject matter but the other dimensions of development. Lillian Katz (1988), a great stimulator of thought in the field of early childhood education, reminds educators that learning is not just knowledge as an accumulation of facts, skills, or the ability to function in a certain way. Knowledge also involves **dispositions**, habits of the mind. Those are the ways that each individual responds to experiences. Some people have the disposition to quit after a defeat or embarrassment. The same situation may cause someone else with a different disposition to try harder, while still another casts blame or reflects on the situation and seeks advice.

The dispositions, feelings, or emotional responses to the fields of mathematics and science affect many early childhood educators. Perhaps it is the nonacademic track through which some have entered the field. Perhaps it is the manifestation of learning-style theory: People with strong logical thinking skills become engineers, while those with interpersonal learning styles and skills become educators. Or it may be the sex role socialization that girls unconsciously absorb from school as the "hidden curriculum," and from the media, family, and peers. Whatever the cause, aversion to math and science has kept many early childhood classrooms from having interesting and challenging math and science learning areas. Consequently, the foundations have not been adequately laid on which children can build knowledge.

In *Last Child in the Woods* (2005), Louv raises our consciousness, saying we are raising a generation of children with a "nature-deficit disorder." Possible reasons could be our busy lives, concern for safety, shrinking natural areas near urban centers, and just plain negligence. Rivkin (1992), an early childhood educator, addresses the emotions of science, urging us to cultivate and nurture a joy in the beauty of nature, a childlike curiosity, and the quest to make sense of things. She urges teachers to examine sexist messages that science is a man's field and to work against the perpetuation of that idea.

Conezio and French (2002) suggest some benefits of science being at the center of an integrated curriculum.

- Science responds to children's need to learn about the world around them.
- Children's everyday experience is the foundation for science.
- Open-ended science activities involve children from a wide range of developmental levels.
- Hands-on science activities let *teachers observe and respond to children's individual strengths and needs.*
- The scientific approach of trial and error welcomes error and interprets it as valuable information, not as failure.
- Science strongly supports language and literacy.
- Science helps children who are English language learners to participate in the classroom and learn English.
- The problem-solving skills of science easily generalize to social situations.
- Science demonstrations help children become comfortable in large-group conversations.
- Science connects easily to other areas, including center-based play, math, artistic expression, and social studies. (p. 16)

REVIEW

STANDARDIZED TESTS

A test in which the administration, scoring, and interpretation procedures are prescribed in the test manual and must be strictly followed. A standardized test is usually norm-referenced.

Types of Information Gathered by Standardized Tests

- Literacy level
  - Vocabulary
  - Comprehension
  - Communication of ideas
- Mathematics concepts and computation
- Science concepts
- Analytical thinking

Such "science process" skills (Lind, 2000) sound very much like authentic assessment of a child's development:

observing—concentrated watching and making field notes
comparing—looking at the changes that have taken place by rereading previous field notes
classifying—categorizing the observed behavior into developmental domains (such as an Anecdotal Recording from dramatic play), possibly providing indicators of social, physical, cognitive, creative, language, literacy, and emotional development
measuring—noting specific, quantifiable changes such as minutes of attention span or letters of the alphabet the child can recognize
communicating—informing the child and the family of the progress the child has made
inferring—using experience to make judgments about those inner characteristics such as self-esteem, coping skills, temperament
predicting—anticipating what milestones will be approaching and planning curriculum to help achieve them

If teachers have feelings of inadequacy and avoidance of math and science, there will be little to observe. The teacher must become conscious of these emotions. The concepts that follow can be used to heighten awareness of what children are doing as they manipulate their environment. They are actively engaging in math and science, even though it may not be on the daily curriculum plan. This will serve also as a curriculum guide of the concepts that can be incorporated into the early childhood program, enriching children's experiences in math and science. Reflective thinking and concept-building encourage the teacher's explorations.

Observing Developing Mathematical Concepts

EXERCISE Which of the following children are learning math?

_____ a) The class is looking at the teacher holding the calendar and counting up to today's date, the 23rd.
_____ b) Two children are setting the table for lunch.
_____ c) Two children are shoving each other at the door to go outside.
_____ d) A child is eating orange sections.
_____ e) Two children are playing with clay.
_____ f) Three children and the teacher are making instant pudding.
_____ g) A child is painting at the easel.
_____ h) The group is sitting on a rug singing, "This Old Man."
_____ i) Four children are picking up the blocks and placing them on the shelves.
_____ j) A child in the housekeeping area is squeezed into a doll high chair.
_____ k) A child is passing out birthday party invitations and has one left over.
_____ l) A child is lining up all the shoes in the dress-up corner.

If you checked all of the items except the first one, you are correct.

a) **Rote.** Counting the calendar with nothing to touch or manipulate has little relevance to the child's life. (Why should the child care if it is the 23rd or the 89th?) This is not how children learn mathematical concepts. More effective ways of using the calendar to support children's concepts of time are with shared experiences (Van Scoy & Fairchild, 1993). Calendars record an event that has happened, like a birthday, with an artifact from that event. Children could record individual experiences, much the same as Show-and-Tell, but drawn, dictated, or written on a calendar by the child. The calendar can be used to plan for anticipated events, how many days until the picnic, and what must be done each day in preparation for it. In this way, calendars are relevant and perform concrete purposes rather than represent merely the recital of numbers and words that have little meaning.

It is through direct interaction with real objects that children construct meaning and make those associations that lead to cognitive development (Figure 8–3). Kamii (1982) has studied Piagetian principles and applied them to mathematics in the early years. She says, "It is good for children to learn to count and to read and write numerals, but a more important objective is for the child to construct the mental structure of number" (p. 25). She advocates teaching number through indirect ways in the environment. "Indirect teaching can

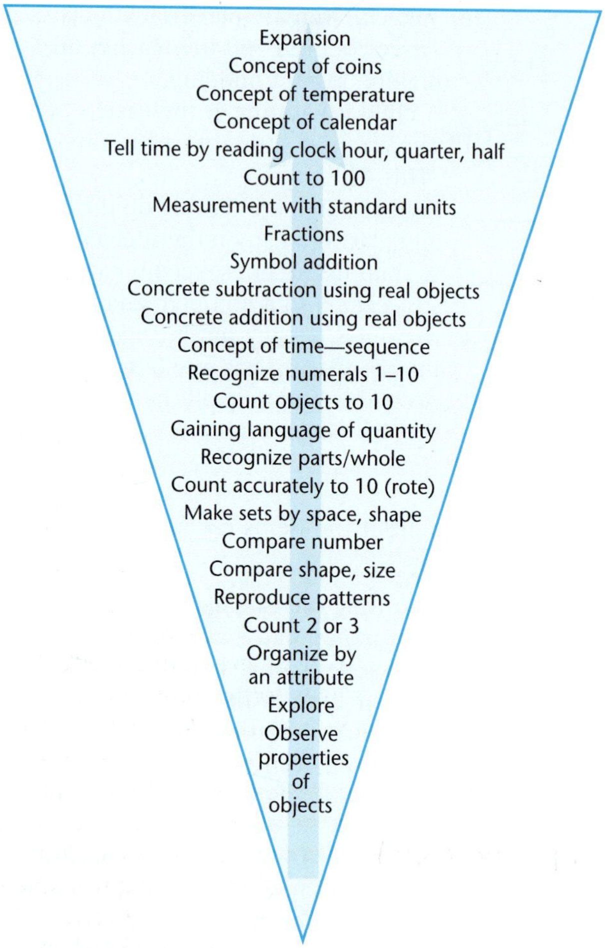

Figure 8–3 Developing Math Concepts.

vary from encouraging the child to put all kinds of things into all kinds of relationships, to asking him to get just enough plates for everybody at his table" (p. 27). While they are working, the observer records and assesses the children's mathematical and physical knowledge.

The activities that follow illustrate children learning math concepts in indirect ways from the environment. Calendar math, while an almost universal part of early childhood daily routine, should be re-examined for its usefulness as a learning strategy in the light of children's cognitive developmental level. Its reliance on teacher-directed, whole group learning of a very abstract principle, especially the concepts of *yesterday, today, and tomorrow,* are not developmentally appropriate (Ethridge & King (2005).

b) **One-to-One Correspondence.** When children are setting the table, placing one cup or one napkin at each place, they are demonstrating the concept of oneness, the most basic concept of number. This is practiced and can be observed in any number of ways. A child puts on a boot and knows she has two feet, so there must be another boot somewhere. She does not try to put the second boot on the same foot. Materials in the classroom with pieces that fit, match, or can be counted if the child is at that level all add to the acquisition of one-to-one correspondence.

c) **Ordinal Numbers.** The idea of **ordinal numbers** (first/second) is learned quickly by children in group settings or in families with siblings. The two-year-old wants his "first." The boys at the door want to be the "first" out. Not that it makes any difference once they get out, but it is the competitive drive for "first" and the disappointment of "last." Would they then tussle to be the "first" in or the "last" in? That would be an indication of their understanding of the terminology of ordinal numbers. In the classroom, the familiarity with the schedule becomes rigidly defined in the lives of two-year-olds. Song time *must* come before the story, and then outside time. If the teacher decides that it looks like rain so today they must go outside "first," many will protest. Having older preschoolers decide which activity to do first, or who will have a first turn, and why, is an excellent way to observe children's understanding of ordinal numbers.

d) **Whole/Part Terminology.** As children interact with the environment, the role of the adult is to observe and provide descriptions for their actions, like, "You've eaten half your orange." By inquiring, the adult can encourage further exploration: "How many sections were in the orange?" "Did each section have a seed, or only some of them?" This type of description can go on incidentally throughout the day. It shows children individual attention by describing ordinary actions. It adds to their vocabulary, raises self-esteem, and promotes thinking.

e) **Conservation.** Clay manipulated into balls and snakes and scrutinized for the concepts of "more" and "less" is an excellent math medium (Figure 8–4). The conservation of volume is the Piagetian concept that the Preoperational child (two to six years old) has not yet attained. The child uses intuition or appearances by centering attention on one attribute and judging volume by that. Two children have clay balls of equal size.

Figure 8–4 The amount never changes even if the shape of the container does—that's Piaget's conservation.

One breaks the ball into several little ones and declares, "I have more." The other one shouts, "Not fair!" There have been efforts to teach conservation with limited results, but the viewpoint now is that it should develop naturally and *not* be taught. However, clay and the water experiments with tall containers and a short squatty one are excellent ways to question children's reasoning to test this hypothesis.

f) **Measurement.** Cooking is an excellent way to apply mathematical principles of measurement, sequence, cause, and effect. In following a recipe, quantities are specified, then measured by different-sized cups and spoons. Johnson and Plemons, in *Cup Cooking* (1993), suggest using multiple measuring utensils, such as three individual teaspoons rather than filling the teaspoon measurer three times. In this way, the child sees the quantity "three" physically present before adding them to the recipe. Recipes are practices in sequencing. The observation of "before" and "after" of cooking or baking demonstrates the cause and effect of heat and prompts description of attributes like hard and soft, liquid and solid.

g) **Geometry of Shape.** The recognition of circle, square, and triangle begins in infancy when the baby reaches out for a ball or a box or a sharp triangular shape. The infant uses all the senses: touching, chewing, seeing, and hearing. Someone says "Ball," "Box." The words are stored, and each experience associates with the prior one. "Is this shape like that one? Yes? Then it must be a ball too." The baby is handed an orange. She says "Ball." She is overgeneralizing in calling all round objects balls. As she absorbs more information, those shapes will be differentiated from one another. They will take on more and more meaning by their various differences. They eventually will be the symbols that are represented in drawing and later writing. Attention to the details and differences are really training for writing skills.

h) **Geometry of Pattern.** A pattern can be the visual image of the regular bars of the crib and the figures printed in a row on the sheets. The repetition of sounds in language and singing also form a pattern. Patterns are expressed in lines painted on the paper at the easel and in the rhythmic clapping of name syllables as the children go to wash for lunch. Materials to form patterns are supplied with a card to guide the sequence of shapes, colors, or beads. They begin with simple two-element patterns and gradually increase in complexity. Scientific observation skills are built as the child notices similarities and differences. The teacher watches and notes how the child uses blocks, buttons, and sound to make patterns.

i) **Classifying.** Sorting is such an important skill to cognitive development that it is taken for granted or overlooked as a cognitive activity. The toddler fills and dumps, then puts some items in this bucket and some in that one. Finally, by some criteria, he purposefully sorts and selects which ones will go into each bucket. He is on the road to classification skills, which are the basis for scientific discovery. In the block area, the shelves are labeled with the shape of the block that belongs there. All the manipulatives have boxes or trays with picture and word labels. Replacing represents more than just keeping the room tidy; it is a cognitive exercise. In the dramatic play area, tools are outlined above the woodworking bench for their replacement. In the art area, supplies are on labeled shelves. Spontaneous classifying occurs at snack time by eating the round pretzels before the straight ones, or separating the peas from the carrots. These all are building cognitive schema against which future associations will be made. Children will sort in ways that are not always predictable. Both this ability to sort the "correct" way as well as the ability to sort the "wrong" way can be observed, noted, and questioned to investigate the child's thinking.

j) **Visual-Spatial Skills.** The estimate of how much space an object will fill sometimes is overcome by strong desire. Fitting into small spaces is a challenge to young children who are still learning the fine art of spatial awareness. They are prone to put fingers into tiny holes, heads through spaces, and bodies into containers. Withdrawing from those spaces sometimes is difficult. This spatial awareness is seen on the playground when a child playing "Duck, Duck, Goose" has difficulty finding the spot to join the circle. It can be observed when a child is doing a puzzle, trying to pound the piece in by force rather than turn it to get it to fit. The sand player fills the container, yet continues to shovel and shovel and shovel. The container overflows with each scoop. Still the child does not indicate a recognition that the space is full and can hold no more. Then comes the day when he lines the containers up and fills each one to the top. Ah ha! A new phase of cognitive development appears.

k) **Problem Solving.** It is James's turn to pass out napkins. Maxine had counted them out because she knows how many children are in the class. "Why do you have one left?" This question invites the child to apply the math skills of how many he started with, how many are in the class, how many children are absent, and then the observation and memory task of deciding who did not receive one. Offering opportunities for problem solving which uses mathematics can show children the usefulness of their newfound knowledge. "There are eight crackers left and four children at the table. How can we decide who can have more? How many can they have?" At the computer there are two chairs, and the rule is two workers, but three people want to use it. Problem solving does not have to have a mathematical solution to be helpful in cognitive development. It is also the logical process of mentally creating the situation, the dilemma, generating possible solutions, and deciding on one by some criteria. Problem-solving strategies are universal.

l) **Seriation.** Placing objects in order according to some rule, such as size, texture, or color, helps the child to look for similarities but also to distinguish differences. The vocabulary of seriation begins with comparisons (big/little, short/long, heavy/light, empty/full) and expands to middle points and closer variations. This shows the ability to center attention on the one critical variable by which the items are being placed in a series. It is a complex skill that can be observed in its progression. Stories like "Goldilocks and the Three Bears" can lead to concrete activities for manipulating props from the hand to the mind. Concepts of small, medium, and large; first and last; and in and out are introduced. Observing what strategies the child uses to come to conclusions about an item's placement also gives clues about the child's thinking processes.

Mathematics and literacy can be combined by incorporating books into the curriculum that have a mathematical theme. Schiro's (1997) example of Pat Hutchins, *A Doorbell Rang* (Hutchins, 1986), gives an example of how this book's story line about more and more visitors to share the tea cookies developed into a 12-day project. It went beyond the obvious exercise in practical division into a critical analysis of the text and illustrations, a dramatization of the book, and a rewrite to incorporate the clarifications suggested by the class. Schiro suggests other titles that can be used in this way: *Alexander, Who Used to Be Rich Last Sunday* (Viorst, 1978), *The Philharmonic Gets Dressed* (Kuskin, 1982), *The King's Chessboard* (Birch, 1988), *Inch by Inch* (Lionni, 1960), and *Caps for Sale* (Slobodkina, 1940/1987). Some of the standards for grades Pre-K–2 from the National Council of Teachers of Mathematics (2000) include:

- *number and operations*—accuracy in counting, number words and numerals, beginning addition and subtraction, strategies for whole-number computations
- *algebra*—sort, classify, and order objects by size, number, and other properties; sequencing; patterns; representations of symbolic notations; symbols for qualitative and quantitative change
- *geometry*—recognize, name, draw, and compare two- and three-dimensional shapes; represent shapes from different perspectives; recognize geometric shapes in the environment
- *measurement*—attributes of length, volume, weight, area, and time; compare objects by these attributes; select appropriate unit and tool for measuring attributes; compare estimates
- *data analysis and probability*—sort and classify objects in sets, represent data using pictures

and graphs, discuss experiences as likely or unlikely

- *problem solving*—recognize, analyze, and strategize how to solve problems that occur in experiences that can be solved through mathematical knowledge
- *reasoning and proof*—use pattern recognition and classifying skills to justify answers
- *communication*—use oral and pictorial language to convey mathematical thinking, listen to others, and evaluate ideas
- *connections*—use experiences to make linkages between one mathematical concept and another and between mathematics and real life
- *representation*—represent understanding through oral and written language, gestures, drawing, and symbols

Observing Developing Scientific Concepts

EXERCISE Check the following science activities that would be appropriate for young children.

______ a) Caves

______ b) Bird's-eye view

______ c) Dolphins

______ d) Making a sandwich

______ e) Let's grow a pumpkin

______ f) The Earth—under, over, on

______ g) Dirty hands

______ h) The food chain

______ i) Shadows

______ j) When will it snow?

Learning activities are appropriate if they are relevant or real to the group of children and if the concept can be tested through investigation. These curriculum ideas may be good ones depending on the context of the children in the group, their age, and their interests. Each of them may be the spark for a project for exploration using the project approach (Katz & Chard, 2000).

Common interests and experiences are the key to curriculum that is meaningful and a springboard for the project approach. If a project comes from the teacher rather than the children, there is a risk that it will become a teacher-telling or teacher-directed experience. "The central feature of a project, as we use the term, is that the children, in discussion and consultation with their teacher, take initiative, make decisions, and take major responsibility for what is accomplished" (Helm & Katz, 2001, p. 12).

a) Learning about caves would be relevant for children in several states, such as Kentucky, West Virginia, and states in other mountainous regions.

b) All children have knowledge of birds, but thinking about what a bird sees involves moving beyond the egocentric view of the world to see it from above the Earth. This would stimulate not only a study of birds but of positional vocabulary, as well as a growing understanding of the Earth as an orb.

c) While children are fascinated with benign animals such as dolphins, unless they live in an area where they can experience them, either in the ocean or in an aquarium, it is a stretch for dolphins to develop into a project where children are constructing knowledge from real, firsthand experiences.

d) Most children have the experience of at least eating a sandwich, but not necessarily making one. It is a familiar food, but the sequence of making a sandwich and the choices available are rich with curriculum possibilities.

e) Growing things from seed, especially large rambling plants like pumpkins, can meet many learning objectives. However, climate, season, and indoor/outdoor environmental factors must be taken into consideration.

f) Children have had contact with the Earth, but to explore by digging into it, studying things above it and things on it, pose interesting questions that can be explored any number of ways. This will bring in language, science, and imagination.

g) What child hasn't experienced dirty hands? This idea brings with it all kinds of reasons for and possibilities to explore what can be done about dirty hands. Dirty hands can act as a springboard for a health and hygiene lesson and more. Sensory experiences that get hands "dirty," different cleaners, and "invisible germs" all would be relevant learning themes.

h) Eating and eliminating are daily activities with which children have an intimate knowledge. Following the cycle for themselves and then thinking about food sources and the whole life cycle chain can be expanded in many different ways.

i) Light and dark, sun and shadows, day and night are all concepts that touch every child.

Using these as springboards for a project can bring about rich learning.

j) Obviously, this is not a topic for temperate and warm climates but for those who await the first snowflake. Children can predict when it will occur, and projects can be derived from observation of the first snowflake and measurement of accumulation.

The same cognitive processes the child uses for math are also used for science (Figure 8–5). Scientific discovery and mathematics awareness come from exploring the physical properties of objects through all the senses and identifying the similarities and differences between objects and events. Meaning is attached to the symbols of the environment, such as day and night, summer and winter. The ability to focus on selected pieces of information while ignoring the irrelevant is developed. Vocabulary is expanded to express the concepts of knowledge in various subject areas (Kostelnik, Soderman, & Whiren, 1993). These processes—matching, discrimination, sequencing, describing, and classifying—have been pointed out as perceptual skills necessary for literacy as well. Science, math, and literacy are all connected to cognitive development. The world of science for the young child contains all of these elements. Their learning is enriched by reading and listening to stories about the natural world, discussing, and hypothesizing. They wonder about how the guinea pig had babies in the night and what happened to the snowman. Small muscles are used in carefully picking up a worm, and large ones are used when they run with paper streamers in the wind. They listen and count the heartbeats of Stephanie's unborn sibling with a stethoscope on her mother's abdomen. Let's get ourselves, then children, excited about science!

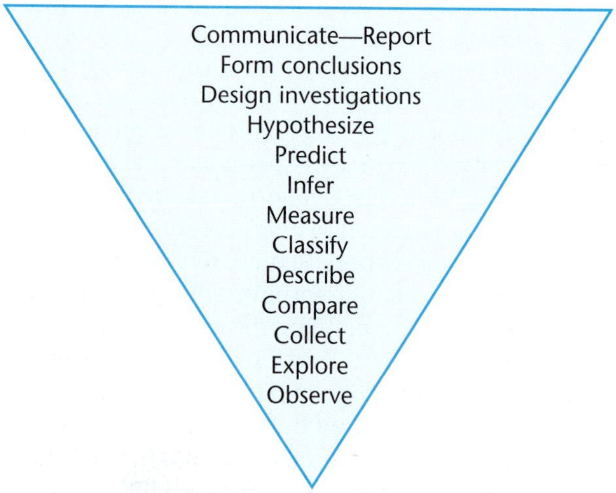

Figure 8–5 Developing Science Concepts.

What are the building blocks of science in the early years? They are the same ones used in chemistry laboratories in real life. The problem-solving skills in science are explored every day by young children as they construct their own knowledge (Charlesworth & Lind, 2003).

DOCUMENTING SCIENCE LEARNING. We can observe, document, and assess science learning in a variety of authentic ways (Jones & Courtney, 2002):

1. Collect a variety of forms of evidence—drawing, dictation, photographs, recording of children's language
2. Collect forms of evidence over a period of time
3. Collect evidence on the understanding of groups of children as well as individuals

This coordinates very well with the Portfolio of work you are gathering on each child using the *Week by Week* system.

EXERCISE **Look at the skills and tasks in the chart in Figure 8–6. Think of activities to provide these kinds of experiences from the child's interests and familiar world.**

SCIENCE FOR YOUNG CHILDREN. Appropriate science content that would have meaning to the young child is suggested in Charlesworth and Lind's useful guide *Math and Science for Young Children* (2003) (Figure 8–7).

Life Science. Life science is the study of plants, animals, and ecology. Appropriate to every early childhood classroom are growing, living things. There are informal ways of incorporating life science into the environment, and hence the curriculum, such as plants on a windowsill, guinea pigs in a cage, fish in a tank, or a recycling bin next to the garbage can. These can become more formalized with specific activities to observe, identify, describe, classify, and so on.

Health Science. The most relevant lesson to all is health science—the human body, its workings, and healthy practices. This is a vital area for foundation building, illness prevention, and promotion of lifelong wellness. Everyday practices, such as hand washing, are probably the most important health lessons that early childhood programs teach. Children are curious about their bodies, the appearance and function, both internally and externally. Measuring, weighing, and charting hair color, eye color, or number of teeth are relevant math and science activities for young children. Having a class baby is a very beneficial activity. At the beginning of the year, the class

SKILL	TASK	ACTIVITIES
OBSERVING	Discriminating alike, different	Observe any two objects for likenesses and differences: clothing, shoes, pinecones, crackers.
IDENTIFYING	Recognizing, naming	Vocabulary games with pictures. "What's this?"
DESCRIBING	Isolating characteristics Using appropriate terms Building vocabulary	Describing objects by shape, color, origin, function, texture, smell, taste, and sound. "How many shape words do we know?" Color words, things that grow, picky things, etc.
CLASSIFYING	Comparing/Contrasting Arranging/Matching Categorizing	Grouping objects together by a rule. Selecting an object that does not belong in the group using a rule.
DESIGNING INVESTIGATIONS	Asking questions Looking for relationships Following procedures	Playing games like "Hot/Cold" and "Twenty Questions." Manipulating objects to find out more about them, like cutting open a coconut. Cooking.
COLLECTING DATA	Taking notes Measuring	Charting the growth of a plant, or the weight and height of each child in the class.
INTERPRETING	Theories of cause and effect Organizing facts	Brainstorming, wondering. "Why does the plant on the windowsill grow faster than the one in the cubbie? Does the plant grow faster in water or soil?"
COMMUNICATING RESULTS	Summarizing Sequencing Describing	Charting, drawing, writing the sequence of events, such as planting a bean seed to picking the bean
FORMULATING CONCLUSIONS	Evaluating Generalizing Analyzing critically Applying to other situations	Theorizing: "If plants grow best in the sunlight, do people need sunlight to grow?"

Figure 8–6 Process Skills in Science.

"adopts" a mom having a baby in a month or two. She visits the class, and they ask questions and learn about the baby growing inside her. After its birth (which is a class celebration!), the mother visits the class regularly for the children to observe, measure, and investigate the baby's growth. By the end of the school year, the baby is sitting up, crawling, getting teeth, and becoming social. The children have learned many concepts in math, science, social studies, language, and physical development.

Physical Science. Physical science is the study of force, motion, energy, and machines. Children themselves are force, motion, and energy in one machine. Their fascination with carrying each other around, moving objects, and what makes things run can be capitalized on in the classroom. Heavy objects (even a teacher sitting on a table) can be moved easily (once they all get moving in the same direction) by a group of 8 or 10 preschoolers. Magnets have always been a part of the classroom, without deep explanation of poles of attraction. Manipulation, exploration, and observation can be augmented with charting what the magnet will pick up or attach to and what it will not. Blocks, a staple area of the classroom, can be augmented with ramps, cardboard tubes, and a facilitator

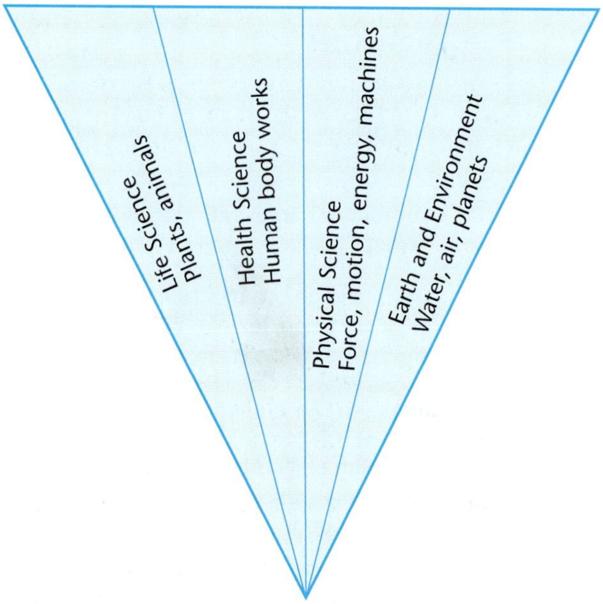

Figure 8–7 Young Children's Science Curriculum.

who asks "what-if" questions to expose children to principles of gravity and to give experiences in making predictions. "From which tube will the ball come out first if we start them both at the same time—the long one or the short one? Does it make any difference if it is a big ball or a small ball? Does it make a difference if we tip the short tube up higher? Why?" These concepts cannot be fully understood at this age. Most adults use electricity and television without understanding the principles behind them. The exploration of the effects of the forces of air, water, and machines are suitable activities for the early childhood classroom to explore and pose questions. The physical science area is important as these children grow up in the technological age, where these skills affect their daily life.

Earth and Environmental Science. All children are in daily contact with weather, water, air, dirt, rocks, sun, moon, and stars. Charting and measuring temperature and rainfall are concrete activities that can be carried on in an early childhood classroom. Experiments with water are carried on naturally as they stick their finger in the faucet to see what happens, or as they plunge a container into the water table and hold it up high to watch the water spill out. The magic of air's invisibility yet power can spark some interesting investigations for young children, laying foundations for the study of aerodynamics or hot air ballooning. Collecting rocks has been done naturally since the child was a toddler, picking up gravel stones from the driveway. Size, color, weight, geography, and effects of the environment all can be

@ it happened to me

Tornados

I was observing a student teacher leading a "science" activity. She had joined two soda bottles at the neck and gave each child in the circle a turn at tipping them over. They watched the vortex of swirling water as it drained from the upper bottle to the lower one. Some waited patiently, others impatiently, as they waited for a turn to make a "tornado." When it finally completed the circle, she asked the question, "And what did we learn about today?" Many were blank and silent, but one dare-to-risk child said "Tomatoes!" There was surprise on the student teacher's face with a "where'd-he-get-that?" look.

Afterward we talked about a child's need to manipulate, a child's inability to wait, and the importance of relevancy. We discussed why the child said "Tomatoes." She had no idea other than it sounded like tornados. For children living in Kansas who had seen funnel clouds and knew the word *tornado,* this lesson might have been more effective. Four-year-olds in New York could make no connection between a tornado and the water in the bottle. Should she not have done it? Possibly. Or perhaps some additional preparations—about wind, funnels, pipes, or even reading "The Wizard of Oz"—would have promoted meaning. This *activity-that-missed* reinforces the principle that learning will only occur in context. There has to be some relationship made to what children already know and have experienced.

Do you have an IT HAPPENED TO ME story about when a plan didn't work because it was out of the children's experience? I'd love to read it. Please send it to WeekbyWeek@thomsonlearning.com

concepts to explore in this area. The sky and its lights have fascinated children and poets. Exploring these from all kinds of curriculum areas begins with familiar stories, such as "Good Night, Moon," and singing "Twinkle, Twinkle, Little Star."

Will children understand all the math and science concepts? Probably not. Most adults do not understand how turning a switch will light a lamp, but it is used. Giving children experiences that provide exploration expands their knowledge and logical thinking processes, posing greater questions that will continue to be explored as they grow older.

Math and science curriculum topics begin with ideas from children's interest, current events, and the natural world around them. Projects and curriculum themes can be webbed or integrated into all of the curriculum areas. These are opportunities to make associations, broaden the experiences, and meet the needs of different learning styles. Here is an example of a curriculum web exploring topics relating to dirt (Figure 8–8).

EXERCISE Select one of the topics mentioned in this chapter and make a web to explore possible activities in each of the learning centers of your classroom or curriculum areas. Use the blank curriculum web in Figure 8–9.

Young Children and Technology

Children today are growing up with electronic technology that some of us only read about in Dick Tracy comic books (if you don't know what that is, ask your parents or grandparents). A child of two years old can manipulate a VCR or DVD player, play games on a computer and watch 24 hours of toddler television programming. The question is, "Should they?" And an even bigger question is about using such technology—computers, videos, and toddler-focused television—in early childhood programs. Teaching and learning has been, and will always be, a human interaction, but tools, even electronic ones, can expand the learning with opportunities and experiences that can reach beyond the classroom environment. The teacher and

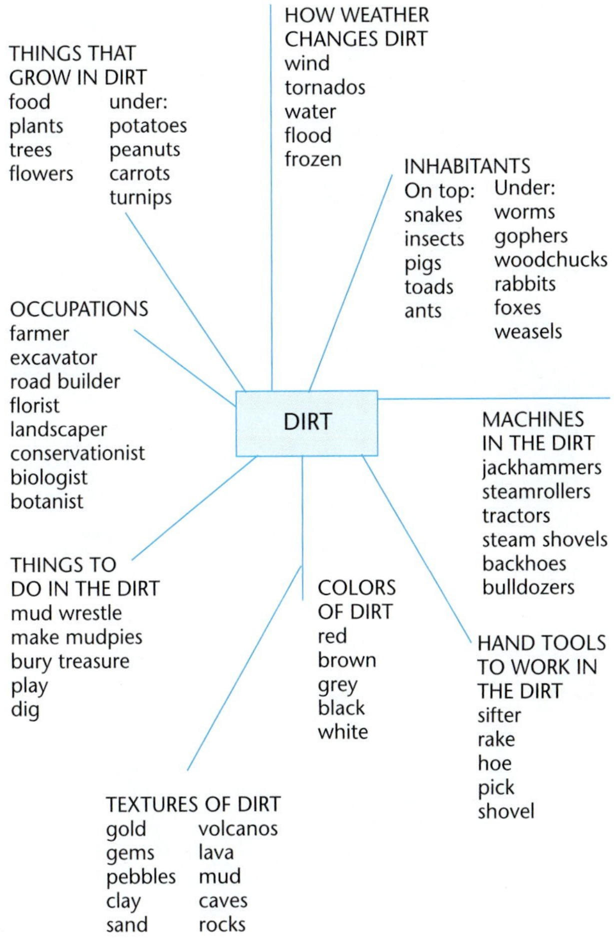

Figure 8–8 Science Curriculum Theme Web.

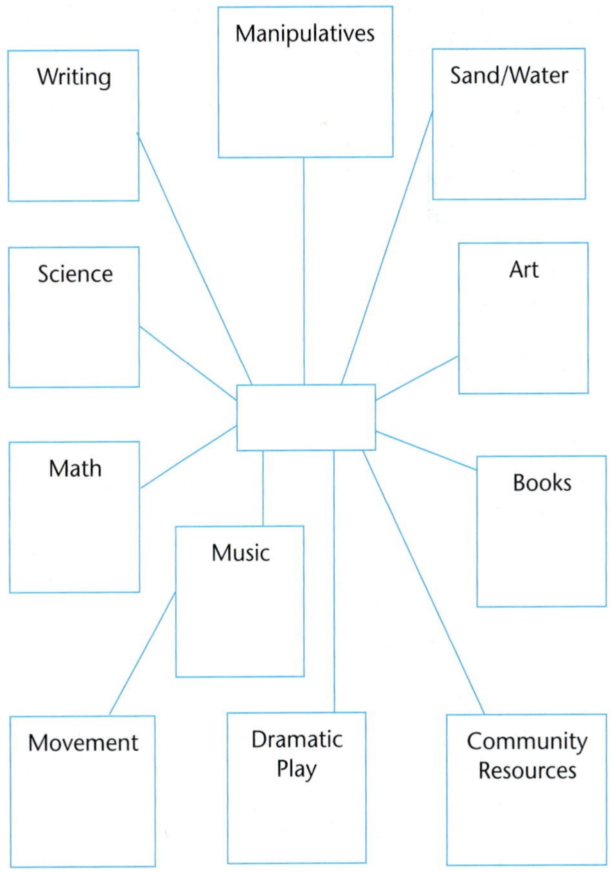

Figure 8–9 Curriculum Area Planning Web.

@ it happened to me

"It's a Record."

A friend of mine has a collection of records (those large black disks that play music) that she still uses in her classroom. One day she was placing one on the record player, one of the children looked up and exclaimed, "Wow, will you look at the size of that CD!"

Do you have an IT HAPPENED TO ME story about technology and today's child? I'd love to read it. Please send it to WeekbyWeek@thomsonlearning.com

program must make wise choices for the appropriate use of software, communication tools such as e-mail and Web pages, cameras, printers and copiers, and audio and video recorders. See the standard regarding the adult's responsibility for appropriate technology included at the end of the chapter.

Mathematics, science, and technology are interwoven into daily life; so math and science concepts are interwoven into the curriculum in much the same way. They are not discrete subjects but useful ways to make connections and meaning. Every individual is affected. Everyone uses mathematics and science in their daily lives.

Assessing Other Developmental Areas While Observing Math and Science Activities

As children interact with math and science experiences in the classroom in integrated curriculum, developmental areas other than cognitive development can be observed simultaneously. The interdependence of development both contributes to and is an outcome of math and science activities.

SELF-CARE SKILLS. The autonomy of doing things for oneself comes as children feel more competent in their environment. When children can count how many napkins they need to set the table for the group, or a child sees her name on the chart as the floor sweeper around the table where marigolds were being planted today, the skills interact.

LARGE MUSCLE DEVELOPMENT. The coordination of the body is observed as the child is running under the parachute to experience the wind or as she follows the game rules to take six steps backward. Both counting to six and walking backward are observed.

SMALL MUSCLE DEVELOPMENT. The child places one shell in each compartment of the egg carton in one-to-one correspondence. He gently picks up the baby chick that has just been hatched. Observation of small muscle skills and math and science come together (Figure 8–10).

LITERACY. Many teachers have explored the use of manipulatives; journals and situational problem solving have been effective in teaching concepts of mathematics and science. The combination of new skills integrates and maximizes the learning (Jones & Courtney, 2002; Whiten & Whiten, 2003).

OTHER AREAS OF DEVELOPMENT. Visual perception and knowledge of size-comparison vocabulary

Figure 8–10 Other areas of development may be assessed during math and science activities.

can be noted when the child picks up the bowling ball and calls it the "heaviest."

Language can be assessed by listening as the child speaks about solving the dilemma of three friends who want to sit by her at lunch. There are only two chairs left. Where will the third child sit? The logical resolution considering number of chairs as well as social interactions are observed while listening for clear speech and complexity of sentence structure.

Sharing Play Doh, dividing cookies, and taking turns on two bicycles are opportunities to observe both mathematical concepts and social development. Cooperation in working together to move a heavy object displays not only scientific principles but an understanding of community.

As children discover math and science concepts in a free environment without fear of "wrong" answers, they do not have to memorize or parrot back "right" answers in reply to closed questions. They can take risks to experiment. That is the basis for all inquiry: the elimination of wrong answers until the right one is arrived at through understanding. Children in the classroom environment dedicated to developmental learning can build and demonstrate that kind of self-concept.

HELPING ALL CHILDREN WITH COGNITIVE DEVELOPMENT

Cognitive development is different for each person, affected by learning styles, strong areas of intelligence, physical characteristics, and experiential factors. Early childhood teachers are faced with the challenge of meeting the learning needs of each child. There are some special populations whose cognitive development presents even more challenges.

Minority and Poverty Effects on School Achievement

Equality of educational opportunity has been the theme of Head Start for over 30 years. The Children's Defense Fund monitors poverty's effect on school achievement and has found that "only 15 percent of those fourth graders eligible for free and reduced-price lunch could write at grade level compared to 42 percent of those who are not eligible" (2005, p. 91). Minority children have higher rates of illiteracy, lower reading levels, and, later on, higher drop-out rates, incarceration rates, and unemployment rates. Schools with the highest percentages of minorities, limited English proficiency, and low-income students had less-experienced teachers, higher class-size ratios, were overcrowded, under-supplied, lacked computer access, and received a smaller per-capita spending budget (Children's Defense Fund, 2005). It's not testing but school improvement that is the important part of No Child Left Behind.

@ it happened to me

Toads

I was observing in a first-grade classroom where the teacher told the children to turn to page 45 in their workbook. She asked, "What is that animal?" One of the children said, "Frog." "No, it's not a frog. It's a toad, /t/, /t/, /t/. The letter of the day is *T*, so this has to be a toad. Now copy the word *toad* at the bottom of the page and you can color it in."

It looked like a frog to me. What is the difference? More importantly, what a learning opportunity was missed for the children and me to learn the difference. Instead, a negative message was sent to the one who answered the question. Do any of those children now know about toads because they wrote the letter or colored it? What if the class had gone out and gathered toads, watched them squirm down into the dirt, felt them wiggle, and measured their jumps? What if they compared them to a frog someone had captured in a pond and to tadpoles (another *T* word to add to their vocabulary)? Then they could have written, drawn, and dictated a story about a toad and a frog. The teacher would have really met her objective to familiarize them with toads and the letter *T* in a way that they would be more likely to remember. Authentic assessment is a real, not contrived, measurement of a real, not contrived curriculum.

Do you have an IT HAPPENED TO ME story about children learning, testing use or misuse? I'd love to read it. Please send it to me at WeekbyWeek@thomsonlearning.com

TOPICS IN OBSERVATION

"Real" Curriculum

Educational advertisements fill teachers' mailboxes, promising easy, fun, ready-to-do activities for every curriculum area, especially math and science. They come with attractive containers, dividers for organization, and free sample plans. Most of these and many idea books for math and science curriculum are adaptations of the workbook format. Directions are given such as, "Draw a line to the one that is the same." "Count the red balloons and select the numeral." "Circle the bead that completes the pattern." The purpose of these activities is to teach and assess cognitive concepts. Visual discrimination and classification, counting and reading numbers, and patterning are appropriate learning objectives for activity plans. Using paper-and-pencil tasks, or even teacher-made paper games, is not showing the teacher's knowledge of child development.

We know the attributes of the young, developing child. By knowing child development principles and observing and assessing the individual child's physical, social, emotional, and cognitive development, we can develop curriculum and teaching practices (Figure 8–11). It is not necessary nor effective to use workbook pages or folder activities to teach or test concepts. Just watch the child, and help the child do real stuff.

BECAUSE WE KNOW . . .	WE DO
Children learn through their senses.	We provide real, three-dimensional objects for them to manipulate.
Children are making associations with previous knowledge.	We provide materials that are familiar.
Children need time to organize their thoughts.	We provide long periods of uninterrupted time for them to explore.
Children cannot share.	We provide duplicates of popular materials.
Children cannot wait.	We do not require them to all do the same thing at the same time.
Children have different attention spans.	We provide a flexible schedule so children can move at their own pace.
Children are egocentric, only seeing things from their own point of view.	We do not force them to internalize someone else's point of view.
Children learn what they want to know.	We listen to them and provide ways for them to learn it.
Children learn from making mistakes.	We allow the mistakes to happen.
Children are frustrated easily.	We provide an environment and materials that are accessible and easy to manage themselves.
Children learn from accomplishing hard tasks.	We let them try without rushing in with solutions.
Children construct their own knowledge.	We provide a way for them to "teach" themselves.

Figure 8–11 Because We Know, We Do.

One in four children in America lives in poverty, and poverty is a strong predictor of poor school achievement, risk for learning disabilities, and need for special education services (Duncan & Brooks-Gunn, 1997; Hart and Risley, 2004). There are many factors contributing to these depressing statistics. It is even more distressing to know that teaching and assessment methods exacerbated rather than helped minority children and children in poverty to learn. The well-known Rosenthal effect (Rosenthal & Jacobson, 1968) may affect these populations. Teachers' expectations, using IQ scores or labels to categorize people, may contribute to the inequities. Jonathan Kozol's *Savage Inequalities: Children in America's Schools* (1991) captured in several vignettes the differences in schools for the haves and the have-nots. Teachers who gave their all to their students under extremely harsh conditions were portrayed along with teachers who did much harm. The book is a call to self-reflection about attitudes and actions by everyone who works with children.

Figure 8–12 Cognitive Development can be affected by many factors, but inclusive programs accept and adapt.

Children Who Are Cognitively Impaired

A whole group of cognitive impairments is categorized as mental retardation, subaverage intellectual function, and adaptive behavior (Figure 8–12). There are many causes, including the following:

- genetic disorders such as Down syndrome
- prenatal influences (maternal illness, drug abuse, fetal alcohol syndrome [FAS]),
- birth complications such as anoxia (oxygen deprivation during the birth process)
- postnatal causes, such as illnesses with high fevers, head injury, and lead poisoning
- environmental causes such as parental abuse and neglect.

The identification and labeling of mild cognitive impairments is difficult in young children because of inaccurate diagnostic methods such as IQ tests and wide cultural definitions of "normal" intelligence.

Some symptoms or clues are

- extremely short attention span
- language delays of more than one year
- social and emotional difficulties

Children with undiagnosed cognitive impairments often are detected first by preschool teachers. Approaching families with suspicions or concerns is a very sensitive task, done with concrete data and surrounded with care, understanding, and tact. The teacher may refer the family first to the pediatrician or a clinic specializing in full developmental evaluations.

After diagnosis, a placement decision is made for the child in the least restrictive environment. It may be the child can function in a regular classroom. Cook, Klein, and Tessier (2004, p. 341) give these recommendations for children who need extra time and spaced practice:

1. Provide concrete, multisensory tasks.
2. Find the child's most efficient mode of learning.
3. Monitor pacing; provide shorter work periods with less information.
4. Provide repetition.
5. Plan for modeling and imitation.
6. Task analyze; use short, simple steps in sequence.
7. Give explicit directions.

Inclusion

Public Law (P.L.) 94-142 specifies that every child must be given access to an *appropriate* education in the *least restrictive environment.* This law and supplementary laws have led to the **inclusion** of children with disabilities into the regular classroom. Children with physical disabilities fare the best in inclusion classrooms. Learning disabilities and cognitive disorders require the teacher to implement an individualized program. With a philosophy that every child is unique, individualizing the curriculum for each child is the goal. There are social benefits as well as social risks to inclusion. Children are forming ideas about *we* and *they* with very basic social skills, so inclusion with peers who may react negatively because they are still learning social skills may bring rejection to the included child. The role of the teacher is expanded here to address social issues and turn inclusion into experiences of greater understanding and caring. Effectiveness in inclusion education depends on the training and support of all people working with the children: teacher, aide, volunteers, and support staff such as bus drivers and lunchroom personnel.

The family of a child with learning disabilities gives the following specific strategies for inclusion but they are really advice for working with all children (Anderson and Weinhouse, 1997, p. 30–31).

1. Never limit your expectations or predetermine the final outcome.
2. Explore all interests and abilities for hidden potential.
3. Include these children in regular education classes and activities whenever possible.

For specific strategies for working with a child with exceptional health, hearing, learning, visual impairments, communication, or physical needs, see *Inclusive Early Childhood Education* (Richey & Wheeler, 2000) and *The Exceptional Child* (Allen, & Cowdery, 2005).

Children Who Are Talented and Gifted

This beyond-the-range-of-normal category, **talented and gifted**, is one of the most neglected in working with children with exceptional needs. While high cognitive abilities characterized by advanced linguistic and reasoning ability, curiosity, and superior memory are the most obvious indicators of cognitive giftedness, other areas also are considered in this category. Children with advanced social skills, physical prowess, and musical ability also are included. The same hindrances to early identification of mental impairments also apply to giftedness. Developmental assessments can indicate advanced attainment of milestones and document behavior that alerts teachers and parents to the child's exceptional abilities. The teacher then individualizes the curriculum to provide enrichment opportunities to support the child's area of strength as well as the areas of normal development.

HELPING PROFESSIONALS FOR COGNITIVE CONCERNS

Families with a child with exceptional cognitive development at either end of the range of normal can first seek help from the following medical personnel:

pediatrician—physician specializing in the health and development of children
neurologist—physician specializing in the nervous system and in brain functioning

Within the educational system, specially trained professionals help the classroom teacher and the family meet the needs of the child, whether cognitively impaired or gifted:

itinerant teacher—visits classroom or home regularly to see that appropriate methods, materials, and services are provided
special education teacher—a specialist trained to work with children with cognitive disabilities; may have further specialties in reading, speech/language, occupational therapy, physical therapy, behavioral, autism spectrum disorders, or talented and gifted
resource teacher—assesses placement and provides instructional time outside of the regular classroom

OTHER METHODS

Other Methods to Record Cognitive Development

Anecdotal/Running Records
Checklists/Rating Scales
Discussions/Interviews
Work Samples
Media such as audio/video and still photography

STANDARDS

Here are selected examples of standards for math, science, and technology for

Young Children
Principles and Standards for School Mathematics (NCTM 2000)
Understand numbers, ways of representing numbers, relationships among numbers, and number systems

Pre-K–2 Expectations

In pre-kindergarten through grade 2 all students should—

Count with understanding and recognize "how many" in sets of objects.

Sub-Standard 4b. Using Developmentally Effective Approaches

Hyson, M., (Ed.). (2003). *Preparing Early Childhood Professionals: NAEYC's Standards for Programs.* Washington, DC: NAEYC. Reprinted with permission from the National Association for the Education of Young Children.

Candidates know, understand, and use a wide array of effective approaches, strategies, and tools to positively influence young children's development and learning.

KEY TERMS

authentic assessment	quantitative scoring
benchmarks	reliability
cognitive	screening
dispositions	standardized tests
high-stakes tests	standard
inclusion	talented and gifted
norm	valid
ordinal numbers	

Go to the Bind-in-Book CD for:

Class List Log form

Plan Week 8 Part A, Obtain, a copy of a standardized test and review it based on your learning from this chapter. Questions to answer concerning the test.

Plan Week 8 Part B, Directions for a Math and Science Assessment for ALL, including What to Do with It, Portfolio Overview Example, Sharing with Child and Family, Actions—Read a Book, In the Environment, In the Curriculum, In the Newsletter

Plan Week 8 Part B, Directions for Work Samples for All

Plan Week 8 Part C, Conversations with Group C for Speech and Language Assessment

Plan Week 8 Part D, Reflective Journal

REFERENCES

Allen, K. E., & Cowdery, G. (2005). *The exceptional child* (5th ed.). Clifton Park, NY: Thomson Delmar Learning.

Anderson, M., & Weinhouse, D. (1997). Learning disabilities—Twice blessed. *Young Children, 52* (4), 29–31.

Bagnato, S. (2006). Quality: Standards, curriculum and assessment, keynote address at NAEYC National Institute for Early Childhood Professional Development, June 4, 2006.

Bayley, N. (1993). *Bayley scales of infant development* (2nd ed.). San Antonio TX: The Psychological Corp.

Benner, S. (2003). *Assessment of young children with special needs.* Clifton Park, NY: Thomson Delmar Learning.

Bredekamp, S., & Copple, C (Eds.). (1997). *Developmentally appropriate practice in early childhood programs* (rev. ed.). Washington, DC: National Association for the Education of Young Children.

Bricker, D., Squires, J., & Mounts, L. (1995). *Ages and stages questionnaires: A parent-completed, child monitoring system.* Baltimore, MD: Brookes.

Brigance, A. H. (1991). *BRIGANC® diagnostic inventory of early development, revised.* Billerica, MA: Curriculum Associates, Inc.

Charlesworth, R., & Lind, K. (2003). *Math and science for young children* (4th ed.). Clifton Park, NY: Thomson Delmar Learning.

Children's Defense Fund. (2005). *The state of America's children yearbook, 2005.* Washington, DC: Author.

Conezio, K., & French, L. (2002). Science in the preschool classroom: Capitalizing on children's fascination with everyday world to foster language and literacy development. *Young Children, 57* (5), 12–18.

Cook, R. E., Klein, M. D., & Tessier, A. (2004). *Adapting early childhood curricula for children with special needs* (6th ed.). Upper Saddle River, NJ: Pearson Education.

Duncan, G., & Brooks-Gunn, J. (1997). *Consequences of growing up poor.* New York: Russell Sage.

Ethridge, E. A., King, J. R. (2005). Calendar math in preschool and primary classrooms: Questioning the curriculum. *Early Childhood Education Journal, 32* (5), April 2005.

Fleege, P. O., Charlesworth, R., Burts, D. C., & Hart, C. H. (1996). Stress begins in kindergarten: A look at behavior during standardized testing. *Journal of Research in Childhood Education,* 7 (10), 20–26.

Greenspan, S. I., & Meisels, S. (1994). Toward a new vision for the developmental assessment of infants and young children. *Zero to Three, 14,* 1–8.

Hart, B., & Risley, T. R. (2004). *Meaningful differences in the everyday experience of young American children.* Baltimore, MD: Brookes.

Hatch, J. A. (2002). Accountability shovedown: Resisting the standards movement in early childhood education. *Phi Delta Kappan, 83* (6), 457–463.

Helm, J. H., & Katz, L. (2001). *Young investigators: The project approach in the early years.* New York: Teachers College Press.

Jones, J., & Courtney, R. (2002). Documenting early science learning. *Young Children, 57* (5), 34–40.

Johnson, B., & Plemons, B. (1993). *Cup cooking: Individual child-portion picture recipes.* Ithaca, NY: Early Educators Press.

Kamii, C. (1982). *Number in preschool and kindergarten: Educational implications of Piaget's theory.* Washington, DC: National Association for the Education of Young Children.

Kamii, C., & Kamii, M. (1990). Why achievement testing should stop. In C. Kamii (Ed.), *Achievement testing in the early grades: The games grown-ups play.* Washington, DC: National Association for the Education of Young Children.

Katz, L. G. (1988). *Early childhood education: What research tells us.* Bloomington, IN: Phi Delta Kappa.

Katz, L. G., & Chard, S. C. (2000). *Engaging children's minds: The project approach* (2nd ed.). Stamford, CT: Ablex Publishing Corp.

Kendall, J. S., & Marzano, R. J. (2004). *Content knowledge: A combendium of standards and benchmarks for K–12 education.* Aurora CO: Mid-continent Research for Education and Learning (McREL). Online database: http://www.mcrel.org/standards-benchmarks/.

Kohn, A. (2001). Fighting the tests: Turning frustration into action. *Young Children, 56* (2), 19–24.

Kostelnik, M., Soderman, A., Whiren, A., Keil, A., & Phipps, A. (1993). *Developmentally appropriate programs in early childhood education.* New York: Merrill.

Kozol, J. (1991). *Savage inequalities: Children in America's schools.* New York: Harper Perennial.

Lind, K. K. (2000). *Exploring science in early childhood education.* Clifton Park: Thomson Delmar Learning.

Louv, R. (2005). *Last child in the woods: Saving our children from nature-deficit disorder.* Chapel Hill, NC: Algonquin Books.

McAfee, O., & Leong, K. J. (2002). *Assessing and guiding young children's development and learning* (3rd ed.). Boston: Allyn and Bacon.

Meisels, S. (1987). Uses and abuses of developmental screening and school readiness testing. *Young Children, 42* (2), 4.

Meisels, S. J., Bickel, D. D., Nicholson, J., Xue, Y., & Atkins-Burnett, S. (2001). Trusting teachers judgments: A validity study of a curriculum-embedded performance assessment in kindergarten–grade 3. *American Educational Research Journal, 38* (1), 73.

Meisels, S. J., Xue, Y., Bickel, D. P., Nicholson, J., Atkins-Burnett, S. (2001). Parental reactions to authentic performance assessment. *Educational Assessment,* 7(1), 61–85.

Meisels, S. J., & Atkins-Burnett, S. (2000). The Elements of early childhood assessment. In J. Shonkoff & S. Meisels, *Handbook of early childhood intervention.* New York: Cambridge University Press.

National Association for the Education of Young Children. (2005). *NAEYC early childhood program standards and accreditation criteria.* Washington, DC: Author.

National Commission on Excellence in Education. (1983). *A nation at risk: the imperative for educational reform; A report to the nation and the Secretary of Education, United States Department of Education.* Washington, DC: Author.

National Council of Teachers of Mathematics (NCTM). (2000). *Principles and standards for school mathematics.* Reston, VA: Author.

Neill, M. (2006). The case against high-stakes testing. *Principal. 85*(4), Mar./Apr. 2006.

Neisworth, J. T., & Bagnato, S. J. (2004). The mismeasure of young children: The authentic assessment alternative. *Infants & Young Children, 17* (i3), 198, July–Sept. 2004.

Neuman, S. B., & Roskos, K. A. (2000). How can we enable all children to achieve? *Early Childhood Today, 15* (2), 21–24.

Pellegrini, A. D., & Bjorklund, D. F. (1998). *Applied child study: A developmental approach.* Mahwah, NJ: Lawrence Erlbaum Associates.

Puckett, M. B., & Black, J. K. (2000). *Authentic assessment of the young child: Celebrating development and learning.* Upper Saddle River, NJ: Merrill Prentice Hall.

Richey, D. D., & Wheeler, J. J. (2000). *Inclusive early childhood education.* Clifton Park, NY: Thomson Delmar Learning.

Rivkin, M. (1992). Science is a way of life. *Young Children, 47* (4), May 1992.

Rosenthal, R., & Jacobson, L. (1968). *Pygmalion in the classroom: Teacher expectation and pupils' intellectual development.* New York: Holt, Rinehart, and Winston.

Schiro, M. (1997). *Integrating children's literature and mathematics in the classroom.* New York: Teachers College Press.

Seefeldt, C. (2005). *How to work with standards in the early childhood classroom.* New York: Teachers College Press.

Shepard, L., Kagan, S. L., & Wurtz, E. (Eds.). (1998). *Principles and recommendations for early childhood assessments.* Washington, DC: National Education Goals Panel, U.S. Department of Education.

VORT Corporation. (1995). *HELP for preschoolers: Assessment and curriculum guide.* Palo Alto, CA: Author.

Wesson, K. A. (2001). The "Volvo" effect: Questioning standardized tests. *Young Children, 56* (2), 16–18.

Whitin, P., & Whitin, D. J. (2003). Developing mathematical understanding along the yellow brick road. *Young Children, 58* (1), 36–40.

Yell, M. L., Katsiyanna, A., Shiner, J. G. (2006). The No Child Left Behind Act, adequate yearly progress and students with disabilities. *Council for Exceptional Children,* Mar./Apr. 2006.

RESOURCES

Calkins, L., Mongtomery, K., & Santman, D. (1998). *A teacher's guide to standardized reading tests: Knowledge is power.* Portsmouth, NH: Heinemann.

Chandler, P. A. (1994). *A place for me: Including children with special needs in early care and education settings.* Washington, DC: National Association for the Education of Young Children.

Charlesworth, R., & Lind, K. (2003). *Math and science for young children* (4th ed.). Clifton Park, NY: Thomson Delmar Learning.

Kamii, C. (1982). *Number in preschool and kindergarten: Educational implications of Piaget's theory.* Washington, DC: National Association for the Education of Young Children.

Seefeldt, C. (2005). *How to work with standards in the early childhood classroom.* New York: Teachers College Press.

Wakefield, A. (1998). *Early childhood number games: Teachers reinvent math instruction, Pre-K through third grade.* Boston: Allyn and Bacon.

CHAPTER

9 Using Rating Scales to Look at Literacy

IN THIS CHAPTER

- Using the Rating Scale
- Looking at Literacy
- Helping All Children with Literacy
- Topics in Observation: Books in the Sandbox
- Helping Professionals for Literacy Concerns

USING THE RATING SCALE

EXERCISE **How hungry are you?**
Starved? A little hungry? Fully satisfied?
How is the temperature?
Too cold? Just right? Too hot?
How well do you sing?
Off key? Comfortably with a group? Soloist?

A **Rating Scale** lists specific descriptions of criteria in a horizontal line from least to most, early developing to later developing, simple to complex, with several choices in between (Figure 9–1).

The Rating Scale shown in Figure 9–1 contains seven sequential milestones or **quality points** in learning to read. A checklist such as displayed in Figure 9–2 contains the same information but in a vertical formation calling for a "yes" or "no" response from the recorder. The Rating Scale visually portrays the stages of development of a skill and can even include notations at the in-between stages.

Once the rater becomes familiar with the instrument and the child or setting, a rating is chosen that most closely describes what has been observed. It could be used by the teacher, a family member, a volunteer, or an outside observer. When more than one rater uses the same instrument on the same child, the validity increases, reducing rater bias. This is called **interrater reliability**. The scores are compared and, depending on the number of raters, the highest and lowest scores are cast out and the remaining

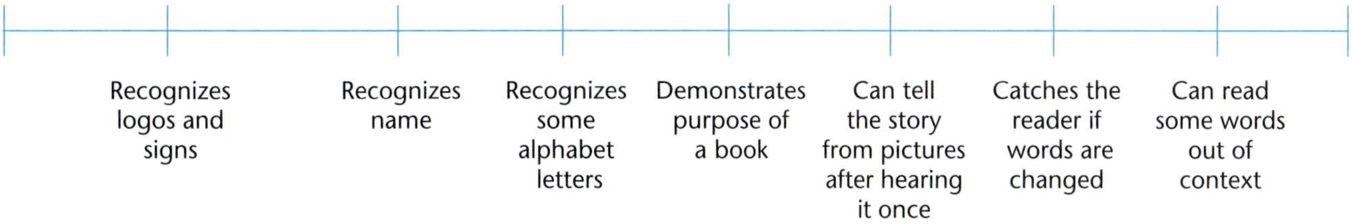

Figure 9–1 Literacy Rating Scale.

scores are averaged. This technique is used in research and in judging Olympic sporting events.

Rating Scales, like Checklists, are self-made or purchased, and are used to measure certain criteria. The criteria can be a child's development or a setting or a program's adherence to certain aspects of quality. When a measurement is made against these criteria, it is an affirmation of what has been attained and an indicator of what to plan for next. In a child's development, this type of measurement indicates progress or reveals lags that may be cause for concern. This tool, like the Checklist, gives the teacher that zone of proximal development (Berk & Winsler, 2002), the not-yet-attained skill that the teacher can scaffold (adult supports the child to accomplish a new task with help). For example, a child who can print the first letter of his name is encouraged to do so at every opportunity, with the teacher finishing the remaining letters. Eventually, the child will write more of the letters himself. When a setting or program rating scale is used, it is an effective self-study tool to measure adherence to guidelines and to indicate areas to be addressed for improvement.

Because the rater is looking for signs of the specific criteria, a Rating Scale is a highly **selective method**. Other observations are irrelevant and not recorded while looking for the specific criteria. A Rating Scale is considered a closed method since no raw data or details are recorded. Exact details of the rater's observation leading to the selection of a rating are not recorded.

A Literacy Rating Scale has been developed to assess the interest, skill, and knowledge of young children's reading and writing. Figure 9–3 is an example of a completed Literacy Rating Scale. Each criterion is rated from observation and dated at its highest level of attainment. When the quality point or milestone is not observed, individualized curriculum or activities are planned for that child to encourage this area of development. It may be that the environment is not conducive for this child's learning style to spawn interest in reading or writing, or the materials are not accessible or meaningful. The tool is a way to accomplish the end result, to stimulate and encourage literacy development and record the progress. See the Bind-in-Book CD for a blank reproducible Literacy Rating Scale.

Rating Scale Examples

The quality points take several forms, depending on the design of the Rating Scale. The scale in Figure 9–1 describes the criteria from which the rater selects the most accurate choice based on observation and the rater's knowledge of the child.

Rating Scales, such as *The Work Sampling System* (Meisels, Dichtelmiller, Jablon, Dorfman, & Marsden, 2001), use quality points of Seldom/Usually/Always or Not Yet/In Process/Proficient. A Rating Scale that uses a similar style is the center evaluation of the *National Association for the Education of Young Children Accreditation Self Study Classroom Observation Tool for Preschool Groups* (NAEYC, 2005). It uses scales with Yes/Yes, but . . ./No (Figure 9–4). It is a closed method because it does not record exactly what has been observed to meet the criterion but does include an area to provide evidence or comments.

Rating Scales can translate the written criteria into a number rating that can be added with others to obtain a quantitative score. *The Environmental Rating Scale* (*ECERS-R*) by Harms, Clifford, and Cryer (1998) has 7 subscales: Space and Furnishings, Personal Care Routines, Language-Reasoning, Activities,

Checklist Example

- ❑ Recognizes logos and signs
- ❑ Recognizes name
- ❑ Recognizes some alphabet letters
- ❑ Demonstrates purpose of a book
- ❑ Can tell the story from pictures after hearing it once
- ❑ Catches the reader if words are changed
- ❑ Can read some words out of context

Figure 9–2 Checklist Example.

LITERACY RATING SCALE Child's Name *Jeremiah Jones*

INTEREST IN BOOKS

No interest, avoids *9/10*	Only if adult-initiated *10/17*	Brings books to adult to read	Looks at books as self-initiated activity

LISTENING TO BOOKS

Wiggly, no attention *9/21 10/6*	Intermittent attention *11/17 can't last thru whole story*	Listens in one-on-one situation	Listens as part of a group, tuning out distractions

INVOLVEMENT WITH BOOKS BEING READ

Little or no response *11/11*	Emotional response, laugh, frown	Comments, asks questions	Joins in during reading

HANDLING BOOKS

No voluntary touching	Rough handling *9/30*	Exploratory manipulation *10/29 Stacking up in piles by color!*	Books as favorite toys

CONCEPT OF BOOK FORMAT

No idea of front/back, up/down *0*	Holds book right side up but skips pages *0*	Demonstrated front/back concept *10/29*	Looks at pages left to right *2/7 He sat & looked at every page of dinosaur book*

CONCEPT OF STORY BOOK *didn't realize he was listening even though he wasn't sitting*

Labels pictures *11/21*	Retells story in sequence from pictures *1/16*	Accurately repeats some story lines	Points to print while accurately re-telling from pictures

PRINT IN THE ENVIRONMENT *no obs. in this area*

Notices signs, labels *0 0*	Asks, "What's that say?" *0*	Reads signs, labels out of context *0*	"Writes" signs to label constructions *0*

BEGINNING READING *a start. "J"*

Recognizes own name *11/15 0*	Recognizes letters in name in other words *3/17*	Reads simple words	Sounds out letters in unfamiliar words

CONTINUED

Figure 9–3 Literacy Rating Scale Example.

LITERACY RATING SCALE (continued)

MANIPULATION OF WRITING TOOLS

Fist hold	High hold on pencil	Adult grip, little control	Adult grip, good control
9/30	11/6	4/17 Work on this!	

COMMUNICATION THROUGH WRITING no interest

Communicates ideas through drawing	Will describe drawing on request	Initiates description of drawing	Draws and writes words
2/16 0	4/20 0 0		

BEGINNING WRITING

Scribbles, no reference to writing	Named scribbles "Says my name"	Single letters, random	Writes name

WRITING IN PLAY

No reference to writing	Asks for signs, words to be written	Asks for adult to spell words	Sounds out words and writes on own

Figure 9–3 *(continued)*.

Interaction, Program Structure, and Parents and Staff. These are broken down into 43 separate rating scales. Each is arranged on a 7-point scale from Inadequate (1) to Excellent (7). In Figure Figure 9–5, each specific criterion under Section 15, "Books and pictures," requires an affirmative decision to attain that score. The quantitative scores are then graphed on the Summary Sheet (Figure 9–6), to report areas of strength and areas that need attention. While the ECERS-R does have a small space for rater's notes that could amplify the rating, it is still a closed method since the outside reader does not have enough data on which to draw her own conclusions, unlike the Anecdotal or Running Record.

Advantages

The Rating Scale is

- fast and convenient. (The rater reads, decides, circles, or checks.)
- efficient for measuring a large number of criteria quickly.
- informative of what "should be" expected.
- useful for tracking progress or warning of developmental lags.
- an assessment measurement against the ideal and used as a plan for improvement (accreditation).
- revisited to see progress over time.

Disadvantages

The Rating Scale is

- not backed up with raw data.
- not objective. (Judgments are made as observation is taking place with little time for considering the criteria and no place for explanation of circumstances.)
- not free of rater bias, with no way for the reader to know that.
- not useful as a method to record spontaneous actions or conversations.
- not sensitive to a wide range of individual differences.

Number	Accreditation Criterion	All Indicators Observed YES	NO
2.E.	*Curriculum Content Area for Cognitive Development: Early Literacy*		
2.E.03	Children have opportunities to become familiar with print. They are actively involved in making sense of print, and they have opportunities to become familiar with, recognize, and use print that is accessible throughout the classroom: • Items belonging to a child are labeled with his or her name. • Materials are labeled. • Print is used to describe some rules and routines. • Teaching staff help children recognize print and connect it to spoken words. Fully met? (circle): Yes Yes, but No Evidence/comments:		
2.E.04	Children have varied opportunities to • have books read in an engaging manner at least twice a day in full-day programs and at least once daily in half-day programs in group or individualized settings. • be read to regularly in individualized ways, including one-to-one or in small groups of two to six children regularly. • explore books on their own and have places that are conducive to the quiet enjoyment of books. • have access to various types of books, including storybooks, factual books, books with rhymes, alphabet books, and wordless books. • be read the same book on repeated occasions. • retell and reenact events in storybooks. • engage in conversations that help them understand the content of the book. • be assisted in linking books to other aspects of the curriculum. • identify the parts of books and differentiate print from pictures. Fully met? (circle): Yes Yes, but No Evidence/comments:		
2.E.05	Children have multiple and varied opportunities to write. • Writing materials and activities are readily available in art, dramatic play, and other learning centers. • Various types of writing are supported, including scribbling, letter-like marks, and developmental spelling. • Children have daily opportunities to write or dictate their ideas. • Children are provided needed assistance in writing the words and messages they are trying to communicate. • Children are given the support they need to write on their own, including access to the • alphabet (e.g., displayed at eye level or on laminated cards) and • to printed words about topics of current interest. • Children see teaching staff model functional use of writing and are helped to discuss the many ways writing is used in daily life. Fully met? (circle): Yes Yes, but No Evidence/comments:		
2.E.06	Children are regularly provided multiple and varied opportunities to develop phonological awareness: • Children are encouraged to play with the sounds of language, including syllables, word families, and phonemes, using rhymes, poems, songs, and finger plays. • Children are helped to identify letters and the sounds they represent. • Children are helped to recognize and produce words that have the same beginning or ending sounds. • Children's self-initiated efforts to write letters that represent the sounds of words are supported. Fully met? (circle): Yes Yes, but No Evidence/comments:		
2.E.07	Children are given opportunities to • recognize and • write letters. Fully met? (circle): Yes Yes, but No Evidence/comments:		
2.E.08	Children have access to • books and • writing materials throughout the classroom. Fully met? (circle): Yes Yes, but No Evidence/comments:		

Figure 9–4 Reprinted by permission, from *NAEYC Self-Study Classroom Observation Tool for Preschool Groups* (2005). Reprinted with permissions from the National Association for the Education of Young Children. All rights reserved.

Inadequate 1	2	Minimal 3	4	Good 5	6	Excellent 7
LANGUAGE-REASONING **15. Books and pictures** 1.1 Very few books accessible. 1.2 Staff rarely read books to children (Ex. no daily story time, little individual reading to children).		3.1 Some books accessible for children (Ex. during free play children have enough books to avoid conflict). 3.2 At least one staff-initiated receptive language activity time daily (Ex. reading books to children,* storytelling, using flannel board stories).		5.1 A wide selection of books† are accessible for a substantial portion of the day. 5.2 Some additional‡ language materials used daily. 5.3 Books organized in a reading center. 5.4 Books, language materials, and activities are appropriate** for children in group. 5.5 Staff reads books to children informally (Ex. during free time, at naptime, as an extension of an activity).		7.1 Books and language material are rotated to maintain interest. 7.2 Some books relate to current classroom activities or themes (Ex. books borrowed from library on seasonal theme).

Notes for Clarification

* Reading may be done in small groups or in larger groups depending on the ability of the children to attend to the story.

† A wide selection of books may include: variety of topics; fantasy and factual information; stories about people, animals, and science; books that reflect different cultures and abilities.

‡ Examples of additional language materials are posters and pictures, flannel board stories, picture card games, and recorded stories and songs.

**Examples of appropriate materials and activities include simpler books read with younger children; large print materials for child with visual impairment; books in children's primary language(s); rhyming games for older children.

Questions

(7.1) Are there any other books used with the children? How is this handled?

(7.2) How do you choose books?

Figure 9–5 Language-Reasoning Rating Scale, 15. Books and Pictures, ECERS-R (reprinted by permission of the publishers from Harms, T., Clifford, R.M., and Cryer, D., 2005. *Early Childhood Environment Rating Scale Revised Edition*, New York: Teacher's College Press).

LANGUAGE-REASONING		
15. Books and pictures	**1 2 3 4 5 6 7**	**Notes**
Y N 1.1 ☐ ☐ 1.2 ☐ ☐	Y N 3.1 ☐ ☐ 3.2 ☐ ☐	
Y N 5.1 ☐ ☐ 5.2 ☐ ☐ 5.3 ☐ ☐ 5.4 ☐ ☐ 5.5 ☐ ☐	Y N 7.1 ☐ ☐ 7.2 ☐ ☐	

Figure 9–6 Score Sheet for Language-Reasoning Rating Scale, 15. Books and Pictures, ECERS-R (reprinted by permission of the publishers from Harms, T., Clifford, R. M., and Cryer, D., 2005. *Early Childhood Environment Rating Scale Revised Edition,* New York: Teacher's College Press).

Pitfalls to Avoid

The Rating Scale recorder should

- make sure the Rating Scale criteria match the goals and objectives of the program and developmental range of the children.
- have more than one person use the same rating scale and compare ratings for inter-rater reliability to limit observer bias.
- become familiar with Rating Scale criteria before using it and be sure that each criterion is observable rather than judgmental: Scribbles/Forms alphabet letters/Writes cursive, *not* Still scribbling/Poor spelling/Good writing.
- be sure the quality points describe behaviors rather than attitudes: Leaves when story reading begins/Stays, plays with toys during story reading/Sits, watching pages displayed during story reading, *not* Not interested/Some interest/Very interested.

Using Technology

Rating Scales that have numerical scoring lend themselves to electronic storage and computation of the results. Personal computers and hand-held computers can store the form in an electronic file, and the observer can enter the numerical rating. Using computer programs that perform computation and graphical reporting, the scores can be saved in individual children's electronic files and also used as aggregate data on the whole group.

How to Find the Time

Completing Rating Scales on individual children's development does take concentrated observation and recording to obtain objective results. Much of this observation can be done during free play time. Remember that it requires a person who is not fully responsible for classroom management. Program Rating Scales such as the ECERS can be done as a self-assessment by the teaching team or by an objective evaluator. See Chapter 13 for more discussion of program assessment.

Go to the Bind-in-Book CD for Literacy Rating Scales, plans, and resources.

REVIEW

RATING SCALE

Criteria are arranged according to developmental stages or range of quality with the recorder making a judgment based on observation.

Types of Information to Record Using a Rating Scale (depends on focus of Rating Scale)

child development stages
environment appropriateness
teacher performance

LOOKING AT LITERACY

EXERCISE What did you read today? What did you write today?

Reading and writing are so natural that they are done automatically. When reading the preceding exercise, thoughts might have gone to formally picking up a book or writing a letter. Do not forget about these:

the numbers on the clock
the name of the toothpaste you used this morning
the on/off light switch
signing a check
jotting down a phone number
reading and writing this exercise

Americans are reading less than ever before. In a survey of more than 17,000 adults, the National Endowment for the Arts found in 2002 less than one half has read a book, short stories, plays, or poetry in their leisure time, down 10 percent since 1982 (2004). If adults are not reading, will children learn to love reading?

"Learning to read and write is critical to a child's success in school and later in life. One of the best predictors of whether a child will function competently in school and go on to contribute actively in our increasingly literate society is the level to which the child progresses in reading and writing" (Neuman, Copple, & Bredekamp, 1999). This is the opening statement of a joint position statement of the International Reading Association (IRA) and the National Association for the Education of Young Children. But how do children learn to read and write? What can families and teachers provide to ensure not just that these vital skills are mastered but that a joy of reading is kindled for a lifetime? It seems to come effortlessly for some, but with great difficulty for others. For most people, though, once it is learned it is there forever, and *very* useful. Becoming literate is like the childhood game of "Mother, May I." It comes in baby steps, tiny little forward motions, then giant steps, leaps that propel it forward. Literacy is not an isolated skill from other development, for it involves motor skills, visual perception, hearing, small muscle development, cognitive development, social interactions, and emotional control. It is simultaneously developing along with language. There are four key components in a home literacy environment that lead to literacy success: value placed on literacy, the press for achievement, the availability and use of reading materials, and parent-child book reading (Snow et al., 1998).

Receptive language skills are greater and earlier than expressive skills (Figure 9–7). This is true in literacy as well. Hearing and understanding words precede speaking them. Reading words usually occurs before writing them. Reading and comprehension ability will always be greater than the ability to write as an expressive form (though some writing seems to be done without thinking). However, exactly how children learn to read and what is the best curricular approach to take is still a matter of debate and research. There is the ecological view. (Go back to the Introduction chapter and reread the Topics in Observation.) This view suggests that every child is a product of biological factors, then is surrounded by relationships of family, friends, peers, and society, all of which affects the child's development, including literacy. The child is exposed to literacy from birth. Researchers are studying how these influences form the basis for learning to read. Then there are the more formal situations such as child care, preschool, and early elementary classrooms and how the philosophy or approach to literacy in these more formal settings affects the curriculum. A few of the approaches:

Figure 9–7 Experiences with books preceed reading and writing.

Basal readers—Books designed for group instruction in teaching whole words that are repeated.

Whole language—Providing a print-rich environment through which children have natural interactions with print and literature.

Literature-based—Using children's literature on which to base reading instruction.

Phonetic reading—Children are taught the sounds (phonemes) of the alphabet letters, then use them to decode words.

Thematic centers—Dramatic play with literacy materials such as library, doctor's office, school, home.

Book reading—Adult reads, children listen.

Dialogic reading—Adult reads and asks questions about the connection between illustrations, print, and plot.

Child narration—The story comes from the child, either in dictation or a combination of drawing and writing and the child sits in the "Author's Chair," where the story is explained to other children who may ask questions or make comments.

Shared drama enactment—Children together construct a dramatic episode, play it out, then the rest of the group asks questions or make comments (Fein et al., 2000).

Most early childhood classrooms use a combination of each of these so that pure research into approach and results has been difficult.

Some imposing evidence offered by Jeynes and Littell (2000) indicates that for low-SES (socioeconomic status) children who are not surrounded by a **print-rich environment** and families who value reading, phonics instruction with a basal reader is more effective.

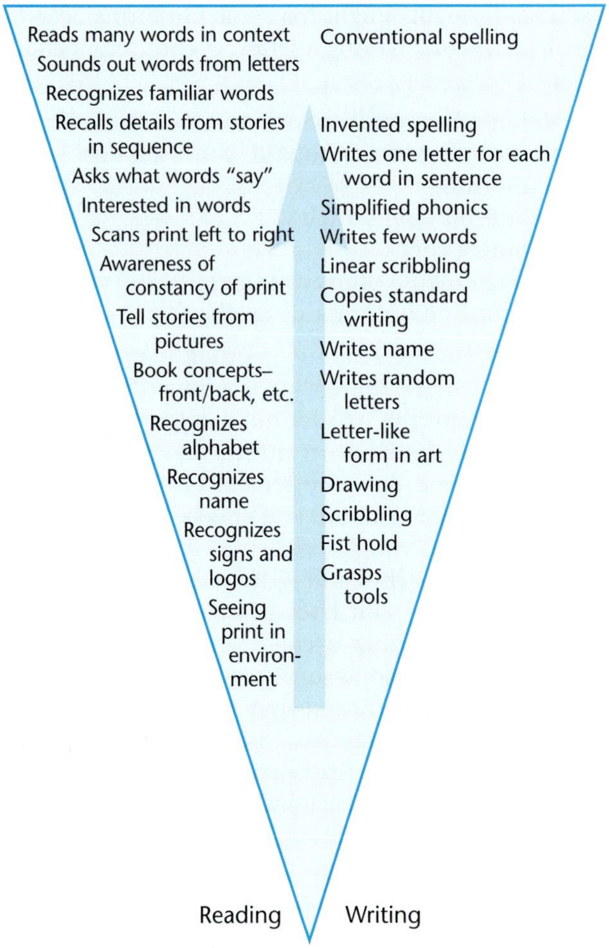

Figure 9–8 Reading and Writing Development.

Literacy Development

The formal instruction of reading and writing formerly began in the first grade. As the field of **emergent literacy** expands, it is now recognized that literacy begins much earlier (Figure 9–8). Children come to school knowing much about reading and writing already.

Print-Rich Environment

EXERCISE **Look around you right now. List all the reading and writing materials in view.**

Probably your list is very long. It may contain labels on the television set, phone books, recipe cards, magazines, and every other form of print, pens, pencils, markers, paper, computers, and brand labels on manufactured items.

Becoming a reader and writer begins by immersion in a world of print. Young children's

@ it happened to me

Permanent Name Writing

A mother came to school one morning and said, "I'm really glad you've been working with name writing and journal writing, but last night Jason wrote his name on the side of the car with permanent marker!" Oops, no guarantees.

Do you have an IT HAPPENED TO ME story about early writing? I'd love to read it. Please send it to WeekbyWeek@thomsonlearning.com

environments are filled with the alphabet on everything including blocks, sheets, and cereal boxes. Colorful logos like McDonald's and Sesame Street are recognized long before the actual individual letters and their sounds are known. This is **contextualized literacy**, words and phrases that can be read because they are defined by their context, shape, color, and position. Besides an environment full of print, children look to role models. They see parents reading the newspaper, the advertising on television, or directions on how to put together the tricycle. They often imitate those actions by picking up papers and babbling or pretending to read. Almost every child has picked up a pencil, pen, lipstick, or permanent marker and made some scribbles in a place not meant for writing.

THE AMERICAN READING CHALLENGE. Despite billions of dollars spent on reading materials, curriculum, studies of various approaches, vast research, and national initiatives, the fact remains that a large number of children in America never learn to read well. This has huge implications because of the connection between poverty and illiteracy. According to Jim Trelease's (2001) findings about the implications of literacy:

1. The more you read, the more you know.
2. The more you know, the smarter you grow.
3. The smarter you are, the longer you stay in school.
4. The longer you stay in school, the more diplomas you earn and the longer you are employed; thus, the more money you earn in a lifetime.
5. The more diplomas you earn, the higher your children's grades will be in school.
6. The more diplomas you earn, the longer you live. (p. xxv)

The connection between language and literacy was discussed in Chapter 6, illustrated so powerfully by the research of Hart and Risley (2004), who studied the gap between the number of words and kind of language used in high- and low-income homes. That gap correlated to the gap in school performance at age nine. It is not early reading skills that matter, but rather the relationships and connections with the spoken word, including vocabulary, open-ended questions, positive feedback, explanations, descriptions, and running dialogue throughout the day, that is vital for true early literacy (New, 2001). The implications of this research are clear; it is too late to begin literacy development in preschool programs. Literacy development begins at birth, so the foundation must be laid by the family and the educators of infants and toddlers.

BABIES AND BOOKS. Literacy begins in infancy through relationships. Four cornerstones that Bardige and Segal (2005) describe are (1) efficacy, the emotional self-confidence built in a child by mastery of manageable challenges; (2) emotional engagement with trustworthy adults; (3) language environment that provides labels for things and feelings; and (4) social supports such as culture, social and economic ties, and community.

The early childhood teacher can address each of these areas by knowing the ecological context of the children and working to build relationships with the child and the family to share the wonder of literacy development, providing access where books are few, and a classroom that values language and literacy.

An important step toward becoming literate is the shared experience of reading a book with bright pictures and simple words about the child's world.

Look at Figure 9–9.

How does this picture make you feel?
What do you think the adult is feeling?
What do you think the child is feeling?

Young babies are at the Sensorimotor Stage, so their books have to be touchable. The small, cardboard books, ones with texture, cloth, or plastic, ones they can pull on and chew, provide those first experiences. Because infants' language development is at a simple stage, one-word books with repeating sounds soon become their favorites. Even if the reading material is the *New York Times*, building blocks of literacy are being cemented together. The bodies are close. There is a difference in the reading voice from the speaking voice. Awareness is growing that those little marks on the page mean something.

As children move into the second year, their memory is lengthening. They are becoming familiar with books and pointing, laughing, and saying words of identification like "Choo choo" and "Wha's dat?"

Figure 9–9 Even very young children enjoy hearing stories.

it happened to me

Taste of Reading

I loaned a book to a student, and when she returned it she made many apologies for the damage to the book. She explained that she was reading and studying and her toddler climbed up in her lap and chomped down on the side of the book. Sure enough, there was a small crescent of punctures in the edge of several pages. I could just see that little one being envious of this thing that had taken mother's attention so took an aggressive action against that thing that had wooed her away. I treasure that book and its bitten pages for the story that it tells.

Do you have an IT HAPPENED TO ME story about baby reading? I'd love to read it. Please send it to WeekbyWeek@thomsonlearning.com

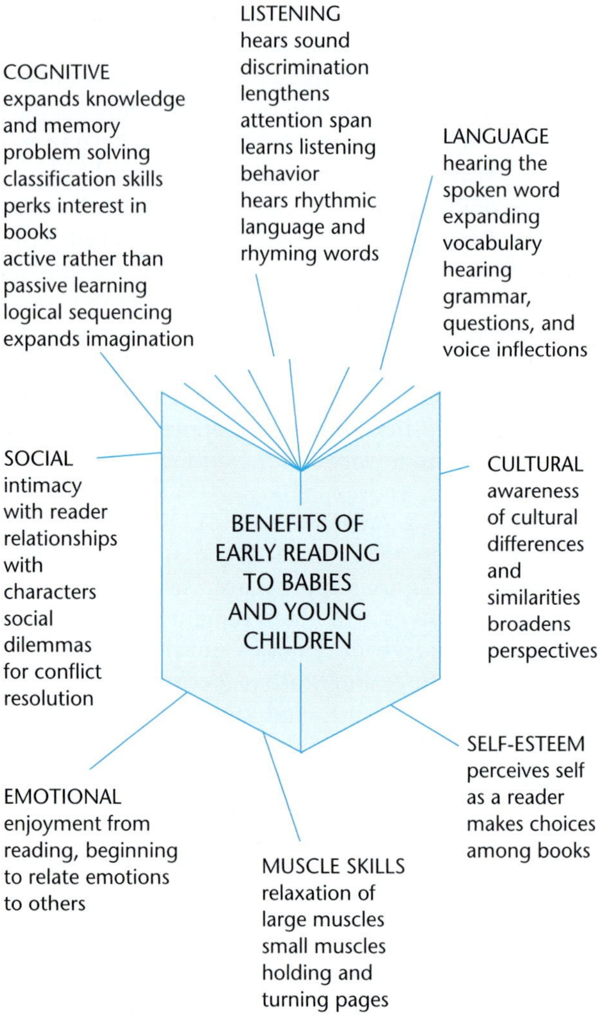

Figure 9–10 Benefits of Early Reading to Babies and Young Children.

They become participants by pretending to read. Words and familiar phrases from favorite books are added to their vocabulary. They ask for their favorites to be read over, and over, and over. When the adult changes a word in a familiar book, the child notices and protests. This shows that they know print and speech are related. By the end of the third year, the child can accurately tell the story from the pictures in familiar books. They will begin to move eyes and fingers along the row of print while saying the words. This is an indication of the child's awareness that those markings below the pictures are a code to be deciphered (Figure 9–10).

READING AND PRESCHOOLERS. Most children learn to listen and speak effortlessly without direct instruction. Traditionally, reading and writing have been taught in formal education. In separate, isolated exercises, the vision, mind, and small muscles were trained for reading with "readiness" worksheets or activities. The term *emergent literacy* is a broader term, differing from isolated skills, coming out of the whole-language movement (Clay, 1975). It fits very well into the paradigm of developmentally appropriate practice—child-centered, developmentally based, using curriculum of themes and projects.

Preschoolers who have had early home literacy experiences that included family involvement in reading and writing, and exposure to receptive language (hearing many words, complex sentences, descriptions, and explanations) are more likely to have high test scores. These are directly related to levels of vocabulary, listening comprehension skills, and reading skills in grade 3 (Senechal & LeFevre, 2002). The common characteristics of these children have most to do with their home environment. They

- were read to on a regular basis.
- had a wide variety of print available in the home, such as books, magazines, and newspapers.
- had paper and pencil available to scribble and draw and copy objects and letters.
- had people in the home who stimulated their interest by supporting reading and writing as a worthwhile activity. (Trelease, 2001)

This is not an endorsement for the "superbaby syndrome." Early reading to babies and young children brings many benefits (Figure 9–10). Forced acceleration of reading training has been shown to have no positive effect on school performance by the third grade. While those two concepts seem in opposition, the difference is in the approach. Young children (as early as two years old) have been taught to read and do mathematics through drill and practice. David Elkind, noted child psychologist, has sent out the warning against such "superkid" practices in his book *Miseducation: Preschoolers at Risk* (1987). These techniques are based on behaviorist philosophies rather than on the work of developmentalists like Piaget and Erikson, on which most early childhood principles and practices are founded.

So how can young children interact with literacy? (See Figure 9–11.)

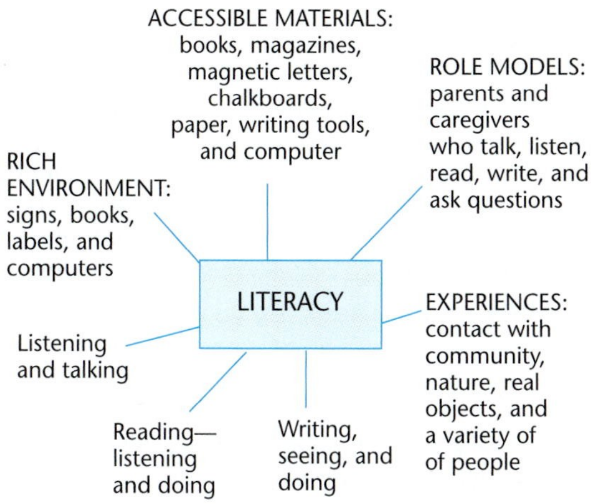

Figure 9–11 Interacting with Literacy.

Literacy begins with communication, verbally and nonverbally. Even the unborn child hears the muffled mother's voice and the rhythm of her heartbeat. Early in the child's life, long before the child can speak to convey thoughts or express feelings, music and visual arts and crafts can be the symbols of thought. Between two and three years of age, children begin to notice and "read" print all around them: McDonald's signs, stop signs, a print advertisement for their favorite cereal box OR television show. This **environmental print** can be the springboard to literacy when it is recognized and followed up with books and activities that build on that knowledge.

EXERCISE Write the alphabet down the side of a piece of paper. Now, begin to think of all the environmental print using the beginning letter. This idea came from *Chicken Starts with CH!* (Xu & Rutledge, 2003). This will get you started:

A—Advertisement
B—Bumper stickers
C—Coins
D—D__________

Children who have been read to begin to recognize the letter names and the sounds of the letters. They know which side is up in a book and the concept of "front to back." In the third year, many recognize familiar logos and signs, their own name, and some short words. They begin to take an interest in the words in books and in the environment, and ask what specific words say. They understand the purpose of a book and begin to turn pages from front to back and scan the pictures from left to right pages. The story sequence of beginning, middle, and end is recognized and can be retold from the pictures. An awareness of rhyming words appears and an association of letters and sounds.

Four- and five-year-old children recognize books as sources of information and entertainment and recognize the difference between story books and "pictionary" or dictionary format. They can fill in story lines from rebus picture books and sometimes read simple stories word by word. They can retell the story from memory. The story is reconstructed from the pictures. Predictions are made about what might happen next or why a certain event happened, relating the concept of cause and effect. Many words are recognized by sight, and the children are also sounding out other words by alphabet letters. This **phonemic awareness** of the sounds of speech in syllables and the relationship of alphabet letters to sounds is a critical stage in the process of learning to read. Children are beginning to notice the space between words and the punctuation marks at the end of the sentence and change their inflection depending on the mark. They act out story characters in their play. Their conversations relate to situations and dilemmas the characters faced and how they solved them. They take an interest in creating and illustrating their own books, either in pretend writing, phonetic spelling, or dictation. Some of them have become readers, either through their families' direct instruction or by natural association of letters and sounds.

Children enjoy and learn different things from different types of books. They should be exposed to many types. Machado (2007) lists the types, the learning possibilities, and why children like them (Figure 9–12).

TYPES	FEATURES TEACHERS LIKE	FEATURES CHILDREN LIKE
Storybooks (picture books) • family and home • folktales and fables • fanciful stories • fairy tales • animal stories • others	sharing moments seeing children enthusiastic and attentive making characters' voices introducing human truths and imaginative adventures sharing favorites easy for child to identify with small creatures	imagination and fantasy identification with characters' humanness wish and need fulfillment adventure excitement action self-realization visual variety word pleasure
Nonfiction books (informational) also referred to as *content books*	expand individual and group interests develop "reading-to-know" attitudes encourage finding out together provide accurate facts contain scientific content	provide facts; allow for discovery of information and ideas discuss reality and how things work and function answer "why" and "how" supply new words and new meanings
Wordless books	promote child speech, creativity, and imagination	provide opportunity to supply their own words to tell the story promote discovery of meanings include color, action, and visual variety
Interaction books (books with active child participation built in)	keep children involved and attentive build listening for directions skills	provide for movement and group feeling promote individual creativity and expression appeal to senses have manipulatable features
Concept books (books with central concepts or themes that include specific and reinforcing examples)	promote categorization present opportunities to know about and develop concepts many examples	add to knowledge visually present abstractions
Predictable books (books with repetitions and reinforcement)	permit successful guessing build child's confidence promote ideas that books make sense	provide opportunity to read along are repetitive build feelings of competence
Reference books (picture dictionaries, encyclopedias, special subject books)	provide opportunity to look up questions with the child promote individualized learning	provide answers are used with teacher (shared time) are resources that answer their questions
Alphabet and word books (word books have name of object printed near or on top of object)	supply letters and word models pair words and objects are useful for child with avid interest in alphabet letters and words can include letter and word play	discover meanings and alphabet letters and words see names of what is illustrated
Novelty books (pop-ups, fold-outs, electronic books, stamp and pasting books, activity books, puzzle books, scratch-and-sniff books, hidden objects in illustrations, talking books)	add sense-exploring variety stimulate creativity come in many different sizes and shapes motor involvement for child many include humor	encourage exploring, touching, moving, feeling, smelling, painting, drawing, coloring, cutting, gluing, acting upon, listening to a mechanical voice, and getting instant feedback

Figure 9–12 Types of Books for Young Children. (From *Early Childhood Experiences in Language Arts, Early Literacy*, 8th edition, by MACHADO, 2007. Reprinted with permission of Delmar Learning, a division of Thomson Learning: www.thomsonrights.com, Fax 800 730-2215.)

TYPES	FEATURES TEACHERS LIKE	FEATURES CHILDREN LIKE
Paperback books and magazines (Golden Books, *Humpty Dumpty Magazine*)	are inexpensive come in a wide variety many classics available	include activity pages
Teacher- and child-made books	reinforce class learnings build understanding of authorship allow creative expression record individual, group projects, field trips, parties promote child expression of concerns and ideas build child's self-esteem	allow child to see own name in print provide opportunity to share ideas with others are self-rewarding
Therapeutic books (books helping children cope with and understand things such as divorce, death, jealousy)	present life realistically offer positive solutions and insights present diverse family groups deal with life's hard-to-deal-with subjects	help children discuss real feelings
Seasonal and holiday books	accompany child interest may help child understand underlying reasons for celebration	build pleasant expectations add details
Books and audiovisual combinations (read-alongs)	add variety offer group and individual experiencing opportunities stimulate interest in books	project large illustrations can be enjoyed individually
Toddler books and board books (durable pages)	resist wear and tear	are easy to use (ease in page-turning
Multicultural and cross-cultural books (culturally conscious books)	increase positive attitudes concerning diversity and similarity	introduce a variety of people
Oversized books (big books)	emphasize the realities in our society have extra large text and illustrations	are easy to see in groups have giant book characters

Figure 9–12 *(continued)*

Owocki (1999) suggests teachers consider providing literacy materials to explore that fill the functions of written language.

environmental print—in the world around us: street signs, instructions, advertising, reference books
occupational print—used in the workplace: health records and appointment books, menus, order pads, and money
informational print—storing and retrieving information: calendars, clocks, recipes, telephone books
recreational print—used for leisure activities: storybooks, poetry books, travel books (p. 58)

Young Children Write

Young children's writing emerges along with language and reading, as well as art. The myth that oral language must be mastered before written language can develop is attacked by Schickedanz. Her book *Much More Than the ABCs: The Early Stages of Reading and Writing* (1999) is a helpful resource for the early childhood educator and families. The first step in writing begins with the small muscle control of the writing tool—pencil, marker, or crayon. This is influenced greatly by the environment that makes these accessible. The adult is a role model for writing lists to remember. Labels are written on items to signify possession. Writing is demonstrated by the adult who says, "This is how you write your name."

Writing is more than mastery of the tools or symbols of reading. In fact, researchers have found that many children actually write before they read, driven by the urge to communicate, although they are limited in the knowledge of writing conventions. Wells (1986) powerfully describes this desire to communicate, this "writing to read," with this statement: "When one has something important to say, and

it happened to me

Office

Walking down the hall, a child in my preschool class asked, "Where's the ice?" "What do you mean, where's the ice?" I asked incredulously.

He pointed to a door with the sign OFFICE. "It says, 'off ice.' I wonder where the ice is?"

He had learned one aspect of print, the decoding of letters into meaningful words, but had not yet mastered the importance of spacing.

Do you have an IT HAPPENED TO ME story about early reading mistakes? I'd love to read it. Please send it to WeekbyWeek@thomsonlearning.com

it happened to me

B L D Z R

This was demonstrated to me by a group of five-year-old boys who dominated a class I had. As we approached the holiday season, they were interested in making their gift wish lists. Having just been inspired by Schickedanz's book (1999), instead of dictating their lists to me, I urged them to write or draw their own. To my amazement, they worked hard at it for many minutes (which was amazing in itself). Even more amazing was that I could really read what they wrote:

B L D Z R (bulldozer)

G N (gun)

2 W E L R (two-wheeler)

They were struggling to communicate meaning, and they had done so!

Do you have an IT HAPPENED TO ME story about children and learning to read and write? I'd love to hear it. Please send it to me at WeekbyWeek@thomsonlearning.com

other people are interested in hearing it, it is then that language and thinking most fully interpenetrate in the struggle to make meaning that captures what one has observed and understood and communicate it to others" (p. 107).

All children, including those from economically disadvantaged settings, can benefit from effective content- and language-rich instruction that includes

- time, materials, and resources that actively build language and conceptual knowledge
- a supportive learning environment in which children have access to a wide variety of reading and writing resources
- different group sizes (large, small, individual) and different levels of guidance to meet in the needs of individual children
- opportunities for sustained and in-depth learning, including play
- a masterful orchestration of activity that supports learning and social-emotional development (Neuman & Roskos, 2005)

STAGES OF WRITING. Writing develops in predictable stages.

Scribbling. The child makes marks as soon as she can hold a writing tool. She begins by stabbing at the paper, the dragging action making lines. She progresses to unclosed circular motions, then to closed circles, vertical and horizontal lines, and eventually boxlike or square shapes. This phase is the preparation for both drawing and writing. Many children extend scribbling into wavy lines that they call writing after observing adults writing cursive (Figure 9–13).

Drawing. Written communication in the form of pictures has its historical roots in the Egyptian pictorials inside the pyramids. Children (and societies) without writing convey meaningful messages by drawing. Young children are hindered by their lack of small muscle coordination and the inability to represent on paper the ideas they have in their head (Figure 9–14). They have a mental image of a horse, but what they draw may not be recognizable as a horse to the viewer. Again, the receptive is greater than the expressive.

Children can express their thoughts by using drawing. This expressive language, known metaphorically as the "100 languages of children" (Reggio

Figure 9–13 Linear scribbles approximate writing.

Children, 1996), has captivated the world through the work of the children of Reggio Emilia, Italy. Carolyn Pope Edwards, who has studied the Reggio approach in detail, calls the various media, such as photography, clay, or drama, "literacies," extending the child's visual expression beyond writing (Edwards & Willis, 2000).

Making Letters. Between the ages of three and four, children come to realize there is a difference between drawing and writing, although it may not be evident to the viewer (Figure 9–15). The first letter they write is usually the first letter of their name. As their knowledge of the sounds and shapes of more letters expands, they will begin to write sentences. The first letter of each word is sounded out and written down, expecting the reader to be able to decipher the message. It is an approximation that is bringing them closer to the symbols that combine to make words in a sentence. They will often ask for words to be written so they can copy them. They try their hand at **invented spelling**, as the boys did on their gift list, by sounding it out and writing the letter sounds that they hear (see "It Happened to Me: BLDZR").

Organizing Print. Writing is more than knowledge of letters and their sounds; it is also the proper sequence, organization on the page, and spaces between that form written language. Random letters will appear in children's paintings and art work whether they have meaning or are just practicing the style.

Name writing can be encouraged with daily sign-in, as Green (1998) suggests. Through this early literacy experience, name writing was a transition routine into the classroom that formalized the children's presence, developed their fine muscle control, and documented their writing progress. Studies such as those done by Haney (2002) are seeing a strong correlation between name writing and cognition and language, suggesting that name writing skills could be used as a part of screening for reading difficulties. Awareness of rhyming and beginning sounds, uppercase letters and the concepts and functions of print is

Figure 9–14 Children's drawings often are the expression of inner thoughts and words before writing has developed.

Figure 9–15 Drawing and writing are beginning to separate from one another.

higher in children who have mastered name writing (Welsch, Sullivan, & Justice, 2003; Foulin, 2005).

Dictation. While a child draws, an adult talking with the child may elicit the thinking that is not revealed in the drawing because of the child's lack of physical ability and representational skills. As the child relates meaning, the adult may ask if the child wants the story written in words that others can read. If so, in the act of dictation the child is seeing oral language translated into written language. It may even help the child add detail to the drawing by thinking about it more concretely in order to express the meaning to another person. This is an example of *scaffolding* (Fields & DeGayner, 2000; Oken-Wright, 1998).

Backward Letters. Preschoolers in their experimentation with letters, and perhaps due to their still-developing visual perception, often reverse letters to their family's alarm. Sulzby, who has studied children's writing for over 15 years, says it is common for preschoolers to write backward and to switch from backward to forward (Sulzby, 1993). They are also beginning to use the conventions of print, such as using the period between every word (Figure 9–16). In first and second grades, depending on the school district, handwriting receives more emphasis. By the end of second grade, letter reversals have all but stopped. If they persist, there may be other things affecting it, so further evaluations should be done.

Writing to Read. Many kindergarten classes are encouraging children to write their thoughts and tell about experiences using invented spelling and illustration preceding formal reading instruction. Children demonstrate a level of phonemic awareness by sounding out the words and writing down the sounds they hear. Look at Figure 9–17 and you can almost hear my grandson carefully writing the letters that he hears to convey the meaning of the story about teeth. You can see he has learned about full sentences with subject and verb and the use of a period at the end of each sentence. The teacher has interpreted his words and written the conventional spelling beneath. The illustration of his family all brushing their teeth completes his story. It is a precious artifact of his pathway to literacy.

Incorporate Writing into Play. By ages five and six, children realize that writing serves the function of conveying information. They will make signs to designate territory or "Do not disturb," print their name on their artwork so they can take it home, and use writing to tell stories or write letters. In the dramatic play area, writing materials are provided as they would appear in context. In housekeeping, put a note pad by the phone, include grocery advertisements, list paper, and a pencil nearby. A shoe store would include sales slip books. A restaurant would need menus with pictures and words, server pads,

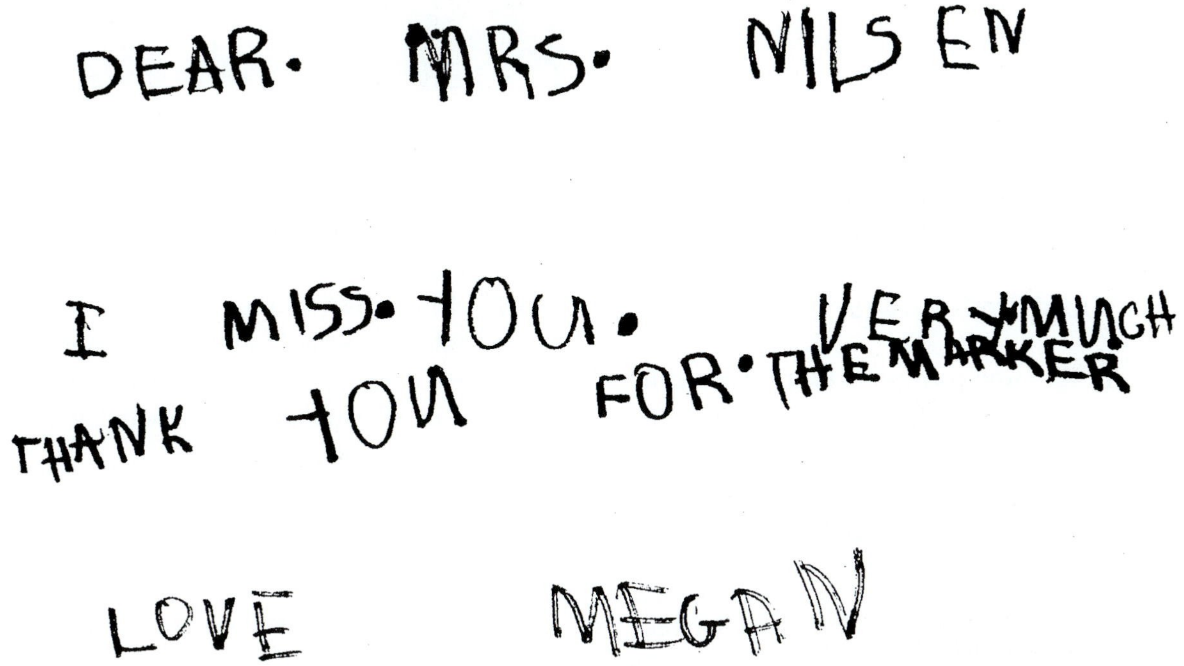

Figure 9–16 Early writing experiments with writing conventions but is precious for its effort and meaning.

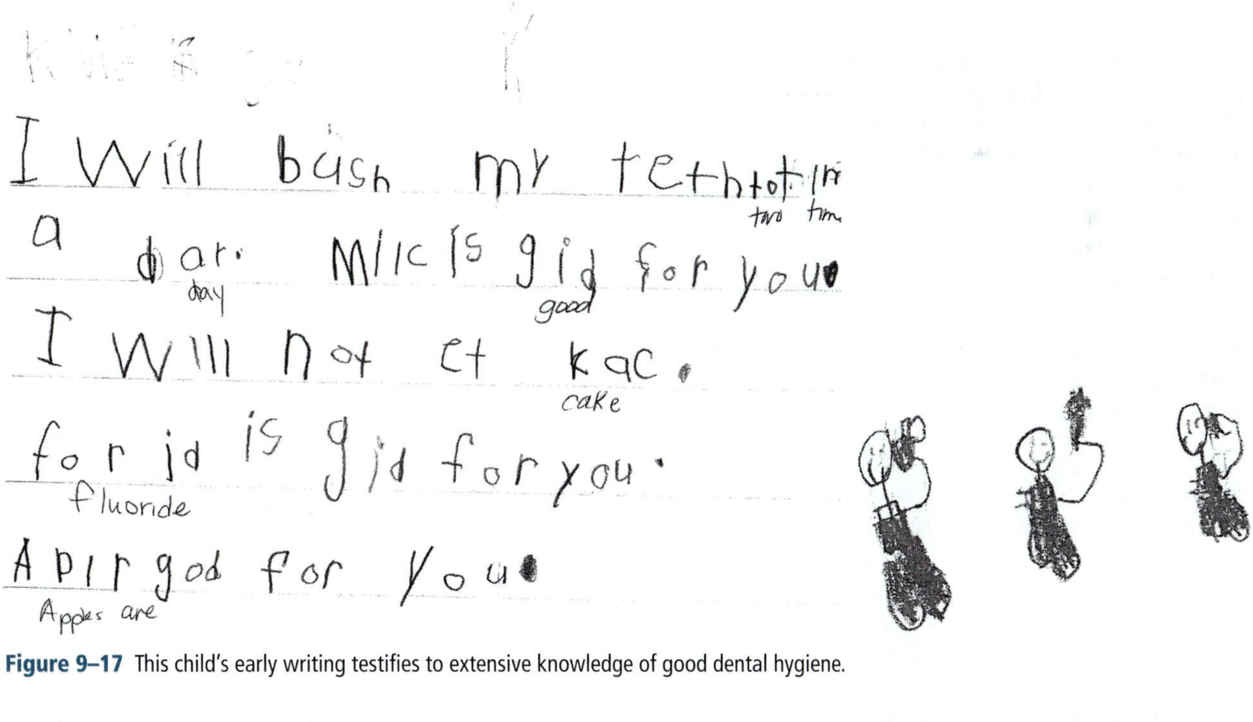

Figure 9–17 This child's early writing testifies to extensive knowledge of good dental hygiene.

and checkbooks. A grocery store would need flyers, "Open" and "Closed" signs, "Help-Wanted" signs, and worker sign-in sheets.

Journal Writing. Many early childhood classrooms have begun daily journal writing for children to make an entry about the day. The daily entries may begin as pictures, but they will move to include or become exclusively print. If the child dictates, or the teachers read and interpret the pictures and print, it is a form of personal communication, but also provides a way of ongoing assessment (Williams & Davis, 1994).

The *Living Classroom: Writing, Reading and Beyond* (Armington, 1997) gives wonderful examples of children's early writing for expression, full of invented spelling and enchanting children's drawings as representations of thought. Journals allow children to control the topics about which they write, use their abilities at any level without risk, and communicate original thoughts (Block, 2001).

Literacy and Technology

EXERCISE **How computer literate are you?**

More than three quarters of children 6 years and under live in a household with at least one computer (Ridout & Hamel, 2006). Young children have a great interest in using them to imitate adults (Figure 9–18). With the myriad of software available, they are actively involved in the manipulation of symbols, pictures, and letters. The explosion of software for young children has addressed this market, but not without controversy. In this age of technology, all advances must be carefully considered for their appropriateness and value to the development of the child.

@ it happened to me

Make Love

Another writing incident is an anecdote I will always remember. A dear, sweet little four-year-old girl came over to me in class one day and said, "Mrs. Nilsen, I know how to make love. Want me to show you?" Gulp! "Sure." She got a sheet of paper and proudly wrote L U V. We rejoiced together!

Do you have an IT HAPPENED TO ME story about invented spelling? I'd love to read it. Please send it to WeekbyWeek@thomsonlearning.com

Figure 9–18 All writing tools begin with manipulation, mastery, then meaning.

Computers can serve the same purposes as any other learning area. They can be explored by manipulation, a vehicle of social interaction with peers, and provide a time of interaction with an adult. These all add to the child's general development as well as literacy competency. With the computer, children produce their own pictures, text, and even their own books. Holdaway (1979) prophetically stated, "The difficulty of handwriting and spelling tend to delay any genuine desire to produce written language for a purpose" (p. 36). The computer removes that obstacle with software that accepts phonetic spelling, spell checks as words are written, and provides picture and word combinations. Preschools inspired by Reggio Emilia have found the computer to be another "language" with which children can organize ideas and represent what they know through documentation of the construction of learning (Hong & Trepanier-Street, 2004).

The integration of computers into the learning environment is their most effective use. This does not mean a computer lab down the hall where children spend a period of time. True integration of a computer in the classroom uses it as a tool for exploration. The computer can enhance language, mathematics, and science, as well as social interactions (Davis & Shade, 1994).

The teacher's role in using technology as an early learning experience is no different than any other experience. First, prepare the environment by safely setting up the computer in a place that is inviting and with software that supports the curriculum goals and allows children to learn at their own individual pace (Vernadakis et al., 2005). The adult models safe and appropriate use, turn-taking, and works with the children and guides them to explore on their own. Facilitating problem solving by pairing children will encourage peer assistance, and observing children as they use the computer will inform the teacher about the child's communication, collaboration, and problem-solving skills (Haugen, 1998).

Children with learning disabilities and different learning styles have been found to use the computer as a way of finding success in learning. Assistive technology devices were included in the Education of the Handicapped Act Amendments of 1986 (P.L. 99-457) and the Individuals with Disabilities Act (IDEA: P.L. 101-476). Computers promise new ways for the disabled to access not only learning and knowledge but focused behaviors. Behrmann and Lahm (1994) also emphasize the use of computers as a play form in special education that allows children choice, independence, and a mode of expression.

The teacher, according to Beaty (2000), observes the child move from manipulation level to mastery to meaning and suggests the Computer Area can reveal development in the following areas:

social—turn-taking and sharing
physical—eye–hand coordination, visual discrimination
large motor activities—exercise activities
cognitive—shapes, sizes, colors, opposites, matching, classifying, counting, measuring, sequencing, memory skills
language—giving information and directions, asking and answering questions, discussing operations with a partner, making exclamations
creative—drawing, problem solving, music
emotional—autonomy

An issue of concern is the inequity of access. In a recent Kaiser Family Foundation Report (2006), 95 percent of high-income homes with a child under 6 had computer access, compared to 54 percent of low-income homes. Blacks and Hispanics had less access at home than whites. Girls were found to use the computers and play video games less than boys, widening the gap in perceived abilities in the math and science areas. Inequality of access is a valid concern that observant teachers need to keep in mind. Technology offers opportunities beyond imagination, but many teachers are still "techno-phobic." Fears of the "teaching machine," however, are discounted by Davis and Shade (1994): "Potentially powerful and stimulating, the computer is only an inert object that can never be a substitute for the personal touch of the classroom teacher."

Remember there is still the caution about the amount of time a young child spends at a computer and the type of programs the child is using (Kelly, 2000). The Alliance for Childhood, a group of educators and professionals concerned about America's children, made this statement in the executive summary of their publication *Fool's Gold: A Critical Look at Computers in Childhood* (2001): "Those who place their faith in technology to solve the problems of education should look more deeply into the needs of children. The renewal of education requires personal attention to students from good teachers and active parents, strongly supported by communities" (p. 4).

Ways to Document Reading and Writing Progress

Literacy involvement can be observed across all learning areas. A multitude of methods, then, are used to observe the various forms that literacy takes.

Class List Logs can survey the group for reading and writing interest, behavior, skill, or participation. Taped on the wall in the book area, it is used to record each time a child selects a book as a choice activity, acting as a Frequency Count. A Class List Log could be used to record a child's listening behavior during story reading time. Time Samples indicate how long a child chooses to spend in the book area or writing center. Interviews or asking questions about a story can document the child's understanding of what was read. Anecdotal and Running Records might contain information about the child's use of literacy in structured and unstructured situations. Photographs and videos capture children's reading and writing graphically while their computer-generated stories provide technological evidence. Tape recordings of a child reading or pretending to read give clues not only of reading ability but speech production.

More formalized assessments like Checklists of specific reading and writing skills can be purchased or self-made. Samples of the child's writing, dictation, and bookmaking provide information about the level the child has attained. Reading records, sometimes called Running Records, are notations made on scripts of book texts during oral reading. This system requires the individual, concentrated attention of the teacher.

Whatever method is selected, a systematic gathering of documentation shows the progress of literacy.

HELPING ALL CHILDREN WITH LITERACY

Language, whether spoken or written, occurs in the context of children's lives. Children who are Limited English Proficient (LEP) may or may not be literacy limited. It depends on the culture and the family circumstances. The family may have limited literacy in their own language. Without literacy materials and role models at home, no matter what the language, children start out at a disadvantage. According to Neuman, Copple, and Bredekamp (1999), children do better adding English while maintaining their home language: "Children who are learning English as a second language are more likely to become readers and writers of English when they are already familiar with the vocabulary and concepts in their primary language." Literacy materials in the classroom should reflect the home language as well as English. All children should be assessed to find the level of development approached as a strength or level of achievement (rather than as a level of deficit), then individualized plans should be made to help the child attain the next level. When literacy materials are placed throughout the classroom environment, this individualization for diverse populations is also possible.

Physical Disabilities and Literacy

When physical or mental limitations are present, literacy development may be affected. Visual impairments will slow or prevent the progression of reading and writing. By providing high-contrast documents and writing tools, along with tactile materials such as sandpaper letters to trace with the fingers, magnetic letters to move on metal surfaces, and raised alphabet letters, children with limited vision can be included in the world of literacy. Reading to them is also an important part of their literacy world. Children with hearing impairments may have affected language development, which also affects literacy. For these children, using visual cues for communication may be even more important. It is a critical component of both receptive and expressive language. With the help of assistive and adaptive technology, computers can help overcome visual, hearing, and physical limitations. Braille keyboards and voice-activated and audio-output computers open the world of literacy. Working with children with hearing deficits in the area of reading and writing is an important facet of the teacher's role.

Learning Disabilities and Literacy

Literacy, the ability to read and write, is the area in which learning disabilities are the most evident. One of the early labels for reading difficulties was **dyslexia**, often characterized by writing alphabet letters backwards or confusing similarly shaped letters like *b* and *p* (which all children do when learning to write and continue this confusion to six and seven years old). This is just one symptom of a larger range of difficulties. The term **learning disabilities** describes people within the range of normal intelligence, without significant behavioral disorders, but failing to reach their potential, often because of the inability to read and write.

The actual causes of learning disabilities are still under study. Neurological (brain) dysfunction is one explanation. Another is that such disabilites are caused by difficulties with vision and perceptual processing, a theory that has spurred some to seek vision training as a remedy, with mixed results. Psychological and emotional causes have been investigated, but academic difficulties affect a child's psychological and emotional well-being, so it has been difficult to determine if this is a cause or an effect. Environmental causes, such as extreme poverty and a lack of cognitive stimulation, have been recognized as connected to learning disabilities; however, there are many middle-class children with learning disabilities, so environmental causes cannot be the total answer either.

A recognized definition, diagnosis, and label were needed to secure services for children with academic underachievement. There are differing and complex definitions of *learning disability.* The National Center for Learning Disability defines it as "a neurological disorder that affects the brain's ability to receive, process, store, and respond to information." Learning disabilities are not limited to but often include difficulties with literacy (Allen & Cowdery, 2005). Young children with learning disabilities are extremely difficult to diagnose because they are in the pre-reading stage. The two primary behaviors characteristic of learning disabilities are impulsiveness and indiscrimination (the inability to tune out distractions or concentrate on a task in an orderly fashion), as defined by Samuel Kirk, who coined the term *learning disabled* (as cited in Hallahan & Kaufman, 1986). These two characteristics are common in all young children. When they are prolonged or exaggerated, learning disabilities may be suspected. They are also characteristics of hyperactivity and ADHD.

The role of the early childhood observer is to closely monitor the literacy progress, along with other areas of development and behavior, aware of indications of difficulties as well as the appropriate referral agents from whom help may be secured.

Literacy and Children Whose First Language Is Not English

Becoming literate and finding school success, overall well-being, and the ability to compete in society is complicated when the child's oral and written language is not English. Children who are language learners in a language other than English come into the early childhood setting with a wide range of literacy exposure. They may have seen a written form of their own language, either by directly observing adults in their family writing it or by seeing it in books, newspapers, and letters. They may have story books printed in that language. Early writing for these children follows the same stages: scribbling, drawing, and forming letters. The writing may appear in another form if the symbols are not alphabetic, with scribbles appearing vertically rather than horizontally for Asian children, for example. Teachers should pay attention to the home language, provide reading material in that language, and encourage families to engage their children in enriching dialogue and language play (Ordonez-Jasis & Ortiz, 2006). They will continue to acquire native language literacy from home and an expanded language and literacy in English from the early childhood setting. Children who have little or no early experience with print come to school at a disadvantage.

For all children, and especially English language learners, picture books are excellent ways to communicate universal messages and to have a shared experience not based on spoken language. Looking at picture books enhances vocabulary growth. Literacy success in the second language depends on the same factors as oral language for all children—an environment filled with materials and activities. Individual interactions enhance both language and literacy. The environment and curriculum include real opportunities to use literacy, such as name lists, drawing and writing materials, story books to look at, and adults reading and pointing to pictures and words. Children will write if they have reason to do so, even if they are not able to speak the language (Urzua, 1987). All children need an social atmosphere accepting of language attempts. Adults who allow and encourage native language speaking and writing demonstrate an overall acceptance of the child and the family. Pictorial and word labels in the classroom will help all children associate the object with the written word. Meaningful opportunities to write give older children with limited English a way to communicate. Young children with limited English proficiency can learn vocabulary, customs, and find enjoyment through books and literacy materials. As mentioned previously, the home may already be literacy-rich with books and writing in the family's language. Families should be encouraged to read to their child in the home language and to involve the child in community activities in the first language and in English (Grant & Wong, 2003). Stories recorded on tapes, dictionaries that have familiar items in both languages, and books in the first language of every child are helpful toward literacy development. Literacy materials can be sent home for reinforcement and enjoyment by the whole family.

Cultural differences other than native language also affect the child's literacy development. Cultural differences also have been found in the amount and

@ it happened to me

Working to Communicate

One of my college students was in a practicum placement in a program in which there was a child from Vietnam who spoke no English. She struggled to communicate. Finally, on her own initiative, she made a book of common items in the classroom from a mail order catalog. She found a translator to write the words for the items in the child's language, as well as phonetic spelling in English so she could pronounce it. That book went back and forth from home to school, aiding both in communicating. Everyone benefited. She received an A.

Do you have an IT HAPPENED TO ME story of a strategy you have used to break through the language barrier? I'd love to read it. Please send it to WeekbyWeek@thomsonlearning.com

TOPICS IN OBSERVATION

Books in the Sandbox

EXERCISE **List the literacy materials (reading or writing) in each of the rooms in your home.**

Kitchen:
Living room:
Bedroom:
Bathroom:

Most homes have some kinds of literacy materials in every room. From cookbooks to magazines to phone message pads, every room has something to read, something to write on. Why then does the early childhood classroom restrict books to the book area and writing materials to the writing center or art area? It probably is for the protection of the books or the walls from indiscriminate writers. What this does, however, is artificially restrict literacy to certain areas, unlike real life. If the classroom is to be a microcosm of the world outside, then perhaps these restrictions need to be reconsidered. Use the placement and proliferation of books and writing materials throughout the environment as an assessment tool of the literacy-rich environment and the teacher's own literacy priority.

How about books about the beach or archaeology in or near the sandbox? In the art area, books about colors, even art books with prints of the masters, could stimulate interest in color, form, texture, and art expression. Books about buildings and skyscrapers, and pencils and paper to trace blocks or sketch buildings will add a literacy component to the block area. Books or magazines on the back of the toilet might capture the interest of a child not ordinarily sitting in one place very long.

In the dramatic play area, books or magazines and writing materials can connect literacy to whatever dramatic play theme is set up there. A medical office would have an appointment calendar, magazines in the waiting room, and books of anatomy or stories about the hospital. The car repair shop would have auto repair manuals, car magazines, order forms for repairs, and invoices.

Another artificial classroom literacy behavior is reading to the whole group of children at one time. In the outside world, reading and writing are usually individual activities. Individualized reading is enhanced when books and reading materials are integrated throughout the classroom environment. That way, the adult can read to every child in the context of their play or can encourage writing as a mode of communication that facilitates the play. Reading and writing are then associated by the children with their play theme, and assimilated and accommodated into their knowledge base. Literacy is connected with real objects and real purposes, not just another isolated routine on the daily schedule.

By desegregating literacy from the library or writing centers, children see the practical use of reading and writing. The adult role is to help fill the span between their actual ability to read and write and a higher level, to provide that scaffold, by suggesting researching books for answers to questions or encouraging writing as a way to communicate ideas or preserve details.

Care of the books and writing materials is a valid concern, but there are some principles to follow that can reduce the worries:

- Once the decision is made that literacy materials will be accessible throughout the environment, preparations are made for book pockets or racks near the sandbox, easels, and other play

TOPICS IN OBSERVATION *(continued)*

areas. A section of the block shelf can just as easily hold books and literacy materials along with wheeled vehicles and block accessories.

- When materials are useful and important to children, they will treat them carefully.
- Adult role models of caring for books and using writing materials in a constructive way will be attended to by the children.

Think about how the opportunities to observe children's literacy skills will be expanded if the materials are included in every area.

type of early vocalization with infants and young children. Middle-class families and teachers are more verbally responsive and referential, giving names to items and repeating them, such as "Doggie. Doggie." Some cultures rely more on body language, teasing, and traditional stories using dialects and nonstandard English. Many cultures do not consider literacy an important component of the young child's world but hold it as a rite of passage into the adult world. This cultural difference will pose challenges to the early childhood program in helping these children reach the level of familiarity with not only the spoken language but the written language as well.

HELPING PROFESSIONALS FOR LITERACY CONCERNS

Children who need further help in the area of literacy development, reading, or writing should begin first with a physical examination. Vision, hearing, or neurological problems may interfere with literacy development. Speech and language difficulties could be contributing factors, so evaluations in these areas may be considered. Helping professionals in the area of literacy include the following:

reading specialists—teachers with specialized training in the teaching of reading, and diagnosis and remediation of reading and writing difficulties

special education teachers—teachers with knowledge of literacy disorders and strategies for overcoming learning disabilities

bilingual teachers or interpreters—people who can translate writing materials and communication in the family's first language

OTHER METHODS

Other Methods to Record Literacy

Anecdotal/Running Records—narrative about a child's interaction with reading or writing, wherever it occurs

Checklist—presence or absence of literacy-related skills

Frequency Count—elements of literacy to measure skills such as recognition of sight words in a passage, hesitations in oral reading, number of misspellings in a passage or list of words

Time Sample—attention span during story time, ability to sustain in self-reading, amount of time spent writing a passage in a journal or working on a literacy computer program

Conversations or Interviews—listening to oral reading, discussions about story themes and characters for understanding, conversations preceding writing in a journal or constructing a story

Work Samples—writing samples, tape recordings of oral reading

Media—photographs or videos of the child engaged in reading and writing behaviors

STANDARDS

Here are selected examples of standards relating to literacy:

NAEYC Early Childhood Program Accreditation Standards

Literacy, see Figure 9–4

Standards for Reading Professionals (IRA 2003)
Creating a Literate Environment
4.3 Model reading and writing enthusiastically as valued lifelong activities

Head Start Child Outcomes (U.S. Department of Health and Human Services [2003]). Domain 2 Literacy—Standards with indicators for Phonological Awareness

- Shows increasing ability to discriminate and identify sounds in spoken language.
- Shows growing awareness of beginning and ending sounds of words.
- Progresses in recognizing matching sounds and rhymes in familiar words, games, songs, stories, and poems.
- Shows growing ability to hear and discriminate separate syllables in words.
- Associates sounds with written words, such as awareness that different words begin with the same sound.

Book Knowledge and Appreciation
Print Awareness and Concepts
Early Writing
Alphabet Knowledge

KEY TERMS

contextualized literacy
dyslexia
emergent literacy
environmental print
interrater reliability
invented spelling
learning disabilities
phonemic awareness
print-rich environment
quality points
Rating Scale
selective method

Go to the Bind-in-Book CD for:

Rating Scales in Literacy form
Plan Week 9 Part A, Directions for a Class List Log on Separation and School Adjustment, including What to Do with It, Portfolio Overview Example, Sharing with Child and Family, Actions—Read a Book, In the Environment, In the Curriculum, In the Newsletter
Plan Week 9 Part B, Conversations to document speech and language development
Plan Week 9 Part C, Reflective Journal

REFERENCES

Allen, K. E., & Cowdery, G. E. (2005). *The exceptional child: Inclusion in early childhood education* (5th ed.). Clifton Park, NY: Delmar Thomson Learning.

Alliance for Childhood. (2001). *Fool's gold: A critical look at computers in childhood—Executive summary.* Retrieved March 21, 2003, from http://www.allianceforchildhood.net/projects/computers/computers_reports_fools_gold.

Armington, D. (1997). *The living classroom: Writing, reading, and beyond.* Washington, DC: National Association for the Education of Young Children.

Bardige, B. S., & Segal, M. M. (2005). *Building literacy with love: A guide for teachers and caregivers of children birth through age 5.* Washington, DC: Zero to Three Press.

Beaty, J. (2000). *Preschool appropriate practices* (2nd ed.). Fort Worth: Harcourt Brace Jovanovich College Publishers.

Behrmann, M. M., & Lahm, E. A. (1994). Computer applications in early childhood special education. In J. L. Wright & D. D. Shade (Eds.), *Young children: Active learners in a technological age.* Washington, DC: National Association for the Education of Young Children.

Berk, L. E., & Winsler, A. (2002). *Scaffolding children's learning: Vygotsky and early childhood education.* Washington, DC: National Association for the Education of Young Children.

Block, C. C. (2001). *Teaching the language arts: Expanding thinking through student-centered instruction* (3rd ed.). Boston: Allyn and Bacon.

Clay, M. (1975). *What did I write?* Auckland, New Zealand: Heinemann Educational Books.

Davis, B. C., & Shade, D. D. (1994). Integrate, don't isolate!: Computers in the early childhood curriculum. *ERIC Digest.* Urbana, IL: Clearinghouse on Elementary and Early Childhood Education. EDO-PS-94-17.

Edwards, C. P., & Willis, L. M. (2000). Integrating visual and verbal literacies in the early childhood classroom. *Early Childhood Education Journal, 27* (4), 259–265.

Elkind, D. (1987). *Miseducation: Preschoolers at risk.* New York: Alfred A. Knopf.

Fields, M. V., & DeGayner, B. (2000). Read my story: Increasing literacy of preschool children. *Childhood Education, 76* (3), 130.

Fein, G. G., Ardila-Rey, A, E., & Groth, L A. (2000). The narrative connection: Stories and literacy. In K. Roskos & J. F. Christie, (Eds.), *Play and literacy in early childhood.* Mahway, NJ: Lawrence Erlbaum Associates.

Foulin, J. N. (2005). Why is letter-name knowledge such a good predictor of learning to read? *Reading and Writing, 18* (2), Spring 2005.

Grant, R. A., & Wong, S. D. (2003). Barriers to literacy for language-minority learners: An argument for change in the literacy education profession.

Journal of Adolescent & Adult Literacy, 46 (5), 386–394.

Green, C. F. (1998). This is my name. *Childhood Education, 74* (4), 226–231.

Greenburg, P. (1998). Some thoughts about phonics, feelings, Don Quixote, diversity and democracy: Teaching young children to read, write, and spell, Part I. *Young Children, 53* (4), 72–82.

Hallahan, D. P., & Kaufman, J. M. (1986). *Exceptional children.* Englewood Cliffs, NJ: Prentice Hall.

Harms, T., Clifford, R. M., & Cryer, D. (1998). *Early childhood environment rating scale* (rev. ed.). New York: Teachers College Press.

Hart, B., & Risley, T. (2004). *Meaningful differences.* Baltimore, MD: Brookes.

Haugen, K. (1998). Using technology to enhance early learning experiences. *Child Care Information Exchange, 123,* Sept./Oct. 1998, 47–50.

Holdaway, D. (1979). *The foundations of literacy.* Sydney, Australia: Ashton Scholastic.

Hong, S. B., & Trepanier-Street, M. (2004). Technology: A tool for knowledge construction in a Reggio Emilia inspired teacher education program. *Early Childhood Education Journal, 33* (2), October 2004.

International Reading Association. (2003). *Standards for reading professionals.* Newark, DE: Author.

Jeynes, W. H., & Littell, S. W. (2000). A meta-analysis of studies examining the effect of whole language instruction on the literacy of low-SES students. *The Elementary School Journal, 101* (1), 21–34.

Kelly, K. (2000). False promise. *U.S. News & World Report, 129* (12), 48–55.

Machado, J. M. (2007). *Early childhood experiences in language arts* (8th ed.). Clifton Park, NY: Thomson Delmar Learning.

Meisels, S. J., Dichtelmiller, M. L., Jablon, J. R., Dorfman, A. B., & Marsden, D. B. (2001). *The work sampling system* (4th ed.). New York: Pearson Education.

National Association for the Education of Young Children. (2005). NAEYC self-study classroom observation tool for preschool groups. National Center for Learning Disabilities. http://www.ncld.org.

National Endowment for the Arts. (2004). *Reading at risk: A survey of literary reading in America.* Research Division Report #46, June 2004.

Neuman, S. B., Copple, C., & Bredekamp, S. (1999). *Learning to read and write: Developmentally appropriate practices for young children.* Washington, DC: National Association for the Education of Young Children.

Neuman, S. B., & Roskos, K. A. (1993). *Language and literacy learning in the early years: An integrated approach.* New York: Harcourt Brace Jovanovich.

Neuman, S. B., & Roskos, K. (2005). Whatever happened to developmentally appropriate practice in early literacy? *Young Children, 60* (4), July 2005.

New, R. S. (2001). Early literacy and developmentally appropriate practice: Rethinking the paradigm. In S. B. Neuman & K. K. Dickinson (Eds.), *Handbook of early literacy research.* New York: The Guilford Press.

Oken-Wright, P. (1998). Transition to writing: Drawing as a scaffold for emergent writers. *Young Children, 53*(2), March 1998, 76–81.

Ordonez-Jasis, R., & Ortiz, R. (2006). Reading their worlds: Working with diverse families to enhance children's early literacy development. *Young Children,* 61 (1), January 2006.

Owocki, G. (1999). *Literacy through play.* Westport, CT: Heinemann.

Reggio Children. (1996). *The hundred languages of children: Narratives of the possible. Exhibit catalog.* Washington, DC: Author.

Rideout, V., Hamel, E., & Kaiser Family Foundation. (2006). The media family: Electronic media in the lives of infants, toddlers, preschoolers and their parents. Author. Retrieved June 5, 2006, from http://kff.org/entmedia/upload/7500.pdf.

Rosen, H. M. (2002). Name writing: A window into the emergent literacy skills of young children. *Early Childhood Education Journal, 30* (2), December 2002.

Schickedanz, J. (1999). *Much more than the ABCs: The early stages of reading and writing.* Washington, DC: National Association for the Education of Young Children.

Senechal, M., & LeFevre, J. (2002). Parental involvement in the development of children's reading skill: A five-year longitudinal study. *Child Development, 73* (2), 445–461.

Snow, C., Burns, M. S., & Griffin, P. (Eds.). (1998). *Preventing reading difficulties in young children.* Washington, DC: National Academy Press.

Sulzby, E. (1993). Encouraging emergent writers. *Scholastic Pre-K Today,* 7 (4), 30.

Trelease, J. (2001). *The read-aloud handbook* (5th ed.). New York: Penguin Books.

Urzua, C. (1987). "You stopped too soon": Second language children composing and revising. *TESOL Quarterly, 21* (3), 279–305.

U.S. Department of Health and Human Services, Administration for Children and Families. (2003). *The Head Start child outcomes framework.* Washington, DC: Author.

Vernadakis, N., Avgerinos, A., Tsitskari, E., & Zachupoulou, E. (2005). The use of computer assisted instruction in preschool education: Making teaching meaningful. *Early Childhood Education Journal, 33* (2), October 2005.

Wells, G. (1986). *The meaning makers: Children learning language and using language to learn.* Portsmouth, NH: Heinemann.

Welsch, J. G., Sullivan, A., & Justice, L. M. (2003). That's my letter!: What preschoolers' name writing representations tell us about emergent literacy knowledge. *Journal of Literacy Research, 35* (2), 2003.

Xu, S. H., & Rutledge, A. L. (2003). Chicken starts with ch!: Kindergartners learn through environmental print. *Young Children, 58* (2), 44–51.

RESOURCES

Beaty, J. J. (2005). *50 early childhood literacy strategies.* Upper Saddle River, NJ: Pearson.

Beaty, J. J. (1997). *Building bridges with multicultural picture books for children 3–5.* Upper Saddle River, NJ: Prentice-Hall.

Burns, M. S., Griffin, P., & Snow, C. E. (Eds.). (1999). *Starting out right: A guide to promoting children's reading success.* Washington, DC. National Academy Press.

Butler, D. (1980). *Cushla and her books.* Boston: Horn Books.

Fisher, B., & Medvic, E. F. (2003). *For reading out loud.* Portsmouth, NH: Heinemann.

Haugland, S. W. (2000). *Computers and young children. ERIC Digest* ED438926.

Machado, J. M. (2007). *Early childhood experiences in language arts* (8th ed.). Albany, NY: Thomson Delmar Learning.

Nelsen, M. R., & Nelsen-Parish, J. (2002). *Peak with books: An early childhood resource for balanced literacy.* Clifton Park, NY: Delmar Thomson Learning.

Neuman, S. B., Copple, C., & Bredekamp, S. (1999). *Learning to read and write: Developmentally appropriate practices for young children.* Washington, DC: National Association for the Education of Young Children.

Roskos, K. A., Christie, J. F., & Richgels, D. J. (2003). The essentials of early literacy instruction. *Young Children, 58* (2), 52–60.

Schickedanz, J. (1999). *Much more than the ABCs: The early stages of reading and writing.* Washington, DC: National Association for the Education of Young Children.

Strickland, D. S., & Morrow, L. (Eds.). (1989). *Emerging literacy: Young children learn to read and write.* Newark, DE: International Reading Association.

The Center for Best Practices in Early Childhood. (2001). *Your preschool classroom computer center: How does it measure up?* Macomb, IL: Author, Western Illinois University.

Trelease, J. (2001). *The read-aloud handbook.* New York: Penguin Books.

VanAusdale, D., & Flagen, J. R. (2001). *The first R: How children learn race and racism.* Lanham, MD: Rowman & Littlefield. Publishers, Inc.

CHAPTER 10

Using Work Samples to Look at Creativity

USING WORK SAMPLES TO OBSERVE A CHILD'S DEVELOPMENT

EXERCISE **What can you tell about the child who created the drawing in Figure 10–1?**

You could probably tell this child has observed a dog closely. The drawing is accurately proportioned and detailed, so the age of the artist could be estimated, by one who knew the usual progressive stages of children's drawing, to be about six years old. Actually, this drawing was done by an active four-year-old with an avid interest in art. Compared to the stages of creative development, it is advanced for the chronological age of the artist.

Creativity comes from within and reveals the self, whether it is a three-year-old with a crayon drawing on the wall, or a great master with oils and canvas. The child's creative products can be used as effective revelations of developmental progress. Almost every developmental area can be assessed from observing a child manipulate creative **media.**

The old saying "A picture is worth a thousand words" is true also of children's creative products. Children's work, done in home or classroom setting, as the child plays and goes through the natural routines of the day, provides information that would take paragraphs to convey. Individual children and groups produce work that can serve as raw data for

IN THIS CHAPTER

Figure 10–1 A drawing can tell a lot about a child.

assessment. They can be collected over time, showing changes in development (McAfee & Leong, 2002). **Work Samples** is the term for any of the child's products, including but not limited to visual arts, all of which reveal many aspects of the child's development (Figure 10–2).

Materials can be contributed to the Portfolio from various sources—the family, the teacher, or the child—depending on its purpose. In the *Week by Week* Portfolio, information and documents are gathered from all three, with equal access as well. The child's access, of course, depends on the age, but even very young children can understand the Portfolio is about them. They often want to see it, just as they love to look at photographs of themselves as babies. By including samples of their work, whether drawing, writing, or photographs, they realize its purpose as a chronicle of their development.

Children should be aware of the Portfolio and its purpose as a receptacle for information about them. They are invited to add to the Portfolio when they have work they feel is important to them. If the Portfolio is a file folder, the child can decorate the four panels of the file folder periodically over the quarters of the school year. This personalizes it, but also makes it an episodic documentation of the child's work. The children can comment on their own work as a way of exploring their thinking. The observer listens to the child describe the memory of the work and comments on the progress from the child's viewpoint.

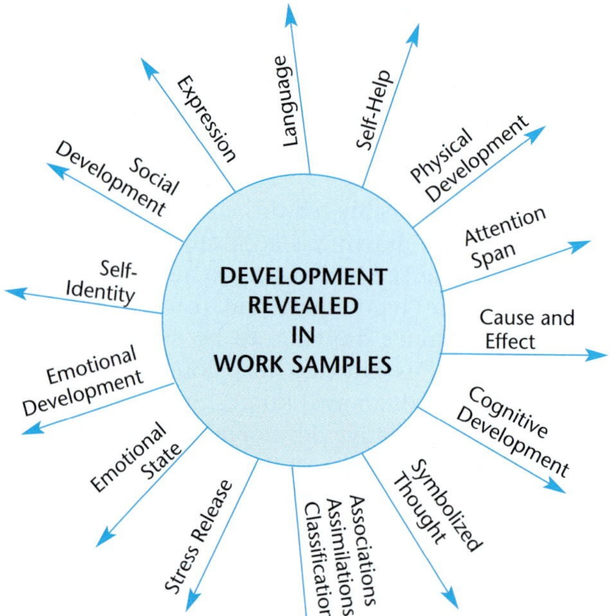

Figure 10–2 Development Revealed in Work Samples.

Children are very possessive of their work (as they should be) but usually are generous in allowing copies to be made on a copier. The color is lost,

@ it happened to me

The Story of the Dog Drawing

The child who made me the drawing in Figure 10–1 was a mischievous boy with freckles and a sense of humor. He gave me the drawing as a surprise gift. It was preceded by a promise that I would display it on my refrigerator door. It has been displayed to a far wider audience as a prime example of a child's creative work going beyond expected stages. The drawing reveals so much about him and his development. His sense of humor is seen in the face of the dog.

The rest of the story: I always wondered what happened to this child. At a college function, I saw his mother, who was there with one of my students receiving an award! It turns out my student was her sister. I asked about her son and explained about the drawing that I had saved and used as an example all those years. It turns out he was a student right here at my college, taking—you guessed it—art. I sent him a letter and a copy of this page and asked him to come by my office. He never did! I will always be disappointed that we didn't get to talk about this. Who knows why he didn't come.

Do you have an IT HAPPENED TO ME story about one of your students from the past and how you have reconnected? I'd love to read it. Please send it to WeekbyWeek@thomsonlearning.com

but the line and form are preserved. Actually having a notebook for each child to draw in over the course of a year is another way of collecting drawings. It is more structured, drawing at the adult's request, and yields less spontaneous and natural art products. It also limits the types of media that can be used.

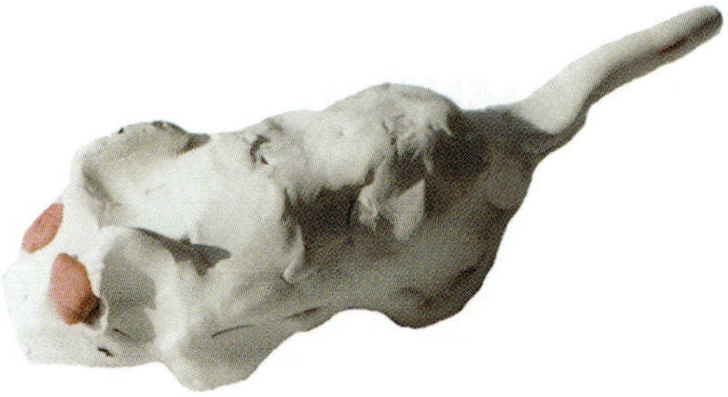

Figure 10–3 Compare the Work Sample photo of a mouse to drawing in Figure 9–14. (From *Growing Artists, Teaching Art To Young Children*, 3rd edition, by KOSTER, 2005. Reprinted with permission of Delmar Learning, a division of Thomson Learning: www.thomsonrights.com, Fax 800 730-2215.

Three-dimensional creations such as sculpture, collages, mobiles, woodworking, sewing, and even movement can be preserved with photographs, documented, and added to the Portfolio (Figure 10–3). Work can be explained with notes attached to the back that include the date. The background of the work, how it came to be done, and any dictation or child's words about the work can be written there. The teacher can make notations concerning the child's development that this work especially illustrates.

Portfolios contain samples of the child's work to document progress and illustrate the child's thinking. Because development is seen in children's graphic art products, they are a concrete way to document development. Children's drawings, paintings, scribbles, and photographs or sketches of their block structures are collected periodically to add to the Portfolio. Genishi (1993) recommends reviewing children's art work Portfolios when it is time to write progress reports or hold parent conferences: "When you review, look to see how well each child's Portfolio captures his or her story of development. . . . For example, include a series of paintings that shows a child's changing use of patterns. Use these stories to inform and enrich your written reports and your conversations with parents" (p. 67).

OTHER WORK SAMPLES FOR THE PORTFOLIO. A wide variety of physical materials can be used as Work Samples beyond the traditional kinds already mentioned. Work Samples can also include child-produced writing, audio, and video products; language samples of riddles, rhymes, songs, or plays; and movement activities such as dances, acrobatic routines, and pantomimes. These products assist in the assessment of other areas of development. Figure 10–4 is the Work Samples Checklist, which includes areas covered in *Week by Week* and some assessment criteria in the creative realm.

WORK SAMPLES CHECKLIST

Child's Name____ Dates ________________

COMMENTS

Separation
- ❑ Separates from adult to work alone
- ❑ Works independently without requiring adult presence or direction

Self-Care
- ❑ Independently selects materials
- ❑ Makes preparations to work (Example: Puts on a smock)
- ❑ Uses materials independently
- ❑ Cleans up spills, messes
- ❑ Writes name on work
- ❑ Places finished product in proper place
- ❑ Washes and dries hands if necessary
- ❑ Replaces materials to storage place

Physical Development
- ❑ Controls whole body movement during work
- ❑ Controls small muscles to hold tool
- ❑ Controls tool to form desired product
- ❑ Draws, prints, paints, pastes
- ❑ Squeezes glue bottle
- ❑ Picks up collage materials
- ❑ Manipulates clay or Play Doh
- ❑ Cuts with scissors
- ❑ Controls body to stay within the space (on the paper, building on a rug, clay on table)

Social Skills
- ❑ Represents important people in his life in his work
- ❑ Desires and can work near other children
- ❑ Shares materials and supplies
- ❑ Engages in positive commentary on other children's work
- ❑ Works cooperatively on a joint project

Emotional Development
- ❑ Uses work to express emotions of happiness, anger, fear
- ❑ Verbalizes feelings about work
- ❑ Enjoys manipulation and creation
- ❑ Controls emotions of frustration when work meets difficulties
- ❑ Uses the media as a stress release, pounding clay, tearing paper, painting

Speech and Language Development
- ❑ Names scribbles, buildings, creations
- ❑ Talks about work using vocabulary connected with materials and design
- ❑ Uses language to describe process, intent, and satisfaction with product
- ❑ Vocabulary reflects knowledge of subject

CONTINUED

Figure 10–4 Work Samples Checklist Example.

WORK SAMPLES CHECKLIST (continued)

COMMENTS

Memory and Attention Span
- ❑ Includes details in work from memories of experiences
- ❑ Focuses attention on project to produce a finished work
- ❑ Tunes out distractions of simultaneous play, talk, and work
- ❑ Gives attention and makes connections between environment and own work

Math and Science Knowledge
- ❑ Includes numerals and quantity in work
- ❑ Shows one-to-one correspondence in work designs
- ❑ Shows perceptual awareness of color, space, form
- ❑ Explores cause and effect and experimentation with variables in media (Example: Sees differences in paint when water and sand are added)
- ❑ Observes similarities and differences, forming theories, and testing them out by manipulating the medium
- ❑ Working with clay or liquid—displays knowledge of the concept of conservation (volume stays the same even though form changes—ball flattened is the same amount)

Literacy
- ❑ Includes literacy in work
- ❑ Recognizes the difference between drawing and writing
- ❑ Uses materials to symbolize ideas
- ❑ Work illustrates or connects with stories
- ❑ Gives attention to art in story books and knows the difference between text and illustrations

Creativity
- ❑ Uses materials in a novel way, displaying flexibility in seeing new possibilities in materials
- ❑ Explores all facets of the medium
- ❑ Draws from experiences to create representations
- ❑ Incorporates creativity into other areas of play, constructing with blocks, drawing and constructing in dramatic play, forming designs in sand and other media
- ❑ Demonstrates creativity in sensory awareness (seeing, hearing, touching, smelling, tasting)

Self-Identity
- ❑ Displays risk-free attitude in work
- ❑ Reveals self in content of work
- ❑ Work shows a sense of identity and individuality
- ❑ Expresses satisfaction in work, confident self-esteem
- ❑ Portrays self, family, world in work
- ❑ Work demonstrates child's sex-role identification
- ❑ Work shows child moving from egocentric view of self to an awareness of self as part of larger society
- ❑ Indicates favorite art medium (singular), media (plural)

Group Time Behaviors
- ❑ Participates in cooperative and collaborative work

Interaction with Adults
- ❑ Involves adults in work as (facilitator, participator, director)

©Nilsen, B. *Week by Week: Plans for Documenting Children's Development,* 4th ed. Clifton Park, NY: Thomson Delmar Learning (2005).

Figure 10–4 (*continued*).

COLLABORATING WITH COLLEAGUES ABOUT THE SIGNIFICANCE OF WORK SAMPLES. Using Jones and Cortney's concept of discussing children's science projects from their book *Documenting Early Science Learning* (2002) as a model, teachers could discuss and collaborate on evaluating children's Work Samples. They suggest using language records (see Chapter 6) and Work Samples, with one teacher presenting the factual evidence of Work Samples, as well as transcripts of conversations with the child about the work. Others review the materials silently, then summarize the evidence, noting questions for clarification. Then the collaborators can discuss and come to consensus on the meaning and indicators of development based on the evidence provided. In this way, several viewpoints consider the work based on their own frames of reference. The child's work is considered a revelation of thought and feelings. This is in contrast to a parent's comment, tossing the art work in the trash can, "I'm only going to drive it around in the back of the car for weeks then throw it away anyway." The painful truth.

Advantages

Collecting Work Samples is an effective recording technique because it is done

- in a natural classroom setting, with the child selecting materials and working at her own pace and direction, illustrating many areas of development.
- over a period of time, showing progress of development.
- as an expression of the child's thoughts and feelings more accurately and powerfully than an observer can describe them.

Disadvantages

Work Samples might

- make the child overly conscious of manipulation or practice.
- lead the observer to draw erroneous conclusions from the work.
- reflect the inferences of the selector, as the teacher may only gather scribbling or experimental pieces when actually the child does much more advanced work.

Pitfalls to Avoid

For Work Samples to be part of an authentic assessment plan, they should be

- dated. (The changeable date stamp comes in handy here. Children can learn to date their work themselves.)
- gathered periodically by joint decision of the recorder and the child.
- accompanied by commentary or narrative concerning the work.
- kept in a separate folder from the Portfolio if they become overwhelmingly large or if children want to submit many pieces.

What to Do with It

Children are possessive of their work, and so they should be. To collect Work Samples, one must either file what the child forgets to take home, make photocopies, or take photographs of the work. There may be a temptation to ask a child to create something for the Portfolio, but that is not what we are seeking here. The purpose is to collect what is called *literacies*, modes of "recording and preserving experiences, reflecting upon, exploring and extending one's thoughts and feelings, and communicating and sharing ideas with others" (Edwards & Willis, 2000). Work Samples are another way of documenting the child's development. They are incorporated into the child's Portfolio with other documents as evidence of development, testimonies from the child that demonstrate physical, social, cognitive, literacy, emotional, and creative development. At the conclusion of the school year, the samples are given to the family. It may be the policy of the school or program to keep copies.

Using Technology

Keeping piles of drawings can get cumbersome and take up valuable storage space. Using technology to file and access Work Samples is becoming easier and easier. Scanners can turn samples such as writings, drawings, and paintings into an easily stored electronic documents. Digital photography can capture three-dimensional works such as collages, sculptures, block building, and other constructions. Digital video recordings can capture not only the product but the process. Electronic storage and access makes it easier to utilize the information for program planning and sharing with the family. It also keeps the whole Portfolio more secure than if it were in a file folder in a drawer or cabinet.

How to Find the Time

Capturing children's Work Samples is relatively time efficient when using a digital camera. A picture tells a thousand words, and the child's work is spoken in a hundred languages or literacies, as mentioned above. Taking photos is less time-consuming than writing descriptions or manipulating Developmental Checklists. It should not be the only method used, but it is very effective.

Observing Creativity with Other Recording Methods

Observing a child during the creative process and preserving the finished product as documentation provides valuable developmental information. The products are not only the outcomes of the child's development but are affected by it as well. **Creativity** is affected by development, yet by observing creativity, development can be observed and assessed (Figure 10–5).

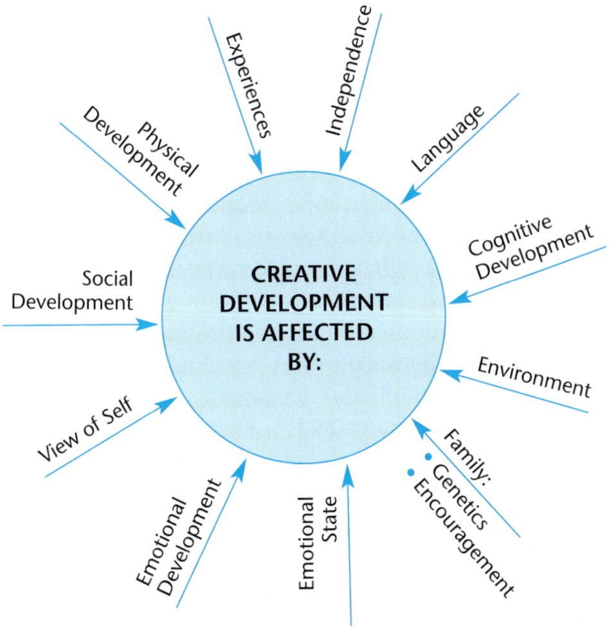

Figure 10–5 Many factors affect creative development.

Developmental Checklists with a section on creative development can be used to quickly gather general observed behaviors for the Portfolio. The actual work or replicas of it serve as the documentation or evidence for the decisions made on the Checklist or Rating Scale.

Anecdotal Recordings, detailed narratives of the action and exact words the child uses during and after the creation phase, are like the caption to the illustration. The dictated words or quotations give the background or setting of the work. The action of the work is documented along with the exact quotes of the artist. It can inform the viewer and reader of the special circumstances that affected the child and the work.

Interviews while a child is working on a project are another way of gathering information. They reveal the child's understanding of concepts and increase the observer's understanding of the child's work. The child conveys the process and intent. That way, it is not misconstrued by the observer. Using what Koster (2005, p. 40) calls *art words*, the teacher can comment on the work in a way that points out concepts:

line—straight, curved, wiggly, zigzag, jagged, crisscross
shape—square, rectangular, round, triangular, irregular, oval
color—red, orange, yellow, green, blue (bright colors); gray, olive, green, deep brown (dull colors); white, beige, gray, tan, brown (neutral colors); pink, coral, sky blue, lavender, pale green (pastel colors); magenta, purple, fuchsia, red-orange, turquoise (intense colors)
texture—soft, hard, bumpy, rough, jagged, smooth, wet, sticky
form—spheres, cubes, pyramids
contrast—light/dark, big/small, top/bottom, front/back, round/square, bright/dull, intense/soft, hard/soft, rough/smooth, patterned, plain, thick/thin, straight/curved
pattern—plaid, polka dot, stripe, floral, all over, border, checkered

Go to the Bind-in-Book CD for Creative Work Samples checklist, plans, and resources.

LOOKING AT CHILDREN'S CREATIVE DEVELOPMENT

Analyzing children's creative work is a visual demonstration of developmental principles. All children, all over the world, in whatever age they have

REVIEW

WORK SAMPLES

Observing and collecting a child's product from which to draw conclusions about development, skills, and behaviors.

Types of Information to Record Using Work Samples

- separation
- self-care
- physical development
- social skills
- emotional development
- speech and language development
- memory and attention span
- math and science knowledge
- literacy
- creativity
- self-identity
- group time behaviors
- interaction with adults

Figure 10–6 Anasazi Indian handprints in New Mexico remind us of fingerpaing handprints that young children make.

Figure 10–7 New Mexico petroglyph carved in rocks a thousand years ago resembles children's experimentation with form.

lived, progress through the same basic stages in art or graphic representation. Historians who have studied pictorials on caves and rocks and alphabetic systems see the same designs that are seen painted by a child in day care in Chicago. Those combinations of circles, squares, straight lines, and curved lines had meaning for those people long ago, just as they do for today's child. Sylvia Fein, in her fascinating book *First Drawings: Genesis of Visual Thinking* (1993), compares artifacts from all over the world with children's first attempts at art. From handprints of the Anasazi Indians on cave walls in New Mexico (Figure 10–6), concentric circles from runic stones in Norway (Figure 10–7), depictions of people from the Caribbean (Figure 10–8), artists in every age use archetypical signs that have universal meaning.

Children's creative work is recognized as a window into their mind. Before a children symbolize in writing, and sometimes even verbally, they use drawing as an expressive outlet. Many intelligence and psychological tests analyze a child's art to gain insight on the child's thinking and feeling. Goodenough's *Draw-A-Man Test* (1926) is a well-known measurement, still used as a prescreener in many schools because it has been shown to correlate well with IQ tests. There have been some complaints that the test is sexist (draw a MAN) (Koster, 2005). Careful study and classification of children's drawings have found predictable stages common to children worldwide, with curiously little variation (Kellogg, 1970; Lowenfeld & Brittain, 1987). This reinforces developmental theory that drawing is the representation of inner thought and connected with stages of development. The same factors that affect all other areas of development also affect the creative: genetic, environmental, and cultural. To accurately observe and assess a child's development from creative expression, then, knowledge of the stages of creative development is vital.

Figure 10–8 Ancient drawings resemble today's children's self-portraits.

Stages of Children's Art

Figure 10–9 illustrates the four stages of creative development.

STAGE I: MARK-MAKING STAGE (BIRTH TO TWO YEARS). The marks are random, done for pleasure and exploration, involving visual and physical movement. The child uses large muscles and whole arm movement. Over time, the marks become more organized and are repeated. The tool is held in a tight fist grip, with a rigid wrist.

STAGE II: SCRIBBLING STAGE (TWO TO FOUR YEARS). Kellogg (1970) analyzed the scribbles of thousands of young children and cataloged them into separate substages. **Scribbling** becomes more controlled with the development of the small muscles, eye-hand coordination, and cognitive abilities. The child uses a finger grip, with small, more-controlled movements. The marks usually are controlled to the confines of the paper. During this stage, the child is still experimenting with line and practicing muscle control. The child intently works and develops designs in variations of the circle. Once language is developed, the child attaches names to the scribbles. She may have a mental image when she draws, but the mind and muscles are not coordinated enough so the drawings are usually not recognizable to others. She might identify drawings, and as the stage progresses they become more representative of her mental image, to the point that the viewer recognizes the object. The first representation of humans begins to appear in this stage.

A definite progression of geometric shapes and representations occurs in this order:

1. *Circles.* As small muscle coordination develops, the circle becomes rounded. Finally, the line connects to close the circle completely.
2. *Vertical and horizontal lines.* These become more deliberate and crosses and Xs become part of the experimentation with the art medium.
3. *Mandalas.* A **mandala** (Figure 10–10A) is a combination of a cross inside a circle. The word means *magical circle* in Sanskrit. In Oriental religion, it is regarded as the symbol of the cosmos. In Jungian psychology, the mandala is representative of the psyche with the collective unconscious (Kellogg, 1970, p. 68; Gardner, 1980). These extended meanings raise the mandala's significance. All children universally pass through this stage.
4. *Suns.* The circle with radiating lines (Figure 10–10B) becomes one of the first symbols children draw.
5. *Radials.* Straight lines radiate from a central point to form a circle-like shape (Figure 10–10C). Radials also occur in the controlled scribbling stage.
6. *Tadpole man.* During the third and fourth years, children begin to represent humans in a curious symbol that resembles a **tadpole man** (Figure 10–10D). They combine the circles and lines into a head with features. This is understandable when the earliest images are considered. For months, the infant concentrates closely on the human face. The arms and legs are added later, just as their awareness of them came later. The circle represents the whole body as they know it, so a circle with dots for eyes and a line for a mouth is the early person

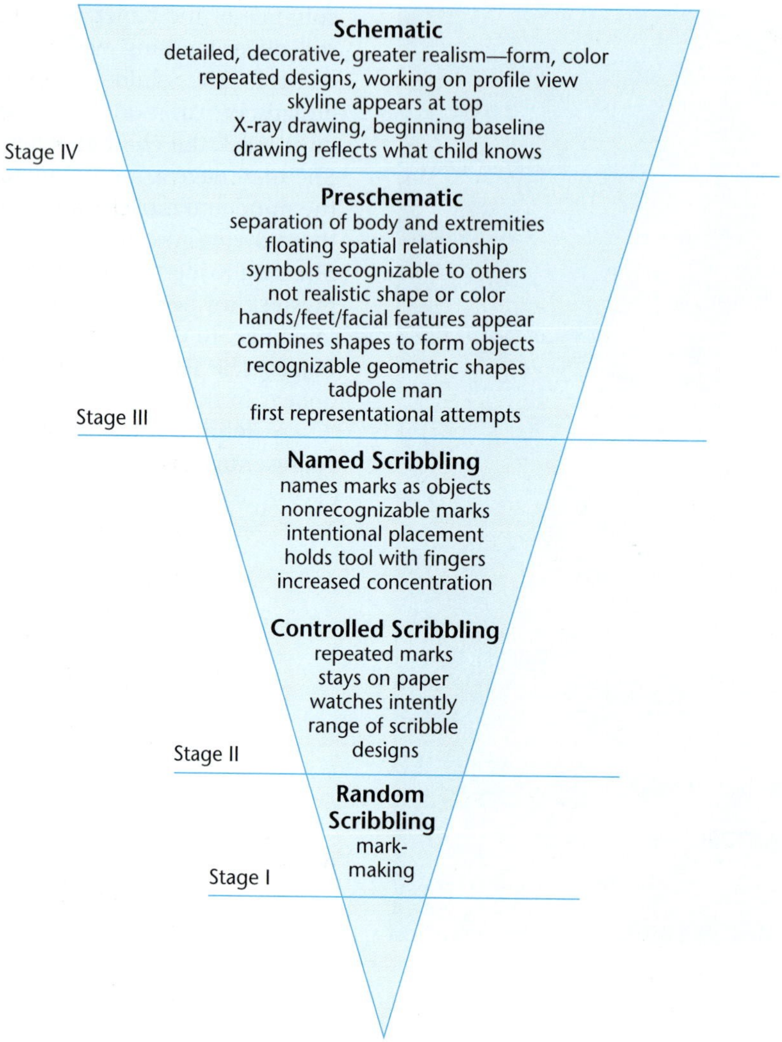

Figure 10–9 The Four Stages of Creative Development. (Adapted from Kellogg, 1970; Lowenfeld & Brittain, 1987; Schirrmacher, 2002.)

drawing. Arms, then legs, then fingers and toes, and more features appear in an orderly progression. This should remind the student of child development of the principle of cephalocaudal and proximodistal development.

STAGE III: PRESCHEMATIC (FOUR TO SEVEN YEARS). Lowenfeld and Brittain (1987, p. 258) call the symbol a child draws for familiar objects a **schema**. The child experiments with drawing through the scribbling and the **preschematic** stages to develop these symbols. They are unique to each child yet similar because they follow the physical and mental developmental stages through which each child moves. Schirrmacher (2006) calls this the "Attempts at Public Representation" stage. These attempts are **nonrepresentational**. It is difficult, if not impossible, for children in this stage to follow instructions like "think of your favorite . . . and draw it." Children at this stage are able to think of a favorite, but they lack the fine muscle skills and cognitive ability to physically represent their thoughts. They are more likely to draw what they can, even a scribble, and say, "This is a butterfly." To the viewer, as well as the artist, it is a blob.

Older preschoolers are trying to represent their mental images to others, yet much of what they create is still nonrepresentational and without realism to the viewer. They draw what they *know*, not what they *see*. They surely see more than they are able to draw. They experiment with the medium and often play with the tools. No message or intent for representation may be present.

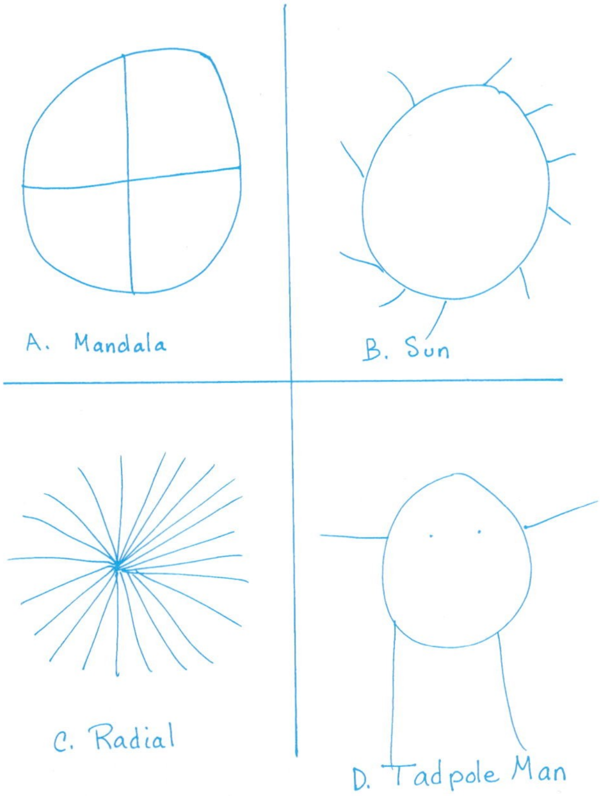

Figure 10–10 Early Stages of Drawing.

At the beginning of this stage, there is little regard for realism in color, size proportion, or exact details. These aspects continue to be more evident as the stage progresses. By the end of this stage, the child can copy a square by bringing a single line back to the beginning with defined corners.

Details on the human figure increase, with the body becoming more like a snowman. The neck separates the head and body circle, and ovals appear, representing the arms and legs. Hands move from single lines to multiple lines, then to accurately drawn five digits, and eventually to more of a glovelike hand. Anatomical representations appear as the child is striving for realism and gaining knowledge of gender differences.

By the end of this period, the child draws an accurate triangle and often uses a repeated pattern or design of symbols. The child begins to use drawings to express feelings, as well as visual images.

STAGE IV: SCHEMATIC (SEVEN TO NINE YEARS). In the **schematic** stage, the child now has a well-developed schema repeated in all drawings to represent humans, homes, trees, clouds—all the relevant, important objects in the child's life. The child's drawing still represents concept rather than perception (what he knows versus what he sees). This is observed in a perspective problem: what to do with the hidden leg of a horse rider or the eyes in a profile view? The child draws these as if by X-ray vision, signifying he knows there are two legs or eyes. Drawing only one is not acceptable mentally to him. The baseline and skyline appear with a partial sun in the corner. Chimneys on roofs are at right angles to the roof line, making them askew to the baseline. As the child's cognitive development improves, the chimney becomes erect. Attempts at three-dimensional representation are beginning by drawing three sides of a building.

EXERCISE Based on the developmental stages discussed, rank Figure 10–11 through Figure 10–16 in order of creative development (number them 1–6).

_____ **Figure 10–11**
_____ **Figure 10–12**
_____ **Figure 10–13**
_____ **Figure 10–14**
_____ **Figure 10–15**
_____ **Figure 10–16**

Figure 10–11 is an example of a tadpole man with the beginning of some features. The circles and firm, straight lines show small muscle control. The artist is four years, one month old.

Figure 10–12 is definitely a scribble, but a controlled scribble. The child left a margin around the

Figure 10–11

Figure 10–12

Figure 10–13

page and confined marks to a located area. The artist is three years, two months old.

Figure 10–13 has separate, distinct body parts, characters on a baseline, and shows representation of thought by drawing the basketball team and the

Figure 10–14

important parts such as the basket, the basketball, and the scoreboard. Note that the child has numbers on the team uniforms not for counting but for realism. There are many signs this child is moving beyond the preschematic stage. The artist is five years, eleven months old.

Figure 10–14 is very realistic. Of course, this was by the oldest artist in the group. The drawing fills the page with the sky, sun, and clouds overhead and rain coming down. There is a definite baseline on which the person is walking and the cage and "Giney pig" are sitting. The artist is attempting a profile—note one eye and no arms drawn—but he just cannot resist the smile, though misplaced. The artist is six years, two months old.

Figure 10–15 was done by the youngest artist at two years, three months. The dots are stabs with the markers, and lines run off the paper as the child is attempting to gain control.

Figure 10–16 is the artist's practice, drawing the same form over and over, changing it slightly by altering the features. Alphabet letters are mixed in with the drawings. The artist is four years, five months.

Your sequence of stages should have been 1) Figure 10–15; 2) Figure 10–12; 3) Figure 10–11; 4) Figure 10–16; 5) Figure 10–13; and 6) Figure 10–14.

Comparing creative work from different children and sorting them into developmental stages is not dependable, but these are representative of the stages, and their ages happened to correspond. It is not always so. The principles of development prevail. The stages are sequential, but children do not pass through them at the same age. Collecting the drawings of

Figure 10–15

Figure 10–16

each child and comparing them to ones drawn previously by that child is dependable documentation of progress.

Blocks as a Creative Medium

Construction materials are open-ended, used in very different ways by each child. This type of material, like any creative medium, gives the observer knowledge about many developmental areas. Blocks are varied in type but provide this kind of experience. Types of block include

plastic interlocking blocks—Legos or Duplos
unit blocks—standard units are multiples of each other
hollow blocks—standard units are multiples of each other but are large; constructed of many pieces nailed and glued together
cardboard blocks—lightweight, often homemade from milk cartons
foam blocks—geometric shapes and units; lightweight

Figure 10–17 Block play areas with accessories, literacy materials, and cross-over play from the dramatic area promote creativity.

special building sets—Lincoln Logs, Erector sets, Tinkertoys, A-B-C blocks, PVC pipes
cube blocks—one unit blocks either of wood or plastic, sometimes with locking features

The placement of shaped blocks on shelves, labeled with exact tracings of the block, builds one-to-one correspondence skills. The association of the shapes—square, rectangle, triangle, cylinder—is made not only with the shape but the word, making the literacy connection. Much of what goes on in the block building area is more than construction. It involves dramatic play, social skills, and language practice. The towers with resultant crashes bring excitement and danger themes to the block area. Accompanying props, such as farm and zoo animals, transportation vehicles, and miniature people, expand the play from functional to symbolic. By including textures, such as rug and fabric pieces, small pieces of turf-like carpeting, and soft pillows, the area becomes a stress reducer as well (Figure 10–17).

There are often physical barriers between the dramatic play area (housekeeping or family area) and the block area. This contributes to gender segregation, which is so common in these areas. Physically removing the barrier and encouraging the crossover of materials can help break down the stereotypes of play materials that are already present in preschoolers. Blocks can be taken to the oven to bake as bread. Block structures become homes where dishes and dolls can be added. By carefully planning the environment, the block area becomes another microcosm of development, affording the observer an excellent view of all areas of development.

STAGES IN BLOCK PLAY. There are progressive stages in the way children interact with blocks, dependent on cognitive, social, emotional, and physical development (Figure 10–18).

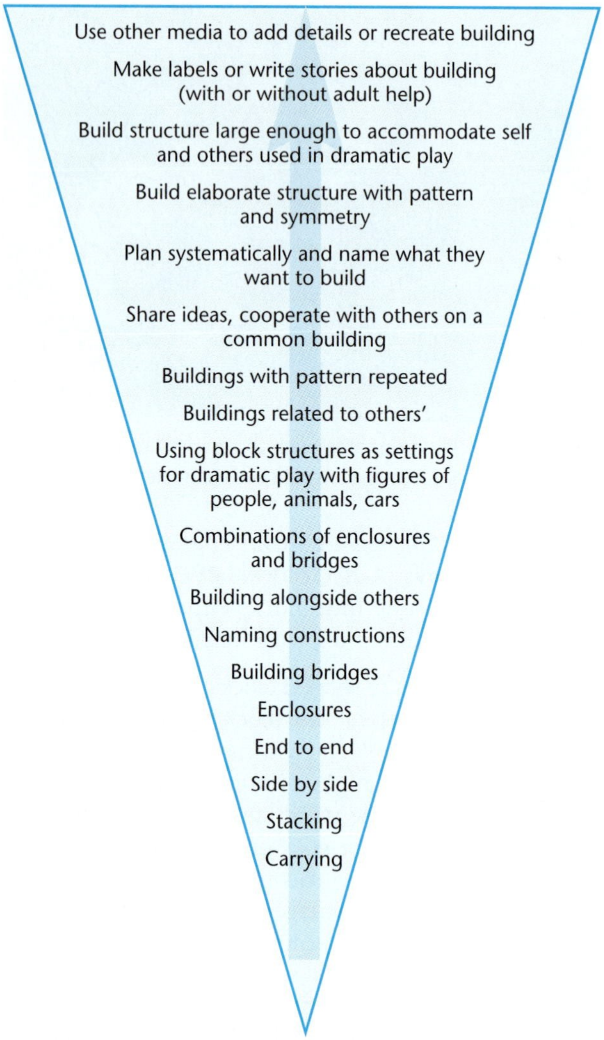

Figure 10–18 Block Play Development. (Adapted from Hirsch (1996) and Day (1994).)

Stage I: Carrying, Filling, and Dumping (Under Two Years). Children are in the sensorimotor stage, so they are exploring the attributes of blocks by feeling, lifting, and moving them from place to place.

Stage II: Beginning Block Building (Two to Three Years). Children make horizontal rows, laying blocks end to end or stacking. They repeat stacking and knocking down. They are beginning to observe the unstable effect of a small base with large blocks piled on.

Stage III: Bridging (Three Years). Two blocks are placed vertically as pillars with a third block placed across the top. This takes visual acuity, small muscle coordination, and balance.

Stage IV: Enclosures (Three and Four Years). Four blocks are placed at right angles to enclose a space. This corresponds to the child's ability to draw a square, recognizing the connectedness of the angles and associating inside and outside concepts.

Stage V: Patterns (Four Years). Bridges and enclosures are repeated to form a horizontal or vertical pattern. Symmetry, a sense of balance and equal proportions, is demonstrated.

Stage VI: Naming Structures (Four to Six Years). Names and functions of buildings are assigned to the structures. Additional pieces like cars, animals, and play people add to the play. The play becomes more symbolic.

Stage VII: Reproducing True-Life Structures (Five Years and Up). This stage is an expansion of Stage VI, with children trying to build more realistically and to incorporate dramatic play into the structures by moving play people and animals according to a script.

These block-building stages parallel the drawing stages: manipulation, simple experimentation, patterns, naming, and realistic reproduction.

Block play can help children in many developmental domains. Wellhousen and Kieff (2001) provide a list of goals to be included in IEP (individualized education program) or IFSP (individualized family service plan), but they really are goals for all children and also give cues for observing specific skills. This list is given in Figure 10–19.

Other Creative Media

Other materials or media such as clay, woodworking, or collage illustrate the child's development through stages similar to drawing. Small muscles interact with creativity to produce three-dimensional products. These often are not preserved (but with a digital camera could be!), since the materials—especially in the case of clay or wood—are often returned to be manipulated in another way. The stages correspond to drawing (Figure 10–20).

Interaction with a tangible, movable medium is sensory, involving seeing, feeling, and often smelling. It helps the development of Logico-Mathematical thinking through manipulation. Physical properties of volume, weight, and length are transformed through play.

Process versus Product

Early childhood teachers are often in a dilemma. Children need time and opportunity to explore and experiment with various art media, but often the

Awareness:

- ❑ Increase body awareness
- ❑ Improve self-concept
- ❑ Increase awareness of individual differences

Creativity:

- ❑ Encourage creativity
- ❑ Encourage creative problem solving
- ❑ Stimulate curiosity

Feelings:

- ❑ Increase awareness of own and others' feelings
- ❑ Provide outlet for expressing feelings
- ❑ Increase feelings of group belonging

Language Skills:

- ❑ Improve expressive language
- ❑ Increase vocabulary
- ❑ Follow directions
- ❑ Increase understanding (receptive language)

Math Skills:

- ❑ Improve measurement concepts
- ❑ Improve number concepts
- ❑ Improve shape concepts
- ❑ Improve size concepts

Motor Skills:

- ❑ Improve large motor coordination
- ❑ Improve small motor coordination
- ❑ Improve eye–hand coordination
- ❑ Improve balancing skills
- ❑ Develop the ability to relax at will

Sensory Skills:

- ❑ Improve auditory association, closure, comprehension, discrimination, identification, memory
- ❑ Improve tactile association, closure, comprehension, discrimination, identification, memory
- ❑ Improve visual association, closure, comprehension, discrimination, identification, memory
- ❑ Localize sound
- ❑ Improve sensory integration

Social Skills:

- ❑ Cooperate with peers/adults
- ❑ Improve ability to take turns
- ❑ Improve ability to share
- ❑ Improve interaction skills

Thinking and Reasoning Skills:

- ❑ Improve color concepts
- ❑ Increase attention span
- ❑ Improve cause-and-effect reasoning
- ❑ Improve classification skills
- ❑ Improve decision-making skills
- ❑ Improve logical reasoning
- ❑ Improve problem-solving skills
- ❑ Make predictions

Figure 10–19 Goals for Block Play. From A Constructivist Approach to Block Play in Early Childhood 1st edition by Wellhousen/Kieff. 2001. Reprinted with permission of Delmar Learning, a division of Thomson Learning: www.thomsonrights.com, FAX 800-730-2215.

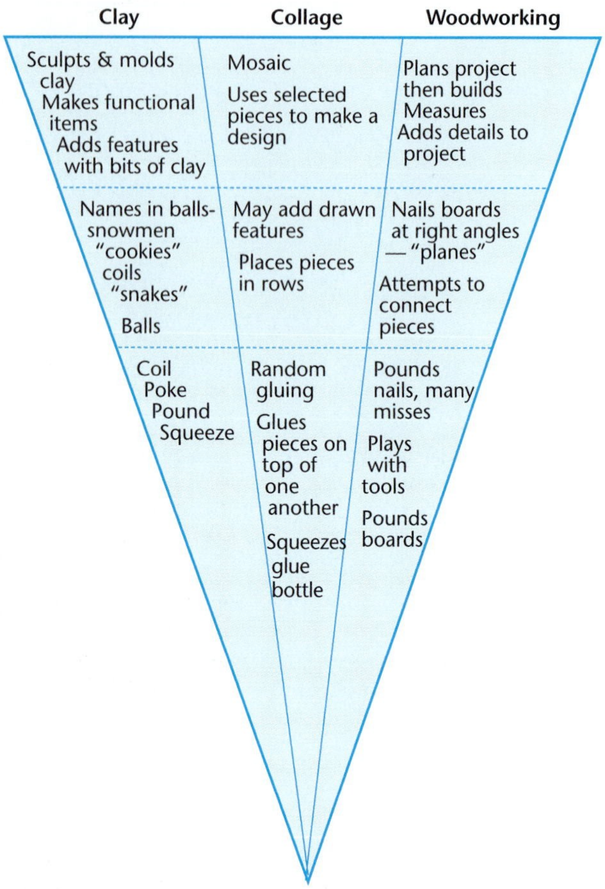

Figure 10–20 Stages of Other Creative Media.

family, the child, and sometimes even the teacher wants it to "look like something." There are cute projects that appeal to adults and to children, but when we are using Work Samples to see the child's development, a pre-cut, directed activity does not suffice. Sometimes these activities are abstract to the child's thinking (does the adult's transformation of an egg carton really look like a caterpillar to a child?), may be beyond their physical ability, and the only "right" way is to follow the pattern. The values and philosophy of the teacher and the program guide these decisions. When the teacher provides art materials as a vehicle for expressing creativity and exploring a medium, they are open-ended activities without an expected product. For older children, following step-by-step directions for a resultant product is important training for mathematics calculations and many other aspects of life. The teacher recognizes the purpose, aligns the project with the skill level of the children, and facilitates the activity so that each child can feel success. Recognizing the difference between the two approaches, the teacher plans activities that meet the purpose and are appropriate for the age and stage of the children.

Creativity and Cognitive Development

Thinking and all the processes that link thinking and learning are integral to creativity. It should not be surprising. There are parallels between the stages of Piaget's cognitive theory (Flavell, 1963), the art stages of Kellogg (1970) and Lowenfeld and Brittain (1987), and the social-emotional stages of Erikson (1950). They correspond to stages of development of language, reading, and writing. The ages of these stages are merely guideposts, not firm transition points (Figure 10–21).

When involved in creative activities, the brain and body can be so focused that it has been called the flow by researcher Mihaly Csikszenthmihalyi (1997). This euphoric feeling is often expressed by athletes when they are pushing themselves to the limit. It stimulates the brain's pleasure centers in such a way that transcends time and space. Creativity is dependent on symbolic thought. It is necessary to have existing structures and beliefs in reality against which to measure new data. It is dependent on cognitive ability, past experiences, and the present environment. Observing children's creative efforts can indicate the following:

- *Long attention span*—When the activity captures their interest, they attend longer.
- *Capacity for organization*—The organization of their creative work indicates their classification skills.
- *Seeing things in a different perspective*—This does not go against the egocentric idea but refers to the child's ability to see things without preconceived notions.
- *Exploring before formal instruction*—They have the need to manipulate first, and later organize into more conventional uses of tools and materials.
- *Using solitary time*—Every parent knows that a quiet child is often one that needs to be investigated, for there may be some trouble brewing. Children get into trouble because they try things they do not know are dangerous or forbidden. This is an aspect of creativity like drawing on the sheets with lipstick or painting on the recreation room wall with tar.
- *Taking a "closer look" at things*—Creative thinking involves manipulation and being close. It could be apples in a plastic bag at the supermarket or a climb to the top cupboard in the kitchen to investigate.

Piaget's Stages of Cognitive Development	Stages of Art Kellogg; Lowenfeld and Brittain; Schirrmacher	Language Development	Writing/ Reading	Erikson's Psycho-social Stages
Sensorimotor (b–24 months) Moving from reflexes to object permanence	Scribbling and mark-making (b–2 years) Random exploration Nonintentional	Pre/Language (b–2 years) Sounds, telegraphic sentences	Book Handling Skills (b–2 years) Right side up, front/back, turn pages	Basic Trust vs. Mistrust (b–2 years) Consistent experiences
Preoperational 2–7 years Egocentric Representation of objects and events by appearances	Personal Symbol and Design (2–4 years) Controlled scribbling, named scribbling	Beginning Language (2–4 years) Acquiring vocabulary, grammar, social speech	Function of print (2–4 years) Reads symbols in context Read pictures Beginning writing	Autonomy vs. Shame/Doubt (2–4 years) Independence, sensory exploration
	Preschematic (4–7 years) Generalized symbols recognizable to others Nonrepresentational	Language (4–7 years) Symbolic language Humor	Readers and Writers (5–8 years) Decode print Invented spelling Word identity	Initiative vs. Guilt (4–7 years) Constructive activities, own decisions
Concrete Operational (7–11 years) Logical, concrete thinkers. Can conserve, classify, seriate	Schematic/Realism (7–9 years) Representation of what he knows, not necessarily what he sees			Industry vs. Inferiority (7 years to puberty) Sense of duty, academic social competence

Figure 10–21 Stage Comparison of Cognitive and Creative Theorists.

- *Using fantasy to solve developmental problems*—Normal aspects of children's thinking are considered frivolous and even deceitful by adults.
- *Creativity*—Children use creative ideas to explain, defend, and problem solve, such as, "The dog must have ridden my bike to the corner and left it there."
- *Storytelling and song making*—Playing with words and music combines mental and creative abilities. Children need opportunities and encouragement to express themselves in the arts.

The child's creativity gives information about her cognitive development. The child does not go to bed one night in one stage and wake up tomorrow in another. It is a spiral moving slightly upward that keeps returning to previous stages to find reassurance, success, and comfort when new stages become too stressful. Kamii (1982) tells the story of the boy setting the table, who moved from one-to-one correspondence to counting out the tableware. When guests were expected, he was not able to mentally add the number of guests to the number in the family. He had to go back to one-to-one correspondence again.

Disequilibrium sometimes invokes a return to a previous stage or strategy. It is seen in the child who has had a traumatic event in her life return to thumb sucking, which brought so much comfort in a previous stage. In creative work, there is the return to the manipulation stage with the introduction of each new medium. The child uses sensory exploration of the materials, play without any purpose other than to get in touch with reality without pressure, before going on to actually represent thought.

@ it happened to me

A professor in the Art Department at a university was asked by his preschool daughter what he did at work. He replied with, "I teach adults how to draw and paint." She came back with, "You mean, they forget?"

Do you have an IT HAPPENED TO ME story about children's comments about art? I'd love to read it. Please send it to WeekbyWeek@thomsonlearning.com

GIFTEDNESS: CREATIVE AND COGNITIVE DEVELOPMENT BEYOND EXPECTED LEVELS. Many parents believe their child is gifted. The definition traditionally referred to an exceptionally high score on an intelligence test, but it has been broadened to include exceptional ability in other areas as well. In 1969, P.L. 91-230 contained a model program provision for gifted and talented children. Because of the limitations of standardized tests (see Chapter 8), many children were not identified as gifted because of the cultural bias of the tests, resulting in low numbers of minorities in gifted programs. Little federal funding has been allocated for gifted programs but much research has been done in trying to define and identify giftedness. Some have to do with **precocity**, early development in areas such as language, music, or mathematical ability. The Renzulli-Hartman scales (in Torrance, 2000, p. 356) are commonly used for assessing creativity in preschool children:

1. The child has unusually advanced vocabulary for age level.
2. The child possesses a large storehouse of information about a variety of topics.
3. The child has rapid insight into cause-effect relationships.
4. The child is a keen and alert observer; usually "sees more" or "gets more" out of a story, picture, film, sightseeing trip, and so on.
5. The child becomes absorbed and truly involved in certain topics or problems.
6. The child strives toward perfection or excellence and is self-critical.
7. The child is interested in many "adult" problems such as religion, politics, sex, race, and so on.
8. The child likes to organize and bring structure to things, people, and situations.
9. The child displays a great deal of curiosity about many things and an intense curiosity about something.
10. The child displays a keen sense of humor and sees humor in situations that may not appear humorous to others.

Divergent thinking is the ability to think of a wide range of possibilities. It is associated with giftedness, rather than **convergent thinking**, the ability to arrive at a single answer. Its identification and measurement at an early age is complicated and inaccurate but close observers of children may see signs of giftedness. Assessment of every child's learning level helps meet the child's needs through curriculum planning. This same reason applies to giftedness.

Using Self-Portraits to Know the Child

EXERCISE **Look at the self-portraits by children four to five years old (Figure 10–22 through Figure 10–25). Describe how very different they are in control, detail, and the mood they present.**

The child's drawings of humans evolve from the beginning circle with dots for eyes. The child is drawing what is known. The human face, with eyes as predominant feature, represents family and self, drawn by hands still developing control. Arms and legs later protrude from this head, and eventually more and more details appear as more "humanoid" drawings in the fourth year. As the child is closer to five, the neck separates the head and body, and limbs begin to take on more substance than just a line. Between five and six, the child usually can outline a drawing of the whole body in one stroke and begin

Figure 10–22

Figure 10–23

Figure 10–24

Figure 10–25

to proportion the height of adults and children more accurately. This is in a predictable sequence (Kellogg, 1970). Three-dimensional work follows a similar sequence. In knowing that sequence, just as in knowing all developmental stage milestones, it helps the observer to recognize change and to anticipate and recognize the next stage when it appears.

The self-portraits in Figures 10–22 through 10–25 were drawn by four-year-old boys. It would be presumptuous to interpret levels of development from one drawing. However, when the observer periodically collects children's self-portraits, along with the child's commentary about the work, the result is a more valid indication of cognitive and creative development.

Reggio Emilia and Children's Art

A discussion of children's creative development would not be complete without mentioning the child care centers and preschools in Reggio Emilia, Italy. They are the model of community and family collaboration and for the project approach to curriculum, but most of all, they represent the incredible level of creativity of which children are capable given such a carefully prepared environment and collaboration between children and adults. Thousands of visitors from all over the world have been enthralled with the visually sensual learning environment that stimulates children to use a vast array of art materials. The image of the child is one of capability and respect. Teachers consider every aspect of the environment as stimulus for learning, for forming mental images that will be called upon to organize and construct meaning. The environment of beauty and light is breathtaking as one enters spaces of reception that welcome families with antique pieces of furniture and cozy sitting areas. Light streams through every possible opening and is reflected in mirrors, shiny surfaces, and translucent panels.

Observation is the adult's most important role, and it is conveyed to the children as well. They are guided to closely observe the details of every physical part of the environment—from the smallest seed to the tracks of an animal in the mud to the patterns of clouds in the sky. The adult follows the children's interests and supports the graphic representation of what the child sees and explores. Documentation panels or booklets illustrate not just the finished product or outcome but the process itself; their only objective is to make the learning public. This kind of documentation records not just what the child knows or knows how to do, but what the child can do with various kinds of environmental support—the contexts, opportunities, and materials offered to the child (Krechevsky & Stork, 2000). Documenting processes as well as outcomes is research that has its application in evaluation and curriculum decisions. Those who have visited Reggio Emilia have changed forever their ideas about the teacher's role as curriculum planner, as well as their ideas about the capabilities of young children to represent their world. When teachers change their approach, the result is children's creative efforts surpassing long-held developmental expectations (Dighe, Calomiris, & Van Zutphen, 1998).

The Hundred Languages of Children (Edwards & Gandini, 1998) brings Reggio children's projects to the world both in book and in exhibit form. Reggio advocates point out, however, that their approach is not about art but using art and other work samples as products of "children's emotional concerns, social relations, and creative and intellectual pursuits as they occur within the context of collaborative problem solving" (New, 1997). The beauty and richness of the colors, the complete absorption of the children in their work, and the planning of each project piques the curiosity of the viewer.

There is much more to the Reggio approach than simply documenting children's work. The approach begins with the image of the child as having legitimate rights, and as an active constructor of knowledge through investigation as a social endeavor. The teacher is not the fount of knowledge but a collaborator, co-learner, guide, facilitator, and researcher. Curriculum develops from the real interests of the children, who decide how to approach learning, then represent what they have learned in a meaningful way (Hewett, 2001). Trust is an important factor in this philosophy, as Linn (2001) points out. First, educators trust children's initiative and intelligence and let them experience things through trial and error, and even allow them to fail. Parents of Reggio children trust the educators without being bound to the necessity of test scores to show that their children are learning. Linn also reminds us that learning is culturally bound and that the lesson from Reggio is not to find ways to duplicate it but to "raise awareness about the connection between culture and educational practice in the United States."

After visiting Reggio Emilia, Carol Seefeldt (1995) describes the Reggio philosophy as one that

@ **it happened to me**

Instinct over Knowledge

I had just discussed the responses to children's art with my college class. The next week, a mother with a newborn came to class to demonstrate the reflexes that were still present. She also brought her preschooler with paper and markers to occupy her while we watched her baby brother. As the demonstration drew to a close, I went over to the big sister and looked at her drawing. Out of my mouth came, "What is it?" The whole class gasped then laughed at my embarrassment at doing what I said not to do. It showed how ingrained those old habits are and how easily the instinctive comments slip out from among the learned behaviors. It takes practice and a concentrated effort!

Do you have an IT HAPPENED TO ME story about children's creativity? I'd love to hear it. Please send it to me at WeekbyWeek@thomsonlearning.com

considers creativity a serious work guided by teachers who

- understand cognitive theories of art.
- motivate children to produce art.
- carefully select teaching strategies. (p. 39)

Assessing Creative Program Goals

When work is not linked to standards and formally assessed, it is seen as less valuable to the educational process and becomes endangered when resources are scarce. It is important for schools and programs to include creativity in goals and to assess creativity systematically as a contribution to cognitive development. Here are some of those efforts.

Dance, Music, Theater, Visual Arts: What Every Young American Should Know and Be Able to Do in the Arts: National Standards for Arts Education (Consortium of National Arts Education Associations, 1994) outlines knowledge and skills children must have to fulfill their personal potential, to become productive and competitive workers in a global economy, and to take their place as adult citizens. In the Goals 2000: Educate America Act, the arts are listed as a core academic subject along with English, mathematics, history, science, and foreign language. These are standards for K–12; they are left to individual schools to implement.

Developmentally Appropriate Practice in Early Childhood Programs (Bredekamp & Copple, 1997) recommends that "children have daily opportunities for aesthetic expression and appreciation through art and music," that they "experiment and enjoy various forms of dramatic play, music, and dance," and that "a variety of art media such as markers, crayons, paints, and clay are available for creative expression and representation of ideas and feelings" (p. 132).

The *NAEYC Early Childhood Program Standards and Accreditation Criteria* (2005) self-study asks programs to rate their opportunities for creative expression and appreciation for the arts.

Koster, in *Growing Artists* (2005), suggests the following for the space designated for art:

- *Layout*—Art activities should be in an area where the activities of the room are visible and influence the artist.
- *Adequate space*—Children need space to spread out and work comfortably.
- *Traffic patterns*—Flexible areas allow more children to explore, both at tables and on the floor.
- *Water requirements*—Location near the water source or movable pans of water for prewashing minimizes messes.
- *Separate from food areas*—Art and cooking activities must be kept separate using separate tables and trays, or at least covers, for surfaces for one or the other, such as a tablecloth for eating or old shower curtain for art (pp. 106–108).

EXERCISE Rate your classroom creative environment according to the preceding criteria.

Unmet Partially Met Fully met

On a separate sheet of paper, write an action plan to improve aspects of the environment to allow for more creative expression.

HELPING ALL CHILDREN WITH CREATIVITY

Creative work is both expressive and receptive. It requires no spoken language to create or enjoy someone else's creation. Even with limitations of language barriers or physical, cognitive, or psychological impairments, creative arts can be a form of two-way communication.

Cultural Diversity

Art is a universal language. The child may not speak a common language with the rest of the people in the group or share a common culture, but creative work can be a vehicle for becoming absorbed in an activity without pressure to speak or conform. Giving children creative materials with a minimum of direction is appropriate for this population and can be a comforting and successful activity in which to engage these children. It also gives them a way to express feelings and ideas nonverbally.

Introducing children to the artists and crafts of various cultures brings a global awareness to the environment and the curriculum. Banks (2001) suggests three ways that this can be accomplished:

- *contributions*—introduction to music and visual artists from diverse cultures

- *additive*—adding projects to the curriculum at the children's developmental level that provide experiences in music and movement and the visual arts using varied materials such as natural clay, coloring agents such as vegetables and plants, and items collected from the natural environment
- *transformation*—looking not just at the creations and creators of European artists but those from Africa, Native America, and Asia, connecting with other aspects of the curriculum such as literature, history, and social studies to see the context in which the works were produced

Ability Diversity

Art plans that are open-ended, designed to explore the medium, can be adapted to meet the needs of special abilities populations. Children with sight or hearing impairments can find great success in manipulating creative materials. Adaptive devices, such as bicycle grips on paintbrush handles, textured finger paint, and Play Doh with scent from powdered, nonsweetened drink mixes, add multisensory aspects to art media. The manipulation of art materials is also soothing and sustaining for children with attention disorders.

Whatever the cognitive or physical functioning level of the child, art plans can be implemented and adapted to the child's capability to encourage creativity and minimize frustration. Creative media are essential parts of every early childhood program. Art involves every developmental area and easily meets the needs of every child, despite their situation. It is a natural place to focus assessment in a nonintrusive way.

HELPING PROFESSIONALS FOR CREATIVE ARTS

Programs or individual teachers who want to enrich the creative environment can enlist the assistance of

art educators—teachers who specialize in the incorporation of the arts into the curriculum

Individual children may be assisted in resolving emotional conflicts or behavior disorders by specialists who use the arts as therapy, such as

art therapist—credentialed professional who helps increase self-understanding and emotional release through art media

music therapist—certified professional who uses music in treatment goals for people with handicaps for physical and mental health

OTHER METHODS

Other Methods to Record Creativity

Anecdotal/Running Records—narratives about a child's approach to work

Checklists/Rating Scales—Work Samples Checklist or the creative portion of a developmental checklist

Conversations and Interviews—recording a child's discussions about work produced

Time Sample—measure the amount of time a child spends on a certain task

Media—use photographs, video or audio recording to document the process or the work produced

STANDARDS

Selected examples of standards regarding young children and creativity:

Preschool Caregivers in Center-Based Programs: Child Development Associate Competencies, Functional Area 7: Creative (Council for Professional Recognition 1996)

Candidate provides opportunities that stimulate children to play with sound, rhythm, language, materials, space and ideas in individual ways and to express their creative abilities.

Head Start Child Outcomes (U.S. Department of Health and Human Services [2003])

Domain 5: Creative Arts

Art

Indicator 1: Gains ability in using different art media and materials in a variety of ways for creative expression and representation.

Indicator 2: Progresses in abilities to create drawings, paintings, models, and other art creations that are more detailed, creative, or realistic.

Indicator 3: Develops growing abilities to play, work independently, and demonstrate care and persistence in a variety of art projects

Indicator 4: Begins to understand and share opinions about artistic products and experiences.

TOPICS IN OBSERVATION

Responding to Children's Work

While observing children working, whether it is just enjoyably watching or observing for a purpose, the adult is often called upon to comment on a child's work. The child may ask, "How is it?" or "Do you like it?" A ready answer is necessary, one that agrees with personal style, program goals, and theoretical philosophy. The following are presented for consideration and practice so that the teacher's repertoire of comments is consistent with beliefs. Different common responses are listed here, along with commentary and suggestions for improvement.

Complimentary

The child may ask or expect a reaction from the adult. A natural response is a generalized, polite praise such as "Oh, lovely," "Very nice," or "Beautiful." The problem with this approach is that they are empty words with no specific reaction. The child's purpose may not have been for it to be "nice" or "lovely." It may be a frightening spider or a bad dream. The adult's comment is a casual remark lacking sincerity. It becomes a denial of the purpose of the artist. It may have been for exploration and practice, not beauty.

> *Instead:* "You worked a really long time at that," "Look how much red you used," or "You really thought about that."

Judgmental

"Great!" "That's wonderful."

Again, these are empty words that may not be truthful or reflect what the child is trying to portray. It is evaluative from the viewer's opinion. It is more important for the viewer to determine the child's opinion of the work or the inspiration behind it. When we consider that young children are egocentric, they only imagine that the viewer will see it just as they do.

> *Instead:* "What do you like about it?" or "Can you tell me how you did it? What part did you do first?"

Valuing

The adult expresses her personal opinion, "I love it." The goal is to help the child find self-satisfaction as the measuring stick of creative work. An outsider's evaluation is not necessary nor advisable. What the *adult* sees or thinks is not important. How the *child* feels or thinks about it is the important point.

> *Instead:* "What do you like about it?"

Questioning

When the adult asks, "What is it?" or "What's this supposed to be?" a loud message is conveyed: "You were supposed to make something I could recognize. I can't see it, so you are not doing it right." The adult should know that young children up to age six and seven are nonrepresentational in their art. They may have a mental image of what they want to draw, but their physical abilities for control of the medium and cognitive development concerning perception and reality are still in the formative stages.

> *Instead:* "Would you like to tell me about it?"

(continued)

TOPICS IN OBSERVATION *(continued)*

Note that with this alternative, the child still has the option of saying "No," an option not given by the more commanding "Tell me about it."

Probing

When the questioning approach asks the significance of every piece of work, it may be overused; it is also probing. From what is known about children's art, much of it is for exploration of the medium. The child is getting the feel of the fingerpaint, or practicing rolling snakes and balls of clay, or watching the glue flow out as the bottle is squeezed.

Instead: Just observe. Watch for indications of what the child is getting from the experience. A simple "Hmmmm" suggests interest, invites the child to comment if she chooses.

Correcting

Of course, early childhood educators should know that children's drawings are unrealistic, so it is inappropriate to tell a child, "Grass isn't orange. Here's a green crayon for grass."

Instead: Allow the child to use materials in any way they wish as long as it is safe for themselves and the environment. Give redirection reminders, such as, "We paint on the paper, not on the wall," or "When you walk around with the brush, you are dripping paint all over. If you want to look at Lizzy's side of the easel, place the brush in the container first."

Psychoanalyzing

Much study has been done on the emotional and psychological meaning of children's creative work. It makes fascinating reading, but it is not for amateurs. Deep psychological significance should not be placed on children's art. It is inappropriate for people without training to make diagnoses about the child's emotional state. Some have said, "She uses black all over the page. She must be depressed." The content of children's creative work and their choice of color is not realistic. A teacher mistakenly commented on the red paint the child used and thought, "He told me this was all the blood from the baby. He must wish his new baby brother was dead. Maybe he's planning to stab him." Forming conclusions about the child's inner mind from one drawing is just as unfair and dangerous as evaluating the whole child from one test.

Instead: Note curious, strange, bizarre creations or comments from the child on a notepad for your own use. If they are repeated or accompanied by behavioral indicators, follow it up. If you are alarmed, talk to your supervisor, then possibly the family, to search for further clarification or evaluation. Sometimes children's art *can be* their way of expressing fears or traumatic incidents that cannot be verbalized.

Modeling

This is an acceptable teaching technique in every other area of early childhood practice *except* art. Modeling in the sense of making a pattern for a child to follow is not good professional practice. Planned art "projects" sometimes present materials for the child to construct the adult's idea of a caterpillar, clown face, or dinosaur. These thwart the whole purpose and theory of children's creative

TOPICS IN OBSERVATION *(continued)*

development and its benefits. Many teachers say, "Well, I'm just providing the materials for the clown face, they can do it any way they want." The child knows the adult's expectation but may not have the experience with a clown's face or the desire to make one.

Instead: Provide the child with rich experiences in the world around him. Provide creative materials that the child can use himself and allow the child to create whatever he chooses from those experiences.

Whereas modeling a pattern for the art itself is not useful, there are some things that can be modeled: Model an accepting attitude to children's explorations. Model an interest in texture, design, and color, using vocabulary words about them such as *rough, smooth, ridges, pattern, balance, horizontal, vertical, swirls,* and *border* and color names like *mauve, lavender, chartreuse*. This makes association between the visual image and the word. Young children love big words. Model processes of using materials by sitting at the clay table and throwing clay to soften it, rolling balls and snakes and pinching pots. This modeling is not direct instruction but scaffolding manipulation techniques that children will adopt when they are ready.

Describing

This is the best *Instead* of the preceding approaches. Every area of development that is seen through creative work can be described (not all at once): physical movement, control of the tools, use of the space, self-help skills in working on the project, social interactions in the art or in the process, control or expression of emotions, vocabulary to describe the product, writing associated with the creations, math and science concepts, self-identity revealed through the art, and interactions with the group and adults through the process.

"You used a lot of red today." (Making the association between the visual color and the word *red.*)

"You covered the whole page with paint. That took a lot of concentration." (Commenting on space and attention span.)

"You made a lot of blue vertical lines and yellow horizontal lines. It made a design that's sometimes called plaid. Look at this. There's the color green where they come together. I don't see any green paint out today. I wonder how that happened?" (Using vocabulary of design, pointing out colors, helping the child observe cause and effect and wonder. If he does not understand it this time, he might the next time. The association has been made and the disequilibrium has been pointed out. The child will accommodate this new knowledge into color concepts.)

EXERCISE **Go back to Figures 10–11 through 10–16, which you may recall were the drawings in the exercise on the stages of art, and practice your comments to the artist who asks, "How do you like it?"**

KEY TERMS

convergent thinking
creativity
divergent thinking
mandala
media/medium
nonrepresentational
precocity
preschematic
schema
schematic
scribbling
tadpole man
Work Samples

Go to the Bind-in-Book CD for:

Class List Log form
Plan Week 10 Part A, Directions for collecting Creative Work Samples on all children, including What to Do with It, Portfolio Overview Example, Sharing with Child and Family, Actions—Read a Book, In the Environment, In the Curriculum, In the Newsletter
Plan Week 10 Part B, Directions for Anecdotal Recording in Creativity for Group A
Plan Week 10 Part C, Reflective Journal

REFERENCES

Accreditation Criteria and Procedures. (1998). Washington, DC: National Association for the Education of Young Children.

Banks, J. A. (2001). *Cultural diversity and education: Foundations. curriculum and teaching.* Boston: Allyn & Bacon.

Bredekamp, S., & Copple, C. (Ed.). (1997). *Developmentally appropriate practice in early childhood programs.* Washington, DC: National Association for the Education of Young Children.

Council for Early Childhood Professional Recognition. (1996). *Preschool caregivers in center-based programs: The child development associate assessment system and competency standards.* Washington, DC: author.

Csikszentmihalyi, M. (1997). *Creativity: Flow and the psychology of discovery and invention.* New York: Harper Collins.

Day, B. (1994). *Early childhood education: Developmental/experiential teaching and learning* (4th ed.). New York: Merrill, an imprint of Macmillan College Publishing Company.

Dighe, J., Calomiris, Z., & Van Zutphen, C. (1998). Nurturing the language of art in children. *Young Children, 53* (1), 4–9.

Edwards, C., & Gandini, L. (Eds.). (1998). *The hundred languages of children: The Reggio Emilia approach: Advanced reflections* (2nd ed.). Greenwich, CT: Ablex Publishing.

Edwards, C. P., & Willis, L. M. (2000). Integrating visual and verbal literacies in the early childhood classroom. *Early Childhood Educational Journal, 27* (4), 259–265.

Erikson, E. H. (1950). *Childhood and society.* New York: Norton.

Fein, S. (1993). *First drawings: Genesis of visual thinking.* Pleasant Hill, CA: Exelrod Press.

Flavell, J. H. (1963). *The developmental psychology of Jean Piaget.* New York: Van Nostrand.

Gardner, H. (1980). *Artful scribbles: The significance of children's drawings.* New York: Basic Books.

Genishi, C. (1993). Art, Portfolios, and assessment. *Early Childhood Today, 8* (2), 67.

Goodenough, F. (1926). *Children's drawings as measures of intellectual maturity.* New York: Harcourt Brace Jovanovich.

Hewett, V. M. (2001). Examining the Reggio Emilia approach to early childhood education. *Early Childhood Education Journal, 29* (2), 95–100.

Hirsch, E. S. (1996). *The block book* (3rd ed.). Washington, DC: National Association for the Education of Young Children.

Jones, J, Courtne, R. (2002). Documenting early science learning. *Young children,* 57 (5), September 2002.

Kamii, C. (1982). *Number in preschool and kindergarten.* Washington, DC: National Association for the Education of Young Children.

Kellogg, R. (1970). *Analyzing children's art.* Palo Alto, CA: National Press Books.

Koster, J. (2005). *Growing artists: Teaching art to young children* (3rd ed.). Clifton Park, NY: Thomson Delmar Learning.

Krechevsky, M., & Stork, J. (2000). Challenging educational assumptions: Lessons from an Italian-American collaboration. *Cambridge Journal of Education, 30* (1), 57–75.

Linn, M. I. (2001). An American educator reflects on the meaning of the Reggio experience. *Phi Delta Kappan, 83* (4), 332–335.

Lowenfeld, V., & Brittain, W. L. (1987). *Creative and mental growth* (8th ed.). New York: Macmillan Publishing Co., Inc.

McAfee, O., & Leong, D. (2002). *Assessing and guiding young children's development and learning.* Boston: Allyn and Bacon.

NAEYC Early Childhood Program Standards and Accreditation Criteria. (2005). Washington, DC: Author.

New, R. (1997). New steps in teaching "The Reggio way." In J. Hendricks (Ed.), *First steps toward teaching the Reggio way.* Upper Saddle River, NJ: Prentice Hall.

Schirrmacher, R. (2006). *Art and creative development for young children* (5th ed.). Clifton Park, NY: Thomson Delmar Learning.

Seefeldt, C. (1995). Art: A serious work. *Young Children, 50* (3), 39.

Torrance, E. P. (2000). Preschool creativity. In B. A. Bracken (Ed.), *The psychoeducational assessment of preschool children* (3rd ed.). Boston: Allyn and Bacon.

U.S. Department of Health and Human Services, Administration for Children and Families. (2003). *The Head Start child outcomes framework.* Washington, DC: author.

Wellhousen, K., & Kieff, J. (2001). *A constructivist approach to block play in early childhood.* Clifton Park, NY: Delmar Thomson Learning.

RESOURCES

Bronson, M. (1995). *The right stuff for children birth to age 8*. Washington, DC: National Association for the Education of Young Children.

Church, E. B., & Miller, K. (1990). *Learning through play: Blocks, a practical guide for teaching young children.* New York: Scholastic, Inc.

Edwards, C., & Gandini, L. (Eds.). (1998). *The hundred languages of children: The Reggio Emilia approach: Advanced reflections* (2nd ed.). Greenwich, CT: Ablex Publishing.

Kellogg, R. (1970). *Analyzing children's art.* Palo Alto, CA: National Press Books.

Koster, J. (2005). *Growing artists: Teaching art to young children* (3rd ed.). Clifton Park, NY: Thomson Delmar Learning.

Lowenfeld, V., & Brittain, W. L. (1987). *Creative and mental growth.* New York: Macmillan Publishing Co., Inc.

CHAPTER 11

Using Technology for Documentation of Sociodramatic Play

IN THIS CHAPTER

USING TECHNOLOGY FOR DOCUMENTATION

Imagine the end of the day. A mother comes to pick up her child at the child care center. She sits for a few minutes with a cup of coffee and puts on virtual reality glasses. Through them, she views her child in selected videotaped segments of the day's activities. The father sitting next to her is doing the same, watching his own child in a virtual reality recording. Each child has been videotaped simultaneously, cued to their movements by the "school button" they put on each day as they arrive. The teacher has ended the day's taped segment with a reminder for an e-mail response to the family survey. Other family members have watched portions of the day from home or their workplace through a classroom video connected via the Internet. Parenting workshop choices are reviewed for reception on their television monitors in the next month. They are also reminded to pay the balance of their tuition bill by electronic bank transfer.

Far out? All of this **technology** exists. Can we afford it? Do we agree with it? Do we want it? These are questions many teachers and administrators will be answering soon.

Using technical or electronic media is not an innovation in classrooms. Tape recorders, cameras, and overhead slide and filmstrip projectors have been used for years. However, electronic and digital technologies have increased the range and quality of products, as well as ease of equipment use.

Lower costs have made electronic media a viable option for documentation in the classroom. Electronic media can capture details that not even the most fluent writer can convey. Tone of voice, nuances of movement, and a visual image all make an incident as alive for the viewer as it was for the original observer. There are legal and ethical considerations that are discussed in the Topics in Observation section of this chapter. A sample release is included in the Plan section.

This recording method section presents the possibilities that are available, although many are out of the question for most programs today. In just the right situation, in the future, however, they may be more realistic options. A few years ago, who would have dreamed that computers would replace typewriters? Who knows what the future holds? Negroponte opens his book *Being Digital* (1995), saying, "Computing is not about computers any more. It is about living."

Types of Technological Media for Observing and Recording

There are many electronic recording devices. With the arrival of computerization, the options and adaptations are wide. Each has its usefulness along with disadvantages. The early childhood practitioner's knowledge, skills, experience, and creativity may extend far beyond direct interactions with children, into the world of multimedia.

AUDIO RECORDING. Recording voices is especially useful for conversations to gather speech and language samples (see Chapter 6). "Transcribing and reviewing these conversations at a later date will provide insights regarding children's learning, thinking, and social skills" (Blagojevic & Garthwait, 2001). Inexpensive tape recorders are available at any electronics supply store. Children's tape recorders make lower-quality recordings but allow the children to record themselves or each other. These can be used as dramatic play props or on project work. Children can record and play back sounds, voices, and music.

Voice-activated **audio recorders** are also available. These can be placed in a selected location where conversations from sociodramatic play, for example, are taking place. The nonintrusive quality is the advantage of this feature, because the teacher does not need to walk over and turn it on. Natural, clear recordings are preserved and may be transcribed and analyzed to assess and evaluate social play level. Problem-solving techniques, learning styles, dramatic play roles, and how the child sustains the role over time can be evaluated.

Parabolic or shotgun microphones (the type sports broadcasts use to catch the coach's instructions and the players' grunts) can be aimed to pick up sound across the room. They can focus on a small, low conversation, screening out all the background noise that is usually going on in an early childhood classroom. They are effective for catching a conversation at the Play Doh table about who has more Play Doh, who made the long snake, or who made all the little balls. Recordings at the sand table might document Caroline's explanation of how she knows which sand is hers and which belongs to Debbie. The self-talk Nicholas uses as he sets the table for snack is captured. His math skills are assessed as he puts out all of the napkins, saying, "Here's one for this chair, one for this chair, one for this chair. Hey, where's the chair for this napkin?"

The advantage of unobtrusiveness can also be a disadvantage. Some regard recording without the subject's approval or knowledge as an invasion of privacy. (See Topics in Observation in this chapter.) Another disadvantage is the cost: approximately $200 to $1,000 and up. It also takes some training to become proficient in its operation. This method would be ideal for the classroom with a separate observation booth. Often the sound quality in a teaching lab observation booth is so poor that the value of the audible observation is lost. Remote control of the microphone would help overcome this problem.

Computer microphones with speech-to-text programs can turn children's words into print to add dialogue to their artwork. They can also help children in describing their thinking process or in problem solving. Text-to-speech software can turn children's printed words into audio so they can hear their written stories read back to them.

What to Do with It. Audio recordings of an individual child are kept in the child's Portfolio. They can be analyzed for speech and language development. Dictated stories or reading abilities, or informal or structured interviews, can be filed there. These preserve an audible record of the child's thinking revealed through language.

VIDEO. Many children are accustomed to being photographed with a **video recorder** today. Cameras are becoming more affordable, and they are smaller, easier to use, and efficient in almost any kind of light and setting. Zoom capabilities allow recording from a distance. Combined with a parabolic microphone, the video and audio can be remotely controlled from across the room. Mounting a camera on the wall, or in a central location in the room, can record all the events happening in one area. The block area could be recorded on one day, and the dramatic play area on another. Children's actions are more natural when captured by a wall-mounted camera than if a person is manually pointing the camera at them. If a videographer is used, it is important for the children to become familiar with the process and the person taking pictures. With familiarity, their self-consciousness decreases. A camera could be present, or have a camera person taking blank pictures, days before the actual "shoot," to allow the children to become accustomed to being videotaped. Cameras have point-and-shoot controls, optional date and time, freeze and fast frames, and a bookmark to find the end. The tape can be viewed immediately on a television monitor through the camera. They have a taping capability of 30 minutes to 4 hours.

Digital video cameras record images and sounds in digital form on a videocassette. The recorded material can then be stored or downloaded to a computer. Most video cameras have a display screen as well, so the event can be viewed on the small screen immediately after it occurs for a playback discussion. Digital photography allows computer editing to zoom in or enlarge portions of the photo. Video printers, which can print up to 30 frames per minute, make it possible to capture small changes in action. These can be used for documentation panels of projects, as discussed in Chapter 10 (Trepanier-Street, Hong, & Bauer, 2001).

Lavalieres (electronic signal devices) can be worn that automatically turn the camera to aim at the subject. These are used in distance learning studios by professors who wander around the room. Extremely small cameras, the size of a pencil, can diminish the awareness of being taped. A teacher could wear one behind his ear or in a pocket. Then he can walk around the room or sit "watching" the children play while he is actually videotaping. Videotaping selected areas could also be done by remote from a control or observation room.

Several companies have combined video and e-mail technologies to provide families a view of their child's day at school. Involved families may want to know more about their child's activities, or concerned families may see this as a protection device. Whatever the motivation, technology is providing the vehicle for electronic observation in the classroom. State-of-the-art child care facilities are outfitted with video cameras in each classroom so that the director has instant access to the day's events and gives some assurance that appropriate actions are taken toward the children there. Surveillance cameras such as baby monitors can enable persons outside the room to view what happening there; however, a word of caution: *they should NEVER be used in place of direct supervision.* Recording capability is useful for the teacher to analyze children's or one's own actions for further study.

Hours and hours of tape are unmanageable. There may be segments that are profound, but much of the taping may yield nothing usable for the purpose of evaluation. Editing the tape can be done by re-taping segments from one recorder to another. This is time-consuming, and the tape is then second-generation quality. Many public or technical schools have videotape editing machines that may be available to perform this function. The digitizing of video converts the analogue video to digital data that computers can read. (Of course, using a digital video camera eliminates the need to convert the video in the first place.) Editing digital video on a computer using basic video editing software is simple, much the same way paragraphs of text are moved with a computer. They also can be manipulated visually and enhanced, and parts can be erased. Captions and background music can be added to make a very professional production with a minimum of technical training. Nonlinear editing allows changes in sequence of segments or individual images. Large amounts of tape can be stored on one compact disc (CD-ROM), useful when cataloging large amounts of information in the computer's memory for sorting, filing, and rearranging. This sophisticated and expensive equipment may be available through the school's affiliations in the community. Families are frequently resources for technical work.

Think About It . . .

Is Video Taping an Invasion of the Child's Privacy?

By Patricia Amanna, Ed.D.

Director, The Children's Center at Purchase College, Purchase, NY

I think media and technology can impose an intrusion upon the "private school life" of a child. School is a place where children get the opportunity to see how they fit into the larger world apart from the family. As they develop, they find out about themselves through their interactions with others. Most importantly, they can and should try many different roles in their exploration. In today's world, we often talk about the "rights" of individuals as though we include children in that framework. Many of us would feel horrified and outraged if we were subjected to the invasion of media and technology into our private and professional lives. If our employers decided to video tape us working or look at us doing our jobs using cameras and the Internet, we would be disturbed, to say the least. Yet, we are using video taping in schools without any regard for the individual child, as long as the parents give permission. Moreover, we often fail to set clear guidelines regarding the usage, access, and storage of these video tapes. Even more alarming is our new use of the Internet to peer into the world of the child in the school setting.

This technological ability brings with it questions regarding its use. Those that come to mind are: Do we have a right to unlimited access to a human being? What good does this information really do anyone or society at large? What damage might it cause in relationships between children and "trusted" adults in their lives? How do we make sure that these data are not used against children?

There are many positive applications of media and technology in the schools, but we must be sure we are not teaching children that the technology ability gives us a right to do it. Otherwise the children of today will be the adults of tomorrow who think they have the right to look in on us electronically because they can. Early childhood professionals should apply the basic principles of the NAEYC Ethical Code of Conduct when using media and technology in their classrooms.

@ it happened to me

Hands in Pants

During a time of extensive videotaping in my preschool classroom by professional videographers, every time one boy was seen on tape, his hand was in his pants. We were accustomed to it, taking into consideration his shyness and hesitancy in social circumstances, especially with unfamiliar people in the room. When his mother viewed the tape for permission to release it for publication, however, she was not pleased. She knew that he did that when he was uncomfortable but did not want the tape, a permanent record, to portray him this way. We discussed his emotional insecurity and, of course, edited him out of the tape at her request. We did some taping of our own later in the school year. We did not see this behavior repeated, so we were able to provide her with some footage of his days at school about which she (and he, someday) could feel more comfortable.

Do you have an IT HAPPENED TO ME story about photographing or video recording children? I'd love to read it. Send it to WeekbyWeek@thomsonlearning.com

Recording for Evaluation versus Surveillance. School is a transitional place from home and the outside world. It is a place where children and adults alike should feel comfortable. Surveillance cameras do not contribute to that atmosphere; they detract from the trust of staff and the privacy or separation of the child's school life from their home life. There may be a place for such technology, but its purpose should be carefully scrutinized and the rights of all protected.

What to Do with It. A videotape is a replay of live action. The episode can be viewed repeatedly, hearing and seeing what took place. Segments can be closely examined for relevance to developmental assessment. An audio commentary can be added for families, other teachers, or referral agents. The accompanying narrative can point out important details: "Watch the way he is picking up that napkin. Watch the movement of the thumb. Let's go back and slow it down. We can stop it right here." Other valuable uses of video recorders in the classroom follow:

- *Historic record*—A videotape can be a memento of a special occasion for the whole class. Later viewing of important events, such as the first day, a special visitor, or a field trip—or just a normal day—serve as enjoyable memories. Events can take on added importance in the future. Looking at the tape, children can see how much they have grown.
- *Replay for discussion with the children*—A play segment could be taped, shown to the children involved, and discussed: "What happened here? When Audrey did this, see what happened? What could she have done instead?" The tape is then used for problem solving and instruction, more real than any puppet play or discussion with no visual connection.
- *Video field trip*—A teacher was going on a trip, so she taped it from the child's viewpoint, as if the child were along with her. She pointed out, "Watch out for that" and "Look over

there, see that." It was very effective when accompanied by her artifacts and books. Video can be a teaching tool.

- *Teacher observation practice*—Teachers can watch a selected segment and practice recording methods such as Anecdotal and Running Recordings, Frequency Counts, Checklists, and Rating Scales. Then the teachers can compare ratings (interrater reliability) to see if they are interpreting the behavior in relatively the same way. This helps them see deficiencies in the system of recording or finding biases that were not realized before. This would make an excellent staff training for improving teachers' professional practice and reviewing child development principles.
- *Reevaluation and referral*—A video recording, authorized with a written release by the family, can be shown to helping professionals for their interpretation or a resource person for an evaluation. It shows the child in a natural setting, capturing usual behavior.
- *Research*—Analyzing videotape can compare small bits of data for research. Ethical principles of voluntary, informed consent are necessary. Family signatures are required after they have been informed of the nature of the research and the techniques to be used. This must be in language they can understand. It is the investigator's responsibility to carefully evaluate the ethical acceptability of the study regarding the "subject at risk" (*American Psychological Association*, 1990, pp. 390–394).
- *Teacher self-evaluation and reflection*—The tape can be used by the teacher to monitor and receive reactions to teaching practices or for personal reflection. The teacher may be unaware of habits revealed on videotapes. The tape may be used to self-evaluate intervention strategies, play involvement, or language usage.

Confidentiality Guidelines. The APA Ethical Principles of Psychologists and Code of Conduct (American Psychological Association, 2002) offers some good advice.

- *Obtain **informed consent***—This must be given (and understood) by the individual, or family consent must be given for minors.
- *Maintain confidentiality*—Take reasonable precautions to protect information storage.
- *Obtain prior permission*—Explicit permission is required for voice or image recording, unless the recordings are naturalistic observations in public places and it is not anticipated that the recording will be used in a manner that could cause personal identification or harm.

EXERCISE Record a segment of your classroom if you work with children, or normal routines of your day. Listen and analyze what the recording reveals about yourself.

PHOTOGRAPHY. Ah, at last something more familiar. Point and shoot. Quality photographs have become much easier to take with automatic focusing, built-in flash, and zoom capabilities. The quality of pictures is *almost* foolproof. Most children are accustomed to being photographed, so photos become a natural documentation of play. That is only true if it is done often throughout the year. This can be expensive, but there are ways to reduce the cost. Buying film in bulk makes it the least expensive part of the operation. Developing has become much less expensive, with many places offering discounts for nonprofit organizations. Check with the developer for what are known as contact sheets. These are small, postage-sized prints, all on one page. When looking for "just the right shot," this allows many, many pictures to be taken and only the selected ones to be printed.

Digital photography is even less expensive than using and developing film. There are few expenses other than the cost of the camera. Photos can be stored and transferred electronically on CD-ROMs that are very inexpensive and can hold up to 43,500 still images. The photos can be made into individual or class photo albums, or into slide presentations for a family night. Photos can be printed out on the printer, copied, and distributed. They can be arranged into a desired order, perhaps to show the step-by-step progression of a project. They can be used to make a book for the children to keep and revisit the memory. These images can be incorporated into the curriculum for a sequencing activity, showing the steps or stages from beginning to end. Printing photos on regular paper is much less expensive than making photo prints, and the size of the print can be varied for the purpose, from postage stamp–size to poster size. Some digital cameras even have the capability of taking small segments of video as well.

What to Do with It. Many teachers use a photo album in the classroom as a pre-reading experience, inspiring children to recall details of past events. It helps children get better acquainted with class members. The teacher sends home a school album with a different child each week. In this way, the family can see the other children in the class and some events that have taken place. Conversations about school now have a focus, and the family feels more of a connection to the school. A Polaroid educational program, "Presenting Bright Ideas for Child Development" (Herr & Libby, 2004), gives many other activity ideas for using photographs in the classroom.

Hosington (2002) suggests using photographs to support children's science inquiry by helping children analyze and synthesize data, revisit and extend their investigations, reflect on previous experiences, and articulate their strategies for problem solving (pp. 27–29).

Photographs can be added to the child's Portfolio to illustrate comments about areas of development. They add visual information to Anecdotal Records. They can also be used themselves as the main observation method, with notes explaining the photograph. For example, what area of development might the photograph in Figure 11–1 document?

Photographs can be used during the year as vehicles to help the child remember and talk about specific incidents. The visual image is a springboard for a description of the event and the feelings surrounding it. The child's narrative could also be taped or dictated, adding a literacy dimension to the experience.

Photographs taken the first week of school of each child can be used in an activity for matching or a concentration game (double prints). This is a personal and unique way for children to get to know each other. Children can dictate captions for photographs taken in the classroom or during special events, adding them to the class album or making a book of their own. Photographs are self-esteem boosters.

Photographs taken throughout the school year are excellent mementos to give the children at the end of the year. They are a lasting reminder of that school year. Photographs taken of the children could be used in an album, a bulletin board, or placed in the Portfolio. At the end of the year, they should be distributed to the children. If the teacher or school is retaining any photographs, a special release form should be signed so the family is aware of that fact and acknowledges consent.

Figure 11–1 What do you see in this photograph?

@ it happened to me

The Gloved Hand

During the days of the taping, our hatched chickens were getting bigger and so were allowed some freedom within a circle of children. It made wonderful footage, but one got out. Not being an animal person, I had to put on work gloves to pick up the chickens. In one short clip of the tape, a black gloved hand appears to scoop up a wandering chicken. Only I know (and now you) the story behind the glove.

Do you have an IT HAPPENED TO ME story about photographing or video recording children? I'd love to read it. Send it to WeekbyWeek@thomsonlearning.com

COMPUTERS AND SCANNERS. As mentioned before, computers can store vast amounts of documentation data, both text and visual, without taking up closet or file cabinet storage space. Data is easily manipulated into various formats for both individual Portfolios and whole group documentation. Handheld computers can easily capture data on-the-spot with some of the forms and Checklists mentioned in earlier chapters programmed into the hand-held computer. Information is later downloaded into the regular computer and stored there or on a CD-ROM. Scanners can take photographs and drawings and transform them into digital files, easily stored and shared. The child's work can be shared with families via e-mail or CD-ROM.

Media as Documentation for Other Areas of Development

Audio recording and videotaping or photography can be used to record and document any area of development. Arrivals and separations can give poignant

it happened to me

Do You Want to Be Pink?

One of the highlights of my days in the classroom was an intergenerational project in which one class of four-year-olds made weekly visits to a nearby nursing home. There are a million stories connected with this project, but my favorite is about Ethel. She was blind and had David for a little friend. He showed empathy that is supposed to be beyond his Preoperational stage.

One spring day we were making drip-dot paintings, so he helped her by placing the paintbrush in her hand and shaking it to make the drips. She got paint on her hand so he asked me for a tissue to wipe it off. As he was wiping, she asked, "What color is it, David?" He answered, "Blue, the color of robin's eggs." (Perceptive, eh?) She sighed, "Oh!" He looked at her and at me and said, "Do you want to be pink?" "I'd love to be pink," she replied. He painted each finger a pastel color, and I snapped the most rapturous photograph of her face glowing, with hand outstretched with pastel fingers. The significance of the incident and photograph was even more poignant when I learned later from the activities director that Ethel's love of her life was painting. That photo is precious but, alas, I have no permission to print it, so it will have to glow in your own imagination.

Do you have an IT HAPPENED TO ME story about a photograph you "wish" you had taken? I'd love to read it. Please describe it and send it to WeekbyWeek@thomsonlearning.com

images of hellos and good-byes. Self-care photos can illustrate the accomplishment of milestone tasks, such as dressing for outside or tying a shoe. A video of outside play could be a delightful reminder of the physical, emotional, language, and social actions of the child. It could show children running down a hill, climbing a slide, or wading in a creek. Social interactions can be preserved with photographs or recorded conversations. Emotionally troubled moments are usually best kept private, but there may be circumstances when these might need to be preserved visually or audibly. Language segments on audio or video preserve not only the words, but facial and body expressions to make them even more illuminating. Visual and auditory reminders of past events help expand memory and attention span. They are good teaching tools and document important events. Creative moments, whether art media manipulation or **sociodramatic play**, are meaningfully captured on video or audio. Incidents illustrating self-identity, group interactions, or relationships with adults in the classroom are more vividly documented with pictures or audio as well. Any observation can be augmented or recorded using these methods. Further commentary will enhance or add the observer's conclusions to the photograph or recording.

Advantages

Photographs and recording audio and video are effective observational recording tools because

- they capture visual or real sound images of the episode.
- they are less subject to the recorder's bias or inferences.
- they allow the viewer to form judgments independent from the recorder's.
- they can be analyzed in a number of ways, for different purposes, at different times.
- they are less time consuming if automatic systems are used.

Disadvantages

Photographs, videotaping, and audio recording can be all of the following:

- expensive
- complicated and time consuming
- intrusive to children and teachers
- a factor causing unnatural behavior
- against families' values

Pitfalls to Avoid

Confidentiality is an issue with any documentation technique. But using audio, video, or photography as an documentation technique carries with it some additional concerns. Children other than the target

TOPICS IN OBSERVATION

Protecting the Rights of the Child

It is essential to receive the permission of each child's family to record their child using audio, video, or photographic recording methods (Figure 11–2). There are instances when this permission may be denied.

- Some religious groups do not allow photographs.
- The child is under protective services in a protected, confidential placement. An innocent newspaper photograph of an activity that included the child may jeopardize the child's safety.
- There may be personal reasons for which the family may deny permission.

AUDIO/VIDEO/PHOTO RELEASE

I give permission for my child to be tape recorded, video recorded, or photographed for educational or publicity purposes while participating in the regular activities of this program.

Date ______________________

❑ YES ❑ NO

Signature ______________________

Figure 11–2 Sample Release Form.

It is important that staff members are aware of the denied photo release. Just as a life-threatening allergy must be made known to all staff, this is important information to be conveyed. Alternative documentation methods must be used if permission is denied. For example, the staff might write down detailed, extensive notes as an alternative to using an audio recording of the child's language sample. If video or still photography is used in the group setting, either for formal or informal uses, the staff is responsible for making the photographer aware of any prohibition. In such cases, sensitivity to the child's feelings is a high priority. The age of the child and reason for prohibition will govern how this exclusion is made. The exclusion from photography or recording should not be obvious to the other children or their families, or even the child, unless it is by the child's request. Techniques of photography could be used to take group casual pictures from the back of the child. All diligence should be given to this serious ethical and legal issue.

Occasionally, photo contests or commercial purposes may arise. If the recordings are used for other than educational or publicity use, the individual child's family should be consulted. A special release form for that specific purpose must be obtained. It is better to be cautious and guard against any possible recriminations.

Any child who does not want to be recorded, videotaped, or photographed has the right to refuse. The staff has the responsibility to respect the child's wishes, even if the family has given permission. No child should be forced to participate in this kind of an activity. This should be a policy in the school, staff, and family handbook.

child may be included in a photo, audio recording, or videotape, thus possibly revealing information about that child's behavior to those who have no need or right to know. This is almost impossible to avoid, especially with video photography. Ethical use of footage is the teacher's responsibility.

Just as equity is important in all other recording methods, it is with audio and video techniques as well. Some children are much more photogenic, do more interesting things, or speak more humorously or in an interesting way than others. When using audio and video, including photography, all children who are allowed to be recorded should be in a fair way, both in number and in content of recording.

View the recording from the family's eyes. Is it embarrassing? Does it show the child in an uncomfortable situation or looking less competent than peers? Reconsider using that recording.

How to Find the Time

It does take time to learn to use new equipment. Just as a child needs to manipulate a new item, you will need to use it and experiment with it before expecting it to perform perfectly. The more you use the technology, the more familiar with it you will become. After some practice, it will become second nature to use that camera or tape recorder. Once you get to that level, you will see how much time it saves in writing.

Go to the Bind-in-Book CD for plans and resources.

LOOKING AT DRAMATIC PLAY

During dramatic play, observers see many interesting scenarios unfold. A child puts on a hat, picks up a briefcase, and says, "See ya, honey, I'm goin' to work now." And off she goes. A toddler holds his sweater coiled up in a ball and strokes it saying, "Nice kitty." A four-year-old at the art bench says to himself, "I need a big piece of paper 'cause I'm gonna make a big truck with a trailer. No, I'll use another piece of paper for the trailer and hitch 'em togedder with a piece of tape." Each of these children is displaying imaginative play through his or her thoughts and actions. They are cute to the untrained observer but meaningful to those who know what each incident reveals about the child's development.

While *play* is the word used for activities that are not seen as having any worthwhile function, for young children (and for us all), it has many benefits. Research on dramatic play, solitary imaginative play (with or without props), and sociodramatic play (a fantasy episode interacting with other children) has important implications for teachers of young children. Studies have found that children who regularly engage in sociodramatic or imaginative play are more friendly, popular, cooperative, verbal, and creative. They are usually less impulsive and aggressive and more likely to take the perspective of others (Fein & Kinney, 1994). These are logical outcomes of having sustained interactions with peers. Other benefits are documented as well. Children between two-and-a-half and five years old who participate in make-believe play are more advanced in general intellectual ability, have better memory, and display higher reasoning ability (Berk, 1994). A review of pretence (pretend play) literature found that "representational skills, problem-solving abilities, and social-linguistic sophistication" were increased by sociodramatic play (Bergen, 2002). Language development and literacy from play-based instruction with dramatic play scenarios are enhanced (Snow, Burns, & Griffin, 1998). Nonparticipants, however, had lower school achievement later and exhibited less self-control in social situations and higher rates of delinquency (Singer & Singer, 1990). Spontaneous sociodramatic play is a setting for cognitive, social, affective, and moral development, with conversations that communicate what is real and what is make-believe between the players (Ortega, 2003) Here are some benefits of dramatic play. It helps children

- develop conversational skills and the ability to express ideas in words.
- understand the feelings, roles, or work of others.
- connect actions with words—actions and words go hand-in-hand in dramatic play.
- develop vocabulary.
- develop creativity—children imagine, act, and make things up as play progresses.
- engage in social interaction with other children.
- cope with life, sometimes through acting out troubling situations, thus giving an outlet for emotion (for example, almost every doll in an early childhood center gets a spanking periodically when children play house).
- assume leadership and group participant roles. (Machado, 2003, p. 398)

With these benefits, can early childhood programs and elementary schools ignore the importance of providing and encouraging this kind of play?

REVIEW

MEDIA

Action preserved in photographs, audio recordings, or videotape

Types of Information to Record Using Technology

- any moment or sequence of a child's day, usual or unusual
- separation and adjustment
- self-care skills
- physical development
- social development
- emotional development
- language and speech (audio or video)
- attention span and interests
- cognitive development
- literacy
- creativity
- sociodramatic play
- self-esteem

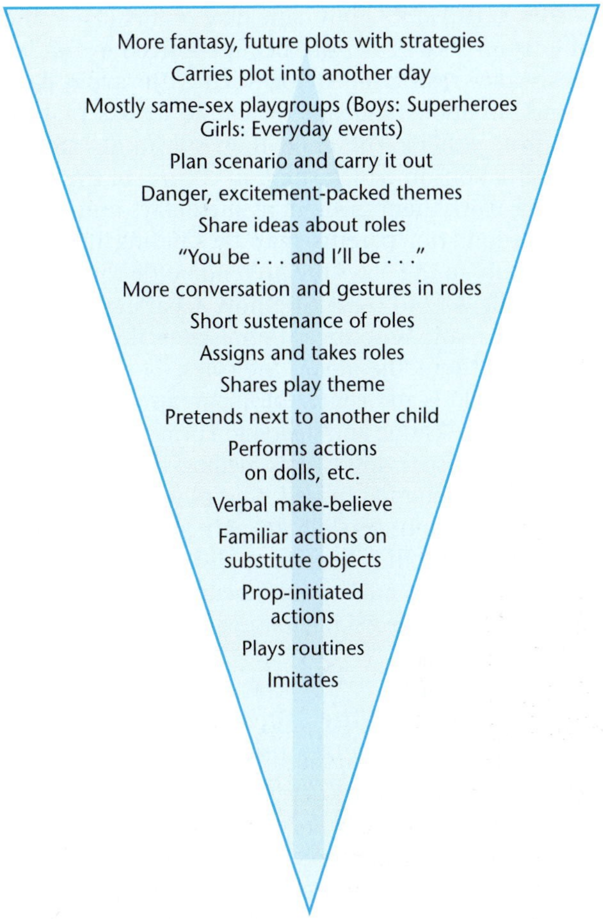

Figure 11–3 Dramatic Play Development.

Stages of Dramatic Play

Children play in different ways at different ages and stages (Figure 11–3). Piaget equated that difference in the way they played with the difference in their thinking (Peterson & Felton-Collins, 1986). The changes in imaginative play are easily observed and do correspond with stages of development by several theorists, including Piaget, Erikson, Smilansky, and Vygotsky.

INFANCY. The infant and adult are gazing at each other intently. As the adult opens and closes his mouth and slowly sticks out his tongue, the infant imitates the action. Imaginative play has begun. This has been documented to occur in the early days of the infant's life, setting the stage for responding to another human and turn taking. The game of peekaboo is really the pretend theme of "I'm going away and now I'm back." The repetition of these adult–child interactions is building the foundation for the later plots of sociodramatic play with peers.

YOUNG TODDLERS. Between 6 and 18 months, the child is exploring the physical world by playing with objects. Close scrutiny of this play illustrates various patterns.

Repetition with Objects. Manipulations are repeated with the objects in every conceivable way. The young toddler takes her bottle and shakes it, throws it, chews on it, sucks on all parts of it, listens to it, and minutely examines it.

Repetition without Objects. The functions she has learned are played out in her imagination without the object. This is the beginning of imaginary play. She puts her fist to her mouth and makes sucking movements and sounds, pretending to suck the bottle.

Substitution. Other objects become stand-ins for the imaginary one. She picks up anything she can handle and puts it to her mouth and pretends (or actually) sucks it like a bottle. She is mentally substituting this object for the bottle.

OLDER TODDLERS. Dramatic play occurs just at the time when social rules are being enforced by adults. These rules restrict behavior, such as to avoid dangerous situations and not to tear up books or take toys from others. The child then substitutes imaginary situations in which she is in control of the rules and can work them through as she delays immediate gratification. Her parents may be offering her milk from a cup, so she plays the pretend bottle routines as a symbolic way to cope. She now separates thought from action and renounces impulsive action in favor of this situation. She makes the rules.

The child is the center of imaginative play, with rituals such as eating and sleeping. The actions become more decentered. Now she is feeding the teddy bear rather than being fed herself. She now can use more language and muscle skills to participate in shared-meaning play with others, but self-control is a problem. Each player must do the acting with the same objects, and none is willing to forego her own desire to possess the toy.

PRESCHOOLERS. The three-year-old has an expanded sense of fantasy using semirealistic props for adult roles. Each player has his own role related to the theme but acts independently. The players are trying to represent themselves in roles with which they are familiar. There are four types of roles common to dramatic play:

- *functional*—performing a common function like feeding a baby or driving a car
- *relational*—representing a family member, friend, or pet
- *stereotypic*—highly predictable based on an occupation such as policeman or construction worker
- *fictional*—taken from a story or media superhero (Garvey, 1977)

Taking roles helps children understand and feel powerful. To be the parent giving the commands, the superhero with super power, or the firefighter as a rescuer, the child takes on the characteristics of another person. They are only able to do this because of expanded vocabulary, experiences with models, and objects that they can mentally transform into props.

Toward the end of the preschool age, the ability to have empathetic thoughts and to want social companionship expands the dramatic play into the Sociodramatic Stage. Most children are becoming less egocentric and more empathetic. They understand others' points of view and feelings. They are in Erikson's Initiative Stage, taking control and leadership of their own play, not dependent on specific props or adult leadership. They are likely to play roles such as family, stereotyped television characters, powerful helpers from the community (firefighter or police), cowboys, pirates, or space creatures. However, now roles are assigned and imaginary experiences are shared through explanations outside the role. Children are frequently heard saying things like, "You be the guy on fire and I'll come with the hose and put the fire out." This often meets with a counterproposal from the victim, "No, *you* be the guy on fire and *I'll* come with the hose." Resolution of the dilemma may indicate language development for negotiation, problem-solving ability, and social status in the group.

YOUNG SCHOOL-AGERS. Sociodramatic play declines in the early school years. The child has a growing contact with reality, feelings of industry, and pride in her motor and intellectual skills. Games with rules are the outlets for these skills and attitudes. Interactions with other children are growing more

@ it happened to me

"You're the Wife, You Stay Home!"

In the "House" dramatic play area, a preschool girl announced, "I'm going to work." She donned a hat, grabbed a briefcase, mounted the rocking horse like a motorcycle, and away she went. A boy in the area went over, grabbed the briefcase, unseated her, and said sternly, "No, you're the wife, you stay home!" One can only imagine a domestic struggle over working wives that this child might have witnessed either at home or in the media. Be careful, though, not to make inferences regarding the child's parents based on dramatic play episodes. What would you have done if you witnessed this drama?

Do you have an IT HAPPENED TO ME story about a dramatic play episode? I'd love to read it. Send it to WeekbyWeek@thomsonlearning.com

competitive. Helm and Katz (2001) call this the age of investigations. They are concrete-operational thinkers, ready for group play. Their investigations may be focused on collections of whatever the fad is this week, though Barbie and sports cards have sustained their favor. Games with rules become the play pattern of this age now that the children can accurately keep score, easily take turns, and strategically plan. The sociodramatic play of the earlier stages has prepared the child for these activities.

Using Play Stages to Assess Sociodramatic Play

The social play stages can be used again when assessing and describing dramatic play (see Chapter 4). A variety of methods can record the play for later analysis, such as Class List Log, Checklist, Anecdotal or Running Record, Rating Scales.

ONLOOKER STAGE. The child watches the dramatic play of others. The child may lack the entry skills and self-confidence to join the organized play of other children. It may be the child's learning style to watch others before he attempts the play, or it may be his shy personality. The adult can give assistance in play entry techniques if it is warranted.

SOLITARY DRAMATIC PLAY. A child of any age may choose to play out dramatic or fantasy play alone. The child selects the props for play and may internally or audibly carry on a dialogue. The observer, just as in the Onlooker Stage, can assess the play and decide if intervention is needed to help the child move to social interaction in the play. The scaffolding of an adult as a parallel player may help the child move to the next stage.

PARALLEL DRAMATIC PLAY. Two-, three-, and four-year-olds are social beings and often play out their dramatic roles alongside other children without interactions. The observer, as in the Solitary Stage, assesses the child's social level and choice of parallel play partners. If it is indicated, she can act as an intermediary, with statements such as, "Suzie, you are a Mommy and Joe is a cook. Maybe you could go to his restaurant and order a Kids Meal."

ASSOCIATIVE DRAMATIC PLAY. In the Associative Stage, children are still each playing parallel but share play theme and conversation. Children are talking, smiling, and offering objects—all corresponding to associative play. It is the stage of social play in which children are playing near each other, in the same play theme, but not together. They do not share props or final results.

COOPERATIVE DRAMATIC PLAY. In the Cooperative Stage, children are working together toward a common goal, contributing parts to the whole. Children engage in social exchanges. They plan and act out make-believe stories.

Smilansky (in Johnson et al., 1999) further defines this level of sociodramatic play as including the following:

- *role playing*—adopting roles
- *make-believe transformations*—symbols stand for objects, actions, and situations
- *social interactions*—directly relating to each other in roles
- *verbal communications*—(1) statements to organize the play designating the situation, assigning roles, planning story lines, and rebuking players who act in an inappropriate way and (2) pretend communication within the role (p. 231)

By using these finer distinctions in describing dramatic play, the observer can make decisions about the need or desirability of intervening in the play. The adult can help dramatic play by role modeling, making suggestions, asking open-ended questions, or giving direct instruction in carrying out the role. Each of these may help the child extend the play and become a more acceptable play partner.

EXERCISE Look at photographs of children in the dramatic play area. Using the stages of Smilansky, determine each child's level or role.

Observing Dramatic Play

The term *dramatic play* refers to the spontaneous play in which a child recreates routines they have seen in real life (Figure 11–4). As the child matures, the role

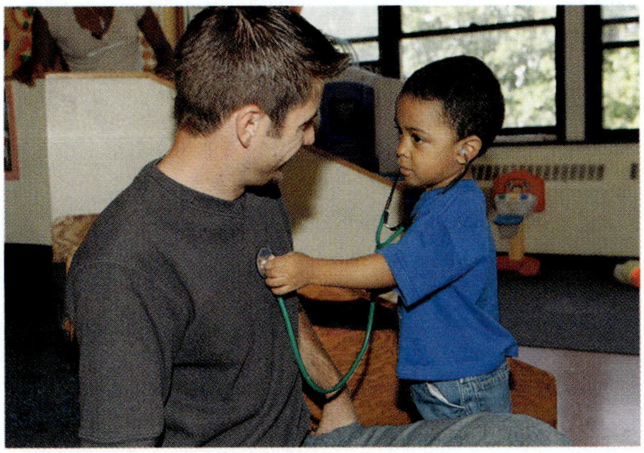

Figure 11–4 Dramatic play offers opportunities to play out familiar roles.

is sustained, is accompanied by a monologue or dialogue with another, and then imaginative new play themes are explored. *Sociodramatic play* is the interaction of two or more children in a play theme with each holding separate roles. This often follows family-life routines such as cooking, child care, and male/female interactions.

A third type of creative play is *story play* (Isenberg & Jalongo, 2001), play inspired by a book or fingerplay. The classic *Three Little Pigs* or *Goldilocks and the Three Bears* are perfect beginning productions. Block (1997) and Edwards (2001) emphasize the added comprehension of the text and its benefits to learning that result from story play. Such play has been very successful in involving children in literature so that they begin exercising cognitive thinking and move out of egocentrism. It helps children work out difficult concepts and their reactions to real-world situations (Howell & Corbey-Scullen, 1997). They tell of using creative dramatics as a follow-up to a field trip to the home of Harriet Tubman in trying to understand slavery with very young children and using a play about animals for conflict resolution. A variation of this kind of dramatic play, **story dictation**, has been documented by Vivian Paley (1984, 1988, 1990, 1997) through her accounts of this kind of play in kindergarten classrooms. Her work highlights the rich learning outcomes of such an approach, especially in both the cognitive and affective domains. One child, or a group of children, write the story line and act as producers and directors, selecting actors to carry out the story line. The rest of the class acts as the audience. The teacher is the facilitator, assisting with the production and presentation, but her more important role is leading the follow-up conversation about the meaning of the play, the conflicts raised, and possible solutions.

When using videotape to record spontaneous sociodramatic play, a followup interview with the players can yield information about the children's thinking and emotions while they played. The tape can be paused and repeated rather than interrupting the play as it is happening. Questions can center on themes, roles, object substitutions, and the distinction between fantasy and reality:

- "Tell me about what you are playing here."
- "Why did you choose that?" or "Why did you say that?"
- "You didn't have a . . . so what did you use instead?" (object substitution)
- "How does it make you feel to be that?"
- "Are there things you don't like to be or play? Why?"
- "If you could play that over again, what would you change?" (Sawyers & Carrick, p. 165)

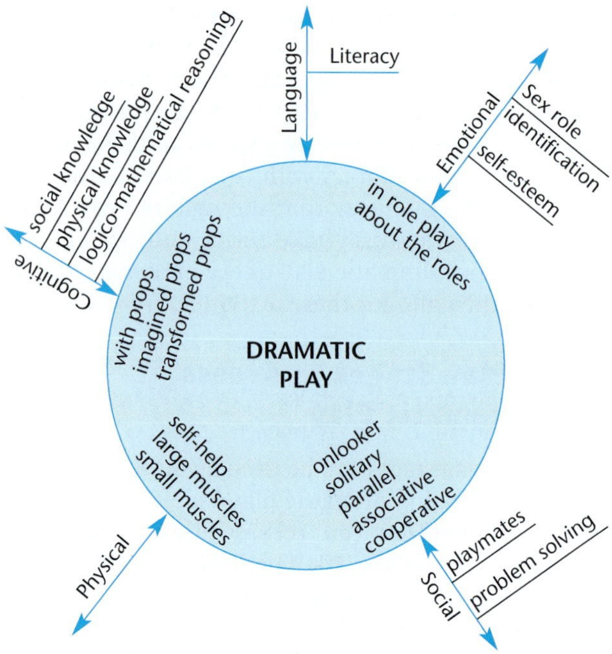

Figure 11–5 Developmental Skills Used and Revealed in Dramatic Play.

Observing Dramatic Play for Assessing Other Developmental Areas

While children are engaging in dramatic play, they are using other skills and behaviors that can be observed and assessed simultaneously (Figure 11–5).

COGNITIVE. Sociodramatic play is a progressive step toward abstract thinking. The movement from the real toy to the symbolic leads the preschooler to abstract thinking. This is the link with Piaget's Concrete Operations Stage. Children who enjoy pretending score higher on imagination and creativity (Berk & Winsler, 2002). During dramatic play, children shift away from self and take the role of another, which helps them see situations from a different viewpoint, moving them out of egocentrism. The reversibility of the role, knowing they can leave it any time, helps develop the cognitive structures for understanding the reversibility of operations such as equal amounts of water in different-sized containers (Johnson et al., 1999). The planning and carrying out of a thematic role through story and fantasy play have been shown to help children's memory for story lines and serve as a foundation for later memory strategies (Kim, 1999).

LANGUAGE. Sociodramatic play promotes vocabulary growth (Block, 2001; Edwards, 1997) and gives children practice in turn taking and using language to plan, as well as teaching them to carry out roles, sometimes with great expression. This shows the child's ability to move out of egocentrism into the role of another, even using different voices, vocabularies, and gestures for the role. The inner speech, or private speech as Vygotsky calls it (quoted in Kraft & Berk, 2002), often is audible as children work through a dramatic play episode, whether alone or with other children. It reveals the child's inner thoughts. It is as if they were being transmitted directly out of the brain, such as, "Now this is my baby and she has to go to the doctor. Oops, her arm just fell off. I think James did that." Accompanying sound effects and directions to inanimate objects, such as, "Get outta here, chair," are often heard in fantasy play.

LITERACY. Sociodramatic play is a natural way to integrate literacy into the child's environment, incorporating it as a natural and important part of the play theme. The use of literacy materials in different learning centers can be observed, such as sign making in the block area, letter writing, and list making in the dramatic play area. Often children will suggest, either spontaneously at the gentle suggestion of the teacher, that a sign or a list could fill a need in the play. It may direct players, like an "Open" or "Closed" sign for a grocery store or labels for buildings with the name of the builder. Watching the use of literacy materials, including books during play, can give the observer clues about the child's understanding of the usefulness of print.

SOCIAL. Dramatic play is encouraged by families who engage in fantasy with their child, provide props, and comment on the play as real. These children tend to be more securely attached and more imaginative. Children's involvement and success with dramatic play depends also on their level of social development (see Chapter 4). When the child is in the Parallel Play Stage, she wants to be near other children playing but does not have the language, emotional, or cognitive development to engage in interactive play. The adult can recognize the child's level of social development, help her find a role that she is capable of, and support her success in that role. Experience in groups greatly affects the child's ability to participate in sociodramatic play. Solving problems in play situations helps children learn the art of negotiation while they divide roles, take turns, and share props. Interacting with an older peer or one more socially experienced will enhance imaginative play. Children seek out familiar same-sex, same-age playmates.

Some children do not participate in sociodramatic play. There are many possible reasons for this, with many implications for the teacher. Some children are more object-oriented than people-oriented, which may simply be their cognitive style (see Chapter 8). They learn through manipulating the physical environment and are convergent rather than divergent thinkers. Children who are withdrawn and do not participate in sociodramatic play may later experience peer rejection, social anxiety, loneliness, depression, negative self-esteem, and even negative school success (Rubin & Coplan, 1998). This emphasizes the importance of facilitating sociodramatic play in the early childhood classroom.

It is well documented that children who are less aggressive are more readily accepted as playmates. The children who introduce wild animal themes and superheroes into dramatic play raise the level of aggressiveness of the play. Research has shown strong relationships between high television viewing (particularly shows depicting violence) and aggressiveness (Johnson, Cohen, Smailes, Kasen, & Brook, 2002; Bushman & Huesmann, 2001; Paik & Comstock, 1994). High levels of television viewing also result in low imagination, more anxiety, and lower reading levels and school performance (Singer & Singer, 1990). These effects can be reduced if adults are mediators of the child's viewing. Talking about the difference between reality and fantasy, and the possible results in real life of aggressiveness and violence, can help children understand cause and effect and hopefully practice self-control. Play themes from television are highly aggressive and antisocial, but television can teach prosocial behaviors with careful adult intervention. The National Television Violence Study (2002) says that children below the age of seven are most vulnerable to television violence because of their limited abilities to differentiate between fantasy and reality.

Should superheroes be banned? There is much discussion and disagreement over this topic (see Slaby et al., 1995; and Levin & Carlsson-Paige, 2006, in Resources). The observer can conduct ethnographic research about the effect of television superheroes on dramatic play through Anecdotal Recordings and Frequency Counts. There is no doubt that children use dramatic play to feel powerful (when they know they are not), feel grown up (when they know they are little), and do dangerous things (when they know they are not allowed). Sociodramatic play can provide a way for a child to behave "beyond his average age, above his daily behavior; in play it is as though he were a head taller than himself" (Sutton-Smith, quoted in Berk & Winsler, 2002. p. 68).

Children more frequently play with same-sex playmates, with girls choosing family themes on everyday experiences whereas boys play physically active, superhero roles (Howe et al., 1993). Studies have been conducted to detect the roots of these differences, biological or cultural. It is the old nature versus nurture question, with the ambiguous answer, "Both." There is no doubt that stereotypical play roles have been reinforced by families, peers, television, storybooks, toy advertising, and even by teachers. This happens overtly in comments like, "You girls might want to play with the new dolls we got for the housekeeping area." Such reinforcement of stereotypes may also be less obvious, for example, by providing only action-hero-type dress-up props for boys in the dramatic play area. Observations of dramatic play roles, routines, and partners will give clues about the child's sex role identity. The role of the adult is also to broaden the child's exploration of play things and themes by providing a variety of opportunities.

EMOTIONAL. Children's emotions are displayed in dramatic play. Observers of young children have heard and seen the pretend crying of the "baby" or the shrill voice of fear as villains chase the good guys. Obvious enjoyment is seen when children are dressing up to go to the dance. Play therapy has been used extensively in the treatment of children's emotional disorders, so the connection between dramatic play as a vehicle for expressing inward emotions is well recognized. Important events to the child, such as a new sibling, mommy going to work, moving, or major changes in the family, often are seen played out in the dramatic play themes. Exact conversations and gestures accompany the actions that help the child physically and mentally reenact what is troubling them inside. Recurring themes of going to the doctor, house on fire, spanking the baby all point to the emotional involvement of young children in dramatic play.

Emotional disturbances can also be observed in children's dramatic play. Curry and Arnaud (1995, pp. 4–9) present three areas of children's play that may suggest an emotional need for intervention:

1. Thematic content: (a) a preoccupation with a single play theme, unchanging and rigid; (b) highly unusual play themes that may be traumatic events the child has witnessed; (c) play with explicit sexual content; or (d) excessive preoccupation with ordinary objects.
2. Style of play: (a) excessively rigid; (b) play in a style of a younger developmental stage; (c) inability to remove himself from the pretend role; or (d) unusual aggressiveness.
3. Social interactions in play: (a) isolated at a stage in the preschool years when sociodramatic play is at its peak; (b) cannot sustain play because of aggressiveness, disruptiveness, or social ineptness; (c) excessively imitative play; or (d) causes rejections.

Even very young children can exhibit complicated and strange behavior. This kind of behavior can be a clue to deeper difficulties or just a unique characteristic of that particular child. Closer observation of the whole child can help make that determination.

Sociodramatic play, with its rules of varying complexity, calls for self-control of emotions and impulses. This does have the developmental effect of practicing in play what is required in real life. The private speech in fantasy play has a major role in the development of self-control. Children use it to regulate their own activity, as in, "I gotta be careful here. I'll pour carefully so I don't spill it" (Berk & Winsler, 2002).

PHYSICAL. The whole body—both the large and small muscles—is involved in dramatic play. Large muscles are put into action when running away from the robbers and lifting heavy boards to construct a fort. Placing tiny horses in a row on a wobbly block wall or buttoning up opera gloves requires small muscle coordination, attention span, and patience.

An environment enriched with interesting props and possibilities expands dramatic play. When children are engaged in imaginative play, they do adapt their own props from whatever is available. Before that stage, however, children first go through the stages of manipulation and exploration. They explore all the physical properties of objects first (Curry, 1992). Two- and three-year-olds require more realistic props to complete their play theme. Children need to physically manage real things in their lives as a significant part of the project approach (Helm, 2003).

Dramatic play incorporates the curriculum areas of art, language, science, math, and social studies. It helps develop interpersonal negotiations, physical coordination, language, and cognitive skills. Children ask their own questions, seek their own answers, and enhance all skill areas with the assistance of the teacher as a support.

Other Techniques for Observing Dramatic Play

Dramatic play can be captured very well through the use of Anecdotal Recording. Some delightful and insightful Anecdotal Recordings of dramatic play comprise the writings of Vivian Gussin Paley. Her book *Boys and Girls: Superheroes in the Doll Corner* (1984) is a wonderful accompaniment to the discussions of this chapter. (See Resources for others.)

@ **it happened to me**

Fan Fascination

A colleague conferred with me about a child who was preoccupied with fans. He watched the ceiling fan at home for long periods of time, his mother reported. At preschool he searched magazines and catalogs looking for pictures of fans. He carried pictures of them around in his pocket and talked about how things reminded him of fans. He was immature socially but linguistically advanced. Curry and Arnaud's (1995) warning signals regarding autism reminded me of this child with the fascination and aberration with fans. He was referred to a psychologist and worked with a play therapist. (See Chapter 7, "Topics in Observation: Autism.")

Do you have an IT HAPPENED TO ME story about a child's interesting behavior? I'd love to read it. Send it to WeekbyWeek@thomsonlearning.com

@ **it happened to me**

Thirty Buttons

I watched in amazement as one of the youngest children in the three-year-old class sat for about 20 minutes in the dramatic play area. She had put on a dress with fabric loops for buttonholes all the way down the front. There must have been 30 of them. She sat and buttoned every one. That was patience, long attention span, small muscle coordination, and one-to-one correspondence. A planned activity would never have taught her the lessons she learned that day. It was an observation full of details about her development.

Do you have an IT HAPPENED TO ME story about an interesting observation? I'd love to read it. Send it to WeekbyWeek@thomsonlearning.com

A Class List Log can be used for a quick check on who does and does not participate in fantasy play. This may be expanded into a Frequency Count over the course of a week or so, as children present a dramatic rendition of *The Three Billy Goats Gruff* or some other story. Repeating the Class List Log or Frequency Count will indicate if more children are engaged in sociodramatic play as the year progresses.

Time Samples will indicate if play is occurring in the dramatic play area. The observer may want to develop a code for the time sample, perhaps a *D* to designate dramatic play occurring in other areas. Under the climber or outdoors, an exciting cops-and-robbers theme may be acted out. In the block area, a city may be constructed in anticipation of an earthquake or a bombing. Children do play out the traumatic events of the news that are even more frightening than the cartoons they watch. While taking the Time Sample, if an event that is interesting or important occurs, the observer could turn the paper over and jot down some notes. Later these could be amplified into a more formal Anecdotal Recording for the Class File or child's Portfolio.

Developmental Checklists and Rating Scales often have one or more criteria for recording the presence, absence, or level of involvement of the child in dramatic play.

Beaty's (2002) Imagination Checklist includes the following items in a developmental progression:

- pretends an action without taking a role
- assigns roles or takes assigned roles
- takes on characteristics and actions related to role
- needs particular props to do pretend play
- can pretend with imaginary objects
- uses language for creating and sustaining plot
- uses exciting, danger-packed themes
- uses elaborate themes, ideas, details (p. 385)

The Reflective Journal is a place to ponder the meaning of what is seen and heard during fantasy play, to wonder about its roots, and to explore possible actions in the future (Figure 11–6). Thought given to possible scenarios and responses may be

Reflective Journal

It bothered me today when the boys kept shouting "NoGirlsAllowed!" but I just couldn't think of a way to let them exercise control of their play but still intervene. I wanted to stop the sexism and exclusion of other children from their play. What would I have done if they said "No BlacksAllowed" or "No Chinese Allowed"? I would have done something! Next time I hear the children voicing bias or discrimination against any group, I will act. I better talk with Betty about it. She always seems to know just what to say.

Figure 11–6 A Reflective Journal is a place to think about what has been observed and make plans for future actions.

considered *before* they occur, to be ready with comfortable, considered answers.

HELPING ALL CHILDREN WITH SOCIODRAMATIC PLAY

It is not surprising that differences exist in the ways children approach dramatic play when they come from diverse backgrounds, cultures, and experiences, as well as varying levels of language, cognitive, and emotional development. Some factors influence the play to such an extent that generalizations can be made that help the teacher reflect on appropriate teaching practices.

Cultural Differences in Dramatic Play

While developmental capacities have individual differences, it is widely held that most are universal. For example, children all over the world begin to talk between the ages of one and two. The social and cultural influences on development, attitudes, and dispositions are evident; however, they are even more obvious in dramatic play, especially in the social-emotional realm. Certain cultures do not value fantasy. Those children enter group situations without the desire or skills to interact in this way. Older Mexican American siblings, however, made expert sociodramatic play partners. In some societies (Russian and East African), fantasy and imaginative play appear to be absent (Johnson et al., 1999). It is difficult to draw conclusions from limited evidence. The observer should cultivate an awareness so expectations are tempered by the consideration of the many possible factors affecting the development.

Socioeconomic Differences in Dramatic Play

Smilansky and Shefatya's (1990) observations of the play of economically deprived children give insight into the play of these children. It was more object-centered, with the object determining the theme rather than the theme suggesting the object. The objects were used in a more rigid way and were possessed with determination. Verbal interactions were more functional, for management and announcement of roles. They rarely took on the "voice" of the role they were playing. The language was more authoritative than democratic. They used less humor, more criticism, aggressiveness, and control in dealing with problems.

Differing Abilities and Dramatic Play

Children with physical challenges participate in all kinds of play in the classroom, including dramatic play. The teacher's role supports a higher level of activity by modifications to the environment.

The adult interprets for the hearing impaired, gives sensory experiences to the visually impaired, and mediates for children with serious learning and behavior problems. The teacher looks for ways that the child with disabilities could participate. The child with limited vision or a child who is blind may need explanations about the nature of the play and suggestions of roles or actions she could contribute. Their play is less imaginative and more concrete than sighted children, and they are more likely to play alone. The teacher needs to orient the child to choices, offer specific suggestions for symbolic play, and provide props that are sensory-rich (Hughes, 1999).

Children who are hearing impaired will use realistic props to join in the play but may need assistance when the play turns to transformational or representational props. The significance of a rope for a fire hose may not be understood. Children with physical disabilities can use their abilities to join in the play but may need the adult's help. Giving other children ideas about how to involve the child, creating roles for the child, and giving a prop to add to the play are ways that the adult can help (Karnes, 1992). The application of private speech for children with self-regulatory problems like ADHD is being explored (Berk & Winsler, 2002).

Since play comes naturally to all children and is a central framework for all development, it serves as a context for intervention strategy. Dramatic play facilitates social interaction and communication, seldom is limited by physical disabilities when there are environmental accommodations, and provides a vehicle for success (Cripe & Lee, 1997).

@ it happened to me

Empty Eyeglasses

One day in my optometrist's office, I offhandedly asked if they ever had any eyeglass frames they could donate to the preschool. They called me in a few weeks with a wonderful collection! These were added to the dramatic play area and at once became favorite props for play. Most of all, they helped all the children relate to a child in the class who wore glasses. It prepared them for that possibility themselves in the future. Sometimes a serendipitous action becomes an important one.

Do you have an IT HAPPENED TO ME story about a dramatic play prop that inspired especially rich play episodes? I'd love to read it. Send it to WeekbyWeek@thomsonlearning.com

HELPING PROFESSIONALS FOR PLAY CONCERNS

There may be children who exhibit no desire or attention to dramatic play experiences. This does not mean that these children are not creative; this is just not an area that interests them. Young children are working out the differences between real and imaginary, and they become very arbitrary sometimes in only wanting to be involved in the real rather than the pretend, rejecting the make-believe as younger behavior. This is usually not a problem, just an observation that one can make from the child's play and interactions with the environment.

On the other hand, there occasionally are some children so caught up in dramatic play and the imaginary world that they lose touch with reality. The causes may be varied, from giftedness in the area of creativity to escape from a traumatic real-world experience. The observer assesses the range of normal expected behavior, alert to excessive or compulsive behavior that may be a clue to a deeper problem. After observation, documentation, and discussion with the teaching team, the family is consulted for advice and insight. If a referral is made, it may be to one of the following psychological professionals:

psychologist—professional trained in human behavior

psychiatrist—physician specializing in social or emotional disorders

OTHER METHODS

Other Methods to Record Sociodramatic Play

Anecdotal/Running Records
Checklist or Rating Scale that has dramatic play criteria
Time Sample—length of time in Dramatic Play area
Work Samples—play written by children, costumes/sets produced

STANDARDS

Selected examples of standards related to technology and dramatic play:

Division for Early Childhood Recommended Practices (Sandall et al., 2005)
Practice 5: Technology applications
Professionals utilize assistive technology in intervention programs for children
5.5 Professionals consider chronological age-appropriateness and developmentally appropriate practices for infants, toddlers, and preschool children when selecting types of assistive technology in assessment and intervention.

Content Knowledge: Theater
Standard 2. Uses acting skills
Level Pre-K

1. Creates and acts out the roles of characters from familiar stories
2. Engages in both fantasy dramatic play and dramatic play that is based on real experiences.

McREL's *Content Knowledge: A Compendium of Standards and Benchmarks for K–12 Education* (Kendall & Marzano, 2004). http://www.mcrel.org/Standards-benchmarks.
Reprinted by permission of McREL.

KEY TERMS

audio recorders
digital video cameras
informed consent
sociodramatic play
story dictation
technology
video recorder

Go to the Bind-in-Book CD for:

Class List Log form
Plan Week Part A, Directions for using technology to document dramatic play on all children, including What to Do with It, Portfolio Overview Example, Sharing with Child and Family, Actions—Read a Book, In the Environment, In the Curriculum, In the Newsletter
Plan Week 11 Part B, Directions for Running Record in dramatic play or blocks or free play for Group B
Plan Week 11 Part C, Reflective Journal

REFERENCES

American Psychological Association. (2002). *Ethical principles of psychologists and code of conduct.* Washington, DC: Author. Retrieved April 7, 2003, from http://www.apa.org/ethics/code2002.pdf.

Beaty, J. (2006). *Observing development of the young child* (6th ed.). Upper Saddle River, NJ: Merrill.

Bergen, D. (2002). The role of pretend play in children's cognitive development. *Early Childhood Research and Practice, 4* (1).

Berk, L. E. (1994). Vygotsky's theory: The importance of make-believe play. *Young Children, 50* (1), 30–39.

Berk, L. E., & Winsler, A. (2002). *Scaffolding children's learning: Vygotsky and early childhood education.* Washington, DC: National Association for the Education of Young Children.

Blagojevic, B., & Gathwait, A. (2001). Observing & recording growth & change: Using technology as an assessment tool. *Scholastic Early Childhood Today, 15* (8), 36–44.

Block, C. C. (2001). *Teaching the language arts: Expanding thinking through student-centered instruction* (3rd ed.). Boston: Allyn and Bacon.

Bushman, B. J., & Huesmann, L. R. (2001). Effects of televised violence on aggression. In D. G. Singer & J. L. Singer (Eds.), *Handbook of children and the media.* Thousand Oaks, CA: Sage Publications, Inc.

Consortium of National Arts Education Associations. (1994). *Dance, music, theater, visual arts: What every young American should know and be able to do in the arts: National standards for arts education.* Reston, VA: Music Educators National Conference.

Cripe, J. W., & Lee, J. M. (1997). Activity-based intervention strategies for serving young children with developmental delays in early childhood programs. In W. H. Brown & M. A. Conroy, *Including and supporting preschool children with developmental delays in early childhood programs.* Little Rock, AR: Southern Early Childhood Association, 49–64.

Curry, N. (1992). Four- and five-year-olds: Intuitive, imaginative players. In V. Dimidjian (Ed.), *Play's place in public education for young children* (pp. 37–48). Washington, DC: National Education Association of the United States.

Curry, N., & Arnaud, S. (1995). Personality difficulties in preschool children as revealed through play themes and styles. *Young Children, 50* (4), 4–9.

Edwards, L. C. (1997). *The creative arts: A process approach for teachers and children.* Upper Saddle River, NJ: Simon and Schuster.

Fein, G. G., & Kinney, P. (1994). He's a nice alligator: Observations on the effective organization of pretence. In A. Slad & D. P. Wolf (Eds.), *Children at play: Clinical and developmental approaches to meaning and representation.* New York: Oxford University Press.

Garvey, C (1977) *Play.* Cambridge, MA: Harvard University Press.

Helm, J. H. (2003). Contemporary challenges in early childhood education. In J. H. Helm & S. Beneke (Eds.), *The power of projects: Meeting contemporary challenges in early childhood classrooms.* New York: Teachers College Press.

Helm, J. H., & Katz, L. (2001). *Young investigators: The project approach in the early years.* New York: Teachers College Press.

Herr, J., & Libby, Y. (2004). *Creative resources for the early childhood classroom.* Clifton Park, NY: Thomson Delmar Learning.

Hosington, C. (2002). Using photographs to support children's science inquiry. *Young Children, 57* (5), 26–31.

Howe, N., et al. (1993). The ecology of dramatic play centers and children's social and cognitive play. *Early Childhood Research Quarterly, 8,* 235–251.

Howell, J., & Corbey-Scullen, L. (1997). Out of the housekeeping corner and onto the stage—Extending dramatic play. *Young Children, 52* (6), 82–88.

Hughes, F. P. (1999). *Children, play, and development.* Boston: Allyn and Bacon.

Isenberg, J., & Jalongo, M. (2001). *Creative expression and play in the early childhood curriculum* (3rd ed.). New York: Merrill, an imprint of Macmillan Publishing Company.

Johnson, M. E., Christie, J. F., & Yawkey, T. D. (1999). *Play and early childhood development* (2nd ed.). New York: Longman.

Johnson, J. G., Cohen, P., Smailes, E. M., Kasen, S., & Brook, J. S. (2002). Television viewing and aggressive behavior during adolescence and adulthood. *Science, 295* (5564), 2468–2471.

Karnes, M. (1992). Dramatic play and children with special needs. *Pre-K Today, 7* (2), 72.

Kendall, J. S., & Marzano, R. J. (2004). Content knowledge: A compendium of standards and benchmarks for K–12 education. Aurora, CO: Mid Continent Research for Education and Learning (McREL). Online database: http://www.mcrel.org/standards-benchmarks/. Accessed July 13, 2006.

Kim, S. (1999). The effects of storytelling and pretend play on cognitive processes, short-term and long-term narrative recall. *Child Study Journal, 29* (3), 176–191.

Krafft, K. C., & Berk, L. E. (1998). Private speech in two preschools: Significance of open-ended activities and make-believe play for verbal self-regulation. *Early Childhood Research Quarterly, 13* (4), 637–658.

Levin, D., & Carlsson-Paige, N. (2006). *The war play dilemma: What every parent and teacher needs to know* (2nd ed.). New York: Teachers College Press.

Machado, J. M. (2003). *Early childhood experiences in language arts.* Clifton Park, NY: Thomson Delmar Learning.

National Television Violence Study. (2002). *Executive summary.* Santa Barbara, CA: Center for Communication and Social Policy.

Negroponte, N. (1995). *Being digital.* New York: Alfred A. Knopf, Inc.

Ortega, R. (2003). Play, activity, and thought: Reflections on Piaget's and Vygotsky's theories. In D. E. Lytle (Ed.), *Play and educational theory and practice.* Westport, CT: Praeger.

Paik, H., & Comstock, G. (1994). The effects of television violence on antisocial behavior: A meta-analysis. *Communication Research, 21,* 516–546.

Paley, V. G. (1984). *Boys and girls: Superheroes in the doll corner.* Chicago: University of Chicago Press.

Paley, V. G. (1988). *Bad guys don't have birthdays.* Chicago: University of Chicago Press.

Paley, V. G. (1990). *The boy who would be a helicopter.* Cambridge, MA: Harvard University Press.

Paley, V. G. (1997). *The girl with the brown crayon.* Cambridge, MA: Harvard University Press.

Peterson, R., & Felton-Collins, V. (1986). *The Piaget handbook for teachers and parents.* New York: Teachers College Press.

Rubin, K. H., & Coplan, R. K. (1998). Social and nonsocial play in childhood: An individual differences perspective. In O. N. Saracho & B. Spodek (Eds.), *Multiple perspectives on play in early childhood* (pp. 144–170). Albany: State University of New York Press.

Sandall, S. R., Hemmeter, M. L., Smith, B. J., & McLean, M. E. (2005). *DEC recommended practices: A comprehensive guide.* Denver, CO: Sopris West.

Sawyers, J. K., & Carrick, N. (2003). Symbolic play through the eyes and words of children. In D. E. Lytle (Ed.), *Play and educational theory and practice.* Westport CT: Praeger.

Singer, D. G., & Singer, J. L. (1990). *The house of make-believe: Children's play and the developing imagination.* Cambridge, MA: Harvard University Press.

Slaby, R., Roedell, W., Arezzo, D., & Hendrix, K. (1995). *Early violence prevention: Tools for teachers of young children.* Washington, DC: National Association for the Education of Young Children.

Smilansky, S., & Shefatya, L. (1990). *Facilitating play: A medium for promoting cognitive, socio-emotional and academic development in young children.* Gaithersburg, MD: Psychosocial & Educational Publications.

Snow, C. E., Burns, M. S., & Griffin, P. (Eds.). (1998). *Preventing reading difficulties in young children.* Washington, DC: National Academy Press.

Trepanier-Street, M. L., Hong, S. B., & Bauer, J. C. (2001). Using technology in Reggio-inspired long-term projects. *Early Childhood Education Journal, 28* (3), 181–88.

RESOURCES

Carlsson-Paige, N., & Levin, D. (2006). *The war play dilemma: What every parent and teacher needs to know* (2nd ed.). New York: Teachers College Press.

Paley, V. G. (1984). *Boys and girls: Superheroes in the doll corner.* Chicago: University of Chicago Press.

Paley, V. G. (1988). *Bad guys don't have birthdays.* Chicago: University of Chicago Press.

Paley, V. G. (1997). *The girl with the brown crayon.* Cambridge, MA: Harvard University Press.

Pugmire-Stoy, M. C. (1992). *Spontaneous play in early childhood.* Clifton Park, NY: Thomson Delmar Learning.

Singer, D. G., & Singer, J. L. (2001). *Make-believe: Games & activities for imaginative play: A book for parents, teachers, and the young children in their lives.* Washington, DC: Magination Press.

Slaby, R., Roedell, W., Arezzo, D., & Hendrix, K. (1995). *Early violence prevention: Tools for teachers of young children.* Washington, DC: National Association for the Education of Young Children.

CHAPTER 12

Using Documentation for Child Abuse Suspicions and Looking at Self-Concept

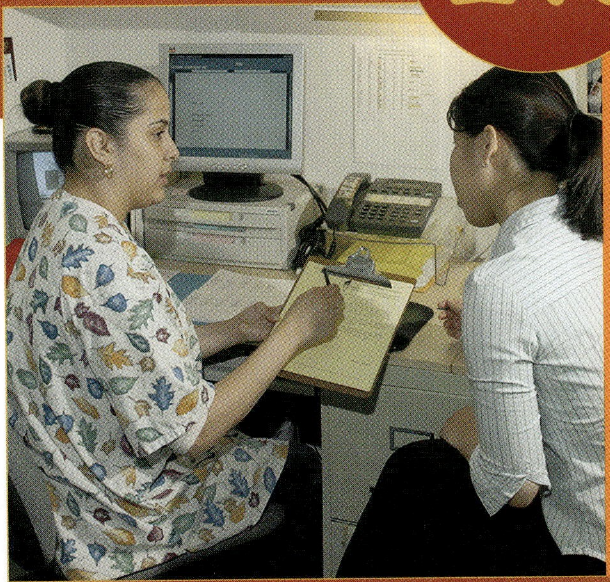

USING DOCUMENTATION FOR CHILD ABUSE SUSPICIONS

Observing children in group settings is not always a pleasant experience. The observer of children has a grave responsibility to fulfill in recognizing and reporting signs of abuse or neglect. This section is one that everyone wishes would not be necessary, but child abuse is a reality. There are people who hurt children physically, psychologically, or use children for sexual purposes.

Neglect is characterized by failure to provide for the child's basic needs, which include physical, medical, educational, and emotional requirements. A form of neglect in infants and young children is organic "failure to thrive," caused by physiological problems (in which case the failure is termed "organic") or lack of proper nourishment (termed "nonorganic"). **Physical abuse** includes any nonaccidental injury caused by the child's caregiver, intentional or nonintentional. **Sexual abuse** includes a wide range of behavior, including exploitation through prostitution or pornography. **Emotional maltreatment** is psychological or emotional abuse through blaming, belittling, or rejecting a child. Child care staff are **mandated reporters**—those individuals who by law must report suspicions of child abuse and maltreatment to specified agencies. Early childhood programs have established policies and protocols that must be followed. Each member of the staff needs to know what to do if abuse or neglect is suspected.

IN THIS CHAPTER

The Abusers

For those who have dedicated their lives to the care and teaching of children, the idea that any adult would knowingly harm a child is unthinkable. Child abusers fit no particular mold, cutting across social class, gender, races, or occupations. They are people just like the rest of us. They could be people without knowledge of the fragility of the forming body or mind. They could be people with such life stresses that their life is out of control, perhaps addicted to substances that lower inhibitions and self-control. They may be victims themselves who resort to inflicting pain according to a pattern established in their own childhood. While this does not excuse anyone from harming a child, we approach the documentation of child abuse and maltreatment not as law enforcement officers, nor to seek punishment, but to protect the child and get help for the family. While it may be one of the most difficult things an early childhood professional must do, it may be one of the most important ones, even saving a life.

As teachers interact with children, they win the child's trust. They have the opportunity to see and hear what children do and talk about the experiences they have had. They may be the one who prevents neglect or abuse from happening again. People who abuse children need help, and the child needs help and protection. Not reporting suspected abuse allows it to continue.

Physical and Behavioral Indicators of Abuse

Teachers and child care workers must be familiar with the physical and behavioral indicators of abuse. Indicators may give very clear evidence of maltreatment, but they also may have other explanations. Some may result from the personality of the child, a new setting with new adults, poverty, different cultural values, accidents, or illnesses. Judgment must be used. For the protection of the child, however, it is better to report those suspicions.

REASONABLE CAUSE TO SUSPECT. The suspicion of child abuse or neglect grows from visual observations, verbal disclosures, or an accumulation of circumstances that build to a reasonable cause to suspect. This does not place the reporter in the position of investigator, interrogator, or prosecutor; it simply means giving an initial alert based on factual observations (Figure 12–1).

THE CHILD'S APPEARANCE. For infants and preverbal children, abuse and maltreatment can be observed in the normal routines of being with the child. By the location and formation of bruises, cuts, and inflammations, concerns are raised. Obvious wounds are usually met by a teacher's empathetic comments—"Ooo, that bruise looks sore"—or interested observations of verbal children—"I notice you holding your arm. Does something hurt?" The child's response may be a first-hand account of what happened, a **disclosure** statement.

THE CHILD'S DESCRIPTION OR DISCLOSURE. The child may say, "My mommy twisted my arm," or "Uncle John hurt me in my goo goo." Comments like these always catch teachers by surprise, but it is important to keep composure so that facial or verbal expressions not reveal the shock, revulsion, or disapproval of what has happened to this child. An appropriate response is, "Would you like to tell me more?" This expresses concern, being open to listen but not probing for more details. These disclosures call for immediate action and documentation (Figure 12–2). Once a mandated reporter has "reasonable cause to suspect," probing for all the details is not necessary. In fact, detailed probing and leading questions may actually place the child in greater jeopardy. Defense attorneys for the abuser may use this as interfering with the witness. The questions should be asked only to answer the question in the reporter's mind: "Do I know enough to *suspect* that this injury or behavior could have been caused by abuse or neglect?" To probe further will inevitably compromise later interviews of the child by child protective authorities. When children must repeat their story to different adults, they may leave out information to protect a loved one. They may recant their story for fear of the consequences, or add untrue details to be more believed. This detailed interviewing must be left to the authorities.

If the child willingly offers and needs to talk about it, by all means be a ready listener, then accurately document both the child's comments and anything you say as well (see Figure 12–3). It is important not to act shocked or disgusted; be willing to listen, and do not deny the child's statements. The less you say in these situations, the better. Leave interrogations to the law enforcement and child protective services professionals.

CIRCUMSTANTIAL EVIDENCE. Suspicious injuries may suggest child abuse or maltreatment. Children's explanations are often protective statements. Behavioral indications by themselves are not sufficient basis for a report, but they should be documented and discussed with a supervisor.

TEACHERS AS REPORTERS. In a review of the research, some of the findings about early childhood

Identifying and Reporting Child Abuse and Maltreatment/Neglect

Type of Abuse/ Maltreatment	Child's Physical Indicators	Child's Behavioral Indicators	Parent's Behavioral Indicators
Physical Abuse	Unexplained bruises and welts • On face, Lips, mouth • On torso, back, buttocks, thighs • In various stages of healing • Clustered, forming regular patterns, reflecting shape of article used to inflict (electric cord, belt buckle) • On several different surface areas • Regularly appear after absence, weekend, or vacation Unexplained fractures • To skull, nose, facial structure • In various stages of healing • Multiple or spiral fractures • Swollen or tender limbs Unexplained burns • Cigar, cigarette burns, especially on soles, palms, back, and buttocks • Immersion burns (sock-like, glove-like, doughnut-shaped on buttocks or genitalia) Unexplained lacerations or abrasions • To mouth, lips, gums, eyes • To external genitalia • On backs of arms, legs, or torso • Human bite marks • Frequent injuries that are "accidental" or unexplained	• Wary of adult contact • Apprehensive when other children cry • Behavioral extremes: aggressiveness, withdrawal, changes in behavior • Frightened of parents • Afraid to go home • Reports injury by parents • Wears long-sleeved or similar clothing to hide injuries • Seeks affection from any adult.	• Seems unconcerned about child • Takes an unusual amount of time to obtain medical care for the child • Offers an inadequate or inappropriate explanation for the child's injury • Gives different explanations for same injury • Misuses alcohol or other drugs • Disciplines the child too harshly considering the child's age or what he/she did wrong • Sees the child as bad, evil, etc. • Has a history of abuse as a child • Attempts to conceal the child's injury • Takes the child to a different doctor or hospital for each injury • Has poor impulse control
Maltreatment/ Neglect	• Consistent hunger, poor hygiene, inappropriate dress • Consistent lack of supervision, especially in dangerous activities or long periods • Unattended physical problems or medical or dental needs • Abandonment	• Begging or stealing food • Extended stays in school (early arrival and late departure) • Attendance at school infrequent • Constant fatigue, falling asleep in class • Alcohol and drug abuse • States there is no caretaker	• Misuses alcohol or other drugs • Has disorganized, upsetting home life • Is apathetic, feels nothing will change • Is isolated from friends, relatives, neighbors • Has long-term chronic illness • Cannot be found • Has a history of neglect as a child • Exposes child to unsafe living conditions • Evidences limited intellectual capacity
Emotional Maltreatment	• Conduct disorders (fighting in school, antisocial, destructive, etc.) • Habit disorders (rocking, biting, sucking fingers, etc.) • Neurotic disorders (speech disorders, sleep problems, inhibition of play) • Psychoneurotic reactions (phobias, hysterical reactions, compulsion, hypochondria) • Lags in physical development • Failure to thrive	• Overly adaptive behavior (inappropriately adult or inappropriately infantile) • Developmental delays (mental, emotional) • Extremes of behavior (compliant, passive, aggressive, demanding) • Suicide attempts or gestures, self-mutilation	• Treats children in the family unequally • Doesn't seem to care much about child's problems • Blames or belittles child • Is cold and rejecting • Inconsistent behavior toward child
Sexual Abuse	• Difficulty in walking or sitting • Torn, stained, or bloody underclothing • Pain or itching in genital area • Pregnancy, especially in early adolescent years • Bruises or bleeding in external genital, vaginal, or anal areas • Sexually transmitted disease (especially in pre-adolescent age group); includes venereal oral infections	• Unwilling to change for or participate in physical education class • Withdrawal, fantasy, or infantile behavior • Bizarre, sophisticated, or unusual sexual behavior or knowledge • Self-injurious behaviors, suicide attempts • Poor peer relationships • Aggressive or disruptive behavior, delinquency, running away, or school truancy • Reports sexual assault by caretaker • Exaggerated fear of closeness or physical contact	• Very protective or jealous of child • Encourages child to engage in prostitution or sexual acts in the presence of caretaker • Misuses alcohol or other drugs • Is geographically isolated and/or lacking in social and emotional contacts outside the family • Has low self-esteem

NOTE: Some behavioral indicators may be common to all children at some time. When indicators are noticeable in a sufficient number and strength to characterize a child's overall manner, they may indicate abuse or maltreatment.

Figure 12–1 Child Abuse and Maltreatment Indicators. (Courtesy of Broome County Family Violence Prevention Council.)

Figure 12–2 Hotline reports need to be made promptly once "reasonable cause to suspect" is determined.

teachers reporting child abuse are surprising (Walsh, Farrell, Bridgestock, & Schweitzer, 2006):

- Teachers are more likely to report physical abuse than emotional abuse or neglect.
- Teachers tend to delay reporting until they feel they have sufficient evidence.
- Boys are more frequently the subject of substantiated abuse.
- Lower socioeconomic groups are more likely to be reported.
- The quality of the relationship with the child and family influenced the willingness to report.
- Male teachers are less tolerant of abuse and neglect, and report more frequently.
- Experienced teachers are more likely to report.
- Teachers' knowledge of indicators and reporting procedures were often inadequate.
- Fear of the negative consequences may prevent or delay reporting.
- The role of the school principal is influential in reporting or not.

TEACHER SUPPORT. The disclosure, recording, and reporting of child abuse all take an emotional toll on teachers, people who have committed their career to the care and education of children. The first area of support should come from the administration through clear policies, responsive follow-through, and empathy. The local child abuse agency can answer specific questions and clear up any misgivings or doubts about suspected abuse. It may be that the adult will need to spend time with a counselor to sort out feelings of loyalty, betrayal, anger, disappointment, or fear. This is a very sensitive area for all the people involved.

When Talking with the Child

DO:

- Make sure the ECE professional is someone the child knows and trusts.
- Conduct the discussion in a place that allows for privacy but is familiar to the child.
- Use only one or two ECE professionals.
- Sit next to the child at his/her level.
- Engage the child in a conversation but do not press the child to talk about the injuries if he/she does not want to.
- Ask the child to clarify words or terms that are not understood.
- Assure the child that he/she has done nothing wrong.
- ______________________________
- ______________________________

DO NOT:

- Suggest answers to the child.
- Probe or press for answers the child does not willingly offer.
- Force the child to remove clothing.
- Display horror, shock, or disapproval of the parent(s), child, or situation.
- Leave the child alone with a stranger.
- Ask "why" questions.
- ______________________________
- ______________________________

When Talking with the Parent(s)

DO:

- Select the person most appropriate to the situation.
- Conduct the discussion in private.
- Tell the parent(s) why the discussion is taking place.
- Be direct, honest, and professional.
- Reassure parent(s) of the program's support to them and to their child.
- Tell the parent(s) if a report was made or will be made.
- Advise the parent(s) of the program's legal and ethical responsibilities to report.
- ______________________________
- ______________________________

DO NOT:

- Try to prove the abuse or neglect; that is not an ECE professional's role.
- Display horror, anger, or disapproval of the parent(s), child, or situation.
- Pry into family matters unrelated to the specific situation.
- Place blame or make judgments about the parent(s) or child.
- ______________________________
- ______________________________

Figure 12–3 Tips for Talking with a Child or Parent. (Reprinted from *Caregivers of Young Children: Preventing and Responding to Child Maltreatment*, 1992, p. 24. U.S. Department of Health and Human Services.)

@ it happened to me

"Private Parts! Private Parts!"

While there is nothing humorous about child abuse, I am reminded of an incident that happened to me. I was teaching a delayed-kindergarten-entry class, mostly five-year-old boys, smart but not "school ready" as the developmental screening used in that school district declared. One day we were doing body tracings with one boy stretched out on a large piece of paper and everyone else around the edge getting ready to color on the tracing. I was making the outline with a marker and as I traced up between his legs he said, "Don't draw my private parts." Five-year-olds love to chant, and that was all they needed. "PRIVATE PARTS, PRIVATE PARTS, PRIVATE PARTS." Every positive guidance technique I had in my bag didn't work. I could just hear them going home and telling that Mrs. Nilsen traced private parts today! So, the only thing I could think of was to declare, "Outside time! Get your coats on!" It stopped the chanting, and I never heard more about it. And I never again did body tracings and discourage teachers from doing so. Think carefully about it.

Do you have an IT HAPPENED TO ME story? I'd love to read it. Send it to WeekbyWeek@thomsonlearning.com

Recording Any Indicators of Maltreatment

The most appropriate method for recording episodes that document suspected abuse or maltreatment is the Anecdotal Record. It is effective for this information because the accounts

- are written shortly after the episode or event occurs, based on notes jotted at the time.
- contain a detailed account, including date and time, people involved in the episode, actions, and exact conversations. This is especially important in situations in which a child reveals to a teacher that someone is hurting him or her. The questions and comments that the adult says must be accurately recorded also. This indicates that the child was not led or influenced in the description of the event.
- contain separate comments by the recorder, such as opinions or questions, from the body of the recording.

In addition to the narrative, diagrams and specific descriptions of the size and nature of wounds should be made. Explanations or conjecture about their cause should be separate from the diagram.

Some states allow the taking of photographs by mandated reporters, but this should be confirmed in the recorder's state. In most cases, however, photographs taken by those other than the authorities are unnecessary and may be very inappropriate. Photographs by authorized persons are considered to be evidence and can be used as such only under controlled conditions. This is best left to child protection, law enforcement, or medical authorities. Further trauma may be added to the child by photographing the injuries. For many sexually abused children, being photographed may be a part of their history of abuse. In any event, photographs, should they be taken, must be turned over to the authorities immediately. *The accurate recording and prompt reporting of suspected child abuse and maltreatment cannot be stressed enough.*

Next Steps

Immediate notification of the supervisor is the first step. Short, accurate notes made as soon as possible preserve vital details. The Child Abuse Hotline, required in every state, should be called immediately by either the supervisor or the witness, depending on the policies and procedures already in place in the program. The local agency may be called to confer if indeed there is enough suspicion to file a Hotline report. The exception to this is if there is suspicion of sexual abuse or the life of the child is in danger. In that case, the law enforcement agency should be called *immediately*. If for some reason the supervisor does not make the call and the teacher has "reason to suspect" there has been possible abuse, then there is a legal and moral responsibility for the teacher to make the call. It is the individual responsibility of each child care professional and teacher to report reasonable suspicion of harm or threatened harm to the child.

LEGAL PROCESS OF REPORTING. Individual states vary in the definitions of child maltreatment, but most include nonaccidental physical abuse, neglect, sexual abuse, and emotional (or mental) maltreatment by a person responsible for the child's welfare.

EXERCISE **According to the laws in your state, reportable child abuse is defined as what?**

Every state has laws for reporting child abuse and a reporting number, many of which are toll-free telephone calls. School personnel and child care workers are mandated reporters by law in every state. A mandated reporter must report any "reasonable cause to suspect" a child has been maltreated. Not reporting suspected neglect or abuse could result in legal action.

it happened to me

"She Made Me Sit in the Puke."

One day toward the end of the school year, a parent came in and said, "I am considering calling the Hotline on you." My heart stopped, my face got red, I got a lump in my throat. She laughed then and said, "My son said you made him sit in the puke." It turns out that we had been practicing for preschool graduation (we did it back then, but I wouldn't do it now) and we were in the church sanctuary where they sat on the front pew while we assembled to sing on the stage. Pew/puke, I could now understand. I did have him sit in the pew, not the puke.

Do you have an IT HAPPENED TO ME story about child abuse and maltreatment? I am not inviting accounts of disclosures, suspicions, or reporting. Perhaps you have an illustration of miscommunication or happy endings. Please send them to me at WeekbyWeek@thomsonlearning.com

Reporters of suspected abuse are not responsible for proving the abuse, just to present the observable facts that led to the suspicions. If the report is **unfounded**—not enough evidence exists to prove it—the reporter is protected from civil action.

EXERCISE **Locate the Hotline or reporting number for child care workers in your state. Find the state and local agency and telephone number to which you could ask questions. Write them on a separate sheet of paper.**

Reporting telephone number:
Agency and telephone number:

WHEN THE HOTLINE OR LAW ENFORCEMENT AGENCY IS CALLED. The reporter will be asked to supply as much of the following information as possible. The lack of complete information *does not* prohibit a report from being made. Requested information includes the following:

- the name and address of the child and his or her parents or legally responsible guardian
- the child's age, sex, and race
- the nature and extent of the child's injuries, abuse, or maltreatment (including any evidence of prior injuries, abuse, or maltreatment to the child or his or her siblings)
- the child's present location
- the name of the person or persons responsible for causing the injury, abuse, or maltreatment
- family composition; others residing in or at the home in regular intervals
- person making the report, where that person can be reached, and where the information was obtained; names of other relevant school personnel who may provide critical information
- any action taken by the reporting source
- any additional information that may be helpful

Though suspicions of abuse or neglect seem obvious by the very act of calling the Hotline, they must hear the reporter's concerns in those terms: "I believe this child to be abused or neglected because. . . . " The report is strengthened if the reporter can (1) detail a pattern (not that a mother was overheard screaming at her child once, but this is how she interacts with her child routinely), *and* (2) state the impact on the child (e.g., behavioral signs, the child is doing poorly in school, and so on).

Needless to say, one would not wait for a pattern of injuries before alerting the authorities.

If troublesome behavior by a family member and/or the child, though not reportable, has been observed, that information may be helpful to set a framework for the report to the Hotline. Documentation of these earlier concerns should be recorded in the style of an Anecdotal Recording and kept in a confidential file.

Once the call is made, the written Report of Suspected Child Abuse or Maltreatment should be completed and filed according to the directions in the state (Figure 12–4). A copy is kept in a confidential file, separate from the child's Portfolio and separate from the Class File, along with any written records referring to these suspicions. For the reporter's own use, a log should be kept of the time of the incident and the witness's exact response (writing an Anecdotal Recording, reporting the incident to supervisor, action taken). Additions to the log should be made as each step in the process occurs ("Made out written report, date," "Answered questions by . . . ," etc.). This should be kept in a confidential file according to the program's policy.

Do not discuss suspicions with the family or the child. This is the one time when what was observed should not be discussed with family or the child after the initial disclosure. The authorities should be allowed to take further action.

If the family member comes to school and asks who made the report, they should be referred to the supervisor. Families should always be treated respectfully and tactfully. When they know a report has been made, they can be referred to the family handbook where it states the policy of the program and the legal responsibility of mandated reporters. They are offered assistance to seek help and given referrals to agencies and support groups in their area. The family member may be angry and abusive, but the child's safety is of the utmost consideration. Arguing with and relating details to the family are inappropriate actions. Supervisors may make a statement such as, "We have observed something that made us suspect the child may have been abused, and we have a legal obligation to report that suspicion. We have done what we think is best for the child. We stand ready to help in whatever way we can." That is all one needs to say, and all one should say, perhaps even *more* than one should say. It all depends on the circumstances.

DIVERSITY AND CHILD ABUSE

Child-rearing customs and practices are not standard between any two families, but they are often even more varied because of racial, cultural, economic, and religious differences. Sometimes these come into conflict with the mainstream practices, and in the case of child abuse, with the legal system. This issue faces people who work with children and families. It is shocking to read child abuse statistics and think about the hurt each statistic represents.

> **REVIEW**
>
> **CHILD ABUSE REPORTING**
>
> Precise, descriptive, immediate note taking is essential to preserve the details of the incident or disclosure. Use the specified state reporting form.
>
> *Types of Information to Report*
>
> indicators of physical abuse
> indicators of neglect
> indicators of sexual abuse
> indicators of emotional neglect

Cultural Differences

Children of families of many cultures are participating in educational experiences. Sensitivity to cultures whose values and customs are different from one's own is an important trait in early childhood professionals. Child-rearing has distinctive differences among various cultures concerning obedience, punishment, dependency, and eye contact. Open discussions about child-rearing will help teachers gain an understanding of other cultures and ethnic groups. The responsibility of the teacher, however, is still to report child abuse and neglect as defined by the state regulations.

Different Abilities

Children with developmental disabilities are also victims of abuse, with some indications that it occurs at higher rates than in the regular population. They are often perceived as an "easy target" with limited defenses or protection. Observation of abuse is even more critical for children with disabilities because they may lack the verbal, physical, or mental skills to protect themselves or disclose what has been happening. The same criteria for signs of abuse are used for children with different abilities. Any questions that need to be asked should be simple and

LDSS-2221-A (Rev. 2/2006) FRONT

NEW YORK STATE
OFFICE OF CHILDREN AND FAMILY SERVICES

REPORT OF SUSPECTED CHILD ABUSE OR MALTREATMENT

Report Date	Case ID	Call ID
Time AM/PM :	Local Case #	Local Dist/Agency

SUBJECTS OF REPORT

List all children in household, adults responsible and alleged subjects. Line # Last Name First Name Aliases	Sex (M, F, Unk)	Birthday or Age Mo/Day/ Yr	Ethnic Code	Relation Code	Role	Lang.
1.						
2.						
3.						
4.						
5.						
6.						
7.						

☐ MORE

List Addresses and Telephone Numbers (Using Line Numbers From Above)	(Area Code) Telephone No.

BASIS OF SUSPICIONS

Alleged suspicions of abuse or maltreatment. Give child(ren)'s line number(s). If all children, write "**ALL**".

____ DOA/Fatality	____ Child's Drug/Alcohol Use	____ Swelling/Dislocation/Sprains
____ Fractures	____ Poisoning/Noxious Substances	____ Educational Neglect
____ Internal Injuries (i.e. Subdural Hematoma)	____ Choking/Twisting/Shaking	____ Emotional Neglect
____ Lacerations/Bruises/Welts	____ Lack of Medical Care	____ Inadequate Food/ Clothing/Shelter
____ Burns/Scalding	____ Malnutrition/Failure to Thrive	____ Lack of Supervision
____ Excessive Corporal Punishment	____ Sexual Abuse	____ Abandonment
____ Inappropriate Isolation/Restraint(Institutional Abuse Only)	____ Inadequate Guardianship	____ Parent's Drug/Alcohol Misuse
____ Inappropriate Custodial Conduct(Institutional Abuse Only)	____ Other specify) ____	

State reasons for suspicion, including the nature and extent of each child's injuries, abuse or maltreatment, past and present, and any evidence or suspicions of "Parental" behavior contributing to the problem.

(If known, give time/date of alleged incident)
MO
DAY
YR
Time : ☐ AM ☐ PM

☐ **Additional sheet attached with more explanation.**

The Mandated Reporter Requests Finding of Investigation ☐ YES ☐ NO

CONFIDENTIAL **SOURCE(S) OF REPORT** ***CONFIDENTIAL***

NAME	(Area Code) TELEPHONE	NAME	(Area Code) TELEPHONE
ADDRESS		ADDRESS	
AGENCY/INSTITUTION		AGENCY/INSTITUTION	

RELATIONSHIP (✓ = REPORTER, X = SOURCE)

___ Med. Exam/Coroner ___ Physician ___ Hosp. Staff ___ Law Enforcement ___ Neighbor ___ Relative ___ Instit. Staff

___ Social Services ___ Public Health ___ Mental Health ___ School Staff ___ Other Specify)

For Use By Physicians Only	Medical Diagnosis on Child	Signature of Physician who examined/treated child X	(Area Code) Telephone No.
	Hospitalization Required: ☐ None	☐ Under 1 week ☐ 1-2 weeks	☐ Over 2 weeks

Actions Taken Or About To Be Taken	☐ Medical Exam	☐ X-Ray	☐ Removal/Keeping	☐ Not. Med Exam/Coroner
	☐ Photographs	☐ Hospitalization	☐ Returning Home	☐ Notified DA

Signature of Person Making This Report	Title	Date Submitted Mo. Day Yr.

Figure 12–4 New York State Child Abuse Reporting Form.

TOPICS IN OBSERVATION

Dealing with Families Suspected of Child Maltreatment

It needs to be said here that discussions with families about their relationship with and treatment of their child is an ongoing dialogue between teachers and families. That basic partnership relationship, which has been emphasized throughout this text, is never more important than in this section. Whether we feel the family just does not know about good hygiene, appropriate discipline techniques, or are deliberately hurting or neglecting their child to the point of placing them in danger, our position is the same. It is one of advocacy for the child and support and assistance to the family. Look again at the Ecological View of the Child from the Teacher's Viewpoint (Figure I–13). While viewing the child in the cold with no socks or boots, or with a nasty bruise the shape of an adult hand, think again of the surrounding factors. This is not to make excuses but to try to understand the context in which the family lives.

The difference between sympathy—feeling sorry for the child and family—and empathy is doing something about it. In cases where it seems that the child does not have the necessities for health and comfort, such as adequate clothing or food, the teacher's first response is not to report the family to the Hotline but to try to supply the need, if there truly is one. It takes all the tact and caring one can muster to determine if the child does not have a coat or just will not wear one. Then, the next step may be some work with the family on parenting skills to help the family take the responsibility for enforcing basic needs (Figure 12–5).

Figure 12–5 The partnership attitude of teacher and families is never more important than when maltreatment is suspected.

Even in cases in which reports must be made for the health and protection of the child, an attitude of empathy for the family still must prevail. The teacher tries not to see the family as ogres or monsters but as people who themselves are so needy or uninformed that these actions are really reactions to their own condition. The reporting then is not "tattling" but an assistance to the family to get the help they all need, as well as protecting the child from harm. This can be communicated again and again to the family, but it is made even more evident by actions that support the family with physical acts of kindness, such as rides to appointments, a home-baked loaf of bread, or a phone call just to see how they are doing.

The teacher is an instrument of change in lives not only of the children in the group but their families. That is an awesome responsibility.

This section was prepared with the help of Jean Rose-Klein, Coordinator of the Broome County Child Abuse Council, Binghamton, NY.

concrete—who, what, when, but *not* why. Drawings, dolls, or a sign interpreter may help the child express the details they want to disclose (Baladerian, 1993). Remember, the observer need not gather all the evidence. All that is needed for a report to try to protect the child is "reason to suspect." Child Protective Services personnel will take the next steps.

What to Do with the Information

Keep your immediate notes, a copy of the report, and a log of the follow-up in a secure place. This is important, but extremely confidential, information. Know the policy of your program or school regarding the storage of this information.

Using Technology

Do not use photographs of the child's body or record interviews with the child. Leave that to the child protective services. By interrogating the child or gathering this kind of evidence, you may be jeopardizing the veracity of the reporting and investigation process. Remember, you need not *prove* abuse or neglect, but you must have reasonable cause for concern. The teacher's role is not to prosecute but to protect.

Pitfalls to Avoid

In such an important situation, it is vital to make sure you avoid doing the following:

- doing nothing when you have strong suspicions
- talking about your suspicions to people who do not have a right to know
- asking the child too many questions or leading questions
- not writing down all the exact details of the disclosure or your observations

Go to the Bind-in-Book CD for Class List Log on Self Esteem forms, plans, and resources.

SELF-CONCEPT AND SELF-ESTEEM

Perhaps no other area of development is more nebulous and difficult to document than self-concept, yet it is at the root of social, academic, and personal success.

Where does the development of **self-concept** begin? This book began the review of child development with attachment and separation. The circle is now complete, coming back to that same important connection between a child's important relationships and the development of self-concept and self-esteem. Whether it is family and child, family and program, or new concepts and established schemata, relationships and connections are what it is all about. The development of healthy **self-esteem** is dependent on certain kinds of relationships. This chapter explores the contributing factors to the development of self-esteem, the stages of the development of a sense of self, and how it can be observed in the classroom. Families and teachers are major influences on self-concept, with the goal of helping the child have high self-esteem based on a truthful vision of the self.

Self-concept resides in the cognitive, what one knows about oneself in many different areas. Self-esteem resides in the emotional realm of how one evaluates and feels about oneself. Physical appearance and ability are very important in American culture, with millions spent on products, clothing, and exercise machines and clubs to improve that appearance. Sports figures are idols because they can jump, throw, catch, or move with outstanding coordination and skill. People measure themselves against others in appearance and physical ability.

Humans are social beings and crave approval, so interactions with other people profoundly affect how people perceive themselves. Connected to that social dimension is the emotional (or affective) side, where feelings sometimes overrule what one knows to be true. One's ability to function mentally affects not only educational achievements but life's decision making, possibly affecting economic status, which also has an effect on the perception of self. All of these parts contribute to one's self-perception (Figure 12–6).

Assessing these areas objectively is the self-concept, what one knows about oneself. It is not, however, simply a matter of assessing those areas. Another dimension enters in, the affective domain, the emotions. For example, a person may know their weight is in the range of normal on the charts (self-concept) but feel they are too heavy. They feel fat and not very good about themselves (self-esteem). It may not be a true measurement, but it is how the person perceives herself. It may be reflected from the appraisal of other people or distorted as in anorexia nervosa.

EXERCISE **Think about yourself in each of these areas (Figure 12–7). In the left column, write three words or phrases that you *know* about yourself in this category. In the right column, write three words or phrases about how you *feel* about yourself in this area.**

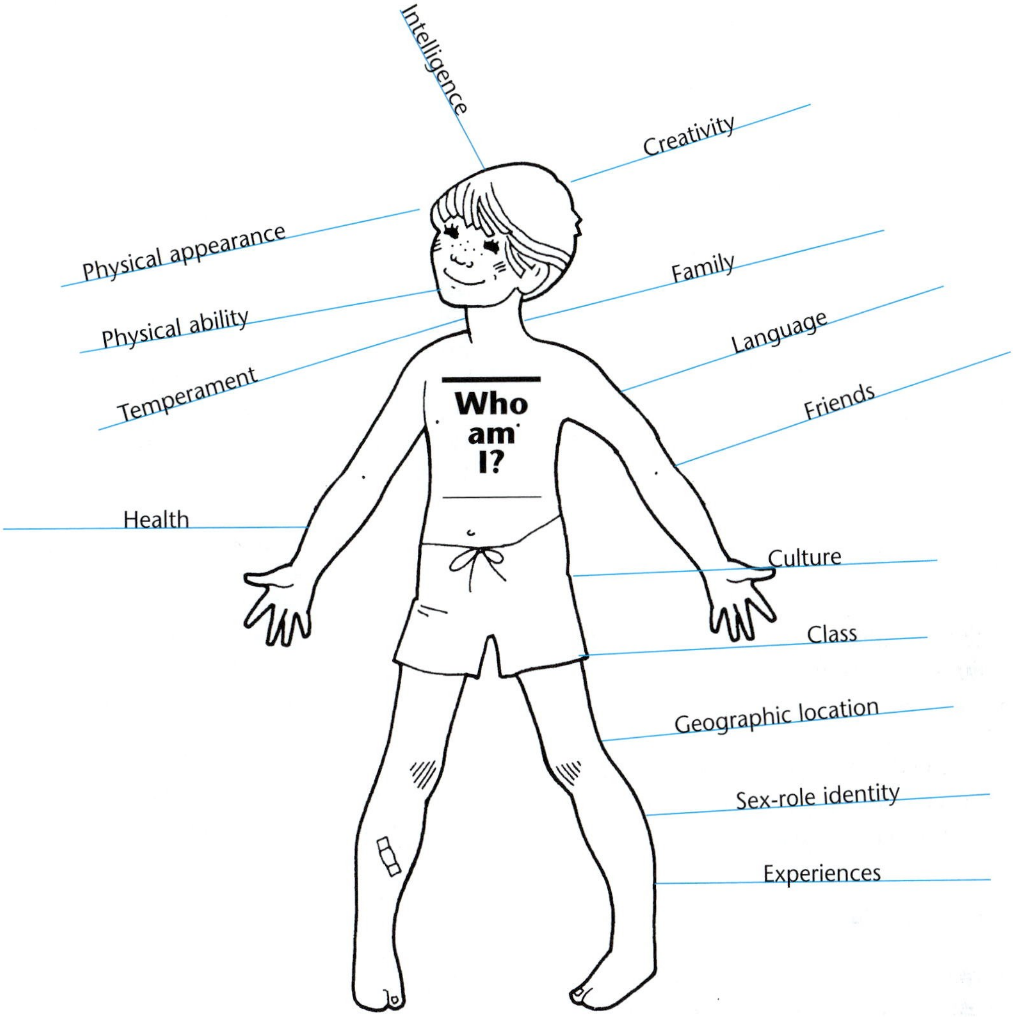

Figure 12–6 Who am I? What do others think of me? How do I feel about myself? All may be different.

Here is the tricky part, the dichotomy as Curry and Johnson (1990) call it, the division or two sides to the issue. They say, "Dichotomous thinking is also evident in the idea that good feelings about the self are always healthy, whereas bad self-feelings are to be avoided. But good feelings about the self can be self-deceptive and narcissistic (excessive pride)" (p. 4). For example, is it always desirable to have high self-esteem?

- High self-esteem about physical appearance is attained when a person finally diets down to 86 pounds?
- High self-esteem in sexual prowess when a man brags he has fathered 12 children by 12 different women?
- High self-esteem in cognitive ability because a person has memorized the phone book?
- High self-esteem in peer acceptance when a high school student gets a 20 on a math quiz because "Dumb is cool"?
- High self-esteem in economic status is proven by lighting a cigarette with a $20 bill?

Feeling good about oneself is only desirable when abilities are accurately assessed, not based on skewed thinking or misplaced values. For example, is low self-esteem always harmful?

- When low self-esteem about physical appearance prods millions of people into diets and exercise programs?
- When low self-esteem from a social encounter shames one into an apology for saying that unkind, hurtful remark?

Describe what you *know* you are like in these areas.		**Describe what you *feel* you are like in these areas.**
	COGNITIVE	
	Language	
	History	
	Math	
	Science	
	PHYSICAL	
	Appearance	
	Abilities	
	Sex role	
	SOCIAL	
	Significant others, including family	
	Peers	
	Culture	
	Socioeconomic status	
	EMOTIONAL	
	Temperament	
	Emotional state	

Figure 12–7 Self-Concept and Self-Esteem Worksheet. Adapted from Shalveson in Owens (1993) and Lively and Lively (1991).

- When low self-esteem over educational achievement motivates work on a high school equivalency diploma, then on a college degree?
- When low self-esteem over computer phobia prompts a person to enroll in a computer workshop?
- When low self-esteem over cultural ignorance encourages one to attend a concert of multicultural music?

When low self-esteem is based on knowing one's shortcomings or inadequacies, *and* brings about action, then low self-esteem "can be constructive and energizing" (Curry & Johnson, 1990, p. 4). Low self-esteem, as a motivator, can raise self-concept and self-esteem.

An interesting study (Kamins & Dweck, 1999) found that praise (and criticism) aimed at the *person* (such as "Good boy," "Bad girl") resulted in more helpless responses and self-blame than praise (and criticism) aimed at the *process* (such as "Great way you picked up your room," "You haven't picked up your room yet"). It makes sense. Specific actions receiving praise or criticism are not personalized and damaging to self-worth as are criticisms that attribute a value to the whole person.

Well-meaning people giving indiscriminate praise for the purpose of raising self-esteem can actually have the opposite effect. Insincerity, whether expressed to a child or an adult, is not believed and tends to be dismissed. When one knows or feels the praise is undeserved, it does not raise self-esteem. If the perception, or self-esteem, is higher than the actual ability, a false pride is present that may prevent future work on this area. This image of self is important to everyone, for it directly affects the motivation to change and learn.

EXERCISE **Now look back at those words you wrote in the previous exercise. Where you see low self-esteem, let it be the motivator for a plan. Work to raise the competency, then the self-concept, then the self-esteem: self-improvement plan!**

Development of Self-Esteem

Development, the progression from simple to complex over a period of time in sequential stages but at individual times, applies to both self-concept and self-esteem (Figure 12–8).

THE FIRST YEAR. The newborn infant is not aware of separateness from the environment. Actions are merely reflexes to stimuli. There is no recognition of self in the mirror, no recognition of people in his life.

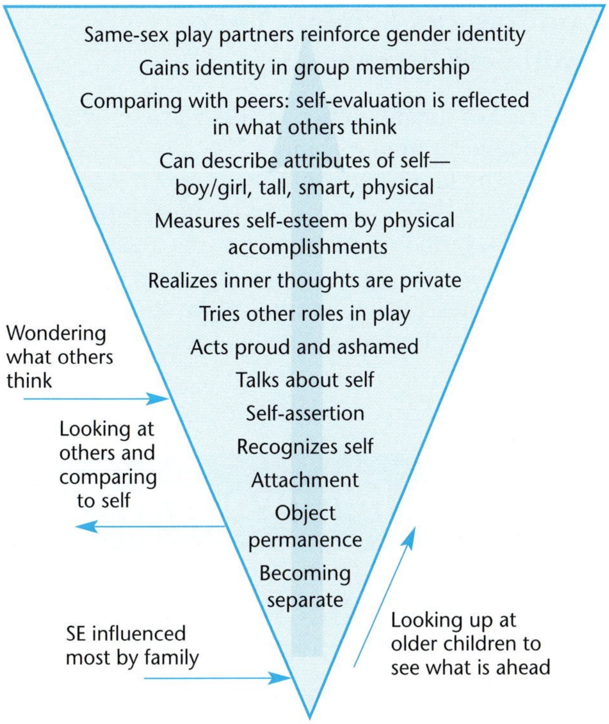

Figure 12–8 Self-Concept Development.

Between two and four months, the infant still has no concept of being separate. Now, however, needs are expressed in signals the family comes to understand. Coos and smiles appear as responses to those people who are cooing and smiling. The child begins to reach toward that image seen in the mirror because it may be something to touch and handle. No, it is just something cold and flat that cannot be put in the mouth to be explored.

By the end of the first year, the knowledge of separateness is attained. The infant now knows he is separate from the people around him and the physical environment. Important people still magically appear and disappear (object permanence). Attempts to keep them present with smiles and sounds work only temporarily. They go away, perhaps never to return. The new mobility of the one-year-old allows the child to go look for those disappearing objects. The knowledge is there that they exist somewhere. If the legs could only support the body, those objects could be found. The baby reaches for the baby in the mirror. When a toy is seen in the mirror, the baby reaches to the mirror to grab it. The long journey of individuation has begun, "the process by which the self or personal identity is developed" (Kostelnik, Whiren, Soderman, & Gregory, 2006, p. 35).

During infancy and toddlerhood, the child's self-concept is primarily influenced by the family and those closest to the child. Information is received about being "good," "cute," "lovable," "capable," "smart," and "accepted." This forms the child's ideas about identity and capability.

THE SECOND YEAR. After walking is mastered, the toddler practices becoming more separate. She now takes journeys away and comes back, farther away, and back again. The toddler is checking each time that a return is possible if necessary. Trust is building that the person will be there when she needs her. Toward the second birthday, if a dot is placed on the child's nose and shown in the mirror, the toddler reaches not to the mirror but to the nose to take it off. Ah, the emergence of self!

Words are multiplying, and some important ones that show an increasing sense of self are "me," "mine," "me do it," and "NO." The child displays great pride when attempts to do a task end in success. If efforts fail, the child expresses disappointment. If scolded, the child shows shame. Sometimes a tantrum erupts when the emotions are so strong they cannot be controlled. It may bring embarrassment or a feeling of unworthiness from those the child knows best. Everyone has witnessed or felt helpless when a child throws a tantrum if his wants are not fulfilled. The child is really helpless also, unable to control their strong emotions.

OLDER PRESCHOOLERS. In the preschool years, children talk about being a boy or a girl, how old they are, how big they are, and what toys they have. Toward kindergarten age, they begin to remember the dreams they had last night and can talk about their thinking. They are beginning to realize their thoughts are part of a private self. No one else can see or know their thoughts unless they are revealed. They used to play with brooms to sweep and trucks to dump, then those brooms became horses and trucks were spaceships. Now they play with their friends in elaborate scenarios in which they leave themselves behind and become other people, talking with other people's words and voices and gestures, doing what grownups do. They constantly read their playmates' faces to look for acceptance. The teacher's words are carefully weighed against what they know they really can do. They are beginning to worry about what others will think of them.

Confronted with many new tasks to try, encouragement and approval of the attempts bring pleasant feelings of competence. This gives motivation to try the next new challenge, expending effort with the confidence of past successes. Success brings more success and even risks at failure. The overall feeling of well-earned, high self-esteem will emerge.

Another child may try as well at all those new things, drawing a circle, tying his shoe, naming his colors. But he is reminded his circle is not round. His shoe does not stay tied. This color is red not green. His attempts at other tasks he is working on may not even be noticed. When he tries again, he feels anxiety because he does not really think he can do it. He could not do it before. Maybe he will not even try, or perhaps he will try but not very hard; then he will not be disappointed when he cannot do it. He looks to see who is watching, but no one is, so he does not even try. Someone comes along and says he did it perfectly and wonderfully, but he knows they are wrong. Even when he tries and it works, he believes it was just an accident. He really did not cause it to work. The child's feeling of incompetence is reinforced by powerful adults, such as family members and teachers, which causes a decline in motivation, willingness to try or risk, and results in lowered self-esteem. This is the beginning of the cycle of failure many children experience in school.

The social comparisons of this age are limited to the child's estimation of performance, mainly physical. They have come so far and can now do so many tasks that they could not do in toddlerhood, still a strong memory. They compare themselves to those big seven-year-olds who can ride a two-wheeler. Because of the successes of the past, they have no doubt they will be able to do it. Social comparisons to older, more developed children only bring hope and confidence of coming accomplishments.

SCHOOL-AGERS. Feedback from formal schooling will be about peer acceptance, academic and athletic competence, and moral worth (Curry & Johnson, 1990). New abilities may be heightened by new challenges or squashed by criticism and labeling. In this stage of Industry versus Inferiority, as Erikson (1950, 1968) called it, much of the self-esteem is dependent on school success. The child is moving into a new stage of cognitive development, Concrete Operations (Piaget, 1968). She is now in new social settings and more interested in the acceptance of friends than family. Most of the abilities in the physical realm will now be used more competitively in sports and in the writing tasks of school. All of these new opportunities can negatively or positively affect self-concept and self-esteem.

This is the age when comparisons to others and the internalization of what other people think is very important. Constant comparisons and competitiveness bring more reality to self-estimations than in the preschool years. The self-esteem is fragile with inside doubts of abilities and acceptance. Clubs, exclusive friendships, and put-downs of others stem from this quest to feel good about oneself.

Families and Schools That Build Self-Esteem

What makes the difference in children's self-esteem? Basic intellect? Innate ability? The family had more money? The family lived in the ghetto? It is all about acceptance. When efforts and independence are praised, they produce internal rewards (Harter, 1999). This gives the feeling of competence and confidence that motivates greater efforts, more independence, and higher self-esteem. The opposite is also true.

@ it happened to me

"Listen to What He Did Now!"

Every day when Jason's mother would come to school, she had a horror story to relate of Jason's latest episode. He had deliberately poured grape juice on the white rug, painted the basement paneling with tar, and pulled up the neighbor's pumpkin patch. I tried to get her not to talk about these things in front of Jason and all the other families and children, but each day she came with a new story of his escapades. One day as the children arrived, I suggested they go check the incubator. "Oh no, you hatched chicks. Don't let Jason go near them. He'll kill them," she exclaimed. Well, you guessed it. Sometime during the free play time, Jason opened the incubator and squeezed a baby chick. Was this Jason's fault? He was just living up to expectations. It is sad that those expectations were not for kind acts, gentle touches, and controlled behavior. I often wonder about what happened to Jason. I wonder what I could have done to try to change his mother's attitude.

Do you have an IT HAPPENED TO ME story about a child you wondered about, feeling that something just wasn't right? I'd love to read it. Send it to WeekbyWeek@thomsonlearning.com

Dependence is increased when efforts are criticized. It is accompanied by feelings of incompetence and a lack of control. Anxiety and doubt fail to motivate. Future efforts are then approached tentatively, expecting failure. External rewards and the approval of others, which is rarely forthcoming, increases dependency. Competency and self-esteem are lowered.

The socialization of the family toward competency sets the course of the path. Owens (1993) reports that children with high self-esteem had mothers who were content with their role, were calm and poised and accepting of others, and led active personal lives. The mothers gave reasons for behavior control, and the fathers took away privileges rather than using punishment. They both used firm follow-through, communicated a commitment to the child's welfare, and expressed a willingness to *listen* to the child's ideas.

Children with low self-esteem, on the other hand, had families who were coercive, rejecting, and controlling by strict restrictions. They were overprotective or neglectful, resulting in the child's feeling of incompetence (Owens, 1993, pp. 399–405). The family has a primary influence over the child's self-esteem.

Schools also have a major part to play in the building of a child's self-esteem. Children need to build a sense of competency, to have an environment with experiences that develop real skills in the cognitive, physical, social, and emotional realms. They need to feel they have the power to make things happen. Involvement in decision making and understanding clear and realistic expectations helps children feel powerful. They thrive in a predictable environment where there are plenty of opportunities to make choices. Their opinions and ideas are accepted as worthy, and the curriculum capitalizes on their strengths. Teachers give informative praise that gives specific reactions and focuses on what they know and do. Negative labels are avoided. The only labels are on the shelves. Children are seen as individuals. That sounds like the teachers *know* each child and their accomplishments. The teachers have watched closely to determine the level of development of each child and have provided an environment where the child can have success. That is a place where a child can go to a Portfolio with his name on it and look at a history of his work. He can even add to it or take something out. He knows it was about all the things he could do.

Self-Concept and Acceptance, Power, Morality, and Competence

Curry and Johnson (1990) present four themes, revisited throughout life as each person seeks to define the self (Figure 12–9).

High Self-Esteem
Acceptance
Power
Morality
Competence

Low Self-Esteem
Isolation
Vulnerability
"Bad" Label
Dependent

Figure 12–9 Self-Esteem Factors.

ACCEPTANCE. From the attachment of the infant to the desire for friendship, **acceptance** is the human quest. Young children desire to please adults and other children. They want to feel they are worthy of being heard. From the crawler tugging on dad's pant leg to the tattler telling of other children's misdeeds, self-concept and self-esteem involve acceptance.

POWER. The infant is exercising **power** when he struggles away from the shirt being pulled over his head. The toddler is exercising power when she says, "No." The preschooler exercises power when he chews his bread into a gun shape to escape the "No guns in school" rule. The teenager exercises power by sporting radical hairstyles or fashions. Adults exercise power through the vote, purchasing power, in any number of ways. It is all saying, "I can make things happen." That is part of self-concept, the knowledge that one has the ability to influence events rather than passively receive or observe them, resigned to accept their consequences.

Empowerment, Wald (2000) believes, is helping children toward self-awareness, encouraging willingness to take reasonable risks and explore their natural curiosity. To shift from teaching to empowering, she suggests the following:

- designing the environment to include child-directed activities
- implementing child-initiated curriculum
- recognizing individual talents
- encouraging peer help
- asking open-ended questions (pp. 14–15)

MORALITY. Morality is the innate desire to be considered "good" rather than "bad," the distinction between right and wrong by society. Self-esteem is affected by knowing the expectations or the rules and following them. The rules may be social, like manners or certain behavior codes (such as being quiet in the movies, or exhibiting a controlled rowdiness at a sports event). They may be legal (such as the speed limit or not stealing), or they may be religious in nature. Self-esteem is increased by following the rules or expectations. Rules and expectation can differ according to their context. Rules may even be contrary to the code of the majority of society, like the Code of Thieves, or in the case of a cult or terrorist group. No matter what the group's expectations, following them gains acceptance, illustrates self-control, and represents a feeling of competence.

Robert Coles adds his advice to the area of morality in *The Moral Intelligence of Children* (1997), combining his stories of children he has interviewed with his thoughts about building character. He explores and wonders about children who are facing insurmountable odds and yet have a basic morality or strong character, and who are concerned about others above themselves. He does not call it self-esteem and in fact eschews self-absorption and self-satisfaction in favor of self-denial and delayed gratification. He says therein lies the power and moral integrity that families and teachers should seek to impart.

COMPETENCE. Satisfaction is the result of accomplishing a task by applying knowledge, skill, and energy and seeing the expected result. This **competence** raises the self-concept and self-esteem. Self-evaluation of positive results brings positive feelings, the feeling of competence, gaining acceptance, demonstrating power, and adding to moral worth.

Acceptance, power, morality, and competence are threads that weave through all developmental areas as we observe children's behavior. Their influence affects self-concept and self-esteem.

Figure 12–10 Sex-role identity is affected by society.

Sex-Role Identity and Self-Esteem

At the moment of birth, the baby's **gender** is announced and the people around the baby begin to form the **sex-role** or **gender identity** (Figure 12–10). In the first few days of life, she receives a name. This distinguishes her sexual identity to the rest of the world. She is held more gently, sometimes covered with a blanket of a certain color, and congratulations to her parents are sometimes tempered with resignation. She receives gifts that are soft and pastel-colored, or toys that inspire nurturing actions instead of construction. She watches her mother to see what women are like and watches her father to see what men are like. Even at two years old, when she pretends to be grown up, she plays the role of mommy, not daddy. By three she tells people she is a girl because she has long hair. She knows that someday she will be a woman, though until she is almost six, she may think she can still change her mind. When she looks at toy advertising, she sees that the girls are playing dolls or the boys are building with blocks. When she watches television, she sees that most of the powerful roles are male. When she has boy playmates, they say, "You can't do this. You're a girl." Her grandma frowns when she climbs a tree and smiles when she pours the tea. She goes to preschool and the teacher says, "The girls can line up first because they're the quietest."

Children are **socialized**, taught the ways to behave in both overt and covert ways. Sexual identity begins with the physiology, the biological indicators of male or female. The view of one's own sexuality is gender identity, the socialized behaviors by parents, siblings, peers, significant other people, culture, and media, communicated by imitation, direct instruction, and reinforcement. Gender enters the subject of self-concept and self-esteem when it is examined according to those four factors that Harter (1999) speaks of as lifelong issues:

- *Acceptance*—Does she feel accepted as a girl, valued for her worth, not just because of her sex, or does she feel like she is valued less because of it?
- *Power and control*—Has she been given autonomy—power over herself—in making decisions, allowed to take risks?
- *Moral virtue*—Has she had opportunities to feel useful and "good," not guilty?
- *Competence*—Does she know about all the things she can do well, given opportunities to show her physical strength, logical mind, self-reliant behaviors?

These are much more at issue for girls than boys, so the choice of using "she" in this section was deliberate. Stereotyping female gender behavior, such as dependency and weakness, has prevented girls from feeling powerful and competent, sometimes in very subtle ways.

Perceptions about the body, even those acquired in infancy and toddlerhood during diapering, can affect self-esteem. When adults use words like *dirty* or *nasty*, genital areas become associated with negative feelings. Children often engage in masturbation for a variety of reasons, most often because it is pleasurable. If the child perceives adults' reactions as negative, they can have an effect on how the child feels about his body, his sexuality, and total self-esteem. Children will also commonly engage in sex play, just as they play out other adult roles. In a similar way, the breadth of experiences will determine how much reality is incorporated into the play. Children often play out explicit television scenes in the preschool classroom or home playroom. Adult reactions to these simulations will also bring value judgments and affect self-concept and self-esteem about their play and ultimately their sexual identity.

Observing Self-Concept and Self-Esteem

All areas of human development contribute to self-concept and self-esteem. Observable behavior demonstrates what a person knows and can do, and the feeling about that knowledge or ability. Self-esteem has defied researchers' attempts to devise measurements for it, especially for young children and those socialized in other cultures. The formation of the concept of self is highly variable in different cultures. Studying Euro-American children, Harter (1990) found two main categories early childhood educators used to define the high self-esteem child:

1. active displays of confidence, curiosity, initiative, and independence
2. adaptive reaction to change or stress

Inferring high or low self-esteem from observing behavior can be highly biased. Indicators of self-esteem in the Euro-American culture are:

- independent and takes initiative
- eager to try new things
- smiles and talks freely
- makes eye contact
- comfortable with peers
- takes pride in work and accomplishments
- uses imagination and takes initiative
- tolerates frustration, perseveres after mistakes (adapted from Samuels, 1977; Fuchs-Beauchamp, 1996)

The child's self-concept is observed while assessing each child's developmental areas. It is revealed in each of the domains of development detailed in the preceding chapters of this book. The Self-Esteem Class List Log will be used in Observation Plans: Week 12 Part A to note these characteristics or behaviors.

SEPARATION. How the child separates from the family member at the beginning of the school year or day depends on the child's self-concept. The child has the sense of belonging and trust in the adult. He feels so worthy of love and care that he is sure his family member would not think of not returning to reclaim this treasure.

SELF-CARE. The child who is secure in self-concept will feel capable and competent and will want to do things independently. She will want to take care of physical needs and not depend on adults. This is observed in the self-care area of toileting, eating, and dressing. The children whose families have given them instructions, let them try, and rewarded their attempts are more likely to be independent and do things for themselves.

PHYSICAL. Physical competence or ability instills pride (Figure 12–11). Climbing to the top of the climber and sliding down, riding the two-wheeler without training wheels, or printing a name can raise a child's self-esteem. The child may have the physical ability but lack confidence in the ability. The resulting behavior is avoidance of the activity, need for assistance, or unsteadiness, resulting in a fall. All these behaviors only end in lowering self-esteem. The observer infers self-esteem while watching the physical skills and recording what the child

Figure 12–11 Abilities contribute to feelings of self-worth.

accomplishes. The reactions when attempts are successful or unsuccessful give clues of self-esteem.

SOCIAL. Excessive withdrawal from social encounters is a sign the child may not feel worthy to be a friend. There may be other reasons, but self-concept is a strong determining factor in a child's social development. By observing children's interactions, the self-concept can be assessed. Self-esteem can be heightened when classroom activities promote prosocial behaviors.

EMOTIONAL. Self-esteem resides in the emotional realm. It is the feeling about the various competencies, the feeling about how capable one is compared to other people, the feeling about how acceptable one is as a playmate. This is observable in the demeanor of the child, the facial and verbal expressions that indicate the emotions inside. Children with good feelings about themselves will appear happy, while those who are uncertain of their competencies and worthiness will appear unhappy, sober, or expressionless. The inborn personality or temperament of the child enters into play here. Care must be taken not to misinterpret a more quiet, introspective person as one with low self-esteem.

SPEECH AND LANGUAGE. When people are in stressful situations, new encounters where they feel uncertain, it is normal to be more quiet and reserved. They may not risk revealing the self by speaking. As one becomes more accustomed to a situation, one feels more free to speak and less concerned about the hearer's reactions or judgments. The child who freely talks to teachers, other children, the janitor, the bus driver, or the UPS delivery person is usually displaying a strong self-concept. "I am important enough for you to listen to what I have to say." Hearing a child constantly say "I can't" will give clues that the child is feeling incompetent and unwilling to risk, indicating low self-esteem.

This is an area in which children who are unsure of their language (especially nonnative language speakers) are observed and often misjudged as having low self-esteem. Because they cannot speak or are unsure about their competencies in communication, they do not speak, even after they have learned many words. These children need to find other areas in the classroom in which to feel competent. Then, language attempts will not be so much of a risk to self-esteem.

MEMORY AND ATTENTION SPAN. Just as emotions govern self-esteem, cognitive abilities govern self-concept. The child is using the cognitive and memory abilities to observe other children's capabilities. She remembers past attempts and failures. Because so many adult–child conversations rely on closed questions like a constant quiz—"What color is your shirt?" "How many crackers are on your napkin?" "What shape is this puzzle piece?"—children form an image very quickly of what they know and do not know in comparison to the adult's expectations. In creating an environment to build cognitive structures and positive self-esteem, opportunities should be presented for divergent thinking, exploring, not reciting.

COGNITIVE. Success breeds success. When a child feels successful and smart, she is more likely to approach challenges with confidence, extend herself to try new experiences, and tolerate a certain amount of less than perfection until the skill or concept is mastered. The success when a difficult task is accomplished raises confidence and self-esteem, so the cycle is on an upward motion. This is the spiral that families, teachers, and schools want for every child. Unfortunately, when a child feels unsuccessful, he is sometimes less willing to try harder, gives in to frustration, and perceives that his self-identity is totally affected by being less competent in one area. This downward spiral is difficult to reverse. The levels and expectations of academic content may not fit every child, so the risk exists for lowering self-esteem. Relative age to other children in the group also has an effect on self-esteem (Thompson et al., 2004). When children are relatively younger than classmates, they may experience lowered self-confidence and self-esteem, and older, age-advantaged children will feel greater confidence when they compare themselves to younger classmates. Older children in a group or grade cohort have been found to be placed in gifted and advanced programs more often. Younger classmates are more likely to be held back, be referred for psychological assessment, and labeled in need of remedial instruction. They may experience depression and hopelessness.

The skillful and aware parent and teacher know the child and give recognition for accomplishments and scaffold areas where competence is close but not yet present. Learning is closely entwined with the emotions, so *feeling* smart is the first step in successful learning.

LITERACY. School is a place of literacy. Watching the child's contact with the written word, whether it is in signs, books, or attempts at writing, can reveal self-concept. The child who has had the advantage of many opportunities with literacy will feel very comfortable in the literacy classroom. The child who has not will exhibit discomfort there, unable to listen and uninterested in stories. No connections are made between the sign in the block area and the sounds the alphabet letters make. It is difficult for the child to find his name on the helper chart. Behavior observations will inform the watcher. What the child is *not* choosing is as revealing as what is chosen. Those areas and activities the child feels the least competent about will not be chosen.

CREATIVITY. Whether it is wondering about what a magnet will pick up, using a variety of materials to glue a design on a piece of tile, or acting as the pilot on an airplane bound for Disney World, children can be observed exhibiting creativity. There may be a child who is unwilling to try the magnet. A pattern is needed for art projects. Dramatic play is avoided. This gives the observer clues about not just creativity but self-esteem. It takes comfort and confidence in oneself to venture away from the tray of metal pieces the teacher has put out and into the room to test out other materials. It takes boldness to try to glue a nail on end to a collage. It inspires others to announce to the passengers on the pretend plane that she is about to have a baby. Creativity is being observed here, as well as self-concept and self-esteem.

ADJUSTMENT TO A NEW SETTING. Because of that secure attachment with the family, the child has the self-esteem to feel lovable. It makes the child feel capable enough to be comfortable in any setting after a nominal settling-in period. The child who learns self-control and follows the routines of the classroom shows confidence. Trust is exhibited that the teacher is a supporter, not an enemy. The child will feel secure enough to want to participate with the group. This gives the observer information, not just about the child's adjustment but about self-concept. Acceptable behavior is assumed and success is expected. This is observable behavior.

Are self-concept and self-esteem observable? Not of themselves, but it appears that by watching the child interact with the environment, peers, and adults, some substantial assumptions about self-concept and self-esteem can be made.

Independence or Interdependence?

Gonzalez-Mena (1997) asks this question and guides the teacher's thinking toward what the family wants for and expects of their child. In homes and cultures that value becoming an independent, autonomous individual, children are encouraged and praised for separation without a fuss, for early self-care, and for high self-esteem. In homes and cultures where **interdependence** is valued and encouraged, children are expected to depend on adults to feed, clothe, and bathe them, are expected to center on serving the needs of others above self, and are encouraged to exhibit humility and a reticence to put self forward.

@ it happened to me

"Bambino"

When I visited the city of Reggio Emilia, I took great pleasure in observing families on the street, in cafes, and in shops. When a two-year-old refused to get on the back of his mother's bicycle and threw a tantrum on the sidewalk, I watched the old people for their reaction. No one looked critical or "tsked, tsked" the mother for not being in control. They were sympathetic of the child and said something like, "Poor bambino." When families were in cafes and restaurants, children of four and five were being fed every mouthful. I was fascinated. It was apparently the mark of good, loving parents to feed their children. In the Reggio Emilia schools, however, these same children were competent in feeding themselves, even using glasses, china, and sharp knives.

Do you have an IT HAPPENED TO ME story about a different culture's view of childhood? I'd love to read it. Send it to WeekbyWeek@thomsonlearning.com

Why Not Ask?

If a person wants the answer to a question, the most logical thing to do is ask someone who is most likely to know. Marshall (1989) suggests some questions an observer might ask a child, probably above four years old, that would get first-person information concerning self-esteem:

> "What can you tell me about yourself? Why is that important?"
> "What can you tell me that is best about you?"
> "What are you good at doing?" (p.46)

This is consistent with the principle of the child as the informant. When the adult asks the child, the child verbalizes what they may have never thought of before. "What am I good at?"

HELPING ALL CHILDREN WITH SELF-ESTEEM

It cannot be ignored that different ethnic, racial, and cultural values affect self-esteem. While the toddler's autonomy and the preschooler's independence may be a Western value, other cultures may hold those same accomplishments with contempt for children in their families. Expectations of competence and styles of interpersonal relations vary between cultures. For example, praising a Middle Eastern boy's ability to clear his dishes and wash the table may not raise his self-esteem in his own culture, where there is a strong division of male/female labor. The child who refuses to participate in a holiday event may not be antisocial but acting according to a religious tradition. Cultural differences affect behavior. They may be misinterpreted as a self-esteem issue. Conversely, expectations in the classroom may conflict with the positive self-concept and self-esteem of a child of a minority group.

Marshall (2001) cautions that behaviors that are valued and interpreted as indicators of high or low self-concept are strongly culture based. The value placed on independence, individuality, and self-assertion in Western society may not be shared by Eastern, African, or Latino cultures, which value harmonious, interdependent relationships. Marshall makes the following suggestions:

1. Be aware of the ways your own culture influences your expectations of children.
2. Consider the cultural backgrounds of the children in your setting and their community.
3. Learn about the cultures from which the children in your program or school may come.
4. Use your basic knowledge of the culture to talk with each family about its values and practices.
5. Build what you have learned from each family. (p. 22)

Even awareness of ethnicity follows a developmental progression. At about three years old, a racial awareness begins, and by six years old it is well ingrained (Derman-Sparks & Phillips, 1997). Young children are in the throes of classification tasks. They are sorting by color and shape, looking for similarities and differences, and making matches of everything in their environment. It is only natural for them to look at each other and compare and contrast. They will notice racial cues, mainly color of skin and texture of hair. While they are classifying, they are also labeling objects. Family and societal labels often have values attached, which the child also absorbs. Experiences and attitudes about groups that bear high or low self-esteem are transmitted. The young child absorbs all this as well.

Observation of racial awareness, especially when it is in the form of children's questions or negative comments, should be addressed right away. Derman-Sparks in *Anti-Bias Curriculums* (1989) recommends:

- Do not ignore.
- Do not change the subject.
- Do not answer indirectly.
- If you are uncomfortable, identify what gets in the way of your responding directly, matter-of-factly, and simply. (p. 33)

Disabilities and Self-Esteem

When disabilities interfere with a child's functioning while included in a regular classroom, self-concept and self-esteem issues arise (Figure 12–12). Peer relations are especially affected when hearing impairment impedes communication. Visual impairment depends on manual contact and results in less smiling. Physical impairments prevent active participation with other children. Mental retardation may reduce responsiveness or limit play options.

For these children, the self-concept and self-esteem issues are acceptance and the power to be independent and feel competent. Children with disabilities who have difficulty developing peer relationships suffer from loneliness, which results in poor self-esteem and increased anxiety and depression.

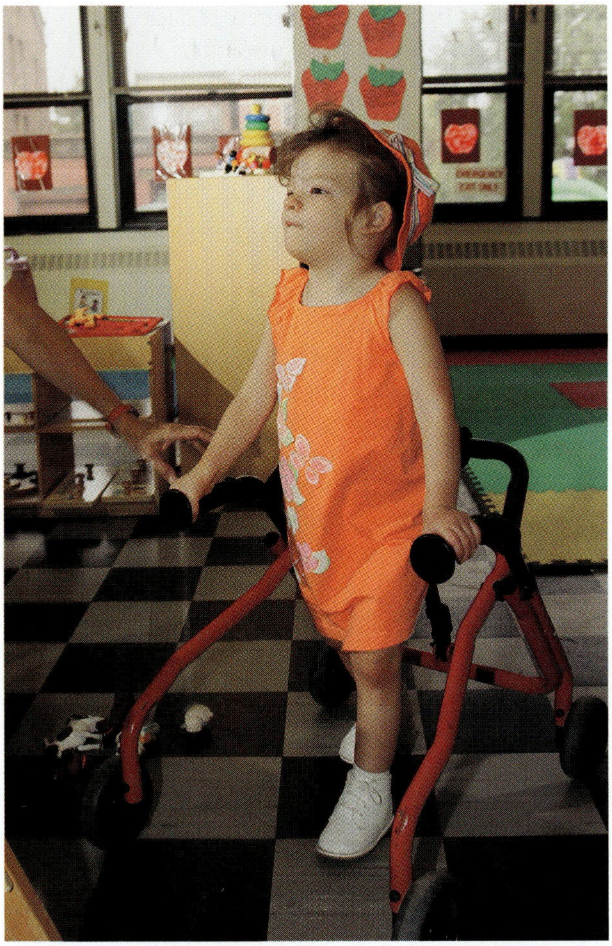

Figure 12–12 Peer relations contribute to self-concept and self-esteem.

This, in turn, prevents satisfactory friendships and may result in even more serious emotional consequences (Pavri, 2001).

It is the children with normal abilities in an inclusive classroom who become very aware of differences when they compare themselves to other children. Observers may see children playing at being visually, hearing, or physically challenged, making up explanations for the disability, and exhibiting fear (Kostelnik et al., 2006). Every child should be recognized for their abilities, rather than their disabilities, the labels applied to them, or the things they cannot do. This attitude or viewpoint will help all gain an understanding of differences, not disabilities, and give the acceptance that they all want. By recognizing the child's abilities and giving clear explanations of limitations, the other children will be made aware of opportunities to help, but the disabled child must have plenty of opportunity to do for himself what he can. It is that old "never do for *any* child what he can do for himself" philosophy. It increases independence, raises competency levels, and ultimately results in positive self-esteem.

These are sensitive, yet vitally important, issues to young children's self-concept and self-esteem. They are challenging.

HELPING PROFESSIONALS FOR CHILD ABUSE AND SELF-ESTEEM CONCERNS

There are many agencies and professionals in most communities to prevent, investigate, advise, protect, and even punish child abuse. Researchers, psychologists, and sociologists are seeking causes and solutions.

Child Protective Services—This is a governmental agency that receives, investigates, and takes action on reports of child abuse or maltreatment. They are a resource for education for mandated reporters, available to answer individual questions and work as advocates for the protection of the child. They protect the confidentiality of all records dealing with the family.

Psychologists and psychiatrists—With specialized training in social and emotional disorders, these professionals work with children and families on issues concerning the causes and results of abuse and maltreatment but also issues dealing with self-esteem. Either abuse or self-esteem issues may interfere with the child's functioning in the social realm. These professionals may serve as educational resources for parenting education for the prevention of child abuse or the development of healthy self-concepts and self-esteem.

OTHER METHODS

Other Methods to Record Self-Esteem

(Be cautious about making judgments about a child's self-esteem. All that can be observed is the outward behavior, which may be interpreted inaccurately.)

Anecdotal/Running Records
Checklist/Rating Scale
Interviews/Conversations
Work Samples—Be careful about interpreting a child's art.
Media

STANDARDS

Selected examples of standards related to child abuse and neglect:

NAEYC Code of Ethical Conduct and Statement of Commitment (NAEYC, 2005)
Principles
P-1.8—We shall be familiar with risk factors for and symptoms of child abuse and neglect, including physical, sexual, verbal and emotional abuse and physical, emotional, educational and medical neglect. We shall know and follow state laws and community procedures that protect children against abuse and neglect.
P-1.9—When we have reasonable cause to suspect child abuse or neglect, we shall report it to the appropriate community agency and follow up to ensure that appropriate action has been taken. When appropriate, parents or guardians will be informed that the referral will be or has been made.
P-1.10—When another person tells us of his or her suspicion that a child is being abused or neglected, we shall assist that person in taking appropriate action in order to protect the child.
P-1.11—When we become aware of a practice or situation that endangers the health, safety, or well-being of children, we have an ethical responsibility to protect children or inform parents and/or others who can.

KEY TERMS

acceptance	physical abuse
competence	power
disclosure	self-concept
emotional maltreatment	self-esteem
gender	sex-role (gender identity)
interdependence	sexual abuse
mandated reporters	socialized
morality	unfounded
neglect	

Go to the Bind-in-Book CD for:

Class List Log on Self-Esteem for all
Plan Week 12 Part A, Directions for a Class List Log on Self Esteem, including What to Do with It, Portfolio Overview Example, Sharing with Child and Family, Actions—Read a Book, In the Environment, In the Curriculum, In the Newsletter
Plan Week 12 Part B, Directions for Anecdotal Recording to observe self-identity for Group C
Plan Week 12 Part C, Reflective Journal

REFERENCES

Baladerian, N. J. (1993). *Abuse of children and youth with disabilities: A prevention and intervention guidebook for parents and other advocates.* Culver City, CA: Disability, Abuse, and Personal Rights Project.

Besharov, D. (1990). *Recognizing child abuse: A guide for the concerned.* New York: The Free Press.

Coles, R. (1997). *The moral intelligence of children.* New York: Random House.

Crosson-Tower, C (2003). *The role of educators in preventing and responding to child abuse and neglect.* Washington, DC: U.S. Department of Health and Human Services.

Curry, N., & Johnson, C. (1990). *Beyond self-esteem: Developing a genuine sense of human value.* Washington, DC: National Association for the Education of Young Children.

Derman-Sparks, L. (1989). *Anti-bias curriculum: Tools for empowering young children.* Washington, DC: National Association for the Education of Young Children.

Derman-Sparks, L., & Phillips, C. (1997). *Teaching/learning anti-racism: A developmental approach.* New York: Teachers College Press.

Erikson, E. H. (1950). *Childhood and society.* New York: Norton.

Erikson, E. H. (1968). *Identity: Youth and crisis.* New York: Norton.

Fuchs-Beauchamp, K. D. (1996). Preschoolers' inferred self-esteem: The behavioral rating scale of presented self-esteem in young children. *Journal of Genetic Psychology, 157* (2), June 1, 1996.

Gonzalez-Mena, J. (1997). Independence or interdependence? *Child Care Information Exchange,* September/October, 1997, 62–64.

Harter, S. (1990). The self-perceptions of uncommonly bright youngsters. In R. J. Sternberg & J. Kolligan, Jr. (Eds.), *Competence considered.* New Haven, CT: Yale University Press, pp. 67–97.

Harter, S. (1999). *The construction of the self: A developmental perspective.* New York: Guilford Press.

Kamins, M. L., & Dweck, C. S. (1999). Person versus process praise and criticism: Implications for contingent self-worth and coping. *Developmental Psychology, 35* (3), 835–847.

Kostelnik, M., Whiren, A., Soderman, A., & Gregory, K. (2006). *Guiding children's social development: Theory to practice* (5th ed.). Clifton Park, NY: Thomson Delmar Learning.

Lively, V. E., & Lively, E. (1991). *Sexual development of young children.* Clifton Park, NY: Thomson Delmar Learning.

Marshall, H. H. (2001). Cultural influences on the development of self-concept: Updating our thinking. *Young Children, 56* (6), 19–25.

National Association for the Education of Young Children. (2005). *Code of ethical conduct & statement of commitment.* Washington, DC: Author.

Owens, K. (1993). *The world of the child.* New York: Merrill, an imprint of Macmillan Publishing Company.

Pavri, S. (2001). Loneliness in children with disabilities: How teachers can help. *Teaching Exceptional Children,* July/August 2001, 52–57.

Piaget, J. (1968). *On the development of memory and identity.* Worcester, MA: Clark University Press.

Samuels, S. C. (1977). *Enhancing self-concept in early childhood: Theory and practice.* New York: Human Science Press.

Thompson, A. H., Barnsley, R. H., & Battle, J. (2004). The relative age effect and the development of self-esteem. *Educational Research, 46* (3), 313–320.

Wald, G. S. (2000). Moving from "I think I can" to "I know I can." *Young Children, 55* (4), 14–15.

Walsh, K. Farrell, A., Bridgestock, R., & Schweitzer, R. (2006). The contested terrain of teachers detecting and reporting child abuse and neglect. *Journal of Early Childhood Research, 4* (1), 65–76.

RESOURCES

Baladerian, N. J. (1990). *Abuse of children and youth with disabilities: A prevention and intervention guidebook for parents and other advocates.* Culver City, CA: Disability, Abuse and Personal Rights Project.

Crosson-Tower, C. (2003). *The role of educators in preventing and responding to child abuse and neglect.* Washington, DC: U.S. Department of Health and Human Services. http://www.childwelfare.gov/pubs/usermanus/educator/index.cfm.

Derman-Sparks, L. (1989). *Anti-bias curriculum: Tools for empowering young children.* Washington, DC: National Association for the Education of Young Children.

King, E., Chipman, M., & Cruz-Jansen, M. (1994). *Educating young children in a diverse society.* Boston: Allyn and Bacon.

Koralek, D. (1992). *Caregivers of young children: Preventing and responding to child maltreatment.* U.S. Department of Health and Human Services, National Center on Child Abuse and Neglect.

Kostelnik, M., Whiren, A., Soderman, A., & Gregory, K. (2006). *Guiding children's social development: Theory to practice* (5th ed.). Clifton Park, NY: Thomson Delmar Learning.

NAEYC. 1996. Position statement on the prevention of child abuse in early childhood programs and the responsibilities of early childhood professionals to prevent child abuse. Washington, DC: Author.

Saifer, S. (1990). *Practical solutions.* St. Paul, MN: Redleaf Press.

CHAPTER 13

Using Program Assessments to Look at Children in Groups

IN THIS CHAPTER

- Assessing Early Childhood Programs
- Topics in Observation: Assessing the Environment—Pointing Back at You
- Looking at the Adjustment of the Child to the Program
- Helping All Children in Group Settings
- Helping Professionals for Program Evaluation and Support

ASSESSING EARLY CHILDHOOD PROGRAMS

The child is enrolled in an early childhood group setting. It could be in a child care center of many types: for-profit, nonprofit, employer-supported family day-care home, or a religiously affiliated program. It may be a part-day program called a preschool, nursery, nursery school, play group, or parent cooperative. Head Start programs serve thousands of three- to five-year-olds across the country, and in some places also serve infants and toddlers. Public and private schools provide educational experiences for children from kindergarten up. Some schools also have programs for prekindergarten and some for infants and toddlers as well. Many school districts and outside agencies provide programs for children before and after school and on school holidays. There are many programs for children with special needs to receive early intervention in separate settings or included within regular classrooms. Some programs draw specific audiences, such as music, gymnastics, and dance schools. No matter what kind of a program in which a child is enrolled, the primary responsibility of that program is to keep the child safe and to deliver the services the family expects.

With the role of the family as the primary educator and socializing agent of children, it becomes increasingly important for all of society to support those roles. When the family is strengthened, society is strengthened. Children's programs providing child care while family members work or are in school also provide respite from the stresses of parenting, strengthen child development, and strengthen the family with positive outcomes for all.

Whenever young children are in group settings outside their home, the program should be evaluated, by some regulating body or agency, for its safety and appropriateness for children. Each state has its own criteria and process for licensing or regulating the care and education of children in groups.

EXERCISE **Identify the regulatory agency for the program in which you work or are doing observations.**

child care—state licensing agency
school—state agency

Obtain a copy of the regulations and look for the method of program evaluation: yearly review or report, on-site visit, or accreditation.

Program evaluations collect information to make informed judgments and decisions about the program. It could be to

- evaluate the program against a standard.
- assess the program's adherence to its stated mission and philosophy.
- receive feedback from various constituencies such as children, families, program administrators, teachers, funders, and community agency personnel.
- assess the program's suitability for an individual child.
- provide measures of accountability. (LaMontagne & Russell, 1998)

Families are the most important evaluators as well as those with the greatest risk, their own child. Families have the right and responsibility to freely access the building in which their child is enrolled. They should ask questions and observe that the program meets their expectations and their child's needs. Families should have a voice in evaluating the program, no matter what type it is. There are many family surveys available that can be adapted to ask specific questions about the program. They typically include questions concerning families' satisfaction with the facilities, program, and staff; communication; interactions between the child and staff; comfort with the policies and procedures; and suggestions or recommendations.

Administrators, staff, and families should regularly evaluate all aspects of the program. There are many organizations that offer an accreditation component to their members (listed in a later section). The common standards against which the accreditation process evaluates the program are:

environment
health and safety
administration
curriculum
staffing
relationships: child to adult and families to program
evaluation

Some sample questions for program evaluation are included in Figure 13–1.

The observation-and-recording method of this section is not focused on the child but on the program. Several program evaluation tools are presented to familiarize the reader with options available to assess the quality of the early childhood program.

A Setting Observation

EXERCISE **Let's take a trip to a child care center or school. You can think about one you have visited or make up one in your mind. No children need to be present. You will observe the setting to see what it tells you. Drive into the parking lot.**

What do you see?/What could it mean? (Record your answers on a separate sheet of paper.)

From the parking lot:
Sign for the program:
Playground:
Entranceway:
Inside a classroom:
Children's spaces:
Learning materials:
Displays:
Adult spaces:

Reactions to a Setting Observation

Without ever observing a program in action, much information is gathered, impressions formed, and judgments made. A program's purpose and practices are readily observed and interpreted from the environment. It is healthy to inspect one's own environment with a visitor's eye. It is also an exercise in professionalism to visit other programs. These bits of information are taken in by the senses and associated with information already stored. Reflection on possible meanings of what is observed may give insight

CHOOSING A TOOL

Evaluation instruments vary with the purpose of the program evaluation. Moreover, a survey of various program evaluations shows that many are designed to be program-specific; that is, the evaluation itself is devised to examine one program only. Individualized assessments are difficult to generalize. However, it appears that most program evaluations assess several, if not all, of the following areas:

The Physical Environment

Are the facilities clean, comfortable, safe?
Are room arrangements orderly and attractive?
Are materials and equipment in good repair and maintained?
Is there a variety of materials, appropriate to age levels?
Are activity areas well defined?
Is cleanup and room restoration a part of the daily schedule?
Are samples of children's work on display?
Is play space adequate, both inside and out?
Is personal space (e.g., cubby) provided for each child?

The Staff

Are there enough teachers for the number of children? How is this determined?
Are the teachers qualified? What criteria are used?
Is the staff evaluated periodically? By whom and how?
Does the school provide/encourage in-service training and continuing education?
Do the teachers encourage the children to be independent and self-sufficient?
Are the teachers genuinely interested in children?
Are teachers aware of individual abilities and limitations?
What guidance and disciplinary techniques are used?
Do teachers observe, record, and write reports on children's progress?
Are teachers skilled in working with individual children, small groups, and large groups?
Does the teaching staff give the children a feeling of stability and belonging?
Do teachers provide curriculum that is age-appropriate and challenging?
How would you describe the teachers' relationships with other adults in the setting? Who does this include, and how?
Can the teaching staff articulate good early education principles and relate them to their teaching?

Family Relationships

How does the classroom include families?
Are family members welcome to observe, discuss policies, make suggestions, help in the class?
Are different needs of families taken into account?
Where and how do families have a voice in the school?
Are family–teacher conferences scheduled?
Does the school attempt to use community resources and social service agencies in meeting families' needs?

The Organization and Administration

Does the school maintain and keep records?
Are there scholarships or subsidies available?
What socioeconomic, cultural, religious groups does the school serve?
What is the funding agency, and what role does it play?
Is there a school board and how is it chosen?
Does the school serve children with special needs or handicaps?
Are the classroom groups homo- or heterogeneous?
What hours is the school open?
What age range is served?
Are there both full- and part-day options?
Is after-school care available?
Does the school conduct research or train teachers?
What is the teacher–child ratio?

The Overall Program

Does the school have a written, stated education philosophy?
Are there developmental goals for the children's physical, social, intellectual, and emotional growth?
Are the children evaluated periodically?
Is the program capable of being individualized to fit the needs of all the children?
Does the program include time for a variety of free, spontaneous activities?
Is the curriculum varied to include music, art, science, nature, math, language, social studies, motor skills, etc.?
Are there ample opportunities to learn through a variety of media and types of equipment and materials?
Is there ample outdoor activity?
Is there a daily provision for routines: eating, sleeping, toileting, play?
Is the major emphasis in activities on concrete experiences?
Are the materials and equipment capable of stimulating and sustaining interest?
Are field trips offered?
Do children have a chance to be alone? In small groups? In large groups?

Tools for program evaluation are woven together to give a more comprehensive look at the total program.

Figure 13–1 Program Evaluation Questions.

@ it happened to me

Where Is Everyone?

I was attending a meeting at the office of a child care director. I arrived on time and walked through the center without hearing a sound, an eerie feeling. What could that mean?

As I walked down the hall, I smelled, then saw, vomit puddles ahead of me. I called out, "Anybody here?" A weak voice from the other end of the hall replied, "In here." It was from the bathroom where two staff people and one child were huddled over sinks. A volatile virus had struck, and all other children and staff had been sent home, some sick, and the rest as a precaution. This little person and two staff were the last ones left but were sick as well. What a pitiful sight! I donned gloves and helped them clean up. The meeting had been cancelled since the director had gone home, too sick to think of calling me. Illness can strike quickly and powerfully when people are in group settings.

Do you have an IT HAPPENED TO ME story about an environment that was especially innovative, welcoming, oh all right, atrocious beyond belief? I want to hear your stories. Please send them to me at WeekbyWeek@thomsonlearning.com

or make inferences about the values, philosophies, economic sponsorship, and even the housekeeping habits of the teacher. Some decisions for action can result, such as:

"Oh, I can't wait to get back to my classroom and use that idea."
"I could really tell they emphasize. . . ."
"I wonder what they did with that? I'll have to ask."
"I wonder how they provide for. . . . ?"
"If that were my room, I would. . . ."
"I certainly don't agree with . . . but they must have a different philosophy."
"I will not comment on . . . but I can talk about. . . . "

As a professional courtesy, write a note of appreciation for allowing the visit and a specific aspect that you liked. Remember the evaluation principles: Look for the accomplishments, not the deficits; specific praise raises self-esteem.

Program Assessments

EXERCISE What do these things tell you?

checkbook balance
bathroom scale
speedometer
wristwatch
windsock
mirror
bookmark
diploma
roadmap
report card

Yes, you guessed it. You are so clever. These are all measurements or visual indicators of important facts. Money, weight, speed, time, wind direction, hair check, last chapter read, course completed, roads traveled, evaluation—constant vigilance is part of life.

In *Week by Week,* many areas of child development have been examined for indicators of progress and possible delays. Programs need evaluation as well for indicators of progress and warning signs of poor quality situations. **Program evaluation** can be informal, such as a staff discussion at the end of the year to recap the successes, the difficulties, and forecasts based on the past. Aspects of program quality can be measured with some of the same methods used to observe children's development (Figure 13–2).

An important measuring stick of a program's effectiveness is the growth and development of the children enrolled. Attendance figures give indicators of the health and safety procedures of the program: Young children in close surroundings do not share toys, but they do share germs, and staff must give constant consideration to infection control. High absence rates could be a sign of lax infection control standards and procedures.

Children require nourishment to grow. If they are nourished developmentally, they will show

Child Observation Method	Program Observation
Developmental Checklists	Checklists: Safety Appropriate programming
Anecdotal Records	Teacher's stories
Frequency Counts	Teacher behaviors Use of slang Negative discipline
Time Samples	Assess learning center use Measure effect of adult presence in learning area
Interviews	Family/child surveys Family/teacher conferences
Work Samples	Examples of teacher projects Bulletin boards Newsletters
Observation	Outside reviewers Licensing agents Accreditation validators

Figure 13–2 Observation Techniques for Program Evaluations.

progress. Portfolios measuring children's progress are one indication of an effective program. Another indicator is children's active involvement with the learning environment. Peeks into classrooms should show children busy working on a variety of activities with the adults facilitating the learning. The rooms should be filled with children's voices—talking and laughing—with a minimum of adult voices. Children can be surveyed to hear what they have to say about the school, the program, and the learning activities. Even very young children can tell what they like about their school or child care center and what they do not. Adults should listen.

Periodic evaluations of early childhood programs are necessary to measure the effectiveness of the program and for accountability. Some indicators stated in the NAEYC, NAECS/SDE position statement (2003) include the following:

Evaluation is used for continuous improvement.
Goals become guides for evaluation.
Comprehensive goals are used.
Multiple sources of data are available.
Sampling is used when assessing individual children as a part of large-scale program evaluation.
Safeguards are in place if standardized tests are used as part of evaluations.
Children's gains over time are emphasized.
Well-trained individuals conduct evaluations.
Evaluation results are publicly shared.

Total Program Evaluations

There are many evaluation instruments available, some determined by the type of the program, others elected for use. All have evaluation as their basic premise: the assessment or measurement of aspects of the program, comparison with an accepted standard of quality, and action implemented to bring the program into compliance or increased effectiveness. An informal program evaluation is one that is a self-study, designed to guide program personnel to assess, evaluate, and raise quality.

Accreditation is a program evaluation completed on-site by an outside body, usually a professional organization, for the purpose of recognizing programs that meet preestablished criteria. The accreditation process usually begins with an extensive self-study that leads to improvements in the program before the validation visit. Fees are charged for accreditation, and usually some kind of periodic reports are required to report the maintenance of the level of quality. Families can use accreditation as a measuring tool when selecting a program. See Figure 13–3 for a comparison chart of some of the systems.

PROGRAM PERFORMANCE STANDARDS. Head Start programs have national **performance standards** by which they are measured. The standards state that the programs must be "developmentally and linguistically appropriate, recognizing that children have individual rates of development as well as individual interests, temperaments, languages, cultural backgrounds and learning styles; . . . support each child's individual pattern of development and learning; provide for the development of cognitive skills by encouraging each child to organize his or her experiences, to understand concepts, and to develop age appropriate literacy, numeracy, reasoning, problem solving and decision-making skills which form a foundation for school readiness and later school success" (U.S. Department of Health and Human Services, 2005).

Crosswalk of Early Childhood Program Standards

	NAEYC Program Accreditation	Head Start Program Standards	National Health & Safety Standards	High/Scope PQA	National Association for Family Child Care Accreditation
Child Development and Education	1. Relationships 2. Curriculum 3. Teaching 4. Assessment	1304.21 Education & Early Childhood Development	2. Program: Activities for Healthy Development 3. 7 IDA Eligible Children	Adult/Child Interaction Curriculum Planning & Assessment Daily Routine	1. Relationships with Children 3. Developmental Learning Activities
Child Health and Safety	5. Health	1304.22 Child Health and Safety	3. Health Promotion & Protection 6. Infectious Diseases	Learning Environment	4. Safety and Health
Nutrition	5. Health	1304.23 Child Nutrition	4. Nutrition & Food Service		4.73 Nutrition and Food Preparation
Mental Health	1. Relationships	1304.24 Child Mental Health			
Parent Involvement	7. Families	1304.4 Family Partnership		Parent Involvement & Family Services	1. Relationships with Parents and Family
Partnerships	8. Community Relationships	1304.41 Community Partnership	9. Licensing & Community Action		1. Provider and the Community
Management Systems	10. Leadership and Management	1304.51 Management Systems and Procedures	8. Administration	Program Management	5. Professional and Business Practices
Staff Management	6. Teachers	1304.52 Human Resources Management	1. Staffing	Staff Qualifications & Staff Development	5. Assistants and Substitutes
Facilities and Equipment	9. Physical Environment	1304.53 Facilities, Materials, & Equipment	5. Facilities, Supplies		2. The environment—Home

Figure 13–3 Program Evaluation Comparison.

HEAD START—PRISM. Head Start programs are evaluated using the *PRISM* (*Program Review Instrument for Systems Monitoring*) developed by the U.S. Department of Health and Human Services (2006). This evaluation tool measures programs against the Head Start Program Performance Standards adopted in 1998. They include standards for the following areas:

- early childhood development and health services
- family and community partnerships
- program design and management
- implementation and enforcement

There have been examples of program standards throughout this book in the "Standards" section. Here are a few more:

HIGH/SCOPE—PQA. High/Scope has developed a program-evaluation tool for all early childhood settings, especially those implementing the High/Scope Curriculum, the *High/Scope Program Quality Assessment,* second edition (2002). It has expanded sections for evaluating the following:

- learning environment
- daily routine
- adult–child interaction
- curriculum planning and assessment
- family involvement and family services
- staff qualifications and staff development
- program management

Potential uses of the PQA include staff training, program assessment and monitoring, observation and feedback, research and evaluation, and information and dissemination.

NAEYC CENTER ACCREDITATION. The National Association for the Education of Young Children (NAEYC) has an accreditation system for early childhood programs, the *NAEYC Early Childhood Program Standards and Accreditation Criteria* (2005), which is the National Commission on Accreditation Reinvention's plan to improve the quality of care and education for young children in early childhood programs. To be eligible for accreditation, programs must serve a minimum of 10 children from birth through age 5 in part- or full-day group programs, have been in operation at least 1 year, and meet state **license requirements** (or be exempt from state requirements). The criteria measure interactions between staff and children and staff and families. They also look at the administration of the program, curriculum, physical environment, health, safety, and nutrition. Staff needs are assessed by criteria for staff qualifications and development, staffing patterns, and program evaluation through a 3-step process in which program personnel and families conduct a self-study rating various standards as unmet, partially met, or fully met. This self-study is designed to indicate areas that need improvements; an improvement plan is implemented and ratings are changed. Classroom staff, administrators, and families have their own components to assess. Once the self-study and ensuing improvements are complete, the administrator submits the program description to the NAEYC Academy and applies for a validation visit. The NAEYC Academy assigns a "validator" to observe in the classrooms and spot check the documentation of the administrator's report to validate or confirm that the ratings are accurate. That validation report is submitted to a 3-person commission for the accreditation decision. Programs are not required to demonstrate 100 percent compliance. The accreditation is valid for 3 years; then the self-study and validation are repeated.

NACCP PROGRAM ACCREDITATION. The National Association of Child Care Professionals (NACCP) serves child care center owners, directors, and administrators regardless of tax status or corporate sponsorship. Their National Accrediting Commission makes the decision to award accreditation to programs following the self-study phase, where improvements can be made, and validation of the self-study report by an on-site observation. The standards' key components are curriculum, interaction, parents, health and safety, and administration.

NECPA PROGRAM ACCREDITATION. National Early Childhood Program Accreditation (NECPA) calls for the owner or director to assemble demographic information and lead a self-paced, self-study evaluation. Surveys are completed by staff and families, along with classroom observations. Improvements are made to the program based on the evaluations, and the program participates in an on-site verification visit by an assigned validator. The scored indicators and program profile are presented to the NECPA's National Accreditation Council for the accreditation decision. The accreditation is valid for three years.

The NECPA's accreditation system is entering the technological age with a new automated process, dubbed *Automated Accreditation Indicator Systems* (*AAIS*).

FAMILY CHILD CARE ACCREDITATION. The National Association for Family Child Care (NAFCC) also has an accreditation system for family child care workers: the *National Association for Family Child Care Accreditation.* These are teachers who provide licensed or regulated care for other people's children in the provider's home for more than 18 months. The standards include relationships, environment, developmental learning activities, safety and health, and professional and business practices. It requires a provider self-evaluation with the assessment profile for family child care, family questionnaires, a family observation, and validator observation. This also is valid for 3 years.

SCHOOL-AGE PROGRAM ACCREDITATION. The National AfterSchool Association has a program-improvement and accreditation process to promote quality in programs serving children 5–14 years old in after school programs. Following a self-study, endorsers conduct an on-site visit to verify the self-study report.

Special Focus Instruments

There are some formal program assessment tools that can be used to evaluate one aspect of a program. This can be accomplished as a self-study, by the administration, or by a consultant. The advantage of a self-study is that the staff considers quality criterion items, standards set by an outside source. These are less threatening and not taken as criticism or a pet peeve but as objective benchmarks against which to compare and consider their appropriateness for the particular situation.

When evaluations are done by the director or administrator, it gives them first-hand information about the program, recognizing the strengths of the program. It also may indicate areas that need attention, from which they can implement change. Often the staff has been aware of the situation and desiring change but were not in a position to make the change themselves. Now that can happen. This type of evaluation, however, can stress the staff and alienate them from administrators if the staff feels they are under scrutiny. Evaluation is only helpful if it focuses on strengths and if plans build on those strengths, not the deficits. They can be addressed in a cooperative way with group decision making more effectively than from edicts or top-down proclamations.

Outside consultants may be enlisted to perform the assessment. This objective outside person can observe, evaluate, and make recommendations without the fear of recriminations from administrators or alienation from the staff. Issues that staff or administrators have been aware of can surface from an outside consultant and can be addressed easier than from within. Whatever the source of evaluation, the outcome should be to discover and proclaim the strengths of the program, and to recommend changes or next steps that are reasonable, attainable, and measurable. This is the same principle that is used in the child's developmental evaluation.

Here are a few program evaluations that may be used and a short description of each evaluation's use.

EARLY CHILDHOOD ENVIRONMENT RATING SCALE—REVISED (ECERS-R). The ECERS-R (Harms, Clifford, & Cryer, 1998) is a comprehensive rating scale to assess personal-care routines, furnishings and displays, language-reasoning experiences, fine and gross motor activities, creative activities, social development activities, and adult needs. Each is rated on a scale of 1 to 7, with quality points of 1, 3, 5, 7 described in detail. ECERS-R's format gives clear criteria and a goal for improvement if a score of less than 7 is determined. The *Infant/Toddler Environment Rating Scale, Revised Edition* (Harms, Cryer, & Clifford, 2002) follows the same format but is specific to younger age groups. Neither one of these rating scales specifically looks at curriculum. The *Family Day Care Rating Scale* (Harms Clifford, 1989) and the *School-Age Care Environment Rating Scale* (Harms, Jacobs, & White, 1995) are two additional rating scales measuring environments for special settings.

NATIONAL HEALTH AND SAFETY PERFORMANCE STANDARDS (2002). The American Academy of Pediatrics, Public Health Association, and National Resource Center for Health and Safety in Child Care have developed an extensive set of performance standards that include educational as well as health and safety guidelines. The standards are based on 13 guiding principles that include program policies and procedures.

STAFF PERFORMANCE. There are many instruments created to measure staff performance. *Measuring Performance: The Early Childhood Educator in Practice* (Elliott, 2002) is a comprehensive guide that can be used for both program performance and spot checks on teacher-demonstrated cognitive, creative, affective, language/literacy, social, and physical behaviors. It also contains separate checklists for measuring child development, diversity, and safety forms for developing staff and program action plans.

ADMINISTRATION. *The Program Administration Scale* (Talan & Bloom, 2004) use the same rating scale format as the ECERS (Harms, Clifford, & Cryer, 1998) with criteria to assess the administration of a child care center.

TOPICS IN OBSERVATION

Assessing the Environment—Pointing Back at You

When I tattled, my mother always said, "When you point your finger at someone else, three fingers are pointing back at yourself." That axiom has applications in observing children's development or lack of it. When we are careful observers, the attention is focused on the child, pointing at characteristics, skills, and behaviors. We tend to lay the source of the problem with the child. "Why is the child like that?" "Why can't she . . . ?" "What's the matter with that child?"

The finger pointing up can be interpreted as, "That's just the way those people are." Substantial elements of a child's development are genetically programmed. The adults in the child's life act as the observers of how that script is played out. However, the three fingers pointing backward are a reminder of the important role the adult plays (Figure 13–4). Rather than blaming the child or the genetic program, some reflection may help. The influence of the adults in the child's life cannot be overlooked.

Figure 13–4 When you point a finger at someone else, three fingers are pointing back at you.

ANTI-BIAS CURRICULUM. Derman-Sparks (1989) lists questions to be answered from videotaped classroom observations. Peers examine interactions between teachers and children that may subtly teach gender, racial, or disability biases. The whole book, *Anti-Bias Curriculum: Tools for Empowering Young Children* (1989), is a self-evaluative, consciousness-raising experience for the reader.

PLAYGROUND SAFETY. Evaluation is more than assessment. It is making a change because of the assessment. Programs periodically should perform safety checks inside and outside using checklists such as the one in Chapter 3. Deteriorating equipment, overlooked hazards, and bad habits can be detected in these checklist formats for the protection of children's health and safety.

Environment and Development

Repeatedly, the influence of the environment, in particular the early childhood setting, has been emphasized as a powerful force in each area of development. The role of the teacher is to provide, modify, enrich, support, supervise, and adapt that environment for each child. It begins with a knowledge of the child's physical development. How large are they? What do they need to be kept safe? What kind of equipment is needed for the routines and activities of the child while in this environment? These decisions are based on the purpose and philosophies of the program. If it is a library story hour, then one kind of equipment and materials is appropriate, whereas a gymnastics program may select different criteria.

The cognitive environment in a developmentally based program will provide materials that prompt children to ask questions. Answers are sought by following the child's level of thinking. Engaging or participating in the actual manipulation of real objects replaces one-dimensional worksheets, watching an adult, or a video explanation of a principle. The adults in the environment support the exploration by asking open-ended questions, such as, "How do you think that happened?" or "Is there another way . . . ?" "What would happen if . . . ?"

The emotional environment of the early childhood setting provides for realistic expectations. Because young children are spillers, mops, paper towels, brooms, and dust pans are handy for clean-up. Group experiences can be noisy and stressful for some children. A quiet, alone space is provided from which to watch the action or withdraw to rest and reduce the adrenaline flow. Because children are learners, approximations for a task are recognized and efforts are rewarded before full accomplishments are attained. Children are made to feel competent by being trusted with responsibility that matches their ability.

The social atmosphere of the environment is monitored constantly to promote cooperation rather than competition, sociability rather than sarcasm, and friendship rather than isolation. Small groups are encouraged to work and play together by the physical arrangement of the furnishings into small areas. Planned and spontaneous activities bring children physically close to one another. This helps them understand the rights and space needs of each person as well as the principle of cooperation. Whenever observing the child, give attention to the environment and note its possible influence on the child. If it is in a negative way, changes need to be made. That is the response of a responsible adult.

Suggestions on the Bind-in-Book CD give the opportunity to assess the environment. The second assignment helps to assess the suitability to the needs of the child by observing the child's interactions with the group. A program may have a wonderful facility, the nicest equipment, materials, and supplies, but for some reason the child is not comfortable or learning there.

Advantages of Formal Program Assessment

By using internal and external evaluation methods, programs measure and maintain the quality necessary for the safety, health, growth, and development of the children they serve. Other advantages include:

- It ensures that the professionalism of the staff is monitored.
- Objective criteria are used to measure this program against others of the same type.
- Staff, administrators, and consultants have an objective instrument with which to measure.
- Evaluation has program improvement as its goal, not revocation of licensing or censure.

Disadvantages of Formal Program Assessment

The disadvantages of formal program assessment include the following:

- There is usually a cost involved.
- They are time consuming.
- Occasionally, when the instrument does not fit the program, erroneous messages are given, which are not really helpful.
- Follow-up is necessary so that the assessment is like seeing a smudge on your face and not washing it off.
- Circumstances, such as economic or leadership, pose barriers to the implementation of evaluation findings.

Pitfalls to Avoid

When considering a program evaluation, the following will help overcome these disadvantages:

- Careful consideration of a good match of instrument to program ensures that the results will be helpful.
- Planning for the added cost not only of the evaluation process but the implementation helps it not be an exercise in futility.
- Using knowledgeable, objective evaluators—they are key components to the success of the evaluation.

Using Technology

Any of the rating systems for program assessments mentioned in this chapter can be tabulated electronically. Using Excel, each of the classroom ratings can be entered and the data can be reported in text or a variety of charts. If you store and use electronic databases for program assessments, strong and weak areas are easily recognized, a quality-improvement plan can be made and implemented, and the ratings revisited to see indicators of improvement. Selecting a program-assessment instrument that fits the program's goals and objectives can be a very useful tool for use in long-range planning, reporting to administrators and decision-making bodies, as well as for justification for grants.

How to Find the Time

The director or administrator has many day-to-day responsibilities, but quality assurance should be at the top of the list. Make a plan for program assessment and do more than go through the motions. This should be one of the most important tasks each year (and it *should* be yearly).

Self-assessments are valuable planning tools, but to ensure the validity of that evaluation, an outside evaluator is usually used. This should be someone who is familiar with the world of early childhood education but is not a colleague, client, or board member. Those individuals may have a conflict of interest, and the evaluation would not be credible for some of the purposes listed above. Some evaluation systems include an on-site validator to verify self-study reports. Evaluation from an outside evaluator not only takes time but involves financial cost, so that is also a consideration. It is a worthwhile endeavor, however.

What to Do with It?

Program assessments should not be done just to fill a notebook and place it on a shelf. The time, effort, and cost involved should bring more benefit than simply completing a necessary task. The report itself should be a dynamic document, used for program improvement so its components are the baseline for an ongoing program-improvement plan. The report results should be communicated to those who have a need to know and those who should know. A report to families about the findings can include favorable ratings—"Our program received excellent ratings in . . . ."—as well as not-so-favorable ratings—"Our program is less effective in . . . and this is how we are working to improve it." This is not only ethical but can help enlist family support in making those improvements, especially those that directly affect them—like record keeping or safety.

Program assessments, especially when they result in an accreditation or certification, should be communicated to the community at large. Many states are now undertaking Quality Rating Scale projects as a way for families as consumers to make choices about child care. Some program assessment awards bring financial gains as well in the form of increased child care subsidies, staff bonuses, and center quality-enhancement stipends. Press releases, press conferences, letters to government officials, and notices to board members and local community agencies all bring positive recognition to the program. Program assessments are used for affirmation, improvement, and recognition.

Go to the Bind-in-Book CD for directions for a Setting Observation, plans, and resources.

LOOKING AT THE ADJUSTMENT OF THE CHILD TO THE PROGRAM

This section is not about measuring a child's development directly but about observing the child's **adjustment** and how the child is benefiting from the program. It ultimately does affect development.

REVIEW

PROGRAM ASSESSMENTS

A measurement tool used to evaluate the program environment, curriculum and administration, staff qualifications and interactions with children, and suitability for an individual child.

Use Program Assessments to Look at

- interactions among teachers and children
- curriculum
- relationships among teachers and families
- staff qualifications and professional development
- administration
- staffing
- health and safety
- environment
- nutrition and health service
- anti-bias policies and procedures

Methods for Assessing Programs

- accreditation process
- checklists
- classroom observations—Running Records
- interviews with children, staff, administration, families
- surveys—staff, families
- data collection—attendance records, accident/incident reports, family participation in center-related activities, staff turnover rates

Figure 13–5 Does the program fit the child?

Children's relationships throughout the day, both with adults and with peers, have great impact on the child's adjustment to the program. The responsibility lies with programs to give careful attention to transitions, mealtimes, small and large group activities, and peer relations (Gable, 2002). Every quality program may not be a good place for every child. Families and program staff evaluate if the child's needs are being met (Figure 13–5). Many of the characteristics that have been discussed already as indicators of development are also indicators of appropriateness of a program for a child. These are reviewed along with the impact of group size, adult/child ratio, and program structure on the child's adjustment to the program.

Child–adult ratios are one of the most basic indicators of adequate care. When there are too many children or the group is too large, a child's adjustment and even well-being are jeopardized. *Caring for Our Children: National Health and Safety Performance Standards* (American Academy of Pediatrics, 2002) recommends:

Age	Child/Staff	Maximum Group Size
Birth–12 mos.	3:1	6
13–30 mos.	4:1	8
31–35 mos.	5:1	10
3-year-olds	7:1	14
4-year-olds	8:1	16
5-year-olds	8:1	16
6–8-year-olds	10:1	20
9–12-year-olds	12:1	24

Compare these recommendations to the state-by-state comparison in Figure 13–6.

Children may not, or possibly cannot, say, "I just love going to this program." There are behavioral signs that the child is emotionally, physically, socially, and cognitively comfortable there. Or the opposite may occur. The child may protest attending strongly or may indicate a lack of comfort through the regressive behaviors of bed-wetting, thumb-sucking, or other earlier stage behaviors. This is not to put the decision of program choice into the child's domain but to give families and teachers an indication that the child is not totally comfortable and further investigation is needed.

Sometimes a program may not meet the needs of children. There may be a discontinuity between the child's home situation and the philosophy of the school. A child from a very structured home that stresses adult permission, obedience, and neatness may have difficulty adjusting to a program that promotes independence and allows choices and sensory exploration. A child from a small family with little contact with other children may find the large group setting a hard adjustment. The high energy of a colorful, noisy, busy center may be too much for a highly distractible child. Consideration should be given to the families' values, the program's goals, and the child's personality and experience.

Families and staff watch for signs of that adjustment to judge if the program is meeting the needs of the child. The use of the Portfolio to document the child's participation can give specific information on areas of development. Periodically, it is necessary to step back and view the whole child. Looking at the child's adjustment to the program does that. These indicators are for toddlers through early school age. Some require an advanced level, especially in language, but behavior can be interpreted even beyond language.

Behavioral Indicators of Comfort

The child gives behavioral indications of the suitability of the program for developmental needs. Some criteria may be answered with a "No" because the child is going through separation anxiety or another emotional upset. It is important for families and staff to give attention to a child's discomfort. It is a form of communication. The program is appropriate when the child

- begins the day at the program without a fuss.
- knows the schedule for the day and can anticipate what is coming next.
- feels an affinity to the school and says things like, "My school," "My cubby," and "My teacher."
- has opportunities to play actively inside and outside every day.

Maximum Number of Children Allowed Per Caretaker and Maximum Group Size in Child Care Centers[1]; Selected Ages, 2004

	Children Per Caretaker			Maximum Group Size		
	9 Months	27 Months	4 Years	9 Months	27 Months	4 Years
Alabama	4:1	7:1	16:1	NR	NR	NR
Alaska	5:1	6:1	10:1	10	12	20
Arizona	5:1 or 11:2	8:1	15:1	NR	NR	NR
Arkansas	6:1	9:1	15:1	12	18	30
California	4:1	6:1	12:1	NR	12	NR
Colorado	5:1	7:1	12:1	10	14	24
Connecticut	4:1	4:1	10:1	8	8	20
Delaware	4:1	10:1	15:1	NR	NR	NR
District of Columbia	4:1	4:1	10:1	8	8	20
Florida	4:1	11:1	20:1	NR	NR	NR
Georgia	6:1	10:1	18:1	12	20	36
Hawaii	4:1	8:1	16:1	8	NR	NR
Idaho	6:1	12:1	12:1	NR	NR	NR
Illinois	4:1	8:1	10:1	12	16	20
Indiana	4:1	5:1	12:1	8	10	24
Iowa	4:1	6:1	12:1	NR	NR	NR
Kansas	3:1	7:1	12:1	9	14	24
Kentucky	5:1	10:1	14:1	10	20	28
Louisiana	5:1	11:1	15:1	NR	NR	NR
Maine	4:1	5:1	10:1	8	10	30
Maryland	3:1	6:1	10:1	6	12	20
Massachusetts	3:1 or 7:2	4:1 or 9:2	10:1	7	9	20
Michigan	4:1	8:1	12:1	NR	NR	NR
Minnesota	4:1	7:1	10:1	8	14	20
Mississippi	5:1	12:1	16:1	10	14	20
Missouri	4:1	8:1	10:1	8	16	NR
Montana	4:1	8:1	10:1	NR	NR	NR
Nebraska	4:1	6:1	12:1	12	NR	NR
Nevada	6:1	10:1	13:1	NR	NR	NR
New Hampshire	4:1	6:1	12:1	12	18	24
New Jersey	4:1	10:1	12:1	20	20	20
New Mexico	6:1	10:1	12:1	NR	NR	NR
New York	4:1	5:1	8:1	8	12	21
North Carolina	5:1	10:1	20:1	10	20	25
North Dakota	4:1	5:1	10:1	8	10	20
Ohio	5:1 or 2:12	7:1	14:1	12	14	28
Oklahoma	4:1	8:1	15:1	8	16	30
Oregon	4:1	5:1	10:1	8	10	20
Pennsylvania	4:1	6:1	10:1	8	12	20
Rhode Island	4:1	6:1	10:1	8	12	20
South Carolina	6:1	10:1	18:1	NR	NR	NR
South Dakota	5:1	5:1	10:1	20	20	20
Tennessee	4:1	7:1	13:1	8	14	20
Texas	4:1	11:1	18:1	10	22	35
Utah	4:1	7:1	15:1	8	14	30
Vermont	4:1	5:1	10:1	8	10	20
Virginia	4:1	10:1	12:1	NR	NR	NR
Washington	4:1	7:1	10:1	8	14	20
West Virginia	4:1	8:1	12:1	8	16	24
Wisconsin	4:1	6:1	13:1	8	12	24
Wyoming	4:1	8:1	12:1	10	18	30
Maximum Recommended Level[2]	3:1 to 4:1	4:1 to 6:1	8:1 to 10:1	6 to 8	8 to 10	16 to 20

NR—not regulated

[1]There may be some exceptions to these ratio and group size requirements in some states under certain circumstaces. For example, some states have different requirements for small centers, classes with mixed-age groups, or different levels of licensing. See original source for details.

[2]Maximum Recommended Level: As recommended in the accreditation guidelines developed by the National Association for the Education of Young Children and in the National Health and Safety Performance Standards developed by the American Public Health Association and the American Academy of Pediatrics.

Sources: State data compiled and posted by the National Child Care Information Center at <http://nccic.org> from licensing regulations posted on the National Resource Center for Health and Safety in Child Care at <http://nrc.uchsc.edu>. "Child Care Licensing Requirements: Child Staff Ratios and Maximum Group Size Requirements" (August 2003). Maximum recommended levels obtained from the accreditation guidelines developed by the National Association for the Education of Young Children (NAEYC) and "Caring for Our Children: National Health and Safety Performance Standards, Guidelines for Out-of-Home Child Care."

Figure 13–6 Child Group Size and Ration by State. Copyright © 2005 Children's Defense Fund. All rights reserved.

- talks freely at school (at maximum of language level).
- is able to make choices from sufficient equipment and materials.
- is not exhibiting stress, such as crying or regressive behaviors.
- has enough time to work at choice activities.
- is warned of impending change in activities and is given opportunity to finish and clean up.
- moves from one activity to the next comfortably.
- does not have to wait before the next activity can begin.
- does not have to receive step-by-step directions for activities but can explore materials independently.
- is not forced to continue in an activity.
- is able to watch or choose not to participate in an activity.
- displays pride in the work brought home.
- can relate what occurred at school when prompted specifically. (Children need a reminder to trigger memory association.)
- talks about playing with other children in the group.
- knows the teachers' names.
- interacts with the teacher on a one-to-one basis several times during the day.
- goes to the adult for assistance and comfort.
- sleeps, eats, and toilets at school without difficulty.

Families and staff should work together to determine if the child is in the right placement, where the child is receiving not just physical care but learns and feels acceptance and belonging.

Looking at the Program through the Child's Eyes

At times any one or more of the previously listed indicators may be answered with a "No." That does not mean necessarily there is an adjustment problem. It may mean that the child is moving through a developmental phase, struggling with the change in thinking or feeling. It may mean there are personality differences between the child and a staff member. The child may feel threatened by an aggressive child in the group. There may be changes happening at home that are affecting the child at school. A child exhibiting such behaviors should be closely observed in an attempt to learn the cause. There are many factors that influence the child's adjustment to the program.

THE MAKE-UP OF THE PEER GROUP. Different activities depend on a certain number of people to be successful.

EXERCISE How many people would you like in your group for the following activities?

Cheering your team at a football game:
Sleeping:
Changing a light bulb:
Taking a shower:
Talking on the phone:
Eating:
Riding in a car:
Birthing a child:
Numbering all the books in a library:
Playing a card game:

Some activities are solitary, or at least intimate. The space and action also determine the number of people who can participate in certain activities. The size of the task at hand and the skill required, or the occasion, are also factors in group size. When thinking of young children in group settings, some of these same factors need to be considered. More than 57 percent of children younger than 5 whose mothers were employed are cared for by nonrelatives. Of those children, 25 percent are in center-based care while 23 percent are in family child care homes (Children's Defense Fund, 2006). Children are grouped together by different criteria in different programs. There are rationales, advantages, and disadvantages to each decision.

Chronological Age Groups. Most center-based child care centers and public schools group children by chronological age. Grouping children by age assumes that children who are in the same age range have similar needs and interests. This is usually the case, especially when curriculum is open-ended so that a range of developmental abilities can all find success. Individual differences, especially of exceptional children (those with disabilities or giftedness), and arbitrary age cutoffs sometimes make decisions about group placement difficult. At 15 months, a child might be advanced physically, walking steadily. She is interested in the wider environment of the young toddler room. Regulations or policies might prevent her advancement into the next group. The wobbly walker may be arbitrarily "promoted" to the young toddler room at 18 months. For a slow-to-walk infant, a room of two-year-olds is a fearsome place. Grouping of children by age has different criteria and functions for the child's interactions in the group setting.

Figure 13–7 Mixed-age groups bring benefits to all.

Continuity of Care. Some early childhood programs have moved away from the arbitrary moving of children from one group to another based on birth date or walking ability. Instead, those children who begin a program around the same time as infants move as a cohort, staying together with the same teachers as well, as they advance toward preschool age. In this way, the children, families, and teachers become very well known to each other. Equipment, materials, and even the room may change, but the group and adults stay together.

Mixed-Age or Multi-Age Groups. **Mixed-age groups**, or heterogeneous grouping, most resembles the family group with members of different ages (Figure 13–7). It gives young children the opportunity to observe, imitate, and learn from older ones. It gives older children occasions to practice nurturing skills, reteach learned skills, and feel competent. Most family child care settings have children of mixed-age groups since they usually care for siblings. The average family child care group age was between five and eight (6.7), according to data gathered by the National Child Care Information Center (Clarke-Stewart & Vandall, 2002). Some centers have mixed-age groups or vertical grouping, with the state regulating the size of the group and the adult–child ratio. Prosocial behaviors, such as giving help, sharing, and turn-taking are elicited in the older children toward the younger ones. Older children exhibit more leadership when they lead younger ones to higher levels of cognitive thinking by assisting in collaborative efforts as "experts." Younger children have seen models of help-giving and nurturing and hopefully will replicate them when they are the older ones. Research shows that even young children can modify the complexity of their vocabulary based on the ages of the persons they are addressing, so mixed-age groupings sharpen communication skills. Mixed-age groupings give older children, who may still be new readers, a nonthreatening arena in which to practice reading aloud (Katz, 1998).

THE SIZE OF THE GROUP. The size of the group and adult–child ratio, both in family child care homes and in centers, matter a great deal. "With too many children for one teacher to attend to, children suffer and so do the adults" (Clark-Stewart & Anhauser, 2005). The class-size-reduction debate has long raged in the public school arena, with teachers and parents advocating it so that children will get more individual attention, whereas economists say the added costs are not justified by learning outcome data (Gilman & Kiger, 2003).

In child care, various states have a wide range of children allowed in groups according to age. Figure 13–6 illustrates an interesting comparison from the Children's Defense Fund (2006).

Infants (Birth to 18 Months). It is common sense that the younger the child, the more care they require, so the size of the group should be smaller. Newborn infants need care and attention from a few of the same people. It is critical that infants receive the required care. The National Institute of Child Health and Human Development (NICHD), in its longitudinal study of children in child care (1996), found that children under two years needed a small group and low staff–infant ratios (Figure 13–8). It also found strong teacher qualifications predicted positive outcomes. Infants should be cared for in groups no larger than six with two adults, or in a group of three with one adult (American Academy of Pediatricians, 2002). The quality and frequency of adult–child interactions are the critical variables in infant care (Cost, Quality, and Outcomes Study Team, 1995). The interaction with adults provides for each infant's individual physical and emotional needs. This includes feeding,

Figure 13–8 Infants need small groups.

diapering, and holding. Infants younger than 8 months interact with the teacher while in close physical proximity to other infants. The space size requirements vary by state regulation, but 35 square feet per child is considered minimum.

Observations of the infant in the group setting would expect to see her looking at other infants, smiling, and touching them. The adult monitors the physical contact, for the infant has no knowledge that her squeezes and hair pulling hurt. She also lacks the self-control to keep from doing it. Other children are part of the world to be manipulated. Once infants become mobile by crawling, creeping, cruising, or walking, they approach other children with simple chase games and peekaboo. They enjoy little finger plays and songs together and a book shared with another child on the lap of the adult. They begin to make vocal exchanges with each other, using vocal signals to invite attention or alert the teacher that they need to be removed from this stressful situation.

The babies' and toddlers' compliance with the adults' requests begin with realistic expectations for children's behavior. Here are some guidelines for behavior from Jennifer Birckmayer (1995):

- Have age-appropriate expectations for children's behavior.
- Tell children what they can do.
- Distraction is a good technique to use with very young children.
- Change the environment instead of the behavior.
- Offer choices only when you can accept child's decision.
- Use words and actions to guide behavior.
- Have a few simple rules consistently enforced.
- Recognize children's efforts.
- Be a friend.
- Be a good role model.

The teacher watches for developmental milestones, which occur almost daily at this age, and marks the developmental checklist the program is using. Daily contact sheets are used to document the amount of time and the type of activities provided for the infant each day. A copy is kept in the child's file. It is desirable to send a copy home at the end of every day (Figure 13–9).

Toddlers (18 Months to 3 Years). The recommended ratio is 5 toddlers to 1 adult and a total group size of 10. This ensures the safety and exchanges with responsive adults needed for this age. Considerations for the toddler in a group setting begin with a safe, healthy environment. The emotional environment provides support, with places to withdraw. The toddler needs consistent teachers and adequate space and materials. He is still developing coordination and has limited social skills. The child is observed as he interacts with the materials, demonstrating his physical development. He can participate in small groups for very short periods of time. This could include songs, finger plays, and short story books. His play with other children is at the functional level, using toys in a repetitive manner but advancing to more make-believe play, simulating grown-up activities. He will pretend to drive a car, bake a cake, and sweep the floor, especially when he sees the steering wheel, cake pans, or broom. Interactions with other children will be stormy because of limited language and the inability to take another's viewpoint. He wants the big ball of Play Doh, so he takes it. When the other player protests, there is little self-restraint in the responses.

Toddlers are fast moving and independent, yet they need much adult assistance with self-care skills. Observations include documentation of the child's ability to dress, eat, and the beginning interest in toileting. Socially, the child is taking an interest in other children, but with little emotional control or awareness of the feelings of others. This leads to aggressiveness and the possibility for physical harm. The child is rapidly developing language skills but often uses biting as an expression of frustration or aggression.

Toddlers have learned the sequence of the events of the day and depend very heavily on its stability. Arrivals and departures are handled in a routine way that allows for a relaxed, unrushed atmosphere. They need programming that allows them mostly freeplay activities from a wide range of choices, including outside play and soft, quiet areas. Sleep and rest time should be adaptable to individual schedules and needs, with some children needing frequent short naps, and others needing long afternoon naps. Eating times are social opportunities, with self-care skills, food exploration, and casual conversation included.

Transitions between periods of play, sleeping, eating, and diapering or toileting should be natural and relaxed. Waiting time should be eliminated and children warned that the end of that phase of the day is coming. When these elements are included in the program, the child is observed as she follows routines, interacts with adults and children, and maximizes the learning environment (Figure 13–9).

Circle times for toddlers include songs, finger plays, creative movement, and short books or

Broome Community College
Child Care Center
607 • 778-5437

INFANT DAILY CARE SHEET

Child's Name: ______________________

Today's Date: ______________________

PARENT INFORMATION

How did your child sleep last night/wake up time? ______________________

Is there medication today? ______________________

What's your child's feeding schedule? ______________________

Is there any other information/last diaper change? ______________________

CAREGIVER INFORMATION

BATHROOMING

Time	Wet	BM	Dry

NAPPING

From ________ to ________

________ to ________

________ to ________

NUTRITION

Bottles:

Breakfast:

Snacks: A.M. P.M.

Lunch: None Some Most All

SOME THINGS WE HAVE OBSERVED TODAY. . . .

________ Sensory Table

________ Dolls

________ Rattles/shakers

________ Outside

________ Babbled/Talked

________ Ball Play

________ Danced

________ Cried, but comforted when held

________ Soft books

________ Climbed

________ Stacking

________ Blocks

Special Activity: ______________________

____

What I Need:

Signed: ______________________

Figure 13–9 Daily Contact Sheet for Infants and Toddlers. (Reprinted with permission from the BC Center, Broome Community College, Binghamton, NY.)

Broome Community College
Child Care Center
607 • 778-5437

TODDLER DAILY CARE SHEET

Child's Name: ______________________

Today's Date: ______________________

PARENT INFORMATION

How did your child sleep last night/wake up time? ______________________

Is there medication today? ______________________

CAREGIVER INFORMATION

Diaper changes/toilet training

Time	Wet	BM	Dry	Tried on potty

Napping: From __________ to __________

Meals

Breakfast:

Snacks:

A.M.

P.M.

Lunch: None Some Most All

Some of the things I did today. . . .

________ Books
________ Climber
________ Outside
________ Puzzles
________ Special games
________ Markers/Crayons
________ Painted
________ Water table
________ Housekeeping area
________ Legos
________ Playdough
________ Movement
________ Music

Special Activity of the day: ______________________

Signed: ______________________

Figure 13–9 (continued).

storytelling. Participation should be optional. It can last as long or as short as they remain interested. Guidelines for group behavior, including self-discipline, depend on a knowledge of child development to be realistic. The young child is egocentric, not able to put himself in someone else's place. The young child is impulsive, without the ability to control emotional urges. Language is not fully developed yet, with vocabulary centered on things rather than on ideas and symbolic actions. It is not developed enough to present a rational point of view or to capably negotiate. The young child's experience in life has been limited, and memory is still developing, so that does not help in self-control. Adults control the environment by placing matches where the child cannot reach them or by placing furniture where a child cannot use it to climb to forbidden objects in cupboards or on shelves. Adults' directions are clear and specific. They give warning of an impending change in activities. It is the child's desire to please adults yet develop autonomy. The two desires come into conflict. The payoff might be a reward or the absence of punishment. Adults may give direct instruction about expectations of behavior in what is called a "personal message" (Kostelnik, Whiren, Soderman, & Gregory, 2006):

- *Rules must be reasonable*—within the capability and knowledge necessary to carry out the desired behavior.
- *Rules must be definable*—specifying the *exact* behavior that is acceptable.
- *Rules must be positive*—telling them what to do rather than "don't . . ." or "stop . . ." (pp. 343–344).

Observing the toddler during play gives information about her concept of right and wrong. She might paint continually on the wall, even after being reminded to paint on paper. It is noted that her inner controls might be missing. She is not understanding the directions. The cause may be emotional in nature, an act of attention seeking, or an example of demonstrating an open defiance to rules.

When the child knows clearly what is expected, observing the child adhere to those expectations gives information about memory, cognitive, and emotional development. The child understands and can resist temptation to do whatever he wants to follow the standard. When adults set firm limits about what behavior is not allowed, children learn to comply, first from outside control, but eventually internalizing the standards. The adults role-model and make suggestions about how the child can meet the standards, giving them choices. By providing children with alternative activities, the adult gives a way for the child to focus his own attention and energies in another direction. When the adult indicates what effect the actions have on others, the child is receiving instruction on cause and effect and the consequences of his actions. Giving the child an outside view of how the actions appear to others begins the movement away from egocentrism.

Preschoolers (Three- to Five-Year-Olds). A total group size of 15 to 20 is recommended, with younger children in the lower range. The recommended adult–child ratio is 2 adults for that size group. Developmentally appropriate practices recommend that the schedule of the day include long periods of uninterrupted involvement in a variety of areas, commonly called learning centers (Bredekamp & Copple, 1997). These usually are set up for independent use to develop physical, cognitive, creative, and social skills. When the integrated curriculum approach or the project approach is used, there is a thematic connection between learning center areas. Woven throughout the schedule are routines for eating, sleeping or resting, toileting, and outside play. Circle time for the whole group, meetings, and small group gatherings may be included, depending on the curriculum model.

SCHOOL AGE. Children attending public school traditionally have been placed in grades by chronological age. The cut-off dates for school entrance may vary by as much as six months. Some are in early summer, and others are not until the end of the calendar year. There are many in between. This makes it difficult when children are moving from one school district or state to another. Attempts to place children in classes by developmental age have met with difficulties (Figure 13–10). There are different opinions on the criteria and validity of the assessment instruments being used to determine developmental age. Questions have been raised regarding screenings

Figure 13–10 Children come in all size, ages, and stages—the teacher's dilemma.

it happened to me

"I Don't Do Naps."

During the orientation to the routines at the beginning of the year, I was explaining the half-day sessions' routines to my new class of four-year-olds. "And after you play then clean up, we wash our hands and have snacks." One boy stood up, stretched out his arms, palms up, and said strongly, "I don't do naps." He wanted it understood right from the beginning what he would do and not do. When I said it clearer, that it was "snacks" not "naps," he was more agreeable to staying.

Do you have an IT HAPPENED TO ME story about children adjusting to being part of a group. Please send them to me at WeekbyWeek@thomsonlearning.com

being used inappropriately as placement tests rather than for their intended purpose.

Children of different ages and at different stages present either a dilemma or an opportunity to the school, depending on the philosophy. Some schools have divided each class into smaller groups by ability. This is to teach lessons closer to the levels of development. Many oppose this early tracking or separating children by abilities. Whole-group instruction is difficult when children are functioning at a wide range of abilities. This is addressed by the selection of curriculum and teaching practices calling for "developmentally appropriate" rather than "age-appropriate" strategies.

WHOLE-GROUP TIMES. A whole-group time may occur at the beginning of the day as a transition between home and school. It welcomes the group and informs them of the choices of the day. It is sometimes held in the middle of the day, usually right before lunch, at which time it serves as a transition to review the work done in the morning and to prepare for lunch and rest time and afternoon activities. At the end of the day, some programs have a whole-group time to summarize the day, recalling the highlights, looking forward to tomorrow, and transitioning to home. Beaty (1996) points out that these whole-group times help children feel a common bond, a sense of community. They can include singing, finger plays, large motor games and musical games, and creative movement. Hohmann and Weikart (2002) say group times should *not* include rigid routines, competitive games, or teacher-led lessons. They recommend group times be held in a spacious location, with a specific plan. The adult should have the materials prepared and draw children in with a transition activity. They begin right away, not waiting until every child is in place. The activity is then turned over to the children. The adult's role is to watch and listen while children are the leaders and to transition the group into the next experience. It is a different vision from the traditional whole-group time.

Unscheduled class meetings may be called to address class announcements, class problems, or mistaken behaviors. Gartrell (2003) refers to Glasser's model (1969) of class meetings that build a sense of togetherness. The general rules are anyone can talk, take turns, be honest, and be kind. Besides the opening, middle, and closing meetings, unscheduled meetings are called out of necessity for spontaneous discussion. Problem solving by the group is underlined by protection of the dignity of the people involved in the problem. The situation is described using "I" messages; solutions are brainstormed and a course of action is decided by the group. This promotes community responsibility and cooperation.

QUESTIONABLE VALUE OF CALENDAR AND SHOW AND TELL.

Think About It . . .

Imagine you are sitting on the floor. The leader says, "Now let's recite the Dow Jones Averages. What was it yesterday? Which stocks sold the most shares? How much was bid for IBM? How much offered? Now say after me, Alco Standard Corp., American Home Products, Apple Computer, AT&T, Bell Atlantic, Chase Manhattan. Now you know the top-selling stocks. Don't you?"

- Do you *really* know them?
- How would you feel if you couldn't remember?
- What if you heard others around you saying them but you couldn't?

Think about this in relation to children reciting numbers from the calendar and days of the week that have no meaning to them.

There are many programs that include counting the days on the calendar and reciting the days of the week and months of the year. These are abstract principles, not readily understood by young children.

This exercise is rote memorization without much value. The time could be better spent on other topics of relevant interest to the children. If counting is the purpose or objective of the group time, there should be concrete objects for the children to count. This is according to child development principles. The association of the numeral is symbolic of the quantity and beyond the level of this developmental stage.

Think About It . . .

Now you are sitting on the rug and it is Show-and-Tell time. Mary brings a full-length mink coat out of her backpack. She puts it on and walks around, but you are told not to touch it. You might get it dirty. Then Gabriel brings out a new shotgun his father just gave him. He is so proud of it, but the teacher is horrified. "Put that away. We don't allow guns at school." Next, it is Katharine's turn. She has an hour-long video of her trip to the Mall of America. There are things all around that you want to do, but you have to sit there and watch it.

Would you

- touch Mary's coat anyway?
- feel disappointed and angry that you did not get to talk about your prized gift?
- wiggle, reach for a toy, pinch a neighbor, and not listen to Katharine's trip monologue?

Show-and-Tell has its champions who claim that it raises the self-esteem of children to bring an object from home and talk about it. They point out the value also of speaking before the whole group. Show-and-Tell usually involves long waiting. The children become disinterested in someone else's object because they are egocentric. The pressure builds to show bigger and better toys. These reasons present contrary evidence of its worth. Many have attempted to resolve the difficulties of Show-and-Tell with creative alternatives, some of which may be successful. Again, a careful consideration should be given to the objectives of the program. This is because of the knowledge of what young children are like:

They cannot wait and watch without touching.
They learn best by doing.
They have limited capacity to describe an object.
They have sensitivity already to the "haves" and the "have-nots."

Teaching practices should be based on what is known about how children learn and develop. Reconsideration of practices sometimes causes resistance and defensiveness in teachers. Calendar and Show-and-Tell are topics for reflection and reconsideration.

SMALL-GROUP TIME. Without espousing any curriculum model, the small-group time of High/Scope gives effective principles for any program's group time (Hohmann & Weikart, 2002). Small-group time is conducted in an intimate place. It is just the right size for a few children and the adult. The same adult and children hold group time every day in that place, where the adult initiates a learning activity with real materials. The children explore the materials, deciding what to do with them. The adult helps the children carry out their plan if they need assistance. At the end, she helps them recall what they did.

TRANSITIONS. Even though a daily routine necessitates many changes, most humans are resistant to change.

EXERCISE **List on a separate sheet of paper all the changes in activities and places you have been today.**

Some people have difficulty getting out of bed, out of pajamas and into clothes, or out of the house and off to work or school. Every change means an adjustment in body position, temperature, and sometimes clothing, a change in social contacts, and perhaps a change in behavior.

This is difficult for adults but even harder for children. They have no concept of time, minutes, hours, or days. They are stationed in the present. "I am doing this now and I want to continue doing it." They may be forced to change activities. There was not enough time to finish what they were doing. They are led to another activity that they are not so sure they can or want to do. They become stressed. This is the time when children act out, cry, or withdraw.

Transition times need planning, with just as much consideration as the activities themselves. Routine signals such as bells, music, gentle whispers, and simple games all give children a clue rather than a command that it is time to make a change. When the schedule of the day is consistent, they quickly come to anticipate and adjust to the changes, especially when they are pleasantly carried out.

When adults consider the child's needs first, plans are made for the program, activities, and interactions to fit those needs. When adults then consider each child as an individual and adapt the plans for that particular child, then the program is truly individually appropriate. If the child is exhibiting adjustment problems, it very likely is the program at fault, not the child.

HELPING ALL CHILDREN IN GROUP SETTINGS

The fit of the program to the needs of the child is vitally important to every child, but for a child with special needs, it is critical. *Mainstreaming, integration, inclusion,* and *least restrictive environment* are all terms related to the legal-legislative postures as well as to child advocates promoting normalizing educational settings for children with special needs. The benefits of regular early childhood settings for children with special needs are many:

- In regular placements, negative views of children with disabilities are reduced because they are not isolated.
- When children of all abilities are grouped together, tolerance and understanding increase.
- Through interactions with typical children, peers become the behavior and skill role models in a demanding environment.
- Early intervention is beneficial for most disabilities.
- Younger children accept others more readily than older children, who may have learned to stigmatize those who are different from themselves.

Planning and consideration of many factors ensure a successful placement for children with special needs in regular classrooms. Cook, Klein, and Tessier (2004) suggest some of the same points of consideration discussed earlier in this chapter:

- *Developmental levels rather than age groupings*—Placing children with special needs with younger children decreases the developmental differences.
- *Ratio of integrated children in the group*—Some have suggested that when only one or two children with special needs are integrated into a group, they still experience isolation. When more than one and up to one-third of the class are children with special needs, true integration is more likely to be successful. The caveat here is dependent on the nature of the special needs, the training of the teacher, and supplemental classroom assistance available.
- *Individualized learning experiences*—The curriculum for all children should be based on their interests and their strengths. Building on what they can do and modifying the environment and activities so that each child finds success is the principle of developmentally appropriate curriculum for all children.
- *Partnerships with families*—The families of children with special needs must be advocates for their own child. They are involved in more educational decisions about their child than other families and must monitor their child's progress closely. This places the relationship and communication between teacher and families in a priority position.

The placement decisions for children with special needs must be carefully considered so their abilities are maximized and needs are met.

HELPING PROFESSIONALS FOR PROGRAM EVALUATION AND SUPPORT

Help can come from referring to experts or from other people who have had a similar experience.

Consultants—The humorous definition of a consultant is someone from more than 100 miles away. A consultant is a specialist who is enlisted, and paid, for their advice. Programs that want an impartial, outside evaluation often contract with a consultant to provide that service.

Support groups—Groups with like concerns often informally or formally band together to discuss, seek answers, commiserate, and give advice to one another. They can become a legislative force for change or a united voice to raise the public's awareness regarding an issue. Many support groups have been formed of families with children who have a specific diagnosed disorder. The program should be aware of these in the local community to make them known to families in the program who may benefit from such an alliance.

OTHER METHODS

Other Methods to Record a Child's Adjustment to Group Settings

Class List Log
Anecdotal/Running Records
Developmental Checklists
Frequency Counts of social interactions
Conversations and Interviews with the child
Time Samples—measuring activity involvement
Rating Scales

STANDARDS

Selected examples of standards regarding program assessment:

Head Start Performance Standards (2005)
1304.51 Management Systems and Procedures
h. (2.1) Program self-assessment and monitoring. (1) At least once each program year, with the consultation and participation of the policy groups and, as appropriate, other community members, grantee and delegate agencies must conduct a self-assessment of their effectiveness and progress in meeting program goals and objectives and in implementing Federal regulations.

Family Child Care Quality Standards (2005)
National Association of Family Child Care
Part 5: Professional and Business Practices
5.14 The provider follows an enrollment process that facilitates an exchange of information between the provider and parent, working to assure a good match. Discussion includes a description of the program and policies as well as parents' values and wishes around such topics as eating, sleeping, toileting, and discipline.

KEY TERMS

accreditation
adjustment
continuity of care
license requirements
mixed-age groups
performance standards
program evaluation
transitions

Go to the Bind-in-Book CD for:
Class List Log form
Plan Week 13 Part A, Directions for Setting Observation, including What to Do with It, Portfolio Overview Example, Sharing with Child and Family, Actions—Read a Book, In the Environment, In the Curriculum, In the Newsletter
Plan Week 13 Part B, Directions for Class List Log on Group Participation
Pan Week 13 Part C, Anecdotal Recording of Group Interactions for Group D
Plan Week 13 Part D, Reflective Journal

REFERENCES

American Academy of Pediatrics. (2002). *Caring for our children: National health and safety performance standards.* Elk Grove Village, IL: Author.

Beaty, J. (1996). *Preschool appropriate practices* (2nd ed.). New York: Harcourt Brace Jovanovich.

Birckmayer, J. (1995). *Discipline for babies and toddlers.* Ithaca, NY: Cornell University.

Bredekamp, S., & Copple. C. (Eds.). (1997). *Developmentally appropriate practice in early childhood programs* (rev. ed.). Washington, DC: National Association for the Education of Young Children.

Children's Defense Fund. (2006). *The state of America's children yearbook, 2005.* Washington, DC: Author.

Clarke-Stewart, K. A., & Vandell, D. L. (2002). Do regulable features of child-care homes affect children's development? *Early Childhood Research Quarterly, 17* (1), March 2002, 52–86.

Cook, R. E., Klein, M. D., & Tessier, A. (2004). *Adapting early childhood curricula for children in inclusive settings.* Upper Saddle River, NJ: Pearson Education.

Cost, Quality & Outcomes Study Team. (1998). *Cost, quality & child outcomes in child care centers.* Denver: Department of Economics, University of Colorado.

Derman-Sparks, L. (1989). *Anti-bias curriculum: Tools for empowering young children.* Washington, DC: National Association for the Education of Young Children.

Elliott, B. (2002). *Measuring performance: The early childhood educator in practice.* Clifton Park, NY: Thomson Delmar Learning.

Gable, S. (2002). Teacher–child relationships throughout the day. *Young Children, 57* (4), 42–44.

Gartrell, D. (2003). *A guidance approach for the encouraging classroom* (3rd ed.). Clifton Park, NY: Thomson Delmar Learning.

Gilman, D. A., & Kiger, S. (2003). Should we try to keep class sizes small? *Educational Leadership, 60* (7), April 2003, 80–86.

Glasser, W. (1969). *Schools without failure.* New York: Harper & Row.

Harms, T., Clifford, R. M., & Cryer, D. (1998). *Early childhood environment rating scale (ECERS-R)* (rev. ed.). New York: Teachers College Press.

Harms, T., & Clifford, R. M. (1989). *Family day care rating scale (FDCRS).* New York: Teachers College Press.

Harms, T., Cryer, D., & Clifford, R. M. (2002). *Infant/toddler environment rating scale (ITERS)* (rev. ed.). New York: Teachers College Press.

Harms, T., Jacobs, E. V., & White, D. R. (1995). *School-age care environment rating scale (SACERS).* New York: Teachers College Press.

High/Scope Press. (2002). *Program quality assessment* (2nd ed.). Ypsilanti, MI: High/Scope Educational Research Foundation.

Hohmann, M., & Weikart, D. (2002). *Educating young children.* Ypsilanti, MI: High/Scope Press.

Katz, L. (1998). The benefits of the mix. *Child Care Information Exchange,* November 1998, 46–49.

Kostelnik, M., Whiren, A., Soderman, A., & Gregory, K. (2006). *Guiding children's social development* (5th ed.). Clifton Park, NY: Thomson Delmar Learning.

LaMontagne, M. J., & Russell, G. W. (1998). Informal and formal assessment. In L. J. Johnson (Ed.), *Early childhood education: Blending theory, blending practice.* Baltimore, MD: P. H. Brookes.

National Association for the Education of Young Children. (2003). *NAEYC and NAECS/SDE position statement: Early childhood curriculum, assessment and program evaluation—building an effective, accountable system in programs for children birth through age 8.* Retrieved July 19, 2006, from http://www.naeyc.org/resources/position_statements/pscape.pdf.

National Association for the Education of Young Children. (2005). *NAEYC early childhood program standards and accreditation criteria: The mark of quality in early childhood education.* Washington, DC: Author.

National Association of Family Child Care. (2005). *Quality standards for NAFCC accreditation.* Salt Lake City, UT: Author.

Talan, T. N., & Bloom, P. J. (2004). *Program administration scale: Measuring early childhood leadership and management.* New York: Teachers College Press.

U.S. Department of Health and Human Services. (2005). *Head Start program performance standards.* Washington, DC: Office of Human Development Services, Administration for Children, Youth, and Families.

RESOURCES

National Association for the Education of Young Children. (2005). *NAEYC early childhood program standards and accreditation criteria: The mark of quality in early childhood education.* Washington, DC: Author.

Quality Standards for NAFCC. National Association for Family Child Care Accreditation. (2005). NAFCC Accreditation Standards. http://www. nafcc.org.

National Early Childhood Program Accreditation (NECPA). http://www.necpa.net.

National Health and Safety Performance Standards. (2002). http://nrc.uchsc.edu/.

U.S. Department of Health and Human Services. (2005). *Head Start program performance standards.* Washington, DC: Office of Human Development Services, Administration for Children, Youth, and Families.

CHAPTER

14 Using the Portfolio to Conference with Families and Looking at the Child's Interactions with Adults

IN THIS CHAPTER

- Communication between Home and School
- Using the Portfolio to Conference with Families
- Daily Contacts
- Looking at the Child's Interactions with Adults
- Topics in Observation: Does the *Week by Week* Plan Meet NAEYC Guidelines for Assessment?
- Helping All Children through Home and School Communications
- Helping Professionals for Home and School Communications

COMMUNICATION BETWEEN HOME AND SCHOOL

Observations have been accumulating in the Portfolio. Their effective use in home and school communication is the final observation topic. "Good information is priceless, but if we can't get to it, it's useless," someone said recently concerning the usefulness of becoming computer literate. This could be extended: "And if we don't do something with it, it's foolish." That applies to all the information and documentation accumulated about the child. At the end of the year comes the question, "What to Do with It?" The future possession of the Portfolio, the Class File, and the Reflective Journal conclude this section.

Families are the authorities on their own children. In group settings, the responsibility for the education and care of children is shared with other people—teachers—who can provide a different perspective on the child. This is an awesome responsibility. Daily contact with families is the preferable mode of communicating the observations and assessments between home and school, and such opportunities should be maximized. Sometimes written communication about the child is the vehicle of transferring information. There are advantages and pitfalls to this mode of exchange. More formal written reports, such as progress reports and child studies, are sometimes warranted, so templates and advice for writing reports about the child are included in this chapter. Combining verbal and written reports in a family conference presents a unique time of sharing between

it happened to me

Families Raising Children

I recently visited an early childhood program during a holiday gathering where families were invited. My eyes were opened to the fact that more than half the adults there were not either of the child's biological "parents." There were grandparents, aunts and uncles, stepparents, foster parents, and other extended family members and some unrelated but caring friends. I was reminded of the statement about every child needing one person who is crazy about him or her.

The world is constantly changing, and so has the configuration of the child's home life. More and more children are living with one parent, or with grandparents or other extended family members as their guardians. Throughout *Week by Week*, the involvement of the parent and the program through interaction with the teacher has been stressed. In this third edition, most of the places where "parent" appeared have been changed to "family," which also includes parents. In many cultures, decisions about the child are made by the whole family, not just the parent. In an effort to be inclusive, I have been retraining myself to use "family" more often, and I find that it fits. I am not making a statement that "anyone will do," because I still strongly believe that a child needs a mother and a father to develop, but I recognize that people who fill that role may not necessarily be related genetically.

Do you have an IT HAPPENED TO ME story about the changing family raising children? I'd love to read it. Please send it to WeekbyWeek@thomsonlearning.com

home and school. Family conferences are more effective with careful preparation and implementation. This chapter gives guidance for successful family conferences. Occasionally, family conferences of a distinct type are necessary, such as conferences for addressing specific problems, questions, or complaints, or an exit interview. Whenever family and program staff have a discussion, there is great potential to benefit the child. That is this chapter's guiding beacon.

Children, entrusted to other adults in other settings, must adjust and adapt to other schedules, expectations, and ways of interacting. Everyone has seen the difference in a child's behavior between when they are with the parents and when they are with the grandparents. How well they know their allies! In this final child development portion of this book, the important topic of the adjustment of the child to other adults is discussed.

A final assessment of the *Week by Week* plan ends this chapter.

USING THE PORTFOLIO TO CONFERENCE WITH FAMILIES

EXERCISE Using a separate sheet of paper, construct a family diagram for a child you know. Draw a triangle with mother, father, and child at each point. Write *M* to stand for Mother, *F* for Father. If there are stepparents, grandparents, or other adults who are responsible for the child, either legally or practically, designate them in the diagram. Let *C* stand for the child. Now draw lines—solid and bold, or dotted and barely visible—for the relationship between these adults and the child. For some the diagram is easy; for other children the diagram is complex. Now place a *T* for yourself (in pencil that can be erased, for you have a temporary part in that family grouping). You are probably not in the center but closer to the child than you are to the family, yet not in between them. Perhaps you are below them as a support. Now draw lines of communication between yourself and the family members. It may be by telephone, written communication, or even e-mail, but whatever form, the goal is to make it a solid, two-way communication to ultimately benefit the child.

Family involvement does not have to be spaghetti suppers, fund-raisers, or discipline classes (though all of those are worthwhile). Involvement,

REVIEW

PORTFOLIOS

A comprehensive collection of teacher observations and children's work to document the child's progress in all developmental areas.

Observation and Recording Methods That May Be Included in the Portfolio

- Class List Log notations (dated)
- Developmental Checklists and Rating Scales
- Anecdotal and Running Records
- Time Sample summaries (dated)
- Frequency Count summaries (dated)
- transcriptions of Interviews or Conversations
- descriptions of Cognitive Task Experiments
- Work Samples
- media documentation such as photographs, audio recordings, or videotape segments
- child study
- Questionnaires about the child filled out by a family member
- Notes inserted by a family member

Portfolios May Include Documentation of

- separation and adjustment to the program
- physical development
- social development
- emotional development
- speech and language development
- attention span
- cognitive development
- literacy
- creativity
- sociodramatic play
- self-concept
- interaction with adults

in its truest sense, is the knowledge families have about their child while in the program. Involved families are familiar with the goals of the program, its policies and procedures, and how those relate to their child. They also know what the child's day is like and how the child is functioning in the group setting. Confidence is built that the staff will keep them informed of important facts about their child.

While the family is the most accurate source of information about their child, it has been found that the public at large has some gaps in their knowledge about children in general. In a national study of 3,000 adults, including more than 1,000 parents of young children, it was found that there are vast overexpectations regarding the behavior of babies and young children (Lally, Lerner, & Lurie-Hurvitz, 2001). These include beliefs about the intentionality of behavior by infants and toddlers: "She knows I just sat down to eat and chooses this time to get fussy." It was also found that adults were misinformed about spoiling and discipline, and had little understanding of the importance of play. The early childhood professional has the opportunity to educate parents and the public about child development, realistic expectations for behavior, and the effects of the environment (including families, media, health issues) on young children. This can be done through every contact, both formal and informal, not by sermonizing but by constantly pointing out children's actions and what the actions reveal about development. That is exactly what observation, recording, and communicating are all about.

The first step is a well-planned intake process, informing families of the facts they need to know. Through their personal contact with the teacher and other program staff, families will build trust in the program. Even if they may not understand all that the program is about, they can tell these people care about them and their child. This trust is extended in various ways during the year, through daily contacts, written communications, progress reports, and conferences. Whatever the mode, these communications should be positive, descriptive, and personal (Figure 14–1).

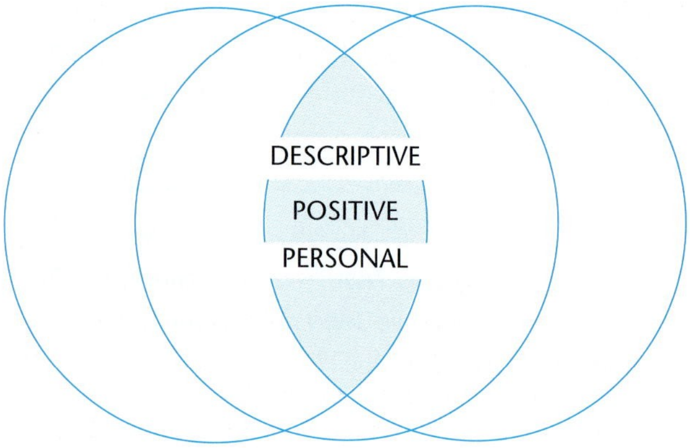

Figure 14–1 Home–school communications must be positive, descriptive, and personal.

DAILY CONTACTS

Personal

The best way for these interactions to be personal is if the staff and families know each other. Through home visits, open houses, visits to the classroom, phone calls, and notes, the staff establishes rapport with each family. This is not to become friends, though that may happen, but to extend friendliness, courtesy, and partnership in a shared interest—the child. The teacher may have to make the effort again and again. It is like the persistent salesperson using different techniques to reach the customer. Many teachers react that it is their job to teach or care for the child, not the family. But they cannot adequately and single-handedly do that job without the family's cooperation, or at least acknowledgment of the role each plays.

Programs that have daily contact with family members who drop off and pick up their children have wonderful opportunities for interaction. Each day, tidbits of information about the child are casually shared. This gives background and breadth to what the teacher knows about the child, helping the teacher to better interpret behavior and help the child develop. Sharing the tidbits of the day with family members at dismissal time gives them insight about the child's day, their accomplishments and near accomplishments. This is an important, crucial part of the teacher's responsibility. The teacher establishes rapport with each family, seeing them day in and day out. Getting to know them and their child should be a priority. Noticing the new hairstyle, or employment badge, or hurried look indicates to the family member they are recognized as human beings. The teacher sees them not just as the client, the tuition check writer, or Amber's daddy. Not all are suited to this task, so the person on the teaching team who is the most adept at personal contacts should be the "doorperson." That person provides a friendly, welcoming face and attitude, a receptive ear, and tactful conversation.

Descriptive

It is a luxury to be able to greet families at the end of the day and complete the circle by relating a bit of the child's day. It gives a springboard for later conversations about the day that may need a little nudge. A flood of talk springs forth when families have a little seed to get the child started. The comments at the door also let the family have an idea of not only what the child did but how she is doing. They make comparisons with other children: "Gee, all the children in Heather's class can put on their own boots. Maybe I better work with her to learn how," or "The teacher said Tamiche played for a long time with the play dough and she gave me a recipe to make it at home. Maybe that would occupy her while I fix dinner." Family education occurs in subtle ways.

It is impossible to give daily detailed comments to every family. Using the many communication modes, descriptive little vignettes like those in the examples in Share with the Family should be communicated to families often. Just as it is important to observe every child in the group, it is important to share information with every family. It is easy to share those shining moments, the ones that really stand out. "Chen wrote his name today for the first time!" For some children, however, remembering to turn the water off after they wash their hands is an accomplishment to be shared. It takes tact and practice to describe daily happenings accurately and without sarcasm. With practice it becomes natural. A little tip: The doorperson can keep a Class List Log in a private spot and jot down who received little "gems" at the door. After a few days, a spot check will show that some children have not had any good news shared for a while. The teacher can then make a conscious effort to observe and share a bit of information.

Positive

All comments shared informally, at the door or by other means, should be *positive* ones. At the end of the day, the family member is tired. The child has long forgotten his mistaken behavior. Other people are present. This is no time to bring out a litany of problems the child had that day. Those conflicts, whether with another child, the staff, or the materials, cannot be solved then and there, so there is no need to talk about them. Staff who relay "bad news" at the end of the day are venting anger. They could be displaying their ineptness at guiding the child's behavior. They seem to be expecting the family to take action on something that happened at school. That is an unfair request. It could even be interpreted as laying blame on the family for raising such a destructive, aggressive, unruly child. Teachers list "tattletale" at the top of the list of characteristics they do not like in children. Telling families about a child's mistaken behaviors at the end of the day is in the same vein. No, the doorperson should only pass on good news (Figure 14–2).

Development is always looked at from the positive viewpoint: "What has the child accomplished

Figure 14–2 Greetings at the door, both at arrivals and departures, should be positive and personal.

so far?" No matter the level of development, an accomplishment has been made and can be shared as good news.

> "Derek made it to the bathroom once today."
> *Rather than:* "Derek had three toilet accidents today."
> "Cecilia used her blanket for comfort today but did let go of it to go down the slide."
> *Rather than:* "Cecilia whined most of the day and didn't play hardly at all."
> "Roshann made an *R* today."
> *Rather than:* "Roshann painted an *R* on the wall."

It may not be possible to relate "good news" stories to every family member at the end of every day, but all families should receive frequent, descriptive, positive messages. If families pick up their children at the center, *every family* and *every child* should be acknowledged as they leave. (This also relieves those anxious moments when suddenly someone says, "I didn't see Serina leave." The doorperson can say, "I was at the door and Mrs. Bigelow was in a hurry so scooted in and out. I saw them leave." A sign-out system also safeguards this possibly dangerous time of the day. Most regulatory agencies require a sign-out at the end of the day.) The personal touch brings closure to the day for the child and reinforces the friendly relationship between the home and program.

High-quality programs make every effort to involve families in a number of ways that fit the families' needs. This emphasizes the partnership, demonstrating the program's recognition of the vital role that families play in the child's life, including their education. Supporting the family's culture is the first step toward this partnership. DiNatale (2002) suggests asking each family to print a welcome sign in their home language for the classroom. Of course, written materials for families should be translated into languages spoken at home, home-language literacy materials in the classroom should be present, and all cultural holidays respected.

Ethical Responsibilities to Families

Teachers and the family have a common interest in the child's welfare. The family is the primary influence on the child. The teacher's role is to collaborate with the family, offering a specialized knowledge, but always approaching interactions with the family with respect and consideration. The National Association for the Education of Young Children expressed these ideals in the Ethical Code of Conduct (NAEYC, 2005). According to these guidelines, the early childhood educator should

- be familiar with the knowledge base related to working effectively with families and to stay informed through continuing education and training.
- develop relationships of mutual trust and create partnerships with the families we serve.
- welcome all family members and encourage them to participate in the program.
- listen to families, acknowledge and build upon their strengths and competencies, and learn from families as we support them in their task of nurturing children.
- respect the dignity and preferences of each family and make an effort to learn about its structure, culture, language, customs, and beliefs.
- acknowledge families' childrearing values and their right to make decisions for their children.
- share information about each child's education and development with families and help them understand and appreciate the

current knowledge base of the early childhood profession.
- help family members enhance their understanding of their children and support the continuing development of their skills as parents.
- participate in building support networks for families by providing them with opportunities to interact with program staff, other families, community resources, and professional services.

Written Communication

EXERCISE Number the following pieces of mail from 1 to 10 in the order you would open them:

______ card-sized envelope with no return address
______ credit card preapproval
______ offer for a free water test
______ newsletter from an organization
______ advertisement for a new early childhood magazine
______ letter from your grandmother
______ letter from the IRS, stamped "Refund"
______ telephone bill
______ letter from the "love of your life"
______ registered letter from a collection agency

A letter from a friend or someone highly regarded is opened expectantly. Those unsolicited pieces of mail are often not even read. Some mail brings apprehension and anxiety as it is opened, causing feelings of depression, anger, or uncertainty.

Written communications from the early childhood program should be closer to the beginning of the such a list than the end. The same points about daily contacts apply to written communications. They should be personal, descriptive, and positive.

FAMILY HANDBOOK. A thorough but reader-friendly Family Handbook is necessary to fully inform families of the philosophy, policies, and procedures the program follows. Educational institutions, from playgroups to universities, have policies or sets of guidelines under which they operate. The people involved with those institutions need to know what those guidelines are before they can follow them. This is the role of the Family Handbook, a guide with all the necessary information parents need to know. It should include the following information and policies (compiled from American Academy of Pediatrics, 2002; Gestwicki, 2004; Berger, 2004; Talan & Bloom, 2004):

information about the program—mission, philosophy/goals, calendar of operation (days, hours, holidays), groups (ages, adult/child ratios), curriculum, child assessments, staffing (qualifications, background checks), payments, fees, refunds, insurance, decision making (board members information), regular evaluation of program by families, modes of communication with families, confidentiality

enrollment and attendance—forms required (health, immunization, family/child information, emergency contacts, consent, photo release), special needs or circumstances information, inclusion of children with special needs, orientation for new child and families, transition to next group or to kindergarten, sign-in and sign-out procedures, late pick up policies, attendance policies

parent involvement—open door policy (parents' right to visit any time), volunteer opportunities, family supports, family conferences, special events, facilities for parent at school (library, suggestion box, bulletin boards)

health and safety—sanitation, hygiene of facility and staff. restricted access of facility, emergency care procedures, illness exclusion policies, medication administration, emergency closings and evacuation procedures, nutrition (meals, snacks, food from home, celebrations), napping procedures and policies, pets and animals on premises, prohibition of alcohol, tobacco, illegal substances, firearms, mandated reporters of child maltreatment

Families are often too busy to read the guide book, or it is too involved and intimidating. Efforts to make it user-friendly, with indexes, graphics, and a concise format, have proven to be effective. Providing in-person orientations where the most important details are presented verbally help the nonreader, the visual learner, and reinforces important elements. Home visits and individual conversations can clarify those points that families need to know most. All of this is done with respect for the families, with an attitude of partnership and consideration for the ultimate benefit of the child.

NEWSLETTERS. A periodic newsletter informing families of current news helps encourage family involvement. Descriptions of past events with short anecdotes from the children give the readers a sense of being there. This should be easy to compile from the Anecdotal Recordings. Names of children and volunteers in a newsletter increases readers' interest. Details families need to know should be bold, concise, not embedded in lines and lines of writing. Short daily or weekly plans in a calendar format will give the families and children a conversation topic. Future events could be anticipated: "It says here that a bunny will visit today. Maybe you want to take a carrot to feed it?" Past events are remembered: "It says here that you had a bee hive and bee keeper visit your class. I didn't know that. Can you tell me about it?" Positive encouragement for families should be the theme of all newsletter writing. Parenting is a tough job. Families are not interested in articles telling them they should be doing more, more, and more.

> "Did you know that we have books to borrow so you don't have to make a trip to the library?"
>
> *Rather than:* "You should read to your child 15 minutes every day. If you don't, they won't be good readers."

There are some commercial newsletters that are very well done which can be personalized by adding pages or by using only edited portions of them. The newsletter should be friendly in tone and fun to read, with short, informative articles. The print should be clear and readable, with one-half as much white space as there is print. That means that drawings by the children, poems centered in columns, and graphics should comprise one-third of the space. These will catch the reader's eye and illustrate the text. They draw the reader's interest to an article a few paragraphs in length (Figure 14–3).

HAPPY NOTES. In situations in which families and teachers do not have daily contact, "happy notes" serve the purpose of comments made at the door. These brief, personal, descriptive, and positive comments about the child that day can be written and tucked in a knapsack or handed to a family member at the end of the day. Every recording assignment could bring out material from which to draw these comments. Finding the time to do these is a consideration. How about one a day? Does that seem manageable? If so, then use a class list and write one a day, focusing on one positive achievement or skill that child displayed today. See Chapter 1 for an example.

DOCUMENTATION PANELS. These are more than bulletin boards with posted announcements and seasonal decorations. **Documentation panels** articulate to the family the philosophy of the classroom and give tangible evidence that children are engaged in active learning. Documentation panels can inform the families of the benefits of play and illustrate the learning that is taking place. While the panels are informational, they also should be aesthetically pleasing. The display may contain photographs, children's artwork and dictation, transcripts of the teacher's observations, and curriculum webs, all outlining step-by-step processes around a central theme. Document panels convey much more information than a newsletter, and they become interactive when the children are the ones explaining the panel, thus enhancing their thinking and language skills.

The documentation panel can communicate information on a variety of topics:

- learning environments
- projects/emergent curriculum
- themes
- special events
- specific curriculum areas
- child development
- skill acquisition (Brown-DuPaul, Keyes, & Segatti, 2001)

TECHNOLOGY. Electronic and technical innovations are changing the way people communicate.

E-Mail. With e-mail, it is possible to send electronic messages, electronic happy notes, digital photographs, and compressed videos to families with Internet access. The day's events or monthly newsletter could be "mailed" to everyone in the class via the computer and a distribution list. However, with the ease of electronic communication, it is important to remember to write sensitively, respecting confidentiality, and being careful that spur-of-the-moment writing is professional.

Voice Mail. Families with voice mail (answering machines) can receive short messages of good news from the program. That would be a good welcome home at the end of the day to hear the teacher's voice say: "Mr. and Mrs. Jones, listen to what James learned today. James, want to sing the Snowman song for Mommy and Daddy?" Answering machines at the school could provide reminders for the next day, little parenting tips, or songs by the children. Anyone who wants to call the program in the evening after hours would hear them and be able to leave a message for the teacher "after the beep."

Traveling Journals. Many programs have made traveling journals that go back and forth between school and home. Some are notes written between the family and the teacher. Several programs have a

CONKLIN PRESCHOOL
MARCH NEWSLETTER

Home is where the heart is, it is as much a state of mind as a physical structure. Children watch construction with fascination, awed by the undertaking of a crew as it creates a structure. At school this month we will be cooperating to build a house, complete with an outside pool! The children will have an opportunity to try some interesting tools and machines, such as pulleys, hammers, and pipes.

This type of hands-on-learning, or play, is a vehicle for the child's mental growth. Play enables children to progress from the sensorimotor intelligence of infancy to pre-operational thought in the preschool years. Play is not only essential to cognitive development but serves important functions in children's physical, emotional, and social development. Come in to PLAY, learn and grow with us at preschool, **we love** to have a mom, dad, grandparent, aunt or uncle on snack day.

FAMILY CONFERENCES

Throughout the school year I have observed your children involved in regular preschool activities. March 15-19 is conference week. There will be no morning classes on the 15th and 16th and no afternoon classes on the 18th and 19th, giving us the opportunity to meet and discuss your child's progress and readiness for school. A sign up sheet for appointments will be posted. If you are unable to make one of these times, we can make alternate arrangements. Call me 775-0511 to schedule an appointment. You are welcome to come early and stay late; we will provide activities and childcare. It is important to be prompt and keep discussions to a maximum of 15 minutes.

TOTE BAGS

On Wednesday, March 17th at 9:00 we will begin to sew tote bags for next year's classes. We need your HELP! We need those who can sew and have sewing machines, those who can iron and pin, and anyone else who can help. Bring sewing machines, pins, white thread, scissors and yourselves. Our goal is to make over 100 bags. The hospitality committee has made arrangements to serve a delicious lunch. Childcare will be provided giving you the opportunity to experience a good old fashion-sewing bee.

CLEANING A ROOM TEACHES ORDER

Did you know that cleaning up a room is a learning activity? It can teach them order and structure. In their room, everything should have a place where it belongs. Toys, for example, each have their place. Teddy Bear goes here, the doll goes there, the ball goes over there. As a child learns about individual objects and the place it goes, they are learning basic lessons about space and how objects are organized in space. Later on in school, this concept will help learn the difference between "b" and "d" and "p" and "q".

Figure 14–3 Newsletter Example. (Courtesy of and reprinted with permission. Conklin Preschool, Conklin, NY)

Rags' first day at my house was very pleasant. Rags took a nap with my brother Christopher. My brother helped me take care of Rags. Rags went with me to my Daddy's house and spent the night.

Rags also went with me to the babysitter's house. I took Rags in my tent with me. I held Rags and hugged him the whole time he was with me. I had a great time with Rags. I even shared Rags with my brother.

Figure 14–4 Journals from home to school are a part of family communication and involvement. (Courtesy of and reprinted with permission. Conklin Preschool, Conklin, NY)

traveling journal in a tote bag with toys or art materials. In one preschool, families were asked to do something with Rags, a cute stuffed puppy, write about it, and then send it back to school for the next child. The responses are delightful, showing families' creativity, and encouraging the child to draw or write as well. While the family has the journal at home, they read the other entries and look at drawing and writing attempts. Figure 14–4 shows a sample page from the story of Rags.

A cassette recorder and a tape on which the teacher has recorded songs sung in school or a short review of projects in progress could be sent home with the traveling journal to inform families of school events. Recordings with each child adding a bit to the tape have also been successful.

Positive, Descriptive, Personal Reports

Why is report card time so dreaded by families, children, and teachers? It is a time of stress. The teacher is placing a value on the child's efforts that may come as a surprise to the families, and sometimes even the child.

Think About It . . .

Imagine going to the doctor for a routine physical examination. You feel fine but they run tests and now you are there for the results. What are you feeling?

There is always some apprehension that tests may reveal some unsuspected problem. If that is the case, there are various reactions. First of all, the patient wants to see the file and the test results to verify that there is no mistake. If the doctor will not show the actual test results, suspicions are raised. The diagnosis may be rejected because there were no previous indicators. The doctor must be wrong. The patient may want to wait a while or have the tests repeated to see if there is a change. A second opinion may be sought to decide exactly what the extent of the problem is

PUPIL *Marcy Johnson* GRADE *2*

Teacher Comment

She is also behind in the independent reading series in the classroom. She must get caught up in these areas as they are a mandatory part of Reading. She has been allowed to take a few books home to catch up. Please see to it that she works on these. She must learn to use her time wisely!

I am not pleased with Marcy's math grade this term. She must practice.

TEACHER: *Mrs. Marshfield*

Dear Parent:
You may keep this for your records. If you wish to reply to the above comment, then please use the reverse side of this sheet and return it in the envelope. You may call to make an appointment with the teacher.

Figure 14–5 Read this note and see how you would feel as a parent or a family member.

and how to remedy it. These same apprehensions and reactions are common in family–teacher interactions.

When there is an ongoing exchange of descriptive information from school to home, there are no surprises when progress reports or report cards are issued. When families see the Portfolio and know they have access to it, they develop trust that the information about the child is based on credible evidence, not just guesses. How often do families say, "She doesn't like my child so she gave him a failing mark." The work in the Portfolio documents educational decisions. Even if they never look at the Portfolio, when they understand what it is about, they have confidence they can look at it if they want. That knowledge brings trust. So-called sunshine laws afford people the right to examine public records, including those of state and local educational agencies and most states' child care regulations. Such laws are only acted upon by a few, but they give everyone confidence to exercise it if the need or desire arises.

The same advice about sending only positive notes home to families applies to report cards as well. Rather than "telling on" the child, if there is a concern or problem, it is best addressed in person, with both parties prepared for the topic. A "bad news note" is like receiving the medical test results in the mail, with no explanation. It leaves a knot of anxiety in the stomach. Most people would rush to the phone for an explanation. That is exactly what families do. They want to know more, usually calling with feelings of anxiety, anger, and frustration at the bad surprise.

Think About It . . .

Read the note in Figure 14–5 that the family of a second-grader received. How would it make you feel if you were the family? What elements do you notice?

This is the second page of what is at least a four-page note. The teacher went on and on and on. If there were so many concerns, a conference could explain this so much better. Did you notice every comment is negative? Not a single positive line! The teacher also is giving a strong order—"Please see to it. . . ." Would a family treasure this note? Would the child feel encouraged to work harder? And what about the impersonality of the opening, "Dear Parent"? What if it is not the parent who is responsible for the child? Either the family member would call for an appointment or be so intimidated that no response but anger or resentment would be felt.

EXERCISE **On a separate sheet of paper, write about a report card you remember as a child.**

Many people still have report cards on which teachers wrote negative, sarcastic comments and made dire predictions that this person was doomed to fail. Thankfully, most of those people did not believe the teacher and went on to succeed and prove her wrong. Remember, what is written is permanent and could be misinterpreted. The teacher must exercise caution, even in happy notes, to make sure that words are not misconstrued or the comments questionable in meaning.

EXERCISE Rewrite the following comments to be positive, descriptive, and personal.

"She usually shares with other children."
"Grady only will play with other children if he can have his own way."
"Stephanie can't write her name, zip her own coat, or tie her shoes."
"Lynn is always the mother giving orders when playing in the dramatic area."

The word *usually* is one to avoid when writing progress reports. It leaves so many questions about what happens at other times. That is an example of the care and caution necessary in writing progress reports.

PROGRESS REPORTS. Progress reports are just what the name implies. They are short reviews of a child's development in written format. They give families a glimpse of the child from another's perspective. They should be positive in tone. They are reporting progress.

Unless there is some serious trauma, all children make progress over time. It definitely is not at the same rate in each developmental area. It most likely is different from any other child. But it is still progress (Figure 14–6). (This form also appears on the Bind-in-Book CD.)

A narrative progress report is a more complete report, following very closely the outline of the Portfolio. Developmental Checklists or charts supply the criteria. A short, descriptive sentence or two in each area is all that is required. An outline and "progress at a glance" can be included in the Portfolio to aid in organizing your thoughts for writing. It should be headed with the child's name, the date, the writer's full name, and the name of the program (Figure 14–7).

A POSITIVE AND NEGATIVE EXAMPLE. Compare the tone and wording of the progress reports shown in Figure 14–7. These reports were written about the same child, each presenting the same information but giving a whole different tone. The first portrays the child as active and imaginative in the beginning stages of socialization. The second typifies the child as an airhead, not able to do many things that are expected. The second uses language such as one-to-one correspondence and cooperative play stage that is not understood by most families and so should be avoided.

TIPS FOR PROGRESS REPORTS. The following suggestions will aid in writing progress reports:

short, concise descriptive statements
positive
child "can do"
positive
no technical terms
positive

Keep a copy in the Portfolio and in the class file.

CASE STUDIES. A comprehensive narrative of the child is called a **case study** or **child study**. It can be used as an end-of-the-year report. It can also be sent with the family as the child moves to another program or as a report to a referral agency, upon the written request of the family. A child study follows much the same format as the **progress report** but amplifies the information given in each area and references comments with the documentation. This referencing is much like the way an author references information from another source. In this way, the reader can go to that source for further information, possibly to examine evidence of what the author said or to learn more about the subject. The reader may then draw a different conclusion from that source.

Figure 14–8 is a sample child study of the same child presented in Figure 14–7 at the end of the year.

After reading the child study and reviewing the documentation, the reader should feel acquainted with the child. The child study is extensive because there are so many specific details, gathered week by week, on which to draw conclusions. The summaries of the child study are also *positive,* relating what the child can do. The documentation is there for proof of the inferences about the child's progress and development. An extensive child study may not be necessary for every child, especially if the child is remaining in the program, moving from one classroom to another. A series of progress reports may be sufficient.

TEMPLATE FOR A PROGRESS REPORT AND CHILD STUDY. The mechanics of preparing the child study are much the same as any term paper. (The progress report is shorter, with only one or two main points

PROGRESS AT A GLANCE Child's Name ______________________

PERIOD 1: Date ____________ Recorder ____________

Strengths ______________________________________

Areas still developing ______________________________________

____

Educational plan to facilitate development ______________________________________

____

____

PERIOD 2: Date ____________ Recorder ____________

Strengths ______________________________________

Areas still developing ______________________________________

____

Educational plan to facilitate development ______________________________________

____

____

PERIOD 3: Date ____________ Recorder ____________

Strengths ______________________________________

Areas still developing ______________________________________

____

Educational plan to facilitate development ______________________________________

____

____

PERIOD 4: Date ____________ Recorder ____________

Strengths ______________________________________

Areas still developing ______________________________________

____

Educational plan to facilitate development ______________________________________

____

____

Figure 14–6 Progress at a Glance (form).

XYC CENTER **NICOLE LIND** **November 29, year** **Age: 4 yrs., 3 mo.** **Sandra Richards, Teacher**	**XYC CENTER** **NICOLE LIND** **November 29, year** **Age: 4 yrs., 3 mo.** **Sandra Richards, Teacher**
ADJUSTMENT TO SCHOOL: Nicole had no difficulty from the first day of school. She hangs up her coat and is ready to participate. SELF-HELP: She can unzip, zip with help. She can pour juice and cut food with ease. She handles the bathroom by herself. She participates in picking up the room. PHYSICAL DEVELOPMENT: She runs with coordination, balances on one foot. She makes circles and lines with markers and cuts slashes with scissors. SOCIAL: She plays primarily with two other girls but joins small groups in organized activities. EMOTIONAL: She smiles a lot and allows herself to be comforted if she is hurt or tired. SPEECH AND LANGUAGE: She can be understood and speaks freely to adults and other children. MEMORY AND ATTENTION SPAN: She spends long times in dramatic play and active outdoor play. She knows the words to songs we sing and knows the sequence of the day's activities. LITERACY: She knows how to look at a book right side up and turn pages. She listens to stories individually read. MATH AND SCIENCE: She can count out loud to 10. She has a wide knowledge about hamsters, including their birth. She has several at home and has provided little ones for the class. CREATIVE ARTS: She fills the page with color and notices lines and shapes in her art. She prefers easel painting to table art like collage, watercolors, or clay. DRAMATIC PLAY: This is the area she chooses most frequently, dressing up, taking on a variety of roles, using her language in an imaginative way. ADJUSTMENT TO SCHOOL: She seems happy here, comfortably follows the routine, and is making progress mainly in dramatic and physical play. WORKING ON: Providing her with dramatic play props that require small hand muscle movement. We are beginning small group storybook reading time into the dramatic play area.	ADJUSTMENT TO SCHOOL: Nicole is indifferent to parent leaving. Arrives in a whirl. SELF-HELP: Can't zip her own coat. Serves self more food than she can finish. Licks the spoon. Needs reminding about washing hands after toileting. PHYSICAL DEVELOPMENT: Runs and climbs. Cannot pedal bicycle yet. Scribbles. Still working on cutting. SOCIAL: Parallel play stage, not cooperative. EMOTIONAL: Happy most of the time, sometimes has bouts of silliness. SPEECH AND LANGUAGE: Talks a lot. Sometimes hard to understand. MEMORY AND ATTENTION SPAN: Does not participate in whole group activities though she listens to the songs. Reminds teacher what should be happening next. LITERACY: Not interested in story time yet. MATH AND SCIENCE: Does not have one-to-one correspondence yet. Often lets hamsters loose in the classroom. CREATIVE ARTS: Paints whole page one color, then paints on lines and circles, mixing the paint. DRAMATIC PLAY: Habitual play area in a fantasy world. Makes up words and imaginary language. ADJUSTMENT TO SCHOOL: She seems happy here as long as she gets to play in the dramatic area or outside. Those are her favorite things to do. Seems uninterested in learning materials or group times. WORKING ON: Zipping, cutting, small manipulatives, language.

Figure 14–7 Progress Report Examples: Positive and Negative.

XYC CENTER **NICOLE LIND** **June 14, year 4 yrs. 9 mo.**

Reporter: Mary McGwinn, 4's Teacher

Nicole is the oldest of three children, all of whom attend the XYC Center. Nicole has been at the XYC Center since September and will be attending kindergarten at Brinker School in the fall. She lives with her family next door to her grandparents with whom she spends much time. She talks about them lovingly. She has many cousins and extended family that make up her social circle. She attends church weekly where she participates in a children's choir. She attends dance lessons on Saturdays and will be dancing in her first recital in a few weeks.

PHYSICAL DEVELOPMENT: She is of average height and weight and in good health as evidenced by her almost perfect attendance record (see attendance record). She was absent for one week with chicken pox and a day occasionally with slight fevers accompanying colds. Her interest in dancing and advanced body coordination skills work together to demonstrate agility and confidence in movement. Her writing and hand muscles for smaller tasks are developing. She can fringe paper with scissors and put together eight-piece puzzles (checklist: physical development). She can write her name in large letters progressing from just the first *N* to the whole name (samples 10/05/0X, 1/17/0X, 4/4/0X).

SOCIAL DEVELOPMENT: Nicole is comfortable with the staff at XYC seeking help mainly for comfort from falls (which are infrequent) or frustration with small muscle tasks. She has little confidence in her abilities and seeks adults to assist her (anecdotal record 11/1/0X, 3/17/0X). With adults holding the paper or providing her with encouragement, she can perform those tasks she tries. Nicole is called *friend* by many children in the class (photo of Nicole and friends taken 2/2/0X). She plays mostly with girls in the dramatic play area, dressing in the various theme props provided there. She had an especially long play sequence when the area was set up as an animal hospital (class video, running record 3/13/0X). Through this interest in dramatic play she has gained negotiation skills. Compare anecdotal record of 10/6/0X and 2/27/0X. She has moved from playing alongside other children along the same theme to interacting and problem solving, assigning, and carrying out intricate play-acting roles, even putting on accents. This is demonstrated on the audio tape.

ADJUSTMENT TO SCHOOL: Nicole has adjusted to the routine of this center since she entered in September. She often goes down the hall "to see how the babies are doing," as she refers to her little sisters. She is welcomed by the teachers and allowed to spend time there, playing with the younger children. She has been observed in a protective, nurturing role captured in some photos (10/1/0X and 12/17/0X). She is comfortable with the routine, using free-play time to be involved in the dramatic play themes. She begins the day with painting since she often arrives before her friends. Her paintings have moved from experimentation with paint (9/29/0X) to more intricate designs (1/6/0X) and on to recognizable forms of people and animals (4/26/0X).

SELF-ACCEPTANCE: She acts independently in caring for her own needs in dressing, eating, and toileting (overview sheet). She independently chooses play areas, companions, and activities (time samples 10/21/0X, 2/03/0X). She exhibits a feeling of competence in physical activities, taking leadership roles (4/7/0X). She has a cheerful temperament. She displays no aggressiveness or antisocial behaviors (frequency counts 10/12/0X, 3/11/0X). She appears to be self-assertive in relations with others. She has a firm sense of self (interviews 11/2/0X, 2/17/0X).

COGNITIVE DEVELOPMENT: Nicole recognizes the letters in her name but not by themselves. She can count to 10 accurately and to 20 if assisted with the "teens." She knows the names of the colors, the names of the geometric shapes, and is beginning to add small numbers mentally (see interview 11/19/0X, 5/2/0X).

She has a wide knowledge of animal life, and a special interest in hamsters. She has raised several litters and provided several classmates with pets along with explicit directions on how to care for them (audio recording 3/22/0X). Her interest and ability in writing is at the beginning stages but her concern for the hamster's care prompted her to write a book. It told her friends how to care for hamsters. She dictated the book then illustrated it (sample, 12/12/0X). This was duplicated and given to each hamster owner. She felt this was a significant work. She talked about it on the tape (12/19/0X).

When listening to Nicole speak on the tape, some irregularities are noticed that are not apparent when talking to her casually (tape 9/29/0X). This was reviewed by her parents and pediatrician and a decision was

Figure 14–8 Child Study Example.

made to wait six months for these sounds to develop. Another tape on 04/6/0X showed those sounds were now present. This was reviewed by her parents and the pediatrician and confirmed. No further action was necessary.

CREATIVITY: Nicole's creativity is centered in the dramatic play realm. She can carry out a role imaginatively and encourage others to do so as well, displaying an advanced degree of concentration and social awareness (running record 1/29/0X). Her drawings are more realistic than her daily paintings, almost methodical in nature from one day to the next (samples 10/30/0X, 10/31/0X, 11/1/0X, 11/2/0X). She called it "practicing." She used scissors, collage, and clay in much the same way by experimenting with the same materials day after day then leaving them for months.

Nicole will enter kindergarten with strong social skills, confidence in her physical abilities, and the beginnings of literacy. Her adaptability to the group setting and helping adults should ensure that her school experience is a good one. She talks of school and all the things she will learn there. Once she saw the loft in the kindergarten rooms with extensive dramatic play areas, she was convinced that it was a good place.

I am happy to answer any questions about this review of Nicole's time at XYC Center. She is a joy to know.

Signed ______________________________

Figure 14–8 (continued)

under each topic and without references to documentation, although they are present.)

1. Begin by calculating the child's age. The child's age is calculated in years and months at the time the report is written. In the life of a young child, much change takes place in a year, so the difference between "just three" and "almost four" is very great. This poses a bit of a mathematical problem to report writers.

EXERCISE **Try these for practice:**

a) The date is October, 2006. Joseph's birth date is July, 2002. How old is he? (Simple.)

2006	10th month
– 2002	– 7th month
4 years	3 months

b) The date is October, 2006. Martha's birth date is November, 2002. How old is she? (Trickier.)

2006	10th month
– 2002	– 11th month

Oops! We have to borrow 12 months from 2006.

2005	22 months
– 2002	– 11 months
3 years	11 months

Rule: When the child has not yet had a birthday in that year, you have to borrow 12 months from the current year to calculate the year and month age. Try some:

Janice was born in August, 2004.
Frederick was born in February, 2003.
Natalie was born in October, 2002.

The correct answers will depend on the month and year you are reading and calculating this equation. Now figure your own age in years and months.

2. Next define the topic. Know about whom you are writing and focus on one child at a time.
3. Assemble the raw data, the research, and the reference material. Have the Portfolio and notes in either chronological order or organized by developmental area.
4. Prepare an outline. Here it is:

   Heading: Child's name, birth date, name of program, name of reporter.

   Family: Birth order, family make-up, contact with extended family, other teachers, community contacts.

   Physical: Appearance, size, build, ways of moving, health, attendance, large and small muscle development.

   Social development: With adults—families, other adult helpers, teachers, visitors to the classroom. With children—stage of play, who the child's friends are, how the child interacts with other children, how the child solves problems with other children.

Adjustment to school: Separation behavior, areas of interest, participation and avoidance, adjustment to school routines, ability to follow directions, mistaken behaviors requiring guidance.

Self-acceptance: Self-care skills, independence, level of self-esteem, emotional development, self-control, aggressiveness.

Cognitive development: What the child knows—numbers, alphabet, shapes, interest in books, language vocabulary, clarity of speech, what the child's attitude toward learning is.

Creativity: Child's use of imagination in art, movement, dramatic play, language.

Closing: Final paragraph, personal best wishes, signature of writer, date of report.

5. Write a rough draft from the outline. Think about the child in relation to each of those topics and jot some notes.
6. Document your statements by making references to sources. Look through the Portfolio and find representative pieces to provide data. Note the type of recording and dates.
7. Prepare final document. This is a document that might be kept by the family for a long time, maybe for the life of the child. It represents the professionalism of the program and the integrity of the writer. It should be written in complete, grammatically correct sentences. Type it, and check for spelling.
8. Proofread. Have a team member who knows the child (for confidentiality, not an outsider) read the document for content, grammar, and tone.
9. Produce the document. Type it as neatly as possible, or, more likely, use a word processor and print the final child study document as perfectly as you can make it.
10. Copy the document. The family should receive the original, either alone or with the Portfolio. A copy should be kept in the Class File. If applicable, file the family's written request for a copy to be sent to a referral agent in the Class File, along with the program's copy of the document.

These 10 steps will become more automatic with experience in writing this type of report. If they are written for the whole class, the task can be divided just as the other observation assignments, with one-fourth of them done each week. The *Week by Week* plan gives you assignments to help you make sure that you accomplish this several times a year. It will come easier.

WHAT TO DO WITH THE CHILD STUDY. Once the child study is printed, two copies are made, one to be kept in the Portfolio and one to go in the Class File.

The child study belongs to the family. It is best presented to them in a conference (discussed later in this chapter). In this way, each section can be discussed using even more personalized anecdotal remembrances. The child study could be mailed if a conference cannot be arranged. There is always the risk that the family may misinterpret the wording or tone. There should always be an opportunity for reply or challenge.

The child study may be included in the Portfolio if it is to be given to the family. With their permission, the child study could be sent to the next program, school, or a referral agent such as a therapist or pediatrician. In that case, copies of the referenced documentation should also be included.

Family Conferences

The family conference's main purpose should be to present and discuss a developmental overview of the child. The early childhood program may be the first contact the child has had with people outside the family. It is a serious responsibility to be allowed to get so intimately acquainted with their child. This conference is not just to allow the teacher to give information to the family; it is also meant as an exchange of information, a discussion, a sharing of points of view. The teacher is seeking feedback from the family for the benefit of the child. By conveying an openness toward the family's input and participation in both word and behavior, the conference has a better chance at success.

Special education and Head Start experiences have proven that family involvement and even guidance in interventions with the child have the best chances for success (Benner, 2003). The strengths-based model (Dunst, Trivette, & Mott, 1994) reminds professionals that families have their own unique strengths and that the professional should work not to "fix" the family but to find ways for the family to take responsibility for any behavior changes.

The progress reports and child study can be the points of reference on which discussion is based. These conferences should be held periodically throughout the year, or any time at the request of the family. Head Start Program Performance Standards 1304.21(2) (2005) state that parents must be

- invited to become integrally involved in the development of the program's curriculum and approach to child development and education.

- provided opportunities to increase their child's observation skills and to share assessments with staff that will help plan the learning experiences.
- encouraged to participate in staff–parent conferences and home visits to discuss their child's development and education.

Much has been written giving advice about family conferences. Their success is fragile and dependent on so many variables. Many preparations and precautions should be taken to guarantee an open, informative, positive exchange.

TIPS FOR FAMILY CONFERENCES. Family conferences can be successful exchanges of information, as well as socially satisfying and affirming for family, teacher, and child. Here are some practical suggestions:

1. Be prepared. Have the progress report or child study complete, with accompanying documentation in an organized system.
2. Make the conference times convenient for the family and provide child care if needed.
3. Prepare the environment by having comfortable chairs, at the same height, next to one another or at right angles with no table between.
4. Make sure the location is private so no one else can hear and there are no interruptions.
5. Begin with social exchange, greetings, small talk.
6. Open the Portfolio and let family know what it holds.
7. Make eye contact, lean forward, nod to their comments, listen.
8. Speak in understandable language.
9. Ask questions, ask for questions.
10. Summarize and make plans for further contact.

CONFERENCES WITH THE CHILD. It is also very useful to discuss the Portfolio with the child. Children above four years old love to look at their own work, and even nonreaders can understand the concept of the teacher keeping notes about them. Looking at work from an earlier stage brings a sense of accomplishment to the child and provides an opening to discuss the meaning of the work and the incidents recorded there. Including the child in the family conference can also be beneficial. Anxiety about what the teacher will say is dissolved. The child hears the teacher review the progress. Of course, this should be a "positive only" conference. This gives the family positive feedback with the child present, hearing what development has occurred this year and indicating the positive effect of their relationship with the child. With so many families feeling blame and heavy responsibility, it is an important role of the teacher to give plaudits for a job well done, to both the child and the family.

FAMILY CONFERENCES WHEN A PROBLEM IS SUSPECTED. Positive stories are related at the door. Positive statements are printed in the newsletters. Positive progress reports and positive child studies are written. But questions arise: "When do you ever tell them the bad news?" "When do you tell them the truth?" "When do you tell them what the child is *really* like?" When? Only after a certain process has taken place should the teacher talk to the parent about a concern (Figure 14–9).

Documented Observations. If there is a concern for a child in a specific area or areas, it is critically important to gather data. This should be done with the methods that are the least inferential, the most accurate. The Anecdotal Record meets those criteria. If possible, have another member of the teaching team also gather data.

Review Developmental Guidelines. The observers should read some basic information about developmental expectations and have a clear understanding based on research.

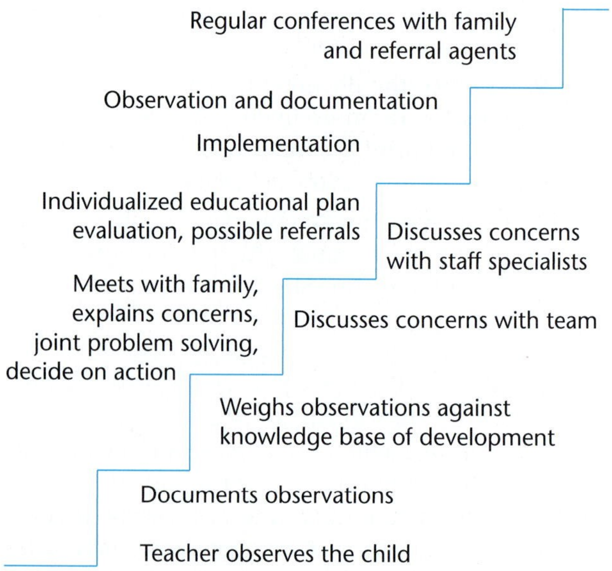

Figure 14–9 Steps in a Problem-Solving Family Conference.

it happened to me

Excuse Me!

I was holding family conferences midway through the year. They were scheduled every half hour, one after another. Between two conferences I had to leave the room. When I came back, the next parent was looking through all the Portfolios I had arranged for the next conferences. I was dumbfounded. What nerve! I got her child's folder and said, "Excuse me! This must be the one you're looking for." My mind raced through what else I could say, but I was so angry that nothing positive came to mind. So I went on with the conference. After all, it was about her child that we came together.

It taught me a lesson that I share with you. Keep all records secure. I did from that day onward.

Do you have an IT HAPPENED TO ME story about a family conference? I'd love to read it. Send it to WeekbyWeek@thomsonlearning.com

Confer with the Team and Your Supervisor. The group should look at the data, review the research, and look again at the child. Theories should be explored, searching for possible causes or influences. Every attempt should be made to eliminate biases, whatever their origin. When it is the consensus of the group that the family should be consulted, the team should decide on the approach and determine who should be involved. Usually the classroom teacher alone is sufficient for the first step in this process. Discussion topics, possible scenarios, and options can be explored. Resources for referral should be researched and prepared for the family, beginning with the least alarming, usually a full physical evaluation.

Approach the Family. In *private,* the teacher conveys concerns and a request for a conference to discuss those concerns. The teacher may ask for the family to be thinking about the areas of concern or may give the family some reading material to think about before that meeting.

"We have been noticing and documenting . . . and wondering if you have noticed this at home? When would it be convenient to get together to discuss it?"

"We've been trying different things to help Robert with . . . but we need some suggestions from you. Can we stop by on our way home tomorrow or could you come by here?"

"The next time you take Lucy to the doctor you may want to ask about. . . . Would you have time later on this afternoon to give me a call so we could talk about it? I really don't think it's serious but it has been nagging at me and I'd like to see what you think."

Try not to get into a discussion at this time. Set a later time whenever possible. Be prepared to have the meeting within 24 hours, but it is best not to have it immediately. This gives the family time to consider the questions and topic.

The Meeting. The meeting should begin with social pleasantries. Even though the meeting is necessary and the topic is a serious one, it is important to remember that both the family and the teacher share a common bond—the child. The basis for the concerns are presented, referring to the documented evidence. This evidence should be available if needed. Then the family should have the opportunity to respond with their thoughts on the situation or topic. The teacher's role is to *listen*. The teacher must remember the family is the authority on the child (Figure 14–10)

The Discussion. The meeting is conducted with attempts at clear communication and empathy.

Figure 14–10 The teacher listens to the family because they know the child best.

Possible solutions can be explored from moderate to drastic. The teacher should be prepared for strong reactions from the family. These may be denial, projection of blame, fear, guilt, mourning or grief, withdrawal, rejection, and finally acceptance (Berger, 2004).

The Decision. The family and teacher come to a decision and to an agreement to carry out the next steps. Referral information should be available if the decision is to seek outside help. The progression is usually to begin with medical personnel to investigate or rule out physical causes. Other agencies may be referred to the family, depending on the nature of the concern.

Follow-Up. The program should make every effort to implement the plan the family has made. It is the responsibility of the program to keep the family informed of the actions taken and the results. If the family is taking an action, they should be asked to keep the program informed.

Documentation. A record of the conference's main points, the decisions made and actions planned, as well as the follow-up should be kept in the school's file. It may be warranted to keep it in the confidential file rather than the Class File, depending on the nature of the concerns.

Pitfalls to Avoid for a Successful Conference of Any Kind

Gestwicki (2004) lists the following pitfalls:

1. Avoid using technical terminology, such as *motor development* or Piagetian terminology.
2. Avoid the role of "expert." Remember the real experts on the child are the family.
3. Avoid negative evaluations. Avoid using words such as *problem, behind, immature, never/can't,* and *hyperactive.*
4. Avoid unprofessional conversation:
    - about other children, families, staff
    - personal topics: marital status, financial, lifestyle
    - taking sides: between family members, between other staff, between this and other programs
5. Avoid giving advice, either requested or unsolicited. It is the teacher's role to enhance parenting skills but also parental self-esteem.
6. Avoid rushing into solutions. See this as a collaborative effort.

Using Technology

Earlier in the chapter, e-mail and voice mail were mentioned as ways to communicate with families. School Web sites and communication listservs not only send out information and news but act as discussion vehicles. Children's electronic Portfolios can be made available to the family by using password-protected areas so that only the family with the password can access the Portfolio. Advances in technology are occurring faster than many of us can adapt; but, rather than become slaves to technology, we can use it to make our job easier and better.

How to Find the Time

It does take time to work with families to keep the lines of communication open. It is essential to value the family as the child's first and foremost teacher and to work in partnership with them for the benefit of the child. That being the case, we will find the time, make the time, use the time for this very important part of the job.

What to Do with the Documentation

At the end of a school year, or when a child leaves the program, the question common to the readers of this book comes to mind, "What to do with it?" Consider the transfer or storage of each child's Portfolio, the Class File, and Reflective Journals (Figure 14–11).

THE PORTFOLIO. The program or school implementing a Portfolio system should set a policy at that time. The family has the right of access to the Portfolio at all times. It remains the property of the school, however, and it is the right of the school to decide when to give it to the family or retain ownership. Any records retained by the school are to be kept confidential. Child studies are retained as comprehensive overviews and are the property of the program, not the teacher. They can be transferred to other agencies only upon the written permission of the family.

The Portfolio could be transferred to the following:

- *Family*—At the close of the year or upon leaving the program, the Portfolio may be

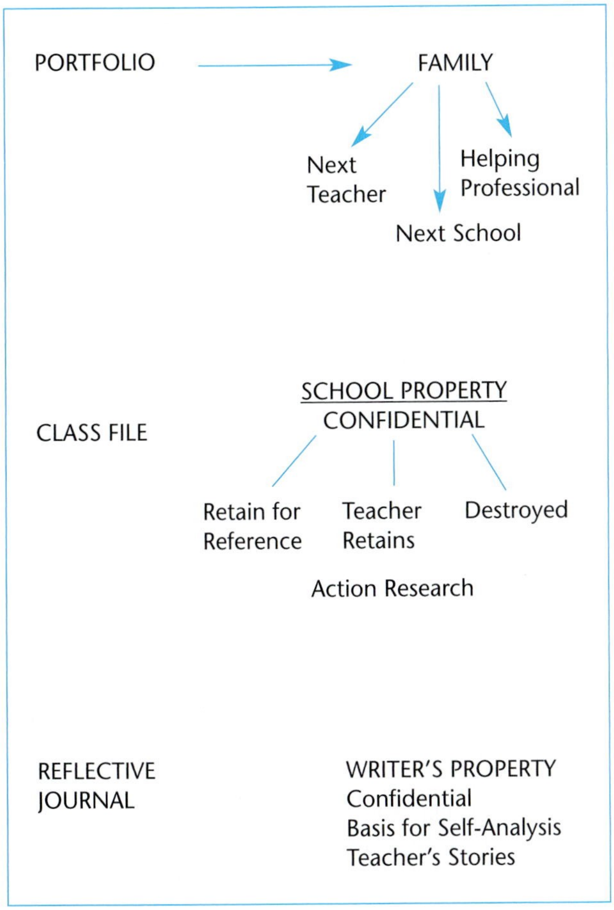

Figure 14–11 What to Do with It.

given to the child and family. For some these become precious mementos. They contain vast amounts of information about the child, along with samples of the child's work.

- *Next teacher within the school*—If the child remains in the school or program, it could be passed on and added to by the next teacher. Because of the large volume of material, it may be sorted and reduced in size. The next teacher can refer to the Portfolio to come to know the child through it. The teacher may decide not to read the Portfolio, opting instead to form an independent viewpoint. That is the teacher's prerogative.
- *Next school*—The family may designate the Portfolio be sent to the child's next school or program. Upon written authorization, that request is carried out.
- *Referral agent or helping professional*—Families may wish to release the Portfolio to medical or psychological personnel. Again, the family's authorization for this must be in writing.

Observations taken periodically through a multitude of techniques can be very valuable for diagnosis of disorders or disabilities.

WHAT TO DO WITH THE CLASS FILES. Again, the school policy is set for the retention of this file. It may be considered the property of the school and retained as a record of that class. It could be used for accountability of the teacher and the program. The Class File may be the property of the teacher, kept as a record of the work done that year. The documentation in the Class Files is of the whole class rather than focused on individual children.

WHAT TO DO WITH THE REFLECTIVE JOURNAL. This, of course, is the property of the writer. It has been used for personal and professional reflection and represents the thoughts and feelings of the writer. From these thoughts may come insights and deeper understandings of self and the profession. This is what is referred to as action research. This process begins with observation, that kind of "child watching" that comes with the pictures the eyes take and the sounds the ears hear. Those observations register against what is known about child development. The thinking about what matches and what clashes is the reflective process. This is frequently shared in an informal way.

Action research is a collaborative effort between observers. They get together to discuss principles and practices of early childhood, new ideas, questions, and theories. They consider the difference between what is seen and what is known. The environment for this collaboration is of primary importance. It must be among people who trust one another, in an intimate group setting where each is free to speak. Time is provided for an unhurried discussion. It is possible that an article, a book, a video, or a report from one person's workshop could stimulate the discussion. Teachers relate difficult experiences without revealing a child or family's identity and try to make sense of the problem. They may decide to go away and experiment with different approaches and come back to report. The lessons learned from reflection and action research make meaningful reading for others, commonly called **teacher's stories**—interesting glimpses into the classroom and the teacher's reflections upon the meaning of the occurrences. The Reflective Journals could be used as a basis for action research and teacher's stories. But the journal itself is a private document, for the writer's use alone, and should be protected for privacy.

Go to the Bind-in-Book CD for plans and resources for this week.

LOOKING AT THE CHILD'S INTERACTIONS WITH ADULTS

When a child enters a child care program or school, it is the beginning of moving out into the world. The child begins to realize there are differences in people and their views on behavior. As the child gains self-control, adherence to the expectations for behavior is possible. The interactions with adults involve a pro-social model by the adult establishing a secure, trusting relationship with the child. Children have been found to be more socially competent with peers and others when they first feel emotionally secure with their teachers (Howes & Ritchie, 2002). When children are from culturally diverse backgrounds, they experience culture shock and can be overwhelmed with the classroom atmosphere. The teacher is an empathetic mediator with the environment, the language, and peers.

The adults also model behavioral guidance by first establishing a secure attachment, setting the boundaries, communicating realistic expectations, and helping facilitate the child's behavior to meet them. By looking at the child through this lens, the observer gets a glimpse of the child's development in all the other developmental areas.

The role of the teacher is different from that of the family. To the teacher, the child is technically the client, to be kept at an emotional distance. That definition is foreign to the intensely personal relationship of child and teacher, but the objective detachment must be recognized. The teacher does not love the child as a family member does. Gartrell (2003) calls this feeling **unconditional positive regard**, describing it as "full acceptance of the child as a developing human being and member of the group" (p. 65). This is in accord with the positive view of the child's development. Observation assessment methods are used, not to catch children who are failing or to find their "weaknesses." Assessment methods measure individual levels of accomplishments and facilitate the next step in the progressive stage for each child.

How Observation and Recording Aids Child-Adult Interactions

The connection with child–adult interactions should be clear. As observations are made and documented, the adult interacts with the child. The child knows the adult is writing about what he is doing because the teacher tells him. She asks questions about his work and writes about it. Samples of his work are collected for the Portfolio the teacher has shown him.

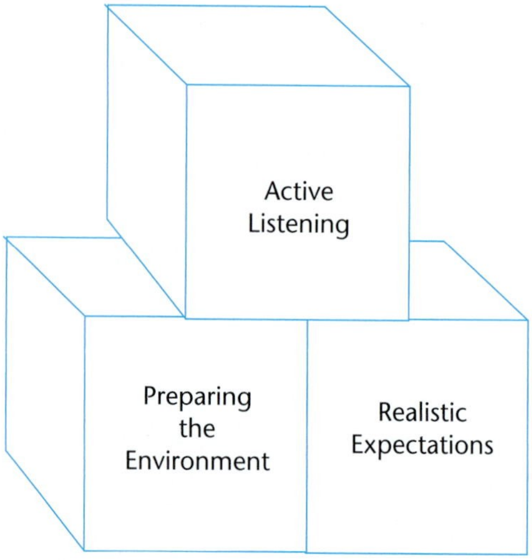

Figure 14–12 Building Blocks of the Teacher's Role in Child Guidance.

He is interviewed, photographed, and recorded. As a result of observations, the adult knows the child from these interactions. The child knows the teacher's unconditional acceptance. She has not told him he is doing it wrong but has just observed and written descriptions of what he is doing without judgment. In classrooms where children are treated and moved as a group, where the whole class does art or science or math or story activities, where the teacher's time is spent giving directions rather than interacting, the teacher does not know the individual child. When the curriculum is appropriate for each child, with the teacher as the facilitator in the learning, then positive interactions between child and adult occur (Figure 14–12).

The various recording techniques can be used to record the child–adult interactions as well:

- Class List Logs allow quick surveys of different aspects of child–adult interactions, often from memory. Some examples of criterion items:

  seeks the adult for comfort
  behavior within state guidelines
  guidance needed in situations of . . .
  still gaining self-control in . . .

- Anecdotal or Running Records are ideal for capturing all the factual information of an incident showing the adult and child interacting.
- A Frequency Count could measure how many times in a day or week the child needed adult intervention.
- Time Sampling could indicate the presence of the adult and the presence of the child,

inferring relationships from contacts with the adult.

- Conversations with the child give information about the nature of the relationship. The child's cooperativeness, comfort with the adult, and willingness to speak indicate a good relationship.
- Work Samples may demonstrate the child's feelings for the adult with love notes and letters, gifts of drawings and work (such as my spotted dog in Chapter 10).
- Checklists and Rating Scales may have criteria regarding adult–child interactions to observe and document. It is the inference of the observer with no details recorded.
- Media, such as photographs, audio, and video, may capture the child and adult interactions. It is hoped that if it is to be preserved, they are positive interactions.

The documentation accumulated in the Portfolio presents a view of the child from the staff's eyes, with contributions from the child with Work Samples. Some ways to use the Portfolio to communicate with families and other individuals comprise this last section of this chapter.

The Teacher's Role in Child Guidance

The adult takes the initiative to get acquainted with the child, recognizing the stages of stranger anxiety, differences in temperaments, and range of experiences the child has had with strangers outside the family. This was discussed in Chapter 1, which outlined strategies for staff members to begin the relationship with the child and family. It was repeated in the discussions on attachment, social and emotional development, and self-concept and self-esteem. With the foundation knowledge of child development and the specific knowledge about the child, and close observation of developing situations, the teacher helps the child develop self-control and independence. Three strategies the teacher uses to help guide children's behavior are the environment, expectations, and active listening.

PREPARING THE ENVIRONMENT. This has been mentioned many times as the first step in planning a curriculum. It is the active involvement of the child with her environment in which she constructs her own learning. The adult's role is to prepare that environment.

It is also prepared to help the children control their own behavior. The equipment and materials are organized, accessible, in good condition, varied, and sufficient for the numbers of children in the group. The space is divided into clearly defined areas from which to choose, with enough floor or table space to adequately use the materials. For example, blocks are organized on labeled shelves next to a carpeted surface, free from people walking through. Thus the builders can be comfortable, undisturbed, and not frustrated by constructions being tipped or knocked down. Blocks of time are needed so teachers are not interrupting play for their own purposes.

REALISTIC EXPECTATIONS. The observer has a knowledge base of child development against which to measure skills and behavior. When adults have inappropriate expectations of children's behavior, it is like expecting an infant to walk and punishing him when he does not. Adults' interactions with children must be based on developmental norms and appropriate practice principles so that children are not expected to behave in a way beyond their years or ability. That phrase "Children can't wait" is so true in many ways. When that principle is understood, the adult modifies his or her own behavior rather than struggling to make children do what they cannot do. For example, the teacher will not make all the children wait until everyone has washed their hands before they begin to eat.

The realistic expectations are stated in terms that children can understand, from the positive, what they can do rather than not do. Because of what is known about attention span, selective listening skills, and cognitive structures, we know that when young children hear "Don't run," they get the opposite message, "Run." It is the word emphasized, heard last and loudest, without the child's knowledge of the negating feature of the word preceding it.

ACTIVE LISTENING. Another facet of adult–child interactions is listening to the child, listening not only to the words they say but how they are said, and using intuitive ears to really hear the intended meaning. **Active listening**, a strategy described in Gordon's *Parent Effectiveness Training* (1975), focuses on what the child is saying, listening actively, and responding to the feelings implied. In the development of emotions, children have strong feelings but lack the vocabulary to express them. They also think that others feel what they feel because they are egocentric. Marian Marion (2003) gives these active listening tips:

- Listen carefully.
- Do not interrupt.

- Try to understand what the message means.
- Listen for what the child is feeling.
- Suspend judgment.
- Avoid preaching, giving advice, or trying to persuade the child to feel something else.
- Label the child's feelings as you interpret them.

The adult manages the environment, sets realistic stated expectations, and actively listens. Then the adult and child interactions can focus on more important topics, such as where butterflies go when it rains, or how this ball can stay on top of the cone collage base.

Adult Intervention of Problem Behavior

The adult role is first to keep children safe. Sometimes in the execution of that role for one child, interactions with another child strain relationships. A child starts throwing chairs, ripping other children's artwork, or yelling obscenities at another child. In the positive guidance model, children are not punished but guided to help control their own behavior and seek solutions and remedies for problems. Gartrell (2007) uses the term *mistaken behavior* as "errors in judgment and action made in the process of learning life skills" and suggests a direct approach that employs the strategy of describe-express-direct:

- *Describe without labeling*—The teacher describes the unacceptable situation: "I heard unfriendly words and saw hitting going on. It has to stop and we'll figure out what to do about the anger."
- *Express displeasure without insult*—The teacher expresses personal feelings without condemning persons: "My job is to keep everyone safe and I am worried about these kinds of actions. I want to help figure out what to do about the anger."
- *Correct by direction*—The teacher not only tells what not to do, but what to do instead: "Our classroom rules are to speak to each other with respect and not hurt anyone. I cannot let you hit each other. Let's take a breath and talk about it. Tell each other why you are upset and I'll help you find a solution." (p. 402)

The first two are considered consistent with positive guidance techniques. As a last resort, unrelated consequences are used. This is more like punishment and does not help the child learn to control her own behavior.

@ it happened to me

The Bare Room

A student teacher warned me of the room's lack of equipment in the setting where she was working. When I visited her, I saw she was not exaggerating. The children were jumping from the top of a play refrigerator, the only piece of equipment in the room besides a table and chairs and a shelf with dittoed coloring sheets and crayons. She told me she was having a terrible time "controlling" their behavior, trying to keep them from climbing and jumping off the refrigerator. The story was that each time the children "misbehaved," the lead teacher took away a piece of equipment, and now they were down to the last piece. Children must play, so they used the refrigerator in place of the large muscle equipment they were missing. Needless to say, the lead teacher and director were not providing an appropriate environment, nor practicing positive guidance approaches. Behavior problems persist when teachers do not adequately prepare the environment.

Do you have an IT HAPPENED TO ME story about an inappropriate environment (no names please)? I'd love to hear it. Please send it to me at WeekbyWeek@thomsonlearning.com

POSSIBLE CAUSES OF PROBLEM BEHAVIOR. The close observer and interpreter of children's behavior looks beyond misbehavior and considers the consequences in light of the child's individual situation. Again, it is the empathetic, reflective professional looking at behavior indicators to seek reasons, causes, contributing factors before blaming the child for deliberately breaking rules. Kostelnik, Whiren, Soderman, and Gregory (2006) suggest these possible causes for behavior problems:

1. Children are not sure of what the rules are or how to follow them.

TOPICS IN OBSERVATION

Does the Week by Week *Plan Meet NAEYC Guidelines for Assessment?*

The National Association for the Education of Young Children (NAEYC) and the National Association of Early Childhood Specialists in State Departments of Education (NAECS/SDE) jointly developed guidelines to evaluate assessment practices. The *Week by Week* system should provide affirmative responses to *all* the guidelines (NAEYC, 2003).

1. Ethical principles guide assessment practices.

   The *Week by Week* system organizes observation documentation so that developmental information is gathered on every child so that no single assessment is the basis of making decisions about the child.
2. Assessment instruments are used for their intended purposes.

   The documentation using various methods can be used to benefit the child, plan for individual children, improve instruction, identify children's interests and needs, and individualize instruction.
3. Assessments are appropriate for ages and other characteristics of children being assessed.

   The documentation methods preserve raw data or are formalized developmental checklists assessing each child on a continuum, compared only to themselves. The assessment procedure reflects individual, cultural, and linguistic diversity.
4. Assessment instruments are in compliance with professional criteria for quality.

   The documentation methods are widely used in early childhood programs and are not linked to a specific curriculum or philosophy. The uses and protocol for various methods are reviewed within the *Week by Week* system so that the most appropriate method is used to record specific developmental domains.
5. What is assessed is developmentally and educationally significant.

   Each child's strengths and capabilities are assessed. The word weakness does not appear in the *Week by Week* system. It is continually emphasized that assessment of development is looking for progress and measuring accomplishment and developing competence.
6. Assessment evidence is used to understand and improve learning.

   The *Week by Week* system not only looks at all areas of development through observation plans giving indicators of development and insights into behavior, but the plan also includes suggestions for enhancing the curriculum in various subject areas, including bibliotherapy or related children's books.
7. Assessment evidence is gathered from realistic settings and situations that reflect children's actual performance.

   The observer using the *Week by Week* system is the classroom teacher, familiar to the child, acting during the normal routine of the classroom environment and activities.
8. Assessments use multiple sources of evidence gathered over time.

(continued)

TOPICS IN OBSERVATION *(continued)*

The *Week by Week* system guides the observer to use at least seven different methods of recording to control bias and meet the objectives for the observation. Interviews and dialogues with the child are included, and the child is informed and can review the Portfolio that contains samples of his or her work gathered periodically over time.

9. Screening is always linked to follow-up.

   When developmental delays or areas of concern are revealed through the *Week by Week* assessments, the teacher has hard data to discuss with the family and referral agents (with the permission of the family).

10. Use of individually administered, norm-referenced tests is limited.

    Norm-referenced developmental checklists are included to not only measure gains but also to give information to the teachers and families about the next milestone in the developmental domain. The *Week by Week* system cautions teachers regarding the use of standardized tests with young children, advocating instead naturalistic assessment methods.

11. Staff and families are knowledgeable about assessment.

    All through the *Week by Week* system, regular communication with families is emphasized. Families are invited to read and contribute to the Portfolio. They are continually reminded in the *Week by Week* system that the Portfolio is a changing collection of documents open for their inspection and comment. Daily contacts concerning the observations are recommended. A periodic narrative report briefly describes the child's accomplishments in each developmental area. These are presented to families in family conferences and become a part of the Portfolio. A child study, covering the whole year, is optional as an additional review of the assessment of the child.

    It appears that the *Week by Week* system meets the NAEYC and NAECS/SDE guidelines. *Week by Week* assessments of every child's development, using a variety of observation techniques, and professional reflection, have been braided together. Together they make the whole strand stronger—the strand of professional practice.

2. Children know that certain behaviors are inappropriate but do not know what to do instead.
3. Children are not capable of following the rule.
4. Children have difficulty controlling impulsive behavior.
5. Children have mistaken perceptions about how to gain acceptance.
6. Other significant adults, siblings, or peers advocate certain behaviors that run counter to those promoted by the caregiver or teacher.
7. Children think that the rule is unjustified.
8. Children have no ownership of the rules and no investment in solving problems that arise.
9. Children have learned that unacceptable behaviors are usually ignored and that it makes no difference whether they follow the rules.
10. Children are trying to figure out the real boundaries of a social situation and whether adults will maintain those boundaries consistently. (p. 358)

Through observation and appropriate professional practice, the child in group settings can be assessed for physical and psychological safety. Nonpunitive, positive guidance techniques are used to help the child gain self-control. In this way, the teacher does not give up on any child and has a career of **liberation teaching** (Ginott in Gartrell, 2003). The teacher sees the child as an individual, recognizing and respecting the cultural differences. Teachers work to help each child be a self-directed, competent, accepted, and moral individual.

HELPING ALL CHILDREN THROUGH HOME AND SCHOOL COMMUNICATIONS

Children from Diverse Backgrounds

Communication is the key component to working in partnership with families. Whether the family speaks a language unknown to the teacher or lives such a different lifestyle that it is almost impossible to comprehend, it is the teacher's responsibility to find some common ground. That common ground is concern for the child and the desire to know and assist the child in development. When that is the motivation, interpreters, schedules, and overlooking lifestyles without judgment all can be managed with creativity and conviction.

Children with Special Needs

Families whose children have special needs must be advocates for their child. They want for their child what every other family wants: an opportunity to learn and be treated equally. In the classroom, for some children to receive what they need, some interventions or modifications must be made. It takes an intense amount of understanding between families and teachers to come to satisfactory arrangements that do not overburden the teacher or the program yet provide for the needs of every child in the group. This may mean adding extra adults who specifically help that child. It may mean the teacher modifies the environment and the routines for one particular child while meeting the needs of the rest as well. This can only be accomplished through open communication between the family and teachers. By regularly sharing information, expressing frustrations, and problem solving together, it *can* be done.

HELPING PROFESSIONALS FOR HOME AND SCHOOL COMMUNICATIONS

Psychologists and social workers can help as intermediaries between schools, programs, and families. They can assess an individual child's emotional state in relation to the adults in the program, how the program is meeting the child's particular needs, and help the family deal with agencies with their own policies and procedures.

No matter what the circumstances of the family, the teacher's first responsibility is to provide for the needs of the child within the goals and objectives of the program. Working with families in a cooperative partnership helps accomplish those goals.

OTHER METHODS

Other Methods to Record the Child's Interaction with Adults

- Class List Log
- Anecdotal/Running Records
- Frequency Count
- Time Sampling
- Conversations/Interviews
- Work Samples
- Checklists and Rating Scales

STANDARDS

Selected examples of standards related to relationships with families:

Child Development Associate—Functional Area 11 (Council for Early Childhood Professional Recognition, 2001).
Candidate maintains an open, friendly, and cooperative relationship with each child's family, encourages their involvement in the program, and supports the child's relationship with his or her family.

NAEYC *Code of Ethical Conduct* Principle 2.2
We shall inform families of program philosophy, policies, curriculum, assessment system, and personnel qualifications, and explain why we teach as we do—which should be in accordance with our ethical responsibilities to children.

@ it happened to me

As I Wrote This Book

These are the "truisms" that have come to me in the process of working out this *Week by Week* plan:

Observations cannot be done occasionally because the novelty of being watched changes children's behavior. Children need to see the teacher writing about them every day.

Writing meaningful observations as they are occurring cannot happen in a teacher-directed classroom. The teacher is too busy.

Useful observations cannot be gathered the week before progress reports or family conferences are due.

A fair assessment of the child cannot be gathered with any one recording instrument.

Every child deserves to be observed and recorded individually.

Observing and recording does no good if it does not change the teacher's practices or individualize the approach the teacher uses with each child.

Because some children in the class have reached a certain developmental level does not mean that others should be there too. They have other strengths.

When we look at what the child cannot do, we fail to see all the child can do. Pointing blame at others—the family, the child, or the program—leaves three fingers pointing back at us. We must reflect on what we could do to make things better for the family, the child, and the program.

Families are the authorities on the child. They lend them to us and we pay them back with interest.

This organized plan comes from a person who is disorganized but enacts plans that get things done.

Teaching is not about transferring knowledge. It is about learning, and the one who learns the most is the teacher. This book could never have been accomplished had I not set *Week by Week* goals for myself. On a calendar near my computer, I plotted chapters, working back from deadlines, so that if I stayed on course I could meet the deadlines. It worked for me. It can work for you!

It is my sincere goal for everyone using this plan to know the child. Because of what we know, this is what we do. In that knowing, we will do what is right for that child.

Do you have a "truism" or value statement that you use to make ethical decisions? I'd love to read it. Send it to WeekbyWeek@thomsonlearning.com

KEY TERMS

- active listening
- case study (child study)
- documentation panels
- liberation teaching
- progress report
- teacher's stories
- unconditional positive regard

Go to the Bind-in-Book CD for:

Plan Week 14 Part A, Directions for a Class List Log on Interaction with Adults, including What to Do with It, Portfolio Overview Example, Sharing with Child and Family, Actions—Read a Book, In the Environment, In the Curriculum, In the Newsletter

Plan Week 14 Part B, Directions for Checklist on Physical Development on all children

Plan Week 14 Part C, Reflective Journal

REFERENCES

Benner, S. (2003). *Assessment of young children with special needs.* Clifton Park, NY: Thomson Delmar Learning.

Berger, E. (2004). *Parents as partners in education: Families and schools working together.* Upper Saddle River, NJ: Pearson Merrill Prentice Hall.

Brown-DuPaul, J., Keyes, T., & Segatti, L. (2001). Using documentation panels to communicate with families. *Childhood Education, 77* (4), 209–213.

Council for Early Childhood Professional Recognition. (2001). *The child development associate: Assessment system and competency standards.* Washington, DC: Author.

DiNatale, L. (2002). Developing high-quality family involvement programs in early childhood settings. *Young Children, 57* (5), 90–95.

Dunst, C. J., Trivette, C. M., & Mott, D. W. (1994). Strengths-based family-centered intervention practices. In C. J. Dunst, C. M. Trivette, & A. G. Deal (Eds.), *Supporting and strengthening families: Methods, strategies and practices, Vol. I* (pp. 115–131). Cambridge, MA: Brookline.

Gartrell, D. (2007). *A guidance approach for the encouraging classroom* (4th ed.). Clifton Park, NY: Thomson Delmar Learning.

Gestwicki, C. (2004). *Home, school, and community relations: A guide to working with parents* (5th ed.). Clifton Park, NY: Thomson Delmar Learning.

Gordon, T. (1975). *Parent effectiveness training: The no-lose program for raising responsible children.* New York: Wyden.

Harms, T., Cryer, D., & Clifford, R. M. (2003). *Infant/toddler environment rating scale* (rev. ed.). New York: Teachers College Press.

Howes, C., & Ritchie, S. (2002). *A matter of trust: Connecting teachers and learners in the early childhood classroom.* New York: Teachers College Press.

Kostelnik, M. J., Whiren, A. P., Soderman, A. K., & Gregory, K. (2006). *Guiding children's social development* (5th ed.). Clifton Park, NY: Thomson Delmar Learning.

Lally, J. R., Lerner, C., & Lurie-Hurvitz, E. (2001). National survey reveals gaps in the public's and parents' knowledge about early childhood development. *Young Children, 56* (2), 49–53.

Marion, M. (2003). *Guidance of young children* (6th ed.). Englewood Cliffs, NJ: Merrill, an imprint of Prentice Hall.

National Association for Family Child Care. (2005). *Quality standards for NAFCC accreditation.* Salt Lake City, UT: Author.

National Association for the Education of Young Children. (2005). *Code of ethical conduct and statement of commitment.* Washington, DC: Author.

National Association for the Education of Young Children and the National Association of Early Childhood Specialists in State Departments of Education (NAEYC and NAECS/SDE). (2003). Early childhood curriculum, assessment, and program evaluation, position statement. Washington, DC: Author.

Talan, T. N., & Bloom, P. J. (2004). *Program administration scale: Measuring early childhood leadership and management.* New York: Teachers College Press.

U.S. Department of Health and Human Services. (2005). Head Start program performance standards. http://www.acf.hhs.gov.

RESOURCES

Gartrell, D. (2007). *A guidance approach for the encouraging classroom* (4rd ed.). Clifton Park, NY: Thomson Delmar Learning.

Gestwicki, C. (2004). *Home, school, and community relations: A guide to working with parents* (5th ed.). Clifton Park, NY: Thomson Delmar Learning.

Marion, M. (2003). *Guidance of young children* (6th ed.). Englewood Cliffs, NJ: Merrill, an imprint of Prentice Hall.

CHAPTER 15

Using the Yearly Plan to Observe and Record Children's Development

STUDENTS

You have used this book as a guide for observing children throughout a semester, but all along you have noticed that this book has a dual purpose. There are extensive directions in the plans on the Bind-in-Book CD. It is the author's intention that this textbook be used as a reference and guide when you have a classroom of your own. What follows is the *Week by Week* plan for compiling documentation on every child, in every developmental area, every week.

PRACTITIONERS

Now you have the tools (the various methods presented in this book). You have the knowledge of how to use the tools (the overview of areas of development). The rest of this book is the building plan for Portfolios that contain documentation of all areas of development, revisited at least three times to measure progress.

The "Introduction and Overview" section of the Bind-in-Book CD contains an "Introduction" file to help you get started using the CD. Also in this section is the schedule for the *Week by Week* plan. (The file for this schedule is titled "Overview.") You will divide the children into groups of three or four children, depending on the size of the class, in alphabetical order by their first name (remember the Class List Log), calling the group A, B, C, or D. This will give you an arbitrary plan so that certain children are not

REVIEW

Here is your last Review Box, a summary of the methods you have in your toolbox. Use the right tool for the job.

Method	Definition	Useful for Recording
Class List Log	Alphabetical first name list to record small, specific pieces of information on each child in the class	Single elements of adjustments to routines Single elements of self-care Single elements of physical development Social development stage Clear articulation of speech Single elements of basic concepts in math/science Single elements of literacy Frequency of choices of Learning Centers
Reflective Journal	Personal diary kept separate and private from children's records	Thoughts Expressions of emotions Questions Self-examination
Anecdotal Recording	Detailed incident on one child, including the setting, action/reaction, exact quotes, and result	Separation and adjustment Self-care skills Physical development Social development Emotional development Language and speech Attention span and interests Cognitive development Literacy Creativity Sociodramatic play Child abuse disclosure Self-esteem
Checklists	Listing of related criteria against which skills, knowledge, or behavior is measured indicating yes or no, present or not present. Can indicate milestones attained and areas yet to be developed	Self-care skills Physical development Stages of social development Stages of emotional development Stages of cognitive development Specific criteria such as "knows colors, shapes, recognizes numbers" Stages of literacy Stages of creative development Stages of sociodramatic play Aspects of self-concept

(continued)

REVIEW

(continued)

Method	Definition	Useful for Recording
Frequency Count	A recording of predetermined frequently occurring behaviors to quantify their frequency, and later used for comparison after a strategy is implemented	Frequently occuring separation difficulties Frequent requests for assistance Frequent prosocial and antisocial incidents Frequency of language used in certain functions Frequency of choices of activities
Conversations or Interviews	Recording a child's verbal interactions either in writing or in audio recording	Informal conversations Interviews to obtain: Child's viewpoint on school adjustment Self-responsibility views Self-evaluation of physical skills Self-evaluation of friendships and social interactions Self-evaluation of emotional difficulties Evaluate speech/language Assess cognitive development Assess literacy development Discuss creative work or play
Time Sample	Recording children's play area free choices every five minutes for a half hour interval and drawing conclusions about interests, abilities, attention span, preferred playmates, level of social play	Presence of child in area Sustained play in that area Interaction with others in that area Presence of adult
Rating Scale	Criteria are arranged according to developmental stages or range of quality with the recorder making a judgment based on observation	Child development stages Environment appropriateness Teacher performance
Work Samples	Collection of child's products from which to draw conclusions about development, skills, and behaviors	Separation Self-care Physical development Social skills Emotional development Speech and language development Memory and attention span Math and science knowledge Literacy Creativity Self-identity Group time behaviors Interaction with adults

REVIEW

(continued)

Method	Definition	Useful for Recording
Technology	Action preserved in photos, audio/video recording	Any moment or sequence Separation and adjustment Self-care skills Physical development Social development Emotional development Language and speech Attention span and interests Cognitive development Literacy Creativity Sociodramatic play Self-esteem
Child Abuse Reporting	Precise, descriptive, immediate note taking, State Reporting Form	Indicators of physical abuse Indicators of neglect Indicators of sexual abuse Indicators of emotional abuse
Program Assessment	Tool to evaluate program environment, curriculum and administration, staff qualifications and interactions with children, suitability of program for individual child	Interactions among teachers and children Curriculum Relationships among teachers and families Staff qualifications and professional development Administration Staffing Health and safety Environment Nutrition and health service Anti-bias policies and procedures

The purpose is to *know* the child in order to fulfill our responsibility to the global village in helping each one develop into a caring, thinking, reliable human being. This plan is only successful if it helps attain that goal by measuring progress, individualizing the environment or curriculum to assist in development, documenting the child's activities, and sharing with families.

overlooked in observations while others are frequently observed. The "Weekly Plans" section of the Bind-in-Book CD contains the plans for weeks 1–40. You may have to adjust for your own program calendar, for vacations, or for necessary suspensions of recording. But like a diet, even if you slip some, just try to get back into the routine in order to meet your goal: a well-developed Portfolio for each child.

The "Forms" section of the Bind-in-Book CD includes the forms you can copy and/or modify for your observations.

The Reflective Journal pages for weeks 1 through 40 are included in the "Reflective Journals" section of the Bind-in-Book CD. You can fill these out week by week to guide your introspection as well as the plans for observing children. Keep these at home, in a private place, and use them to reflect on your own attitudes, practices, and feelings.

The Bind-in-Book CD also includes separate sections containing the Learning Activities associated with each chapter; PowerPoint slides for each chapter for use in note-taking during lectures; and Internet Resources associated with each chapter.

Go to the Bind-in-Book CD for more plans and resources.

Glossary

A

acceptance—the feeling of being loved and appreciated, contributes to self-esteem (12)

accommodation—takes in new information, balances with previous knowledge, and adjusts response (7)

accreditation—voluntary submission to a standard through a review process, usually consisting of a self-study and verification (13)

action research—informal collection of information about a child or children, nonstandardized (6)

active listening—technique for clarifying the message and the feelings (14)

ADD, ADHD—attention deficit disorders, professionally diagnosed impairments that affect attention span and cause impulsivity and distractibility (7)

adjustment—ability of a child to adapt socially and emotionally (13)

aggression—actions that injure people, things, or emotions (5)

Anecdotal Recording—factual narrative of an incident (2)

animism—preoperational child believes natural world is ruled by willful intent like humans (7)

articulation—the sounds of speech (6)

artificialism—preoperational child believes that humans create and influence nature (7)

assessment—process of observing, recording, and documenting a child's actions, skills, and behaviors (I)

assimilation—information received that adjusts previously related information (7)

association—information received that matches previously related information (7)

associative play—play that is similar, in the same theme but still with each player playing individually (4)

attachment—the emotional bond that infants show to a person (usually the mother) with whom they have had a stable, trusting relationship (1)

attention deficit—inability to focus; medical diagnosis, may or may not be accompanied by hyperactivity (7); see also ADD/ADHD

attention span—focus perceptual processes on a specific aspect of the environment (7)

audio recorders—device that makes a taped or digital reproduction of sound (11)

authentic assessment—measurement of knowledge or skill in context, in as realistic a setting as possible (8)

autism—pervasive spectrum disorder with a range of effects on several domains (7)

autonomy—the process of governing oneself (2)

B

benchmark—descriptions of knowledge, skills, development that are measurable outcomes of standards (8)

bias—preconceived attitudes that may affect objectivity, either positively or negatively (3)

brain hemisphericity—two hemispheres, or sides, of the brain deal with information and function in different ways (7)

C

case study (child study)—a comprehensive written overview of the child; it may be documented by written evidence and the child's work (14)

cause and effect—ability to perceive the link between two events with one as a result of the other (7)

centration—focus of attention on one attribute, ignoring other variables (7)

cephalocaudal—sequence of the development of muscle control from head to toe (3)

Checklist—a method of documenting the presence or absence of a skill or behavior in a developmental sequence (3)

Class List Log—method of gathering a specific piece of information on every child in the group (1)

classification—matching or grouping similar data (7)

closed method—the recorder makes a judgment from observation and records it with a check, slash, few words. Raw data is not available for the reader (3)

closed question—one expected answer, like a test (6)

cognitive—knowing, thinking, reasoning, and remembering (8)

competence—the feeling of capability, independence, and autonomy; contributes to self-esteem (12)

Concrete Operational Stage—period of development (7 to 11 years old), using logic and reasoning; mental actions are still related to "concrete" objects (7)

confidentiality—the professional attitude and practice of preserving the privacy of information (I)

conservation—understanding that volume or measurability of objects remains the same if nothing is added or subtracted but the form is changed (7)

constructive play—manipulating objects, such as blocks, to create a physical product (4)

contextualized literacy—ability to read words when other clues are present, such as cereal names, restaurants, and traffic signs (9)

continuity of care—practice of child care advancing children as a cohort, staying together with the same teachers as well (13)

convergent thinking—the ability to arrive at a single answer, more difficult for young children with still-developing classifying, listening, and attending skills (10)

cooperative play—play where players are in the same theme and working toward a common goal (4)

coping mechanisms—strategies for overcoming uncomfortable circumstances (1)

coping skills—strategies to overcome emotional traumas (5)

core emotions—basic emotions present at birth from which other emotions evolve (5)

creativity—novel thinking or product (10)

criterion-referenced—method that provides a predetermined standard or guideline to look for and measure against (e.g., Checklist, Rating Scales) (I)

D

daily log or journal (also called **diary**)—end of the day account from recall (1)

development—change that takes place in a predictable sequence, from simple to complex, but at a different pace for individual people (2)

diagnostic interview—conversations designed to yield developmental information about a child (6)

digital video cameras—devices that record images electronically (11)

disclosure—a statement that indicates the speaker has been a victim of abuse or maltreatment (12)

disequilibrium—cognitive conflict when new information does not associate or match previous data (7)

displacement—turning angry feelings away from the source of the anger (5)

dispositions—the feelings or responses to a body of knowledge (8)

divergent thinking—ability to think of a wide range of possibilities, associated with creativity and giftedness (10)

diversity—broad range of differences, individual uniqueness (6)

document (verb)—the action of preserving data for later review; documentation (noun)—the product that preserves the data (I)

documentation panels—displays of children's work that show the process of their thinking and planning and the resulting product (14)

dramatic play—symbolic play, pretend (4)

dysfluent—speech disorder in which the speaker repeats a beginning sound or a word (6)

dyslexia—an impairment of the ability to read (9)

E

Ebonics—nonstandard English spoken by some (6)

ecological view—consideration of all aspects that influence a human being (I)

egocentric—the cognitive stage in which the child is not able to take another's point of view (4)

egocentrism—preoperational child's inability to understand that others do not share his or her perspective (7)

emergent literacy—continuous process of becoming a reader and writer (9)

emotional intelligence—type of intelligence that motivates oneself, persists in frustration, controls impulses, delays gratification, and empathizes with others (5)

emotional maltreatment—psychological damage from blaming, belittling, or rejecting a child (12)

environmental print—the signs and labels that appear on everyday objects in homes, media, and neighborhoods (9)

ethics—the moral principles and practices under which an individual operates (I)

evaluation—comparison of information gathered against a standard or set of criteria (I)

executive function—ability to self-regulate thought, action, and emotion because of the development of cognitive and neural skills (5)

expressive language—messages that are communicated through words and gestures (6)

F

failure to thrive—developmental delays caused by physical or emotional factors (3, 5)

family—the group of related or unrelated adults who are legally responsible for a child (I)

file access log—a form in a Portfolio that records the name, purpose, and date of each person who views the file (I)

frame of reference—individual point of view influenced by many factors (3)

Frequency Count—recording method to measure how often a specified event occurs (5)

functional play—manipulation of objects with no particular goal other than to examine and practice repetitive motions (4)

G

games with rules—play where players take turns and act according to a mutually understood standard (4)

gender—general term for the social and cultural constructions of sexual identity, whereas sex is the term for the biological distinction between male and female (12)

gender identity—*see* sex-role identity

good-bye rituals—established routines to help the child with separation (1)

growth—quantitative change that can be measured in numbers (3)

H

high-stakes test—on the basis of the tests, decisions are made that affect the child, the teacher, or the school (8)

holographic—one-word sentences that have meaning (6)

I

inclusion—the practice of including children with special needs within the least restrictive environment (8)

inference—conclusion; judgment; explanation (2)

informal conversations—spontaneous conversations between adult and child that yield information (6)

informed consent—ethical practice of obtaining permission before using a person as the subject of a study or in photos, audio, or video recordings (11)

interdependence—serving the needs of others above self, and a humility and reticence to put self forward (12)

interrater reliability—two or more raters use the same instrument on the same child to control bias (9)

invented spelling—phonetic spelling with a letter for each sound (9)

invulnerable child—child who escapes from childhood psychological trauma without harm (5)

L

language—the meaning of the words and gestures that are communicated (6)

large muscle (gross motor)—muscles used in moving the body from one place to another (3)

learned helplessness—feeling of inadequacy results in lack of motivation and increased dependence on others (2)

learning disabilities—an interference with the ability to process written communication (9)

least restrictive environment—legal term referring to the educational placement of exceptional children in regular settings to the maximum extent possible (3)

liberation teaching—theory that the teacher, by seeking to meet the child's needs, does not give up on any child (14)

license requirements—required standards, usually set by the individual states (13)

logico-mathematical knowledge—understanding principles of the nature of matter by reasoning rather than intuition or appearances (7)

M

mandala—universal symbol combining circle and intersecting lines (10)

mandated reporters—those individuals who by law must report suspicions of child abuse to specified agencies (12)

matching—recognizing the similarities of an attribute of an object (7)

media—art materials (singular: **medium**) (10)

mixed-age groups—also known as heterogeneous, multi-age, vertical, ungraded, nongraded, and family grouping; groups of children not separated by chronological age (13)

morality—characteristic of making choices based on a set of standards set by social group (12)

morphemes—smallest unit of language, words (6)

multiple intelligences—individual ways of processing information (7)

N

narrative—method that tells a story, includes all the details of an incident (e.g., Anecdotal Recording, Running Record) (I, 2)

neglect—the withholding of basic survival needs of food, water, shelter, clothing, medical care; constitutes maltreatment (12)

nonrepresentational—young child's drawing a symbol of mental image; not able to "represent" a recognizable symbol; difficult to draw what they are thinking (10)

norm—standard against which others are measured (8)

O

object permanence—the cognitive understanding that objects and persons continue to exist even out of sight (4)

objective—detached, impersonal, unprejudiced, data-only recordings (I)

observing—watching children to know more about their development (I)

one-to-one correspondence—ability to count objects accurately by assigning one number to each object (7)

onlooker play—watch others play; may talk or ask questions (4)

open method—recording method that preserves the raw data; only records actions and words so separate conclusions can be drawn (2)

open question—no single correct answer, creative answers (6)

ordinal numbers—indicating the order or succession, such as first, second, or third (8)

overgeneralization—early stage in grammar construction where child adds "s" to all words for plural and "ed" to all words for past tense (6)

P

parallel play—play that is near, maybe even doing the same actions or using the same equipment or toys, but not interacting (4)

performance standards—criteria by which individuals or programs are measured (13)

phonemes—basic unit of sound in spoken language (6)

phonemic awareness—child's understanding and conscious awareness that speech is composed of identifiable units, such as spoken words, syllables, and sounds (9)

physical abuse—any nonaccidental physical injury caused by the child's caretaker (12)

physical knowledge—knowledge about the general properties of the physical world: gravity, motion, and nature (7)

Portfolio—a systematic collection of documentation about the child's development (I)

power—the ability to control one's actions and destiny, rather than depending on outside agents (12)

precocity—exceptional early development in cognitive or creative ability (10)

Preoperational Stage—stage of cognitive development with distinct characteristics, according to Piaget's theory, ages 4–7 (7)

preschematic—stage in drawing development before the child has attained the small muscle coordination and cognitive abilities to draw recognizable symbols (10)

print-rich environment—literacy materials available to promote recognition of symbols of alphabet and their sounds, phonemic awareness (9)

program evaluation—the process of examining all the components of a program to measure effectiveness and quality (13)

progress report—a periodic written overview of short-term goals the child has achieved (14)

proximodistal—development of muscle control from center of body to extremities (3)

Q

quality points—milestones or measurement intervals on a rating scale (9)

quantitative—method that provides a numerical count of individual or group actions (e.g., Frequency Counts, Time Samples) (I)

quantitative scoring—an assessment tool that reports results with a numeric score (8)

R

Rating Scale—measuring a specific behavior, skill, or attribute by choosing from three or more descriptors (9)

receptive language—that which is heard, taken in (6)

record—documentation of an event, may be written, recorded as audio or video, or photography (6)

recording—a system or method of writing down what has been observed (I)

referral—a recommendation made for further evaluation by a helping professional (I)

reflection—thoughtful consideration of past events for analysis (1)

Reflective Journal—a private, written record in which to express feelings; not a part of child's record; property of the writer (1)

reflexes—muscle reactions to stimuli, not controlled by intent (3)

reliability—quality of tests that will produce a similar score by the same individual on the same test (8)

reversibility—the concrete-operational child understands that any change can be mentally reversed, for example, think of an ice cube as water (7)

rote counting—counting by memory, may be inaccurate or out of sequence (7)

Running Record—detailed account of a segment of time; recording all behaviors and quotes during that time (4)

S

schema—symbol in art that is repeated over and over representing a real object (10)

schematic—stage in which symbolic representations go through modifications as child develops cognitively (10)

screening—a test given to a broad population to indicate possibilities that are evaluated further (8)

scribbling—experiments with drawing media, can be uncontrolled or controlled (doodling) (10)

selective method—the recording instrument dictates what is to be observed (9)

self-care—ability to eat, toilet, dress, keep clean, and keep safe (2)

self-concept—the qualities one attributes to one's self, self-identity (12)

self-esteem—the valuing of that knowledge based on self and social comparisons (12)

Sensorimotor Stage—stage from birth to age two when the child "takes in" information mainly by sensory means and gains differentiation of self from the environment (7)

separation anxiety—distress when a parent leaves an infant's presence, beginning at 8 or 9 months and usually disappearing at about 24 months (1)

seriation—the ability to order objects by some standard rule, height, weight, shade, or tone (7)

sex-role (gender identity)—socialized preference of behavior identified with one gender or the other (12)

sexual abuse—sexually explicit conduct with a minor (12)

shyness—hesitance in social situations, self-consciousness (5)

small muscle (fine motor)—muscles that control hands and fingers (3)

social competence—ability to maintain interactions, to have friends (4)

social conventional knowledge—information gathered from influential adults about general rules of conduct acceptable to that group (7)

socialized—behavior learned to adapt to the expectations of the social group (12)

sociodramatic play—fantasy play episode with others involved (11)

solitary play—play that is focused on objects or movements, not involved with others (4)

speech—the sounds produced to make words, phonemes (6)

standard—description of knowledge, skills, and development that children should acquire by a certain age/stage/grade (8)

standardized tests—scores are measured against the norm group that has taken the test (8)

story dictation—children write and produce a story or episode (11)

stranger anxiety—distress when approached by an unfamiliar person, beginning at seven to nine months and ending around one year (1)

stress—physiological reactions to emotional events (5)

structured interview—planned conversations to find out specific information about a child (6)

subjective—influenced by state of mind, point of view, inferential, interpreting the meaning, or cause of an event (1)

summative observation—cumulative evaluation describing progress (1)

syntax—order of words in a sentence that give them meaning; grammar (6)

T

tadpole man—beginning drawings of humans with lines protruding from circles (10)

talented and gifted—designation for higher than average cognitive, linguistic, social, creative development (8)

teacher's stories—the relating of classroom experiences to child development or professional practice principles; may be related orally or in written form (14)

technology—tools used to perform a task (11)

telegraphic—few-word sentences that have meaning (6)

temperament—inborn personality traits (5)

Time Sample—method of recording where children are by choice at a certain time, measuring attention span and interests (7)

transitions—period between activities, time periods, or programs; may be problematic without planning (13)

U

unconditional positive regard—feelings a teacher should have for a student (14)

unfounded—child abuse reports that upon investigation lack evidence for criminal or civil charges (12)

unoccupied play—not interested in play, wanders around room (4)

V

valid—describes quality of a test that measures what it proposes to measure (8)

video recorder—device that makes a taped reproduction of image and sound (11)

W

Work Samples—method that preserves the child's work as a documentation of development (e.g., drawings, writings, constructions, media-preserved work such as audio or video recordings or photographs) (I, 10)

Working Portfolio—includes selected but typical Work Samples along with teacher documentation to show the child's progress (I)

Z

zone of proximal development—behavioral levels that can be approximated with assistance (5)

Index

D

E

F

Q

S

T

U

V